BLOODY STREETS

The Soviet Assault on Berlin, April 1945

A. Stephan Hamilton

Helion & Company Ltd

For Dad
His words of caution about the past intensified my historical drive.

Helion & Company Limited
26 Willow Road
Solihull
West Midlands
B91 1UE
England
Tel. 0121 705 3393
Fax 0121 711 4075
Email: publishing@helion.co.uk
Website: http://www.helion.co.uk

Published by Helion & Company 2008

Designed and typeset by Helion & Company Limited, Solihull, West Midlands
Cover designed by Bookcraft Limited, Stroud, Gloucestershire
Printed by Cromwell Press Ltd, Trowbridge, Wiltshire

Text and maps © A. Stephan Hamilton
Photographs © as individually credited within book.
Colour AFV profiles © Wydawnictwo Militaria.

Front cover images:
Soviet troops following the capture of Berlin 1945 (Ullstein Bilderdienst),
T-34/85 tank from the 55th Armoured Brigade 7th Guards Armoured Corps
Third Guards Tank Army, Germany, April 1945 (Wydawnictwo Militaria).

Rear cover image:
In the stark ruins of Berlin a broken bust of Hitler surveys all that remains of his
1,000 Year Reich (Author's collection)

ISBN 978-1-906033-12-5

British Library Cataloguing-in-Publication Data
A catalogue record for this book is available from the British Library.

For details of other military history titles published by Helion & Company Limited contact the above address, or visit our website:
http://www.helion.co.uk.

We always welcome receiving book proposals from prospective authors.

CONTENTS

ACKNOWLEDGEMENTS

I wish to express my sincere appreciation to everyone that assisted me over the long years of research, writing, and editing of this book. Without your help, I would not have completed this project.

In Germany, I wish to thank Frau Kuhl at the Bundesarchiv in Koblenz who identified excellent photographs for this book. C. Notzke at the Bundesarchivs-Militärarchivs in Freiburg made unit order-of-battles and other textual documents regarding German units that fought in Berlin available to me during my brief visit. In addition, Herr Gerd-Ulrich Herrmann, who is the director of the Seelower Höhen Gedenkstätte, provided useful information and access to the museum's archive.

Many thanks go to the staff at the U.S. National Archives. In particular, I wish to thank Mr. James Kelling whose knowledge of the Captured German and Related Records on microfilm is surpassed by few. Mr. Kelling also assisted in finding a variety of often overlooked additional sources located in the archive's Special Collection. Mr. R. F. Cookson made available much information on 'Eclipse' as well as other relevant files declassified in the last decade from the Office of Strategic Services collection. The Cartographic Division assisted in locating all of the hard-to-find, and rarely accessed period aerial imagery of Berlin used in this book. Richard H. Smith located and made available the Lage-Ost daily situational maps that offered significant insight into German and Soviet unit dispositions during the fighting.

This book benefited the greatest from Mr. Doug McCabe and his staff who oversee the Cornelius Ryan Collection, Mahn Center, Alden Library, at Ohio University. Mr. McCabe granted my request for access to all of Cornelius Ryan's research material accumulated for his book *The Last Battle*. I will argue that Ryan's accumulated research is one of the greatest single collections of historical documents and interviews about the battle for Berlin, and the final days of the Third Reich. Ryan utilized very little of the material at his disposal for his book and I am perhaps the first author to access this material since the 1966 publication of *The Last Battle*. No author writing about the battle for Berlin can afford to ignore the material at the Mahn Center. By extension, I offer my thanks to the hundreds of German and Soviet veterans that shared their experiences of war with Ryan's research staff four decades ago—may their account's incorporation into this book fill a historical void.

Translation assistance of the numerous German, Russian, and Latvian source materials came from Frau S. Hartman in Germany, C. P. Falotico in the United States, as well as others from across the World Wide Web who graciously gave their time to this effort.

The editing process was greatly enhanced by the enormous historical knowledge of Franz Schwuchow and his stern attention to detail that revealed issues of nomenclature and technical specification. His former experience as a M1A1 tank crewman served the text well. Retired U.S. Army Colonel Steve Rundle provided significant input on the text's thematic consistency and overall concepts. I also want to thank Major Tony Lee (USAR), and many others who offered their comments and insights over the years.

M. Hamilton transcribed hundreds of pages of primary documents and interviews, and offered clarifying comments throughout select chapter drafts. Her transcriptions drastically reduced the amount of time required to prepare portions of this text.

Duncan Rogers of Helion receives special thanks for supporting me in my first publication effort over the long years of research and writing. He continually answered my questions, and routinely gave me support, in addition to undertaking research for many of the photographs from Eastern Europe. In that respect, thanks must also be extended greatly to Kamen Nevenkin, who uncovered a number of rare images. The colour profiles and some of the very rare images from Russia appear due to the great help of Janusz Ledwoch. Finally, in respect of photographs, thanks must also be extended to Martin Månsson, Lennart Westberg, Chris Habisohn and Charles Trang.

I must thank my wife Kim most importantly. She never realized the amount of time, effort, and cost required to prepare this book, yet she continued to support me through its six long years of development. This book might have remained nothing more than an outline in a notebook without her commitment.

Due to the controversial nature of some topics within this book, it must be made clear that I alone am responsible for the content and tone contained in the following pages.

Doug McCabe (left) and the author (right) stand in front of a display case in Mahn Center, Alden Library Athens Ohio, that contains information related to Ryan's production of *The Last Battle*, March 2005. Author's collection.

PREFACE

The political, social, economic, and military power shift in Europe ushered in after Berlin's fall to the Soviets in 1945 has few corollaries in European history. Other European capitals were attacked, besieged, and fell over the years to be sure—some with significant power shifts, others without. The fall of Constantinople in 1453 forever ended the Byzantine Empire and established an Islamic presence on mainland Europe. Constantinople's fall was followed by the unsuccessful sieges of Vienna in 1529 and 1683 that would arguably have brought Islamic domination over Central Europe; however, both sieges were defeated. The siege of Paris in 1870 ushered in the fall of the Second French Empire under Napoleon the III and saw the birth of the *Deutsches Reich* (German Empire) also known as the Second Reich—an event that brought a significant shift in power that shaped European and world history over the next 60 years. During World War II in Europe capitals were attacked or captured with immediate consequences for the local population or governments; but only London, Moscow, and Berlin were key strategic targets that held the potential to dramatically change the course of events in the war, and by extension European and world history. London and Moscow while attacked—the former by air and the latter by land—did not fall. Berlin, however, did fall in the largest urban combat operation in human history. *Who* captured Berlin strategically, is as important as *how* Berlin was captured operationally and tactically. Both the political-social and military ramifications shaped the postwar world in ways still being felt today, though often not attributed to the cataclysmic events that took place during the 16 days of Spring 1945.

The genesis for this book began in 1992 when as a young U.S. Army Cadet I stepped off a tour bus outside the Pergamon Museum in what was East Berlin and immediately confronted the visible scars of street fighting that occurred almost half a century earlier. My fascination with the street fighting in Berlin germinated over the next decade as I watched modern military forces engage in brutal urban combat in places such as Grozny, Gaza, Mogadishu, and Sarajevo, never realizing how the military events in Berlin foreshadowed the tactics, weapons, and vehicle modifications that would be employed as 'improvisations' in these later conflicts. Not until the U.S.-led invasion of Iraq in 2003 that culminated in the commitment of a predominately mechanized force into the capital of Baghdad did I decide to write this book. Baghdad is the second largest city in the Arab world behind Tehran, boasting a pre-war population of nearly 7 million people spread out over 700 square kilometers. Running through the city is the Tigris River, numerous waterways, and irrigation channels. These characteristics bear striking similarities to the operational environment the Soviets faced in their assault on Berlin. After U.S. forces captured Iraq's capital, I decided to write a short comparative military analysis of mechanized urban operations between Berlin and Baghdad, citing Berlin as the first example of modern asymmetric urban combat.[1]

Prior to WWII there were few examples where asymmetrical combat was employed within major cities. History is replete with sieges to be sure, but the fight was over once the walls were breached, and an attacking force entered the city. From the time of the Greeks, well into the Twentieth Century, the goal of combatants was to defeat your enemy outside of your city and avoid its subsequent destruction. Cities are unnatural places to conduct military operations and were avoided for this reason. WWII witnessed a dramatic increase in urban combat operations where combatants planned and conducted military operations *within* a city. At the start of the war belligerents fought in cities using conventional forces that were primarily made up of regular infantry supported by limited numbers of tanks—the Battle of Stalingrad is a classic example. Artillery and aircraft assets were plentiful to be sure, but the opposing forces were not highly mechanized and ground operations were executed conventionally. By the end of the war changes in technology brought changes in tactics. Specialized designed tanks and equipment, coupled with the availability of new and lethal high-tech anti-armor and anti-personnel weapons changed the face of urban combat forever. Today, small well-armed unconventional infantry and civilians are often employed asymmetrically in urban combat with success against larger conventional mechanized forces. In recent battles like Grozny in Chechnya, Mogadishu in Somalia, and Fallujah in Iraq, the enemy *wanted* the opposing force to be drawn into the city where numerical and technological advantages by the attacker could be minimized.

Urban combat in Berlin was complex and both Soviet and German forces were forced to adapt to the changing operational environment rapidly. The Soviets tried to initially apply standard operational manoeuver doctrine during their assault and failed as their losses in men and equipment grew exponentially. The overall lack of joint training between independent tank and infantry formations before the battle proved to be a critical factor that contributed to increased Soviet losses. Soviet commanders had to adjust to their urban environment and the asymmetrical German tactics. A few inspired commanders applied new tactical methods that proved very effective. One development was the creation of combined arms battle groups at the battalion level (a Soviet battalion was equivalent to a German company in terms of manpower) with infantry, artillery, and tanks working in mutual support to advance and take the city block-by-block. Units that employed this force mixture decreased their losses and maintained survivability, whereas other units simply degenerated and became combat ineffective. Unfortunately, few Soviet commanders found themselves capable of making this tactical adjustment. The ever-present drive to capture the city quickly retarded most tactical ingenuity. The Germans too, suffered and adapted. Soviet firepower was so devastating that large combat forces could not effectively operate in the city. Division and even regimental structures lost cohesion as units blended together in favor of small company-sized *Kampfgruppe*. Without realizing it, the Germans began employing a flexible application of force along interior lines. German soldiers came together at a particular point forming a nexus of resistance only to quickly melt away and reform later; avoiding superior Soviet firepower in the process. All means of urban terrain were used for movement and combat. Existing rubble, sewers, U-Bahn, S-Bahn stations, railway embankments, canals, culverts, as well as both residential and government buildings became defensive bastions. It must also be noted that German civilians took to the streets in their city's defense, especially young men and women who only had rudimentary weapons training and no affiliation to regular combat formations. German efforts, however, suffered under the weight of competing commands and a lack of effective coordination. The German defense, executed asymmetrically by a mixture of regular combat infantry formations, irregular paramilitary forces, and even civilians, took on a superior, predominately mechanized force and caused considerably enemy losses in the process. It might be argued that other examples in WWII exist to illustrate modern asymmetrical urban combat, most notably the Warsaw Uprising of 1944, or the Battle of Manila in 1945, though there are key differences.[2] One difference in Berlin, unique to modern asymmetrical urban combat, was the use of a revolutionary weapon system—the *Panzerfaust*.

The image that most accurately reflects what the Soviets faced in Berlin is that of a lone enemy soldier, predominately an adolescent or young man, firing a rocket projectile known as the *Panzerfaust* at approaching Soviet armor from a hidden corner of rubble. This weapon demonstrated versatility in a variety of tactical situations like house clearing, wall breaching, and general hand-to-hand combat. The devastating impact that the *Panzerfaust* made on Soviet forces was so great that it was copied and turned into what is now one of the most infamous weapon systems of modern warfare, the Rocket Propelled Grenade (RPG).

The RPG and its variants have become the hallmark of all modern asymmetrical conflicts, not just those that occur in cities. The RPG played critical roles in the various Arab-Israeli conflicts, with the Egyptian defense of the Chinese Farm in October 1973 being a defining moment for the Israeli Army. Mujahedeen used the RPG extensively to devastate Soviet combat operations during the 1979–1989 Soviet occupation of Afghanistan, and the weapon has again seen extensive use in the Chechen Wars that began in 1994 and are ongoing today. In particular the 1994–95 Battle of Grozny proved lethal to the Soviet attempt to quickly take the city as their mechanized assault was immediately defeated by the Chechen's employment of asymmetrical tactics based in part on the RPG. The U.S. Army is not immune to the effects of this weapon or its versatility in employment. The ability of individuals with relatively little formal military training to use RPGs to damage and eventually down two modern Special Forces Black Hawk helicopters in Mogadishu in 1994 shocked the U.S. military establishment. The Soviet RPG inherited a deadly legacy from the German *Panzerfaust* that remains the bane of modern mechanized armies operating in urban environments today.

Soviet tankers encountered the *Panzerfaust* in vast numbers for the first time during the operation to clear Pomerania and Prussia in 1945, then again on their axis of advance across the Seelow Heights toward Berlin. This devastating weapon could be employed by anyone with little training. The Soviets could not afford to worry only about German soldiers with this weapon, as old men, women, and children were given rudimentary training and used the *Panzerfaust* with good effect. This prompted some Soviet units to adopt the use of adding manufactured 'bed spring' screens, hanging chain link, or even metal shields around tank turrets and hulls to impede the forming of the penetrating jet generated by the *Panzerfaust's* concave hollow shape charge. This practice (also undertaken by some U.S. tank units along the Western Front) was cheap and effective, but was never fully grasped by the Soviet or Western Allied armies. Despite the additional armor protection, there was no substitute for combined infantry and armor operations that offered the best protection for tanks and other armored vehicles while operating in urban centers—a tactical change in doctrine that only some Soviet tank units experimented with during their fighting in Berlin. The Soviet Army later lost a large number of tanks during their retaking of Budapest from revolutionaries in the 1950s that armed themselves with captured Soviet arms, including the RPG–2 first deployed to the Soviet Army in 1949. This suggests that the lessons of Berlin were even neglected by the Soviets in the immediate post-war years. It was the Israeli Defense Force that quickly adopted what became known as Explosive Reactive Armor (ERA) in the 1970s based on their experience in the 1973 Yom Kippur War. They realized their armor was especially vulnerable to missiles and shoulder-fired RPGs in general, and particularly while operating in urban enclaves. ERA was used for the first time in combat operations during the 1982 Israeli invasion of Lebanon that culminated with their armor driving into Beirut. Despite ERA's effectiveness, the Israelis still found it necessary to employ dismounted infantry to protect their vehicles by flushing out and killing the enemy infantry before they fired a RPG. The Soviet Army, which had the earliest experience in countering hand-held hollow shaped rocket projectiles, finally took notice. The Soviets adopted ERA in the 1980s where it was applied to their T–64BV main battle tanks deployed throughout Europe. U.S. Army doctrine, based on the Cold War scenario of long-range engagements outside of cities, never adopted add-on armor until it found itself locked in urban pacification operations in Iraq. The U.S. Army now finds itself in need to counter the effects of shoulder-fired RPGs, and improvised explosive devices (IEDs), employed through asymmetrical urban combat tactics. The application of steel cage bar protection for Stryker vehicles in 2005 was never an initial design consideration. These were added *after* their deployment into Iraq's urban environments. In addition, the U.S. Army is now fielding ERA on certain combat vehicles. Despite the added protection on combat vehicles, the experience of U.S. Forces has shown that combined infantry and armor operations in urban terrain offer the best survivability. These developments are often written about in news and military trade journals in the terms of the changing 'face of modern war'. This view is disingenuous. The experience of mechanized forces in modern asymmetrical urban combat is a legacy handed down sixty years earlier during the Soviet assault on Berlin.

I planned to explore parallels between the problems associated with the employment of mechanized forces in urban combat and analyze asymmetrical tactics utilized by the defenders to defeat these forces. During my research, however, I unearthed new and previously unused material that required me to forego the purely comparative military analysis and recast Berlin's fall as a major turning point with broad political-social implications for Europe—if not the world—and very specific military lessons completely ignored for almost half a century. To cast Berlin's fall as simply the end of Adolf Hitler's Nazi Germany and WWII in Europe is to grossly oversimplify the magnitude of the event.

I began to see the fall of Berlin not just as the key battle that ended the war in Europe, but a foundation for Stalin's Communist dominance of Eastern Europe, the Soviet Union's rise to world power, and its eventual collapse nearly 45 years later. Understanding the political implication of this battle is critical to understanding the operational nature of the Soviet assault on the Third Reich's capital. The Soviet *military* plan to assault Berlin was driven by Stalin's *political* desire to capture the city before the Western Allies, and claim victory over Nazi Germany. Stalin's goals resulted in the subsequent ruthless speed of combat and unrestrained destruction that characterized the subsequent Soviet operation.

Berlin's fall brought an end to Nazi domination of Europe, but it did not bring freedom for all Europeans. WWII in Europe did not neatly end in 1945 with the Soviet flag waving in the wind from the roof the burnt-out Reichstag. A prearranged demarcation line existed between the Western Allies and the Soviet Union that ran like a fault line through Berlin, Germany, and Europe. To the west of that fault line freedom was truly gained. There were hardships in the immediate postwar period to be sure, but for Europe's citizens, including Germans, which came under the Western Allied zones of occupation, self-determination was the rule. To the east, brutal postwar Communist oppression reigned for nearly fifty years, killing millions of East European's citizenry, denying millions more the very self-determination that so many had sacrificed their lives to secure in WWII. This suffering continued until the collapse of the Soviet Union began with a catalyst—the fall of the Berlin Wall.

Historians are now beginning to realize that the political-military events of 1945 cannot be compartmentalized and simply packaged as the closing act of WWII. The fall of Hitler's Nazi Germany and the rise of Stalin's Communist Russia are arguably inseparable events with far reaching consequences few historians have explored. Professor Norman M. Naimark wrote in his study *Fires of Hatred: Ethnic Cleansing in Twentieth-Century Europe* that "There is a clear and apparent relationship between, on the one hand, the rise to power of Nazism and its domination of the continent and, on the other, the ascendancy of Stalin and Stalinism."[3] Naimark's statement is meant to focus attention on the social and ethnic implications of postwar Europe's new regime, rather than how it came to dominate during that period. Historian Gregor Dallas, however, tackles the point directly in the introduction to his book *1945: The War That Never Ended*. Dallas presents the observation that "Very few works have examined that transition from war to peace [in 1945] in a systematic manner—the majority of books available to date end abruptly with the defeat of the Nazis. Or there is that other kind of book which, after a superficial survey of the events of the war, plunges into 'the Origins of the Cold War'. Yet the two topics are inseparable."[4] Norman Davies in his monumental study of the 1944 Warsaw Uprising titled *Rising '44* states unequivocally that "Since the Western Powers enjoyed a clear-cut victory over Germany in their part of Europe, Western readers invariably make a clear-cut mental distinction between the wartime and the post war years .... But in many countries of Central Europe, where one totalitarian occupation was succeeded by another, the significance of VE-Day is greatly reduced."[5] These three views, while politically oriented, are relevant to the military events that follow in this text. Only by understanding the postwar impact of Berlin's capture by the Soviets—a military act politically accepted by the Western Allies—does the city's fall in 1945 become more than a just a military afterthought, a foregone conclusion as some have argued, to the end of WWII. The Soviet assault on Berlin resonates as a decisive military engagement that marks a political-social watershed in Twentieth-Century European history.

Bloody Streets: The Soviet Assault on Berlin, April 1945 specifically uses the word *assault* and not *battle* to describe the Soviet military campaign for good reason. The Oxford English Dictionary defines *battle* as "a prolonged fight between armed forces." It defines *assault* as "a violent physical or verbal attack [or] ... rape." The Soviet offensive against Berlin was an act of unrestrained violence in the employment of firepower *and* behavior. While I believe the use of *assault* accurately reflects the nature of the fighting in Berlin, the word *battle* is not excluded when placing Berlin the wider context of urban military actions during and after WWII.

The book's Introduction establishes the significance of Berlin's fall within the context of both WWII and broader European history. Particular attention is given to the Soviet cost in taking Berlin and the nature of the campaign that was driven by both an inherently brutal military command structure and the political demand for a quick victory. Focus is placed on Zhukov's command performance in particular, as his decisions, perhaps more than any others, directly contributed to the horrendous losses in men and material suffered by the Red Army during the assault. The book is then divided into three parts: Prelude, Battle, and Aftermath. In Chapter 1 the relevance of Berlin's strategic importance is traced with a focus on why the Western Allies left Berlin to the Soviets and how the Third Reich's capital fit into both Adolf Hitler's and the *German High Command's* strategy during the last few months of the war. Chapter 2 provides an in-depth review of the defense plans for Berlin and relates how unprepared the city was for a protracted, let alone, brief battle. Chapter 3 reviews the German preparations to defend the Oder River line—as the first and last line of defense for Berlin; and the organizational state of the *Wehrmacht* in April 1945. There is a focus on the *LVI Panzer Korps*, as this unit represented the broad-cross section of combat formations deployed along the Eastern Front and it ultimately became the core of Berlin's military defense. Chapter 4 recounts the creation and expectations of the Soviet operational plan to capture Berlin. This chapter also relates the Soviet Army's organizational preparation for the final battle with Nazi Germany by reviewing the training and equipment of key formations. Chapter 5 details the day-to-day fighting for the Seelow Heights from 16–20 April. Again, the focus is on the *LVI Panzer Korps* sector of battle because this formation defended the main line of the Soviet assault toward Berlin. Chapter 6 takes the reader through the daily street fighting in Berlin that began along the eastern outskirts of the city starting on 21 April and ends with the finding of Hitler's charred remains on 3 May. As there are so many books written about the last days of Adolf Hitler and the inhabitants of the *Führerbunker*, little attention is given to their machinations in this book. I chose instead to focus the majority of research and writing effort on the operational and tactical aspects of the street fighting not readily known. Readers will see that Chapter 6 alone takes up more than half the book as much of the information and analysis found in this chapter is new. Great effort was spent to reconstruct aspects of the battle on period aerial imagery that allows readers to trace the fighting across the actual city streets of Berlin. This was a painstaking process that resulted in significantly new conclusions based on unit dispositions and movements not easily discerned by reading text alone. To help the reader make sense of the various combat actions that take place in and around Berlin, each day is broken into a series of subsections that generally correspond to the major commands and districts of the city. Chapter 7 offers a unique glimpse into the trauma and trials of the German defenders who elected not to capitulate with their commander on 2 May. The majority of the military forces that conducted the defense of Berlin didn't capitulate in the city. Instead they left the city in different breakouts with the goal of reaching the Western Allies along the Elbe. The reader is treated to various individual accounts about the breakout and their attempt to flee to the West—with several accounts taking place over the course of years. The accounts reveal what life in and around Berlin was like after the city's capture by the Soviets. Readers will immediately see why so many individuals didn't surrender to the Soviets but continued to find a way to the West. Chapter 8 assesses the military and political impact of the Soviet assault on Berlin. The chapter attempts to define the battle's many enduring legacies; as a watershed in both European political-social history, and post-war asymmetrical urban combat.

A note about style is in order. German place and street names used throughout the book are based on what was in existence in 1945. A reprint copy of the 1944 Pharus-Plan Berlin No. 54 was referenced as my primary guide for Berlin's street names. The term 'German' is used when referring to both German and non-German satellite forces or volunteers fighting for Nazi Germany. Likewise, I use 'Soviet' and 'Russian' interchangeably, though the reader should be clear that by the war's end a large portion of the Red Army was made up of non-Russian speaking conscripts drafted out of the eastern provinces of the Soviet Union. 'Panzer' is used to reference German armored vehicles and 'tank' is used to reference Russian armor. 'Pioneer' is also used to reference German combat engineers, while 'engineer' is used to reference their Soviet counterparts. *Italics* are used when referring to a German unit, either by direct name or inference. German spelling is used for unit designations and military ranks to clearly differentiate between their Soviet counterparts. I selected to reference *OKW* and *OKH* as simply the *German High Command*. I do this to avoid confusing the reader because in reality *OKW* and *OKH* maintained a special relationship that often blurred their traditional roles. By the time the Russians encircled Berlin, both staffs were combined into one command. I do, however, reference them individually in specific cases. The reader will also find that I tend to use *SS* and *Waffen-SS* interchangeably. I do this for two reasons. First, I agree with historian Bernd Wegner's concluding remarks in arguably the best academic study of the *Waffen-SS* written to date that " … the analysis of SS ideological model conceptions had made clear that the history of the *Waffen-SS* cannot be considered isolated from the history of the *SS* as a whole, which in turn is inseparable from the story of national socialism. The political and ideological closeness of the *Waffen-SS* to national socialism was the precondition of its very existence …."[6] In many interviews and some primary documents, the nomenclature for the *Waffen-SS* was simply *SS*. Second, *SS* and *Waffen-SS* forces tended to blend together in the street fighting. It is an important fact that the *SS* and *Waffen-SS* drew a very divisive line between their forces and commanders and those of the *Wehrmacht* that negatively impacted German operations in Berlin. One final note on nomenclature: *Heeresgruppe Weichsel* translates into *Army Group Vistula* and was the name of the primary German Army Group defending the Eastern Front at the time of the Soviet assault. Most Western readers are more familiar with the translation of Vistula than the original German *Weichsel*, named for the river running from the Baltic Sea through the Polish capital of Warsaw. Since the former translated name is used extensively throughout the book I chose to reference it in its better known and abbreviated form as *AGV* instead of *HGW*.

There are few primary documents regarding the Soviet assault on Berlin. The few available German primary sources are the War Diaries of *AGV* available in the U.S. National Archives, though they do not specifically discuss operations in Berlin. Russian sources are few and not easily obtained. The majority of source material for this book came from an unusual location—Athens, Ohio. Ohio University became the benefactor of all of writer-historian Cornelius Ryan's research that he and his virtual army of assistants compiled for all his historical works on WWII battles: *The Longest Day*, *A Bridge Too Far*, and *The Last Battle*. All of Ryan's research is now housed in the Cornelius Ryan Collection, Mahn Center, Alden Library, Ohio University, in Athens, Ohio. What I found regarding Berlin was a treasure trove of first person interviews from German and Soviet veterans never used in the publication of his book *The Last Battle*. The vast majority of them were first-person recollections recorded by Ryan's associates in the early-mid 1960s. The human mind does not easily reconstruct twenty-year old memories in precisely the right sequence or with uniform clarity. Many accounts often diverged, even when telling of the same event.[7] This required extensive cross-checking of sources to determine whether a specific event actually occurred and on what date. For purposes of consistency, an account's recorded event might have been shifted to a different day in order to place the reference correctly within the historical timeline of the ongoing fighting in Berlin. I did this based on the simple criteria of how many accounts corroborated a specific event, and what primary documents, if any, supported the accounts. Source citations for documents derived from the Ryan Collection are marked in the endnotes as (RC: box #/folder #). While this book took five long years to research and write, the analysis of these first person accounts took up almost three of those years alone. Anyone thinking they can reach back in time and take a person's recollection at face value, especially when concerning a veteran that experienced a psychologically jarring event like urban combat should be warned.

The Soviet assault on Berlin was complex to reconstruct in the detail depicted in this book. I only hope that I have done justice to the spirit of the material I accessed and provide new insights into a savage battle that turned the page on one brutal European tyranny to reveal another.

A. Stephan Hamilton
Virginia, U.S.A.
April, 2008

Notes to Preface

1   For the purposes of this book modern asymmetrical urban combat is defined as one force's operational intent to employ unconventional weapons, tactics, and terrain to negate another force's superior numbers, conventional warfare training, tactics, and technology during urban combat operations.

2   The Battle of Manila was a relatively set-piece battle between predominantly conventional infantry forces. The Japanese Naval Infantry had no intention of surrendering during their defense of the Philippines capital, and tended to set up fixed strongpoints they defended to the death versus employing a flexible defense along interior lines. In addition, there was a complete lack of mechanized forces within the city. The Warsaw Uprising of 1944 did set the tone for the evolution of modern asymmetrical urban combat operations employed in Berlin eight months later and offered a glimpse into technical innovations that would not be seen again for nearly half a century. The Germans in particular deployed small remote-control German Panzers known as 'Goliaths' armed with cameras for reconnaissance or explosives to destroy fixed sites—concepts that have come to the forefront of urban tactical thinking only in the last decade with the use of Unmanned Aerial Vehicles (UAVs). The Germans also employed specialized rocket-equipped Panzers designed to destroy fixed enemy strongpoints. Today, this would be accomplished with air-dropped laser-guided munitions. In fact, the Germans employed Panzers in the fighting in large numbers (though still relatively small) for the first time in direct urban combat operations, but quickly learned their folly. The Polish use of small unit asymmetrical tactics to conduct hit-and-run attacks while using the urban landscape to negate German advantages in firepower and mechanization proved effective beyond their belief. They also utilized home-made petrol bombs (a.k.a. Molotov Cocktails first used by the Finns and employed against Soviet tanks in the 1939-1940 Winter War) against German Panzers with deadly effect. Warsaw, however, was not Berlin in either size or scope of forces used. The majority of German forces that fought in the reduction of the Polish Home Army were in fact irregular *SS* forces themselves and not standard combat trained and tested soldiers. Overall numbers of forces engaged were in the end very small compared to Berlin. The Germans force consisted of 50,000 soldiers and a small number of armored vehicles, while the Polish Home Army boasted 15,000 men, boys, and women. It also should be noted that the Polish Home Army did not receive wide support from the civilian population of Warsaw. The civilian atrocities committed by the *SS* in the opening weeks of the fighting served to drive many into the ranks of the Home Army, however, most civilians left Warsaw either on their own or by German force. See Davies, pp., 254, 257, 259, 282, 288, and 419.

3   N. M. Naimark, *Fires of Hatred: Ethnic Cleansing in Twentieth-Century Europe*, pp. 11-12.

4   G. Dallas, *1945: The War that Never Ended*, p. xv.

5   N. Davies, *Rising '44: The Battle for Warsaw*, p. vii.

6   B. Wegner, *The Waffen-SS*, p. 360. Individual motivations for joining and fighting in the *Waffen-SS* were as complex and varied as its half-million members drawn from across Europe. Early in the war most members were ideologue volunteers, however by the war's end many were not as the *Waffen-SS* relied on conscription to fill out their diminishing ranks both from within Germany and without starting as early as 1943. This was especially true in and around Berlin in March–April 1945.

7   The interviews are quoted extensively throughout the book. They are unedited and may contain spelling and grammatical mistakes that are resident in the original documentation.

TERMS AND ABBREVIATIONS

AA—Anti-aircraft.
Abteilung / Abt.—Battalion / Btl.
AGC – Army Group Center.
AGV—Army Group Vistula.
Armee—Army.
Armeegruppe—Army Group.
Artillerie—Artillery.
AT—Anti-tank.
Aufklärung—Reconnaissance.
Bataillon / Btl.—Battalion.
Batterie—Battery.
BDA—Berlin Defense Area
Brigade—Brigade.
CBDA—Commander Berlin Defense Area.
CCS—Combined Chief of Staffs.
Chef des Generalstabes—The Chief of General Staff.
Division / Div.—Division.
Fallschirmjäger—Paratrooper.
Fliegerabwehrkanone or Flak—Anti-aircraft guns.
Freiwillige—Volunteer.
G1—Chief of Personnel in the US Army.
G2—Chief of Intelligence in the US Army.
G3—Chief of Plans in the US Army.
Gruppe—Group.
Guards—Honorific title given to Soviet infantry and tank formations.
Hauptkampflinie / HKL—Main defense line.
Heer—Army.
Heeresgruppe—Army Group.
Hilfswillige / Hiwis—Foreign Auxiliary Volunteers.
Hitlerjugend / HJ—Hitler Youth.
Ia—Chief of Operations in a German division.
Ic—Chief Intelligence in a German division.
IIa—Adjutant in a German division.
Infanterie—Infantry.
Kaserne – Barracks.
Kompanie—Company.

Korps—Corps.
Kriegsmarine—German Navy.
Luftwaffe—German Airforce.
Marine—German Naval Infantry.
Maschinengewehr—Machine-gun.
Nebelwerfer—Rocket Artillery.
Narodnyy Komissariat Vnutrennikh Del / NKVD—People's Commissariat for Internal Affairs.
Oberkommando der Wehrmacht / OKW—*Wehrmacht* High Command.
Oberkommando des Heeres / OKH—*Germany Army High Command.*
Panzerabwehrkanone / PAK—Anti-tank gun.
Panzer / Pz.—Armor or armored.
Panzerfaust—lit. 'Armored fist'. First hand-held rocket propelled grenade.
Panzergrenadier / PzGr.—Armored Infantry.
Panzerjäger / PzJg.—Tank hunter.
Pionier—German Army engineer.
Reichsarbeitsdienst / RAD—Reich Labor Force.
Regiment / Rgt.—Regiment.
Rifle—Soviet designation for regular infantry formations.
Schützenpanzerwagen or SPW—German armored halftrack personnel carrier.
Schwere—Heavy.
Sicherung—Security.
SMERt' Shpionam / SMERSH—Soviet Army counterintelligence service.
SS—*Schutzstaffel.*
Sturmabteilung / SA—Storm Trooper detachment of the Nazi Party.
Sturmgeschütz / Stug.—Assault Gun.
Volkssturm—lit. 'People's storm' infantry, the German home guard or militia.
Wach—Watch or guard.
Waffen-SS—Armed *Schutzstaffel.*
Wehrmacht—German Armed forces.

MAP SYMBOLS

Unit Symbol Abbreviations

23N - 23.SS.Rgt.Norge
24D - 24.SS.Rgt.Norge
AH - Anhalt
BK - Babick
CH - Charlemagne
DR - Danmark Regiment
Funk - Radio
FB - Fantasma Bataillon
FJ - Fallschirmjäger
FT - Flak Tower
Gal - Galician
GD - Grossdeutschland
GT - Guard Tank
HJ - Hitlerjugend
HvS - Herman von Salza
JS-2 - Joseph Stalin 2 Heavy Tank
KG - Kampgruppe
KT - King Tiger
LAT - Latvian
MB - Müncheberg
RAD - Reichsarbeitsdienst
R - Rifle
P - Panther
Pol - Polizei
Solar - SS Regt Solar
S - Shock
SP - Self-Propelled
SS - SS / Waffen-SS
Stug - Sturmgeschütz
T - Tiger
TH - Theimer
WR - Wachregiment

Unit Size
XXXX - Army
XXX - Corps
XX - Division
X - Brigade
III - Regiment
II - Battalion
I - Company

... - Platoon

.. - Section

. Squad

Unit Symbols

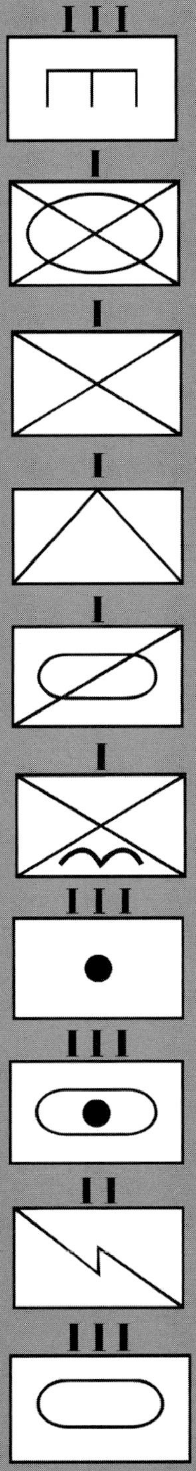

Engineer / Pioneer

Mechanized Infantry /
Panzergrenadiers

Rifle / Infantry

Anti-tank

Reconnaissance

Fallschirmjäger

Artillery

Self-Propelled Artillery /
Assault Gun Unit

Communication /
Signals

Tank / Panzer

Sample Unit Symbols

408 Artillery Brigade of
the LVI Pz. Korps

1.Bataillon of the
2.Pz.Gren.Regt. of the
Müncheberg
Pz.Division.

1.Company of Tiger I
panzers from the
Müncheberg
Pz.Division.

302 Regiment of the
303.Division

920.Assault Gun
Brigade

8th Guards Mechanized
Corps of the 1st Guards
Tank Army

236 Guards Regiment
of the 74th Guards
Division

xi

INTRODUCTION

Adolf Hitler's Nazi Germany and the underlying genocidal political-social strata that supported the regime had to be destroyed. Europe and the world became a better place for it, though a high price was paid. That price cannot be measured solely by the human and material cost of the war in Europe that ended in May 1945, but by the continued suffering of Eastern Europe under Soviet domination wrought by Joseph Stalin's postwar agenda. European deaths at the hands of Soviet or Eastern Bloc Communist forced labor and purges exceed tens of millions in the period from 1945–1989.[1] The war didn't end in 1945 with liberation for hundreds of millions of Europeans who looked to the Allies to bring them freedom. Europeans east of the demarcation line between the Western Allies and Soviet Union would not see *their* freedom for almost fifty more years once an equally vile ideology—known as Soviet Communism—collapsed in on itself. This is the paradox of the world's victory over Nazi Germany; that from the ashes of Hitler's tyranny, Stalin's arose from the bloody streets of Berlin to claim dominance over Eastern Europe.

The official name for the final Soviet offensive against Germany and Berlin is the 'Berlin Strategic Offensive Operation 16 April–8 May 1945'. This operation was one of the largest and costliest offensives undertaken by the Soviets during what their historians call the Great Patriotic War. Berlin's fall and the subsequent victory over Nazi Germany represent arguably the single greatest military achievement in the collective memory of Red Army veterans, the current Armed Forces of the Russian Federation, and Russian national history to this day. Berlin's importance to the Soviets during the war and its role in post-war dominance of Eastern Europe are clearly linked. This importance resonated from Stalin down to the lowest ranking member of the Red Army. The capture of Berlin took on the character of a divine right intrinsically linked to Soviet power and stature. The operational planning and execution of the final battle for Germany and Berlin was forged by Stalin's political ambitions, and his victory subsequently shaped post-war Soviet politics. This is important in understanding both the battle's importance and its relevance in Twentieth Century military history. It is no coincidence that the rise and fall of the Soviet Union as a political force in Europe and the world is bound historically to the capitulation of Nazi Berlin and the eventual removal of the Berlin Wall that brought reunification to that divided city.

Stalin wanted the Soviet Union to be the sole military power on mainland Europe once the German 'Fascist Beast' was defeated. Communist parties would replace the ageing monarchies and fledgling democracies in every country overrun by Russian armies. There would be no free elections, and no challenge to Soviet dominance.[2] Dr. Earl F. Ziemke, former U.S. Marine veteran of the Pacific Theatre of Operations, and military historian, wrote in his preface for *Stalingrad to Berlin: The German Defeat in the East* that "Save for the introduction of nuclear weapons, the Soviet victory over Germany was the most fateful development of World War II. Both wrought changes and raised problems that have constantly preoccupied the world in the more than twenty years since the war ended."[3] Ziemke wrote those words in 1966, yet they held true through the end of the century nearly 50 years after the Red Army ushered in the death of Adolf Hitler's Third Reich and the birth of the Cold War in the ruins of Nazi Germany's capital.

No single military victory brought greater dramatic political-social change in the Twentieth Century than the Soviet conquest of Berlin. The immediate result was the polarization of the world between Communism and Democracy. A secondary effect was the complete political, social, and cultural subjugation of Eastern Europe. WWII began with the German invasion of Poland that prompted a declaration of war by France and Great Britain September 1939. Despite the end of the war in Europe, freedom for the Poles did not come for nearly 45 more years. In arguably one of the seminal accounts of brutality that Communism unleashed on Russia after 1917, and the world after 1945, Martin Malia writes in the Foreword to *The Black Book of Communism* that:

> … the ways in which Eastern Europe was "liberated by the Red Army remain largely unknown in the West, where historians assimilate two very different kinds of "liberation," one leading to the restoration of democracies, the other paving the way for the advent of dictatorships. In Central and Eastern Europe, the Soviet system succeeded the Thousand Year Reich, and Witold Gombrowicz neatly captured the tragedy facing these peoples: "The end of the war did not bring liberation to the Poles. In the battlegrounds of Central Europe, it simply meant swapping one form of evil for another, Hitler's henchmen for Stalin's. While sycophants cheered and rejoiced at the 'emancipation of the Polish people from the feudal yoke,' the same lit cigarette was simply passed from hand to hand in Poland and continued to burn the skin of the people." (S. Courtois, et al., *The Black Book of Communism*, p.22.)

Polish anti-communist resistance flared up immediately in 1944 as many Poles loyal to the Polish Government in exile in Great Britain took up arms against the Soviets.[4] From 1944 through the mid-1960s armed partisan rebellion occurred throughout Poland. During that period an estimated 20,000 Poles would loose their lives, followed by another 50,000 deported to Siberia.[5] Unfortunately, Soviet killings and deportations didn't start or end with Poland.

The war for European freedom did not end with the expulsion of the *Wehrmacht* by the Red Army from Eastern Europe. What ensued was a series of long and often bloody struggles, many still unknown or not fully appreciated by Western historians who continually cast the Allied victory in terms of 'freedom' for all countries liberated from Nazi or Imperial Japanese oppression. In the Baltic States where independence was gained after World War I, armed rebellion against the Soviets began immediately after the withdrawal of German forces in 1944. The Lithuanian resistance boasted over 30,000 partisans that fought the Soviet occupation from 1944–1953.[6] The death toll in this particularly bloody guerilla conflict was over 100,000.[7] Armed and unarmed conflicts continued throughout Eastern Europe that included the 1953 East German workers rebellion in Berlin, the 1956 Hungarian uprising, and the 'Prague Spring' that caused the 1968 Warsaw Pact invasion of Czechoslovakia. At the center of the conflict was the ever-present tension between East and West, Communism and Democracy, in the divided city of Berlin.

The Soviets understood that the presence of a free West Berlin within the heart of their post-war conquests was a blight that required removal. No less than three major post-war crises arose from the ruins of a destroyed Berlin, each one with the potential to generate a Third World War between the members of the North Atlantic Treaty Organization (NATO) and the Warsaw Pact. There was the Berlin Airlift in 1948–1949 caused by the Soviet economic blockade of the city; Soviet Premier Nikata Kruchev's 1958 proposal that Berlin become a 'Free City,' thereby forcing the Western Powers out; and finally, the dramatic building of the Berlin Wall in August 1961.

Berlin was a prize that the Soviets viewed as their right to take after four bloody years of combat against the bulk of Nazi Germany's armed forces. Stalin knew the political power of 'inviting' the Western Allies into a conquered Berlin even though the pre-determined zones of post-war occupation were already agreed upon. German social historian Erich Kuby wrote in his book *The Russians and Berlin 1945* that Stalin "looked upon Berlin as a central power station, with his hands on the main switch."[8] The nearly 50 years of joint occupation of Berlin demonstrated how central this city was to the ebb and flow of post-war politics dominated by the Cold War. Berlin's status within the post-war world was correctly articulated by the one-time Mayor of Berlin and Chancellor of West Germany, Willy Brandt, who, writing in 1959, stated before the building of the Berlin Wall, that " … the fate of Berlin depends on the world['s] problems and to what extent Berlin is a problem of world policy. What will be decided here is more than only the life of Berlin and its inhabitants, even more than the development of Germany as a whole."[9] It is not surprising then, that the end of the Cold War, the collapse of the Soviet Union, and the self-liberation of Eastern Europe came after the fall of the Berlin Wall and unification of that divided city.

Multiple postwar crises centered on Berlin opened the debate as to whether the Western Allies should have advanced on Berlin instead of leaving the city to the Soviets during the final weeks of April 1945. Western authors consistently argued that the decision to leave Berlin to the Soviets was correct based on the assessment that the cost in U.S. soldiers' lives might be too high, the city fell within the Soviet postwar zone of occupation, and that it lost significance as a strategic target in the final weeks of the war.[10] The Soviets clearly understood the political necessity to conquer the Nazi capital before the Western Allies regardless of the cost. They also understood how important it was in their political control of Central and Eastern Europe. It is by no means a coincidence that European freedom rose like a tidal wave on the historic 9 November 1989 evening that brought the collapse of the Berlin Wall. This was soon followed by the reunification of Germany on 3 October 1990 after the signing of *The Treaty on the Final Settlement with Respect to Germany* in Moscow between The Federal Republic of Germany, The German Democratic Republic, United States, Great Britain, France, and the Soviet Union on 12 September 1990.

The Soviet political collapse began in early 1990 and continued through 1991 with the recognized independence of all Baltic States on 6 September, followed by Ukrainian independence on 1 December, and finally the official absolution of the Soviet Union and creation of the Commonwealth of Independent States on 8 December 1991. Free elections also began in earnest throughout the European countries once occupied by the Soviets. It is no coincidence that at the center for these dramatic events was Berlin—a city whose capture by the Soviets arguably was the cornerstone to Stalin's, and subsequently the Soviet Union's, postwar dominance of Eastern Europe.

The Soviet cost to take Berlin during the last weeks of WWII is significant and revealing. Until recently the true nature of Soviet losses was purposely hidden from public disclosure. Under the wartime generation that led the postwar reconstruction in the Soviet Union, few officers wanted to reveal wartime losses. Marshal Ivan Koniev in particular stated in 1964 that as long as he lived no one would ever know the nature of Soviet losses.[11] Not until the mid-1990s did two Russian Staff Officers finally publish a volume that consisted of previously classified material on Soviet combat losses. The book *Soviet Casualties and Combat Losses in the Twentieth Century* offers the western reader an authentic record of wartime Soviet losses for the first time.

In terms of manpower alone, the Berlin Strategic Offensive Operation represents the fourth largest operation in the Great Patriotic War. It can be argued that based on the small frontage where the offensive took place there was no previous Soviet operation with a higher force concentration per square kilometer undertaken from 1941–1945. Based on losses alone the Berlin Strategic Offensive Operation had one of the highest daily casualty rates of any offensive during the war. Only twice before did the daily loss rate of Soviet soldiers exceed that of Berlin, and that was during the defensive operations in Byelorussia and Western Ukraine that occurred in the first 18 days of July 1941. This meant that in nearly four years of combat, the Russians had not seen casualty rates as dramatic or disastrous since the opening phase of *Barbarossa*, the June 1941 German invasion of the Soviet Union.

Table 1.1   Total Soviet Losses in the Berlin Strategic Offensive Operation

	Numerical Strength	Irrecoverable Losses	Sick and Wounded	Total	Total Average Daily Losses	Total % of Force Lost
2nd Byelorussian Front	441,600	13,070	46,040	59,110	2,570	13
1st Byelorussian Front	908,500	37,610	141,880	179,490	7,804	20
1st Ukranian Front	550,900	27,580	86,245	113,825	4,949	21
Dnieper Flotilla	5,200	16	11	27	1	0.5
Baltic Fleet	—	15	8	23	1	—
Total	1,906,200	78,291	274,184	352,475	15,325	18
1st and 2nd Polish Armies	155,900	2,825	6,067	8,892	387	0.5

Source: *Soviet Casualties and Combat Losses in the Twentieth Century* p. 158. "Total % of Force Lost" column added by the author

The Soviets incurred losses of 17.5% of their total force. This represents the average loss of 15,000 soldiers per day or the equivalent of one WWII U.S. Infantry Division per day of operation. Marshall Georgi Zhukov's 1st Byelorussian Front bore the brunt of the assault through the Seelow Heights and into Berlin. His forces suffered nearly 20% casualties of the total force. Marshal Ivan Koniev, who not only fought his way into Berlin but also had to contend with the German *12.* and *9.Armees,* suffered 21% casualties. It must be stated that the Soviets calculated their loss rate based on the operation ending on 8 May.[12] As the majority of all combat was over by 2 May one can argue that the loss ratio was perhaps even higher than the opening battles of 1941. This argument places Berlin's capture at the top of the list of the Soviet's most costly battles of WWII. Soviet equipment losses were also monumental.

Table 1.2   Comparison of Soviet Arms Losses between Berlin and Kursk Operations

	Berlin Operation 16 April–8 May (23 days)	Kursk 5–23 July (19 days)
Small Arms	215,900 (9,400 per day)	70,800 (3,700 per day)
Tanks and Self-Propelled Guns	1,997 (87 per day)	1,614 (85 per day)
Guns and Mortars	2,108 (92 per day)	3,929 (207 per day)
Aircraft	917 (40 per day)	459 (24 per day)

Source: *Soviet Casualties and Combat Losses in the Twentieth Century* p. 262–263.

The Berlin Strategic Offensive Operation exceeded even the battle of Kursk in terms of losses across almost all categories of equipment. This too is revealing as Kursk is generally considered the largest mechanized battle in history. Comparing the losses of these two titanic Eastern Front engagements is telling. In all categories except 'Guns and Mortars,' the Berlin Strategic Offensive Operation resulted in significantly higher losses. Again, considering that the majority of the fighting for Berlin was over by 2 May the daily loss rate in 'Tanks and Self-Propelled Guns,' as well as 'Aircraft' was arguably closer to 124 and 57 per day respectively. This equates to approximately 69% higher losses in 'Tanks and Assault Guns,' and 42% higher losses in 'Aircraft' during the Berlin operation than experienced at Kursk. What is striking about the figures is that in 1945 the Soviets were not up against a fully-equipped, well-trained, or even well-supplied enemy like they faced in 1943. The *Wehrmacht* opposing the Soviets in 1945 was largely a composite of patchwork units, men, and equipment that simply was not the same caliber as their 1943 counterparts due to the years of attrition. These drawbacks aside, the *Wehrmacht* employed their meager resources effectively during the opening stages of the assault. In addition, the complex terrain of the Oderbruch and Seelow Heights, and the sprawling urban complex of Berlin contributed significantly to the defense. Yet, these reasons are not sufficient to justify why a modern, numerically superior force suffered such heavy losses in men and equipment. Analysis reveals that the key contributing factors to Soviet losses were a lack of operational planning and intelligence preparation of the battlefield, no coordination between the infantry and armor, unsound military decisions in the face of tactical adversity, and a brutal, if not caustic disregard for the loss of the lives of Soviet soldiers. Many of these reasons fall on Zhukov, the chief architect of the Soviet operational plan to capture Berlin.

Zhukov's assault on Berlin was arguably not his best operational performance as a military commander during the war. His operational plan proved unsound, inflexible, and improperly executed. His disregard for his own casualties and inability to apply even the rudimentary aspects of the art of war to counter adversity on the battlefield clearly demonstrated his own brutal nature and the inflexibility of the Soviet Army. In one of the least known, if not understood aspects of the battle, Zhukov ordered his own forces into direct conflict with Koniev's forces driving into Berlin from the south. Instead of coordinating forces with his rival, Zhukov's decision caused significant incidents of Soviet fratricide and undoubtedly led to Zhukov's postwar isolation by both Koniev and his subordinate commander Marshall Vasili Chuikov. Both Koniev and Chuikov rose to prominence within the post-war Soviet hierarchy as Zhukov was relegated to backwater commands.

Zhukov was a product of a brutal and inflexible command system. The nature of this brutality is not fully grasped by the average student of military history unfamiliar with the national characteristics of the Soviet Army during WWII. It is important that Western standards of military application are not applied when rationalizing decisions made by Zhukov that led to the significant losses by the Red Army during their operation to take Berlin.

Shortly after the war Supreme Allied Commander General Dwight D. Eisenhower, met with Zhukov and discussed a variety of military topics to include tactics. The discussion revealed to Eisenhower the clear difference between Zhukov and the Soviet Army's view of their soldiers and tactical practices and those practiced by the U.S. Army. Eisenhower wrote:

> Highly illuminating to me was [Zhukov's] description of the Russian method of attacking through mine fields. The German mine fields, covered by defensive fire, were tactical obstacles that caused us many casualties and delays. It was always a laborious business to break through them, even though our technicians invented every conceivable kind of mechanical appliance to destroy mines safely. Marshal Zhukov gave me a matter-of-fact statement of his practice, which was, roughly, "There are two kinds of mines; one is the personnel mine and the other is the vehicular mine. When we come to a minefield our infantry attacks exactly as if it were not there. The losses we get from personnel mines we consider only equal to those we would have gotten from machine guns and artillery if the Germans had chosen to defend that particular area with strong bodies of troops instead of with mine fields."

This Soviet approach to a tactical challenge clearly surprised Eisenhower who knew this type of tactic would never be tolerated by the U.S. Soldier or the American public. There was no tactical subtlety in Soviet operations; no concern regarding the human cost of war. Eisenhower also noted a key difference in the application of morale between the U.S. and Soviets:

> Americans assess the cost of war in terms of human lives, the Russians in the overall drain on the nation. The Russians clearly understood the value of morale, but for its development and maintenance they apparently depended upon overall success and upon patriotism, possibly fanaticism.

>   As far as I could see, Zhukov had given little concern to methods that we considered important to the mainte-
> nance of morale among American troops: systematic rotation of units, facilities for recreation, short leaves and
> furloughs, and, above all, the development of techniques to avoid exposure of men to unnecessary battlefield risks, all
> of which, although common practices in our Army, seemed to be largely unknown in his.[13]

This comparison illustrates clearly how Zhukov's command decisions, while a product of an overall military organization that by Western standards was brutal, was a key contributor to the losses incurred by his forces.

Against this backdrop the cost of Zhukov's military decisions are measured. His key decisions that contributed to increased Soviet losses are broken down as follows:

>   Zhukov ignored all intelligence on German positions, troop strength, and defensive plans. He assumed that his
> offensive would simply be a repeat of the wildly successful Vistula-Oder Operation launched in January 1945.

>   His operational concept was too aggressive in terms of timelines and ignored the realities of terrain.

>   Zhukov kept a strict adherence to Soviet offensive doctrine and did not alter any aspect of the standard plan. This
> cued the Germans off to the start of the Soviet offensive and allowed them to counter Zhukov's opening attack.

>   Soviet pre-battle training lacked coordination between independent Soviet infantry and tank formations.

>   Zhukov prematurely ordered the 1st Guards and 2nd Guards Tank Armies into the front lines during the opening
> the battle for the Seelow Heights before his infantry took the difficult terrain as originally planned, and without any
> coordination with his front line armies already engaged in combat. The resulting battlefield chaos caused significant
> confusion and losses.

>   When Zhukov learned that his rival Koniev entered Berlin on his own drive to reach the Reichstag, he ordered
> Chuikov to reposition his forces across Koniev's front, and across the inter-front boundary approved by Stavka. This
> order was done without Koniev's coordination and served to generate significant instances of fratricide among Soviet
> troops.

Berlin's importance to the Soviets, Stalin's desire for a rapid capture of Berlin, and Zhukov's brutal command nature conspired to forge an unsound military operation that increased Soviet losses. Overall Soviet success in the Berlin Strategic Offensive Operation was given significant aide by the actions of Hitler and the *German High Command*.

Hitler practiced a strategy of strategic diffusion during the final months of the war. He created operational situations that often ran contrary to reality and moved his remaining divisions around to support the defense of unlikely military places. *Wehrmacht* units were scattered in Northern Italy, the Balkans, Norway, and Kurland that could have been recalled, as some were, to better defend Central Germany and Berlin. When Germany surrendered on 12 May, the vast majority of German combat divisions surrendered outside the pre-war boundaries of Germany. There were only 15 divisions in Central Germany while over 400 surrendered in all other parts of Europe.[14] This reveals the extent that Hitler was either in denial or simply despondent with the overall strategic situation of Germany and Berlin during the first four months of 1945.

There was no master plan to defend Berlin. Defense preparations for Berlin began far too late to make a decisive difference in the coming assault, but the effects of what little defense planning was done contributed to significant Soviet casualties. The *German High Command*, not Hitler, stepped in after the start of the Soviet offensive and orchestrated what was supposed to be a final decisive battle for the Third Reich's capital. Hitler went along with the plan fueled by the idea that he might gain some political victory by defeating Zhukov outside Berlin. The last minute plan to defend Berlin highlighted the need to have troops to defend the city while the *9.* and particularly the *12. Armees* outside Berlin were readied to launch their attacks into Zhukov's southern flank. The forces that defended Berlin were designated by chance and not by plan. The *LVI Panzer Korps* was *en route* south to the *9.Armee* lines when through a series of unlinked events it now became the defender of Berlin. Its inclusion in the battle served to significantly increase the city's defense and illustrates how a small defending force, operating primarily asymmetrically in a large urban environment, can exact a heavy toll on a large attacking mechanized force. Indeed, if Berlin was properly reinforced and defended then Zhukov's offensive might have faltered along the city's outer defensive zone drawing the Western Allies over the demarcation line running along the Elbe River into the Soviet Occupation Zone to assist Stalin's armies.

What makes Hitler's strategic thinking so devoid of reality was the fact that his forces captured the Allied strategic plan for Germany known as 'Eclipse.' This plan clearly showed the future division of Germany and the main political fault line running down the length of the Elbe River. Chief of *OKW* Operations Heinz Guderian and the newly appointed commander of *Armeegruppe Vistula (AGV) Generaloberst* Gotthard Heinrici understood that the war was lost and what 'Eclipse' really meant for Germany.[15] There was only one real strategic option left in their minds—save Eastern Germany from the Soviet onslaught and prevent Stalin from taking Berlin. The experiences of German refugees and soldiers flooding west over the Oder River brought with them a sense of utter fear and dread that that reinforced the resolve of these two men to take action on their own. Guderian's concept, which Heinrici translated into an operational plan, was simple. Defend the Oder River line long enough to force the Western Allies over the Elbe River to assist the Soviets, forcing the Western Allies to take the remaining territory of Eastern Germany and Berlin the process. In fact, if the defense of the Oder River failed then the orders were clear: retreat west around Berlin. Berlin would then be declared an open city in order to prevent giving the Soviets any reason to attack and destroy Germany's historic capital. Heinrici ensured all his subordinates knew his intent regarding Berlin. The fact that Berlin was defended at all was the product of an act of chance and not design.

The ferocity of fighting in Berlin is unmatched in Twentieth Century military history. The reason is that the war on the Eastern Front was far more than a politically motivated conflict, it was a race war.[16] Prisoners were rarely taken by either side during the assault. The Germans in particular were in no position to keep Russian prisoners in or around Berlin. Once the interrogation of a Soviet soldier was over they were simply shot. Both German and Russian forces demonstrated a disregard for cultural or commercial centers in the city as unrestrained firepower was exercised. The Russians in particular were well stocked with ammunition and employed whole train loads in blasting known and suspected German positions into oblivion. The Soviets boasted that while the Western Allies dropped 45,000 tons of

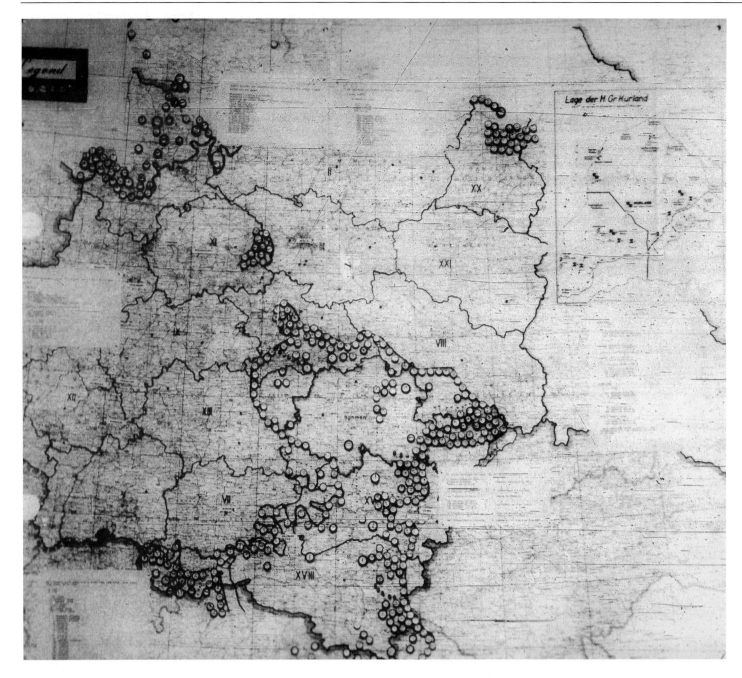

This *OKW* map depicts the location of all German divisions that surrendered on 12 May, 1945. Note the complete lack of divisions within the prewar German borders except for the *12.* and *9.Armees* west of Berlin and the remaining divisions under Dönitz's command to the northwest around Kiel. The majority of German divisions were deployed outside of Germany's prewar borders through the end of the war. Courtesy of US National Archives.

bombs on Berlin during the war, the Soviets fired 40,000 tons of artillery shells into the city in two weeks. Soviet aircraft ranged across the city attacking targets almost at will. Blanket devastation occurred across huge residential sections. The indiscriminate firing of artillery shells, the resulting collapsed buildings, and raging fires they caused was an ever-present part of the daily environment that both German and Russian soldiers operated.

The brutal retribution by many Soviet soldiers against German women was another unique facet of the daily operational environment in Berlin. As Professor Norman Naimark wrote in his landmark study *The Russians and Germany: A History of the Soviet Zone of Occupation, 1945–1949* the number of reports available points to systematic violence against Berlin's women that can't easily be dismissed as random acts of rogue soldiers. He states that "Even as they entered bunkers and cellars where Germans hid from the fierce fighting, Soviet soldiers brandished weapons and raped women in the presence of their children and men."[17] Rape came up time-and-time again German soldier's accounts both as a function of the environment that they found themselves fighting in, and as a motivational factor to continue fighting, or end fighting early. Naimark concludes that "the taking of Berlin was accompanied by an unrestrained explosion of sexual violence by Soviet soldiers."[18] This sexual violence continued for weeks. Soviet soldiers, often with the knowledge and participation of their officers, went out into residential districts and apartment complexes to conduct nightly gang rapes, in many cases in front of the woman's male relatives. Girls aged 10 to 75 years were violated repeatedly. The intent of describing the brutal acts of the Soviet Army in Berlin is not to alleviate or diminish the crimes committed by the *SS*, *Wehrmacht*, or the Nazi Government. It is intended to convey to the reader that Berlin's conquest was more than a military battle; it was an act of brutal vengeance that clearly impacted operations.

Stalin—the conqueror of Berlin—being greeted by worshipping Soviet soldiers at a Berlin airport. From the movie *Fall of Berlin*.

The civilian population of Berlin often participated in the combat, and sometimes against their German defenders. Amidst the military violence that occurred in the streets of Berlin, some civilians rose up against the teetering Nazi political and military structures. Communist elements of Berlin, repressed since the Nazi rise to power, now armed themselves and conducted either overt or covert operations against German soldiers. German defenders often had to deal with sniper attacks from German civilians and outright collaboration with Soviet forces. These efforts brought Berlin's Communists no leniency from the attacking Soviet soldiers who viewed all Germans as 'Hitlerites' and treated them accordingly.[19] There was little sympathy for the German population caught in the maelstrom. No considerations were made for the protection of civilian life by either side. The pace of Soviet operations precluded such considerations. Stalin wanted Berlin to fall quickly—and at any price.

In 1949 Russian director Mikhail Chiaureli released the film *The Fall of Berlin*.[20] This movie is a masterpiece of postwar Soviet propaganda that spared no expense in production. It also provides a window into how Stalin wanted the final climatic battle to be viewed. During the course of the movie, Zhukov's forces are shown stalled along the Seelow Heights. Zhukov tries to justify this by telling Stalin that according to a captured German enlisted soldier, Hitler had given orders to his German forces to hold the line against the Soviets until the Western Allies arrived. Stalin dismisses Zhukov's excuse as enemy propaganda and tells him that there is only one course—'Take Berlin!' It is Stalin, who upon completing his terse conversation with Zhukov, that orders Rokossovskii to launch his offensive across the and follows that with a phone call to Koniev, telling him to turn his forces toward Berlin as Zhukov required assistance. At the end of the movie a Soviet military transport plane delivers an impeccably dressed Joseph Stalin formal military uniform into the recently conquered Berlin. Stalin is immediately surrounded by cheering Russian soldiers hailing him as a hero of the Soviet Union. He is even greeted by released British and American prisoners-of-war waving their own national flags in joyous celebration of their liberation by Soviet forces. After striding triumphantly down the ranks of Red Army soldiers, Stalin reaches his senior military commanders. He then takes turns thanking each of them—Chuikov, Koniev, and Rokossovskii—for delivering Berlin to the Soviet people. Zhukov is unceremoniously and quietly sidelined from the film's culminating celebration of Berlin's fall. There is only the image of Stalin; as commander, conqueror, liberator, and statesman, forever intertwined with *his*—and by extension the *Soviet Union's*—conquest of Berlin.

Notes to Introduction

1   R. J. Rummel, *Lethal Politics: Soviet Genocide and Mass Murder Since 1917*, pp. 201, 221.
2   G. MacDonogh, *After the Reich: The Brutal History of the Allied Occupation*, pp. 8-9.
3   E. Ziemke, *Stalingrad to Berlin: The German Defeat in the East*, p. v.
4   T. Piotrowski, *Poland's Holocaust*, pp.88-90. Stalin ordered that the Red Army engage and destroy the Polish Home Army, or resistance movement, in combat once Poland was entered as early as 1943.
5   Rummel, pp. 193-194.
6   *War after War: Armed Anti-Soviet Resistance in Lithuania in 1944-1953*, p. 3.
7   Rummel, p. 193.
8   E. Kuby, *The Russians and Berlin 1945*, p. 7.
9   Otto M. von der Gablentz (ed. on behalf of the Research Institute of the German Council on Foreign Relations), *Documents on the Status of Berlin 1944-1959*, R. Oldenbourg Verlag, Munich, 1959, p. 5.
10 S. Ambrose, *Eisenhower and Berlin, 1945: The Decision to Halt at the Elbe*, pp. 67,

70, and 98. Ambrose's conclusions about Soviet intentions on Berlin are, in the opinion of this author, completely wrong and intended solely to support Eisenhower's decision not to attempt a drive on Berlin.
11 G.F. Krivosheev ed., *Soviet Casualties and Combat Losses in the Twentieth Century*, p. vii.
12 8 May is the date that unconditional surrender of the German military was symbolically signed in Berlin at the Soviet's request.
13 D.D. Eisenhower, *Crusade in Europe: A Personal Account of World War II*, pp. 467-468.
14 RG 242, T-77/1432, 424.
15 *Heeresgruppe Weichsel* was named after the river that runs from the Baltic through the center of Poland. This is where the German front line ran from the summer of 1944 until the Soviet Operation known as the 'Vistula-Oder Operation' that commenced in January 1945. 'Weichsel' translated from the German means 'Vistula', which is the more common name for this German Army Group. Due

to the fact that the translated name is used so widely in secondary western texts, the translated name is utilized throughout this book.
16 Geoffrey P. Megargee, *War of Annihilation: Combat and Genocide on the Eastern Front, 1941*, pp. 33-41 and Omer Bartov's, *Hitler's Army: Soldiers, Nazis, and War in the Third Reich*, pp. 152-164. The role that race played on the Eastern Front is beyond the scope of this book. It might be argued that terms such as "total war," "war of annihilation," or "ideological war," might be more appropriate. In any case the reader should understand that the Nazi invasion of the Soviet Union and subsequent retribution by the Soviets was the product of a brutal war conceived and executed by Adolf Hitler, but ultimately won by Joseph Stalin.
17 N.M. Naimark, *The Russians in Germany: A History of the Soviet Zone of Occupation, 1945-1949*, p. 80.
18 Ibid, p. 79.
19 Hastings, Max, *Armageddon: The Battle for Germany 1944-45*, pp. 479-480. M. Chiaureli, *The Fall of Berlin*.

PART I: PRELUDE

1

OBJECTIVE BERLIN

A natural objective beyond the Ruhr was Berlin. It was politically and psychologically important as the symbol of remaining German power. I decided, however, that it was not the logical or the most desirable objective for the forces of the Western Allies.

Supreme Commander Allied Expeditionary Forces, Dwight D. Eisenhower

Who will take Berlin, us or the Western Allies?

Generalissimo Joseph Stalin to Marshalls of the Soviet Union Georgi K. Zhukov and Ivan S. Koniev

Who should succeed to be in possession of Berlin? Western powers or Stalin? For every German it was, insofar as one could determine decided: No-one wished to see the Russians as master of Berlin.

Generaloberst **Gotthard Heinrici, Commander of** *Army Group Vistula*

Berlin's status as a military and political objective shaped the strategic plans of the Allies and their German counterparts during the last months of the war. These strategic plans shaped the nature and course of the final battle for the Third Reich's capital, Eastern Germany and Central Europe. On the one hand, the continued debate between senior U.S. and British officials over the importance of taking Berlin before the Soviets fueled Generalissimo Joseph Stalin's mistrust, especially when the Western Allies declared they had no intention to take the city. Stalin's view of Berlin's importance as a political cornerstone to his post-war plans, and general mistrust of Western Allied intentions, generated what became a poorly planned and executed operation that pitted the two senior Soviet military commanders, Marshalls of the Soviet Union Georgi K. Zhukov and Ivan S. Koniev against each other in a dangerous contest. Their rivalry, masterfully managed by Stalin, caused significant instances of fratricide between Soviet forces on the streets of Berlin.

On the German side, there was never any formal plan to defend Berlin or eastern Germany. Hitler's strategic procrastination led to an unrealistic dispersal of the majority of German combat formations away from the main battlefields of western and eastern Germany. Hitler's strategic ineptness caused several of his senior generals to devise their own final strategy to save Berlin and eastern Germany without his knowledge. In the end, when the final battle for Berlin reached its zenith, the *German High Command*, not Hitler, decided on a bold, yet unworkable strategy to defeat the Soviets outside the city in the hope of creating a rift between the Western Allies and the Soviets that might still save Hitler and the National Socialist State. This final strategy benefited from the accidental incorporation of the *LVI Panzer Korps* into the defense of the city, which prolonged the final assault. Potential conflict between the Western Allies and the Soviets ran like an undercurrent throughout the final drama played out over Berlin. It was, in the end, the Soviets that stormed the capital of Nazi Germany at a significant cost as the Western Allies sat on the banks of the Elbe River and waited for the battle's outcome to be decided. The assault on Berlin ushered in the death of Adolf Hitler and the elimination of the Nazi hierarchy, leading to a rapid political collapse of Germany. This chapter outlines these broad themes and sets the context necessary to understand how they affected the final battle for Berlin.

Stalin met with his two senior Front Commanders, Zhukov and Koniev on 1 April 1945 in Moscow to answer one of the most important questions posed to either general since the German invasion of the Soviet Union. Chief of Main Operational Administration S.M. Shtemenko read a brief that began " … the Anglo-American command was preparing an operation to capture Berlin, setting themselves the task to capture it before the Soviet Army could do so." After Shtemenko's brief was complete, Stalin turned to Zhukov and Koniev and asked "So, who will take Berlin, we or the Allies?" [1]

When Stalin asked this question to his two senior military commanders, the Soviet Army was located on the banks of the Oder River 50 kilometers from Berlin, while the Western Allies completed their crossing of the Rhine River and started operations to encircle the Ruhr some 500 kilometers to the west. What prompted Stalin's question to his commanders was an unprecedented and controversial communiqué from the Commander and Chief Allied Expeditionary Forces General Dwight D. Eisenhower directly to Stalin on 28 March.[2] In his communiqué, Eisenhower outlined his strategy for the final phase in the conquest of Germany. Eisenhower stated that after he closed the Ruhr pocket his next goal was to drive his forces on the axis Erfurt-Leipzig-Dresden in order to join forces with the Soviets and break any further German military resistance. There was no mention of Berlin and Eisenhower's concept of operations took his forces away from the Nazi capital.[3] Instead of being taken at face value as a means of coordinating the final military effort between the Western Allies and the Soviet Union, Eisenhower's communiqué fueled the already inherent mistrust of Stalin who could not believe the Western Allies would not want to drive toward Berlin—the focal point of seven years of fighting in Europe.

Berlin was never an immediate object of strategic planning among the Western Allies during the war. There was no mention of it during planning of Operation Overlord or during the breakout of Normandy. The first mention of Berlin as a potential objective came during the crossing of the Rhine River.[4] While not an immediate objective, Berlin did factor into the occupation plans of the Allies. The first mention of Berlin and zones of occupation was in a secret protocol issued on 12 September 1944. The protocol states "1. Germany, within her frontiers as they were on the 31st December 1937, will, for the purposes of occupation, be divided into three zones, one of

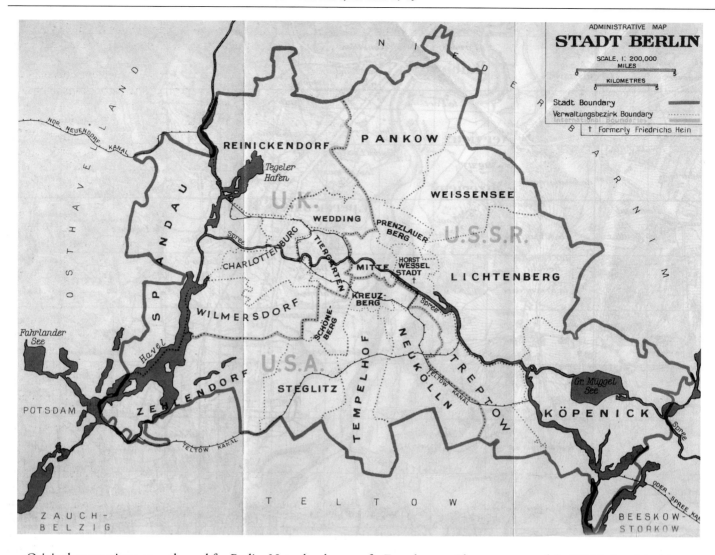

Original occupation zones planned for Berlin. Note the absence of a French zone. Photo courtesy of the US National Archives.

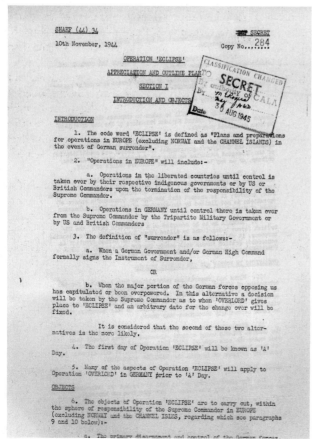

Operation 'Eclipse' dated 10 November 1944. This document was captured by the Germans during *Wacht am Rhein* in January 1945 and was known to Hitler and the *German High Command* who did very little with this strategic intelligence coup until it was too late. Photo courtesy of the US National Archives.

which will be allotted to each of the three Powers, and a special Berlin area, which will be under joint occupation by the three Powers."[5] This document developed into the Top Secret 'Eclipse' plan by November 1944 and was further ratified during the Yalta Conference that took place in February 1945.[6]

'Eclipse' was the code word for the specific zones of occupation that came into effect once Nazi Germany collapsed. This plan was issued to Allied Headquarters in November 1944. The document suggested that an internal overthrow of the Nazi Government was unlikely and that ultimate collapse would not occur until Germany suffered additional military defeats. The document went on to suggest that "if this defeat occurred in the WEST, the Eastern front would not necessarily collapse until its position became untenable owing to *our* [author's emphasis] advance; on the other hand a major defeat on the Eastern front would probably cause a rapid collapse of the WEST."[7] This assessment demonstrated the correctness of Western Allied thinking that the Nazi leadership, and in particular the *Wehrmacht*, would continue to resist the Soviets until a rapid defeat along the Eastern Front occurred either through a future Soviet offensive or a rapid advance of the Western Allies into the rear area of German forces fighting in the east. Only after a collapse of Nazi Germany was assured did 'Eclipse' factor in Berlin. It stated that the purpose to occupy Berlin was "to gain control over the enemy capital and foremost administrative and transportation center, to secure important intelligence centers and installations, and to display our armed strength."[8] The Western Allied halt along the Elbe River in the beginning of April 1945 contradicted the spirit of 'Eclipse's' strategic assessment. Instead of launching an attack across the Elbe toward Berlin to foster a quick military collapse of the Eastern Front and quickly end the war, the Western Allies choose to halt their advance allowing a bloody and costly drama to unfold in and around the Nazi capital.

Eisenhower understood that pressure might be placed on him to capture Berlin and he gave the idea serious thought during the month of March. As he began his planning he decided to keep the operational details secret and not share them with any of his subordinate commanders including Field Marshall Bernard Montgomery or even the Combined Chiefs of Staff (CCS).[9] Eisenhower was briefed by his Chief of Plans (G–3) to be cautious when it came to the *Wehrmacht*, especially their resilience in battle. This caution was based on the surprise Ardennes offensive launched by the Germans known as *Wacht am Rhein* December 1944 after it was thought by the Western Allies that the *Wehrmacht* had no operational reserves and were all but defeated. On the question of Berlin itself, Ike was also cautioned by General Omar Bradley that the amount of casualties to take Berlin would be approximately 100,000.[10] Later Ike discussed this with Major General Kenneth Strong, his Chief of Intelligence (G–2), who stated "if I were to seize Berlin at a very great cost of lives and a day or two later we were ordered to withdraw with the postwar occupation plan [Eclipse] what would the troops think of it and what would the American people think?" (Reprinted by permission of Sll/Sterling Lord Literistic Inc. Copyright 1978 by James Gavin.)[11] Even more important, Ike was warned that if he chose to take Berlin there was a very real threat of fighting breaking out in the streets of the Nazi capital between the Western Allies and the Soviet Union at the last moment. It was Strong's opinion that open conflict would ensue between the two sides if Berlin was taken by the U.S.[12] On top of this discussion was the growing concern of a new threat–the National Redoubt.

The National Redoubt was a belief that the remaining Nazi leadership and hand-picked divisions of the *Wehrmacht* and *Waffen-SS* would retreat to a mountain fortress along the Alps in southern Germany to draw out the war as long as possible. In the post-war investigation of the legitimacy of the National Redoubt, interrogated Germans cited that the idea for a defensive plan was driven not by any thinking on the part of Hitler or Nazi leadership, but by an Allied memorandum that fell into the hands of German military officials through the Swiss legation.[13] The Germans dubbed this 'Redoubt Psychosis' and attempted to draft plans to exploit this idea both as a real defensive position and as a strategic bluff in order to potentially break the Allied desire for unconditional surrender. In either case, Hitler gave no firm decision on how to exploit the 'Redoubt Psychosis' and nothing came of it from the German side. Without much effort on the part of Germans, the Western Allies convinced themselves that southern Germany was the new strategic priority.

A G–2 study on the National Redoubt from the Headquarters of the U.S. 7th Army reached Eisenhower on 25 March 1945 and highlighted the prevailing concern over what might happen. The five page report detailed troop and supply movements spotted in southern Germany, and the disposition of German troops in Italy, the Balkans and Czechoslovakia as factors contributing to the fear that something was being prepared. The report cites among other things the continued deployment of the *6.SS Panzer Armee* in the area of Vienna despite the loss of significant territory in Silesia and East Prussia as further justification that a last stand was being prepared in the south.[14]

The reality was quite different. When General Kurt Dietmar, the German High Command radio spokesman, surrendered to the U.S. 9th Army across the Elbe at the end of April, he told his U.S. captors that "the Redoubt is a myth." He prophetically explained that "Hitler is still in Berlin. But when Berlin will fall an[sic], and Hitler will either be killed or will commit suicide. Then the war will end in a few days."[15] While Dietmar's comments proved to be true, four weeks earlier anything seemed possible to U.S. Army Intelligence officers assessing the possibilities of a regime they predicted would collapse in the summer of 1944 only to be brutally surprised by an undetected German winter offensive in the Ardennes. With the specter of significant Allied losses and the National Redoubt at the forefront of his mind, Eisenhower made a decision to leave Berlin to the Soviets.

The disclosure of Eisenhower's operational plan to Stalin was kept secret for fear of upsetting Prime Minister Winston Churchill and Montgomery who he knew desired to capture Berlin before the Soviets. This message sparked a controversy lasting years after the end of WWII.[16] While Eisenhower waited for a reply from Stalin, Churchill raised concerns over Eisenhower's communiqué for two reasons: he was overstepping his authority by intervening in decisions of political nature; and that Berlin's importance as a prestige target was being ignored. This prompted Eisenhower to issue a 'For Your Eyes Only' cable to CCS General George C. Marshall stating that "Berlin as a strategic area is discredited as it is now largely disrupted .... It is so near to the Russian Front that once they start moving again, they will reach it in a matter of days."[17] Eisenhower had no intention of being pressured into changing his mind by Churchill.

Eisenhower received Stalin's reply confirming that the future Soviet offensive would be launched mid-May in the direction of Leipzig as per his suggestion and that Berlin was simply not a worthwhile target anymore.[18] Stalin's reply was purposely deceptive because he feared the Western Allies were planning their own offensive against Berlin an attempt to capture the city before the Soviets. Stalin's concern regarding the possibility of a Western Allied capture of Berlin was based in part on the existence of 'Operation Talisman'. 'Talisman' was the Allied plan to conduct an airborne drop on Berlin as part of 'Eclipse'.[19] The airborne drop on Berlin was a plan kept alive beyond all necessity in order to pacify Churchill and the British according to Commanding General 82nd U.S. Airborne Division James Gavin, who would have led this operation if ever carried out.[20]

Fueled by Stalin's desire to take Berlin first, his military commanders and soldiers viewed the capture of Berlin as a divine right. In his post-war memoir Koniev is quite clear on this point: " ... Berlin was for us the object of such an ardent desire that everyone experienced, from soldier to general, to see this Fascist Berlin with their own eyes, to capture it by the force of their arms."[21] This 'desire' to capture Berlin manifested itself militarily through Stalin's manipulation of the rivalry between Zhukov and Koniev. During his planning session with the two generals he purposely drew the inter-front boundary only to Lubbe, a mere 80 kilometers south east of Berlin. Beyond that point, it was up to his generals to define the boundaries based on the progress of Zhukov's 1st Byelorussian and Koniev's 1st Ukrainian Fronts. This opened up the way for Koniev to drive toward Berlin if Zhukov appeared to be slowed by German defenses.[22] Militarily speaking, this was a flawed operational concept that caused the troops of both Soviet Fronts to loose their lives in unnecessary fratricide while maneuvering for better positions to strike at the Government Quarter and the Reichstag in the center of Berlin. The Soviets became even more alarmed over the next few weeks as American and British forces appeared to drive without serious enemy resistance across western Germany.

In the days between 1–15 April the U.S. 9th Army advanced over 320 kilometers to the Elbe River securing a bridgehead on the east bank. This drive was across relatively uncontested enemy territory against all possible reasoning.[23] One day before the Soviet offensive to Berlin began, the U.S. 9th Army received the final word that there would be no further advance toward Berlin.[24] Despite the lack of coordinated resistance in western Germany after the surrender of the Ruhr Pocket, Ike refused to change his decision concerning Berlin. It is interesting to note that the drive across western Germany, against virtually no opposition, did not constitute an official collapse of Germany under the 'Eclipse' guidelines. In fact a SHEAF G–3 report dated 14 April declared "With our armies on the Elbe, it is clear the ultimate defeat of GERMANY is assured. Therefore, considering military factors alone, the objective of our operations should be to complete the defeat of the remaining German forces as rapidly as possible."[25] The primary method, the document continued, " ... to destroy enemy will to resist would undoubtedly be to destroy the leaders of the NAZI Party, in particular Hitler ... "[26] Still this prompted no further Western Allied move toward Berlin, even knowing that the Soviet offensive, as stated by Stalin, was still a month away and not even focused on Berlin. Even on 17 April, the CCS, perhaps trying one last time to prod Eisenhower into moving toward Berlin, sent a communiqué that stated "prior to this date the CCS had interpreted Allied movements as not entering the ... 'ultimate' zone of Soviet occupation even though it might still be in German hands, and vice versa. This

Operation 'Talisman' dated 4 November 1944. This was the Top Secret Allied Airborne drop on Berlin and Kiel that kept Churchill pacified but continually worried Stalin that the Western Allies might try to take Berlin first.
Photo courtesy of the US National Archives.

concept has now been changed and any portion of the enemy's territory can be entered by the Anglo-American or Soviet forces having military interests therein."[27] As Command-in-Chief of all Western Allied Forces, Eisenhower was given the military authority to cross the Elbe River into the Soviet Zone of Occupation in order to pursue the stated goals of destroying the remaining military formations of the German Army along the Eastern Front, thereby forcing a final collapse of the German forces within eastern Germany. Eisenhower, however, made no further move across the Elbe, let alone toward Berlin. The collapse of the Western Front warranted, if not demanded, a continued move east to facilitate a collapse of the Eastern Front and the capture of Berlin based on the guiding principles of 'Eclipse'. Eisenhower chose not to do so. Eisenhower selected a more conservative plan allowing his forces to drive southeast instead, and ensure that the creation of a redoubt did not occur.

The unprecedented drive by the U.S. Army across Germany caused the Soviet High Command to place pressure on Zhukov to finalize his operational plans and start his offensive. The rate of the Western Allied advance, coupled by the belief that the Germans were trying to make a separate peace with them, forced the Soviet Union into a potential offensive posture toward the Western Allies on the approach to Berlin. Koniev stated after the war:

> ... we could not help but consider the circumstances that the German command [and] the German government had persistently conducted a policy of splitting the anti-Hitler coalition, and in recent times had resorted to direct searches for separate agreements with our allies, hoping as a result ... to transfer their troops from the Western front to the Eastern front against us.[28]

Koniev was cautious in his tone toward the Western Allies, yet he did not hide his mistrust as he continued " ... we did not want to believe that our allies could enter into any sort of separate agreement with the Germans. However, in the atmosphere of the time, which abounded not only in fact, but also in rumors, we, as military men had no right to exclude absolutely the possibility ...."[29] Koniev concluded in his memoir that " ... we had to consider the entirely realistic possibility that, the Fascist leaders nevertheless would prefer to surrender Berlin to the Americans and British rather than to us; before them the Germans would open a way but with us they would fight fiercely to the last soldier."[30] No Soviet documents to date have been found suggesting that the Soviet military leadership issued written orders preparing their forces for a potential hostile engagement with the U.S. or British during the offensive to take Berlin. Some circumstantial evidence exists, however, that suggests some planning was given to this possibility by Soviet Commissars. One Soviet POW from the 49th Rifle Division captured on 15 April outside of Frankfurt-on-der-Oder told his German interrogators that the "Soviets will not let British and Americans take Berlin." The Russian prisoner suggested that the Soviets would engage the Western Allied units with their artillery, specifically their Katushya rockets, possibly as a warning not to advance any further.[31] A Russian Officer captured outside of Küstrin, along the main Soviet line of advance toward Berlin, reported that the Russians expected to encounter the Americans on the route to Berlin and that the Western Allies were to be attacked with Soviet artillery to halt their advance eastward.[32] Other official Soviet actions surrounding coordination with the Western Allies regarding Berlin also suggest ulterior motives.

Soviet deception about the Berlin offensive continued even after it began. On 16 April, the first day of the Soviet assault toward Berlin, the U.S. Military Mission in Moscow confronted Stalin with information gained from German sources that the Soviets were planning to attack toward Berlin. Stalin, who was dealing with Zhukov's reports of slow progress in taking the Seelow Heights, slipped and stated he would attack toward Berlin, then caught himself and as an afterthought confirmed that it would simply be part of a general offensive against Dresden.[33] Even after the Soviets broke through the Seelow Heights and drove toward Berlin their mistrust in the Western Allied intention did not diminish. Still believing that they would run into U.S. or British units along the way, Stavka agreed with Eisenhower that Soviet tanks should be painted with a white stripe around the turret and a white cross on the top.[34] It has been suggested that stripe was designed for recognition of Soviet tanks and self-propelled guns during the street fighting in Berlin, but in reality it was to differentiate their vehicles from the Western Allies. Studies of late war photos of Russian armor depict no vehicles outside of the fighting for Berlin carrying the white stripe. By the end of April the Soviet tank recognition marking changed from the white stripe to a small triangle on the turret. This change was caused by German Panzers in the *9.Armee* painting their tanks with the Soviet recognition stripes in an attempt to fool the Soviets during their breakout west.[35] Again, a study of late war Soviet photos show the small triangle marking on vehicles involved in the Berlin fighting but nowhere else. This poses the question as to why only Soviet vehicles in Berlin were painted with the recognition markings if the Soviets didn't expect to encounter the Western Allies along the Berlin axis or in the city itself. Perhaps more revealing is that the Soviets did not officially admit to their drive on Berlin until after the encirclement of the capital on the 25 April. An article published in the English language edition of *Pravda* in London titled 'Forward to Berlin' provided the world with the first admission that the Soviets were on the way to the Nazi Capital.[36] That same day the Soviet High Command officially declared their intention to take Berlin to Eisenhower.[37] This declaration came after the first full day of the Soviet encirclement.

Eisenhower elected not to drive on Berlin despite the protests of his British counterparts. This allowed the Soviets to take the city in the heart of their post-war occupation zone. Between these would-be conquerors were the plans for a final defense of Germany architected by the German High Command and bolstered by Hitler's belief in some form of political victory. In addition, the commander of *AGV* was secretly charged by the Chief of Staff of *Oberkommando des Heeres (OKH)* to ensure that the Soviets never saw Berlin. This was a strategy separate and unknown by Hitler. It was designed to force the Western Allies over the Elbe River into the postwar Soviet occupation zone in order to take Berlin.

Hitler declared Berlin a 'Fortress' on 3 February.[38] His declaration came several days after Soviet soldiers of the 2nd and 3rd Battalions of the 266th Rifle Division's 10006th Regiment crossed the frozen Oder to take the German village of Kienitz in the pre-dawn hours. These soldiers were the vanguard of the 5th Shock Army's, 26th Guard Rifle Corps. They were now across the last natural barrier to Berlin and only some 50 kilometers from the Nazi capital.[39] Berlin's declaration as a 'Fortress' was the first time during the war that any strategic consideration of the city occurred.

Not surprisingly, *Oberkommando der Wehrmacht (OKW)* had no plan to defend Berlin. This lack of foresight derived from Hitler's belief that it was equivalent to defeatism to prepare for a defense west of the Oder as long as the German Eastern Front was still holding the west bank of the river.[40] Hitler's intelligence service netted a document that should have influenced all future deployment of German forces in preparation for the final battle for central Germany. During the fighting in the Ardennes the German's found a copy of 'Eclipse' on a British officer. This document marked 'State Top Secret' by Hitler described the strategic assessment of Germany's future accompanied by an Allied map with various zones of occupation portioning Germany.[41]

The capture of 'Eclipse' had little effect on overall German strategic planning. This document outlined what Germany would look like after the war and offered a means to develop remaining strategic options.[42] The document seemed to confirm that the Allied declaration of 'unconditional surrender' was a reality and this was of paramount importance to *Generaloberst* Alfred Jodl who was the head of the Operations Section of *OKW*.[43] The Allied conference at Yalta confirmed 'Eclipse' in the minds of the German High Command. German Intelligence Services reached out to all available contacts to determine if unconditional surrender was still valid, and the state of the relationship between the Western Allies and Soviet Union.[44] Reports soon came back suggesting a possible clash between the Western Allies and Soviet Union. One report read: "The conviction had been reportedly expressed that the unrestrained Soviet urge for expansion and the worthlessness of any agreement contracted with the Soviets had become clear to the British and the Americans at the Yalta Conference and that their own interests would force them to make military and political preparation to meet the inevitable clash with Moscow."[45] 'Eclipse' and the potential for a clash between the Western Allies and Soviets made little impact on Hitler and German strategy.

'Eclipse' offered Hitler the ability to devise a late war strategy focused on splitting the Allied coalition. This strategy required the deployment of the majority of German combat forces into central and eastern Germany in order to create defensive bastions necessary to drag out the conflict along the political fault line of the Elbe River.

Hitler illogically dispersed his military power to seemingly remote areas of his Greater German Reich (as pointed out in the Introduction) instead of focusing on defending central Germany following the failure of operation *Wacht Am Rhein* launched in December 1944 against the Western Allies. After that offensive, he sent the *6.SS Panzer Armee* from the Ardennes front to Hungary where they engaged in the defense of the Hungarian oil region. It was here that 80% of Germany's oil reserves existed.[46] To Hitler, this made *Heeresgruppe Süd (Army Group South – AGS)* more important than the central or northern *Heeresgruppe* defending Germany and Berlin. This caught the attention of Allied Intelligence who noted that by their estimates there were "twice as many divisions available for the defense of south Germany as for the north. By far the greater part of the enemy's armor and the bulk of the SS Divisions will be in the south."[47] Hitler realized too late that Berlin, as a planned divided city in the middle of the postwar Soviet Zone of occupation, may have served as the catalyst fsplitting the coalition and developed a strategic plan that focused on exploiting this potential weakness.

The known partition of Germany, unconditional surrender, disagreement between the Allies at Yalta, and the fact the Soviets were only 50 kilometers from Berlin caused no change in Hitler's strategic thinking. Berlin received no defensive plan until the Soviets reached the Oder River and Hitler declared the city a Fortress. Up to that point the military needs of Berlin were responsible to *Wehrmacht* Area HQ, subordinated in turn to Deputy *HQ II Korps*, the *Replacement Army* and then to *OKW*.[48] Based on the Fortress declaration, the Commanding General of *Wehrkreis III* now became responsible for Berlin's defense. The question of Hitler staying or leaving Berlin became a key discussion point with many of his close advisors now that the city was declared a Fortress. In most cases, once a Fortress was declared then no one was allowed to leave. Soldiers that found themselves in a designated Fortress were expected to fight until the very end. By the second week of February Hitler still had not decided whether or not to stay or head south to command from the area of Berchtesgaden as his advisors suggested in taking advantage of the 'Redoubt Psychosis.'[49] As Hitler procrastinated, military events were outpacing his ability to make timely strategic decisions.

By mid-March German forces were being defeated across Europe. The Western Allies were surrounding the last sizable force of *Wehrmacht* units in the west within the Ruhr Pocket and looking for a Rhine River crossing. In the east, the *6.SS Panzer Army* was conducting a fighting retreat through Hungary toward Austria after it failed to relieve the Soviet siege of Budapest. Zhukov's main forces continued their buildup in the east unabated while other Soviet forces completed the conquest of East Prussia and Silesia. The only defense between the Soviets and Berlin was the remnants of the battered German *3.Panzer Armee* commanded by *General der Panzertruppen* Hasso von Manteuffel and the *9.Armee* command by *General der Infanterie* Theodore Busse that fought daily to keep the Soviets in check along the Oder River. Both armies fell under the command of *AGV*, which was at that time, arguably the single most important command within *OKH*. *AGV* was the last organized line of defense between Berlin and the advancing Soviet Armies. The weight of this command was not in the hands of a capable military commander, but rather a political appointee with no military experience—*Reichsführer-SS* Heinrich Himmler.

Himmler was in command from 25 January until 20 March before being replaced by a more capable military commander *Generaloberst* Gotthard Heinrici. Himmler demonstrated a complete lack of command ability.[50] The *OKH* Chief of Staff, *Generaloberst* Heinz Guderian knew that Himmler's continued appointment in his role as commander of *AGV* would only lead to immediate defeat in the east. Guderian had read 'Eclipse'. In his last act as Chief of Staff before being sacked by Hitler on 28 March, Guderian decided to ensure that Himmler was replaced by a competent military commander. With the change of command Guderian wanted a strategy to help save eastern Germany and Berlin from Soviet occupation.

On 22 March Heinrici was summoned to meet with Guderian in his command HQ at Zossen. The German High Command HQ was located in a picturesque Brandenburg town south of Berlin that housed the underground bunkers of the *OKW*, the *Wehrmacht* Operations Staff, and the German General Staff. In Guderian's office hung a large map of Germany with partition lines drawn marking zones of occupation for the Western Allies and Soviet Union. Heinrici stared in stunned silenced remarking after the war that "it stood there plain and stark for all to read that the opponents of Germany, that is the Allies, were prepared to cut Germany into pieces, to root out Naziism [sic] and militarism to the roots, to de-militarize the divided land and to turn it into an agricultural economy."[51] According to Heinrici, everyone in the German High Command knew of the existence of 'Eclipse' and most had an opinion of what it meant. Guderian was blunt on this point, tasking Heinrici to hold the Oder River line at any cost. The objective was to stall the impending Soviet offensive along the Oder River forcing the Western Allies to cross the Elbe River into eastern Germany and take Berlin—potentially saving the lives of millions of refugees, civilians, and soldiers.[52]

The strategy to hold the Soviets back and force the Western Allies across the Elbe River was not Hitler's. In fact Hitler and the *German High Command* never knew what their two senior generals planned. Guderian and Heinrici set a course that recognized Germany's inevitable defeat and chose to try and prevent the Soviets from conquering the rest of Germany. There is no evidence to suggest that German commanders expected that U.S. or British forces would join their side against the Soviets, even though wild rumors of such a scenario abounded. Hitler, in particular, would not settle for any agreement that ended his leadership of a National Socialist Germany. While he hoped for a falling out between the Allies, there was no consideration of 'joining' forces with them against the other. Hitler's only strategic goal was to continue to defend Germany militarily without any consideration of overall strategy.

Hitler finally decided that Berlin would be the next target of the Soviets by the end of March.[53] Hitler, however, had a change of mind that uncannily followed the false strategic plans that Stalin fed Eisenhower. This suggests that German Intelligence Service may have known of the communiqué from Eisenhower, although no documentary evidence of this possibility exists. In reaction to Stalin's plan to drive southeast, Hitler decided to take three key Panzer divisions from the *3.Panzer Army* and move them to *AGC* against the protests of Heinrici.[54] On 30 March Hitler moved the *10.SS Panzer*, followed by the *Führer Grenadier Division* on 2 April, then finally the *25.Panzer Division* on 3 April, to *AGC*. These moves seem to confirm his strategic policy to prevent the collapse of Nazi Germany by defending occupied territory for political and economic reasons. The real reason might have been that the commander of *AGC*, *Generalfeldmarschall* Ferdinand Schörner, who was an ardent support of Hitler and his policies, was able to exert some influence on the dispositions of the remaining Panzer divisions.[55] Krebs justified this move to a complaining Heinrici by stating that Panzer divisions could be used by both army groups.[56] This policy was compounded by Hitler's 21 January order requiring all Commanding Generals and Divisional Commanders to report directly to him before they issued any operational orders. This order usurped all roaming freedom of movement within the *Wehrmacht*, paralyzing operational flexibility.

Hitler decided on a final strategic course of action on 25 April. By this date the Soviets completed their encirclement of Berlin. Realizing that the decision to leave Berlin was now made for him, Hitler drew inspiration from desperation and 'decided' to remain the city and oversee the final battle. By 22 April Chief of *OKW* Field Marshall Wilhelm Keitel believed an opportunity existed to use the forces around Berlin to launch a concentric attack designed to both relieve Berlin and possibly defeat the attacking Soviet forces. This plan was handed to Hitler who approved it and believed that he might still defeat the Soviets and win National Socialist Germany's continued existence. With renewed fortitude he declared that every last soldier would go to battle in Berlin and that in Berlin the final battle of the war would be decided.[57]

The operational plan to save Nazi Germany prepared by *OKW*, called for the already battered *9.Armee* to launch a combined offensive with the newly formed *12.Armee* commanded by General Walther Wenck toward the southern part of Berlin, while in the north *SS Obergruppenführer und General der Waffen-SS* Felix Steiner's new *Heeresgruppe Steiner* would launch an offensive from the *3.Panzer Armee*'s flank into Berlin's northern suburbs. This plan was based on the ability of Berlin to avoid capitulation to the Soviets. Unknown to

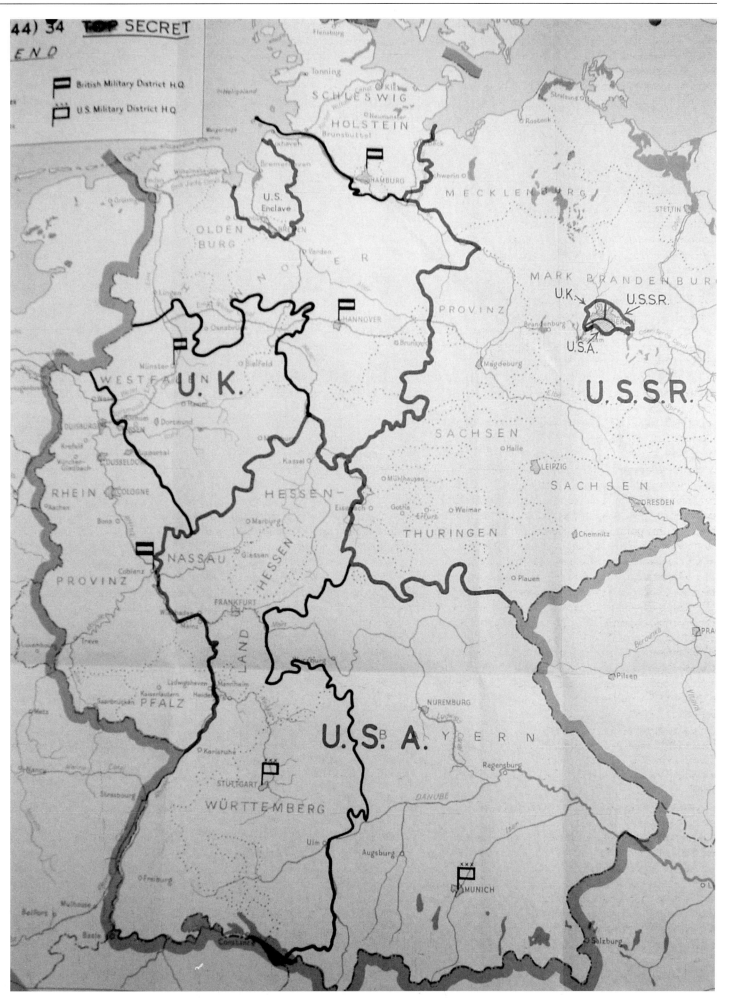

The original occupation zones planned for Germany. Note the absence of a French zone.
Photo courtesy of the US National Archives.

General der Artillerie Alfred Jodl.
Photo courtesy of the Bundesarchiv.

Generalleutnant Hans Krebs.
Photo courtesy of the Bundesarchiv.

Heinrici and against his wishes, the commander of the *LVI Panzer Korps* was ordered by Hitler to pull his forces into Berlin—against all military reasoning. In the end the plan failed, as the commanders of the various German armies arrayed around Berlin showed little intention of sacrificing their men for a lost cause. Instead, the commanders of the *3.Panzer, 12.* and *9.Armees* focused their remaining resources on rescuing as many German soldiers and refugees as possible from Soviet captivity by retreating toward the Western Allied lines along the Elbe River.

The failure to defend Berlin was rooted in the desire of Heinrici not to have forces dragged into the capital, but instead to defend the city well to the east and hold the Russians off long enough for the Western Allies to cross the Elbe and take the remnants of Germany. As Heinrici stated after the war:

> The question whether the Americans and the Englishmen would halt on the Elbe or advance further was one which agitated [*Army Group Vistula*] severely ….it had always been announced that Germany must be completely beaten to her knees and that she must be forced to unconditional surrender. That had already been decided at Casablanca and once again it had been restated at Yalta. And therefore, it was a matter for some speculation that the enemy was taking absolutely no steps in the west in order to push his attack forward and to bring this hope into reality. They only needed to jump out of their bridgeheads ….and then by all accounts they would have been in Berlin about two days.[58]

Heinrici believed in the mission assigned to him by Guderian. Once he realized that he could not hold back the Soviets his focus shifted on saving the soldiers in his command and rescuing refugees. Heinrici ordered Manteuffel's *3.Panzer Armee* to retreat from the front after the Soviet breakthrough and told Busse's *9.Armee* to avoid the 'Fortress' fate and breakout to Wenck's waiting *12.Armee*. Wenck, for his part, never planned on participating in Hitler's final battle but rather to provide a corridor to rescue the surrounded defenders of Berlin. Heinrici's lack of responsiveness to Hitler's plan caused him to be relieved on 29 April for insubordination.

Zhukov wrote after the war that the Berlin Strategic Offensive Operation accelerated Nazi Germany's unconditional surrender and the end of the war in Europe.[59] The fact that Hitler remained in Berlin and committed suicide there during the Soviet assault was a key factor in ensuring the complete collapse of Nazi Germany. This collapse supported the 17 April SHAEF Intelligence appraisal that stated the quickest way to end the war was to take out the Nazi leadership, especially Hitler. This intelligence assessment was ignored by Eisenhower who opted to avoid increased losses and potential confrontation with the Soviets.

The potential for open conflict between the Western Allies and the Soviets in the final weeks of the war was possible. Mistrust ran high among all participants. If Guderian and Heinrici's plan to hold the Soviets along the Oder River or Keitel's plan to defeat the Soviets outside Berlin were successful then the Western Allies may have been forced to reevaluate strategic priorities and drive over the Elbe River to take Berlin themselves forcing a potential conflict with the Soviets. These ideas were not lost on the Soviets who perceived much of the final strategic decisions made by the Germans at the end of the war in this light. Chuikov wrote after the war that "all the Nazi leaders could hope for was that contradictions would build up, to the point of actual armed conflict, between the Allies—the Soviet Union on the one side and the British and Americans on the other."[60] Contrary to the well publicized and popular meeting of U.S. and Soviet forces at Torgau, examples of overt or perceived hostility between the U.S. and Soviets existed that suggest it would not have taken much for open conflict to occur.

During the pursuit of fleeing German civilians and soldiers to the Elbe River in the last days of April and beginning of May, U.S. and Soviet forces did occasionally clash. On 25 April in the sector of the U.S. 9th Army's XIII Army Corps, Major General Alvan Gillem, Jr. watched astonished as German soldiers, officers and women swam across the Elbe to escape the pursuing Russians. "At this point three Russian fighter planes came down and strafed along the both banks of the river." Officially there were no U.S. casualties but it seems likely that some occurred. His observations were recorded after the war:

> … it was obvious that the Russians knew that they were firing on American troops. Gillem promptly picked up his radio microphone and contacted the Tactical Air Command assigned to his Corps and told them to clear the air of the Russian planes. Next he radioed the 29th Infantry Division and told them to lift their artillery fire and to drop a lot of it several miles behind the far bank of the Elbe. This was where the Russians were supposed to be. After a 'great deal of artillery fire' Gillen told the 29th to stop firing. Then he got his interpreter to contact the Russians on the radios and delivered the following message: "I have adequate divisions to fight you and we are ready. If that's what you want come ahead because I'm waiting for you." From that point on Gilen had no problems with the Russians.[61]

This was not the only instance. During the crossing of the Elbe by the German *12.Armee* the Soviets unleashed artillery barrages against both the east and west banks of the river forcing the U.S. to pull back to avoid casualties. Despite the possibility of open conflict with the Soviets, Gillem believed that the U.S. forces should have been allowed to cross the Elbe and drive toward Berlin. "I had always assumed that the strategic objective of our advance across Europe was to be Berlin. We knew the Russians might be coming in from the other side but it didn't bother us. We were all saying to each other—we're in, let's go on."[62] According to Gillem, not going on to Berlin was a strategic mistake.[63]

Generalfeldmarschall und Chef des Oberkommandos der Wehrmacht Wilhelm Keitel.
Courtesy of the Bundesarchiv.

It is important to realize that strategic decisions about Berlin directly impacted motivation, attitudes, and tactical decisions that shaped the fighting in and around the city. While the proceeding chapters will focus on the preparation of Berlin's defense, the final battle along the Oder River, and finally the ferocious street fighting in Berlin itself, it all needs to be understood in the context of the varying motivations that affected all those concerned. Hitler's inability to gain strategic insight from 'Eclipse' and foster a workable defensive strategy to potentially wear down the Allies was at least consistent with his pattern of strategic despondency after *Wacht am Rhein*. Keitel's last grasp at victory against the Soviets around Berlin was too little too late and none of his commanders considered pursuing this idea. Guderian and Heinrici's plan to hold of the Soviets and force the Western Allies across the Elbe had potential, but Heinrici needed the additional combat divisions dispersed inconceivably throughout Europe to have a chance. He summarized the key political issues regarding 'Eclipse' after the war:

> The inactivity of the Americans had perhaps a number of reasons to explain it. After such a long approach march up to the Rhine perhaps it was necessary that they had some kind of breathing space before they undertook new operations. But perhaps they wanted to wait just for that period of time so that the Russians themselves would move forward and thus both sides together would be able to strike the Germans so much more easily and so much more effectively. Or perhaps it was thought better or indeed it might have been preferred, that Western and Eastern troops should not make contact with each other, as it were, moving towards each other on the battlefield, and this take up undesired contacts or perhaps merely to avoid the error of them shooting at each other? Such a resolve obviously worked on the Russians in the fighting out of the battle, with all its consequences and its losses. But to halt, that was not a military but rather a political solution. And it was evidently this that Roosevelt himself had decided upon. The end of the war dragged on for some three weeks. Americans had it in their power to finish the end battle of the Third Reich quickly, that is in a shorter time and without so much pain than in fact actually took place.[64]

Ending the war early was a laudable goal that Eisenhower did not pursue by crossing the Elbe to take Berlin, but left it as a fait accompli to the Soviets. The cost in making this choice exceeds half a million dead and wounded (see Chapter 8). The more controversial issue at hand is how important Berlin's capture-by either side-was to shaping the political and social landscape in postwar Europe. In this context, it is clear that Berlin in Stalin's hands meant domination and subjugation of Eastern Europe under Communist rule. It was these final political-military decisions made by dictators and generals that pitted German and Soviet soldiers against each other in the largest urban assault in history; a final bloody street fight between two forces whose outcome not only destroyed much of Germany's capital, but reshaped the political-social landscape of Europe and the world.

Notes to Chapter 1

1 I. Koniev unpublished memoir, pp. 54-55.
2 J. Gavin, *On to Berlin: Battles of an Airborne Commander 1943–6*, p. 301, and C. Ryan, *The Last Battle*, p. 214.
3 Gavin, p. 302.
4 Ibid, p. 298–9.
5 Gablentz, p. 18.
6 Ryan, p. 102.
7 RG 331, *Eclipse*, p. 3. This logic was based on the understanding that the Germans considered the Russians their primary enemy in the conflict. The collective fear of the Russians, and genuine anti-communist sentiment fostered over years of Nazi Propoganda caused 'Eclipse' planners to surmise that the Germans would not stop fighting the Russians unless they were defeated by *them*. This made a rapid collapse of the Eastern Front a priority, regardless what happened on the Western Front.
8 Ibid, p. 6.
9 Gavin, pp. 299–300.
10 O. Bradley, *A Soldier's Story*, p. 535.
11 Gavin, p. 300.
12 Ibid.
13 F. Hofer, *MS #B-458 National Redoubt*, p. 9.
14 HQ, 7th U.S. Army, G-2 Study on National Redoubt, Mar 25, 1945 (RC: 65/4). Paradoxically these troop dispositions were occurring due to Hitler's strategic ineptness and not because of a grand strategic vision to drag the war out by defending a 'Redoubt.'
15 J. Wellard, *"When Berlin goes, all is over: Hitler is there"* (RC: 65/2)
16 Ryan, p. 236.
17 Gavin, p. 303.
18 Gavin, p. 307 and Ryan, pp. 252–3.
19 Ryan, p. 249. See also SHAEF G3 "Operation Talisman-Targets for Specialist Personnel," 4 November 1944, and SHAEF G3 "Eclipse Outline Plan," 28 February 1945 in RG 331: Box 72.
20 Gavin, p. 299.
21 Koniev, p. 60.
22 Ibid, pp. 59-60.
23 Gavin, p. 310 and Ryan, p. 279.
24 Ryan, p. 279.
25 SHAEF G3 "Operations after reaching the River Elbe," 17 April 1945 (RC: 42/3-4).
26 Ibid.
27 CCS to Eisenhower communiqué, 17 April 1945, (RC: 42/1-2).
28 Koniev, p. 62.
29 Ibid.
30 Ibid.
31 "Fremde Heere Ost," pp. 12. RG 242, T-78/503-11/215.
32 Ibid.
33 Military Mission, Moscow to War Department communiqué, 16 April 1945 (RC: 42/1-2).
34 SHAEF file "Liaison with Russians," 21 April 1945 (RC: 42/3-4).
35 In addition, the Soviets would use white flares to identify their forces. Archer & Olsen (Moscow) to SHAEF, 29 April 1945 (RC: 42/1-2).
36 Soviet War News, "Forward into Berlin," 24 April 1945 (RC: 74/14).
37 Military Mission Moscow to War Dept, 25 April 1945 (RC: 42/3-4). "Please tell Ike that the immediate plan of the Soviets forces is to occupy Berlin and clean up the elements troops on the Eastern banks of the River Elbe. . ."
38 W. Wilmer, MS #P-136, *The German Defense of Berlin*, p. 7.
39 T. Le Tissier, *Zhukov on the Oder*, pp. 34–5.
40 MS #P-136, p. 10.
41 Ryan, p. 97.
42 It is an interesting sidenote that Hitler spent several late nights pouring over the captured material. Hitler had a first hand glimpse of what his war of aggression was going to bring Germany in the end. Despite this realization, he made no effort to stop it from happening. In fact, 'Eclipse' probably fueled his despondency and no history of the end of World War II can be written without taking into account Hitler's complete lack of strategic action even when confronted with arguably the single most important intelligence coup the Germans had during the war.
43 Ryan, p. 101.
44 "German view of Yalta Conference," RG 246, Box 441, NO 855.
45 "German Discussion of Yalta Conference Results," RG 246, Box 441, NO 969.
46 G. Maier, *Drama between Budapest and Vienna*, p. 113.
47 SHAEF JIC Report Prepared 20 April 1945 (RC: 42/3-4).
48 MS #P-136, p. 14.
49 Ziemke, p. 462.
50 MS #D-189, *The Pomeranian Battle and Command in the East*, pp 20–3.
51 Heinrici interview.
52 Ibid, p. 6.
53 Ziemke, p. 463.
54 Ryan, pp. 256-257, and Ziemke, pp. 469.
55 Schörner was a particularly brutal commander favored by Hitler who instituted and supported flying court-martials for any solider caught in the rear areas that did not have written orders. He was imprisoned by the Soviet Union and DDR for over 12 years. After his release to the West German government in 1958 he was tried for the illegal execution of German soldiers and served 5 more years before being released in 1963.
56 Heinrici interview.
57 Glantz, p. 722.
58 Heinrici interview.
59 G. Zhukov, *Marshal Zhukov's Greatest Battles*, p. 267.
60 V. Chuikov, *The Fall of Berlin*, p. 180.
61 A.C. Gillem Interview. (RC: 44).
62 Ibid.
63 Ibid.
64 Heinrici interview.

2

FORTRESS BERLIN

No cohesive, overall plan for the defense of Berlin was ever actually prepared. All that existed was the stubborn determination of Hitler to defend the capital of the Reich. Circumstances were such that he gave no thought to defending the city until it was much too late for any kind of advance planning. Thus the city's defense was characterized only by a mass of improvisations. These reveal a state of total confusion in which the pressure of the enemy, the organizational chaos on the German side, and the catastrophic shortage of human and material resources for the defense combined with disastrous effect.

Generaloberst **Franz Halder**

I n 1939 Berlin was the greatest industrial and commercial city on the continent of Europe and the sixth largest in the world with a population of 4.3 million.[1] Greater Berlin, established in 1920, consisted of 549 square kilometers, running 37 kilometers north to south, and 45 kilometers east to west. Berlin is surrounded by thick pine forests, numerous lakes, and waterways. Over 200 kilometers of waterways run through the city.[2] By January 1945 Berlin could now boast that it was the most bombed city in Europe. Only 2.25 million people were left in the city, a significant reduction from the prewar total.[3] The raids on Berlin only increased in 1945 with the start of Allied daylight bombings on 6 March.

Berlin endured 450 raids that dropped 45,517 tons of bombs causing 78% destruction within the central district by the end of the war.[4] For a perspective, the Germans dropped less than 75,000 tons of bombs (both aerial bombs and V-Weapons) across the *whole* of England during the war; Berlin endured more than 85,000 tons of aerial bombs and artillery shells—the entire city of Berlin received more explosive tonnage than all of England! The bombing, while hindering efforts to fortify the city actually assisted the German defenders significantly during the upcoming street fighting as many side streets were blocked by rubble. The carcasses of apartment complexes and government buildings made excellent defensive positions. These added 'benefits' were hardly in the mind of the new Commander of Berlin Defense Area (hereafter referred to as *CBDA*). The responsibility of defending Berlin belonged to the *Wehrmacht* Area Headquarters until 1 February 1945. This headquarters was subordinate to the Deputy HQ, *III Korps* and in turn to the Replacement Army. Once Berlin was declared a Fortress the Deputy HQ, *III Korps* was then designated the Office of Commander of Berlin Defense Area.[5]

Contrary to popular belief, few people expected or even wanted to fight the Soviets in the streets of Berlin. Berlin could never be defended with the meager forces at the city's disposal and it lacked all of the key stores necessary for a protracted defense. Weapons, ammunition, fuel, and other equipment were in short supply or non-existent. Effective command structures were not in place. Perhaps more important, key military leaders had no plans to defend Berlin. Despite their knowledge of 'Eclipse', Hitler and the German High Command viewed the defense of Berlin as a non-essential task while others actively planned to bypass the city and retreat to the west if the Soviets broke through the Oder River line.

Barely any defensive preparation took place in Berlin from the time Hitler declared Berlin a Fortress in February to the time *Generalleutnant* Helmuth Reymann was ordered by Hitler to take over as *CBDA*.[6] Reymann's title was officially known as Deputy Commander General in Military Zone III and Commandant *BDA*.[7] The only work completed under Reymann's predecessor, the sickly General Ritter von Hauenschild, was the construction of defensive positions along the eastern city limits that consisted of a series of trenches and dragon's teeth.[8] Reymann drove into Berlin on 7 March and observed that "as we neared the Berlin city limits, I looked in vain to find any kind of defenses. Aside from a few trifling tank traps, which hardly presented any obstacle to an enemy advance, there was nothing in sight which could lead one to the conclusion that Berlin had the status of a fortress."[9] A primary reason for the lack of defensive works was Hitler's inability to conceive or approve a strategy for defending Berlin and eastern Germany in the last six months of the war.

Reymann's appointment placed him directly under Hitler.[10] The defense staff consisted of Reymann, Hans Reifor as Chief of Staff, *Major* Sprotte as Operations Officer fresh from the war academy, and several junior officers.[11] Reymann and his staff met with Hitler once in mid-March for the first and last time. Reymann met Hitler alone on several more occasions, but never again with the entire staff. Typical of Hitler's leadership style, he did not issue any specific orders to Reymann but left the management of the defense planning entirely up to him.[12] Without any orders, the staff began to plan for the defense of the city from their new headquarters in the Military Zone III building on Hohenzollerndamm.

Reymann interpreted his orders in historical terms. He drew on the successful defense of Vienna against the Turkish siege in the late 17th Century as inspiration. Reymann reviewed the operational situation and tried to draw parallels he might be able to use for guidance in his planning. "I thought of Vienna," he stated "which had been defended successfully against the oncoming Turks, and which thus saved Europe from a dismal fate."[13] While this provides insight into the motivations of the planners of Berlin's defense, Berlin like Vienna in 1684, could not be defended without outside assistance. Reifor concluded that the staff's job was " ... and had to, be the assembly of all available manpower and materials in Berlin, and the *preparation* of the defense of the Reich capital to such an extent, that under emergency conditions an army coming from outside the city would only need to place itself in the ready-made [defensive positions]."[14] The immediate problem with this plan was the lack of strategic or operational purpose in defending Berlin. Other German cities were declared

Generalleutnant Helmuth Reymann (in the trench), Commander Berlin Defense Area inspecting trench works in the city with his staff and local *Volkssturm*. German Propoganda Kompanie (PK), photo courtesy of the Cornelius Ryan Collection, Mahn Center, Alden Library, Ohio University, Athens, OH.

Reymann (on the far left) and his staff inspecting a newly constructed anti-tank barricade. German PK, photo courtesy of the Cornelius Ryan Collection, Mahn Center, Alden Library, Ohio University, Athens, OH.

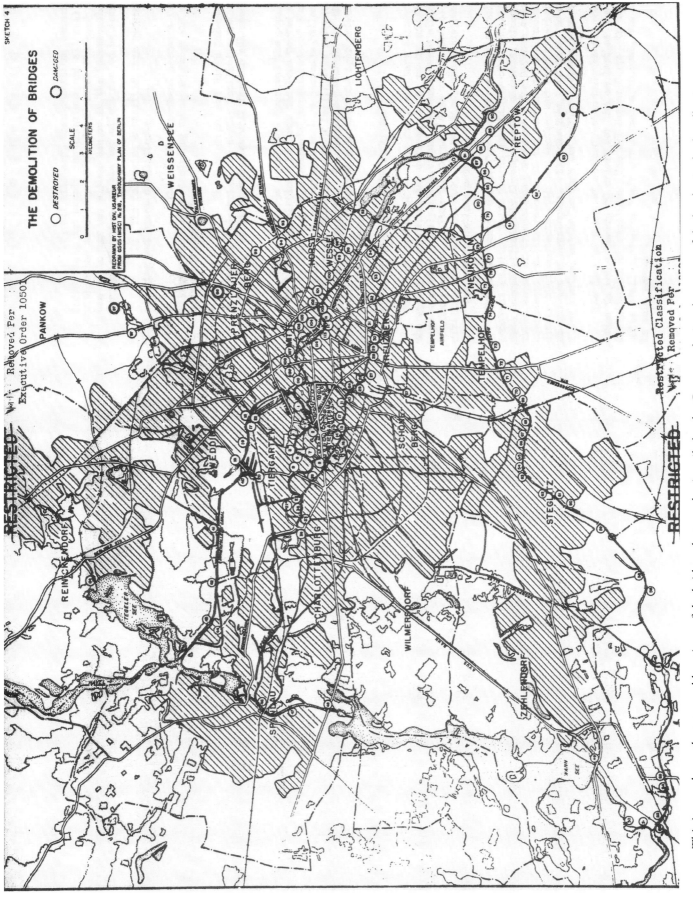

This image shows the type and locations of the bridges destroyed primarily by the Germans during the course of the battle. Author's collection.

Fortresses in the east like Königsberg, and Breslau. The purpose of defending these Fortresses was to tie down Soviet troops and slow their westward advance. But this was not a practical reason to defend Berlin.

The *CBDA* immediately ran into personality conflicts as they began to deal with both local and party personalities. The most important was Dr. Joseph Goebbels who was Reich Defense Commissar and *Gauleiter* of Greater Berlin. He believed that he alone was responsible for the defense of Berlin. The second person was *Gaufürung* of the *Volkssturm* who had nominal, administrative authority over the various *Volkssturm* units within the city.[15] In addition, most state and party agencies provided little support to Reymann and Reifor. These agencies believed that while the Soviets were on the Oder in defensive positions, they didn't need to prepare for a future assault. When the situation became critical in a month, many of the heads of these agencies fled to the West.[16] The behavior of the city officials was quite different from those in Königsberg and Breslau where they offered considerable help in defense planning. Berlin officials were simply in a state of denial about the coming assault.

Goebbels required a daily war council meeting with Reymann where he often issued orders that conflicted with the General's military planning. In one such meeting, Reymann recommended the evacuation of Berlin's civilian population, but Goebbels refused stating it was too soon to suggest this and he didn't want to alarm the population.[17] Goebbels stated that he already had a plan for just such an emergency. His plan, Reymann later found out, consisted of no more than two red lines on a map that marked an evacuation route. There was no planning on how to move the population. Control points, sanitation points, etc., were all lacking. No thought was given to the lives of the men, women, and children that might be trapped in the front lines when the Soviets launched their assault.[18]

Hitler issued several directives that shaped the defense planning for Berlin, despite his apparent despondence over the city's defense. On 19 March Hitler issued a 'Scorched Earth' order regarding Germany.[19] This order was largely ignored except that it demonstrated Hitler was not looking for a strategic solution to ending the war. He was going to take Germany down fighting with him in defeat. This decision was perhaps based on his knowledge of 'Eclipse'. If Germany was going to be conquered, he might have decided to leave the conquerors nothing usable. Berlin was impacted by the new order as all bridges and some overpasses were ordered rigged for demolition on 7 April.[20] The exact language in Hitler's order was "1. Bridge installations which are operationally important must be so destroyed that there is no possibility of them being used by the enemy."[21] Explosives were available in limited quantities only due to the needs of the front. During the battle, several key bridges were detonated but were not destroyed because of the lack of quality demolitions. During the course of the battle, 120 of the 248 bridges in Berlin were destroyed and 9 damaged. Only a few overpasses were blown up. Two U-Bahn tunnels were also destroyed under dubious circumstances.[22] It should be noted that none of the orders to destroy the bridges originated from the *CBDA*[23]. In almost every case, the destruction of the bridges offered little military value as their destruction was not tied to a defensive strategy. Once the battle for Berlin began, the only hope that the destroyed bridges offered was to slow, not stop the Soviet assault.

The most significant decision the *CBDA* issued was the creation of three defensive belts and eight defense zones in Berlin with assigned commanders.[24] These defense zones helped organize the existing resources and offered a skeletal command system that was used to some effect by the German forces that entered the city from *AGV* after the Soviet assault began. The primary defensive line, or *Hauptkampflinie (HKL)*, consisted of the perimeter of Greater Berlin, the second line ran along the raised S-Bahn track in the middle districts, and the third defensive line was the Government Quarter bordered by the Tiergarten in the west, the Spree River to the North and East and the Landwehr Canal to the south.[25] The entire city was then carved up into eight Defense Sectors, running from A-G and Z being the Government Quarter.[26] Each zone was commanded by at least an *Oberst* or higher. Reymann and his staff tried to find officers with battle experience to fill in the positions.[27] They were supposed to fall under *CBDA* but in reality they all worked and acted independent of each other, often in a very counterproductive way. Each sector commander differed in energy and political connections. These differences uniquely shaped the combat readiness and local defenses.

Table 2: 1 Initial Berlin Defnse Sector Commanders

Defense Sector	Designated Commander
A	*Oberstleutnant* Erich Bärenfänger (Knight's Cross w/Swords)
B	*Oberst* Clausen (Knight's Cross)
C	*Oberst* Mootz
D	*Luftwaffe Generalmajor* Scheter
E	*Oberst* Thede
F & G	*Oberst* Eder (Knight's Cross)
Z	*Oberstleutnant* Seifert (Knight's Cross)

While it cannot be said for certain what each military commander heard about 'Eclipse' or the demarcation lines, it appears that Reymann did not fear an Allied advance into Berlin from the west. His focus on the Russians may have been shaped by their proximity as the Western Allies were still far to the west struggling to cross the Rhine and close the Ruhr Pocket. At a distance of 30 kilometers east of the HKL an obstacle ring was built to delay the Soviet advance. All large towns were to become tactical strong points.[28] An anti-tank line ran north-south in a 100 kilometer arc in front of Berlin. This line consisted of 'dragon's teeth' and a tank ditch and was one of the only times that the Germans established a fixed defensive line of this nature in the east.[29] The construction of the defensive positions required about 100,000 laborers but only 30,000 were available at any given time due to transportation and other logistical issues.[30] It appears that this number occasionally increased to 70,000.[31] Undoubtedly the Allied air raids took a toll in March as rail service was interrupted and construction equipment was needed for clearing rubble in Berlin and not building fortifications. Promises of additional support from the *Gauleiter* never materialized.[32] Hitler also wanted every large town designated a 'tactical strongpoint' equipped with road blocks and defense positions. Reymann understood the magnitude of this and quickly convinced Hitler that the idea was not possible and had no real military value.[33]

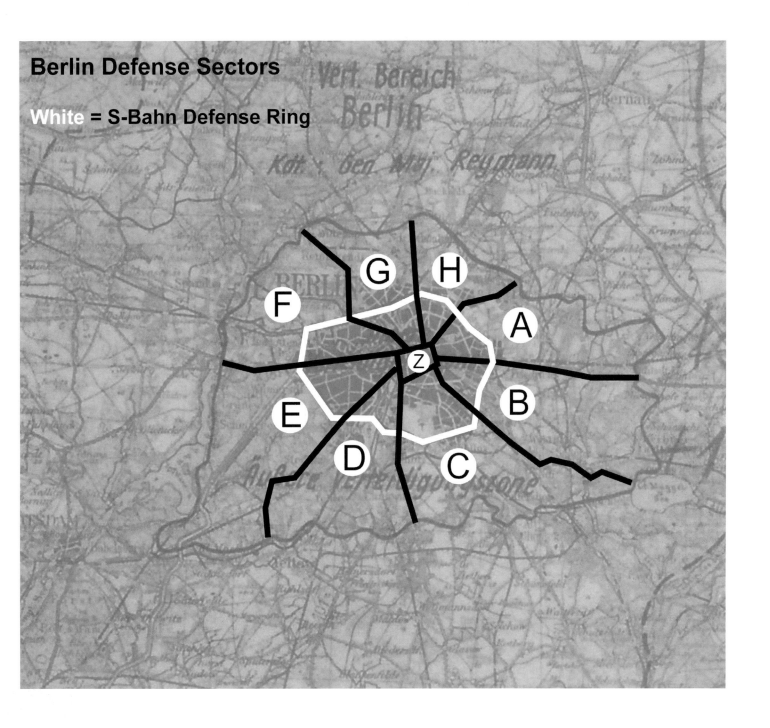

Berlin Defense Sectors

White = S-Bahn Defense Ring

Dragon's Teeth awaited Soviet tanks on the first defensive belt along the eastern approaches to the city. Soviet accounts suggest that these did not slow them down much in their advance. Photo courtesy of RGAKFD Moscow.

The Germans constructed a few reinforced strong points along the eastern approaches to Berlin. These defensive points were typically not integrated, allowing the Soviets to either bypass them or easily knock them out. Photo courtesy of RGAKFD Moscow.

Volkssturm constructing an anti-tank barricade at the S-Bahn station on Hermannstrasse in Neukölln on 10 March 1945. Photo courtesy of the Bundesarchiv.

Another view of the barricade on Hermannstrasse. Photo courtesy of the Bundesarchiv.

Volkssturm constructing an anti-tank barricade at an unknown location in Berlin. March 1945. Note the use of steel girders to form the outer frame. Photo courtesy of the Bundesarchiv.

A second view of the steel reinforced anti-tank barricade. Photo courtesy of the Bundesarchiv.

Street bunkers were often built at the entrance of key U-Bahn stations and other tactically important intersections. Note the firing ports around the bunker that were sized to allow the use of Panzerfausts. Early February 1945. Photo courtesy of the Bundesarchiv.

A photo taken early in April 1945 of an anti-tank barricade erected at the western end of Leipzigerplatz. In addition to the barricade street cars were placed in front and behind of the barricade for reinforcement. Barricades like this prevented the Soviets from quickly advancing down key avenues. Photo courtesy of the Bundesarchiv.

An unidentified barricaded bridge crossing over the Teltow Canal into Neukölln. Photo dated 13 April 1945. Photo courtesy of the Bundesarchiv.

The second defensive line that ran along the S-Bahn constituted the main-line of resistance inside Berlin. Trenches were dug along the street and embankments on the eastern and western flanks.[34] Each train station was solidly built and turned into ready-made strong-points. The S-Bahn itself ran both above and below ground where Germans used the raised portions as observation and firing points, while the deep culverts became impassible barriers to the advancing Soviet forces. Behind this defensive line, twenty permanently fixed local artillery and mobile anti-aircraft artillery batteries were distributed.[35] Fixed tank obstacles were constructed across many road intersections. These stationery concrete obstacles consisted of moveable sections to allow the passage of street cars and other vehicles.[36] The openings were closed after dark and strongly guarded in some sectors. Eder, Sector F's commander, was apparently well connected politically. His connections allowed for better defensive construction than many other sectors.[37] In Charlottenburg, for example, twelve barricades were erected along the main roads that were three meters high and consisted of steel girders rammed into the street and covered with heaps of rubble. Throughout the sector local defensive positions were established. Machine-gun emplacements were setup in upper stories of houses near key intersections. Passageways and trenches were constructed from cellars into the streets as positions that allowed quick *Panzerfaust* attacks. In general, cellars were converted into shelters by local residents and connected with one another so that troop movements could be carried out under cover. Roofs in key tactical positions also saw preparation as sniper posts.[38] As previously noted, defensive preparations were not consistent among the varying sectors. In Sectors A & B trenches were built daily by workgroups numbering 500–600 people. These sectors faced east where it was assumed that the primary Soviet assault would appear so most unified efforts at constructing positions went to Bärenfänger's area of responsibility. Bärenfänger was also a close fried of Goebbels. His friendship guaranteed better support for the sectors under his command. During the battle his relationship with Goebbels also cause significant friction with other commanders and prevent any unified defensive coordination.

There was a shortage of building materials in Berlin despite all the defensive building activity. It was out of the question to construct bunkers of reinforced concrete as the Allied bombing wrecked havoc on German raw material production. Only very small quantities of mines and barbed wire were available to be placed due to the lack of supplies.[39] This caused problems during the battle as many of the bridges in the city rigged for demolition were only damaged and not destroyed in the resulting explosions. Partial demolitions allowed Russians passage across the wide canals. Much of the defense along the inner perimeter of Berlin was based on positions that consisted of preexisting rubble caused by years of relentless Allied bombing. These natural defensive positions offered better cover and concealment from the Russians who easily identified and destroyed many of the fixed emplacements in the city.[40]

Three massive Flak Towers anchored the Berlin defense. The Flak Towers were arguably the most sophisticated defensive structures built by any nation during WWII. They were never intended to be used as fixed sites for ground defense but their ability to destroy Russian armor and fend off Soviet infantry assaults with their accurate firepower surprised German and Russian soldiers alike. Hitler ordered the construction of the Flak Towers immediately after the first British RAF bombing raid of August 1940.[41] The first built was the Zoo Tower, so named for its location in the Berlin Zoo. This tower was followed by the Humboldthain and Friedrichshain Flak Towers, with each built in the park they were named after. All three locations were selected to help provide added concealment due to the surrounding foliage and to keep the weapons platform as far away from residential areas as possible. The original plan called for six towers to protect Berlin, but only three were built in the period 1941–1942. One of the future six towers was to be built on the burnt-out carcass of the Reichstag.[42] The 100,000 ton structures were impregnable steel and concrete fortresses that presented a serious problem for attacking Soviet troops (and post-war attempts to destroy them). Each tower was built in pairs with a G-Tower or Gun Tower and a nearby smaller L-Tower or Fire-Control Tower. The ground surface of the G-Towers measured 70.5x70.5 meters with outer walls 2.5 meters thick. The G-Tower had a cellar, a ground floor, and five upper floors linked by concrete spiral staircases in the corners and center of the tower. There were two freight elevators and several armored ammunition elevators that could lift 10 tons to the gun decks.[43] On the roof were two gun platforms. The upper most gun deck consisted of four dual 12.8cm Flak 40s. These massive guns were considered one of the most effective AA platforms of the war. The shot height was 14,800 meters with a maximum range of 20,950 meters. Rate of fire was 20–24 rounds per minute for the twin version mounted on the top gun platform. The gun had a 360 degree traverse and an elevation of −3 to +88 degrees allowing them to fire over open site and hit ground targets.[44] They were so powerful that their firing caused a dramatic pressure change inside the Flak Tower requiring soldiers to leave their helmets unbuttoned to prevent injury.[45] Just below the main gun deck was a second gun deck that housed 3.7cm Flak Guns on the corners and 2.0cm Quad Flaks on the sides. The Flak Towers also had their own water and communication supply. Even the foundation was elastic to absorb the shock generated by the 12.8cm guns.[46] This design feature helped the survival of the towers when they came under direct fire from Soviet aircraft and artillery during the battle.

During the Soviet assault on Berlin the G-Towers participated in all aspects of the defense. The Zoo Tower's 12.8cm guns reached as far away as Gatow Airfield in the west and supported the defenders there. They fired at Soviets tanks in Moabit well north of the Spree. The 12.8s were so powerful that Soviet tanks hit by their shells practically disintegrated. The smaller 3.7cm guns switched to armor piercing ammunition during the battle that easily punched through the sides of Soviet armor that got in the way.[47]

By 1945 the gun crews were manned by young *Hitlerjugend* and *SS* Cadets from White Russia and Galicia. These cadets wore a yellow armband with a Lion's Head in the center. They were supposed to be replacements for the *14th Waffen-SS Grenadier Division (1st Galician)* but were reallocated to Berlin's immediate manpower needs. They had a strong hatred for ethnic Russians and the Communist system. They were among the staunchest defenders in Berlin.[48] Many of these boys joined volunteer tank hunting teams and launched sorties from the towers into the surrounding streets during the battle.

The Flak Tower's served significant multi-purpose roles during the Soviet assault on Berlin. They were defensive platforms, command-and-control centers, bomb shelters for tens of thousands of civilians, active military hospitals, and storage centers for significant art and antiquities from Berlin's many museums. An anti-tank warning system designed to alert of a surprise breakthrough by Soviet armor was established within Berlin.[49] The code word to activate the warning system was 'Clausewitz.' By the end of March the switchboard of the tank warning system moved into the Zoo Bunker where it could be managed reliably within the bunker's communication center.[50]

Supplying Fortress Berlin was a difficult problem in March 1945. Available war material was sent to the front causing shortages of all types. Ammunition was particularly lacking, while supply trains requisitioned from other parts of the Reich never made it to the city. Ammunition production could not occur in the city due to a lack of skilled labor.[51] Much of the weapons stockpiled in the city were not even of German manufacture. Three large ammo depots already existed in Berlin: Depot Martha in the Hasenheide Volks Park; Depot Mars in the Grunewald; and Depot Monika in the Jungfernheide Volks Park. These depots were at most 80% full. Smaller depots were set

TIERGARTEN

Command Tower

Flak Tower

Zoo Flak Tower complex. Note that from a height of over 10,000 feet you can still see the plumes of smoke generated by the powerful twin 12.8cm AA guns. When these guns were used on Soviet ground targets any tanks hit by these shells disintegrated upon impact. Aerial image courtesy of the US National Archive.

The steel shutters protected the occupants of the Flak Towers from almost all outside attack. Photo courtesy of the Bundesarchiv.

The roof of the Zoo Flak Tower looking east toward the L-Tower. Photo courtesy of the Bundesarchiv.

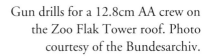

Gun drills for a 12.8cm AA crew on the Zoo Flak Tower roof. Photo courtesy of the Bundesarchiv.

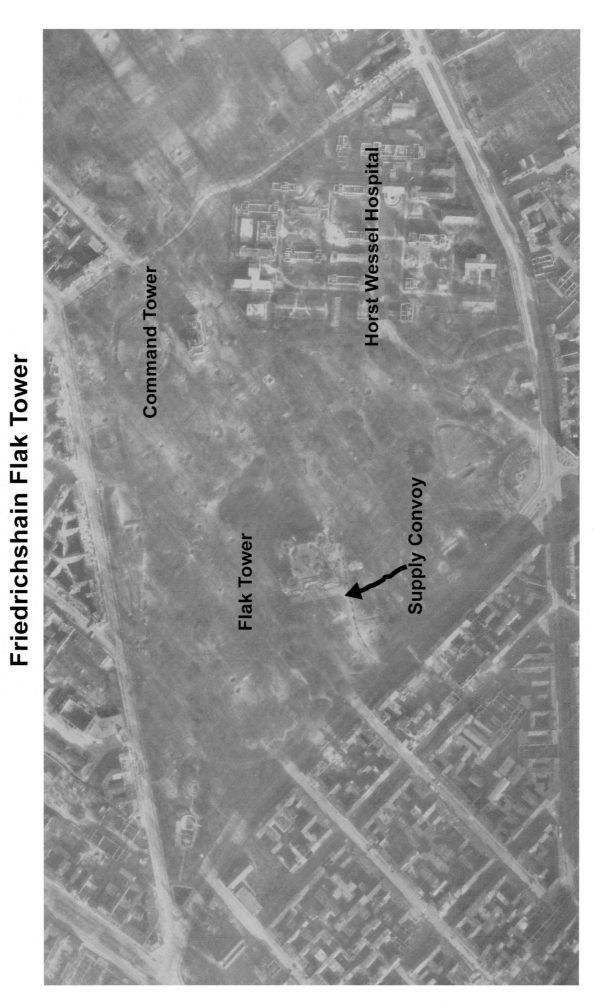

Friedrichshain Flak Tower

Command Tower

Horst Wessel Hospital

Flak Tower

Supply Convoy

Note the supply column lined up outside the entrance. Aerial image courtesy of the US National Archive.

Humboldthain Flak Tower

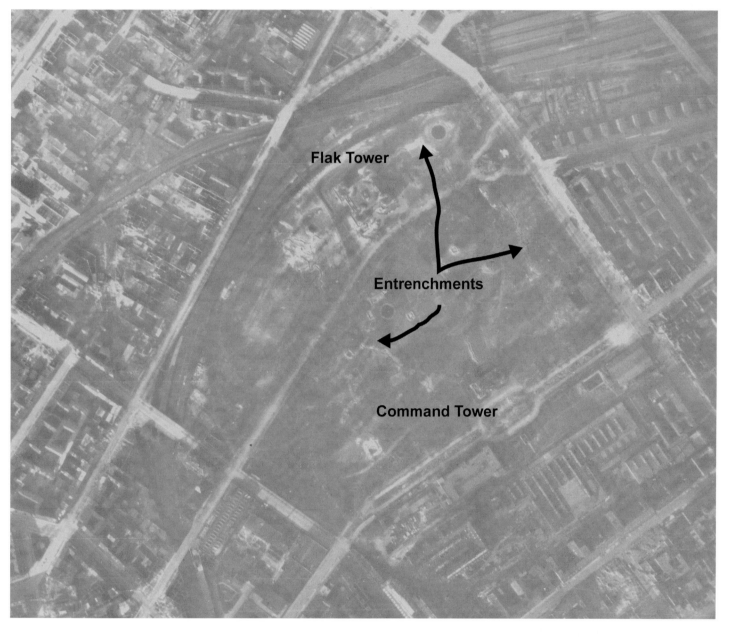

Note the trench lines built for defense. Aerial image courtesy of the US National Archive.

Defensive positions erected around the Funkturm (Radio Tower) located just south of Kaiserdamm Strasse. This area remained in German hands until 2 May. This photo was taken in March 1945. Photo courtesy of the Bundesarchiv.

up around the Tiergarten in Sector Z. Almost two-thirds of Depot Monika was transported by horse and cart to Depot Mars as the Soviet advanced into Berlin. The effort, however, was wasted as both Depot Mars and Martha fell into Russian hands on 25 April. Ironically, Reymann and his staff did not realize these depots existed until it was too late to properly distribute and store the contents to other locations.[52]

Petrol was also in extreme short supply within the city.[53] Lack of fuel resulted in tanks and military vehicles becoming immobile, hampering their effective military employment. Many units kept their own stocks and used whatever means necessary to acquire additional fuel for their independent uses. Unfortunately, no stockpiles of fuel existed and none were able to be set out before the Soviet assault. The only petrol the defenders could count on is what they brought into the city.

Lack of food and water were another problem for soldiers and civilian alike. The *BDA* staff brought in *Oberst* V. Hauenschildt as Quartermaster General. He previously setup the supply for the Silesian city of Breslau where German defenders were putting up successful resistance against Russian forces besieging that city. Trying to supply a city of Berlin's size turned out to be beyond even Hauenschildt's ability. It was thought that Berlin's soldiers could feed themselves for up to two weeks from their issued food stores. The few food storage facilities setup on the outskirts of Berlin were quickly overrun by Soviet troops like the ammunition dumps.[54] Water was available in quantity due to the lakes, canals, and wells throughout the city. The most disconcerting aspect of the defensive planning was trying to account for the needs of the estimated 120,000 children in Berlin. Goebbels suggested that they could drink canned milk in a siege. He even offered to bring in cows to provide fresh milk. When confronted with the question of how to feed the cows during the siege, Goebbels offered no reply.[55] Attention soon turned to supplying Berlin from the air once the Soviet assault on the city began.

Berlin had two major airports that could be used for supplying the city. The airports were Tempelhof in the southeast and Gatow in the west. As an additional precaution the *BDA* staff recommended that the East-West axis from the Siegessäule (Victory Column) to the Brandenburg Gate be cleared as a runway. This required both trees and lamp posts on either side of the street to be cleared allowing aircraft the size of Ju–52s to land.[56] Coordination for pre-planned aerial supply never materialized, however. Emergency ammunition supply drops occurred by parachute during the siege as no supply planes ever landed on the East-West runway during the assault.[57] Reinforcements did arrive using the makeshift runway on at least one occasion.

Medical supplies, with the exception of gauze, were available in quantity within Berlin. Vast medical supplies were stored in hospitals and *Wehrmacht* medical depots in Heeressanitätspark, Wahrkriegssanitätspark, Luftgausanitätspark, and Zentraler Park der Technischen Nothilfe (The Technical Emergency Aid Central Depot). Bandages, however, were non-existent. Gauze simply didn't exist due to production shortages. Soldiers and civilians alike were left to their own devices to create makeshift bandages.[58]

Perhaps the most problematic aspect of Berlin's defense was the lack of a unified communication system. A serious shortage of trained signal personnel and equipment existed.[59] This was in part due to the constant manpower shortage that placed highly skilled technicians into the role of infantry. Berlin's civilian telephone system only partially made up the difference as constant Allied bombings in March caused whole telephone grids to loose power for days at a time. The primary answer to the communication problem was the traditional military use of messengers. Messengers were relied on extensively to carry orders between units. Messengers, however, "often took hours to

Levy I *Volkssturm* armed with Panzerfaust in front of an anti-tank barricade. Photo taken on 10 March 1945.
Photo courtesy of the Bundesarchiv.

proceed a few hundred meters through the rubble strewn streets" according to a postwar assessment of the battle.[60] In one instance, orders sent from the *Führerbunker* to the Defense HQ on Bendler Strasse took two hours—this was normally a 15 minute walk.[61] During the battle, the shots of Soviet snipers, concentrated artillery fire, frontal assaults, and friendly fire conspired to limit the effectiveness of German messengers.

All of Reymann's defensive planning was based on the availability of trained and equipped soldiers that could occupy the fixed emplacements under construction. The defense of Berlin and the perimeter along the *HKL* required 100,000 battle-trained soldiers according to Reymann's estimates. Within the city of Berlin the *CBDA* could draw on only a small force of mixed combat formations that were ill-trained and equipped.[62] The actual number of German troops available for the defense in Berlin can never be known. The rapid course of battle combined with the ferocity of fighting created an environment where accurate records were not kept. Likewise, most unit records were burnt before surrender to the Soviets. The Soviets on the other hand did not bother to accurately ascertain who their adversaries were. After capitulation they simply took every able-bodied male in uniform and marched them east. The actual number of defenders in Berlin, excluding those forces that ended up in Berlin from the Oder Front, is lower than previously thought. The units already located in Berlin and available to *CBDA* are listed below. Chapter 3 will detail the forces that retreated into Berlin along with the *LVI Panzer Korps*.

The main force available to the *CBDA* consisted of *Volkssturm*—otherwise known as Home Guard Units. Hitler ordered the creation of the *Volkssturm* on 25 September 1944.[63] They reported directly to individual *Gauleiters* who were in control of the various *Gaues*. In *Gaue 3* (Berlin), the *Volkssturm* came under the control of *Gauvolkssturm Führer SA-Obergruppenführer* Graenz.[64] Graenz reported directly to Goebbels. Graenz, like so many other Nazi political appointees, disappeared while visiting a defense sector during the first Russian attack. The *CBDA* exercised only tactical control of these units in Berlin and they remained under Goebbels command for armament, equipment, provisions, and administration. The *Volkssturm* in Berlin were different from the *Volkssturm* formed in the last months of 1944.

The original *Volkssturm* battalions consisted primarily of World War I veterans that organized and fought as homogeneous units. These units showed little combat value in practice and were often defeated in the first attack by enemy forces. During the assault on Berlin it became practice to infuse the *Volkssturm* with young *Hitlerjugend* recruits, typically led by a veteran *SS* officer or senior non-commissioned officer (NCO).[65] This was based on Hitler's 28 January order called 'Employment of the *Volkssturm*' that recognized the inherent weakness in the *Volkssturm's* fighting value and now required them mixed with regular units to assist in bolstering their combat effectiveness.[66]

The *Volkssturm* in Berlin were organized into two separate levies. Levy I consisted of all men born between the years of 1884 and 1924. These men averaged 52 in age and were mainly World War I veterans. They had some weapons and equipment and conducted regular training. Levy II were men of the same age bracket that were currently engaged in essential civilian employment.[67] These men could not be called up until the Soviets were actually fighting in the city. In Berlin they were primarily meant as replacements for Levy I. It is generally accepted that a total of 40 *Volkssturm* battalions were organized, with 20 in Levy I and 20 in Levy II.[68] The total number of men represented by both levies is approximately 40–60,000; however, this number has to be understood in context.[69] The battalions

Volkssturm receive instruction on the Panzerfaust in the Grunewald on 9 April 1945. Photo courtesy of Bundesarchiv.

numbered widely in men. They ranged anywhere from 600–1,500 men.[70] Based on a careful review of all available sources, perhaps 30,000 men were available for service and less than 15,000 saw any real combat.

Equipping the *Volkssturm* was a significant challenge faced by the *BDA*. The *Volkssturm* were equipped primarily with captured Italian rifles with only 20 rounds of ammunition for each weapon. Weapons from every country Germany occupied could be found in the ranks of the *Volkssturm*.[71] This was due to an 11 March order from Hitler that specified *Volkssturm* units had to give up their weapons to the *Wehrmacht* in order to fill massive shortages of weapons now being experienced in the German war economy.[72] Most battalions were equipped with at least one Machinengewehr 08. The MG 08 was a WWI vintage 7.92mm water-cooled, belt-fed weapon that fired 600 rounds per minute. These were designed by the American Hiram Maxim and manufactured locally in Spandau. The factory in Spandau apparently had hundreds left over in storage and provided them to the *Volkssturm*. Other battalions were given significant numbers of weapons based on the affiliations that the battalion commander had with local arms factories. Several battalions in Spandau boasted as many as twenty Machinengewehr 42s.[73] The MG 42 was a modern weapon system when it was deployed during WWII that fired a 7.92mm round up to a rate of 1,500 rounds per minute. Another battalion funded by the Siemens Factory numbered 770 men and deployed with three complete rifle companies, a support weapons company, and an infantry gun company. It was also commanded by a WWI veteran and received excellent training—this was the exception, not the rule.[74] Attempts to cross levy excess weapons across all battalions in Berlin failed because local Nazi officials refused to relinquish control of what amounted to their own private armies.[75] No known units were armed with modern assault rifles although some were equipped with the Voksssturmgewehr 1–5. This was also known as the VG 1–5 and was a 7.92mm semi-automatic weapon that began production in January 1945. Only 10,000 were produced and the majority was rushed to the *Volkssturm* units fighting in Pomerania and Prussia. Most were armed with the German Karabiner 98k.[76] This was the standard German issue rifle at the start of the war. It held a 5 shot magazine of 7.92x55mm ammunition and was very accurate out to 500 meters. This weapon was great in open terrain but in urban combat where lethal engagements with the enemy occurred at ranges of 25 meters or less, it was not very useful. In addition, ammunition was in short supply for all weapon systems employed during the battle except the *Panzerfaust*. This weapon was in significant supply and almost every *Volkssturm* battalion had an allotment and received regular training on how to use them effectively in an urban environment.

The *Panzerfaust* is synonymous with the Battle of Berlin. No other weapon was used with such deadly effect by *both* sides. Men, women, and boys all received some rudimentary training on this weapon system that was lightweight, easy to use and very effective against tanks, enemy soldiers, or just about any fixed target. The *Panzerfaust* was designed in November 1942 at the request of the *Wehrmacht* weapons office for a hollow shaped charge that could be hand fired. The first 350,000 *Panzerfaust* were delivered in 1943 and could penetrate 200 mm of armor at a maximum range of 75 meters. Improvements in design and production occurred throughout the war. By November 1944 the *Panzerfaust* 100 was introduced. This new model could penetrate 200mm of armor plate with an immediate effective range of 100 meters. It also boasted a trajectory height of 3.5 meters that extended the range out to 280 meters. Production reached a staggering 1,295,000 units in December 1944 alone, though it had a 5.5% misfire rate.[77] The importance of this weapon's employment during the fighting in Berlin and subsequent impact on the future of anti-tank and urban combat has gone almost unrecognized over the last sixty-two years.

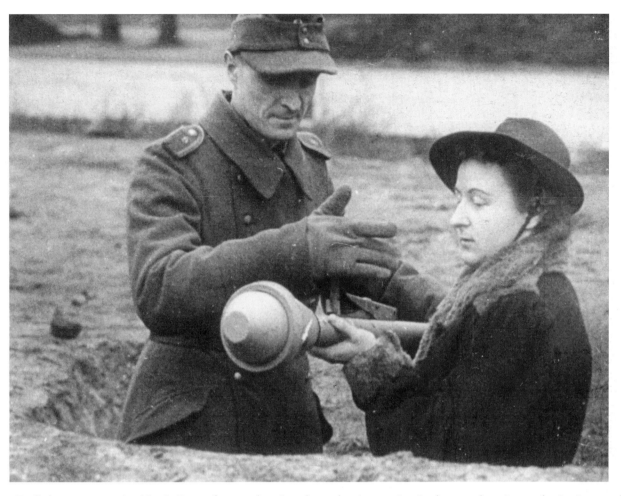

Even Berlin's women received basic Panzerfaust and anti-tank combat instruction in the months prior to the Soviet assault. Photo courtesy of Bundesarchiv.

Volkssturm digging a fighting position near an S-Bahn line and nearby bridge. Photo courtesy of Bundesarchiv.

The *Volkssturm* called up in Levy I participated in regular training drills. Units usually received training on the weekends or in the evenings after work from 1700–1900 hours.[78] The ability to train effectively was a product of the unit leadership and weapons available. Some units were sent to the Grünewald (a large, densely wooded park district in the southwest of Berlin) 2–3 times a week for training.[79] During the fortification construction in the month of March the *Volkssturm* were used extensively in the labor role. This dramatically reduced their training time although they continued to receive political lectures to foster morale.[80] Some *Volkssturm* draftees responsible for construction even practiced passive resistance as a means to protest their call to service and use as labor.[81] Levy II *Volkssturm* participated in no known training and were not equipped with weapons. These men were supposed to draw equipment from the various Levy I units when they reported as replacements.

The conflicts caused by political infighting wrecked havoc with the *CBDA's* ability to control and employ the few *Volkssturm* units left in Berlin. For example, two of the original 20 battalions slated for the defense of Berlin were commanded by the Brandenburg *Gauleiter* Stürtz. His area of charge was the city of Potsdam. He refused to provide the two battalions to the *CBDA* because of his dislike for Goebbels, sending them to the *9.Armee* independently stating " … Berlin is of no interest to me!"[82] During the battle *Volkssturm* battalions often received simultaneous orders from both military and party officials that were often contradictory.[83]

The actual number of *Volkssturm* that fought in Berlin will never be known with 100% accuracy. If we use the conservative figure of 1,000 to represent the strength of each battalion in Levy I then we have approximately 20,000 men under arms in the *Volkssturm*. One German source states that no more than 24,000 *Volkssturm* were available in April.[84] More than half of these battalions were ordered to the Oder Front at the request of Heinrici on 18 April and were destroyed by the Soviets. Few battalions remained intact after their first encounter with the Red Army in the open, although perhaps a few retreated back into Berlin intact as a cohesive fighting force.[85] In most cases many of the battalions were co-mingled and reconstituted as *Kampfgruppe* in Berlin. According to the *AGV* daily operational map there were 2 *Volkssturm* battalions already operating behind the *9.Armee* on 18 April, presumably sent from Potsdam, and another 11 battalions on their way to the front.[86] This represents 13,000 or 65% of Berlin's *Volkssturm* available for the city's defense now moving into the frontline of *AGV*. According to Soviet sources, the Soviets encountered the following twelve *Volkssturm* battalions during the battle: 3rd, 16th, 17th, 39th, 93rd, 103rd, 107th, 109th, 121st, 205th, 260th, and 721st.[87] Soviet sources appear to be in line with the German sources in this case. While there were another 20,000 available for call up in Levy II, all first person accounts suggest that due to lack of weapons and training, this reserve *Volkssturm* pool offered no military value to the *CBDA*. Based on all calculations, a conservative estimate of the number of *Volkssturm* that actually fought in Berlin is between 7,000–10,000 men. Their combat performance varied widely.

Some of the *Volkssturm* simply evaporated in the face of Soviets attacks, while others fought well alongside their integrated *Wehrmacht*, *Waffen-SS*, and *Hitlerjugend* counterparts. These soldiers consisted of the largest combat force available to the *CBDA*.[88] For example, the *Volkssturm* that defended the Teltow canal south of Tempelhof was mixed in with *Wehrmacht* units in a well-constructed defensive perimeter. Here the *Volkssturm* were able to hold off assaults by elements of the Soviet's 8th Guards Army for nearly two days.[89] Several *Volkssturm* battalions led by Wolfgang Skorning operating in Sector D conducted well-organized defensive operations by employing hit-and-run tactics using *Panzerfaust* against Soviet armor.

The *CBDA* also had thousands of *Hitlerjugend* available for incorporation into the various *Volkssturm* battalions and as stand-alone formations. These boys typically did not receive better training than their *Volkssturm* counterparts (though their membership in the *Hitlerjugend* organization naturally focused on military exercises), but were, by most accounts, fanatical in their motivation and quickly picked up their military instruction. The *Hitlerjugend* were under the organizational command of *Reichsjugendführer* Artur Axmann who was present in Berlin until the end. Axmann continued to exercise some control over the *Hitlerjugend* formations, like Goebbels did of the *Volkssturm*. Like the *Volkssturm*, no accurate period information on the total number of *Hitlerjugend* that fought in Berlin is available.[90] The estimates range from 3,500 to more than 6,000.[91] The actual number of *Hitlerjugend* that fought may actually be higher. The argument for a higher number of *Hitlerjugend* participants is primarily based on the fact that several *Hitlerjugend* Anti-Tank Brigades were raised and fought along the Oder Front. After engaging with the Soviets many of the boys retreated back to Berlin with the front line combat units. How many actually made it back into the city is simply unknown. In addition, regular sweeps of the city's residential districts by the *SS* forced boys not previously associated with any military units into service. If 6,000 *Hitlerjugend* were in Berlin at the start of the assault than perhaps another 2,000–3,000 can be added to this number. The *Hitlerjugend* formations that were affiliated with Berlin were initially organized into a regiment under command of *Gebietsführer* Harmann, a Spandau division under *Oberst* Marreck, and a battalion under *Oberbannführer* Schlünder.[92] Most of these boys were transferred into the *Volkssturm* during the battle. Not all *Hitlerjugend* saw combat as many found a place as 'runners.' Other commanders did not welcome the enthusiastic boys in their units or rear areas and fought hard to have them removed from the combat zone. In either case all accounts of the *Hitlerjugend* in Berlin are unanimous as to their fighting capability and impact on the battle. One of the most widely viewed films from the last days of the war is propaganda footage of Hitler awarding members of the *Hitlerjugend* with Iron Crosses. In that same film footage, Axmann was also awarded the Golden Cross of the German Order by Hitler in recognition of his *Hitlerjugend's* exploits in battle. According to one participant in the ceremony Hitler looked at Axmann and stated "Without your boys the battle could not have been carried through, not only here in Berlin, but in the whole of Germany."[93] Putting aside the morally repugnant aspect of using boys to fight in combat aside (many pre-teen), the *Hitlerjugend* represented an important pool of combat manpower.

Various combinations of *Allgemine SS*, *Waffen-SS* and *Gestapo* forces existed in Berlin. The *SS* troops were almost exclusively based in Sector Z. Many individual *SS* commanders and senior NCOs became commanders of *ad-hoc* units drawn from stragglers as well as independent *Hitlerjugend* formations. They numbered approximately 3,000–4,000 men. All *SS* troops, regardless of affiliation, fell under the command of *SS Brigadeführer* Wilhelm Mohnke. Mohnke was also the defense commander of the Government Quarter directly reporting to Hitler. He had the responsibility of ensuring the protection of the area around Voss and Wilhelm Strasse down to the Hallesches Tor.[94] Mohnke's primary responsibility was to ensure the protection of the Reich Chancellery and the *Führerbunker*. He operated as a separate command and did not coordinate with either the *CBDA* or any *Wehrmacht* authority.[95] Mistrust and even open hostility existed between many *SS* and *Wehrmacht* soldiers during the battle. The *SS* in Berlin were organized into two regiments from elements of *Leibstandarte SS Adolf Hitler* (*LSSAH*) *Wachregiment*, *LSSAH Ausbildungs-und Ersatz Bataillon* from Spreenhagen, the *Führer-Begleit-Kompanie*, and the *Reichsführer SS Begleit Bataillon*. The *1./Regiment* was known as the *SS Regiment Anhalt*, named after the unit's commander *Standartenführer* Günther Anhalt who served with distinction in the ranks of *LSSAH* under Mohnke then in the *SS Polizei* where he won the Knight's Cross while fighting in Russia. His regiment numbered 1,500 men that consisted of the remnants of the *LSSAH Wachregiment* that contained seasoned frontline troops.

SS-Brigadeführer Wilhelm Mohnke commanded the forces in the Government Quarter.
Photo courtesy of Charles Trang.

A rare photo of an abandoned German experimental anti-tank assault vehicle Borgward B IV Sd Kfz 301 armed with 4-6 Panzerscherck launchers in Berlin, May 1945. Photo courtesy of ASKM.

Other members of the *Waffen-SS* stationed in Berlin also fell under this unit. The *2./Regiment* consisted of primarily *Allgemine SS* that served as administrative staff in various buildings around the Government Quarter.[96] Various *Gestapo* units were organized as local fighting units assigned to specific buildings like the Gestapo HQ on Prinz Albrecht Strasse. The *SS* units were well-equipped, motivated, and trained; however, they were poorly integrated into the overall defense. Individual *SS* combat leaders, regardless of rank, often demonstrated considerable worth when integrated into *Volkssturm, Hitlerjugend,* or other *ad-hoc* formations, as they brought leadership, motivation, and combat expertise.

The *Wachregiment Grossdeutschland* was another ceremonial unit based in Berlin. This unit had a primary mission of guarding the surviving members of the old German Royal family in Berlin. As the air raids over Berlin continued they became more involved with the rescue of civilians. They also played a key role in managing the increasing numbers of foreign laborers forced to work in the many local factories.[97] A portion of the unit was formed into an independent regiment that became part of the *309.Berlin Division* and was sent to the Oder Front. The rest of the unit stayed in Berlin. These soldiers were well-equipped, trained and motivated. Many of the soldiers had recent battle experience while serving on the Eastern Front in one of the component of the *Panzerkorps Grossdeutschland.* The remaining elements of *Wachregiment Grossdeutschland* in Berlin numbered no more than 300–400 trained soldiers, although accurate figures are not available.

Supporting the above combat formations were a wide variety of localized, smaller forces. Local Defense Forces, School Cadets, *Wehrmacht* Replacement units, Plant Protection Troops, Alert Units and local Police Battalions were found in every defense sector. They were not numerous and their combat effectiveness varied significantly.[98] In the case of the organized Police Battalions, Reymann never saw them at all during their defense planning as they were busy with their daily jobs.[99] Presumably they conducted business as usual, but their lack of participation in the planning process prevented better integration in the German defense during the Soviet assault. Among the best units that the *CBDA* drew on were a variety of important combat support units.

The *1.Flak Division* was based in Berlin under *Luftwaffe Generalmajor* Otto Sydow. The command post of the *1.Flak Division* was located in the Zoo Bunker's L Tower located across the Landwehr Canal in the Tiergarten. This division consisted of 4 Anti-Aircraft (AA) regiments with 4–5 battalions (2.0cm–12.8cm) of older guns of German and foreign makes.[100] The AA battalions were deployed across the city's perimeter, primarily along main avenues of enemy approach. Many of the crews were well-trained and motivated while others were conscripts and could not fire the guns effectively in a ground defense role. A number of the guns were encased in concrete and could not be moved and were quickly abandoned in the face of approaching Soviets. Many of the *Luftwaffe* schools were combed for additional guns during the month of March. Under the leadership of *Oberstleutnant* Plantho, another 7 light and 7 heavy training batteries were located and deployed along the city perimeter. In addition, various rocket units were located at key avenues of approach for psychological effect. Due to their low ammunition, they could only fire one salvo each.[101]

Among the most unusual units that were available to the *CBDA* was an experimental Anti-Tank (AT) detachment. This unit consisted of a Detachment HQ and three companies that consisted of 3–5 Borgward vehicles. These vehicles were either Volkswagen or older Panzerkampfwagen I chassis mounted with 6 Panzerschrecks that fired simultaneously through an electric ignition.[102] The Panzerschreck was a cousin to the *Panzerfaust* and based on the U.S. Bazooka captured by the Germans in Tunisia in 1943. During the battle elements of this unit fought as mobile strike teams, striking at the flank of a Soviet armor column then falling back before a counterattack was launched.

Berlin resembled an armed camp by the end of March. Training of existing forces was seen with more frequency throughout the Grunewald and various *Wehrmacht* barracks. The weapon of choice was the *Panzerfaust. Wehrmacht* replacement troops were training with this weapon at practice tanks around various *Kasernes.*[103] By the order of Goebbels, even women began receiving 5 hours a week of weapons training.[104] Barricades, road blocks, and armed patrols were prevalent in all Defense Sectors. AA guns and fixed *Pazerstellung* (Panzer turrets dug-in and placed at ground level along key intersections) were now moved near the S-Bahn rings crossing points. While the *CBDA* receives credit for providing the only coherent command structure across Berlin, serious conflicts over resources, training, deployments and tactical placement of units occurred. The *CBDA* appointed Defense Sector commanders, *Volkssturm* commanders, Axman's *Hitlerjugend,* various *SS* under Mohnke and other local units all operated independently. As Reifor stated in his diary, no one wanted to be responsible to Hitler, so they refused to subordinate themselves to the *CBDA.*[105]

Reymann's team continued to struggle for guidance and support from Hitler. When Reymann didn't receive effective guidance from Hitler he went to *OKH* but was told that "we are only responsible for the Eastern Front, apply to *OKW* if you want orders!" When he went to *OKW* they said "Berlin faces East and *OKH* is responsible for you."[106] At the end of March the *BDA* was subordinated, although temporarily, to *AGV.* In case of a Soviet breakthrough, Berlin was now to become part of *AGV's* frontline, where arguably it should have been placed months ago.[107] The *CBDA* staff looked at this development with new promise. Now it appeared they might be able to draw on real combat units for support and work this possibility into their defense plan. They knew that their defense plan required an estimated 100 battle ready divisions—an unrealistic number given the military situation—but they hoped that they could count on some units to bolster Berlin's defense in a time of crisis.[108] Reifor reiterated in his diary that "it was clear to us from the very beginning that Berlin could never be defended with the available forces ….we still had to consider ideas for the direction of the battle in the event of encirclement … "[109] In a preliminary phone conversation with the new commander of *AGV,* Reymann made it clear that he expected to have some of Heinrici's units retreat into Berlin if necessary. Heinrici immediately dispatched his Chief of Staff *Generalmajor* Kinzel, and Operations Officer *Oberst* Eismann to meet with the *BDA* staff and review the defense plans for Berlin. Kinzel and Eismann listened with unease at Berlin's lack of preparedness to withstand a major ground assault by Soviet forces. Perhaps most shocking was the absolute lack of reason demonstrated by the various political and military departments on the issues of coordination. At the end of the *CBDA* brief Eismann said to Reymann that "as far as I am concerned those madmen in Berlin can fry in their own juices."[110] Eismann soon informed Heinrici that Berlin could not be properly defended without the necessary forces from *AGV.* Heinrici then placed *CBDA* operationally under command of General Busse's *9.Armee.* Heinrici, however, did not plan on providing *CBDA* with any combat formations.

Heinrici realized that defending Berlin directly was simply impossible if not outright madness. He planned to avoid drawing Berlin into frontline combat. Heinrici's goal was to pursue the course of action directed by Guderian: defend against the Soviet offensive along the Oder Front long enough to bring the Western Allies across the Elbe into eastern Germany and Berlin. To support this effort he decided along with Reymann that all the forces in Berlin must be drawn out of the city to bolster the defense along the Oder Front. Heinrici subsequently ordered Busse and all subordinate commands of the *9.Armee* to retreat west around Berlin if the Soviets did break through along the Oder Front. Heinrici told Busse bluntly " … to avoid [Berlin] with its troops and it was to fall back on two sides towards Mecklenberg."[111] Busse's Chief of Staff, *Generalmajor* Hölz, echoed Heinrici's reluctance to be involved in any protracted struggle for Berlin when he subsequently met with Reymann and reiterated that the final battle will be along the Oder and not Berlin. He stated that "the 9th Army stays and will stay on the Oder. If necessary we will fall there, but we will not retreat."[112] In essence, no combat units of *AGV* under Heinrici's command were allocated for Berlin's defense. Eismann wrote after the war that "the worst thing that could happen in my opinion was for the *9th Armee* to fall back to Berlin. This would give Hitler the opportunity to [enforce] one of his 'fort[ress]' orgies which had started with Stalingrad and was to end in Berlin. This had to be prevented in any case. Seen from a military viewpoint, there was no point in defending Berlin."[113] The command staff of *AGV*, to which Reymann and the *CBDA* were now subordinated, made the final decision that Berlin would be defended along the Oder Front and not be turned into a battleground.

Reymann and his staff exercised their meager authority to develop a battle plan to be used when Berlin was surrounded. The planning revealed two key weaknesses. First, that Berlin needed troops to be defended and they simply didn't exist. Second, there was no clear goal in the defense plan. Was Berlin to be defended until a relief force arrived? Was Berlin simply going to be a strong point used to bleed the Soviets until they stopped attacking? Was the defense of Berlin to draw the U.S and British forces across the Elbe River in order to create open conflict with the Soviets? None of these discussions occurred. The defense of Berlin existed without any context to the overall strategic situation. What was clear was that no support was going to arrive from the only place it could—Heinrici's *AGV*. Heinrici had his own mission to plan and carry out. He was now in charge of the single largest formation of German soldiers within Germany facing one of the largest concentrations of Soviet forces during the war. If Berlin was going to be saved from direct assault by the Soviets then it would happen during the final battle for Germany along the Oder Front.

Notes to Chapter 2

1   J. Ethel and Dr. A. Price, *Target Berlin, Mission 250: 6 March 1944*, p. 3.
2   U. Hellweg, "Berlin: The Rebirth of Public Transport on Water," Public Transportation International, April 2000, p. 6.
3   T. Le Tissier, *Race for the Reichstag*, p. 11.
4   Le Tissier, *Zhukov on the Oder*, p. 11.
5   MS #P-136, p. 14.
6   No work was done during the preceding month because the BDA had two successive changes of commanders and the need to reinforce the front along the Oder was given top priority.
7   H. Reifor, Mein Berliner Tagebuch! RH 53-3/24 and H. Reifor, My Berlin Dairy, p. 1. (RC: 67/11)—hereafter referred to as HRD.
8   H. Reymann interview. (RC: 67/12).
9   Reymann interview.
10 HRD, p. 2.
11 Ibid.
12 Ibid, p. 3.
13 Reymann interview.
14 HRD, p. 3.
15 Ibid, p. 10.
16 Ibid, p. 12.
17 Ibid, p. 7.
18 Ibid, p. 8.
19 MS #P-136, pp. 34–7.
20 HRD, p. 12.
21 Translation of "Führer Order, 7 April 1945," (RC: 65:9).
22 MS #136, pp. 33-34.
23 HRD, p. 12.
24 Reymann interview.
25 HRD, p. 5.
26 Ibid, p. 6.
27 MS #P-136, p. 16.
28 Ibid, p. 26.
29 HRD, p. 9.
30 Ibid.
31 MS #P-136, p. 26.
32 HRD, p. 10.
33 MS #P-136, p. 27.
34 Ibid, p. 28.
35 Ibid, p. 29.
36 HRD, p. 10.
37 MS #P-136, p. 33.
38 Ibid, pp. 31-32.
39 MS #P-136, p. 27.
40 Ibid, p. 38.
41 M. Foedrowitz, *The Flak Towers in Berlin, Hamburg and Vienna 1940-1950*, p. 3.
42 Ibid, p. 6.
43 Ibid, p. 7.
44 Ibid, p. 10.
45 T. Le Tissier, *With our Backs to Berlin: The German Army in Retreat 1945*, p. 125.
46 Ibid, p. 126.
47 Ibid, MS #P-136, p. 31.
48 Le Tissier, *With our Backs to Berlin*, p. 126.
49 HRD, p. 6.
50 Foedrowitz, p. 11.
51 HRD, p. 17.
52 MS #P-136, p. 48.
53 Ibid, p. 49.
54 HRD, pp. 16–17.
55 MS #P-136, pp. 50–1.
56 HRD, pp. 11–12, see also Reymann interview.
57 Ibid, p. 17.
58 G. Drost interview, (CR: 69/28).
59 MS #P-136, p. 22.
60 Ibid, p. 46.
61 HRD, p. 40.
62 MS #P-136, p. 26.
63 H. Kissel, *Hitler's Last Levy: The Volkssturm 1944–45*, pp. 8, 17.
64 HRD, p. 13.
65 Ibid, p. 18.
66 Le Tissier, *With our Backs to Berlin*, p. 204.
67 Kissel, pp. 26–7.
68 HRD, p. 13. Some accounts cite as many as 92 battalions; see MS #P-136, p. 40. This number is unrealistic and all other published accounts point to the lower number.
69 MS #P-136, p. 40.
70 Ibid.
71 Reymann interview.
72 Kissel, p. 35.
73 HRD, p. 13.
74 Le Tissier, Race for the Reichstag, p. 23.
75 HRD, p. 14.
76 W. Venghaus, Berlin 1945: *Die Zeit vom 16. April bis 2 Mai*, p. 159. This VS Battalion was only armed with the K98 and a few hand grenades, nothing else.
77 W. Fleischer, *Panzerfaust* and other German Infantry Anti-Tank Weapons, pp. 28, 47.
78 MS #P-136, p. 40.
79 O. Haaf interview. (RC: 69/30).
80 MS #P-136, p. 32.
81 H. Hellriegel interview. (RC: 69/33).
82 Ibid, p. 15. From Reymann's perspective the best of his *Volkssturm* units were sent to the Oder Front at the request of Heinrici. See Reymann interview.
83 MS #P-136, p. 20.
84 H. Holztträger, *In a Raging Inferno: Combat Units of the Hitler Youth, 1944–5*, p. 65.
85 HRD, p. 21. See also Le Tissier, Race for the Reichstag, p. 10, and MS #P-136, p. 27.
86 Heeresgruppe Weichsel "Lage Ost" (Eastern Theatre) 1939–45, 18 April 1945 in RG 242: Box 47.
87 Platonov, *The Second World War 1935-1945*, p. 24. (RC: 74/10). Soviet sources reviewed for this book were all unreliable for detail on German forces so this has to be taken in that context.
88 DTV, *Der Kampf um Berlin 1945* cites 42,531 *Volkssturm* and 3,532 Hitlerjugend available in Berlin for the defense, pp. 228. About 90% of the available fighting force in Berlin was *Volkssturm*, see H. Eismann interview. (RC: 68/12).
89 MS #P-136, p. 29.
90 Ibid, pp. 44–5.
91 Holztträger, p. 71.
92 Ibid.
93 Ibid, p. 73.
94 Le Tissier, *Race for the Reichstag*, p. 25.
95 MS #P-136, pp. 21, 43.
96 Le Tissier, *Race for the Reichstag*, p. 25.
97 H. Spaeter, *The History of the Panzerkorps Großdeutschland vol. 2*, pp. 93–5.
98 MS #P-136, p. 42.
99 Reymann interview.
100 MS #P-136, p. 44.
101 Ibid, p. 42.
102 Reymann interview.
103 H. Altner, *Berlin Dance of Death*, pp. 8.
104 Ibid, p. 15.
105 HRD, p. 18.
106 Ibid, p. 19.
107 MS #P-136, pp. 17–18.
108 Ibid, pp. 25–6.
109 HRD, p. 5.
110 Ibid, p. 19.
111 Heinrici interview.
112 HRD, p. 19.
113 Eismann interview.

3

ARMY GROUP VISTULA

The Oder is the HKL. Not one step back.

Generaloberst* Heinrici to the soldiers of *AGV

Guderian had a serious problem as Chief of *OKH* overseeing the Eastern Front. The most important command to the defense of Germany and Berlin was in the hands of *Reichsführer-SS* Heinrich Himmler. This was a man who had no military experience and led from behind the frontline in a personal armored train. Himmler made no positive contribution to *AGV* or the defense of Germany during his two months of command that started on 25 January. Himmler lost Pomerania to the Soviets and was unable to eliminate or contain the expanding Soviet bridgeheads along the Oder. He demonstrated a complete lack of military organizational ability. He failed to actively ensure a steady flow of replacements and equipment to *AGV*. Himmler did nothing to bolster the depleted divisions or prepare *AGV* for the final battle for Germany and Berlin.[1] Guderian realized the importance of this command. With the background knowledge of 'Eclipse', he made the decision to replace Himmler at any cost with a general that had a proven ability to defend against a Soviet attack. He immediately lobbied Hitler to replace Himmler with Heinrici. This was the last key decision Guderian influenced as Chief of Staff before Hitler sacked him at the end of March.

Heinrici came from a family with a long history of military service to Germany. A direct descendant served with Gustav Adolphus during the Thirty Years War in the mid 1600s. Heinrici served with distinction during the First World War where he participated in combat in Russia, France and Galicia. He remained in the post-war Germany Army known as the *Reichswehr* during the inter-war period. He then saw service first in France during the 1940 campaign, then in Russia where he fought to a position south of Moscow by 6 December 1941. He was a devout Protestant who never joined the Nazi Party. This caused him to be passed up for promotion to *Generaloberst* when his time came, but his ability to hold the *4.Armee* front against Soviet attacks in the winter of 1942 caused Hitler to give him his promotion. Later, he would come under scrutiny for not obeying the 'Scorched Earth' policy when he retreated from Russia. He was ordered to destroy the Smolensk Cathedral as his forces retreated, but he issued orders preventing it from being burned. His refusal

Generaloberst Gotthard Heinrici, commander of *Army Group Vistula*, in winter 1944-45. Photo courtesy of the Cornelius Ryan Collection, Mahn Center, Alden Library, Ohio University, Athens, OH.

Heinrici reviewing a map with several Hungarian Officers during operations in Southern Russian 1944.
Photo courtesy of the Cornelius Ryan Collection, Mahn Center, Alden Library, Ohio University, Athens, OH.

to follow orders caused him to be removed from command temporarily in late 1943. In the summer of 1944 he took over command of the *1.Panzer Armee* and the attached *1st Hungarian Army* retreating from the Ukraine. His ability to hold these formations together, and conduct a tenacious defense after they were temporarily encircled by the Soviets won him the Swords to the Oak Leaves of his Knight's Cross on 3 March 1945.[2] Heinrici's character and noted ability to command in defense resonated with Guderian who saw in Heinrici a commander worthy of the most important military assignment in Germany at that time.

The *Wehrmacht* was on the defensive since the summer of 1943 and Heinrici's skills at organization, planning and execution of complex defensive maneuvers were exactly what were required in the current situation. Heinrici understood the predictable pattern of a Russian attack and how to defeat the heavy opening artillery bombardment by withdrawing his frontline forces just prior to the barrage. He was able to preserve his frontline strength to fight from secondary defensive positions by conducting this complex maneuver. Soviet attack doctrine was so regimented and inflexible that Heinrici easily recognized the signs that signaled an impending attack days before it began. This was clear in Guderian's mind when Heinrici was appointed commander of *AGV* on 22 March. Guderian explained *AGV's* operational situation to Heinrici along with his new orders when they met in Guderian's underground office in Zossen where *OKW* and *OKH* were based. Guderian stated:

> I was concerned that you should be appointed because this is a situation where we need a man who has had actual combat experience of operations against the Russians. With Himmler it is simply impossible to carry on any further work. He has simply no idea of how military things go. He has no concept at all of tactics or operational questions. Things simply go over his head. It is high time that there should be some kind of change because we can reckon on a Russian attack against Berlin a very short time. It is not possible to say with any certainty at the moment when this will begin. Nevertheless it could be in a few days. The mission, to which [sic] you have been assigned, is extraordinarily difficult. Operations must be so handled that in every circumstance our worst enemy, that is Stalin, must be prevented from seeing Berlin.[3]

Heinrici left Guderian's office with an extraordinary responsibility. He had to reorganize *AGV* and prepare a defense that might have a chance to stop one of the Soviet's largest offensives seen during the war—and save Berlin.

AGV formed at the end of January after the *9.Armee* retreated back across the Oder River in the face of the Soviet's successful January 1945 Vistula-Oder offensive. *AGV* consisted of the *3.Panzer* and *9.Armees*. Manteuffel commanded the *3.Panzer Armee* along the northern sector of the front that ran from the Baltic to the heights around Eberswälde. The *9.Armee*, under Busse, continued from Eberswälde south into Silesia where it bordered *Armeegruppe Schörner*. Ferdinand Schörner, who was promoted to *Feldmarschall* on 4 April, was an adherent to Hitler's operational principles and well liked by the Führer. His relationship with Hitler allowed Schörner to request additional Panzer divisions from *AGV* during the month of April in a move that shocked Heinrici. Heinrici understood from intelligence and prisoner-of-war reports that the majority of Soviet forces arrayed against *AGV* were located between Küstrin and Frankfurt-an-der-Oder—directly opposite Busse's *9.Armee*.[4] In addition to favoring Schörner, Hitler believed, as discussed in Chapter 1, that the next major attack was going to happen toward Prague and not Berlin. This may have been a cover to provide the needed argument to

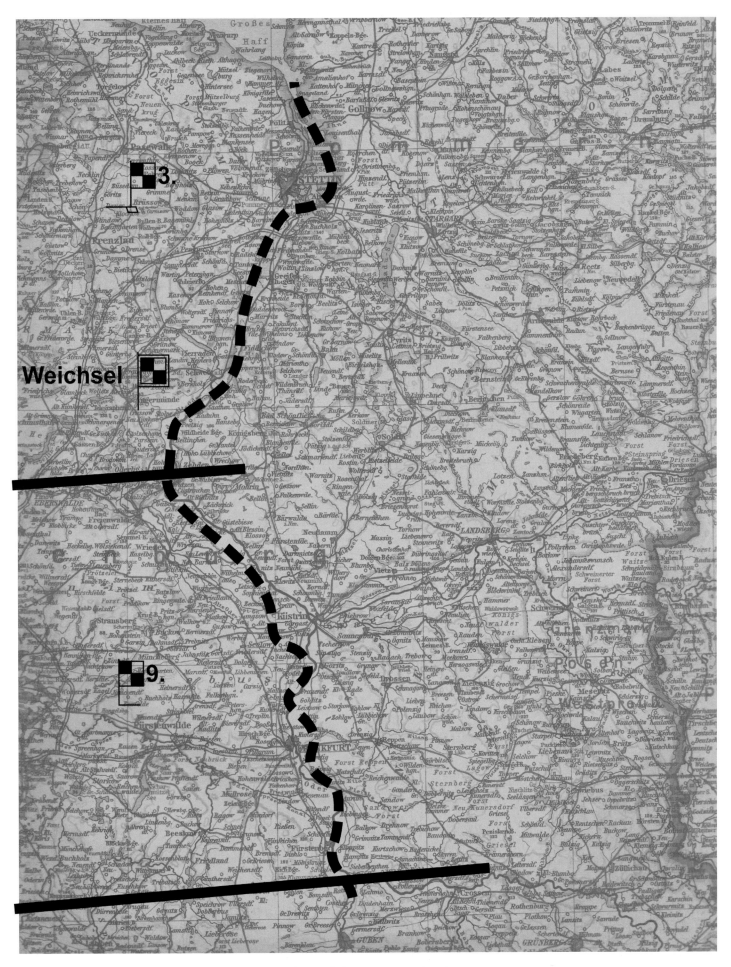

Boundaries of the *3.Panzer* and *9.Armee*.
Courtesy of the US National Archives

General Theodore Busse, *9.Armee* commander. Photo courtesy of the Cornelius Ryan Collection, Mahn Center, Alden Library, Ohio University, Athens, OH.

General Hasso von Manteuffel, *3.Panzer Armee* commander. Photo courtesy of C. Habisohn

shift the divisions although it is no mere coincidence that Hitler's decision followed Stalin's note to Eisenhower regarding the direction of the Soviet's future offensive in the direction of Prague. Krebs assured Heinrici that the shifted divisions were available to both army groups if the need arose. The army group's remaining divisions were in no shape to fight a protracted defensive battle.

Both armies under Heinrici's command suffered from losses incurred during the defensive battle for Pomerania. The majority of the units in the *3.Panzer* and *9.Armees* consisted of either units almost destroyed in recent fighting or newly-raised formations with little combat experience. There were hardly any reserves of notable strength. New units sent to *AGV* were remnant formations that arrived from recent combat in Kurland or East Prussia.[5] The arriving units were simply shuffled into the frontline as there was no plan for the defense of the Oder River that Himmler or his staff maintained. Heinrici immediately took assessment of the situation. He didn't fear a major Soviet assault north of Eberswälde due to the high flood zone along the Oder River caused by the spring thaw.[6] He knew from intelligence reports that the main Soviet thrust would come from the direction between Eberswälde and Frankfurt-on-der-Oder, most likely along Reichsbahn 1 opposite the Seelow Heights. The Soviets were not on the defensive as they continued to expand their bridgeheads and probe German lines forcing *AGV* to maintain an active defense, particularly along the *9.Armee*'s sector opposite Zhukov's 1st Byelorussian Front. The areas north and south of Küstrin were particularly active. This was where the main action was taking place during Heinrici's change of command with Himmler as the Soviets just closed off the land route into the ancient Prussian fortress of Küstrin.[7]

The *9.Armee* conducted an active defense against the Soviets since the beginning of February that included launching a number of costly counterattacks. Busse's troops attempted to eliminate the Soviet bridgeheads across the Oder, defend the Reitwein Spur (16–18 February), prevent the closure of the Küstrin corridor (20–23 March) and then attempt to reopen it after the Soviets closed the corridor (25–26 March). In all cases the *9.Armee* failed.

The last ten days of March witnessed significant operational activity centered on the Küstrin bridgehead. The Soviets maintained twenty bridges over the Oder River, but the single most important one was the bridge linking Küstrin to the west bank. This bridge had the only rail line running east-west on the Berlin access. Soviet ownership of the bridge and the Küstrin fortress were required to allow a significant increase in logistical support for the Soviets involved in the future Berlin operation.[8]

On 25 March Heinrici launched the last mandatory counterattack to reopen the Küstrin corridor that failed with heavy losses for both sides.[9] The failure, however, demonstrated the difficulty of using heavy armor in the saturated terrain along the west bank of the Oder—a lesson lost to the Soviets who would soon repeat the mistake in their coming attack. Küstrin, now surrounded, was ordered by Hitler to hold out to the last man as an official Fortress. The *SS-Grupenführer* in command soon broke out with 800 men against orders

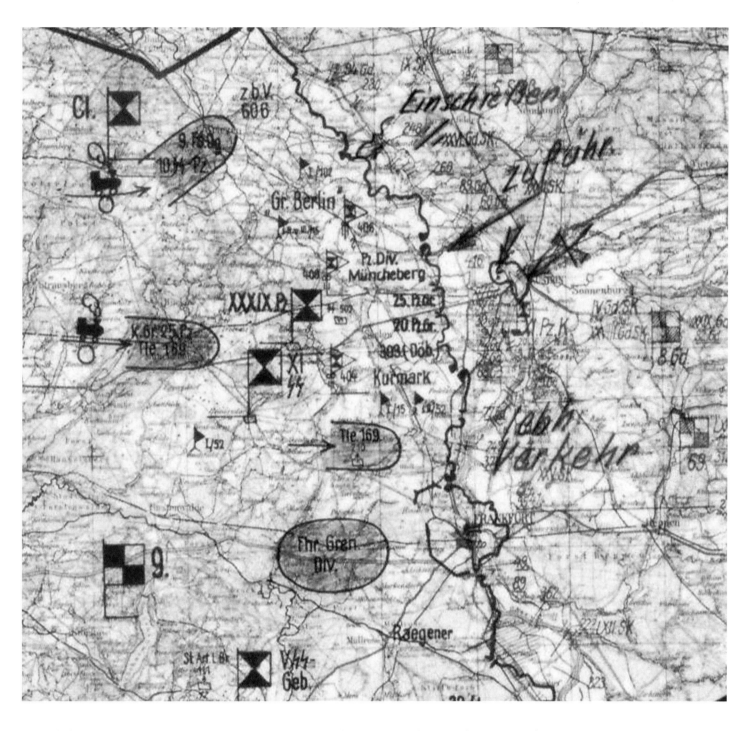

AGV daily operational map dated 23 March 1945 showing the Soviet attack to cut the land corridor to Küstrin and expand the Soviet bridgehead on the western bank of the Oder. Courtesy of the US National Archives.

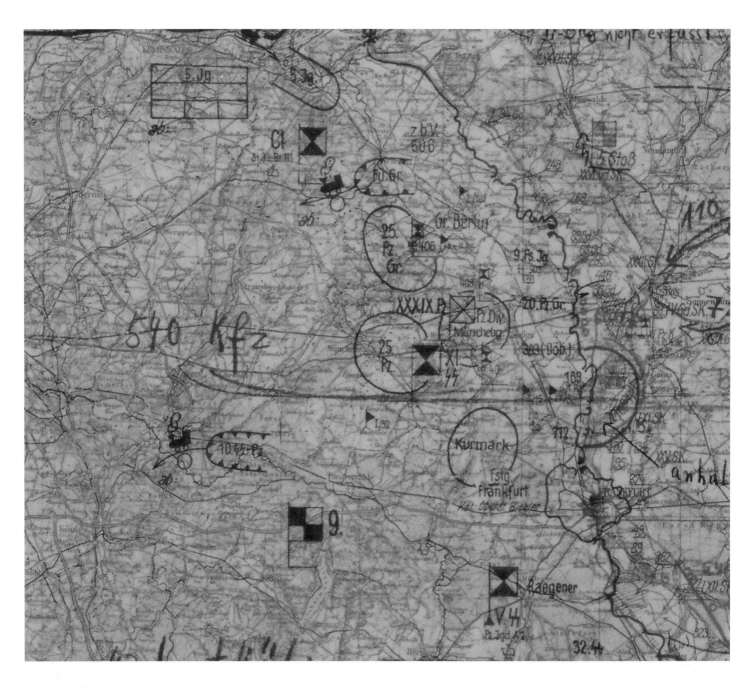

AGV daily situational map dated 1 April 1945 showing the movement of two of the three key Panzer divisions away from the most critical sector of *OKH* at that time. Courtesy of the US National Archives.

the next day.[10] Heinrici ordered his arrest but he had connections with Himmler so nothing came of the arrest order. Calls from Hitler to launch a new counterattack quickly came on the heels of Küstrin's loss. Heinrici, upset at the constant orders from the *Führerbunker* to attack the Soviets, argued to Krebs (who replaced Guderian on 28 March) that he had no chance of defending the Oder unless the attack orders stopped. Krebs understood that Heinrici needed to a period of operational rest to refit and rebuild the weakened *9.Armee* and immediately issued orders halting any further offensive action.[11]

Heinrici now took the full assessment of *AGV's* situation at the end of March once the fighting for Küstrin was over. All intelligence predictions called for a Soviet assault to occur by the middle of April. Heinrici had little more than two weeks to rebuild his army group and prepare for a protracted defense. This was a near impossible feat, but Heinrici pursued his desperate assignment with vigor and purpose. First, he created a new staff of officers that never worked together. All of Himmler's staff members that were *SS* left with him except for the sole *Wehrmacht* member, *Oberst* Hans Georg Eissman, who stayed on to assist Heinrici. Heinrici gave his new staff three major priorities. They were: 1) establish a viable defense in-depth; 2) obtain new replacements and reorganize existing units; and 3) obtain large quantities of supplies to support a prolonged defensive battle. On 21 March Heinrici issued his now famous *Kampfführung in der Groâkampf-HKL* (Conduct of Operation in the Great Battle on the Main Line of Resistance).[12] This document described guidance on how *AGV* prepared itself for the coming Soviet assault. Heinrici's most important directive was the establishment of the Oder as the HKL followed by a subsequent defensive line that his frontline troops could occupy through a rearward movement prior to the expected Soviet opening artillery barrage.

The guidance presented in his order stipulated that the time of the Soviet attack must be established, followed by a timetable stating when the rearward movement would occur. Heinrici laid out four principles of his strategy that explained his reasoning to the soldiers along the front. First, that if the troops are well organized they will be able to extract themselves successfully and keep their morale intact. Second, the enemy will waste a portion of its ammunition stocks on undefended positions. Third, the enemy's attack will drive into 'nothingness' causing confusion and disorder. Finally, the enemy's timetable to deploy reserves will be thrown off.[13] Heinrici stressed the importance of coordination, control, and unity of effort of this maneuver. His order stated that no subordinate unit except his staff had authority to issue the order to occupy secondary positions. The maneuver was planned to start at 2200 hours the night prior to the Soviet attack. If no attack came, then the German forces would reoccupy their original positions. All subordinates units were to be trained to carry out the maneuver independently and be able to prevent a rout in the process. Heinrici's plan was bold, innovative, and played directly on the inherent weakness of Soviet operational planning and execution.

Few commanders liked the idea of giving up terrain or significant forward defensive structures in favor for less prepared positions to the rear. Heinrici stated after the war that:

> I gave the order that the proper dispositions were to be made for this evasion movement. I knew that this method of operation was extremely difficult to employ, because it induced the danger that our own troops while in the course of their rearward movement were brought into it at a run, and also that it was not simple to choose the correct point of time to set the operation into movement. So that the effect of the evasive movement should not be lost, so must it be put into operation at that point during the night—before the beginning of the enemy's offensive operations.[14]

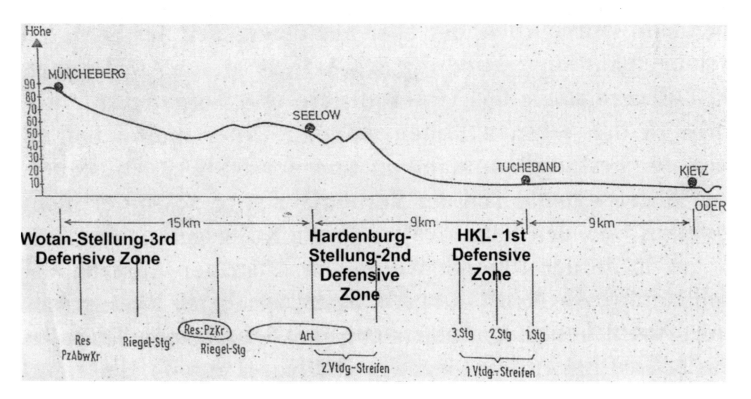

This wartime document illustrates how Heinrici maximized his use of the commanding terrain along the Seelow Heights. The 1.Stg and 2.Stg in the HKL were evacuated before the initial Soviet artillery strike on 16 April. As the main Soviet forces advanced across the Oderbruch they began to encounter German resistance in the 3.Stg along the base of the heights. Note the placement of the artillery and Panzers in depth. The height of the terrain the Soviets faced was challenging and favored the defender.

German Luftwaffe Flak Crew building a defensive position in the Oderbruch for their 8.8cm gun. Note the young age of these soldiers. Photo courtesy of the Bundesarchiv.

Heinrici was no stranger to the Soviet operational art of offensive operations. The Soviets were rigid and methodical in their application of military doctrine (a peculiarity that continued until the collapse of the Soviet Union). The Germans gained enough experience to recognize the preparation for a Soviet offensive and predict when it would start. Heinrici also knew that he had no other way to defeat the initial massive artillery bombardment that everyone expected based on daily intelligence reports. Heinrici had neither the requisite number of German artillery to act as counter-battery fire to suppress the Soviet artillery or the *Luftwaffe* resources capable of sustained attack operations against the Soviet guns. Heinrici unfortunately found a lack of desire by subordinate commanders to order soldiers to dig defensive positions in the rear and little construction material to help assist in this effort. Both the soldiers and necessary equipment were ordered to help the local farmers harvest food.[15] Food crops were in short supply within the Reich and farming needs apparently trumped military necessity in the spring of 1945. Heinrici ultimately ordered commanders to obey his instructions. Heinrici remarked that he could not understand how these men were oblivious to the fact that if they stayed in those forward lines they would be pulverized by Soviet artillery. Despite their grumblings, construction began on multiple defensive lines both within the HKL and well to the rear.[16]

The German High Command did not practice layered defensive planning during the war. They relied instead on flexibility and mobile reserves to counter-attack and defeat the enemy. Layered defense was prohibited by Hitler because it was believed that German soldiers would look "toward the rear and consequently did not present strong enough resistance" as one German commander relayed after the war.[17] The primary factor that gave the Soviets such a success in the Vistula-Oder operation was the 'thin crust' approach to typical German defense that dominated planning at that time. The Soviets easily penetrated the initial defensive line and continued to drive west with their mobile forces preventing the outmaneuvered German formations from being able to establish a secondary defensive line. The lack of operational mobile reserves was another significant factor contributing to the Soviet's success. Heinrici understood this and was not about to see it happen again.

The German defensive line was made of three primary zones starting with the HKL. The HKL ran along the German front lines with the Soviets and reached back 8–12 kilometers to the base of the Seelow Heights. Within this line divisions were to deploy in echelon with secondary fallback positions prepared 3–6 kilometers behind the main positions to allow the forward deployed units to occupy when the order was given. The secondary defensive positions known as the Hardenberg-Stellung ran along Seelow Heights and the Alte Oder.[18] In the secondary line the German artillery and anti-tank guns were deployed with overlapping fields of fire designed to support the forward deployed units in the Oderbruch.[19] The Seelow Heights proved a formidable obstacle that the Soviets simply did not factor in their planning. The Heights were about 40 meters high but offered a spectacular view of the Soviet bridgeheads and operational area with great fields of fire for the anti-tank 88s placed in position there. The mobile reserves were placed behind the HKL in a natural fault between Diedersdorf and Lietzen. Directly behind the mobile-reserves were the various *Hitlerjugend* anti-tank brigades aligned in a third defensive line known as the Wotan-Stellung. The Wotan-Stellung marked the final defensive boundary that ran through both the *3.Panzer* and *9.Armee* lines. The Soviets were not permitted to breach this line. If they did, no further defenses existed before Berlin or the rest of eastern Germany to the Elbe River.

The primary defensive line consisted of continuous trenches with mixed pillboxes located along natural strong points. In one sector the foxholes were 12–15 meters apart, with the Russian frontline only 30–40 meters away.[20] The primary and secondary defensive lines within the HKL ran almost exclusively within the Oderbruch during the spring floods. This caused the water table to rise so that many trenches and foxholes could not be dug below 50cm. Most of the front line defensive works opposite the Soviet positions consisted of earthen bunkers with rocks on top while the fallback line that ran along the base of the Seelow Heights were nothing more than shallow foxholes with minimum protection. This was due to both the lack of time and building resources available to AGV.[21] In front of the HKL were scattered minefields that consisted of anti-personnel mines intertwined between anti-tank Teller 43 mines. The Teller 43s were magnetic mines used by specifically-trained German soldiers to place on the sides of Soviet tanks that had a timed trigger device. The minefields were wired together where possible.[22] The secondary positions were little more than foxholes scraped out of the ground. In some cases they were built on the west bank of the numerous canals that ran through the Oderbruch. Terrain, lack of equipment, and lack of manpower all conspired to prevent the building of significant defensive positions in the rear. The result, however, worked to the Germans advantage as Soviet reconnaissance aircraft and ground patrols were unable to identify any secondary defensive positions in the HKL. Zhukov and his commanders had no knowledge of the fall-back line built in the Oderbruch. The appearance of a secondary defensive line completely took the Russians by surprise when they attacked.

Heinrici's strategy supported the overall goal of keeping the Soviets from penetrating the Germans lines in the HKL and reaching Berlin. This defensive posture ran contrary to much of the recent operational orders issued by Hitler. Heinrici met with Hitler and convinced him that if he was to defeat the Soviets along the Oder then he needed to plan and carry out defensive operations in depth. Hitler agreed to the feasibility of Heinrici's approach. In an unusual display of confidence in a traditional Prussian Officer this late in the war, Hitler issued a complimentary order on 30 March that stated among other things that "The battle for Berlin must and will then end in a decisive victory for the defense."[23] In addition Hitler echoed Heinrici's plan that a secondary defensive line within the HKL be built that his troops would occupy at the commanders discretion before the planned Soviet assault to avoid casualties. The importance of the Oder as the HKL and the coming defensive battle was ingrained in the vernacular of the troops through its daily repetition at the end of almost every order. This became a running joke with many soldiers. Fritz Haas, a *Rottenführer* of the *11.SS-Nordland Panzergrenadier Division* in army group reserve commented that the "Oder is the HKL and not one foot backwards" caused funny situations as troops began to utter it at the end of simple verbal commands. It was not uncommon to hear phrases like "wish to step out for a second. Oder is the HKL and not one foot backward" or "ammunition for 20 guns has arrived. Oder is the HKL not one foot backwards."[24] No matter how silly this sounded, the repetition of this simple phrase brought new purpose to many German soldiers now joining the front lines from across Germany—many of whom were probably wondering why they were still fighting.

The battered *Wehrmacht* and *Waffen-SS* divisions were not organizationally up to the task of a protracted defense at the end of March. Continual combat stretched the ability of each unit to field cohesive combat battalions. In the period from 1 February to 15 March alone the *9.Armee* suffered the loss of 35,376 killed, wounded and missing. They received only 9,990 replacements during that same time period.[25] In contrast, the *3.Panzer Armee* suffered 49,381 and received 24,745 replacements in the same time period. The average strength per division was down to 3,770 men.[26] Most of the men were not the skilled professional soldiers of 1939–41. Many were recent draftees that were younger or older than their 1939–41 counterparts. Few experienced NCOs and officers existed from earlier campaigns to train or guide the new recruits. The *Waffen-SS* also suffered under years of continued attrition. Many units drafted anyone they could find into their ranks, particularly *Volksdeutsch* from various parts of Europe as well as the *Hitlerjugend*. Himmler was in charge of the Replacement Army, but this did not generate new manpower for the *Waffen-SS* who continued to rely on other sources for recruitment when volunteers did not fill out the ranks. Their élan remained high, especially in the Panzer and Panzergrenadier divisions. It was almost impossible to determine the actual strengths of *AGV* as Heinrici had to deal with various commands under the *SS* and *Luftwaffe* that refused to provide their actual strengths. In most cases these organizations hoarded men and equipment to bolster their own forces. For example, *Kriegsmarine* forces were now being employed as infantry under Heinrici, but they were under the direct control of *Oberbefehlshaber der Kriegsmarine* Karl Dönitz.[27] The most accurate numbers are derived from the postwar study *MS R–69 The End of Army Group Weichsel and Twelfth Army, 27 April–7 May 1945*. This postwar study cites a strength report that *AGV* had a total available strength of 394,067 men on 1 April. Based on the documentary evidence, *AGV* had an authorized strength of 481,428 and was now operating 88,000 men short. Heinrici was also concerned about the non-German, non-*Wehrmacht* units under his command. It should also be noted that only 104,162 soldiers were considered 'Combat Effective.' This was only 26% of his total force.

Table 3.1 *AGV* Manpower as of 1 April 1945

	German	Hiwi	Combat Effective
AGV HQ & GHQ	23,803	2,776	1,864
3 Panzer Armee	69,637	3,258	27,595
9. Armee	168,413	2,765	74,703
Subtotal for entire *Armee Gruppe*	**261,853**	**8,799**	**104,162 (a)**
Personnel consisting of Luftwaffe, SS, Foreign Units, Field Training Divs., *Kriegsmarine* and *Volkssturm*	123,451 (b)	—	—
Total personnel	385,268	8,799	**394,067**
Autorized TO&E	462,312	19,116	481,428
Personnel vacant	(77,044)	(10,317)	(87,361)

Source: MS # R-69 Appendix G.

A *Waffen-SS Sturmbannführer* directs a unit of *Volkssturm* or *Panzerjäger's* in anti-tank training along the Oder River in March 1945. Photo courtesy of the Bundesarchiv.

Hitler makes a rare Eastern Front visit to bolster morale along the Oder Front in March. From left to right, *General der Artillerie* Wilhelm Berlin, *CI Korps* commander, *General der Luftwaffe* Ritter von Greim, commander of *Luftflotte 6*, another staff officer of *Luftflotte 6*, and *General* Busse, *9.Armee* commander. Photo courtesy of the Bundesarchiv.

a. Combat Effective refers to those soldiers capable of conducting combat operations based on equipment, training, and current duty assignment in a combat role. This total in included in the counts to the left and below and included to show the 'tooth-to-tail' ratio.

b. Heinrici tracked his purely German Heer unit strength separately from overall strength he received through other services. He found non-Heer and non-German units particularly unreliable.

Weapons, equipment, ammunition and fuel were all in short supply. While the Germans increased overall production of war material by late 1944, they were unable to get the supplies to the troops due to problems with a rail network under constant Allied aerial bombardment. The supplies the soldiers did receive were sub-standard due to the shortages in raw materials. For example, there was a shortage of brass for the carbine cartridges so most were now made of steel. The steel cartridges were coated with a protective lacquer to prevent rust that melted when the weapon heated from use. This caused the cartridge to become stuck in the weapon while firing in battle. Soldiers had to force it from the carbine with an entrenching tool, often while under enemy fire.[28] Fuel for tanks and armored vehicles was now made from synthetic blends after the loss of the primary refineries in Romania and Hungary. The new blend was a mixture of ethyl that often caused tanks and other armored vehicles to frequently stall at inopportune times. All through *AGV* shortages of machine guns, assault rifles, ammunition, transport, horses, wireless sets, and field kitchens existed.[29]

Heinrici tried to gather additional stocks of weapons, ammunition, and supplies from the various Gaus in his area by exercising military control over the political governors. He was particularly interested in gaining command over the Gauleiters of Brandenburg and Mecklenburg in order to ensure access to the quantities of supplies horded by these Reich agencies. This request was refused by *OKH*. Many of the Gau leaders saw themselves as their own commander-in-chiefs complete with private armies to justify their political power. This attitude, prevalent in National Socialist

SS-Obergruppenführer und General der Waffen-SS Felix Steiner, commander of the *III.SS-Germanic Panzer Korps* and subsequently *Heeresgruppe Steiner*.
Photo courtesy of Lennart Westberg/Martin Mansson archive.

Germany, worked against the ability of military authorities to acquire needed supplies to support their soldiers. In the case of Gauleiter Schwede in Stettin, he decided to become the defender of Pomerania and stockpiled quantities of needed supplies and equipment. Schwede fled when the Soviets attacked, and the supply stocks were captured intact.[30] Like Reymann's struggle with the political agencies and personalities in Berlin, Heinrici faced these same issues on a larger scale. Heinrici's efforts to materially prepare for the defensive battle ahead yielded only modest results as he could only amass sufficient ammo for 2–2.5 days for his artillery and anti-aircraft guns. Fuel reserves were small and would last not more than a day of prolonged combat. German aviation was also in bad shape. The *Luftwaffe* hoarded their meager supplies of aviation fuel and hoped to fulfill their combined mission of interdiction and destruction of Soviet artillery concentrations in the first two to three days of battle.[31]

Replacements for *AGV* received individual training in Berlin before they were sent to the Oder Front for integrated unit training.[32] Brandenburg and Berlin supplied many of the reinforcements to *AGV*. Hitler chose to levy new recruits instead of shifting existing, battle proved combat formations from remote areas of the Greater Reich to the main operational areas. Extensive *Panzerfaust* training occurred during mobilization in Berlin at various military barracks or converted sports fields where immobile tanks were towed in for target practice.[33] Once the soldiers reached the Oder Front, new recruits were instructed by the few senior NCOs or officers on KAR 98s and MG 42s. Training was hard and realistic in most cases. When the troops weren't training they were improving their fighting positions or on watch. Concern for security was paramount given the proximity of Soviet front lines. Soldiers slept mainly during the day for about 4 hours and stayed up all night.[34] Russians routinely fired over the lines with artillery during training, especially when they heard movement.[35]

The Germans attempted to hide troop dispositions as much as possible to avoid pre-targeting by Soviet artillery. Supply truck drivers were maintained at different areas knowing that supply movement provided a key tip off to the Soviets about unit types and location. Drivers were notified of their delivery location by field telephone a few minutes before they were supposed to move out. Supplies were quickly loaded into trucks then driven at night with blackout lights along unfamiliar roads to their destination. After delivering supplies, they turned back around to await the next call.[36] In addition, dummy anti-tank and anti-aircraft positions were installed all over the front using cut logs meant to look like 88s from the air. The hope was to draw the attention of Soviet artillery and aircraft spotters leaving the real positions intact after the initial Soviet barrage. While new recruits and supplies filtered into *AGV*, training continued.

The motivation and morale of German and non-German soldiers serving the Third Reich this late in the war was varied and complex. Over the course of the month of March *AGV* suffered 1,396 casualties a day with the *9.Armee* bearing 1,064 of that number. This number was almost 2.5 times the amount of casualties suffered by the *3.Panzer Armee*.[37] Total casualties for the *9.Armee* in March were over 33,936—nearly one-third of the army's overall strength.[38] The problem this created was a lack of general cohesion and traditional military bonds that translated into poor morale and military performance. Many of the divisions within the *9.Armee* collapsed after several days of

A typical German 8.8cm flak position situated along the Seelow Heights. This photo was taken in February 1945.
Photo courtesy of the Bundesarchiv.

General der Artillerie Helmuth Weidling, *LVI Panzer Korps* commander. Photo courtesy of the Bundesarchiv.

fighting as they disintegrated under the massive Soviet attack toward Berlin. The importance and proximity of the Oder Front prompted Hitler to make his third and last visit to the Eastern Front in his life. The first was in 1942, and the second time was in February 1943. Both of these visits were at the urging of his field commanders. Only in March 1945 did Hitler make a surprise visit to the front on his own. He visited the *606.Infanterie-Division*, where he met with Busse, his staff, and several other divisional commanders in a small house in Neuhardenberg. The visit had a positive affect on morale as Hitler gave the impression that he understood their situation and was going to ensure their success by providing additional resources for the defense.[39] Despite Hitler's visit and the promise of new reinforcements, equipment, and secret weapons, fear continued to be a prime motivator for many German soldiers. Fear of unconditional surrender,[40] fear of Soviet atrocities,[41] and fear of draconian punishment all provided motivation.[42] Soldiers without orders found in rear areas were summarily shot. As one veteran recalled " … for this is the rear boundary for front combatants, where the military police reign, casting a ring of fear and horror in the hearts of the men at the front."[43]

Hope that the Western Allies would cross the Elbe and join forces with the Germans against the Soviets was another motivation German soldiers' and commanders' looked to for strength. This was driven by rumors circulated by officers that knew of 'Eclipse'. According to Heinrici, 'Eclipse' was known all over, and no one believed that the Western Allies would let the Russians take Berlin.[44] This turned the upcoming battle into an important, historic fight of monumental importance to Germany. This belief was clearly reinforced by commanders in *AGV*. Heinrici viewed the upcoming battle as a struggle that represented the "Life or Death of the [German] state."[45] Steiner, commander of the *III Germanic SS-Panzer Corps*, stated the importance of the upcoming battle clearly on several occasions to his troops. In one instance he said "Germany's fate will be decided here. If we manage to beat the Russians here, everything will still be all right. If we fail, the entire West will become Communist."[46] Steiner also commented to a group of soldiers that "If the western Allies do not cross the Elbe, the biggest drama of the century will take place between the Elbe and the Oder." [47] Busse, the commander of the *9.Armee* stated that "if we can hold the Oder long enough until the Americans arrive, we will have fulfilled our mission before our people, our country and history."[48] Down to every German soldier a mixture of fear, and hope abounded.

There was particular concern over the motivations of various non-German formations in the area behind the front. Heinrici was alarmed at the Russian defectors coming out of the Vlassov Army. "Already during the preparations it had been apparent that those Russian troops who were operating on the German side had no great wish to fight against their countrymen," wrote Heinrici after the war. According to Heinrici, "The Russian troops were therefore taken out of the front and taken to Bohemia where the General Headquarters of General Vlassov was located in Carlsbad."[49] He also had concerns with the various foreign volunteers of the *Waffen-SS*. He ordered most of these units disarmed and had their equipment passed over to German reinforcements moving to the front. [50] Heinrici believed that in the final battle for Germany, Germans should be in the front line.

The majority of reinforcements arrived in the first two weeks of April. Table 3.2 offers a view of the number of tanks and self-propelled guns available to *AGV* on 8 April, followed by a table listing all known guns. Heinrici dispersed the majority of his guns into the 'Hardenberg-Stellung' line. The status of forces improved with each passing day.

Table 3.2   *9.Armee* Heavy Equipment

Artillery Guns

Light Field Howitzers (12.5 cm)	228
Heavy Field Howitzers (15 cm)	84
1. *Volksartillerie Korps*	
AA 8.8 cm Guns	9
Light Field Howitzers	9
21 cm Mortars	6
15 cm Cannons	2
10 cm Cannons	2
15 cm Cannons mounted on RR Wagons	2
24 cm Cannons mlunted on RR Wagons	2
21 cm Mortars mounted on RR Wagons	9
Total Artillery	**353**

8.8 AA/AT Guns

AA 8.8 cm guns	176
AA 10.5 cm guns	24
AT 8.8 cm guns	40
Küstrin (AA guns)	24
Frankfurt-an-de-Oder (AA guns)	24
Fürstenwalde (AA guns)	24
Werneuchen (AA guns)	24
Total AA/AT	**336**
Grand Total of Heavy Equipment	**689**

Source: Heinrici Report 17 July 163, Ryan Collection 68:3

As the reorganization of the army group continued Heinrici turned his focus to the coming battle. He asked his staff to address two key operational questions.

> The first was this: would the troops prove equal to the human demands which the forthcoming massive Russian attack would make upon them? Above all, how would the troops stand up to the first great prepatory fire which the Russian artillery would direct against the German positions, and then the aerial attacks which would be mounted with increasing violence? From long previous experience I knew the shock effect that such a massed concentrated artillery preparatory barrage could have. I had seen many newly formed divisions, although they were equipped with everything they needed, break under the effect of this fire. How would my makeshift Divisions stand up to this? Would they be able to hang on?

The second question was this: How long would the Russians be able to push their attack, days, one week, two weeks, or more? All this was very relevant to whether the resources of the Army Group would last out and whether they would be able to match the unavoidable expectant losses.[51]

Heinrici was skeptical of his troop's ability to hold out against the Soviets. His concerns were particularly heightened after the surrender of Küstrin by a *Waffen-SS* commander who had all the supplies necessary for a protracted siege.[52] This event made an impact on him and he continued to have nagging doubts about his ability to carry out Guderian's assigned task. Yet, it was clear to Heinrici that based on experience his army group might loose 4–5 battalions per day and that he could not rely on simply shifting forces to fill that gap. In fact he didn't believe he could rely on *OKH* to supply the needed replacements once the battle was engaged. In his final analysis he realized he would have to rely on his experienced troops to ensure that losses were kept at a minimum.[53] Despite these doubts, Heinrici never wavered in his focus to build up his army group and prepare them for the Soviet assault.

Table 3.3 *AGV* **Panzers and Assault Guns**

	8 April			13 April		
	Panzers and Assault Guns	*Short-term Repair*	*Long-term Repair*	*Panzers and Assault Guns*	*Short-term Repair*	*Long-term Repair*
3. Panzer Armee	220	4	20	232	5	13
9. Armee	489	34	46	512	25	30
Total	709	38	66	**744 (a)**	30	43

Sources: Heinrici Report 17 July 1963, Ryan Collection 68:3 and T-311, 171 7223 305-08

a. The increase in Panzers and assault guns came almost exclusively from short- and long-term repairs. There were no new shipments of Panzers or assault guns to *AGV* after 8 April.

Heinrici's hard work began to payoff as the *9.Armee* was slowly revitalized. By the middle of April the *9.Armee*'s manpower and operational armor increased. Overall the total number of operational armor in the *9.Armee* grew from 527 to 587. The German soldiers gained some reinforcements in the form of untrained *Kriegsmarine,* and *Luftwaffe* forces. Approximately 30,000 arrived in the first week of April[54] but their assimilation remained problematic before the planed Soviet offensive. Total strength almost reached 200,000 men. There were a total of 658 batteries with a total of 2,625 guns including 695 flak guns. The *Luftwaffe* had close to 300 aircraft available to the *9.Armee* as well. One formation in *AGV* that played *the* central role in the battle for the Oder and Berlin was the *LVI Panzer Korps* [hereafter referred to as *LVI Pz. Korps*].

By 16 April the *LVI Pz. Korps* was the strongest formation in the *9.Armee*. The corps was placed into the line in the Oderbruch and along the Seelow Heights. Its position was directly across the main line of Soviet advance along Reichsbahn 1. The *LVI Pz. Korps* was

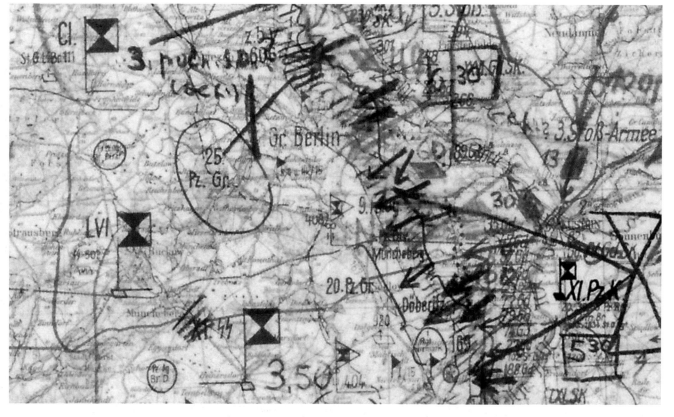

LVI Panzer Korps sector on 14 April 1945 showing the start of the Soviet reconnaissance in force. This regimented pre-offensive activity of the Soviets alerted Heinrici that the main Soviet offensive was 24-48 hours away. Courtesy of the US National Archives.

Volkssturm training on the bank of the Oder River opposite Frankfurt-an-der-Oder. Note the Volkssturmgewehr 1-5 and the *Panzerfaust* to the far right. The soldier on the left is a Zugführer (Section Leader). Photo courtesy of the Bundesarchiv.

reconstituted in mid-March with a new command staff after being surrounded and destroyed in Upper Silesia several months earlier.[55] The reconstitution of the *LVI Pz. Korps* was done for primarily propaganda reasons as this corps was well known in the *Wehrmacht*. It won distinction in the Crimea in 1942 as part of *Feldmarschall* Erich von Manstein's forces as well as during other significant battles on the Eastern Front.[56] By March of 1945 only two soldiers were left that served under von Manstein and neither of them were senior officers.[57] The command staff was reconstituted slowly, starting on 13 March with the appointment a Chief of Staff *Oberst* Theodor von Dufving. Not until around 11 April—five days before the Soviet assault—was the *LVI Pz. Korps* assigned to the front and given combat divisions. The new corps commander, *General of Artillerie* Helmuth Weidling did not arrive until the eve of the Soviet offensive.[58]

By 12 April the *LVI Pz. Korps* had under its direct command most of the strongest formations in the *9.Armee*. The combat formations included the *9.Fallschirmjäger Division*, *20.Panzergrenadier Division*, and *Müncheberg Panzer Division*, as well as *Panzerjäger.Abteilung.920 Döberitz*. Assorted independent combat teams included *Volkssturm*, *Hitlerjugend*, and *Kriegsmarine* soldiers. Weidling's defense sector ran from just south of Letschin the north, to Friedersdorf in the South. Bordering the *LVI Pz. Korps* in the north was the *CI Korps* and in the south was the *XI SS Korps*. The *9.Fallschirmjäger Division* [hereafter to referred to as *9.Fallschirmjäger* or *9.Fj.Div.*] deployed from the edge of the corps' left wing to the village of Gusow just north of Reichsbahn 1. The *20.Panzergrenadier* [hereafter referred to as *20.Pz.Gren.Div.*] and *Müncheberg Panzer Divisions* [hereafter referred to as *Müncheberg*] deployed their units intermingled in an overlapping fashion from Gusow to the corps' right flank. The *Panzerjäger.Abteilung.920 Döberitz* [hereafter referred to as *PzJg.Abt.920*] remained in reserve behind the town of Seelow. Along the crest of the Seelow Heights ran a belt of 8.8cm anti-aircraft guns placed in positions well suited for the dual use anti-aircraft, or anti-tank role. In the immediate rear area supporting Weidling's forces was the *408.Volksartillerie Korps*. Not one of these formations was at full strength and they all recently suffered from heavy fighting.

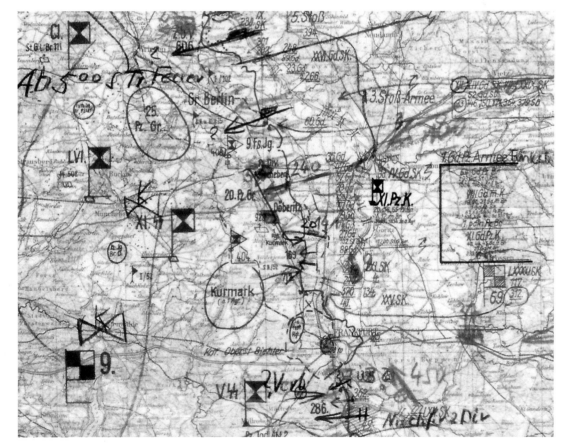

LVI Panzer Korps sector on 15 April 1945. The Soviet reconnaissance in force continues though greatly reduced in operational scope. The Germans did a good job at identifying the Soviet units opposite their front. Courtesy of the US National Archives.

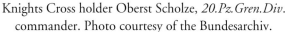

Knights Cross holder Oberst Scholze, *20.Pz.Gren.Div.* commander. Photo courtesy of the Bundesarchiv.

Knights Cross holder Generalmajor Mummert, *Müncheberg* commander. Photo courtesy of the Bundesarchiv.

During the course of the battle, additional combat formations released from *AGV* reserve were assigned to the *LVI Pz. Korps*. As the corps retreated toward Berlin, it picked up stragglers and remnants of other divisions destroyed in the Soviet offensive. Below is a description of all formations of the *LVI Pz. Korps* and *AGV* that fought in Berlin.

9. FALLSCHIRMJÄGER DIVISION

The *9.Fallschirmjäger* was formed in February 1945 and was a formidable combat division this late in the war. It initially consisted of three regiments; *Fj.Rgt.25*, *Fj.Rgt.26* and *Fj.Rgt.27*. Additional support elements were added in the form an artillery regiment, an anti-tank battalion (*Fj.PzJg.Abt.*) that consisted of 8 Jagdpanzer 38(t) Hetzer self-propelled guns, a pioneer, and an anti-aircraft battalion.[59] The Hetzer was a light tank destroyer designed to replace the interim solutions of both towed and self-propelled anti-tank guns. These were built on modified Panzerkampfwagen 38(t) chassis and armed with a 7.5cm Pak 39 L/48 gun very effective against Soviet armor at ranges of 700 meters or less. The Hetzers were normally organized into companies of 12 tank destroyers and assigned independently to infantry formations. This division initially contained 6,758 soldiers, many of whom were experienced and well trained. *Fj.Rgt.25* was ordered to *AGV* ahead of the other regiments and gained experience fighting in Pomerania alongside the *Waffen-SS* formations of *SS-Obergruppenführer* Felix Steiner's *III SS Panzer Korps*.[60] *Fj.Rgt.25's* battalions were a unique composite of veteran soldiers. The *I./Fj.Rgt.25* consisted of members of Otto Skorzeny's Special Unit that fought in the Ardennes and more recently along the Oder River south of Stettin. The *II./Fj.Rgt.25* was made up of members of the famous *Brandenburg Special Operations Unit*. Finally the *III./Fj.Rgt.25* consisted of fully trained parachutists—unusual for this period in the war.[61] The *Fj.Rgt.26* consisted of only two battalions as the *III./Fj.Rgt.26* was flown into Breslau on 22 February to bolster the defense of that city surrounded by Koniev's forces.[62] The *9.Fallschirmjäger* was inserted into *9.Armee's* lines at the end of March.[63] The *Fj.Rgt.25* was placed into the frontline just south of the hamlet of Steintoch along with *Fj.Rgt.26* that was centered on Buschdorf. The *Fj.Rgt.27* was placed in division reserve near Neuenhauser, just outside of Platkow where the Commanding *General* Bruno Bräuer established his divisional headquarters.

20. PANZERGRENADIER DIVISION

The *20.Pz.Gren.Div.* was given the responsibility of defending the main Soviet approach to the Seelow Heights running along Reichsbahn 1 in the Oderbruch as well as the town of Seelow. This division numbered 4,848 and was equipped with 13 Panzerkampfwagen IV's (various models), 3 Quad Flak Panzers (excellent in the anti-infantry role) and 16 Jagdpanzer IVL/70(A) self-propelled guns.[64] The Panzer IV

This photo illustrates a standard Pz IV (L) of the period. Note the addition of side skirt armor to help protect the vulnerable area of the chassis.
Photo courtesy of the Tank Museum.

was a medium tank and the most widely produced German tank during the war. It had many variants. In 1945 the variants primarily in use were the H and J versions that had armored skirts applied around the body and turret. This tank was equipped with the effective 7.5cm KwK 40 L/48 gun. The Flak Panzers typically consisted of the 2cm quad anti-aircraft gun mounted on older Panzer IV chassis. These were very effective in the anti-personnel role. The Jagdpanzer was a low-silhouetted tank destroyer also built on the Panzer IV chassis. Variants could come with side skirts or no side skirts and were armed with the 7.5cm Pak 42L/70. This division was in action for most of March suffering 1,367 casualties.[65] Both Panzergrenadier regiments, *Pz.Gren.Rgt.90* and *Pz.Gren.Rgt.76*, were placed in the Oderbruch along the base of the Heights. Each regiment was less a battalion as they were given to an *ad-hoc* command set up to defend the town of Seelow. The *8.Panzer Battalion* [hereafter referred to as *Pz.Abt.8*] interspersed the majority of its armor among the defensive positions of the two Panzergrenadier regiments.

This photo illustrates a typical early war Tiger I. To make up for losses in panzers, many early war training vehicles were dispatched to the front. *Müncheberg's* Tiger I's were almost all early war versions. Photo courtesy of the Tank Museum.

This photo illustrates a standard Panther Ausf. G of the period.
Photo courtesy of the Tank Museum.

Major Helmut Wandmaker was appointed the combat commander of Seelow. He was ordered to let the Soviets surround the village if necessary and hold it to tie down as much of the enemy force as possible.[66] The force under Wandmaker's command consisted of one battalion from each of the two Panzergrenadier regiments combined with *Kriegsmarine* sailors whose ships were shot out from under them in the Baltic. Two *Volkssturm* companies from Berlin were also added to this force.[67] The forward deployed company of this force was commanded by *Hauptmann* von Wartenberg. This company numbered 136 soldiers divided into three rifle platoons and a mortar platoon. Most men were new recruits and inexperienced in combat. Morale was good despite everyone being aware of their situation and impending Soviet assault. The defense perimeter ran from a semicircle of 1,500 meters in front of Seelow with a secondary defensive ring of connecting trenches running 700 meters between houses. The mortar platoon was divided into two sections and deployed to cover the eastern and northeastern exit roads. On the slopes in front of the railroad embankment were as many as eight 8.8cm anti-aircraft guns being used in the anti-tank role.

MÜNCHEBERG PANZER DIVISION

Müncheberg was an *ad-hoc* Panzer division formed on 5 March under the command of the very capable *Generalleutnant* Werner Mummert.[68] The order creating the Panzer division showed two Panzergrenadier regiments with *Pz.Gren.Rgt.2* consisting of two battalions including one mounted on bicycles! It was planned that *Pz.Gren.Rgt.1* was to consist of at least one battalion of the *Leibstandarte SS Adolf Hitler (LSSAH) Wachregiment* located in Berlin.[69] The Panzer battalion initially consisted of *I./29 Coburg* and was planned for two companies of 10 Panthers, one company of 10 Tiger Is, one company of Jagdpanzer IVs and one company of Hetzers. The Panzerkampfwagen V Panther was the standard medium tank of the *Wehrmacht* by 1945. It was versatile, and well armed with the 7.5cm KwK 42 L/70 main gun. Several versions of this tank were produced with the most common being the G models. Armored skirts were applied along the sides to protect the vulnerable area around the wheels. This tank was designed as a counter to the Soviet T–34 that the Germans encountered in 1941. The sloped armor offered the Panther better protection than other German tanks that had straight armor, even if the straight plate armor was thicker. The Panzerkampfwagen VI Ausführung H (PzKpfw VI) or simply Tiger I remains arguably the most famous tank of WWII. Its thick frontal armor and 8.8cm KwK 36 L/56 main gun adopted from the fearsome 8.8cm anti-aircraft gun, coupled with the hydraulic turret, and outstanding optics made this a feared weapon system on the battlefield. The main gun of the Tiger I could penetrate between 84–110mm of sloped frontal armor at 2,000 meters.[70] One drawback to the Tiger was its lack of sloped armor. Soviet tests showed that the sharp nosed armor-piercing ammunition of the 122mm main gun of their JS–2 heavy tanks could only penetrate the sloped armor of the Panther at ranges of 700 meters or less, while a well trained and experienced gunner under optimal situation could penetrate the flat armor of a Tiger I at ranges of 1,200 meters.[71] It was unusual for units to receive their own Tiger Is. *Müncheberg*, however, was an unusual Panzer formation. Based on photographic evidence, the Tiger Is received by this division were early versions formerly used for training at Kummersdorf and pressed into frontline service.

This unit saw immediate action in the counterattack to relieve Küstrin at the end of March and lost three Panzergrenadier battalions in the Alt Bayern pocket during the counter attack.[72] This reduced *Müncheberg* considerably, even losing a company of Hetzers that joined the Küstrin garrison.[73] The authorized strength of the division before the battle was over 6,836 men but it suffered after the losses during the counterattack to reopen the corridor to Küstrin at the end of March. It was taken out of the line at the end of March and refitted. As reinforcements, this division gained an Infra-Red equipped (I/R) Panther company but it never made up for its Panzergrenadier losses. The infra-red devices were mounted primarily to the Panther commander's copula and allowed visibility out to 100 meters at night.[74] Based on all available evidence it does not appear that the contingent of *LSSAH* soldiers was ever sent to the division, but if they were, they were no longer assigned to *Müncheberg* in mid-April. By 15 April the division consisted of 1,986[75] men along with two companies of 21 Panthers and 10 early model Tiger Is.

On the evening of 15 April *Müncheberg* deployed behind the Hauptgraben water obstacle east of Seelow with the majority of its Panzers and Panzergrenadiers in mutual support of the *20.Pz.Gren.Div*. A small reserve of both Panzers (probably the Tiger Is) and Panzergrenadiers were kept in corps reserve.[76] The *920.Panzerjäger Battalion Döberitz* [hereafter referred to as *PzJg.Abt.920*] was also assigned to *Müncheberg* in early April. This formation consisted of 17 Sturmgeschütz and 7 Jagdpanzers and was placed in reserve of the *LVI Pz. Korps* as a mobile counterattack force.[77]

OTHER COMBAT FORMATIONS

To the north of the *9.Fallschirmjäger* was the *309.Infanterie-Division,* otherwise known as *Groß Berlin Division* [hereafter referred to as *Berlin Division*]. This division was an *ad- hoc* composite like so many German divisions of late 1945. One regiment was made up of two battalions of the *Wachregiment Großdeutschland* from Berlin.[78] The remnant of this division would come under the command of the *LVI Pz. Korps* during the retreat to Berlin.

A number of *Hitlerjugend* Tank Hunting Brigades were formed by *Reichsjugendführer* Artur Axmann. These consisted of young boys organized into 4 battalions of 480 boys each. These units were interspersed throughout the rear areas and were designed to act a bulwark against Soviet tank breakthroughs. Armed with *Panzerfausts*, these boys had the job of destroying enemy tanks at close range.[79] Many of these boys, some as young as 12 years of age, were recruited by *Waffen-SS* officers and highly motivated. Active recruitment from the frontline units occurred up until the eve of the Soviet attack.[80] Many of the boys in these units were swept back to Berlin after the Soviet breakthrough along the Seelow Heights.

Norwegians, Danes, French, Spaniards, Hungarians, and Ukrainians, were found fighting alongside their German counterparts in Berlin. There is a belief that the battle for Berlin attracted a multitude of foreign volunteers from the *Wehrmacht* and *Waffen-SS* whose Nazi zeal for anti-communism drew them into a final battle for Europe's 'Freedom' in the streets of Berlin. The reality could not be farther from the 'truth.' No foreign volunteers willingly went into Berlin to fight and die in Hitler's final battle except for the *Waffen-SS* Spaniards. All were either ordered into the city or were caught in the retreat and ended the war there by accident. The troops of *Nordland* were under orders by Zeigler to get out of Berlin; while the French were ordered into the city before the final avenues of approach were sealed by the Soviets. The few Hungarians were already at the various training Kasernes in the city and represented remnants of former units that fought on the German side in Hungary. Ukrainian boys serving in the *Hitlerjugend* and *Luftwaffe* were already located at training schools and the Flak Towers. Perhaps two of the more interesting groups were the Spaniards and Latvians. Several hundred Spanish volunteers joined the *Waffen-SS* against official policy of both the Third Reich and Spain after the disbandment of the *Spanish Blue Division* in May 1944. All Spanish troops were supposed to be repatriated back to Spain. While most did, 600 volunteers formed the *Bataillon Fantasma* (Ghost Battalion).[81] By the time they retreated into Berlin they were down to about 100 soldiers and could be found guarding

Generalleutnant Josef Rauch, *18.Pz.Gren.Div.* commander. Photo courtesy of the Bundesarchiv.

This photo, taken during the Battle of Arnhem, illustrates a typical period Sturmgeschütz found in German formations fighting in and around Berlin. Photo courtesy of the Bundesarchiv.

key bridges across the Spree. The Latvian contingent initially attempted to escape to the west. Many were caught in the retreat and ended up in Berlin instead. In March 1945, Latvian units, crossed the Oder at Swinemünde (now *Svinoscje*) and were deployed in the Neubrandenburg area as the reserve of *AGV*. Per Heinrici's orders the Latvians gave up all their automatic weapons, leaving only a few rifles for guard duties, in order to arm German reserve units going to the front. The Latvians used their situation to prepare forced marches across Central Germany in order to reach the Western Allies, 150 kilometers to the west. This was concealed from Heinrici and the German High Command. Wartime law was in effect, and this meant that even the slightest disobedience to orders was a possible death sentence.[82] In the end a number of Latvian soldiers were swept into the city during their westward movements. The lack of desire of Foreign Volunteers to fight in Berlin did not impact their fighting ability or zeal as they all demonstrated military skills and professionalism that often rivaled their German counterparts.

The following formations were assigned to the *LVI Pz. Korps* by Heinrici during the battle of the Seelow Heights. Both units were swept back into Berlin.

18. PANZERGRENADIER DIVISION

The *18.Panzergrenadier Division* [hereafter referred to as *18.Pz.Gren.Div.*] was under the command of *Generalleutnant* Josef Rauch. This division, like almost all German divisions, suffered major losses causing it to be reconstituted after the Soviet winter counteroffensive in 1941–42 and again during the Soviet Summer offensive Bagration in 1944. During the Soviet offensive, the *18.Pz.Gren.Div.* was encircled at Minsk and destroyed. The divisional commander, at that time, *Generalleutnant* Zutavern, committed suicide rather than surrender to the Russians. The remnants of the division continued to fight in Pomerania. By mid-February the division lost an estimated 65% of its combat soldiers as well as all of its tanks. It was placed in *AGV* reserve and reformed during the next four weeks. According the *Colonel* Friedrich Böttcher, the division's Operation Officer, "by the time the refitting period was over, the division was once more completely filled up, with its contingent of Panzers and other vehicles. Its soldiers and officers were all well trained, battle experienced and once more the *18.Panzergrenadier* was a first-rate division."[83] The *18.Pz.Gren.Div.* was the most powerful division in *AGV* and control and consisted of approximately 6,000 soldiers as well as 25 armored half tracks known as Schützen-Panzer-Wagen (SPWs), the *Panzer Bataillon Schlesien* [hereafter referred to as *Pz.Abt. Schlesien*] with 27 Panzer IV G & H model Panzers, and the *Panzerjäger Bataillon Schlesien* [hereafter referred to as *PzJg.Abt. Schlesien*] with 19 Hetzers and 8 Jagdpanzers. This division remained in reserve around Eberswalde until it was released on 18 April to plug the gap in the *LVI Pz. Korps* sector and was immediately caught in the flank by elements of the 2nd Guards Tank Army.

11. FREIWILLIGEN-GRENADIER-DIVISION 'NORDLAND'

This division was also in *AGV* reserve under the command of *SS-Gruppenführer* Joachim Ziegler. This division along with the *34.SS-Freiwilligen-Grenadier-Division 'Nederland'* [hereafter referred to as *Nederland*] made up Steiner's *III SS Germanic Panzer Korps*. *Nordland* was also ordered to reinforce the *LVI Pz. Korps* front. The division consisted of the *23.SS-Panzergrenadier Regiment Norge* [hereafter referred to as *SS-Pz.Gren.Rgt. Norge* or *Norge*] and the *24.SS-Panzergrenadier Regiment Danmark* [hereafter referred to as *SS-Pz.Gren.Rgt. Danmark* or *Danmark*] along with the *11.SS-Panzer Abteilung Hermann von Salza* [hereafter referred to as *SS-Pz.Abt. Hermann von Salza*]. This division had engaged in heavy defensive fighting in Pomerania during the preceding months and was in the pro-

SS-Gruppenführer Joachim Ziegler (on the right), *11.Freiwilligen-Grenadier-Division 'Nordland'* commander. Photo courtesy of Lennart Westberg/Martin Mansson archive.

cess of refitting. The total strength of the division was about 3,000 men, although the number of actual combat effectives was less. The division's Panzer battalion contained 24 Sturmgeschütz III and 10 Jagdpanzer IVs. The Sturmgeschütz III acted as both an assault gun for the infantry and a tank destroyer. They were moderately armored, and often had added side skirts typical of German Panzers late in the war. They were armed with either the standard 7.5cm Stuk 40 L/48 guns, or the powerful 10.5cm StuH 42 L/28 main guns. This unit suffered a lack of effective leadership at the division command level. The division's leaders became despondent to their assigned mission of Berlin's defense. The unit fought mainly as regimental *Kampfgruppe* during the battle.

SCHWERE SS-PANZERABTEILUNG 503

Schwere SS-Panzerabteilung 503 [hereafter referred to as *s.SS.Pz.Abt.503*] was under the command of *SS-Sturmbannführer* Friedrich Herzig. During the short for months that this unit existed it managed to score more hits per day than any other Tiger battalion during the war. The fact that *s.SS.Pz.Abt.503* claimed to score an estimated 500 kills while deployed against Zhukov's forces in Pomerania, along the Oder, and Berlin suggests that the fighting was ferocious in those final months of the war.[84] The unit was formed in July 1943 but did not deploy for combat until January 1945. The battalion consisted of 39 Panzerkampfwagen VI Tiger II Ausf. B Königstiger (King Tiger). The King Tiger, when properly employed in the defense, was a virtual fortress. It boasted frontal hull armor of 150mm and frontal turret armor of 180mm. The 8.8cm KwK 43 L/71 main gun, like the Tiger I, could easily penetrate the frontal armor of the heaviest Soviet tanks on the battlefield. Its longer barrel gave the King Tiger added velocity and a higher penetration factor at long range allowing the King Tiger to engage and knock out enemy armor at ranges of 1,500 meters or more. Due to the sloped armor of the King Tiger, Soviet armor had to close within 700 meters or less to penetrate even the side armor of the Tiger II. The unit fought in a series off vicious battles in Pomerania, where it lost much of its equipment in the process. By 16 April the unit was down to 12 operational King Tigers and a few Wirbelwind quad flak guns that mounted quad 2cm anti-aircraft guns. This unit operated as part of *Pz.Abt. Hermann von Salza*.[85]

The following two photos taken of Henschel model King Tigers issued to s.Pz.Abt.503 (the *Heer* not *SS* heavy tank battalion) during Operation Grief in Hungary are good illustrations of the King Tiger model that operated with *s.SS-Pz.Abt.503* in Berlin. One key difference: the *SS* King Tigers had no Zimmermit coating.
Photos courtesy of the Bundesarchiv.

408th VOLKSARTILLERIE CORPS

The *408th Volksartillerie Korps* were formed on 29 September 1944 and was little more than an overstrength artillery regiment. There were six battalions equipped with a variety of guns, many of which were captured Russian artillery pieces. The 408th was in direct fire support of the *LVI Pz. Korps*.

German divisions were equipped with a wide variety of weapons, equipment, and armored fighting vehicles in 1945. Much of the equipment came from training facilities around Germany, or captured weapons from any number of nations that Nazi Germany conquered during the early war years. German units typically were equipped with more wireless communications equipment than their Soviet counterparts that gave them a distinct tactical advantage. German weapons were excellent, although they were not the predominant models found in frontline units. The *Panzerfaust* was among the most numerous weapons available to the Germans. The Panzerschreck, a German copy of the U.S. Bazooka first encountered in Tunisia, was also available, though not in wide numbers. The MG42, considered one of the most effective machine-guns of WWII, was a main support weapon. The MP 40, and its replacement the Sturmgewehr 44, represented the standard German machine pistol and assault rifle available to the German soldier. The single shot of a KAR 98k or other bolt-action rifles was ineffective in assault or defense this late in the war as the Soviet soldiers relied heavily on automatic weapons, including captured German ones. The KAR 98k was very effective as a sniper rifle when fitted with the Zielfernrohr 40 and 41 scopes. In addition the Germans produced a semi-automatic rifle in the class of the U.S. M1 Grand known as the Gewehr 41 and 43. This weapon was also found among the troops and was used in the role of sniper rifle.

The *Wehrmacht* experimented with a variety of Panzer variants during the war. Many of them were located at various training or test sites all around Germany. As the need for replacements grew many of these training sites were stripped of their operational or experimental armor and they were sent to various Panzer battalions through *AGV*. This is why there was such a variety of armor present among the various German divisions. Panzers in the same battalion might have different camouflage schemes or equipment. Two Jagdpanzer IVs tank destroyers from the same unit might look completely different, one sporting side skirts and the other without any. German armor also carried different paint schemes. Panthers in *Müncheberg*, for example, probably relied on their factory applied red-oxide primer followed with angled stripes of both yellow and green to break up the image. King Tigers had ambush colors consisting of green, yellow, and dark brown along with speckled spots. German ammunition emitted a smokeless, green hued discharge when shot, making detection by enemy observation very difficult. This combination allowed the King Tigers of *s.SS.Pz.Abt.503* to score impressive kills against masses of Soviet armor caught in the open. The Soviets simply could not locate the well-camouflaged King Tigers nestled into the pine tree covered wood line. One key drawback to the German Panzers was that late in the war German companies had to switch from manganese to high-carbon steel alloy with nickel that made the armor very brittle.[86] *AGV* clearly consisted of a wide variety of non-standard individual weapons and varying armored fighting vehicles. It was truly an amalgamation of everything available at that time and the reliance on so many vehicles from training grounds demonstrates how damaged the German war economy was by March-April 1945.

On 6 April aerial reconnaissance observed 1,000 Soviet vehicles moving west from Prussia to the Oder.[87] On 8 April a memorandum sent to the *AGV* and *AGC* stated that the 'Soviet Groâangriffes' would begin on 15 April based on all available assessments.[88] By 10 April it was clear that the Soviets were planning to attack soon. Changes in their deployment were observed. Russian POWs, however, gave little detail of when the attack would commence.[89] On 12 April the Soviets began operations to expand their bridgeheads and Heinrici realized that the attack would come soon. Heinrici knew from recent experience that the Soviets always preceded a major offensive with strong reconnaissance.[90] Reports flooded into the *AGV* from the *9.Armee* that Soviet tank concentrations were seen building in the bridgeheads. In addition the Soviets were zeroing their artillery.[91] During 13–14 April the Soviets launched their probing attacks west of Küstrin opposite the Seelow Heights designed to confuse the Germans of their new troop dispositions as well as hide the timing of their attack. During this phase their artillery began to zero in on clumps of trees or noticeable landmarks like church steeples. All this activity read like a page from a Soviet Field Operations Manual to the German Army now long accustomed to the typical preparations made by the Soviets before a large attack. The German High Command was confident that the Soviet attack would occur on the 16 April that a prior prepared special order by Hitler was released to the soldiers of *AGV*. Hitler's order read:

Führer's Order-of-the-Day

Soldiers of the Eastern Front!

For the last time our deadly enemies, the Jewish Bolsheviks, have rallied their massive forces for an attack. They intend to destroy Germany and to exterminate our people. Many of you eastern soldiers know well the fate that awaits above all German woman and children; the old men and children will be murdered, the women and girls turned into barrack room whores, and the rest marched off to Siberia.

We have been expecting this attack, and since January this year have done everything possible to build up a strong front. The enemy will be received with massive artillery fire. Gaps in our infantry have been filled by countless new units. Our front is being strengthened with emergency units, newly raised units and *Volkssturm*.

This time the Bolsheviks will meet the ancient fate of Asia, which means that they will bleed to death before the capital of the German Reich.

Whoever fails in his duty now behaves as a traitor to our people. Any regiment or division that abandons its position will be acting so disgracefully that they will be shamed by the women and children braving the terror bombing in our cities.

Above all, be on your guard against those treacherous officers and soldiers, who, in order to preserve their pitiful lives, fight against us in Russian pay, perhaps even wearing German uniform. Anyone ordering you to retreat, unless personally known to you, will be immediately arrested and, if necessary killed on the spot, no matter what rank he may hold.

If everyone on the Eastern Front does his duty in these coming days and weeks, the last assault of Asia will crumble, just as the invasion by our enemies in the west will fail in the end, despite everything.

Berlin stays German, Vienna will be German again and Europe will never be Russian.

Table 3.4 *LVI Panzer Korps* Strength

	Manpower 10 April	AFVs 13 April
From *9. Armee*		
9. Fallschirmjäger Division		
Strength 6,758		
Pz.Jg.Abt.		
Stug III		0
Jagdpz 38		8
20. Panzergrenadier Division		
Strength 4,848		
Pz.Abt. 8		
PZ IV		13
PZ IV Flak		3
PZ IV (L) A		16
Müncheberg Panzer Division		
Strength 1,986		
I/Pz.Abt.29		
PZ III		1
PZ IV		1
PZ IV (L) A		2
PZ V		1
PZ VI		21
Jagdpz. IV		10
920.SPG Trg Bde (Döbertitz)		
Stug III		17
Pz IV (L)		7
From 3. Panzer Armee		
11. Waffen-SS Panzergrenadier Division Nordland		
Strength 3,000		
Stug III		22
PZ IV (L) V		10
schwere.SS-Panzerabteilung 503		
PZ VI		10
Pz. (Flak)		8
18. Panzergrenadier Division		
Strength 6,000		
PZ IV		27
PZ IV (L) A		8
Jagdpz. 38		19
Total Strength	22,592	
Total Panzer and Assault Guns	204	

Sources: Lakowski, Seelow 1945, p. 49, T-311, 171 7223305-08, T-311, 169 7221230, and T-311, 169, 7220993, Weidling Interrogation Report, p. 2. In his post-war interrogation Weidling told the Soviets that before the attack on 16 April his corps numbered about 50,000 soldiers. This may have been purposely worded by his captors to justify their costly efforts to take the Seelow Heights. By totaling the three divisions under Weidling's command (not counting the two divisions released to him from the 3.Panze Armee) a total number of only 13,592 soldiers were available for the immediate defense. For comparison, on 17 March there were only 50,000 soldiers in the entire 9.Armee!

Form yourselves into sworn brotherhoods to defend, not just the empty concept of a Fatherland, but your homes, your wives, your children, and with them our future.

In these hours the whole German nation looks to you, my eastern warriors, and only hopes that by your resolution, your fanaticism, your weapons, and under your leadership, the Bolshevik assault will be drowned in a blood bath.

In this moment, in which fate has removed from the earth the greatest war criminal of all time, will the turning point of the war be decided.

Adolf Hitler[92]

A 14 April daily report issued by *AGV* stated that the opening phase of the Soviet attack began, outlining the combat actions occurring throughout the various division sectors.[93] On 15 April a *Fremde Heere Ost* daily report called for the attack to be launched on 16 April.[94] After two days of strong Soviet reconnaissance, Heinrici decided that the Soviet attack would indeed commence in the early morning of 16 April. There was nothing else Heinrici could do to prepare the German soldiers of *AGV*. His efforts over a four week period dramatically increased the strength and readiness of the German forces despite the difficulties in obtaining replacements and material. Heinrici operationally planned to follow Guderian's orders and attempt to hold the Russians along the Oder and force the Western Allies over the Elbe River into eastern Germany. The Western Allies might then take Berlin first. The belief that "Better that the Americans come to Berlin but, in no circumstances, the Russians" resonated through Heinrici's command staff and subordinate commanders.[95] If that plan failed, Heinrici issued verbal orders to Busse and Manteuffel to fall back to the Elbe on either side of Berlin. There would be no fight for the German capital.

Notes to Chapter 3

1 Heinrici interview.
2 MS #P-136, p. ii.
3 Heinrici interview.
4 Ibid.
5 Ibid.
6 Ibid.
7 RG 242, T-311: 169/7221263 "Es könne sodann später überlegt werden, wenn der feindliche Grossangriff unmittelbar vor seine Losbrechen stünde, ob man die Spitze von Kustrin in diesem Falle usf eine Grosskampf - HKL wieder zurücknehme, die Zuge der augenblicklichen Stellung zu suchen sei."
8 Heinrici interview.
9 Le Tissier, *Zhukov on the Oder*, pp. 90–7.
10 Heinrici Memoir, p. 17, (RC: 68/3).
11 Heinrici interview, and T-311: 169/7221263 "General Krebs erkannte die Nachteile, die eine Stellungsvergrösserung durch Angriff uns bringen würde."
12 T-311: 169/7221216
13 Ibid.
14 Heinrici interview.
15 Ibid.
16 Ibid.
17 MS #D-189, *The Pomeranian Battle and the Command in the East*, p. 12.
18 Le Tissier, *Zhukov on the Oder*, p. 120.
19 T-311: 169/7221378 "Einsatz der Artillerie für den Grosskampf" 31.3.45, and T-311: 171/7223310-11.
20 Le Tissier, *With our Backs to Berlin*, p. 18.
21 H. W. Arnold and H. Jansen interviews, (RC: 69/9 and 11).
22 Le Tissier, *With our Backs to Berlin*, p. 28.
23 MA DDR, WF-13433, Sheet 055 cited in Le Tissier, *Zhukov on the Oder*, pp. 117–18.
24 F. Haas interview, (RC: 69/18).
25 T311: 169/7221401.
26 T-311: 169/7220993. The actual number is 4,209. It includes the 9,039 soldiers in 'Fortress Frankfurt-an-der-Oder'. If these are removed from the calculation then the number drops to 3770.
27 Heinrici interview.
28 Le Tissier, *With our Backs to Berlin*, p. 34.
29 Heinrici interview.
30 Ibid.
31 Ibid.
32 Altner, p. 37.
33 Ibid, p. 8.
34 Le Tissier, *With our Backs to Berlin*, p. 22.

35 Ibid, pp. 18–19.
36 W. Bensch interview.
37 T-311: 169/7221534-35.
38 Ibid.
39 Eismann interview.
40 Heinrici interview.
41 Henrici interview.
42 Altner, p. 7. See also OKW Messages and Documents, March 8 Directive, (RC: 62/8).
43 Altner, p. 32.
44 Heinrici interview.
45 Heinrici interview.
46 Haas interview. Also see F. Bottcher interview (RC: 68/8).
47 H.H. Lohmann interview, (RC: 66/2).
48 T. Busse interview, (RC: 67/17).
49 Heinrici interview.
50 Ibid.
51 Heinrici interview.
52 Heinrici interview.
53 T 311: 169/7221376 "Infanterie-Ersatz im Groâkampf".
54 Heinrici interview.
55 T. von Dufving interview, (RC: 69/1).
56 Eric von Manstein commanded the force that took Sevastopol in the summer 1942. Sevastopol was considered impregnable and boasted the strongest fortifications in Europe at that time.
57 One was actually just a driver. v. Dufving interview.
58 v. Dufving interview. *AGV* daily operational maps do not show the Panzer Korps at the front until 11 April.
59 H.M. Stimpel, *Widersinn 1945*, pp 12–13. See also T-311: 171/7223306.
60 G. Ramm, *"Gott Mit Uns:"Kriegserlebnisse aus Brandenburg und Berlin*, p. 192, and Stimpel, p. 35.
61 Le Tissier, *Zhukov on the Oder*, p. 127, and Stimpel, p. 38.
62 Stimpel, p. 37, and Ramm, p. 192.
63 Le Tissier, *Zhukov on the Oder*, p. 78.
64 R. Lakowski, *Seelow 1945*, p. 49. T-311: 171/7223305.
65 T-311: 69/7221537 "Gesamtverluste von 22.6.41 – 31.3.45 15.4.1945"
66 Le Tissier, *With our Backs to Berlin*, p. 96.
67 Ibid, pp. 95, 98.
68 RH/10, Schultz-Naumann, p. 158.
69 RH/10, Le Tissier, *Zhukov on the Oder*, p. 128.

70 Peter Chamberlin, Hillary Doyle, and Thomas Jentz, *Encyclopedia of German Tanks of WWII*, p. 245.
71 "Development History of the JS-1/JS-2," p. 9. www.battlefield.ru.
72 Le Tissier, *Zhukov on the Oder*, p. 128.
73 Ibid, p. 86.
74 The effectiveness of the IR devices cannot be verified through identified primary or secondary sources. It is plausible that these devices may have helped the Panthers engage Soviet armor at close range, there is no operational evidence to corroborate this assertion.
75 Le Tissier, *Zhukov on the Oder*, p. 273 and Lakowski p. 49.
76 Le Tissier, *With our Backs to Berlin*, p. 92.
77 Le Tissier, *Zhukov on the Oder*, p. 128.
78 Le Tissier, *With our Backs to Berlin*, p. 33.
79 W. Feldheim interview. (RC: 70/12).
80 Altner, pp. 47, 51.
81 W. Bowen, "The Ghost Battalion: Spaniards in the Waffen-SS, 1944–5," p. 2.
82 A. Pçtersons, *Mums jâpârnâk: Latvieðu karavîripçdçjie Berlînes aizstâvji*, p. 68–73.
83 Böttcher interview.
84 C. Wilbeck, *Sledgehammers*, p186.
85 W. Schneider, *Tigers in Combat II*, p. 296–8.
86 "Development History of the JS-1/JS-2," p. 9. www.battlefield.ru
87 Heinrici, interview.
88 T-311: 169 7221541 "Am 15.4 wahrscheinlich Beginn des Groâangriffes." Vermerk über Ferngespräch zwischen Ia H.Gr. Mitte und Ia H.Gr. Weichel.
89 Heinrici interview.
90 Heinrici interview.
91 Eissman interview.
92 T-311: 169/7221733 and (CR: 62/8). By 15 April it was understood throughout the command that the final military battle for the Third Reich and for Berlin was abut to begin. Hitler's order prepared in advance was released to the soldier of *AGV*.
93 T-311: 169/7221669. "Gegen die 9. Armee trat Feind in den heutigen Morgenstuden zu den seit Tagen erwarteten Vorangriffen an."
94 T-314: 1445/000229 "Wichtigste Feindfeststellungen v. 15.4.1945"
95 Heinrici interview.

4

BERLIN STRATEGIC OFFENSIVE OPERATION

Berlin was a tempting target to the Soviet Army as its forces extended precarious bridgeheads across the frozen Oder River at the end of January 1945. The Soviet proximity to Berlin was the product of a wildly successful winter campaign that routed the *Wehrmacht* from Poland. The speed the Soviets showed in defeating and exploiting the fragile German defense stunned even the Western Allies according to German intelligence reports.[1] The Soviet success was as much the German's fault as it was any significant development in Soviet doctrine or technology. The German defense was thin and contained no mobile reserves. Much of the German reinforcements went west in preparation for the Ardennes Offensive known as *Wacht am Rhein*, leaving the defenses along the central corridor into Germany lacking. Even after the Soviets reached the Oder River the German High Command sent forces from the Ardennes to Hungary and not to the most threatened sector of the front. The Soviets, however, were not in a position to risk a push further into Germany despite the lack of strong, organized German defenses along the Oder.

Many factors prevented the Soviets from launching a renewed assault into eastern Germany to take Berlin February 1945. Lack of supply, the need for replacements, extended and exposed flanks, German Fortresses, and politics all weighed in on Stavka's decision to hold. In a postwar interview Chuikov stated that "if our communications, our lines of communications, had not been so spread out and so strained in the rear, in February we could have struck out for Berlin itself; but we needed ammunition, fuel and pontoons for forcing the Oder and then the canals which lay in front of Berlin itself."[2] The Soviets could not easily supply the units that reached the Oder because the German rail gauge was different. The Soviets rail lines worked off two pins instead of three causing a weaker rail that required more maintenance.[3] This required the Soviets to rely heavily on motor transport to support the needs to two complete Soviet Fronts that moved more than 500 kilometers in 20 days of offensive action. In Koniev's sector alone, 15,000 trucks crisscrossed his front ferrying troops, ammunition, fuel, and towing guns and tanks. All 15,000 motor vehicles in this case were U.S. and British trucks supplied to the Soviets through the Lend-Lease program.[4] Petrol became so critical that vehicles were abandoned due to lack of fuel. Every second truck that returned from delivering supplies to the front had to be towed back. Even captured German alcohol stocks were being used as fuel, although this proved problematic under best circumstances.[5] On the north flank, all of East Prussia and Pomerania remained in German hands. The Germans in Silesia clung to a variety of Fortresses and offered significant resistance in Breslau. Soviet infantry units, made up of ethnic Russians, and ethnic groups from central and eastern districts began to suffer serious morale problems. The Russians were now fighting on German soil and acted accordingly. Mass rapes, intoxication, and looting, all coupled by the exposure to the 'bourgeois' life style eroded control and disciple among the Soviet soldiers.[6] In addition, the frozen Oder River would start to thaw in 4–6 weeks preventing easy supply of any Soviet forces on the west bank unless significant transportation arteries at Küstrin or Frankfurt-an-der-Oder were immediately captured.

Any Soviet attempt to seize Berlin February without further preparation ran the risk of failure. A failure to seize Berlin quickly by the Soviets might have forced the Western Allies to eventually cross the Elbe River into eastern Germany and take Berlin instead—a possibility Stalin did not want to see. In addition, Himmler launched Guderian's *Operation Sonnenwende* into the flank of Zhukov's forces south of Pomerania. *Operation Sonnenwende* was planned to be a large-scale counterattack across Zhukov's northern wing, but Hitler changed the scope until the operation became a local counterattack, contrary to Guderian's wishes. The initial success of *Operation Sonnenwende* highlighted many of the key shortcomings the Soviets were facing. Stavka quickly ordered the reduction of German forces in Prussia and Pomerania. Guderian's offensive certainly helped remove any lingering doubts with the Soviet High Command whether to halt or advance toward Berlin.[7]

Stalin and Stavka quickly became dismayed at the pace of Western Allied operations across Germany after they crossed the Rhine. While the Soviets continued to struggle against fanatical and determined German resistance in farming hamlets and district towns in Prussia, Pomerania, and Silesia, the Germans were surrendering major industrial and transportation hubs like Kassel and Manheim without a shot. In the Soviet view, the Western Front ceased to exist as a military front and the fact that the Germans did not shift a single division from the Eastern to the Western Front only fueled their suspicions. Stalin's view was clear. The Western Allies would be invited into a Berlin conquered by Soviet force of arms, not the other way around.[8] The only way to accomplish this political feat was to take Berlin first. Stalin decided after receiving Eisenhower's memo at the end of March that the time was now to seize Berlin before the Western Allies jumped across the Elbe to take the city and disregard the zones of occupation outlined in 'Eclipse'.

Stalin ordered Zhukov and Koniev back to Moscow on 1 April. Upon entering Stalin's office in the Kremlin, both men found him seated at the end of a long table, where portraits of the Russian military heroes Suvorov and Kutuzov hung on the wall. Around the table with Stalin were Molotov, Voroshilov, Malenkov, Beria, Kaganovich, Vaoznesenskiy, Mikoyan, General A. I. Antonov and Chief of the Operations Directorate of the General Staff S. M. Shtemenko.[9] Almost immediately Shtemenko began to read an intelligence assessment of the strategic situation that outlined the planned Western Allied drive toward Berlin under a main grouping of forces led by Field Marshall Bernard Montgomery. The intelligence assessment continued to outline the expected Western Allied forces involved and expected timetables. At the end on the assessment, Stalin looked at Zhukov and Koniev and asked who would take Berlin first, "We or the Allies?" It was Koniev that answered the question first, ignoring Zhukov's presence. Stalin allowed a slight smile then responded to Koniev

Marshall Ivan S. Koniev. His independent assault into
Berlin's southern districts ensured Zhukov's success.
Photo courtesy of the Cornelius Ryan Collection,
Mahn Center, Alden.

Marshal Georgi Zhukov, 1st Byelorussian Front commander.
He is often considered to be the overall commander of the
Berlin Strategic Offensive Operation, however, this is false.
Zhukov exercised no command influence over his rival Koniev
advancing from the south. Photo courtesy of the Bulgarian
Ministry of Defence.

that Koniev was far to the south and a large re-grouping of his forces was required first. Koniev quickly responded that he required no significant movement. He would easily effect the required re-grouping within his Front boundaries and launch the assault from there. Zhukov now responded that his forces would launch the assault on Berlin since they were on the direct axis and the shortest distance from Berlin. Stalin clearly achieved his intent at pitting his two senior commanders against each other and now required them to prepare their operational plans over the next 24 hours.

Koniev and Zhukov worked as they would later fight, independently and with little coordination. Only on a few occasions did either man consult with one another and exchange opinions. Neither plan developed serious operational detail. There was no time for that. Instead their plans focused on basic directions, and the start date for the operation. On the morning of 3 April, both men presented their plans to Stalin. Zhukov went first, then Koniev. In both cases Stalin offered no additional comment. Next, the question of the start date of the operation was discussed. Koniev initially proposed a very aggressive date that was only a week away; however, he also requested more forces to be deployed to his Front. Stalin agreed to the initial date and offered the 28th and 31st Armies that were now completing their operations in East Prussia. Then it was discovered that both those armies could not reach Koniev in time to participate in the assault on Berlin due to the situation with the conversion of rail line gauge. A new start date was proposed by Koniev to account for the time needed to incorporate the new armies. Stalin agreed, and the start date for the assault on Berlin was moved out to 16 April. Stavka then issued two directives. The first gave Zhukov's 1st Byelorussian Front the responsibility to take Berlin, and then reach the Elbe in 12–15 days. Koniev's 1st Ukrainian Front was now given the assignment to capture the line Beelitz-Wittenberg, then capture the east bank of the Elbe River up to Dresden, with a notable exception. If Zhukov's forces encountered any difficulty along the Küstrin-Berlin axis then Koniev's forces might be tasked by Stavka to assist Zhukov by turning his tank armies in a north-west direction. The inter-front boundary between both commanders' forces was drawn only to Lübben, erasing the original boundary that kept Koniev south of Potsdam.[10] In addition, Stalin gave the 2nd Byelorussian Front under Marshal K. K. Rokossovskii, who was still engaged in the reduction of Prussia and Pomerania, a warning order to take over positions on Zhukov's right flank and prepare for an offensive across the Oder River to begin sometime after 18 April.[11] The addition of Rokossovskii provided extra support for the operation.

Stavka prepared three directives that outlined Operation Berlin. Zhukov's and Koniev's were prepared and issued while both men were still in Moscow. The third, Rokossovskii's, was prepared several days later. The 1st Byelorussian Front under the command of Zhukov had the primary responsible of taking Berlin as outlined in the 2 April Stavka Directive signed by Stalin on 1 April. It read as follows:

General V. I. Chuikov (2nd from the left), 8 Guards Army commander (the photo is taken during the battle for Stalingrad).
Photo courtesy of the Bulgarian Ministry of Defence.

Stavka directive to Front commander (2 April 1945):
> To prepare and to conduct operations for the capture of the capital of Germany, BERLIN
> To reach the line of the River Elbe not later than the 12th–15th day of operations
> Operational deployment:
> > Main blow to be mounted westwards from the Küstrin bridgehead with 4 field and 2 tank armies
> > To secure the main assault group of the **1st Byelorussian Front** from the north and south, to mount two supporting blows each with 2 armies …
> > The two tank armies operating with the main assault group to be employed – after the break-through – to exploit successes in the northerly and north-easterly outflanking of Berlin.[12]

Koniev's orders signed by Stalin on 2 April and issued on 3 April left no doubt as to his potential role in the conquest of Berlin.

Stavka Directive to Front commander (3 April, 1945):
> To destroy enemy forces in the Cottbus area and south of Berlin
> To reach Beelitz/Wittenberg line and thence the line of the Elbe up to Dresden not later than the 10th–12th day of operations
> Operational Deployment:
> > Main blow to be mounted with 5 field and 2 tank armies, from the area of Triebel advancing in the general direction of Spremberg/Belzig …
> > Field and tank armies of the second echelon to exploit successes of main assault group
> Additional directive to **1st Ukrainian Front**:
> > To overcome the powerful enemy defense on the Küstrin/Berlin axis, the **1st Byelorussian Front** was directed to assemble the maximum density of troops per kilometer of front – 1 division per 7 kilometers of front; nevertheless, in the event of the rate of advance of the **1st Byelorussian Front** being slowed down, the **1st Ukrainian Front** would switch its mobile forces on to Berlin, and thus be in a position to assist **1st Byelorussian Front** in the encirclement of the Berlin garrison and the storming of the Fascist capital.[13]

The 2nd Byelorussian Front's directive read:

Stavka directive to Front commander (6 April, 1945):
> To force the Oder,
> To destroy the Stettin group of enemy forces
> To reach line Anklam/Dammin/Waren/Pritzwalk/Wittenberge not later than the 12th–15th day of operation
> Operational deployment:
> > To operate from the region north of Schwedt in the general direction of Strelitz;
> > To co-operate with the right flank of the **1st Byelorussian Front** in destroying enemy by the Oder
> > To mount the main blow with 3 field armies, 3 tank corps, 1 mechanized and 1 cavalry corps[14]

Stavka also mandated an artillery density of no less than 250 barrels of 76mm and larger per 1 kilometer of front! In total the Soviets amassed 20 Field Armies, 4 Tank Armies and 3 Air Armies for the offensive totaling more than 42,000 guns and mortars, 6,300 tanks, and 6,600 aircraft.[15] More than 2 million soldiers were being organized for the operation. In terms of manpower, the Berlin Strategic Offensive Operation ranked fourth out of all Soviet operations conducted during WWII. This operation came behind the Dnieper-Carpathian

Strategic Offensive Operation of 24 December 1943–17 April 1944, the Byelorussian Strategic Offensive of 23 June–29 August 1944, and the Vistula-Oder Strategic Operation 12 January–3 February 1945. The Berlin Strategic Offensive Operation, however, was conducted across a smaller frontage and contained more units than the previous offensives. This caused new command-and-control challenges on the existing Soviet command structure. It should also be noted that Berlin exceeded Stalingrad in personnel losses incurred during the city fighting, and exceeded Kursk in the amount of armor lost. The Soviets fielded a superiority of 5.2:1 in manpower and 8.2:1 in tanks and assault guns against *AGV*.

Table 4.1 Soviet Soldier and Equipment Totals for Berlin Operation

	2nd Byelorussian Front	*1st Byelorussian Front*	*1st Ukrainian Front*	*1st and 2nd Polish Armies*	*Total*
Soliders	441,600	908,500	550,900	?	2,056,900
Tanks	644	1,795	1,388	?	3,827
Self-Propelled Guns	307	1,360	667	?	2,334,
Anti-Tank Guns	770	2,306	1,444	?	4,520
Artillery 76mm and higher caliber	3,172	7,442	5,040	?	15,654
Mortars 82mm and higher caliber	2,770	7,186	5,225	?	15,181
Rocket Launchers	807	1,531	917	?	3,255
Anti-Aircraft Guns	801	1,665	945	?	3,411
Motor Vechicles	21,846	44,332	29,205	?	95,383
Aircraft (Fights, Bombers, Reconnaissance, etc.)	1,360	3,188	2,148	NA	6,696

Sources: Krivosheev, *Soviet Casualties and Combat Losses in the Twentieth Century*, p158 and Tieke, *Das Ende Zwischen Oder und Elbe: Der Kampf um Berlin 1945*, quoted from *Voyenno-Istoricheski Zhurnal* 1965, p. 506. Compare with the Red Army Order of Battle found in Ryan 71:9.

Marshal K. K. Rokossovskii, 2 Byelorussian Front commander. Photo courtesy of the Bulgarian Ministry of Defence.

One interesting point about the directives was how the 2nd Byelorussian Front was ordered to co-operate with Zhukov's forces, while the 1st Ukrainian Front was not. The directives were written in such a way to purposely foster the competition between Zhukov and Koniev and clearly spell out that Koniev had the green light to go to Berlin if Zhukov was held up. When Zhukov became aware that Koniev's forces were indeed in Berlin at the height of the assault on Berlin, he showed more concern with whose forces reached Berlin first rather than coordinating their operations. This also explains how his decisions in Berlin were clouded by his rivalry. Zhukov ordered his own forces across Koniev's front lines without Koniev's knowledge precipitating considerable confusion and unnecessary fratricide among Soviet formations fighting in Berlin.

Zhukov and Koniev were different men that shared similar traits. Both men fought in World War I then later served in the Red Army during the Russian Civil War. During the early years of the war, Koniev served under Zhukov as an Army, then Front Commander, first during the defense of Moscow in 1941, then during the disastrous attack against *Heeresgruppe Mitte* in the fall of 1942 known as Operation Mars. It is not known what their feelings were toward each other during the early part of the war, but it is clear that Koniev developed a dislike toward Zhukov's style and execution on the battlefield. Zhukov, like most commanders under Stalin, was arguably a brutal leader. Zhukov understood the technical aspects of war, but his operational application was far less artful and more direct. He was aggressive and demonstrated little regard for human life, especially his own soldiers' lives. David Glantz, renowned historian of Russian military affairs wrote in his introduction to Zhukov's memoirs:

When assessing Zhukov's long and illustrious career, several distinct attributes emerge. First and foremost, his iron will and strong stomach made him tenacious on offense and defense and unsparing of himself and his subordinates. Recent archival evidence serves only to reinforce Harrison Salisbury's judgment that "Zhukov never fought a battle in which he was sparing of the lives of men. Only by expenditure of life, he believed, could the military goals be achieved."[16]

Contrary to popular history, Zhukov did not win every battle.[17] In the fall of 1942, before he executed the counterattack at Stalingrad known as Operation Uranus, Zhukov planned and launched Operation Mars against the German *Heeresgruppe Mitte* opposite Moscow. That offensive failed and cost the still-recovering Soviet Army significant casualties that it could not afford. It took almost another two years for the Red Army to recover sufficiently to launch another major attack against the Germans opposite Moscow. Zhukov's behavior during that battle foreshadowed many of his less than perfect attributes that he demonstrated again during the assault on Berlin. In particular, Zhukov's failure in Operation Mars was based largely on his penchant for underestimating the German forces, his own overoptimistic assessment of his operational plans, and his insistence on more sacrifice by his troops in the face of adversity.[18] Glantz records that "Once Operation Mars commenced, Zhukov was preoccupied with achieving success, and his own innate stubbornness (tinged with jealousy of Vasilevsky) [a rival commander] prevented him from realistically scaling down his goals and expectations to accord with existing conditions. Instead … he demanded his commanders and troops fight on with even greater resolve."[19] Greater resolve often meant significant carnage for the troops under his command.

Koniev served under Zhukov for the first three years of the war. He demonstrated many of the key characteristics of Zhukov. Koniev was noted for his aggressiveness in battle, his temper with subordinates, and was prone to moments of jealousy of his peers. Koniev's operational planning and execution, however, was much different than Zhukov's. He demonstrated significant thoroughness and did not fall into the trap of underestimating his enemy and overestimating his own abilities like Zhukov. Perhaps the most striking difference was Koniev's flexibility in battle. Where Zhukov focused on the application of military science, Koniev was clearly rooted in the application of military art, presumably credited to his love of military history.[20] This distinction is of some interest as Koniev started his career as a Political Commissar instead of as a career military officer like Zhukov. By 1945 both commanders had demonstrated success and failure in battle. Koniev rose out of a sea of potential rivals by a combination of force of personality and proven capabilities to be selected by Stalin to directly confront Zhukov by developing a rival plan to take the most prestigious target of the war—Berlin.

Zhukov and Koniev were now dismissed to finalize their operation plans with their respective subordinate commanders. There were only twelve days left to prepare the fourth largest Soviet operation of the war. The Berlin Strategic Offensive Operation was designed to beat the Western Allies to Berlin and deliver the Nazi capital and control of Central Europe into Stalin's hands. Even though a date was selected, the Soviets had much to prepare. In fact they had eight days left before the reconnaissance in force began in preparation for the offensive. The rush was felt by everyone at the front. Even after the war it was noted by Chuikov that "In the existing military political situation, the strategic task had to be fulfilled in the shortest possible time."[21] Chuikov continued: "In the preparation of the plan for the offensive one could sense haste and underestimate of the enemy forces. This came out in both the opening stage of the operation and the process of its further execution."[22]

Upon leaving Moscow, Zhukov called all his Army, Corps, Independent Cavalry and Tank Formation commanders from the 1st Byelorussian front to a staff meeting in a school at Landsberg around 5 April. The meeting room was filled with aerial reconnaissance

View from the German side of the Seelow Heights looking east down the tree lined Reichsbahn 1. On the other side of the open clearing just beyond the tree line is Alt Tucheband from where the Soviet 47th Guards Rifle Division of the 4th Guards Rifle Corps launched its assault on the morning of 16th April. The Soviets ran right into the *76.Pz.Gren.Rgt.* supported by Panzergrenadiers of the *Müncheberg Pz.Div.* The wide open terrain made the Soviets easy targets. Author's collection.

View of the Seelow Heights looking west from the Soviet side near Hackenow and Reichsbahn 1. The Soviet advance was dominated by the German 8.8s positioned along the crest of the Heights. No Soviet movement could happen in the Oderbruch without the Germans noticing. Note the Church spire in the distance—the Soviets used this as an aiming point to zero their artillery guns before the battle. Author's collection.

photos, maps, and a massive terrain table of Berlin built by his staff in two days.[23] In dramatic fashion, Zhukov briefed his subordinate commanders on their mission:

> Comrades, I have been with the Supreme Commander [Stalin]. The situation is such that I found it necessary to summon you here urgently. Earlier we had proposed that the Berlin operation should begin later … now the timetable has changed!
>
> The little allies [sarcastic reference] are pressing us with requirements that aren't quite 'allied.' [Reference to Yalta]
>
> Eisenhower in April intends to surround and destroy the Ruhr concentrations of the enemy – and then advance to Leipzig-Dresden, and just 'on the way' take Berlin. All this will look like helping the Red Army. But the Stavka knows very well that taking Berlin before the arrival of Soviet troops is Eisenhower's main aim. The Stavka also knows that two Allied airborne divisions are being rapidly readied for a drop on Berlin. [Reference to Operation Talisman]
>
> The Germans, evidently, help this on: they offer us stubborn resistance in every urban centre, but in the west they surrender towns by telephone.[24]

Zhukov challenged his subordinates in the room by telling them the going might be tough against the Germans despite the fact that Berlin was only 70 kilometers away. He reminded them that this was a shorter distance than his armies covered in one day during the Vistula-Oder offensive of January (Zhukov unrealistically planned for an average rate of advance of 35–37 kilometer per day by his armor and 11–14 kilometers per day by his infantry formations).[25] He reviewed the three known main German defensive lines on a map to his commanders then dramatically pulled back a tarp that covered a huge relief map of Berlin complete with three dimensional buildings created by his engineers. In the center of the relief map were numbered buildings that represented the Government Quarter.[26] Pointing to building 105 in particular, Zhukov raised his voice and with emphasis bellowed "And there is the Reichstag. Who will get their first? … Who will be the first to raise the Victory Banner?"[27] The Reichstag was the primary target. Why the Soviets chose to focus on the Reichstag is not documented, but it began after their successful defense during the Battle of Kursk in 1943. What is certain is that the Reichstag's mystique as a Soviet goal was related to the burning of the Reichstag in 1933 that initiated Hitler and the Nazi Party's seizure of power. "On to the Reichstag!" was now the cry that focused the energies of Zhukov's subordinates as they began to wargame their offensive with Zhukov over the next two days. At the end of the briefing he revealed the date for the attack 16 April—everyone in the room applauded.

Zhukov and Koniev were confronted with very different tactical and operational circumstances based on their Front's geographical locations. Each tackled their problems differently. Zhukov was confronted with a narrow operational area based on the availability of bridgeheads, and limited maneuver area caused by spring floods of the swelling Oder River. Geographically speaking, Zhukov had a significant challenge to overcome. Both banks of the Oder River consisted of marshy terrain. The river itself was between 200–300 meters wide, but due to spring flooding, reached closer to 380 meters in width. His engineers built 20 bridges that were constantly attacked by *Luftflotte 6* under the command of *General Feldmarschall* Robert Ritter von Greim. The Soviet engineers demonstrated significant skill at bridging the flooded Oder as they were able to maintain the majority of their crossings. The Soviets engineers maintained the bridges despite attacks by *Luftflotte 6* that reached upwards of more than 1,000 sorties a day.[28] On the west bank of the Oder was a flat marshland that ran 10–15 kilometers to the base of the Seelow Heights. The marshland, known as the Oderbruch, was crisscrossed by canals, and streams. Small villages dotted the expanse; otherwise the flat terrain was without any significant vegetation or tree cover. The Seelow Heights rise up over 60 meters in some places with only a few improved roads winding a steep ascent to the top of the ridge. In most places the Seelow Heights could not be navigated by tanks due to the steepness of the terrain. Beyond the Seelow Heights were dense pine forests with narrow tracks that crossed both hill and lake country before reaching Berlin. Only one main improved road existed that ran directly from the Oder River to Berlin, and that was Reichsbahn 1. The difficulties the terrain posed to the Soviets were not new.

During the last two months, Zhukov's forces had fought on the western bank of the Oder to expand their bridgeheads at Kienitz, Görlitz, and successfully captured the highest elevation in the area known as the Reitwein Spur. They gained direct experience with the problems of launching armor attacks across the Oderbruch when several German formations, including *Müncheberg*, and *schwere SS Panzerabteilung 502* counterattacked the Soviets over open terrain March to relieve Küstrin. The German attack demonstrated to the Soviets the difficulty in moving across boggy open terrain, especially at night.[29] The role of the terrain the defeat of the German counterattack did not influence the Soviet operational or tactical thinking at all.

It was believed that the *Wehrmacht* planned to defend along the Seelow Heights the way they defended Poland during the Vistula-Oder Operation in January. Soviet planners expected that the Germans would defend in their positions immediately opposite the Soviet frontline without executing any tactical repositioning. The Soviets were optimistic that the Germans were all but defeated and that overwhelming firepower could easily overcome any significant resistance. It appears that the three defensive belts shown on Zhukov's planning map meant little to Soviet commanders. In addition it appears that Soviet intelligence, usually very good, offered no help now that the Soviets were operating on German territory. According to senior Soviet commanders the operations planners had very little combat intelligence about the Germans.[30] Soviet planners either did not identify the new German commander of *AGV*, or if they did they made no connection between Heinrici and his past ability to counter initial Soviet artillery barrages with an elastic defense. The Soviets dropped agents behind German lines to spy on troop movements, but their operations were not very successful. In most cases German security forces were able to capture them.[31]

The Soviets did employ a large number of Germans in both covert and direct combat actions to assist them in gaining intelligence, misleading German forces, and launching attacks. These German soldiers were known to the German High Command as Seydlitz Troops. They were named after *General der Artillerie* Walther von Seydlitz-Kurzbach who was captured at the battle for Stalingrad. Seydlitz was a key Soviet collaborator and soon became the leader of the Bund deutscher Offiziere (League of German Officers) and a prominent member of the Nationalkomitee Freies Deutschland (National Committee Free Germany). A comprehensive history of this organization and its membership does not exist, but what is known is that potentially thousands of German POWs captured in Russian served in this organization against their counterparts still fighting in the *Wehrmacht*. Now that the war was brought to German soil, many of these Communist sympathizers and anti-Nazi soldiers were employed against their fellow countrymen. In some cases they had a significant effect at the tactical level. Their appearance on the battlefield and activities to mislead German formations led *OKH* to issue an order to *AGV* that they take strong measures against any unknown or unauthorized German soldiers, officers or generals found in their area of operations.[32] Another key disadvantage that the Soviets could not overcome was the ability of the Germans to see almost all of the Soviet movement within the Oderbruch, whether through direct observation from the Seelow Heights or through aerial reconnaissance.

Zhukov's planning demonstrated a complete lack of operational or tactical understanding of the situation his forces faced. The overall plan called for Zhukov to use four rifle and two tank armies to smash the German defense along the Oder and storm Berlin. Along the main axis of attack were the 3rd Shock, 5th Shock and 8th Guards Armies. Chuikov's 8th Guards Army had the responsibility of taking the Seelow Heights by the end of the first day. All three armies had the responsibility of making a hole in the German defense that the 1st and 2nd Guards Tank Armies could exploit. All the rifle armies were expected to reach the Havel Lakes and Gatow district west of Berlin by day six of operations. The 47th Army was to launch its attack and drive northwest around Berlin toward Nauen—Rathenow and reach Schönhausen on the Elbe on day eleven of operations. On Zhukov's right flank the 61st Army and 1st Polish Army were expected to drive north than west of Berlin across Liebenwalde and reach the Elbe on day eleven of the operation. On the left flank the 69th and 33rd Armies were given orders to drive toward Potsdam and Brandenburg then sweep north into the Berlin suburbs. The 3rd Army would be committed as a reserve force along the main line of advance.[33] This overall plan called for taking the Seelow Heights by 16 April, assaulting and capturing Berlin by 21 April and completing the entire operation by reaching the Elbe River on 27 April.[34] Perhaps in a conscious acceptance of the difficulty his forces faced, Zhukov's operations staff opted for a three-phased approach they believed offered the best opportunity to demoralize Heinrici's forces.

The operational plan was simple and brutal. Zhukov's assault began two hours before daylight on 16 April. Over 8,900 artillery pieces were to open fire in an initial ten minute artillery strike, followed by ten minutes of battery fire, then a second ten minute artillery strike. The infantry and supporting armor planned to advance across the Oderbruch towards the Seelow Heights after the initial thirty-minute barrage while supported by a double rolling barrage out to 2,000 meters and up to 4,000 meters by a single barrage. In order to support Chuikov's 8th Guards Army, that was responsible to conduct the direct assault against the Seelow Heights, the double rolling barrage was followed with a massed fire against the heights at the start of the assault.[35] A key problem for the Soviet artillery was that they were firing in the dark and in many cases within close range of their own forward Soviet formations. Immediately after the artillery barrage, Zhukov and his operations staff decided upon a novel concept that believed would solve the problem of illuminating the battlefield for their soldiers and frightening the Germans that may have survived the initial bombardment. It was decided to illuminate the Oderbruch with a total of 143 anti-aircraft searchlights. The searchlights were sited 150–200 yards apart, some 400–500 yards from the German positions. Sweeping the landscape in front of the advancing Soviet troops the Germans forces would be blinded and their defensive positions illuminated in the intense light.[36] Once the Seelow Heights fell on the first day of battle, it was then decided that the two Soviet tank armies would not launch a combined offensive to the north around Berlin, but instead split their force and conduct a dramatic

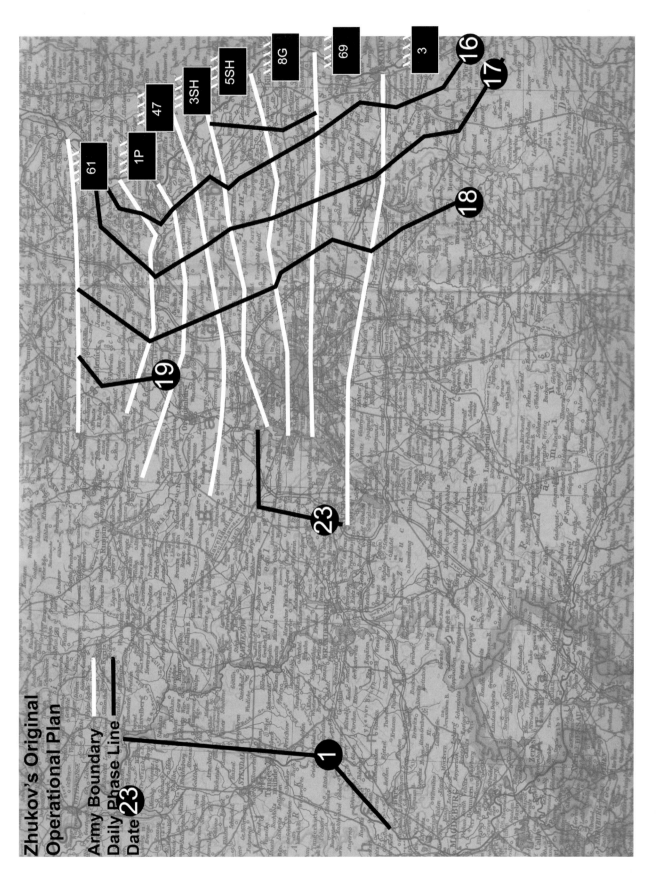

Zhukov's Original Operational Plan

Army Boundary
Daily Phase Line
Date **23**

Zhukov planned to reach Berlin within 2-3 days of the start of his offensive. Berlin was to fall after another 3 days of combat ending with the capture of Potsdam 7 days after the start of operations on 23 April. The Elbe River was expected to be reached by 1 May. This plan was unrealistic. Also note the lack of any involvement from Koniev's forces to the south or even the Polish Army operating to the north of Berlin.

encirclement of Berlin with the 2nd Guards Tank Army circling to the north and the 1st Guards Tank Army to the south, finally linking up in the Charlottenburg suburb of Berlin.[37] This change in plan was approved directly by Stalin.

In direct support of ground operations was S.I. Ridenko's 16th Air Army. The 16th Air Army's 3,188 combat aircraft, along with 800 bombers from the 18th Air Army, were to support the Soviet assault from the start. Zhukov demanded that his air assets be arranged in three ground-attack aviation corps and one ground-attack division. Operational control was assigned to the infantry during the initial assault and the tanks during the breakthrough. From the start of the operation through 1950 hours on the first day the 16th Air Army would launch non-stop attacks against German positions.[38] Forward air controllers were assigned directly to join the staffs on the rifle and tank armies in order to facilitate tight coordination.

Zhukov's plan was ambitious, complex, and large. He arrayed an impressive density of artillery, armor, and men. In the Küstrin bridgehead where the main effort was planed, there were 41 of his 79 total infantry divisions, along with another 4 waiting on the east bank to move forward once the assault developed. Behind these divisions were the tank brigades of the 1st and 2nd Guards Tank Armies. Zhukov's operational plan was detailed only for the first twenty-four hours despite the enormous concentration of infantry, tank, artillery, and aircraft.[39] Zhukov and his operations staff clearly believed they were dealing with a defeated enemy that would not resist under the weight of their immense firepower. Zhukov expected that after the first day of combat the Germans would simply be defeated and the road to Berlin would be wide open. In his mind, additional coordination and detailed planning was simply not necessary.

North of Zhukov, the 2nd Byelorussian Front prepared to play a supporting role to Zhukov's main effort. Rokossovskii had to launch his attack across two branches of the Oder in his sector where the river was so wide and shallow that assault boats could not be used because they would simply ground themselves on the sandy shallows. Scheduled to begin his offensive on 18 April, Rokossovskii decided to attack on a wide front using his three main armies. The 65th, 70th, and 49th Armies supported by three tank, one mechanized, and one cavalry corps would attack along a 50 kilometer front. Wherever the breakthrough occurred would then become the main effort of advance. Rokossovskii's mission was to destroy the *3.Panzer Armee*, protect Zhukov's flank then reach the Elbe on day 15 of the main offensive or 1 May.[40]

Koniev's operational plan for his 1st Ukrainian Front was very different from Zhukov's. Unlike Zhukov, Koniev's three rifle, and two tank armies enjoyed no bridgehead on the western bank on the Neisse River. In addition, 35 kilometers beyond the Neisse was the Spree River. Koniev's success depended on rapid, yet complicated movement. His forces had to make a quick river assault under fire, followed with a rapid breakthrough of prepared German defenses on the west bank. Koniev's forces had to drive to the Spree River once the German positions were breeched and conduct another rapid assault crossing in order to prevent any retreating Germans from consolidating their defense along the far bank. Koniev opted for a 190 minute artillery barrage during the daylight hours of morning using 7,733 guns of all calibers. The first artillery strike would last one hour and strike German defensive positions directly along the Neisse, followed by a forty-five minute smoke screen barrage that would be immediately followed by the river assault. The third artillery barrage, lasting another forty-five minutes would target German positions between the Neisse and the Spree.[41] Koniev's artillery plans were detailed and he personally checked every one.[42] The assault plan was impressive and Stavka assigned 485 battalions of combat engineers to assist in the preparation and actual crossing of the Neisse. The plan was not as simple as Zhukov's. Once crossing points were established on the western bank then the engineers were tasked to start building pontoon bridges across the Neisse and establish ferry crossing points to allow the tanks of the 3rd and 4th Guards Tank Armies to move across.[43] The soldiers of the 1st Ukrainian Front knew that their orders included a possible assault on Berlin based on the Stavka directive. Koniev also knew that Stalin had suggested he might be able to group his tanks to launch an assault north if Zhukov's advance toward Berlin slowed. Koniev was not going to wait for the situation to present itself before he reacted with new orders to move north. He immediately planed for the 3rd Guards Tank Army to drive north toward Berlin with infantry support from the 3rd Guards Army immediately after crossing the Spree River.[44] In addition he organized his artillery assets into powerful regimental groups directly assigned to his mobile units. The mechanized and tank corps commanders had full control over the application of fire support in their area of operations.[45] His later success in executing a complex turn northwest was based primarily on his advanced planning. Unlike his rival to the north, Koniev did not underestimate his enemy and developed an operational plan that went well beyond the first twenty-four hours.

The Berlin Strategic Offensive Operation was an impressive undertaking. Between the three fronts they amassed 41,600 artillery pieces and mortars, 6,300 tanks and self-propelled guns, and 8,400 aircraft. Even the official Soviet history concedes that the amount of time allotted to prepare for an operation of this size was inadequate.[46] The planning for the assault on Berlin was rushed and incomplete. Zhukov and Koniev had less than two weeks to plan and prepare the entire operation. The pressure on them to begin the assault on Berlin was strong given the existing military-political situation with the Western Allies. As Eisenhower's forces began their drive across Germany it became apparent that the Germans were simply not resisting U.S. and British forces the way they were against the Soviets in the east.[47] On 11 April reconnaissance forces of the U.S. 2nd Armored Division were already on the eastern bank of the Elbe River. The U.S. 2nd Armored and U.S. 5th Armored raced across Germany closing the 320 kilometers from their start positions to the Elbe in just twelve and eleven days respectively—without any significant combat. The Western Allies were now a mere 56 kilometers from Berlin. This feat by U.S. forces confirmed Soviet fears and served to heighten tension among senior commanders. Even Soviet soldiers now began to view the upcoming operation with a two-fold purpose of defeating Hitler and preventing the Western Allies from stealing their rightful prize. Soviet preparations for the upcoming assault on Berlin were accelerated as the Western Allies advanced closer towards the Elbe River.

Soviet Armies had little time to prepare a coordinated offensive against Berlin. In most cases, individual armies only received their written orders on 12 April as in the case of the 3rd Shock Army.[48] The 3rd Shock Army was ordered to break through the German lines on the west bank of the Oder and drive westward to assault Berlin and capture the area of Spandau-Kladow on the west bank of the Havel while remaining in direct contact to the 47th Army on its right flank and the 5th Shock Army on the left flank. In order to achieve this operationally, the staff of the 3rd Shock Army decided to break through a 6 kilometer section of their bridgehead on the west bank of the Oder with an operational depth of 10 kilometers. Two rile corps, the 79th and 12th, were tasked to conduct the initial assault. A third rifle corps, the 7th, was planned to be held in reserve until the first two rifle corps reached the outskirts of Berlin. The 3rd Shock Army was given four days to prepare for this! Soviet intelligence placed the German forces opposite the Soviets at numbering 12,700 soldiers, equipped with 59 machine-guns, 80 mortars, 207 guns, and 40 tanks and self-propelled guns. It was believed that the majority of German forces were in the first line defensive positions directly opposite the Soviets. Against this potential German force the 3rd Shock Army arrayed 12,000 soldiers, 150 tanks and self-propelled guns, 450 guns and mortars. Soviet intelligence overestimated the number of

Germans soldiers and equipment that opposed them in their sector and placed the majority of the defenders in the first echelon defense. This showed a complete lack of understanding of their enemy's strength, capability and intent.

The 3rd Shock Army offers an excellent view into the steps that took place to prepare the Soviet troops for the assault on Berlin and highlights several key organizational problems. Stavka ordered the preparation of a new planning and training program for the front line troops in the middle of March that focused on "offensive operations and the securing of a passage over large rivers."[49] This training lasted through 6 April when the 3rd Shock Army was ordered to cross the Oder and deploy within the Küstrin bridgehead. Once they crossed over into their new area the focus of training turned on the breakthrough of fortified positions and combat in large urban areas. Two key problems stood out with the training. The first problem was that there was simply no way to instruct any Russian soldier in the tactics of urban warfare because there was no training environment that could even come close to replicating the immense scope of operational and tactical problems Berlin presented. Historians often cite Chuikov's memoir regarding Soviet preparations for the coming assault because Chuikov makes a point of stating that he provided his soldiers an urban training manual, perhaps based on his experiences in Stalingrad.[50] This manual could offer little to help Soviet troops as Stalingrad was not Berlin and there was really no way to prepare for the intensity or chaos of the coming battle. The second problem was that no pre-battle training or coordination between independent Soviet armor and infantry formations occurred. Each Soviet tank brigade contained their own sub-machine gun company, typically referred to as the classic Soviet 'Tank Riders.' Soviet doctrine called for independent action of their armor once the breakthrough was achieved so they contained their own integrated infantry company. This meant that as per doctrine, Soviet tank units were not required to train with independent infantry formations. The theory was that once a breakthrough occurred the armor would drive out ahead of the infantry, relying on the composite sub-machine companies to provide immediate support to the armor. In the coming battle Soviet tank regiments and brigades found themselves fighting side-by-side with infantry regiments and divisions without the ability to effectively coordinate operations due to a lack of training.

Throughout this period particular focus was placed on the training and rebuilding of the Soviet Officer Corps after they suffered heavy losses, especially in the lower ranks, during the recent operations.[51] Soviet commanders were particularly concerned at overcoming the morale issues they were facing among their soldiers. This was caused by three key factors: exposure to a higher standard of living encountered in Central Europe; mass rapes of German and non-German women; and overcoming a manpower crisis now acute after four continuous years of conflict.[52] The first two issues were environmental and could be controlled by the current deployment of forces in the bridgeheads. The third was more difficult. New replacements and their quick integration into existing units were critical to formulating strong soldierly bonds and cohesive fighting units. Many of the new recruits were ethnically diverse as they were drawn from the Central and Eastern districts of the Soviet Union. The Soviets began to mobilize Russians liberated from Germany territory and the western districts of the Ukraine, Byelorussia and Moldavia where strong anti-Russian feelings existed prior to the war. Many replacements never

Soviet ISU-152 crew hastily camouflages their assault gun during an administrative halt as new Russian reinforcements are driven to the front in preparation for the 16 April offensive. Soviet Army photo courtesy of the Cornelius Ryan Collection, Mahn Center, Alden Library, Ohio University, Athens, OH.

Nikita Khruschev and General Rybalko (the commander of the 3rd Guards Tank Army) behind, shown in an earlier phase of the war, in a village near Tarnopol, May 1944. Photo courtesy of RGAKFD, Moscow.

Two Soviet ISU-152s ford a stream. The ISU-152's short barrel, large shell caliber, and excellent frontal armor made it well suited for fighting in the streets of Berlin. Photo courtesy of the US National Archives.

received military or partisan training at all. One group of 3,460 replacements to the 3rd Shock Army never received military training.[53] The only way to bring these groups together as a functioning unit quickly was through focused attempt to reinforce both ideological training and instill military esprit de corps.[54] According to the official Soviet history, "It was necessary, therefore, to help troops to adjust themselves properly to the new situation, to enable them to distinguish the external glitter of capitalism and the inner rottenness of the Capitalist way of life, and once more to kindle in them such a burning pride of the whole of our great fatherland."[55] Propaganda lectures were provided nightly on topics such as "The Victory of the Red Army, the Victory of Soviet Society," "The Communist Party: the organizer of the victory of the Soviet people in the Fatherland War."[56] Speeches were issued tying political-military themes together. For example "Party Political work in securing of the cooperation between the crews of self-propelled guns with the infantry" or "Work of Party bureau of the regiment on order to fulfill the directions and orders of the military."[57] The increase in morale, however, could not make up for the overall shortages in manpower and lack of military training of new recruits.

The Soviet Army was undergoing a manpower crisis in 1945 that directly impacted military operations. During the fighting at Kursk in July 1943, a reinforced Soviet Rifle Division typically contained 8,000 soldiers. By April 1945, Guards Rifle Divisions were lucky to have 6,000 soldiers on hand if they were engaged in a major assault operation.[58] The rule was that by 1945 a regular Soviet division was now down to an average of 3,600 men or less with few exceptions.[59] A rifle company by Soviet regulations attacks in a line on frontage of up to 350 meters. By 1944 entire Rifle divisions attacked on a frontage of 2,500 meters while individual companies attacked on frontages less than 100 meters. By late 1944 many of the Soviet Rifle Companies were no bigger than the rifle platoon of 1942 when at full strength.[60] The lack of soldiers figured greatly into the final offensive as the Soviets tried to increase firepower to make up for a lack of infantry. In fact it was emphasized by the Soviet High Command that if a Rifle Division's manpower had to be reduced, that the reduction was to be taken from the division's rifle regiment first before reducing manpower from any of the supporting weapons battalions or companies. Even if manpower was drawn from the supporting weapons sections, it took the form of reducing a crew member from an artillery gun instead of removing the whole weapon system.[61] For example, the 126th Rifle Division's 2nd Battalion, 550th Rifle Regiment organized into two assault groups for the 16 April attack. Each assault group was based on one understrength Rifle Company with only two rifle platoons. The two platoons of the company were in turn supported by 1x heavy weapons company, 2x platoons of the 175th Sapper Battalion, 2x platoons of the 266th Independent Flamethrower Company, 2x 280mm siege guns and 2x ISU–122 self-propelled guns.[62] Significant firepower indeed! Their German counterparts could boast of no such support.

There was also little difference between Guard and Regular formations by war's end. During 1942 and early 1943, it was Soviet Guards units that were entrusted with even basic military tasks like moving from place to place without fouling up the rear areas with traffic jams or getting lost.[63] Well into 1943, the creation of Guards Regiments falls off dramatically, the reason being that 900,000 new officers, NCO and enlisted personnel left various training camps and schools to fill out the depleted ranks of the Soviet armed forces bringing a certain level of consistency across all formations. By 1944, the combat performance between Guards and Regular army units was so small that Soviet Regular army units began to receive the heavy weapons before Guards units.[64]

A review of several key Soviet units follows with a brief discussion of their equipment.

150th RIFLE DIVISION of the 3rd SHOCK ARMY

This division was reformed on 8 September 1943 for the second time in the war near Staraya Russia. It joined the 3rd Shock Army in January 1944 where it was assigned to the 70th Rifle Corps. This division consisted of the 469th, 674th, and 756th Regiments with an initial total strength of approximately 5,000 soldiers. By April 1945 this division's ranks were probably down to no more than 4,000 total soldiers. Select assault rifle divisions in the Berlin Strategic Offensive Operation, however, were given additional direct support to make up for the manpower reduction. In the case of the 150th Rifle Division, they were allotted the following units: 868th Light Artillery Regiment (24x 76mm canon), 1956th Antitank Regiment (24x 76mm canon), 23rd Guards Light Artillery Brigade (72x 76mm canon), 1203rd Self Propelled Regiment (21x SU–76 self-propelled guns), and the 351st Guards Heavy Self-propelled Regiment (21x ISU–152 self-propelled guns).

Under the command of Major-General V.M. Shatilov, this division led the vanguard of the assault across the Oderbruch and into Berlin. It was one of the first Soviet units to cross the Moltke Bridge over the Spree into the Government Quarter, storming the Ministry of Interior and raising Red Banner No. 5 on the Reichstag. A standard rifle company contained one sub-machine gun platoon and two rifle platoons. The sub-machine gun platoon was armed with the PPSH–41 and 43 models firing a 7.62mm round bullet from a 35-round magazine. These were durable, reliable, and lethal at close range. The standard infantry rifle was the Mosin-Nagant, a bolt-action, 7.62mm rifle that had a 5-round magazine. This weapon was prized by Soviet snipers for its accuracy. Soviet standard divisional artillery and anti-tank support was the dual use 76.2mm ZIS–3. It was one of the most effective artillery pieces of the war. When firing the Soviet standard armor piercing projectile this weapon could easily penetrate the side armor of all German medium tanks like the Panther at ranges of 1500 meters.[65] A series of self-propelled gun platforms were produced by the Soviets that included the SU–76, SU–85, SU–100, ISU–122, and ISU–152. These were designed to provide direct support for the infantry assault during breakthrough operations and act in the role as tank killer when organized into regiments as part of a mechanized or tank corps. The two main weapon systems found during the battle of Berlin were the SU–76 and the ISU–152. The SU–76 series were based on a lengthened T–70 chassis. The SU–76 was not well armored and mounted the standard 76mm ZIS–3 cannon. It was effective in the infantry support role but was easily outgunned by almost all German anti-tank weapons. The ISU–122 and 152 were heavy self-propelled howitzers/tank killers. Their heavy armor provided good survivability at medium and long range. Their armament was either the A–19S or the 152mm howitzer. The long barrel of the ISU–122 made this self-propelled gun very hard to maneuver during urban combat and less effective than the ISU–152.

266th RIFLE DIVISION of the 5th SHOCK ARMY

Formed on 26 August 1942, this was the second 266th Rifle Division formed during the war. The first 266th Rifle Division was caught and destroyed in a German pocket during the 1942 battle for Kharkov that opened the drive to Stalingrad. The second 266th Rifle Divi-

Soviet T-34/85s cross one of the many waterways that surround Berlin. Note the white triangle on the turret. This suggests that this photo was taken well after the start of Soviet operations. Soviet Army photo courtesy of the Cornelius Ryan Collection, Mahn Center, Alden Library, Ohio University, Athens, OH.

A Soviet heavy JS-2 rolls over the Oder River across one of the many bridges emplaced by Soviet engineers. Soviet Army photo courtesy of the Cornelius Ryan Collection, Mahn Center, Alden Library, Ohio University, Athens, OH.

One of the remaining search lights emplaced in fixed or mobile positions that swept the German frontline with light after Zhukov's initial Soviet bombardment. The search light proved to be a significant hindrance to advancing Soviet riflemen as the powerful anti-aircraft lights were reflected back into the eyes of advancing Russians due to the enormous clouds of dust and smoke that their artillery kicked into the air.
Author's collection.

sion consisted of the 1006th, 1008th, and 1010th Rifle Regiments boasting over 10,000 officers and soldiers in its' ranks. This unit participated in the December 1942, 'Little Saturn' offensive and was given honors for its performance in battle. By late October 1944 the division was preparing for the upcoming Vistula-Oder offensive in Poland and was assigned to the 26th Guards Rifle Corps of the 5th Shock Army. During the assault on Berlin the division initially fought in the heavy factory districts along Frankfurter Allee. They later engaged a battalion of *SS-Anhalt Regiment* for control of the Schlesischer S-Bahn station, followed by a grueling room-to-room battle for the Polizeipräsidium (Berlin's main Police HQ) in Alexanderplatz. Finally, the division ended the war after taking the Armory and State Library on Unter-den-Linden.

Under the command of Major-General Fomichenko, the unit had an approximate strength of 3,000–4,000 men and was assigned additional assets to include the 728th Signals Battalion, and 360th Self-Propelled Artillery Battalion. By the time of the Vistula-Oder offensive this division contained 80 artillery pieces and howitzers of all types, 72x 82mm mortars, 12x SU–76s, 141 anti-tank rifles, and 374 machine guns. During the Vistula-Oder operation in January 1945, the division placed 30 men into 18x U.S. 2.5 ton trucks and motorized most of the heavy weapons of the 1006th Regiment using Lend-Lease vehicles. This improvised force supported Soviet tank units pursuing German units across Poland. By this time most of the division's artillery was also motorized by U.S. M3A1 halftracks. Lend-Lease played a significant role in the motorization of the Soviet Army. The Soviets received 1,000 US M17 Gun Carriers, as well as 3,112 U.S. M3A1 halftracks during the war.[66]

This unit was also equipped with a variety of small arms weapons utilized in the fighting for Berlin. The standard soviet anti-tank rifle was the PTRS–41. It reportedly penetrated 40mm of armor at 100 meters using its standard 14.5mm armor piercing round. The PTRS–41 was employed against a variety of targets including fixed German machine-gun positions, mortars, and even bunkers or building walls. The Soviet employed several crew served machine guns, the most widely used being the gas operated SG–43 Goryunov medium machine gun that fired the standard 7.62mm ammunition between 500–700 rounds per minute.

8th GUARDS MECHANIZED CORPS of the 1st GUARDS TANK ARMY

This unit was formed on 23 October 1943 and would find itself in constant combat for almost a year before being withdrawn by Stavka, and placed into reserves for refitting in September 1944. In preparation for the assault on Berlin, the Corps, under the command of Major General I.F. Drygemov, consisted of the 19th, 20th, and 21st Guards Mechanized Brigades each with 41x T–34/85 tanks and three Rifle Battalions; 1st Guards Heavy Tank brigade with 65x T–34/85s; the 48th Guards Heavy Tank Regiment with 21 x Joseph Stalin II tanks; the 353rd and 400th Guards Self-Propelled Regiment with ISU–152 and ISU–100 self-propelled guns; 265th Mortar Regiment with 36 x 120mm mortars; 358th Guards Antiaircraft Regiment with 24x 37mm guns; 405th Guards Mortar battalion with 8x BM–13 rocket launchers; 8th Guards Motorcycle Battalion with a tank company; and finally the 27th Sapper Battalion. This corps, like the rest of the 1st Guards Tank Army, would suffer heavy losses in armor during the breakout from the Oder bridgehead. The unit's forces were subordinated to the 8th Guards Army and operated in support of them during the assault on Berlin. They participated in the fighting for Tempelhof and the Landwehr canal crossings.

The three standard tanks found in the Soviet tank corps were the T–34/76, T–34/85 and the Joseph Stalin or JS–2 heavy tank. The T–34/76's sloped armor was a revolutionary feature when it entered service. By 1945 the T–34/76 was outclassed in terms or armor and armament, with the T–34/85 providing only better lethality with its 85mm canon. The T–34 was plagued with mechanical problems, contrary to much of the post-war myth regarding its design superiority. In a recent study of the T–34, *T–34: Mythical Weapon*, it appears that not only was the wartime model of the T–34/85 plagued with mechanical problems, but the S–53 85mm gun under-performed against both the Western Allied and German 76mm main gun. The T–34's turret drive was electric, compared to the German's hydraulic version, and in comparing the ability of the turret traverse the T–34/85 could be beaten by the German Panther by as much as 2 seconds. In fact the authors of the study, Robert Michulec and Miroslaw Zientarzewski, conclude that when one compares the employment of the T–34/85 against the T–34/76 the T–34/85 was not an improvement over the earlier model. The T–34/85 offered less survivability to Soviet tankers on the battlefield in 1944–45 than the T–34/76 did in 1941.[67] Soviet tank manufacturers failed to modernize the T–34/76 sufficiently enough in the 85 variant to be a competitor against the German Panther, let alone the heavier German models encountered on the battlefield at the end of the war.

By mid 1944 the Soviets introduced the JS–2 heavy tank. This tank was equipped with a 122mm cannon, and heavier and improved slopped armor over its counterparts. Its welded design could boast 120mm armor along the front of the hull. The JS–2 was a formidable opponent against all German tanks. It had drawbacks, however, such as limited ammunition stowage, slow rate of fire due to the separate storage of projectiles and propellant, and a slow turret traverse. These tanks were organized into Heavy Breakthrough Tank Regiments as part of the tank corps, but also assigned to Mechanized Corps. Soviet Mechanized Corps were powerful formations but limited within the Soviet Army. They were truly mechanized, meaning that in Soviet terms their composite infantry battalions were motorized and they had a substantial armored force assigned. To field a full strength Mechanized Corps the Soviets had to be able to identify skilled manpower and that was not readily available. In addition, there were significant equipment shortcomings. For example wireless radios were in short supply and there might not be enough to make the formation function. In one example the 5th Guards Tank Army could only boast at having 254 radios. This was less than the amount of radios found in an entire U.S. Division.[68] Transportation was also a key shortage for the Mechanized Corps. Lend Lease supplied about 100% of the armored personnel carriers (APCs) and 50%–75% mobile AAMG. Without Western Allied Lend Lease the late war Soviet Army could not have reached the levels of mechanization it enjoyed—a fact sometimes ignored by historians.

The Soviet Corps was the basic operating formation. Corps formations were employed in an independent fashion with the intent that they managed their operational goals without coordination from neighboring units. This may have worked well during combat operations in the open, but in an urban environment the lack of coordination and the capability of mutual support cost the Soviets dearly. It should be understood that Soviet formations can be compared to the next lowest combat formation in the *Wehrmacht* for organizational purposes. What this means is that in theory a Soviet corps, was equivalent to a German division, a Soviet division was equivalent to a German regiment, and a Soviet brigade was equivalent to a German battalion. An important distinction needs to be made between nomenclature and employment. A Soviet Mechanized Corps might be compared to a German Panzergrenadier Division. In the

Wehrmacht a Panzergrenadier Division was a motorized infantry division. In the Soviet Army a Mechanized Corps was a motorized infantry division with a significant combined arms force of armor and artillery.

Training was accelerated all across the 1st Byelorussian Front. Tanks, artillery, self-propelled guns, material and soldiers began to move at a hectic pace across and behind the Oder. Many Soviets were trained on the *Panzerfaust* as large stocks were captured in Pomerania by the 1st and 2nd Byelorussian Fronts.[69] The Soviet army encountered the German *Panzerfaust* in the past, but never in the numbers experienced in Prussia and Pomerania. The weapon made a lasting impression on Soviet commanders as their official history relates:

> Thus, from the first days of the preparation for the Berlin operation in formations of the army there were organized instructional courses on the *Panzerfaust* and also instruction in the methods of fighting the German *Panzerfaust*. In each section of every rifle company there were prepared a tank-busting unit. Their assignment was to instruct the rank and file in the use of this captured German weapon. Five-day courses were run by the specialists in the anti-tank weapons who were assigned to the units. Then the soldiers in the sections in their turn became instructors.[70]

The *Panzerfaust* proved deadly to Soviet tanks. The *Panzerfaust* accounted for 24% of all Soviet armor loses.[71] Soviet infantry also became accustomed to its value as an effective weapon they could employ against German Panzers. This weapon was a key component to their successful defense against the German relief attempt at Küstrin March destroying both German Panzers and SPWs.[72] Soviet tankers came to fear the weapon and attempted to devise effective countermeasures.

The Soviet tanker was considered an extremely tough opponent. German soldiers noted how the crew often stayed with their tank even after it was knocked out. One early report by the *33rd Panzer Regiment* of the *9th Panzer Division* in July 1942 stated many immobile Soviet tanks that were hit five or six times had to be destroyed by anti-tank teams on foot because Soviet tank crews continued to fire their tank's main guns. Soviet tanker morale was described by the Germans as being "fantastic."[73] The key factor that allowed the Soviets to sustain their armored force even after severe losses was the introduction of the maintenance company. The Soviets became masters of managing to repair their armor that either broke down or where hit by tank or anti-tank fire. Stavka placed all tank maintenance under one command in November of 1944. This reorganization increased armor repairs by 50% as revealed by their employment during the Vistula-Oder operation. During the first six days of fighting in January the 8th Guards Army had 159 tanks and self-propelled guns disabled by enemy fire and for other reasons, with 85 quickly repaired and sent back into front line service. Statistics reveal that during the whole Vistula-Oder operation the 1st Byelorussian Front conducted 3,786 tank and self-propelled gun repairs while the 1st Ukrainian Front conducted 4,267 repairs. Many Soviet vehicles were being disabled by enemy fire and repaired more than once.[74] The ability of the Soviets to quickly repair vehicles was a key component to their success on the battlefield at the end of the war.

It was difficult for the Soviets to conceal their preparations for their assault, as the Oderbruch was exposed to viewing from the Seelow Heights. The trees were not in bloom so foliage cover was lacking. Digging in proved difficult as well, due to the spring flooding that soaked the ground with water. Most movement was done at night but the Germans mounted searchlights on the heights that routinely swept across the Oderbruch at intervals followed by flares.[75] On 14 April, reconnaissance in force operations started pushing on the forward German positions on the extreme flanks of the *9.Armee* in an attempt to confuse the Germans as to the real direction of the main assault. The reconnaissance attacks by the Soviets only served to alert the Germans of an impending attack. Soviet offensive preparations were completed by mid-day on 15 April. For the first time in months the Soviets halted all artillery and mortar fire of German positions that created an uneasy quiet that hung in the air. In the assembly area of the 1st Guards Tank Army, Colonel General of Tank Troops, M. Y. Katukov watched his tank formations move into their final positions. Tank after tank had slogans that read 'Moscow to Berlin' painted on their sides in large white Cyrillic letters. One T–34/85's crew seemed particularly enthusiastic. The side of their tank was marked with the slogan 'Bridgehead zero—Müncheberg—Berlin and the Reichstag!' Witnessing this tank roll by, General Katukov, perhaps with a sense of humor, leaned over to his staff and said "that's not a combat vehicle, that's more like a moving advertisement platform."[76]

The Soviet attempt to hide both their final preparations and date for their offensive failed. Zhukov met with Chuikov, and Katukov in Chuikov's underground HQ nestled atop the Reitwein Spur overlooking the battlefield. The time was approximately 0100 Moscow Time 16 April. Zhukov asked Chuikov if his battalions were all ready for the assault. Chuikov replied that his battalions were ready and that they had carried out Zhukov's orders to conduct reconnaissance for the last two days. Despite the reconnaissance, Chuikov confirmed to Zhukov that he really didn't have significant combat intelligence about the Germans other than that they retired into their defensive line. In addition, he informed him that the Germans knew the Soviets offensive was about to begin. Zhukov, now with a tinge of concern asked Chuikov about the details of their operational planning (this seems to be a very poor time to bring up the fact that the Front Commander and the Senior Commander leading the vanguard assault against the Seelow Heights and Berlin still had not discussed operation details). Chuikov responded by stating that "I suppose we will merely repeat the tactics of our break-through on the Vistula." However, "the direction of the main blow is perfectly plain to the enemy … They are quite aware of the time period this blow will fall."[77] Chuikov cited an interrogation report obtained from a German soldier who stated that the Germans knew the current reconnaissance wasn't the main offensive and that the main Russian offensive would be launched in two days with the expectation of reaching Berlin a week and ending the war in two.[78] Chuikov then apparently dismissed the concerns, and perhaps feeding Zhukov what he expected he wanted to hear, exclaimed that even though the Germans might know the time and place, " … they won't expect that we will once again employ our old tactics; and this fact will come as a complete surprise to them." "Just imagine for yourself: a massive artillery preparation, the blows mounted by our aviators – and then suddenly quite expectedly the search lights are switched on. That is a blow with light if that is what I could call it!"[79] If this conversation between Zhukov and Chuikov occurred as witnessed by Major General N. K. Popiel, the Operations Officer for the 1st Guards Tank Army, then one can already see the potential for disaster in the Soviet offensive about to begin. Poor operational planning, lack of coordination between tank and infantry units, and a belief that the Germans simply would not withstand the coming Soviet assault conspired to adversely impact Zhukov's final offensive of the war. The Berlin Strategic Offensive Operation was now ready to commence.

Notes to Chapter 4

1. RG 226/441 NO 880 "German Evaluation of Allied Military Affairs Feb 1945".
2. Chuikov interview. (RC: 71/7)
3. Le Tissier, *Zhukov on the Oder*, pp. 13–14.
4. J. Erickson, *The Road to Berlin*, p. 539.
5. Le Tissier, *Zhukov on the Oder*, p. 39.
6. C. Duffy, *Red Storm on Reich*, pp. 122–3.
7. See Zhukov's comments in his article "Taking Berlin," Military Historical Journal #6, 1965 (RC: 73/11). Zhukov comments that the potential for attacks from Pomerania were a primary deterrent to advance any further toward Berlin, and that Himmler's offensive forced Stavka to now commit the 2nd Byelorussian Front to include the 1st and 2nd Guard Tanks Armies in the immediate reduction of Prussia and Pomerania.
8. Erickson, p. 540.
9. I. Koniev, Marshal of the Soviet Union, "Forty Five" in *Noviy Mir*, #5 1965 Voroshilov, Molotov, Voroshilov, Malenkov, Kagonovich were purged by Kruschev. Beria was shot by post-Stalin leaders, and Voznesenskiy was shot by Kruschev. A testament to the violent internal politics of communist Russia. (RC: 72/3).
10. Ibid, Erickosn, p. 533.
11. Erickson, p. 533.
12. "Red Army Order of Battle for 15 April, 1945," (CR: 71/9).
13. Ibid.
14. Ibid.
15. Ibid.
16. Zhukov, p. pxxvi.
17. Ibid, p. pxviii-xx.
18. D. Glantz, *Zhukov's Greatest Defeat: The Red Army's Epic Disaster in Operation Mars, 1942*, p. 303.
19. Ibid, pp. 303–4.
20. D. Glantz, *Red Storm Over the Balkans: The Failed Soviet Invasion of Romania, Spring 1944*, p. 28.
21. Platonov, p. 4.
22. Chuikov, p. 140.
23. Le Tissier, *Zhukov on the Oder*, p. 137.
24. G. V. Ivanov interview. (RC: 72/2).
25. Le Tissier, *Zukov on the Oder*, p. 138.
26. Zhukov, "Taking Berlin," (RC: 74/11).
27. W. Tieke, *Das Ende Zwischen Oder und Elbe: Der Kampf um Berlin 1945*, p. 355. The Soviets assigned numbers to their targets in Berlin: 105 Reichstag; 108 Foreign Ministry Building; and 106 Reich Chancellery, for example.
28. Heinrici interview, and Jansen interview. The Soviet bridges were attacked by a new suicide squadron formed by *Luftwaffe* volunteers that used planes loaded with explosives to be flown into the bridges by their attached FW-190 pilots.
29. Tieke, *Tragedy of the Faithful: A History of the III. (germanisches) SS-Panzer Korps*, pp. 416–18.
30. N. N. Popiel interview. (RC: 74/12) and V. Chuikov, *The Fall of Berlin*, p. 29.
31. Army Group Weichsel War Diary, Apr 20-29, p. 4 (RC: 64/3).
32. T311: 169/7221626-7. "Bezug: Diess. Befehl R 30/44 G. Kdos vom 6.2.44. - Anzeichen haeufen sich, das feind macht, um eigene truppe zu taeuschen. Truppe ist zu erhoehter wachsamkeit und staerkstem misztrauen gegen jeden unbekannten soldaten, einerlei ob mann, offizer, oder general, anzuhalten. Bei nicht sofortiger." [from *OKH* to *AGV*].
33. Zhukov, "Taking Berlin," 35–6, and Le Tissier, *Zhukov on the Oder*, pp. 138–9.
34. Le Tissier, *Zhukov on the Oder*, p. 139.
35. Erickson, p. 538, 556.
36. Ibid, p. 537.
37. Zhukov, "Taking Berlin," and Erickson, p. 535.
38. Ibid, p. 557.
39. Le Tissier, *Zhukov on the Oder*, p. 145.
40. Erickson, p. 559.
41. Ibid, p. 538 and 556.
42. Koniev's unpublished memoir, p. 9 (RC: 72/3).
43. Ibid, p. 71.
44. Ibid, p. 66.
45. Erickson, p. 556.
46. Platonov, p. 5.
47. Ibid, pp. 3-4.
48. Yedenskii, *The Berlin Operations of the Third Shock Army*, pp. 37–8, (RC: 74/10) and Erickson, p. 562.
49. Yedenskii, p. 32.
50. Le Tissier, *Zhukov on the Oder*, p. 138.
51. Yedenskii, pp. 32–3.
52. Le Tissier, *Zhukov on the Oder*, p. 148.
53. Yedenskii, p. 36.
54. Le Tissier, *Zhukov on the Oder*, p. 147.
55. Yedenskii, p. 36.
56. Ibid, p. 33.
57. Ibid, p. 35.
58. C. Sharp, *Soviet Order of Battle World War II: Volume X 'Red Swarm': Soviet Rifle Divisions Formed From 1942-1945*, p. 143.
59. Ibid, p. 142-143.
60. C. Sharp, *Soviet Order of Battle World War II: Volume IV 'Red Guards': Soviet Guards Rifle and Airborne Units 1941-1945*, p. 105.
61. Sharp, *'Red Swarm'*, p. 142.
62. C. Sharp, *Soviet Infantry Tactics in World War II: Red Army Infantry Tactics from Squad to Rifle Company from the Combat Regulations of November 1942*, p. 121.
63. C. Sharp, *Soviet Order of Battle World War II: Volume IV 'Red Guards': Soviet Guards Rifle and Airborne Units 1941–45*, p. 34.
64. Ibid, p. 35.
65. "Fire and Movement," RAC Tank Museum, pp. 22–5.
66. C. Sharp, *Soviet Order of Battle World War II: Volume III 'Red Storm': Soviet Mechanized Corps and Guards Armored Units 1942–1945*, p. 10.
67. R. Michulec, M. Zientarzewski, *T-34: Mythical Weapon*, pp. 245–59.
68. Sharp, *Red Storm*, p. 6.
69. Yedenskii, p. 35.
70. Ibid, p. 36, and Platonov, p. 37.
71. C. Duffy, *Red Storm on the Reich*, p. 349.
72. Chuikov, p. 132.
73. C. Sharp, *Soviet Armor Tactics in World War II: Red Army Armor Tactics from Individual Vehicle to Company According to the Combat Regulations of February 1944*, p. 90.
74. Duffy, p. 349.
75. Chuikov, p. 144.
76. Popiel interview, p. 2.
77. Ibid, p. 3.
78. Ibid.
79. Ibid.

PART II: BATTLE

5

BATTLE FOR THE SEELOW HEIGHTS

16 APRIL
MONDAY

A tense quiet hung over the Oderbruch on the night of 15–16 April. The Soviet guns stopped zeroing, infantry patrols were non-existent, and the rumble of tank tracks were no longer heard in the Soviet bridgeheads. Around 2000 on 15 April Heinrici gave the order for the *9.Armee* to pull back out of the front line. He knew that the Soviet attack was imminent in the early morning hours. The code word filtered down throughout the front line formations as thousands of German soldiers were on the move or settling into their secondary positions along the HKL as ordered. Meanwhile hundreds of thousands of Soviet soldiers braced for the order to launch the final offensive against Berlin and end the war. An hour before the Soviet assault began Soviet officers passed out Zhukov's proclamation:

> To our comrades:
> The last nest of wolves is in front of us. We shall today cross the Oder and we must reach our objective. Our aim is to plant the [Soviet] flag on the Reichstag. You have already fought bravely and you have the courage to fulfill the order of comrade Stalin. For Fatherland and Stalin, ahead!
> Signed Zhukov and the war council[1]

Thirty minutes before the opening barrage Soviet commanders opened their sealed envelopes marked "Open at 0330 16 April."[2] The message inside read only "Signal will be given at 0400 to attack."

In the Oderbruch, a squad of *Fj.Rgt.27.* from the *9.Fallschirmjäger* led by Gerd Wagner left their forward positions and began moving through the dark to their secondary line near Gusow. They received Heinrici's order to pull back later than most units. Suddenly the eerily dark and quiet landscape around Wagner's section was shattered in a crescendo of brilliant flashes and ear splitting explosions. Wagner recalled that in seconds all "ten comrades of my section had fallen, and I found myself in a still smoking shell hole, wounded, a fact that I did not notice until I reached the second line. As far as the eye could see were burning farms, villages, smoke and clouds of fumes. An inferno."[3] The Soviet assault was now underway.

The ensuing artillery barrage blew out eardrums and damaged sinus cavities of both German and Soviet soldiers. It was the strongest concentration of artillery and rocket fire seen anywhere on mainland Europe during the war. A Soviet war correspondent on the east side of the Oder recalled how the banks of the river were packed with masses of Soviet infantry. He could "feel the soldiers almost trembling with excitement." Katushya Rockets opened first with hundreds of rocket salvos. Then the 'Gods of War' – the artillery opened up. As soon as the artillery barrage began "everyone started firing even though they could not see anything, and cheering their heads off as though they were actually, at that moment, fighting hand-to-hand."[4] Svishchev Nikolai Alexsandrovich, Senior Sgt. Commander of one of the artillery guns that participated in the barrage recalled that "it was one of the most powerful [barrages] from large to small; for those who were not accustomed to the noise the blood ran from their ears, for that reason we kept our mouths open while we were firing. After the artillery preparation, powerful searchlights were turned on."[5] In one sector of the front a Soviet soldier recalled the amazing view that the Soviet crossing of the Oder River presented.

> I saw soldiers swimming across the 600 meters over the flooded Oder, on empty gasoline tanks, on blocks of wood, on tree trunks, on empty boxes—I even saw my friend the doctor, who was supposed to stay in the hospital, behind the line dragging a very small rowing boat down [to] the river. His name was Nicolaieff, he was a huge man. He got into the boat which was a tiny thing and rowed like hell across the river. There were very few rubber boats. The river was suddenly alive with bobbing heads, boats of all sorts—it looked like a huge army of ants crossing the flooded water. There was no holding anybody [back]—everybody wanted to get over.[6]

All along the *9.Armee* front the Soviet barrage pummeled the empty forward German defensive positions.

Karl-Hermann Tams of the *20.Pz.Gren.Div.* witnessed the opening Soviet barrage and fifty years later recalled that precise moment with vivid clarity:

> The whole Oder valley bed shook. In the bridgehead it was as light as day. The hurricane of fire reached out to the Seelow Heights. It seemed as if the earth was reaching up into the sky like a dense wall. Everything around us started dancing, rattling about. Whatever was not securely fastened down fell from the shelves and cupboards. Pictures fell off the walls and crashed to the floor. Glass splinters jumped out of window frames. We were soon covered in sand, dirt and glass splinters. None of us had experienced anything like it before, and would not have believed it possible. There was no escape. The greatest concentration of artillery fire in history was directed immediately in front of us. We had the impression that every square yard of earth would be ploughed up. After two or three hours the fire was

suddenly lifted. Cautiously we risked a peep over the Heights down into the Oderbruch, and what we saw made the blood run cold. As far as we could see in the grey light of dawn came a single wave of heavy tanks. The air was filled with the noise of tank engines and the rattling of tank tracks. As the first row came closer we saw behind them another, and then hordes of running infantry.[7]

Kurt Keller, a member of *Müncheberg*, recalled how after the bombardment the Soviets turned on searchlights and drove toward the German lines. Members of his unit used the searchlights as aiming points and after shooting several out began a retreat to a rally point at the company command post.[8] Despite the enormity of the Soviet artillery barrage, Heinrici's ploy was overwhelmingly successful. The majority of German combat formations were now in a position to effectively engage the unprepared Soviet formations advancing in the early morning hours. Zhukov's entire operational plan was now rendered null and void.

Colonel General Vassili Chuikov, commander of the 8th Guards Army and veteran of the defense of Stalingrad, watched the battle unfold from his headquarters that occupied the highest elevation in the Oderbruch. Writing after the war, he stated how Zhukov's plan was executed strictly and when the searchlights were turned on after the initial artillery barrage they came up against smoke, dirt, and debris floating in the air. The lights could not penetrate more than 150–200 meters due to the dense smoke. This had the effect of reflecting the light back onto the Soviet soldiers, blinding them, and eliminating their night vision. The lights also marked the main Soviet avenues of approach and focused German fire on them.[9] Chuikov's forces continued to move forward making slow but steady progress for the first several kilometers. As his forces neared the Seelow Heights the infantry separated from the accompanying armor as the Soviet tanks had to contend with negotiating numerous water obstacles. Without direct fire support the Soviet infantry quickly became bogged down by German defensive fire.

As daylight came, the Soviets were able to identify the German secondary positions. Soviet artillery had to switch targets, taking up valuable time. Soviet aircraft were retargeted to attack the new German positions but in the confusion of battle and lack of direct communication with the ground forces they attacked Soviet force concentrations by mistake. Along the main avenue of approach Chuikov's forces were confronted by fierce resistance at the Hauptgraben Canal.[10] The canal was defended by elements of the *Pz.Gren.Rgt.76* and *Pz.Gren.Rgt.90* of the *20.Pz.Gren.Div.* as well as the Panthers and Tiger Is of *Müncheberg*. Captain Horst Zoebel, who commanded the *Müncheberg* armor, claimed the destruction of 50 Soviet tanks this first day before pulling back over the Seelow Heights.[11] By mid-morning it was obvious that the Soviet objective of taking the Heights along Reichsbahn 1 on the first day was now in crisis and not making the expected progress against the resistance of the *LVI Pz. Korps*.

Zhukov was co-located with Chuikov during the opening phase of the battle and was not happy with the reports he was receiving. Chuikov informed Zhukov that his forward units were encountering "heavy enemy resistance on the Seelow Heights. Heavy [German] artillery fire. [Soviet] infantry deprived of support tanks: part of these, that is part of the tanks have been burned out [destroyed], some are stuck in bogs and in the irrigation canals round about the flooded areas." Zhukov reportedly replied that "you mean the attack is pinned down? Is that what you want to say?" Chuikov's response was well measured given the weight of the political ramifications Zhukov placed on his subordinate's next words. "Comrade Marshal, whether it's pinned down or whether it's not pinned down we will continue the offensive operations!" A second attack on the Seelow Heights was quickly ordered for early afternoon.[12]

The German defense along the Seelow Heights continued in its ferocity during the late morning and early afternoon. The 8.8cm anti-aircraft guns positioned along the crest of the Heights knocked out tank, after Soviet tank, while firing over open sights. Soviet infantry riding on the armor were swept off with severe losses. Panzergrenadiers defending along the Hauptgraben Canal and the base of the Heights used *Panzerfausts* to knock out the few Soviet tanks that managed to reach that far. In preparation for the next attack the Germans in the secondary line now withdrew and occupied their positions along the crest of the Heights. This was executed without Soviet knowledge.[13] Chuikov hit previously identified German secondary positions with a new artillery barrage lasting thirty minutes before ordering his soldiers forward. Like the opening Soviet barrage, the artillery strike fell on empty enemy positions. When the second Soviet assault began it was quickly repulsed by the entrenched and relatively intact German forces.

There is no doubt that by mid-afternoon the overall Soviet offensive was halted and suffering unexpected losses. There is no known record of the phone calls that took place between Stalin and Zhukov during the day but one can assume that these were not pleasant conversations for Zhukov. Zhukov came under extreme pressure to take the Seelow Heights and continue the offensive toward Berlin. Zhukov now made the first of several poor operational decisions. In the face of adversity he elected to throw more firepower at the German positions. He overrode his own operational plan and directed the immediate introduction of the 1st and 2nd Guards Tank Armies into the assault without consulting either commander. At 1400 hours, without any notification to forward units or their commanders, the 1st and 2nd Guards Tank Armies advanced into a confused and difficult situation.[14]

Zhukov's decision demonstrated a complete lack of military judgment that fits perfectly well with his authoritarian and brutal leadership style. The massed tanks clogged the remaining maneuver space on the few available roads and presented dense targets for waiting German guns. His decision illustrates a complete lack of understanding regarding the terrain and operational realities that confronted his forces along the Oderbruch. Zhukov's order fits a pattern of throwing bodies at an operational problem without any pause for losses. He offered no innovative or creative solution to the tough tactical situation that his soldiers faced.

The 5th Shock Army, operating on Chuikov's right flank, also ran into unexpected resistance from the northern wing of the *LVI Pz. Korps*. In this area the *9.Fallschirmjäger* and *Pz.Gren.Rgt.2* of *Müncheberg* were located in the defense. The forward elements of *Fj.Rgt.25*, *Fj.Rgt.26*, and the Hetzers of the *Fj.PzJg.Abt.* ambushed and destroyed the leading Soviet formations. Once the Russians appeared to become passive in the wake of the stiff resistance, the aggressive Fallschirmjägers launched repeated counterattacks during the day effectively holding back the forward divisions of the Soviet 26th Guard and 32nd Rifle Corps.[15] The counterattacks, however, exposed the forward German units to heavy Soviet artillery fire and aerial bombardment causing considerable, if not unnecessary, casualties among the Germans. The Soviets regrouped and then launched their next attack between 1500 and 1800 in the afternoon. The renewed attack finally breached the Fallschirmjäger's secondary positions. By the end of the first day the *Fj.Rgt.25* was shattered after bearing the brunt of the Soviet assault. The regiment's survivors that included Skorzeny's veterans and the special forces of the *Brandenburgers* now formed small combat groups and started to retreat northwest on their own. *Fj.Rgt.26* lost an entire battalion, along with a battalion of *Fj.Rgt.27* that was deployed forward in the main defensive line. Both regiments remained relatively intact but began to commingle in the confusion of battle.

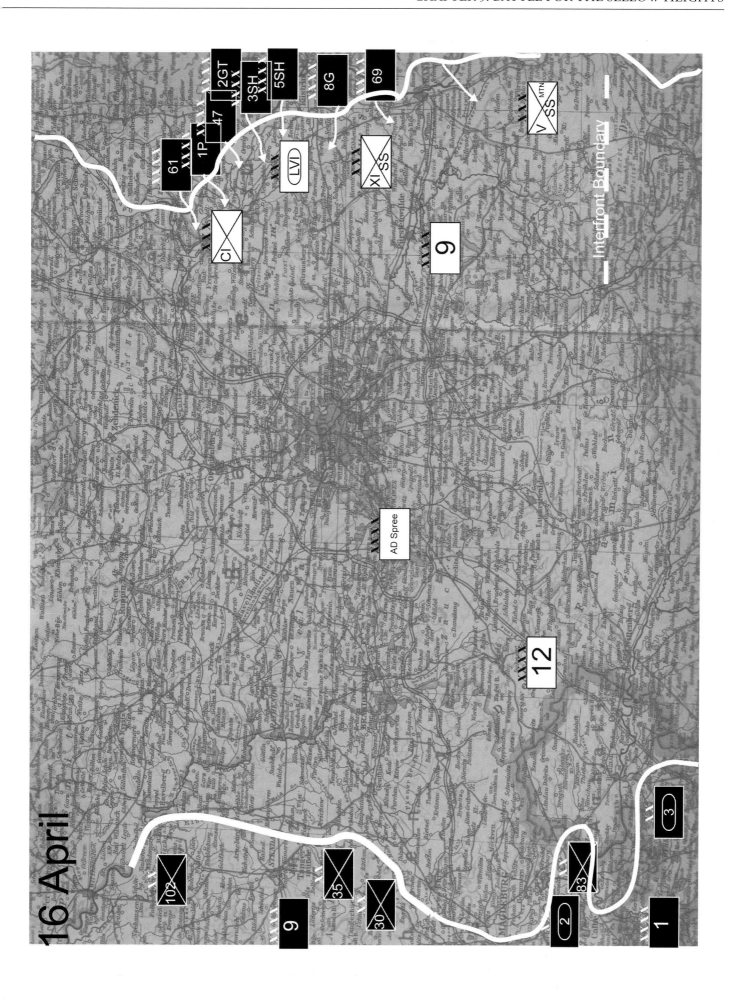

16 April

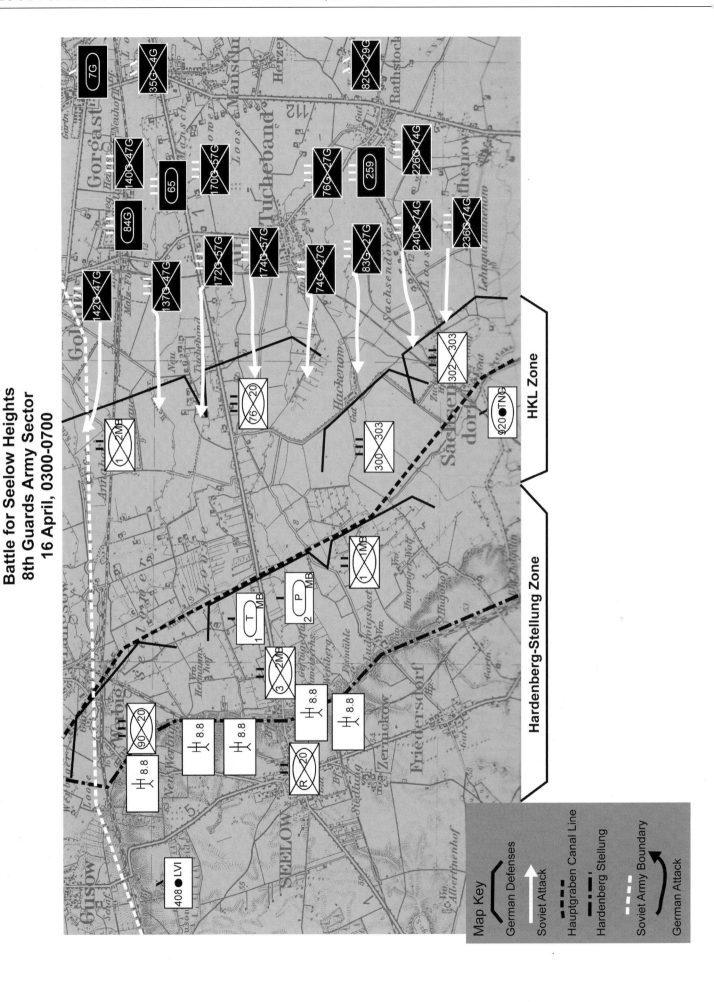

Battle for Seelow Heights
8th Guards Army Sector
16 April, 0300-0700

Map Key

German Defenses
Soviet Attack
Hauptgraben Canal Line
Hardenberg Stellung
Soviet Army Boundary
German Attack

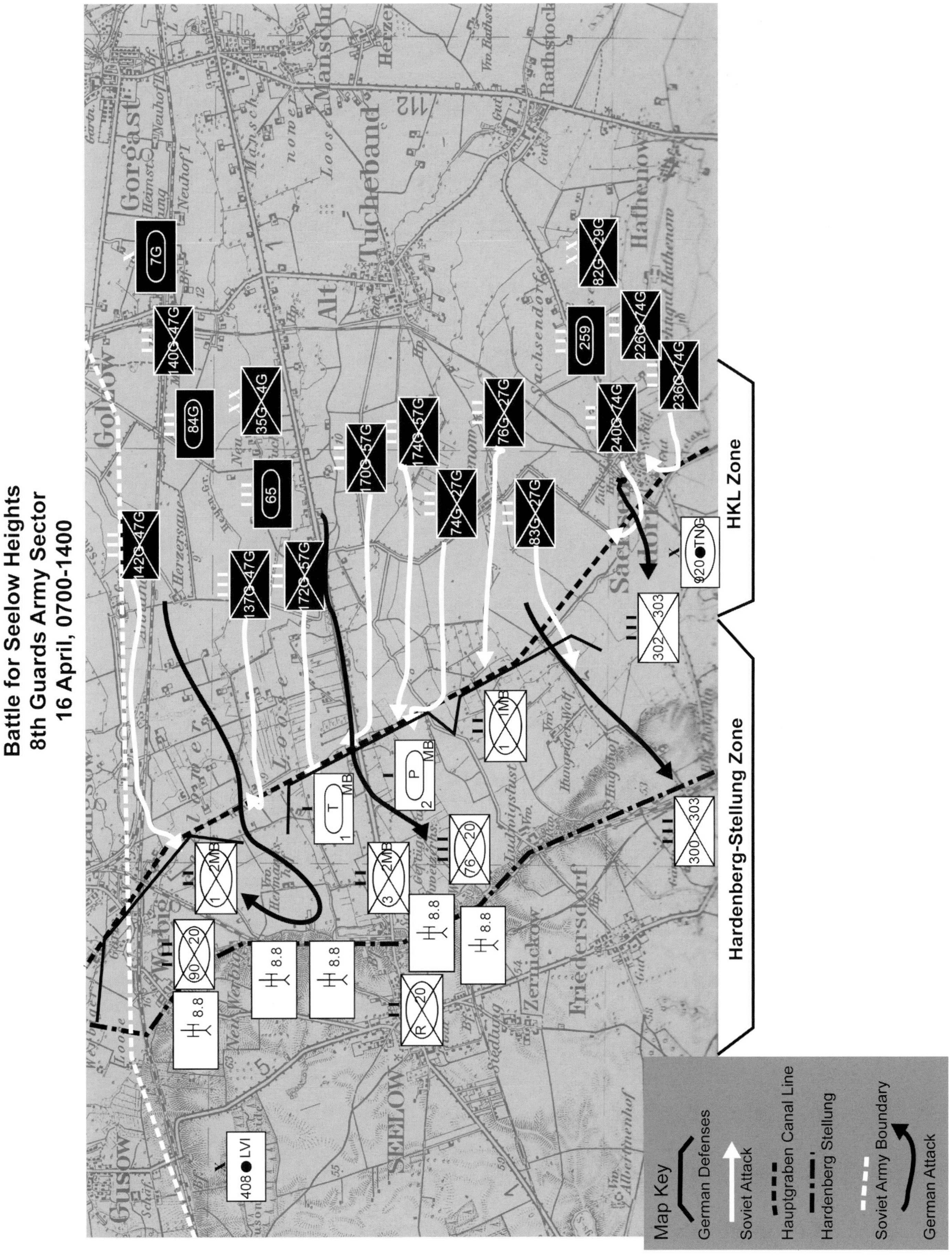

Battle for Seelow Heights
8th Guards Army Sector
16 April, 0700-1400

HKL Zone

Hardenberg-Stellung Zone

Map Key
German Defenses
Soviet Attack
Hauptgraben Canal Line
Hardenberg Stellung
Soviet Army Boundary
German Attack

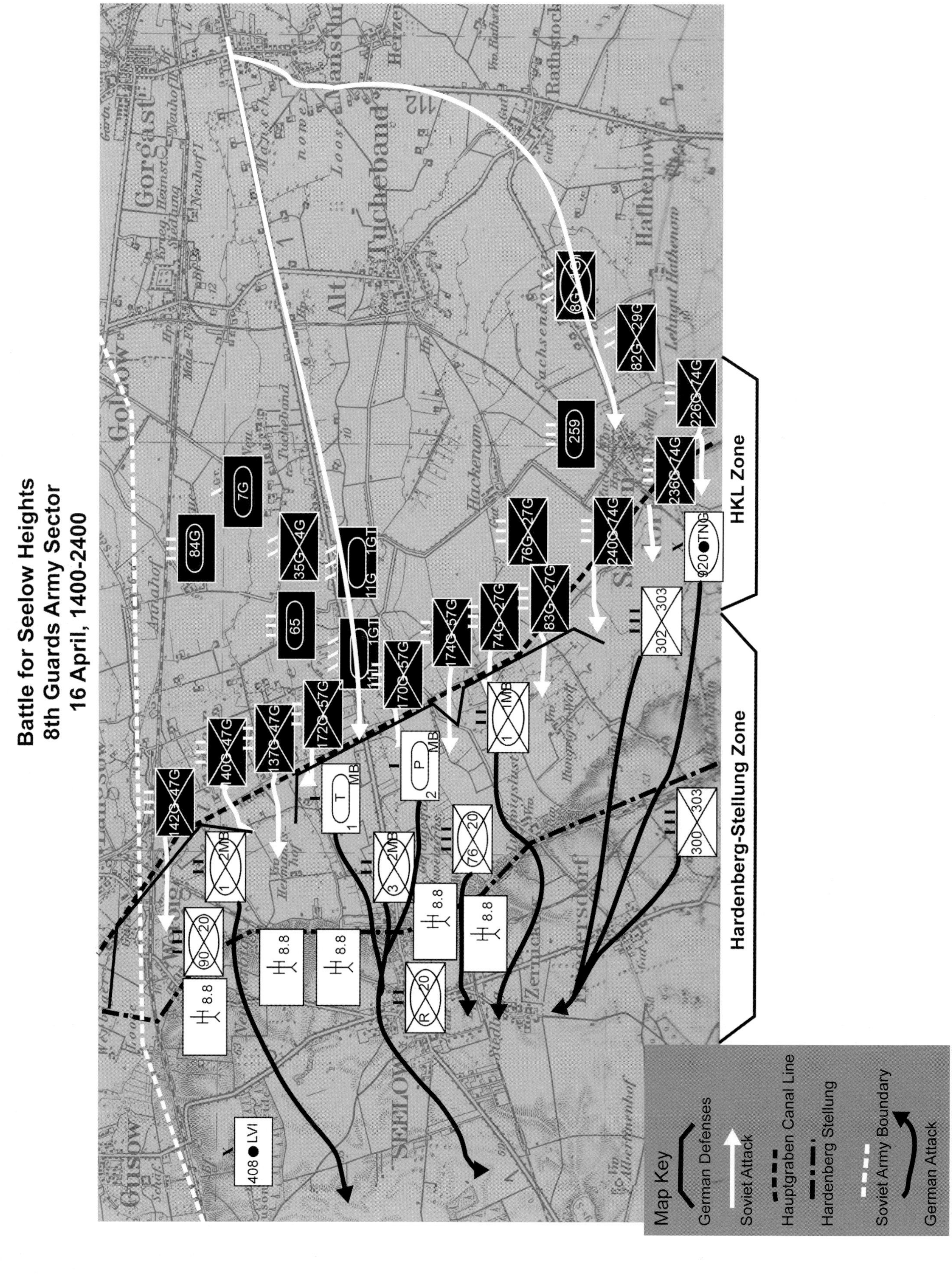

Battle for Seelow Heights
8th Guards Army Sector
16 April, 1400-2400

Map Key

German Defenses
Soviet Attack
Hauptgraben Canal Line
Hardenberg Stellung
Soviet Army Boundary
German Attack

HKL Zone

Hardenberg-Stellung Zone

Ammunition in this sector now became scarce and by the end of the day the remnants of the *9.Fallschirmjäger* slowly pulled back toward Platkow to consolidate.[16]

German units north of the *9.Fallschirmjäger* maintained their positions under the strain of brutal Soviet assaults that lasted all day. *Panzergrenadier Regiment 652* of the *Berlin Division* was located on the northern edge of the 5th Shock Army zone. This single regiment fought fiercely, forcing the 5th Shock Army to commit its second echelon force into the front line earlier than originally planned.[17]

The soldiers of the 3rd Shock Army noted the absence of German forces along the expected enemy defensive line in their sector. As they advanced the 3rd Shock Army's soldiers quickly noted the increase in German resistance along a second, previously unidentified defensive line.[18] The multi-echeloned defense, along with the numerous canals and drainage ditches, prevented the 3rd Shock Army from moving their tank units forward into the 'breakthrough' zone as defined by Soviet operational guidance. By dawn on 16 April the 3rd Shock Army commander decided to deploy the 9th Tank Corps to pass through the forward combat echelons but this proved impossible due to terrain and poor coordination with the infantry.[19] This demonstrates how poor operational judgment permeated Zhukov's command. The 3rd Shock Army planned to reach a point 15 kilometers behind the first German line but advanced only 3–9 kilometers by the end of the day. The price that the Germans paid in this sector for blunting the 3rd Shock Army was heavy. The *606.Infanterie-Division* [hereafter referred to as *606.Div.*] and remaining regiments of the *Berlin Division* suffered severely during the first day of battle. Both divisions, cobbled together from a variety of composite units quickly fractured under the Soviet pressure. Their ability to avoid the initial Soviet artillery barrage was the primary factor that allowed them to offer significant resistance against the assaulting Soviets. Both divisions did not last long after their first combat engagement with the Soviets. The *606.Div.* almost immediately became combat ineffective and the *Berlin Division* lost about 60% of its forces during the first day of combat.

In Chuikov's sector the 1st Guard Tank Army's armor started to cross the Hauptgraben Canal by late afternoon. The German defenders could simply not engage every moving Soviet target in the Oderbruch as leading tanks managed to finally cross the German canal and approach the base of the Heights below the town of Seelow. The Soviet tankers that began to find a way up the slopes on either side of Reichsbahn 1 found that their armor was incapable of climbing the steep slopes and were forced to locate other avenues of approach while under continued German defensive fire. It appears that Zhukov's intelligence failed to warn him that the slope's gradient below the town of Seelow was not capable of supporting his armor. Chuikov's forces were tired, confused, and stuck in the Oderbruch under the withering German defensive fire bearing down on them from the German positions. All around them were their wounded or dead comrades lying amidst the smoking hulks of burning Soviet tanks. It is not unreasonable to suggest that Zhukov's forces suffered in excess of 10,000 casualties in the first twelve hours of combat.

Zhukov's assault on Berlin was turning into an operational fiasco. "Keep moving forward! Do not stop!" were the orders of the day. Chuikov's infantry finally scaled the Heights several kilometers south of the town of Seelow in the evening dark. This enabled them to secure a small foothold at the southern end of the town. They were not able to exploit that success as the German *Kampfgruppe* under the command of *Major* Wandmaker continued its counterattacks through the night.

Overall the first day of operations went poorly for the Soviets. The addition of the 1st and 2nd Guards Tank Armies did not achieve the decisive breakthrough that Zhukov expected.

General Katukov stated to his Chief of Staff, General Nikolai Kirillovich Popiel, that "I have never seen such resistance in the whole course of the war. These Hitlerite devils are standing and fighting! We have been ordered [presumably by Stalin] to press on with the offensive day and night, to drive forward, taking no account of anything!"[20] Reports from the forward Soviet tank brigades stated that "the forward elements had managed to break through [to] the Heights by traveling at top speed, but the Seelow Heights had not proved really to be tank country. They had come across the opposition of [*Panzerfausts*] and German anti-aircraft guns which had been depressed and were firing at open sights—almost in every irrigation ditch and this was seriously impeding their progress."[21] A general lack of training and coordination before the assault with both infantry and air units contributed to Soviet losses and confusion. An assessment by the 3rd Shock Army is likewise revealing:

> Moreover the first day of these operations revealed considerable shortcomings in the organization and the conduct of military operations. Further, not all commanders were able to utilize their manpower for the out-flanking of enemy positions and breaking into their rear. Some of them resorted to frontal attacks on defensive positions which did not give the desired results. They did not utilize to the full the shock and fire power of the tanks. Some tank units and elements did not show flexibility in their operations or otherwise showed too little a degree of activity. To a certain degree the political organs were to blame for this because in the first place they had not paid sufficient attention to the tank units and formations, nor had they shown sufficient attention to the question of co-operation between the various kinds of troops, especially to the co-operation between infantry and tanks.[22]

The above official assessment is very critical of Soviet combat leadership and training inefficiencies that resulted in poor tactical execution. The assessment goes on to state that Soviet aircraft did not conduct any pre-battle exercises with the Soviet tank formations. During the assault Soviet pilots misidentified Soviet tank formations as German and routinely attacked them in the Oderbruch.[23]

General Popiel met with three generals of various Soviet tank corps during the evening of 16 April and asked for their opinion of initial Soviet operation. Their collective response foreshadowed the problems that Soviet forces encountered during the street fighting in Berlin. General Shalin of the 1st Guards Tank Army stated that:

> … the actual composition of the battle formations of the enemy at the very beginning of the Soviet offensive was unknown to us. The basic German forces and the basic elements of the German equipment had been moved from the first defensive position and had been placed in the second defensive line, that is on the Seelow Heights themselves. This re-grouping of the German forces was not entirely clear to the Soviet Front Command.[24]

Lieutenant General Getman, another Corps Commander of the 1st Guards Tank Army stated that in regards to the employment of the searchlights they merely " … illuminated our infantry support tanks to the Germans! We simply didn't blind the main forces of the enemy and that was the disastrous thing!" Finally, Colonel General Kuznetsoz of the 3rd Shock Army concluded that the complete failure of the Soviet operation was caused by:

> … sticking to the book! The Germans knew just too well what our traditional method was—that after the reconnaissance actions then there would come the general assault. And so they were able to withdraw their main forces into the second line of the defenses, that is they were able to pull back some eight kilometers from the main combat line. Thus we were directing all our artillery fire on covering detachments but we were not striking at the main body of the enemy … [25]

The official Soviet history of WWII recorded the failure of 16 April:

> … the commander of the front [Zhukov] threw into offensive operations the mobile forces of his front but the tank troops were not able to break away from the infantry …. In spite of the fact that artillery and aviation with subsequent blows on the intervening positions and the sectors of enemy opposition … the troops of the assault groupings were only, at the close of 16 April, able to break through the first field of enemy defense on a narrow sector. [26]

The previous assessments by Soviet commanders relate key factors that contributed to the poor results of the first day of the Soviet offensive toward Berlin. These factors included lack of planning, intelligence, training, ineffective leadership, and a general lack of coordination between rifle, tank, and air formations. While Zhukov bears the weight of responsibility for the operation's overall shortcomings and flawed execution, these factors point to more systemic organizational shortcomings of the Red Army. At the heart of the Soviet failure was their organizational rigidity in offensive execution that allowed Heinrici to effectively predict with uncanny exactness the precise time to order his forward deployed formations to withdraw. In addition the *9.Armee's* execution of Heinrici's reward movement to their secondary line of defense prior to the opening Soviet artillery barrage was masterful and can be considered an extremely difficult maneuver to do in a training environment let alone during wartime. This deceptively simple tactical maneuver demonstrated that even late in the war the *Wehrmacht's* organizational effectiveness remained high and under the right commander could still be utilized to execute difficult missions. Zhukov found his overwhelming advantage in firepower was negated by Heinrici through his simple but extremely effective ploy.

Table 5.1 *LVI Panzer Korps* and Soviet Force Comparison

	16 April		Comparison	24 April		Comparison
	LVI Panzer Korps	1st Byelorussian Front		LVI Panzer Korps	1st Byelorussian Front and 1st Ukrainian Front	
Strength	22,592	400,000	1:18	27,644 (11,644 LVI Pz.Korps + 15,000 Volssturm and Hitlerjugend approx.)	1.0 million (approx.)	1:36
Panzers/Self-Propelled Guns	204	2,000	1:10	80	3,000 (approx.)	1:36

This table shows the approximate difference in soldiers and tanks between the two adversaries on 16 April at the start of the Soviet offensive and on 24 April when the *LVI Panzer Korps* took up the defense of Berlin. Despite the enormous difference in manpower and equipment the *LVI Panzer Korps* held their ground against overwhelming odds. Without understanding the differences in equipment, organization, tactical doctrine, commanders, and of course the use of terrain between the two adversaries, it is difficult to comprehend how such a smaller force could maintain cohesion for 15 days of non-stop combat.

The *9.Armee* believed it had done a good job in the defense under the circumstances. The Germans claimed the destruction of 106 enemy tanks by the end of the day.[27] Heinrici understood that based on the rate of German losses and the expenditure of ammunition the *9.Armee* could not last long in a static defense despite the apparent success of holding the Soviets off the Seelow Heights. Amazingly the *LVI Pz. Korps* blunted the combined forces of the Soviet 5th Shock and 2nd Guards Tank Armies on its left wing as well as the 8th Guards and 1st Guards Tank Armies on the right. Weidling's divisions were confronted by no less than four reinforced Soviet armies along the main axis to Berlin. This was an uneven contest. Now that the Soviet's main axis of attack was confirmed, Heinrici ordered the release of the *18.Pz.Gren.Div.* at 2300 hours from *AGV's* reserve with the initial intention that it would join with the *25.Panzergrenadier-Division* [hereafter referred to as *25.Pz.Gren.Div.*] and counterattack the vanguard of the 5th Shock Army in the area of the collapsing *Berlin Division*. This intention, however, appeared to be overruled by Hitler who ordered the *18.Pz.Gren.Div.* south to the *9.Fallschirmjäger* positions instead.[28] Hitler's tactical intervention robbed *AGV* of an opportunity to strike the weak right flank of the Soviets. The time it took to deploy into the combat zone further south prevented the *18.Pz.Gren.Div.* from effectively contributing to the battle raging along the Seelow Heights.

Soviet T-34/85 crosses a water obstacle in the Oderbruch. It appears that a bridge may have been under construction to the right of the tank. Photo courtesy of the Bulgarian Ministry of Defence.

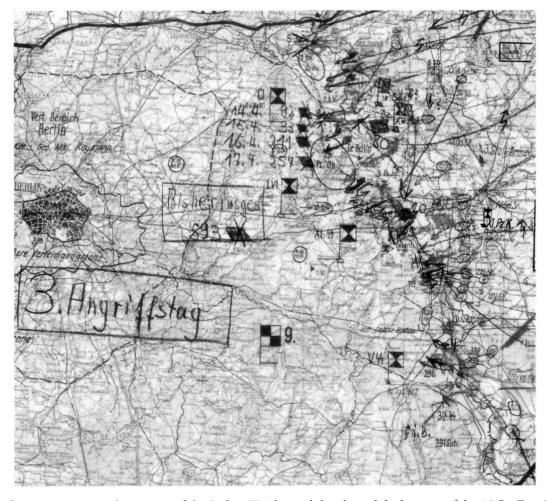

Note the lack of Soviet progress in the vicinity of the Seelow Heights and the planned deployment of the *18.Pz.Gren.Div.* to the east of Muncheberg. 16 April *AGV* Daily Situational Map. Courtesy of the US National Archives.

A knocked out German 8.8cm anti-tank gun along the Seelow Heights. Photo courtesy of RGAKFD, Moscow.

A super-heavy 203mm Soviet howitzer in action along the Oderbruch. Photo courtesy of RGAKFD, Moscow.

17 APRIL
TUESDAY

The news of the Soviet offensive reached Berliners on 17 April. As Berlin's citizens ventured out into the streets of the capital and reached for the morning paper many read the headlines of the *Völkischer Beobachter* that declared " … Bolshevists have launched the decisive battle … "[29] After several months of waiting the expected Soviet assault was underway.

While the *LVI Pz. Korps* actions were pivotal in blunting the Soviets, Weidling found his Corps in an increasingly difficult position by the evening of 16–17 April. Based on reports coming in from the *9.Fallschirmjäger* and *20.Pz.Gren.Div.* he knew the Soviets were fighting desperately to force a breach between his corps and the *XI SS Pz. Korps* on his right and the *CI Korps* on his left. Some relief was felt with the arrival of the *18.Pz.Gren.Div.* that deployed in the early morning hours. Weidling ordered the arriving Panzergrenadiers to take up position 6–8 kilometers north east of the town of Müncheberg with the task of counterattacking the Soviet breach between the *CI* and *LVI Pz. Korps*.[30]

In the area of the 8th Guards Army the town of Seelow continued to present a challenge for Chuikov. German anti-aircraft guns along the heights raked the Soviet armor until the German guns were either knocked out or destroyed by their crews after they ran out of ammunition. German leadership in the Seelow defense changed shortly after midnight as *Hauptmann* Rosenke of *I./Pz.Gren.Rgt.76* took command of *Kampfgruppe Wandmaker* on orders of the Regimental Commander. *Pz.Gren.Rgt.76* had pulled back over the Heights during the night and placed itself just south of Seelow where the main threat by the Soviets 57th Guards Rifle Division appeared. The German defenders in Seelow were now called *Kampfgruppe Rosenke*.[31] Tams's company was now down to 80 men. Elements of the 11th Tank Corps finally fought up the Heights several kilometers north of Seelow by late morning where the gradient didn't offer a significant challenge to their mobility. The Soviet armor finally reached a point just north of town by the afternoon. The Soviets pummeled Seelow with artillery then attacked again with aircraft causing at least one member of Tams' Company HQ to suffer a mental breakdown under the stress of the Soviet bombardment.[32] Soon T–34/85s appeared heading into Seelow from the north via the Guzow road causing alarm. During the night the German *3.Platoon* responsible for this area apparently disappeared. The situation along the south edge of town also began to deteriorate.

Pz.Gren.Rgt.76 now came under increased pressure from a renewed Soviet assault. The Soviet 27th Guards Rifle Division attacked the Panzergrenadiers' defensive positions with the support of tank brigades from the 11th Guards Tank Corps that pushed up the Heights to the south of Seelow. During the fighting the Regimental Commander *Oberst* Stammerjohn was killed sometime during the early morning hours.[33] The increased Soviet pressure coupled with the news of *Oberst* Stammerjohn's death apparently left the remainder of the *Kampfgruppe* staff in a defeated mood. By evening the German defenders were ordered to retreat to the hills in front of Diedersdorf several kilometers to the west. Under massive Soviet pressure the German defenders finally pulled out of Seelow under cover of darkness. By 1900 hours the Soviets slowly occupied what was left of Seelow. The command staff of the 1st Guards Tank Army now occupied a small house just to the north of town and waited for orders.[34]

North of Seelow *Pz.Gren.Rgt.90* was still in the Oderbruch on the morning of 17 April. Soviet forces of the 5th Shock Army pushed north of the unit and engaged the *9.Fallschirmjäger* while the main elements of the 8th Guards Army passed the Panzergrenadiers to the south during the drive to the Heights. By 0400 the command post was moved back to the Gusow railway station. Soon Soviet tanks of the 1st Guards Tank Army moved up the road without firing and caused havoc at the command post. The Soviets now began to ignore pockets of Germans and press west due to the slow pace of the first day of operations. Zhukov wanted no more delays and urged his subordinate commanders forward at any cost. The Soviets soon penetrated behind the rear of both the *I.* and *II./Pz.Gren.Rgt.90*. The *III./Pz.Gren.Rgt.90* fell back on its own to avoid being encircled. By 0900 the entire regiment started a withdrawal under cover of the *Pz.Abt.8's* self-propelled guns. The regiment soon reached the area around Görlsdorf and the command element began to move up the slopes of the Heights as pursuing Soviet forces were forming up opposite the regiment's positions. The Soviets launched another attack on the regiment's flanks at dusk and were able to get behind the bulk of the *20.Pz.Gren.Div.* An immediate counterattack was organized with the help of a 20mm anti-aircraft gun and tanks of the *Pz.Abt.8* but the Germans were unable to push the Soviets back.[35] The remainder of the Panzergrenadiers conducted a fighting withdrawal to the Wotan Defensive line that ran west of Müncheberg. The reward movement of *Pz.Gren.Rgt.90* now exposed the right flank of the remaining elements of the *9.Fallschirmjäger* as the Soviets moved into the building breach.

The remnants of the *9.Fallschirmjäger* continued to resist the 5th Shock Army in a series of small unit actions. The terrain favored the defense as the flooded Alte Oder on the division's left front forced the 2nd Guards Tank Army to find a suitable crossing father north. On the right part of the division's front the intact two battalions of *Fj.Rgt.27* were situated in that town of Gusow. Gusow was nestled among gently rolling slopes that gave way to heavily forested patches where only winding, narrow dirt roads traversed. The Soviet 248th Rifle Division managed to surround Gusow from the rear splitting the remnants of *Fj.Rgt.26* and *Fj.Rgt.27* while the 301st Rifle Division combined with elements of the 11th Tank Corps launched a frontal attack on the village. Situated around the village were 8.8cm anti-aircraft guns manned by 15–16 year old *Luftwaffe* crews. Their guns fired on the Soviet armor until their ammunition ran out and the guns were destroyed by their crews.[36] By 1300 hours the village fell to the Soviets. The remnants of *Fj.Rgt.27* retreated through the forests to Wulkow, passing the arriving lead elements of the *18.Pz.Gren.Div.* on their way. The Soviet armor wasted no time in pursuit. According to Gustav Herbster, a *9.Fallschirmjäger* veteran, he was in Wulkow for only 5 minutes with his company when 18 Soviet tanks broke through the woods nearby.[37] These tanks were counterattacked and many probably destroyed as Wulkow held out for another day. The Fallschirmjäger now formed *ad-hoc* formations and continued a fighting withdrawal west. *Fj.Rgt.25* was already shattered with its composite battalions retreating north. Elements of *Fj.Rgt.26* withdrew northeast after being split from *Fj.Rgt.27* earlier that day, although some remnants from the regiment fell back west and joined with the *Fj.Rgt.27* during the retreat toward Berlin.[38]

The 3rd Shock Army continued to fight their way forward against determined German resistance. They crossed the Freidlanderstron Canal by the evening of 17 April. Not until 18 April did the 3rd Shock Army reach a position 15–16 kilometers west of their start line—the objective they were assigned to reach in the first day battle. The surviving elements of the *Berlin Division* continued to fall back. The division's elements retreated from one town to another until they ran into the military police who tried to maintain order and force soldiers back into line. The military police routinely let staff clerks and supply personnel through their screen, but soldiers with weapons were ordered to turn around and head back into the frontline.[39] The north wing of the *LVI Pz. Korps* was now being flanked while the southern wing began to buckle under Soviet pressure. The situation was compounded by the failure of the *18.Pz.Gren.Div.* to maintain a defensive line and launch a successful counterattack to seal the breach on Weidling's left wing. The lead elements of the *18.Pz.Gren.Div.* that entered the line in the area around Wulkow were now forced to retreat as *Fj.Rgt.27* fell back.[40] Heinrici again had to shore up Weidling's front. By the evening *AGV* ordered *Nordland* south into the *LVI Pz. Korps* area of operation to take up position on the disengaging left wing of the *9.Fallschirmjäger*.[41] *Nederland* was also released from reserve and ordered into the line behind the *XI SS Pz. Korps* area south of Seelow.[42]

Weidling now had to order a general retreat of his forces back to the line Didersdorf—Alt Rosental—Hermersdorf.[43] In addition *Müncheberg's* Panzers and Panzergrenadiers were ordered to disengage from the Soviets and move west to reach the Wotan defensive line. This was done presumably at Weidling's request to maintain a solid front and preserve his armor forces for a counterattack. As a testament to the ferocity of fighting the *9.Armee* claimed an additional 211 Soviet tanks destroyed during the day's fighting bringing the two day total to 317 across its entire front.[44]

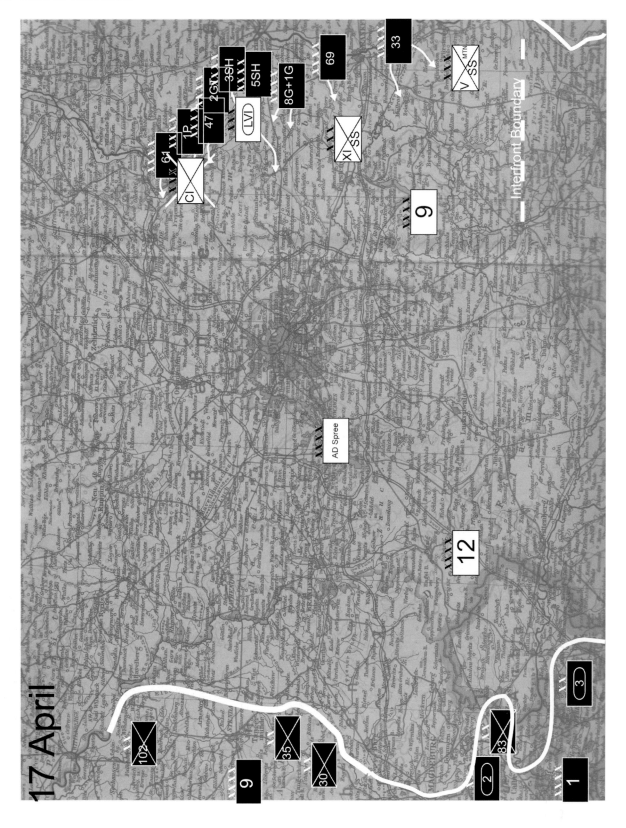

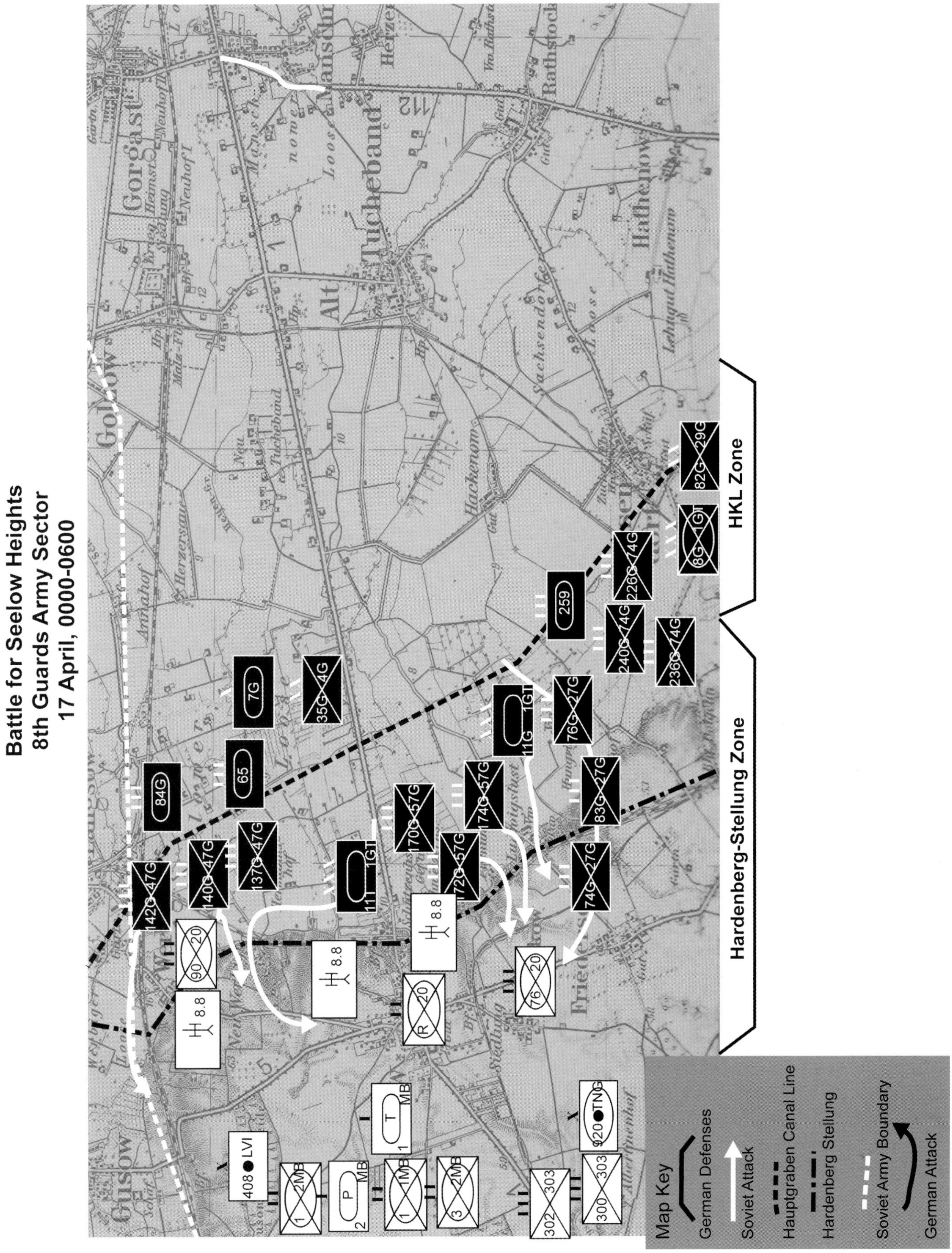

**Battle for Seelow Heights
8th Guards Army Sector
17 April, 0000-0600**

HKL Zone

Hardenberg-Stellung Zone

Gorgast

Golow

Gusow

Alt Tucheband

Hackenom

Sachsendorf

Hathenow

Rathstock

Herze

Friede

112

259

7G

4G
35G

65

84G

47G
42G

47G
140G

47G
137G

1G
111

1G
11

47G
170G

57G
174G

57G
72G

57G
74G

27G
76G

11G
11G

27G
83G

27G
74G

14G
240G

14G
236G

14G
226G

29G
82G

1G
8G

8.8

8.8

8.8

90
20

R
20

76
20

MB
T

MB
P
2

MB
1
1

2MB
1

1MB
1

2MB
3

TNG
20

303
302

303
300

LVI
408

Map Key

German Defenses

Soviet Attack

Hauptgraben Canal Line

Hardenberg Stellung

Soviet Army Boundary

German Attack

109

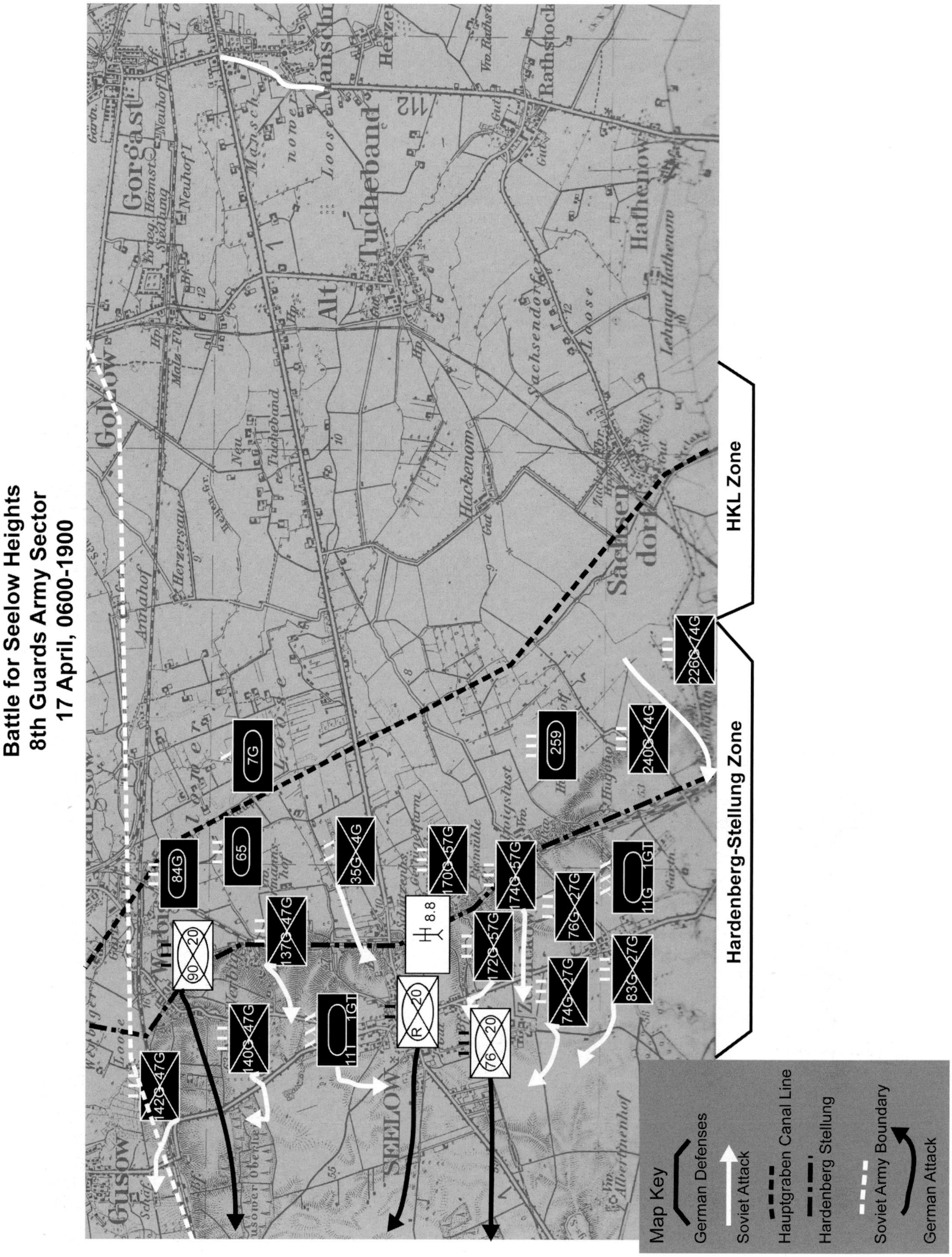

Battle for Seelow Heights
8th Guards Army Sector
17 April, 0600-1900

HKL Zone

Hardenberg-Stellung Zone

226G-74G

259

240G-74G

7G

65

35G-4G

84G

137G-47G

90/20

11 GT

140G-47G

11 GT

R 20

42G-47G

170G-57G

8.8

76/20

172G-57G

174G-57G

76G-27G

74G-27G

11G 1GT

83G-27G

Map Key

German Defenses

Soviet Attack

Hauptgraben Canal Line

Hardenberg Stellung

Soviet Army Boundary

German Attack

German 8.8 firing in a ground support role presumably outside a village along the Seelow Heights. If well camouflaged and in dug-in positions, these units took their toll on Soviet mechanized forces. The young German *Luftwaffe* crews often manned their guns until they fired all but the last shell. The last shell was used to destroy their gun before retreating. Photo courtesy of the Bundesarchiv.

A Polish JS-2 prepares to cross the Oder River. Photo courtesy of the Bulgarian Ministry of Defence.

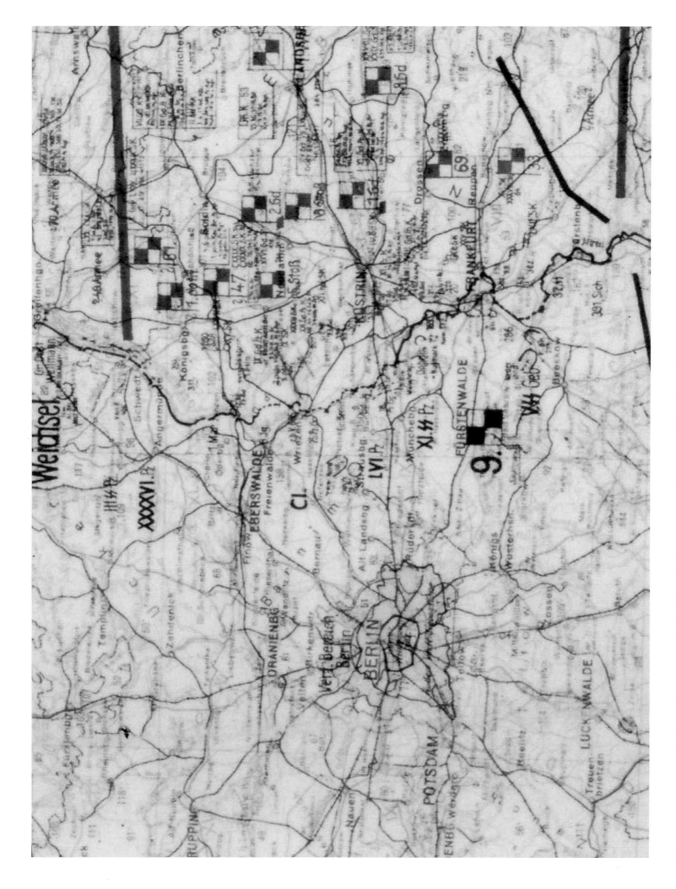

The majority of the *9.Armee* front is marked with dash lines noting the uncertainly of actual German unit positions. 17 April *AGV* Daily Situational Map. Courtesy of the US National Archives.

A knocked out Panther Ausf. G from the *3/10.SS-Pz.Rgt* from the *10.SS-Panzer Division "Fründsberg"*, Cottbus area, April 1945. Note the heavy camouflage. Photo courtesy of ASKM.

18 APRIL
WEDNESDAY

18 April was a critical day for the *LVI Pz. Korps*. The town of Seelow and the accompanying heights around the Stein-Stellung finally fell into Soviet hands almost two days after Zhukov planned. Breaches on both flanks of Weidling's corps were now imminent. He hoped that the expected reserves released from *AGV* would prove capable of reinforcing the line. On the Soviet side Zhukov's force pushed forward recklessly. They tried to find ways around the German defensive positions but often ran head-on into the enemy without any coordination or knowledge of the terrain. Confusion continued throughout the Soviet frontline. In one example, an *ad-hoc* formation of the *9.Fallschirmjäger* known as *Kompanie 'Blumenthal'* was situated at Hermensdorf when it was forced to fight off a series of frontal Soviet tank attacks from the 11th Tank Corps. The Fallschirmjägers of this *ad-hoc* company destroyed five T–34/85s as well as one Joseph Stalin tank in close quarter defense.[45] Amazingly the Soviet tankers were pushing ahead without any accompanying rifle divisions for support. There was no coordination with any Soviet formations operating on the right or left flanks. The 11th Tank Corps then tried to bypass the German defenders without any effective reconnaissance and encountered heavy German resistance in the nearby woods.

The vanguard of *Nordland* drove south during the night toward the *LVI Pz. Korps'* sector through roads clogged with thousands of refugees and German soldiers heading west. The immediate area behind the HKL was evacuated of civilians before the battle but the area west of the Stein-Stellung was not, and the approaching Soviets forces caused many civilians to flee on foot for the west. German soldiers, many of whom were shocked by the Soviet assault began to throw down their weapons and head west in an attempt to avoid further combat. Other soldiers lost contact with their commands and were wandering looking for leadership and orders. This was especially true in the area behind the *CI Korps* where the *Berlin Division* continued to rapidly disintegrate. The drive took almost two days and Soviet aircraft continually harassed the moving formations of *Nordland*.[46]

Nordland's commander issued orders to his division to move out just after midnight in the early morning hours of 18 April. Weidling expected that this division would launch an immediate counterattack from the region southeast of Jahnsfelde. This attack was designed to strike into the inter-front boundary between the Soviet 5th Shock and 8th Guards Armies along Reichsbahn 1 east of Müncheberg. One of the first units on the move was the *SS-Panzer Aufklärungs-Abteilung 11* [hereafter referred to as *SS-Pz.Aufkl.Abt.11*] that drove all night to be in position to counterattack the Soviets.[47] As the lead elements of *Nordland* arrived, their regiments soon came to a halt in the area around Protzel with some of the Panzergrenadiers reaching the woods east of Buckow—well to the north and west of Jansfelde. The division, with the exception of *SS-Pz.Aufkl.Abt.11*, ran out of fuel and could not complete their deployment. It took over twenty hours before the division received enough fuel to motorize its remaining formations.[48] It was clear that Weidling was not happy by this development as he kept Zeigler at his command post all day.[49] Zeigler's motives were dubious as subordinate commanders revealed after the war that

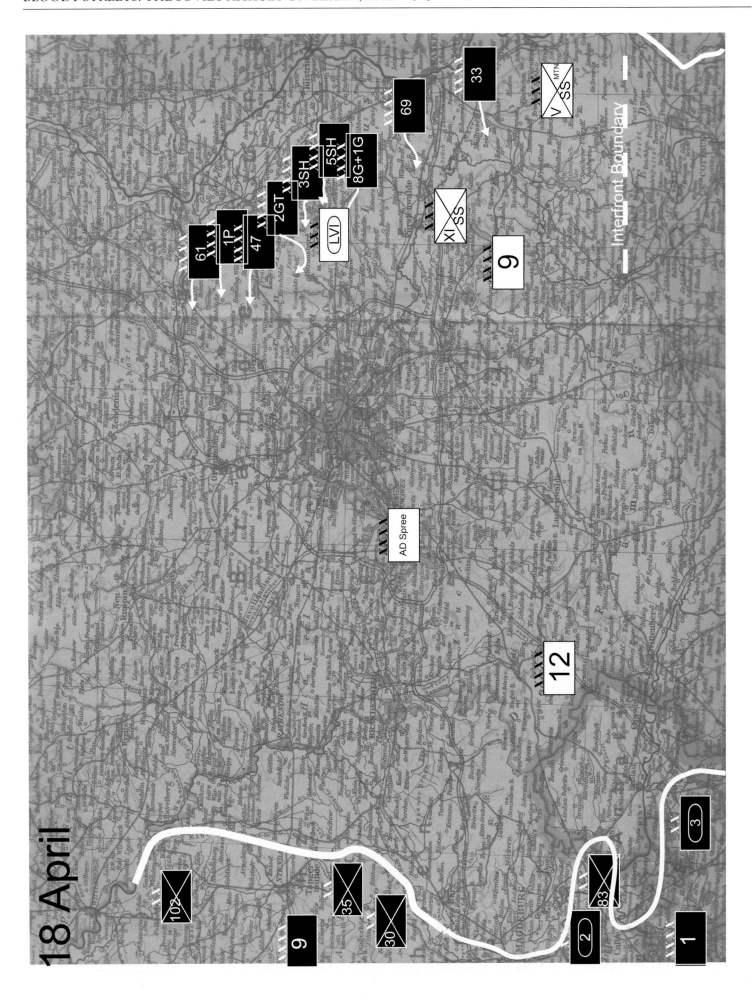

18 April

The east-west rail line in Trebnitz, east of Müncheberg where Zobel's Panther's and Tiger I's ambushed and destroyed a Soviet armor column advancing west. Author's collection.

The road looking east from Buckow. This photo shows the typical road network running east-west from the Seelow Heights that Soviet armor had to negotiate. One-lane unimproved roads, like the one pictured here, ran through dense woods where German infantry easily ambushed and destroyed lumbering Soviet tank columns. Author's collection.

This is a rare photograph of a T-34/85 tank from the 3rd Guards Tank Army fitted with side screens from the German Pz. IV, April 1945. Only a few Soviet tank units took the time to adopt the precautions to protect from the deadly Panzerfaust's hollow-shaped charges employed against them during the fighting around Berlin.
Photo courtesy of ASKM.

A knocked out Pz IV/L presumably in the vicinity of Seelow.
Photo courtesy of RGAKFD, Moscow.

A knocked out German 10.5cm leFH18M (foreground) and Hummel (background). These self-propelled artillery appear to be somewhere in the Oderbruch. Photo courtesy of RGAKFD, Moscow.

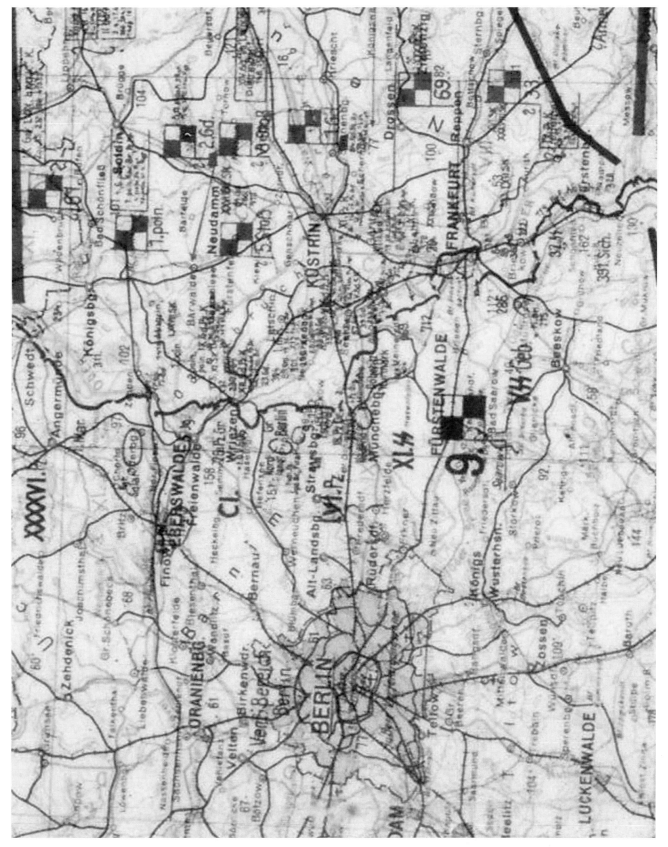

The German defense line buckles in the center. The situation overall is unclear as no Soviet movements are marked on the map. 18 April *AGV* Daily Situational Map. Courtesy of the US National Archives.

Zeigler did not want to fight under a *Wehrmacht* commander, and later ordered his units to flee to the west on their own disobeying direct orders from Weidling and Hitler. It is clear that in the case of the *SS-Pz.Gren.Rgt.24 Danmark*, they received written orders to move out at 0700—nearly eight hours after Heinrici ordered the division south—and their orders did not contain any mention of a counterattack, but instead they stated to establish a defensive line west of Straussberg in an east and north east direction.[50]

The Soviets completely occupied Seelow after two days of hard fighting. The tired, weary soldiers of the 8th Guards Army occupied every corner of every house in the town. The German artillery of the *408th Volksartillerie Korps* had the town zeroed and continued to fire into Seelow all day from their positions to the northwest. Rare appearances of the *Luftwaffe* occurred during the day as strafing and bombing runs were made against the town. Chuikov didn't rest his men long and by morning the 8th Guards Army and 1st Guards Tank Army attacked down Reichsbahn 1 hitting the boundary between the *LVI* and *XI SS Panzer Korps* hard. The regiments of *Müncheberg* and the *20.Pz.Gren.Div.* continued to hold the right wing of Weidling's front while *Nederland* (which apparently didn't run out of fuel) along with *Panzer Division Kurmark* and the King Tigers of *s.SS-Pz.Abt. 502* from the *XI SS Pz. Korps* held the area just to the south of the road.

Chuikov's forces moved along the easiest avenues of approach available toward the town of Müncheberg as they were being driven at a frenzied pace by Zhukov. No attempt at reconnaissance was made and the 1st Guards Tank Army's armor soon formed a single line back-to-back moving down Reichsbahn 1, while other Soviet units began winding down secondary roads on the flanks. They quickly ran into the defending Germans. The ensuing fighting was fierce as German Panzers, anti-tank guns, and soldiers engaged the strung out Soviet formations. Chuikov temporarily halted his advance in order to bring up the 3rd Guards Cavalry Corps from his reserve to assist in the reduction of the Germans. Soviet artillery now zeroed in on the German positions after moving up to positions along the Heights. The Soviets practiced a 'boxing' technique with their artillery that they used regularly in Berlin. When they reached a German strongpoint their artillery fire formed a wall of steel preventing any reinforcements while the infantry moved in to destroy the defenders. In one vivid example Russian artillery bombarded the line behind Tam's positions while Soviet infantry engaged in hand-to-hand fighting for his unit's trench line. Tam recalled the image that still haunts him in his sleep despite witnessing frontline combat during his three and a half years of service: " … I had never experienced anything like this, nor believed it possible. Men were fighting with clubs and knives just like in the Middle Ages."[51]

Weidling had no choice but to order immediate counterattacks as the 8th Guards Army continued to grind down against his front. *Müncheberg's I./Pz.Rgt.29* was refitting in the woods west of Diedersdorf during the late afternoon as the Panzers were replenished with ammo and fuel. *Hauptmann* Zobel received immediate orders to recover the village of Trebnitz that was recently occupied by elements of the 1st Guards Tank Army. When Zobel's forces arrived they found that Soviet infantry had already occupied the village. Since Zobel's counterattack force had no accompanying infantry he positioned his armor along the railroad embankment east of the village. He was soon rewarded by a large Soviet armored column that emerged from the woods to the east crossing his front. The Soviets were trying to find a way around the stubborn German positions after encountering fierce resistance along Reichsbahn 1 and found themselves channeled into one of the east-west dirt lanes that crossed the area. Zobel's force destroyed nearly 50 Soviet tanks with one of their senior NCOs scoring 17 kills alone before he was severely wounded in the face.[52] The battalion withdrew to its starting position by early evening where it was attacked by Soviet artillery. It was then ordered back to the village of Müncheberg—Chuikov's next objective.

Lead elements of *Nordland* finally reached positions in the Hühnerberge hills by evening then stopped to coordinate their positions with identified German units already in the area. An assault company commanded by Gunnar Illum arrived in the forests east of Buckow and immediately began to look for the elements of the *9.Fallschirmjäger* in his area in order to coordinate for a unified defense.[53] Illum was commander of an assault company numbering 44 soldiers from the *SS-Pz.Gren.Rgt.24 Danmark*. They were heavily armed with Sturmgewehr assault rifles, one light machine gun, and *Panzerfausts*. These soldiers moved into the woods east of Bollersdorf and Buckow. Illum and his messenger found the *9.Fallschirmjäger* Command Post, presumably in Printzhagen, and identified themselves to its commander. Illum and his runner were surprised when they suddenly had machine pistols placed at their back, their pistols removed, and had a German *Major* demanded to see their identifications papers and pay books. After examining them, and feeling everything was in order, the Fallschirmjäger *Major* explained that Seydlitz Troops were operating all along the front and no one unfamiliar could be trusted.[54] This was the first time Illum heard of the organization, although he would hear much more about it during the course of the fighting in Berlin. After reviewing maps and making final coordination he then began to place his men in defensive positions for the night.

Limited Soviet progress was made overall due to a total lack of coordination as many units to become mixed up in huge traffic jams along the few available dirt roads among the heavily fostered hills behind the Seelow Heights. The slow pace of Soviet offensive operations continued to drain Zhukov of all patience. Again, Zhukov received reports of high armor losses as his tankmen were caught either in the open or along narrow dirt lanes by crippling German anti-tank fire. Zhukov realized that no firepower could overcome this situation and he attempted to address the problem creatively. He immediately organized a traffic control service, increasing coordination between the rifle divisions and tank brigades trying to maneuver along the same roads. Next he removed all support vehicles from the roads. He now required mechanized infantry to move on foot presumably to reduce the losses he was receiving by getting them to comb the woods for Germans. He reinforced his desire to get his forces moving forward by issuing an order stating that any commanders not fulfilling their duty would be replaced on the spot.[55] It must be noted that Zhukov's orders demonstrated that he gave no prior thought to movement coordination before the operation. Particularly paradoxical was the order to dismount the mechanized infantry to clear the woods. This countered his earlier direction for his forces to move west as fast as possible and didn't address the fact that his armor was already operating ahead of the infantry formations so clearing the woods of Germans served little operational benefit. Finally, his order regarding the removal of his subordinate commanders only served to perpetuate an already reckless drive west by his units who now labored under Zhukov's threat.

The struggling Soviet advance managed to gain 3–6 kilometers on 18 April but failed to break Weidling's frontline. Weidling's flanks, however, were in poor shape. The *9.Fallschirmjäger's* poor operational state finally came to Weidling's knowledge when its commander had to be replaced by *Oberst* Harry Hermann. Brauer apparently radioed the *LVI Pz. Korps* HQ and asked for a 24 hour period of rest for his division.[56] This request was clearly out of desperation. The *20.Pz.Gren.Div.* pulled back farther west under significant Soviet artillery pressure, while *Müncheberg* continued to hold its positions in Müncheberg despite receiving initial losses. The *18.Pz.Gren.Div.* deployed intact but the fluid situation along the left flank of the *LVI Pz. Korps* forced the division to pull back west. This precipitated a Soviet penetration from Wriezen all the way to Tiefensee. This success was not initially realized by the Soviets in their confused and uncoordinated advance. Much to Weidling's anger, *Nordland* arrived piecemeal into an area different from where he expected them to deploy. Communications with the *XI SS Pz. Korps* on his right flank was severed by the evening as the 1st Guards Tank Army pushed behind *Nederland* to the southwest of Reichsbahn 1 and Müncheberg.[57]

19 APRIL
THURSDAY

In the early morning hours of 19 April Weidling called the Operations Officers from all his divisions together to discuss the current situation. Weidling had arrived to the front shortly before the battle started and he was probably not fully aware of either 'Eclipse' or of Heinrici's desire not to defend Berlin case of a Soviet breakthrough. He stated that "On our northern flank as well as our southern flank the Russians have broken through. Schörner will hold his position down south. The *3.Panzer Armee* has not yet been seriously attacked. It is clear that the Russians are trying to reach Berlin as fast as possible. It is our intention to defend Berlin."[58] Böttcher, the Operations Officer from the *18.Pz.Gren.Div.* countered that fighting in the streets of Berlin was madness and that tanks were useless in an urban environment. He stated that the *18.Pz.Gren.Div.* should make for the south and link up with *Heeresgruppe Schörner*. Weidling listened to this, and in a change of heart, stated that he now believed Berlin should be declared an open city and that the situation was simply too unclear to make a final decision. Weidling's final guidance at the meeting was that for the moment there was nothing they could do but hold the line where they were.[59] This discussion would come back to haunt Weidling and Böttcher in the next several days with effects that neither men could foresee at the time.

On this morning the Soviets launched a strong artillery attack on the wooded area where *Danmark* positioned itself the night before.[60] Illum's company was in the vanguard at the eastern perimeter of the woods. Soon an attack developed by the 12th Guards Tank Corps operating on the extreme left of the 3rd Shock Army's front.[61] As the Soviet attack began, the clanking of Soviet tank tracks immediately alerted the Danes who quickly took up defensive positions. In Illum's sector he watched a Soviet heavy tank brigade appear across his front. The Soviets wanted to breach this area and placed their heaviest armor forward to conduct the breakthrough as per Soviet doctrine. Illum counted 28 JS–2 tanks with infantry riding on them. His company was equipped with *Panzerfausts* and backed up by a Nebelwerfer (rocket launcher) company from the *9.Fallschirmjäger*. A fierce battle began that raged all morning. Illum's soldiers were reinforced by elements of a *Hitlerjugend Panzerjäger Regiment K* [hereafter referred to as *Hj.PzJg.Rgt.K*] led by *Wehrmacht* and *SS* NCOs.[62] During the fighting one of the Soviet tanks succeeded in breaking into the woods. Illum sent two men to deal with the tank but one was soon seriously wounded. Illum then set out himself to destroy the tank armed with a *Panzerfaust* and pistol. While stalking through the rough woods he turned to see a Soviet soldier with an automatic rifle only 10 meters away. Illum jumped to the side, dodging the first spray of bullets. He then dropped the *Panzerfaust* and readied his pistol. Suddenly a shot rang out and the Soviet soldier dropped to the ground. The shot was fired by his companion, a Hungarian farm boy named Zlucki, who was attached to the company. Illum went back for the dropped *Panzerfaust* and stalked closer to the Soviet tank. He aimed and fired the *Panzerfaust* but the hollow shell glanced off the thick side armor and the tank promptly withdrew having barely survived the encounter.

The Soviets attacked again the afternoon. Heavy Soviet artillery hit the area where the 200–300 *Hitlerjugend* were positioned. Many were killed along with several members of Illum's company. By nightfall they were ordered to pull back to the village of Hohenstein where they rested for the night in the woods east of Straussberg. While this fight was going on during the day, Soviet tank brigades of the 2nd Guards Tank Army attempted to pass to the north, around the forests of Bollersdorf, outflanking the *Nordland* troops and remnants of the *9.Fallschirmjäger*.

Lead elements of the 1st Mechanized and 9th Guards Tank Corps pushed recklessly west and immediately ran into the single deadliest tank engagement during the Soviet assault on Berlin. These tank corps of the Soviet 2nd Guards Tank Army continued to move north to cross over the Alte Oder, finally crossing just north of Alt Friedland, then drove west through secondary dirt roads leading toward the area between Protzel—Grunow from Ihlow. Their lead elements, advancing without reconnaissance or infantry support, drove right into an ambush by the King Tigers of *s.SS-Pz.Abt.503* that recently arrived from *Nordland's SS-Pz.Abt.11 Hermann von Salza*. *SS-Unterscharführer* Hans Dier's King Tiger (314) was in position in the hills northeast of Klosterdorf when the lead Soviet tanks appeared driving east across the Protzel—Grunow road. Dier's King Tiger engaged the Soviet T–34s and began knocking them out one by one until a hit by a Soviet gunner on Dier's turret damaged the fire control system of his King Tiger.[63]

Southeast of Diers were five additional King Tigers of *s.SS-Pz.Abt.503* under the command of *SS-Obersturmführer* Müller. His forward three heavy Panzers were in a blocking position on the heights near Grunow west of Ernsthof covering the open fields from the forested hills. The King Tiger's green and brown swabs of camouflage paint that covered the tanks, coupled by the smokeless discharge of their deadly 8.8cm shells, and advanced optics gave the heavy German Panzers a distinct advantage from a stationary position. Over a hundred Soviet tanks moved into the open from the east. The three King Tigers opened fire too early, however, and caused some of the shots to fire wide. Due to the range, effective camouflage, limited visibility, but most importantly a lack of wireless communication inherent in the Soviet tanks, the Soviets were not able to tell the direction of fire. In immediate reaction they began to scatter as they drove erratically west to avoid being targeted. This was not the first time the Germans encountered this Soviet tactic. According to an intelligence report of the *I./Pz.Rgt.33* dated 19 January–15 February 1945 Soviet tank tactics in recent mobile battles proved ineffective. The report cited that when a Soviet tank formation was encountered in the open they tended to scatter due to a lack of effective command-and-control. They tried to make up for this weakness by making swift, unplanned cross-country moves to avoid being targeted.[64] In addition, the Soviets were under direct orders to advance as fast as possible and avoid any German strongpoints. The three King Tigers soon ran out of ammunition and two King Tigers of the reserve element under command of *SS-Oberscharführer* Körner were ordered to join the fight. Together the five King Tigers knocked out or left burning in the open fields over 70 Soviet tanks. The Soviets finally zeroed in on the King Tiger's position and launched a counter attack with Stalin Organs. The Soviet rockets rained down around the assembled King Tigers killing Müller who was outside of his tank at the time of the rocket barrage. The tank killing wasn't over for the Germans.

A German counterattack east around Bollersdorf developed in support of *SS-Pz.Gren.Rgt.24 Danmark* engaged in keeping back the Soviets from advancing through the woods. As the Danes retreated west to their new positions east of Straussberg, Körner's three King Tigers advanced east and spotted a company of JS–2s that previously drove through Illum's position and were now forming up in line along the narrow, pine tree-lined road leading from Bollersdorf to Straussberg. These JS–2s may have belonged to the 79th Guards Tank Regiment of the 12th Guards Tank Corps. In addition, forming up outside of Bollersdorf were more than 100 T–34/85s representing

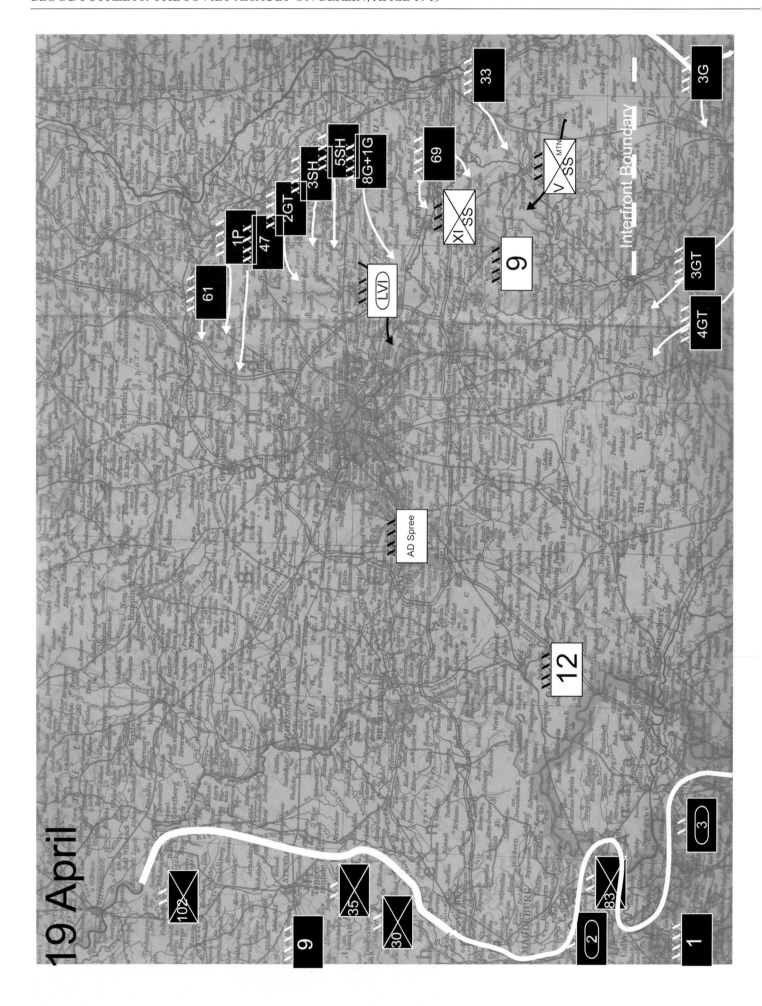

The road west to Strausberg through Bollersdorf. It was in these woods on either side of the road where Illum's Panzergrenadiers of *Nordland*, along with *Hitlerjugend* tank hunters fought off the initial attempt of Soviet JS-2 to breach the German defense line. Author's collection.

As Soviet armor and mechanized forces emerged from the thick forest to the east they immediately entered the wide open fields for the first time since the assault began and were immediately engaged by German King Tigers and assault guns from *Nordland* deployed along the hills to the west. This photo shows the open fields to the northeast of Grünow. Author's collection.

King Tigers of *s.SS-Pz.Abt.503* were in camouflaged, hull down positions along the hills to the north-west of Bollersdorf. As elements of the 12th Guards Tank Corps emerged from the woods to the east they were immediately engaged at range by German King Tigers firing across these open fields. Author's collection.

Battle for Bollersdorf
2nd Guards Tank Army Sector

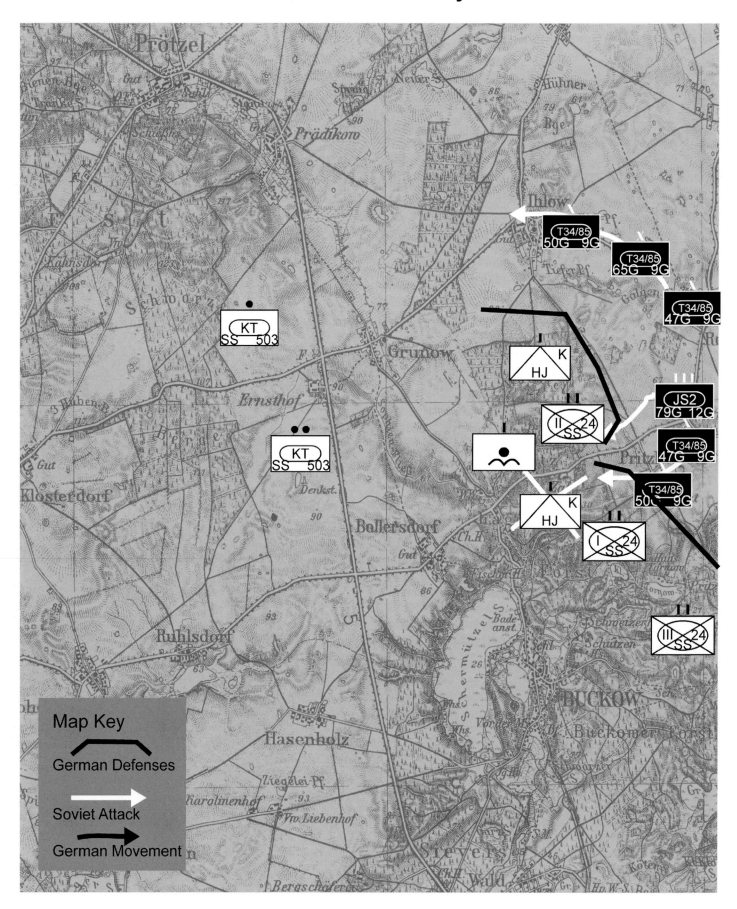

Map Key

German Defenses

Soviet Attack

German Movement

Battle for Bollersdorf
2nd Guards Tank Army Sector
19 April, 0600-1200

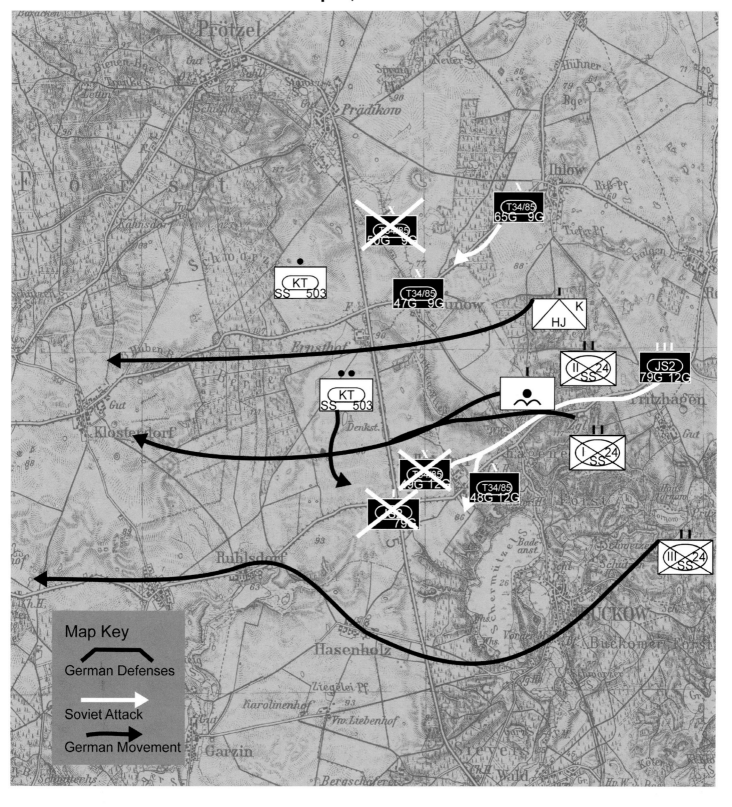

Map Key

German Defenses

Soviet Attack

German Movement

The center of Müncheberg looking south. Little of the pre-war buildings are intact as the town was heavily bombed, then destroyed during the subsequent Soviet assault. This town is now north of the main east-west road between Berlin and Seelow.
Author's collection.

either the 48th, 49th or 66th Guards Tank Brigades also of the 12th Guards Tank Corps. Due to the reported number of tanks, it is likely that that the 12th Guards Tank Corps completed their push through the woods to the east and were now forming up for a continued west-ward advance with their surviving JS–2s in the lead followed by the better part of two tank regiments. Körner's King Tigers opened the engagement by destroying the first and last JS–2 in the column preventing the rest from moving. Due to the limited ability to traverse their turrets on the tree-lined road the JS–2s were knocked out in detail. The German Panzers now engaged the mass of Soviet T–34/85s and began to knock them out. It is not reported whether these Soviet tanks engaged the King Tigers during their action against the JS–2s. At least 64 additional Soviet tanks were claimed to be knocked out.[65]

The three King Tigers retreated back toward Straussberg for resupply. After arriving at their depot they were immediately ordered north then northwest to Werneuchen. Here they engaged an additional thirty T–34/85s and Soviet infantry. This armor column was presumably the survivors of the 9th Guards Tank Corps that engaged the King Tigers earlier in the day and was ordered north then west around the German positions. A fourth King Tiger was brought up and all enemy tanks were knocked out or destroyed while the infantry assault was stopped with delay-fused rounds.[66] During the evening JS–2s tried to push through to Straussberg under cover of night but the King Tigers again halted the attack. The Germans used flares to illuminate the main road approaching the town and in their eerie glow opened fire on the JS–2s. *Hitlerjugend* from the *Hj.PzJg.Rgt.K* along with members of *SS-Pz.Gren.Rgt.24 Danmark* located in the surrounding woods also participated in destroying Soviet armor.[67] During the night the Soviets hit the *III./SS-Pz.Gren.Rgt. Danmark* lines hard with artillery and rockets, setting the woods on fire. The order was soon given to pull out of the burning woods and head to the Straussberg airfield. The Soviets lost approximately 200 tanks from the 12th Guards Tank Corps while trying to push through the dense woods on the Weidling's left flank.

The amount of Soviet tanks losses at the hands of a half dozen German panzers and assorted infantry were extraordinary. Evidence to support the losses claimed by the Germans comes from Soviet sources. Between the 18-21 April the 12th Guard Tank Corps maintenance section repaired forty-eight T-34/85s, five JS IIs, twelve SU-100s, and two SU-76s tanks. Given that the Soviets were able to turn around and repair 77 tanks their irrecoverable losses were easily equal to or more than the number repaired.[68] While the Germans may have doubled counted their kills, the Soviets often repaired their tanks multiple times making an accurate total from either side nearly impossible. The 12th Guard Tank Corps probably suffered irrecoverable losses of over 100 tanks just over the last three days of combat. That meant a reduction of more than a third of this operating force. Given that repairs could be major or minor, the 12th Guards Tank Corps was probably not operating at more than 60% of its authorized strength of 270 tanks and self-propelled guns. Soviet sources state that without the ability to repair these tanks, the 12th Guards Tank Corps would never be able to accomplish its mission in Berlin. Despite their horrendous losses the 12th Guard Tank Corps pushed 9 kilometers west to the outskirts of Straussberg by the evening.

Chuikov launched his attack against Müncheberg along Reichsbahn 1 with the 242nd Regiment of the 82nd Rifle Division in the vanguard. The regiment's commander, Colonel of the Guards Ivan Fyodorovich Sukhorukov, avoided a frontal assault and instead moved

This Sturmgeschütz appears to have driven into a drainage ditch and became disabled presumably in the outskirts of Müncheberg. Note that the Soviets knocked out the church steeple to prevent the Germans from using it as an observation point.
Photo courtesy of RGAKFD, Moscow.

This Pz IV/L from *Pz.Div. Müncheberg* was knocked out in fighting presumably in the outskirts of the town of Müncheberg. Note the two German corpses in the foreground. Photo courtesy of ASKM.

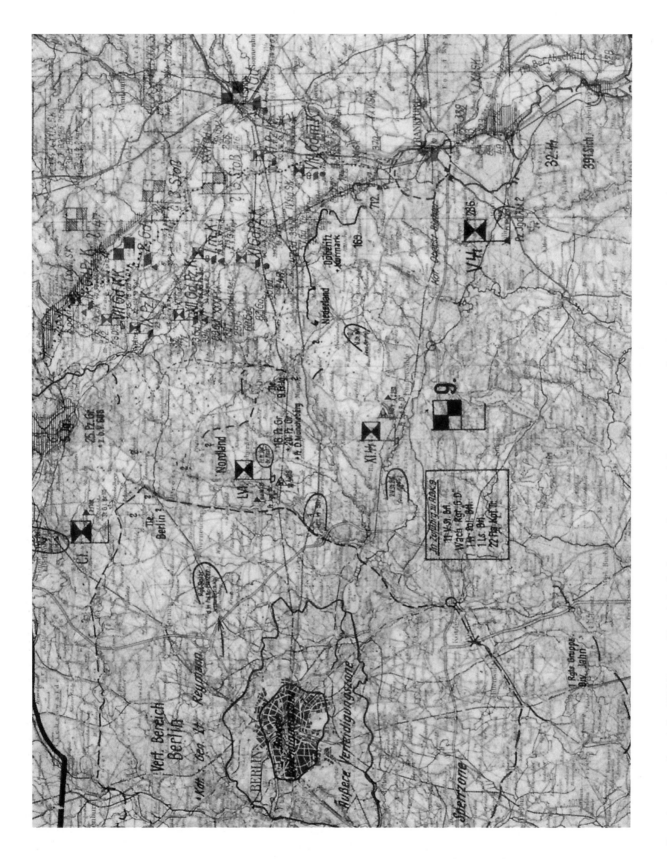

The German front is ruptured and the *LVI Panzer Korps* is backed up to the outer defense perimeter of Berlin. Note the movement of forces from Berlin to the threatened sectors of the *9.Armee*. This shows Heinrici's attempt to empty Berlin of all military forces to avoid any fighting in the streets and subsequent destruction of the city. Also note that there is no knowledge of *Nordland's* location. 19 April *AGV* Daily Situational Map. Courtesy of the US National Archives.

northwest into the woods to outflank the town. Using small combined forces of infantry, assault guns, and armor they took the town after several hours of street fighting.[69] A more contemporary Russian account suggests that the 1st Guards Tank Army was ordered to make a frontal assault on Müncheberg but refused, presumably after suffering losses at the hands of Zobel's defending Panthers, and Tiger Is. The 1st Guards Tank Army instead moved south to avoid the German defenders, leaving Chuikov to deal with the problem.[70] This is credible as *Müncheberg's* Panzers claimed that 53 Soviet tanks were knocked out along the approaches to this sleepy German town.[71] In any case the town fell by late afternoon. Chuikov wrote that once Müncheberg fell he started to move his forces southwest as ordered by Zhukov, but his armor encountered strong German resistance in the woods that effectively brought his attack to a halt through the use of *Panzerfausts*.[72] Here the rearguard of *Müncheberg's* Panzergrenadiers and elements of the *20.Pz.Gren.Div.* held back Chuikov's advance.[73]

The deployments of *AGV's* reserves proved ineffective and only served to deflect and not block the Soviet armor penetrations. The main problem for Weidling and Heinrici was the 30 kilometer wide exposed left flank of the *LVI Pz. Korps* that appeared in the wake of the disintegrating *606.Division* and *Berlin Divisions*. There was no longer a cohesive front between the *9.Armee* and *3.Panzer Armee*. By the evening of 19 April the Soviets finally pushed behind Weidling's forces. His left wing was broken and his right was under considerable strain. With the fall of Müncheberg Weidling now had to face the possibility that if he stayed where he was he would either be surrounded in place or be forced to retreat back into Berlin. Weidling now made his decision—withdrawal south to the *9.Armee* lines before the Soviets cut off his only means of retreat—and above all, avoid fighting in Berlin.

Zhukov had to develop a new operational plan in the wake of the disastrous several days. Zhukov now ordered Katukov's 1st Guards Tank Army and the 8th Guards Army under Chuikov to combine forces and continue on the direct line along Reichsstrasse 1 to Berlin, and there swing south over the Spree and Dahme Rivers to encompass the southern suburbs along an arc extending from the Spree to the Havel River. It was thought that the combining of the two forces offered the potential of better coordination. Although the original plan had been for Bogdanov's 2nd Guards Tank Army to provide the northern armored pincer enveloping Berlin, the three component corps were now allocated individually to the three combined-arms armies in that sector. Major-General A.F Popov's 9th Guards Tank Corps was given the task of pushing straight through to the Havel in support of Lieutenant-General F.l. Perkhorovitch's 47th Army that was further reinforced by Major-General M.P. Konstantinov's 7th Guards Cavalry Corps, and the 1st Polish Motorized Mortar Brigade from Lieutenant-General S.G. Poplawski's 1st Polish Army's Reserve. Lieutenant-General S.M. Krivosheina's 1st Mechanized Corps and Major-General M.P. Teltakov's 12th Guards Tank Corps were now ordered to approach the northeastern suburbs, acting as the spearheads of the 3rd and 5th Shock Armies respectively. The 2nd Guards Tank Army was to re-form with these two latter tank corps to take over the northern arc of Berlin's suburbs. Colonel-General V.I. Kutznetsov's 3rd Shock Army was given the responsibility to attack the northeastern suburbs of the city, while General N.E. Berzarin's 5th Shock Army operated on the left flank and drove directly into the eastern suburbs of Berlin. Zhukov wanted to minimize further risk to his tank forces by forcing them to become subordinated to his rifle corps, hoping that this would force the two to work together.[74]

20 APRIL
FRIDAY

20 April was Hitler's last birthday. He arose at 1000 and received birthday greetings from the Americans who conducted a bombing raid at noon with nearly 300 B–17 bombers.[75] As he received his morning briefing he learned that the code word 'Clausewitz' was issued at 0400 with full power going to the *CBDA*.[76] Hitler received his birthday greetings during a small celebration arranged in a bombed-out hall of the New Reich Chancellery.[77] It was generally believed that Hitler would leave Berlin on 20 or 21 April and during the course of the day he was encouraged to leave by all his confidantes. Hitler refused all requests to leave reiterating his instructions issued on 14 April that in case Germany is split in two that *Groâadmiral* Karl Dönitz would take command of the north and *Generalfeldmarschall* Albert Kesselring the south.[78] Goebbels argued through passionate pleas with Hitler, the night before, that he had to stay in Berlin to see out the fight. Convinced by this, Hitler rebutted all calls for his departure by stating that "How can I motivate the troops to wage a decisive battle for Berlin if I escape to a safe place?"[79] This is presumably the first time Hitler mentioned waging a decisive battle for Berlin suggesting that he now began thinking of the Soviet drive on the capital in terms of a final battle that was tied to his own mortality. Perhaps inspired by Hitler's words, one of his guests, Heinrich Himmler, took time from the celebration to issue a communication to his two *Waffen-SS* divisions, *Nordland* and *Nederland,* now engaged in the fight to the east of Berlin. It read: "You are standing in the decisive battle in the east. There is no withdrawal or retreat. We have to stand to the last man or we have to attack. The fate of Europe is in your hands. Think of your dead comrades or the millions of Teutonic women and children. I expect ruthless conduct of battle and fullest performance of duty."[80] It is doubtful the communication was ever sent to the divisions by Heinrici's headquarters who were contending with frantic phone calls from subordinate commanders fighting for survival.

Heinrici's staff built an operational picture of Soviet movements and objectives opposite the *LVI Pz. Korps*. Based on intelligence gathered from captured documents, Russian prisoners (including spies dropped behind German lines from Soviet aircraft), and reports sent by the *9.Armee's* Operations Officer, Heinrici could see that the Soviets were attempting to use their tank armies to pierce the *LVI Pz. Korps* on either flank and drive northwest and southwest around Berlin. Soviet armored units of the 2nd Guards Tank Army including the 1st Mechanized Cavalry Corps, 9th Tank Corps, and 8th Guard Cavalry Corps were recorded advancing from Proetzel—Steinbech to the northwest. The 1st Guards Tank Army including the 11th Tank Corps and 2nd Guards Cavalry Corps left Müncheberg to the southwest in the direction of the Spree River.[81] The Soviets perceived that the German forces were weakest in the area northeast of Protzel and there is where they focused their air attack efforts with the hope of quickly gaining freedom of movement. During the night 713 bombers of the 18th Air Army and Po–2s of the 16th Air Army bombed German positions north and northeast of the city, softening them up for the advancing ground forces.[82] The movements of the Russians alarmed Busse who called Heinrici at 1050 and asked for instructions on conduct in the Battle for Berlin case his Army was split.[83] With news that 'Clausewitz' was issued, *CBDA* now fell under the responsibility of Heinrici who telephoned Reymann by 1500 and issued orders that no bridges should be blown unless *AGV* gave permission.[84]

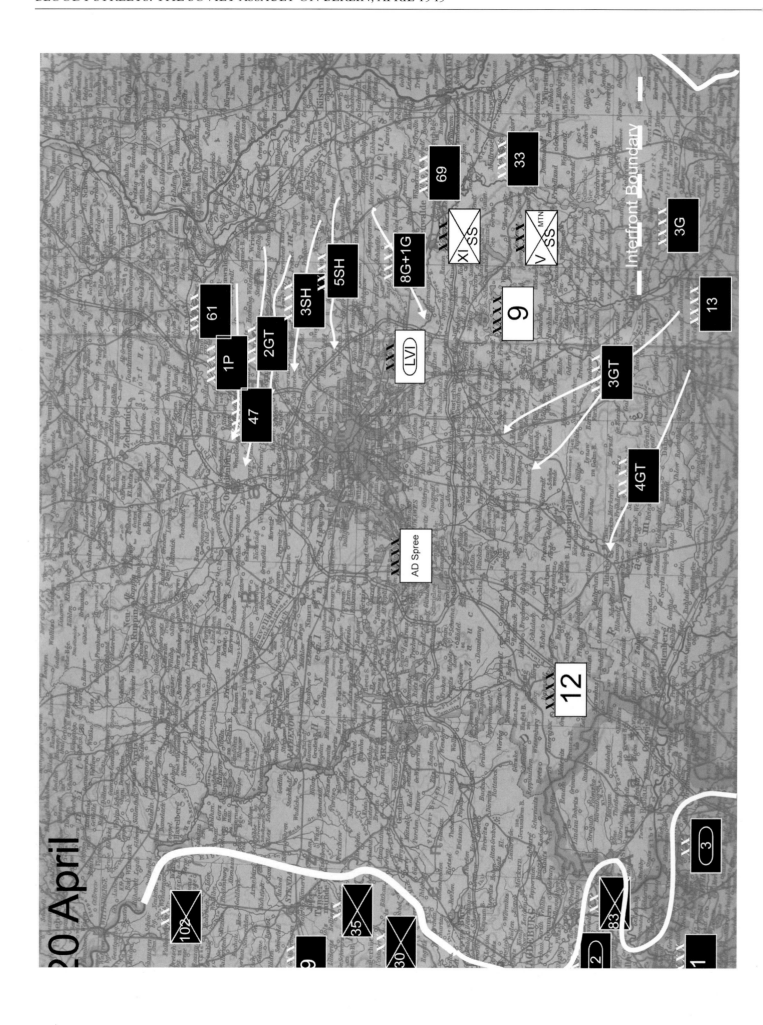

Heinrici's headquarters now received disturbing reports from the *3.Panzer Armee*. In the north the 2nd Byelorussian Front began its attack across the Oder with an artillery barrage starting at 0530.[85] By 0700 a full-scale attack was underway.[86]

The heavy losses on the direct route to Straussberg received the day before convinced Zhukov to alter his operational plan.[87] During the night the 12th Guards Tank Corps was ordered to reposition to the northeast for a drive southwest towards Werneuchen then to Altlandsberg behind the northern wing of Weidling's forces situated around Straussberg.[88] The 12th Guard Tank Corps arranged itself into two separate squadrons to give it flexibility in independent operations and to conserve force after the near disastrous losses over the last three days. Soviet corps acted without coordinating with units operating on their flanks. This was due to a lack of wireless communications and poor training. The 12th Guards Tank Corps was no exception, and reorganized its forces into two self-supporting squadrons. When one squadron ran into German resistance the other squadron could be called upon to encircle the force and strike from behind. The 49th Tank and 24th Independent Motorized Brigade were organized into the 2nd Squadron and the 66th and 48th Guards Tank Brigades were organized into the 1st Squadron. The assembly was done by 1300 hours. By 1600 hours 1st Squadron reached Werneuchen and was stopped by a combination of stiff resistance from the local *Volkssturm* and *Wehrmacht* defenders in the town, the remaining King Tigers of *s.SS-Pz.Abt.503* that kept the vanguard of the 9th Guards Tank Corps at bay the day before, and by artillery fire from the *408th Volksartillerie Korps* to the south. The 2nd Squadron was then ordered by Colonel Schevtschenko to drive southeast toward the village of Wesendahl, which was located west of Straussberg. The 2nd Squadron quickly took this undefended village and turned southwest and drove toward Alt Landsberg. Alt Landsberg was the last town outside of Greater Berlin and it now became the focus of the 5th Shock Army's drive. Artillery and aircraft were quickly sent to support the 12th Guards Tank Corps drive and at least 100 Soviet aircraft hit German positions around and inside the town. A 15-minute artillery barrage also struck the town. The 49th Tank Brigade drove into the southern section of the town, while the 34th Guards Motorized Brigade struck the north side. The German *Volkssturm* and *Hitlerjugend* defenders fought back fiercely using *Panzerfausts*. The 12th Guards Tank Corps came under heavy fire by *Panzerfausts* for the first time. This clearly shocked the Soviets as they ordered the 1st Squadron to reposition itself and combined forces with the 2nd Squadron in order to capture Alt Landsberg.[89] Despite the resistance, the 12th Guards Tank Corps was now well behind Weidling's north flank. Most of the German troops in Straussberg were cut off from behind as the Soviets began to shift forces from the 3rd Shock Army into the breach made by the Soviet armor. Meanwhile, the 5th Shock Army prepared to continue a push through the German resistance around the forests surrounding Grunow and drive directly into Straussberg.

The Soviets shelled the *SS-Pz.Gren.Rgt.24 Danmark* positions as well as Strausberg all day. East of Straussberg, the Soviets pushed through the weakened German positions in an effort to continue their drive west. Walter Timm, a *Leutnant* in the *SS-Pz.Abt.11 Hermann von Salza* was stationed just below a rise at the top of a hill near Klosterdorf and watched mass formations of T34/85s push through German lines and headed toward Straussberg.[90] The Soviets fought their way through the lines of *SS-Pz.Gren.Rgt.24 Danmark* killing the regimental commander von Klotz and his driver when an explosive shell from a JS–2 hit their staff car. *SS-Sturmbannführer* Per Sörensen now took over command of the regiment.[91]

Destroyed and abandoned German Sturmgeschütz, Pz.Kpw. IV/L, and SPWs lost during the fighting along the eastern approaches to Berlin. The Sturmgeschütz in the center-right appears to have received several hits in its lower hull.
Photo courtesy of RGAKFD, Moscow.

A panoramic view of captured German artillery guns after the battle of the Seelow Heights was over. The pace of Soviet operations ensured that many German units simply left the field without their guns as there was not enough motorized transport in the *Wehrmacht* at this stage of the war. Photo courtesy of the Bundesarchiv.

By 1900 the Soviets launched an assault on Straussberg with both armor and infantry taking the southern edge of town while hitting the eastern edge with rocket fire.[92] The *Nordland* division was ordered to retreat to Alt Landsberg. The NCOs of *Nordland* struggled to maintain an orderly retreat while forces were placed in blocking positions. As the units neared Alt Landsberg they found that the 12th Guard Tank Corps had already reached the town. The Germans could do nothing but retreat west. *SS-Untersturmführer* Henseler commanded the *3.Kompanie* of *Nordland's* engineer battalion. It took him two days to reach the area east of Straussberg. On the morning of 20 April he watched military police patrols gathering stragglers heading west from the Oder and forming them into combat groups. He also watched the remnants of the *9.Fallschirmjäger* retreat across his front in disorder. He was ordered to build a security line in the woods and also gather up stragglers but Russian artillery fire hit his positions in the woods forcing Henseler and his men to pull back. By evening they began to bed down for the night but soon heard tank tracks from the nearby road. When they investigated they saw a huge column of Soviet tanks heading toward Berlin. The hopelessness of the situation continued to affect *Nordland's* commander adversely as he celebrated his birthday. It was on this day that Zeigler decided the best thing to do was to avoid combat in Berlin and make for the west with his division. Zeigler ordered his staff to burn their pay books and papers identifying themselves as *Waffen-SS*. He also told his staff that they had to make it to the west and that this was the only chance for survival. Zeigler now devised a plan to escape west that he prepared to be briefed to his engineers.[93]

The collapse of Weidling's left wing forced many of his subordinate units to retreat toward southwest Berlin without orders or direction. Remnants of the *9.Fallschirmjäger,* and *Berlin Division* retreated southwest through Waldsieversdorf where they were joined by remnants of *Hj.PzJg.Rgt.K.* These soldiers began to move toward Reichsbahn 1.[94] The *Hitlerjugend* in particular demonstrated a significant zeal for combat and they constantly tried to stop the retreating German forces in order to reform the line and continue the fight. A member of the *Berlin Division* witnessed one engagement where the 16–17 year-old boys rounded up stragglers moving to the rear and forced them back into line. These particular *Hitlerjugend* were not heavily armed and already suffered losses at the hands of the Soviets. Despite these facts, they engaged Soviet armor with apparent zeal, knocking out several tanks at the extremely close distances of four or five meters. They did not retreat until the Soviets brought up reinforcements and attacked them from three sides.[95] There was no rest for the German or Soviets engaged in the battle. The momentum of operations began to move beyond human endurance after four days of non-stop fighting.

To the south the *20.Pz.Gren.Div.* continued to have trouble maintaining a front line during its withdrawal. Most of the division was strung out along roads leading west. The supply column was combed through for 90 men to establish a combat ready company. Even the signals platoon was broken up and the men used as frontline infantry. These soldiers were ordered to hold a position in the woods by evening. Soon 30 men of the newly formed company deserted on their bid for freedom. The Soviets now used incendiary shells in the wooded areas to set them on fire and drive out the German defenders. After the Soviet artillery barrage finished there was no sign of the other 90 men of the regiment. This force was then relieved by a mechanized infantry company equipped with a SPW and two Panther tanks from *Müncheberg.* A JS–2 broke through the lines destroying one Panther. As it drove up the lines it was knocked out by *Panzerfausts* and the second Panther waiting in ambush.[96]

The *LVI Pz. Korps* was completely cut off from neighboring units. The remnants of the *Berlin Division* were officially subordinated to Weidling, increasing his operational responsibility.[97] The *AGV* war diary recorded the Soviet's breakthroughs. The 1st Guards Tank Army "pierced our front in the area of the Autobahn Frankfurt-Berlin and the road Kustrin-Berlin by leaving behind its infantry … "[98] Despite Zhukov's orders for subordination and cooperation the tankers of the 1st Guards Tank Army were clearly in no mood to play second string to Chuikov's forces. The 2nd Guards Tank Army "succeeded in tearing up the forces of the *LVI Pz. Korps* and *CI Korps* and in breaking through in the section Straussberg-Bernau and in reaching the outer defense of area of Greater Berlin."[99] Weidling wrote on 20 April "that indeed [it] was a bitter day for my corps and to tell the truth for the whole of German formations. Having suffered enormous losses in continual battles, being broken into pieces and pressed to the extreme, they could no longer hold the powerful thrusts of the superior Russian forces … "[100] Concerns grew at *AGV* HQ that Berlin might become a battleground and it wanted no units to retreat into the city. Orders were issued by *AGV* to Weidling to hold in place, even though that meant being encircled.[101] The *LVI Pz. Korps*, despite the orders, was not in a state to continue a static defense. Ammunition was running out, fuel shortages were a problem, communication was inadequate and its subordinate formations were moving west and southwest trying to keep ahead of the next Soviet envelopment. Weidling ordered a general retreat southwest to begin on 21 April in order to rejoin the northern shoulder of Busse's *9.Armee*.[102] Due to rapid developments along Weidling's front all communications between the *LVI Pz. Korps* and its higher HQ ceased at 2000 hours. The lack of communications started a chain reaction that had terrible consequences for Weidling and Berlin.

Zhukov's forces finally broke through *9.Armee* defensive lines into the outer defensive belt of Greater Berlin. Now that 'Clausewitz' was declared in Berlin significant mobilization activity occurred throughout the city. *Hitlerjugend* and Levy I *Volkssturm* were mobilized and sent to the Oder Front. Local sports fields became mobilization centers for new recruits drafted from the local population as well as from *Wehrmacht* stragglers appearing in the city streets bringing tales of massive destruction by the Soviets. Signs called for a *Frontleitstelle* (collection points) at the Von Seekt barracks in Spandau where Martin Günzel arrived with an *Unteroffizer* and seventy-six survivors of the recent fighting east of Berlin.[103] In Spandau a mixture of 2,000 men of all services were already gathered and being organized into *Alarm Units* consisting of 167 men, 1 officer, and 1 NCO. They were armed with rifles only. A few of the soldiers were issued steel helmets if any were missing theirs. His unit received orders to integrate into the defense of the Friedrichshain Flak Tower that housed 15 officers, 60 NCOs and 1,500 soldiers. Most of these soldiers were *Luftwaffe* cadets between 15–16 years old armed with K98s, a few grenades, and plenty of *Panzerfausts*. During the following days Günzel's unit and other *Alarm Units* would operate against the Soviets that advanced into the eastern Defensive Zones. It was obvious to Berliners that the war was rapidly approaching their streets as they watched their young and old march east, and the dirty, tired, shell-shocked remnants of the *9.Armee* wandering through the city heading west.

KONIEV'S OFFENSIVE

Marshal Koniev launched his attack across the Niesse at 0610 Moscow time. Koniev's plan was to suppress the Germans on the far bank with his artillery and air forces while laying a thick smokescreen for his assault crossing that consisted of his 3rd Guards, 13th and 5th Guards Armies. The Soviet engineers worked tirelessly to provide crossing points. In the area of the main assault of the 3rd Guards and 13th Army there were twenty bridges, nine ferries, twelve assault landing points, and seventeen assault bridges.[104] The 3rd Guards and 4th Guards Tank armies began their crossing operations as soon as the lead infantry echelon cleared the far bank. Koniev's assault hit the northern end of the *4.Panzer Armee* that was part of *Armeegruppe Schörner*. Koniev knew that he had the authority to drive toward Berlin and he made sure that his forces knew it before the battle. He issued an addendum to the Stavka orders that read "Bear in mind that part of the forces of the right wing of the front will aid the troops of the 1st Byelorussian Front in capturing the city of Berlin."[105] In particular he singled the 3rd Guards Tank Army for this effort by issuing a specific order to "have in mind attacking Berlin from the south with a tank corps, reinforced with a rifle division from the 3rd Guards Army."[106] The *German High Command* expected an attack by Koniev but Hitler believed that he would drive south toward Dresden. Koniev, however, had other plans.

Koniev's forces met less prepared German defenses compared to Zhukov. Schörner did not have Heinrici's operational abilities and made no preparations for a fall back prior to the opening artillery engagement by the Soviets. Schörner was an ardent supporter of Hitler and appears to have generally disliked fixed defenses favoring mobile counterattacks. Schörner's formations defending against the immediate breakthrough were the *214* and *275.Infanterie Divisions* along with Kampfgruppe of both the *35.* and *36. Waffen-SS Divisions* in the first defensive line with the *10.SS-Panzer-Division Frundsberg* positioned as a mobile reserve. To the left of these formations were the *342.* and *545. Infanterie Division* along with the *Führer-Begleit Brigade* in reserve. These units were part of the *V Korps*. In reserve behind the front was the *21.Panzer Division [hereafter referred to as 21.Pz.Div]*. The rapid advance of Koniev's tank armies split the northern wing of the *4.Panzer Armee* forcing the *V Korps* along with the *21.Pz.Div.* into the *9.Armee* lines. The other units hit by the Koniev's onslaught disintegrated and split into small groups either heading north with the *V Korps* or west.

In the first twenty-four hours of operation Koniev's forces reached the Spree River where the 3rd Guards Tank Army proceeded to conduct an assault crossing using shallow water fords.[107] Koniev was now over both main water obstacles and in a position to strike north toward his ultimate goal. Koniev spoke to Stalin about his progress during an evening phone call and suggested turning his forces north toward Berlin.[108] In a well-recorded exchange, Stalin immediately asked if Zhukov might be able to reposition his forces and head south to take advantage of Koniev's success. Koniev quickly rebutted stating that such a move was impractical as his tank armies were already positioned for the assault. Stalin agreed and gave Koniev the go ahead to turn his forces toward Berlin. Koniev now informed his tank commanders to open the sealed envelopes in their pockets. As Koniev stated in a postwar interview "they had their orders in their pockets" before he issued the new direction of attack toward Berlin.[109] Unlike Zhukov, Koniev planned carefully before the battle to position his forces for just this moment. His operational plan was detailed out for the first 2–3 days with the goal of making the broad turn toward Berlin.

The 3rd Guards Tank Army was now ordered to drive toward Teltow and the 4th Guards Tank Army toward Potsdam and capture the southwest portion of Berlin. Koniev issued specific orders that this would be a fast drive—or a race. "In the main direction, with a tank spearhead, move ahead courageously and decisively. Bypass the cities and frontal battles. I require that you firmly understand that the success of the tank armies depends upon courageous maneuver and rapidity in their actions."[110] By the end of 19 April the 3rd Guards Tank Army advanced 35 kilometers while the 4th Guards Tank Army advanced 50 kilometers. In the south, pockets of German forces continued to resist in his rear area as well as in the large towns of Spremberg and Cottbus.

AGV watched these movements with great concern and sent meager *Luftwaffe* resources south in aerial reconnaissance flights to monitor the situation. On 20 April they reported that on the Cottbus-Lübben road there were 800 tanks and 500 motorized vehicles with infantry marching northwest. On the Kalau-Golsen road were an additional 300 tanks with 500 motor vehicles and infantry marching northwest.[111] Later that day these sightings were again updated by the reports of infantry on the ground and additional aerial reconnaissance dismissing ideas that there were over 1,000 enemy tanks on the move toward Berlin. The real number was still high. To the west of Lübben were indeed 360 tanks and 700 motor vehicles in two columns that advanced 37 kilometers that taking Baruth during the afternoon and almost reaching Zossen before disaster struck. The reports that Heinrici received noted that Koniev's column was halted and that they most likely ran out of fuel. These latter reports were correct as the 3rd Guards Tank Army did run out of its petrol supply. The leading brigade of the 6th Guards Tank Corps stopped cold without petrol and was destroyed piecemeal during a German counterattack

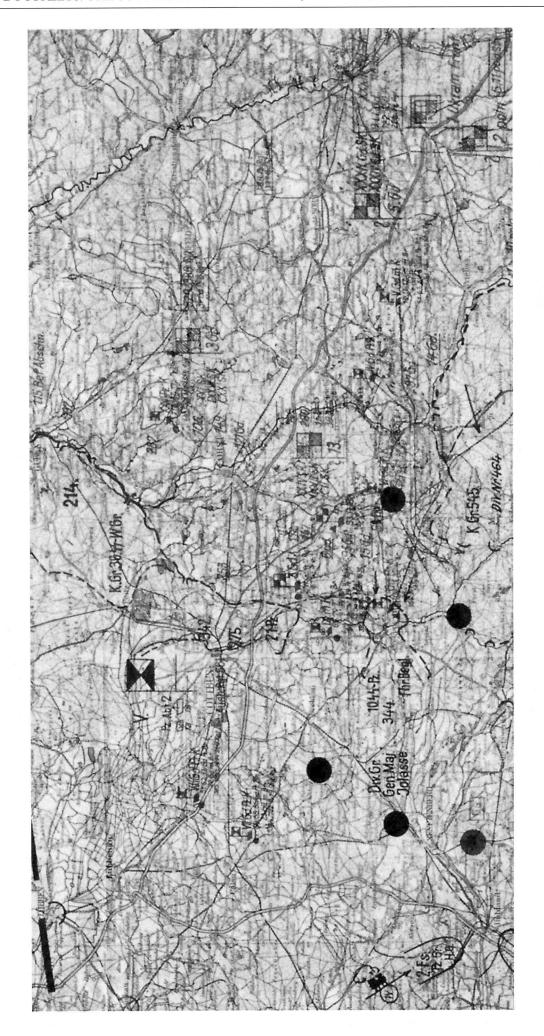

19 April *AGV* Daily Situational Map. Far to the south of Zhukov's main effort, Koniev's forces have breached the northern wing of *AGC* and lead elements of the 3rd Guards Tank Army are on their way northwest toward Berlin. Courtesy of the US National Archives.

As the Soviet reached the outer defense zone of Berlin they encountered fortifications and Dragon's Teeth for the first time along Eastern Front. Soviet Army; photo courtesy of the Cornelius Ryan Collection, Mahn Center, Alden Library, Ohio University, Athens, OH.

by soldiers armed with *Panzerfausts*.[112] Without petrol no other support could be dispatched from the column. Koniev, like Zhukov was not above pushing his forces beyond their capabilities even if it meant risking the lives of his own soldiers.

Hitler and the *German High Command* now realized that there was no attack toward Dresden or Prague. Berlin was Koniev's target.[113] New formations were called up to stem Koniev's approach. The *Friedrich Ludwig Jahn RAD Infanterie Division* and 6–8 Panthers from the Wünsdorf training area were sent south of Zossen to engage the Soviets. As these reinforcements arrived and were forming the Soviet 4th Guards Tank Army attacked and scattered the division. The division's commander was captured and one regiment lost. Krebs now ordered them back to Potsdam.[114] Other formations were thrown together around southern Berlin. A special armored halftrack company was formed in Spandau that consisted of three platoons with a total of 14 Sd.Kfz. 251s consisting of various models to include the 251/1 Nebelwerfer Rocket Launcher model, the 251/9 with the 7.5cm StuK 37 L/24 anti-tank gun, and the 251/16 flamethrower model. Several *Kampfgruppe* were also organized. *Kampfgruppe Möws* was joined with *Kampfgruppe Kaether* near Zossen and consisted of a variety of unusual combat vehicles drawn from local German military depots and ordnance facilities. The *Kampfgruppe* consisted of the *II./Panzer Regiment.36, 4./Panzer-Regiment.11, Panzergreandier-Kompanie Ülzen, Panzer-Kompanie Kummendsdorf, Panzerjäger-Kompanie Dresden*, and *schwere Panzerjäger-Kompanie.614*, which was equipped with Elefant tank destroyers. The Elefant was also known as the Panzerjäger Tiger (P) Ferdinand. This fixed turret weapon platform consisted of the 8.8cm Pak 43/2 L/71 main gun and had massive frontal armor of 200mm+ and side armor of 100mm+. The Elefants were effective in the defense but prone to mechanical failures. Two of the Elefants made their way into Berlin and fought in the central districts.[115] On 22 April, another formation called *Kampfgruppe Ritter* formed taking over the Panzer elements of *Kampfgruppe Kaether* after it suffered losses by the Soviets.[116] Despite the last ditch efforts to throw forces in Koniev's way, Soviet armor continued to push forward. Koniev's avenue of approach into Berlin was wide open by 22 April.

BEYOND THE ODER

The battle for the Oder Front was over. The assault on Berlin was about to begin. Heinrici was unable to hold the Soviets along the Oder River long enough to entice the Western Allies across the Elbe and into Berlin first. After four days of continuous fighting Busse's northern wing collapsed under the massive Soviet pressure. Zhukov's forces ripped a gap in the German lines and were now pouring through an ever-widening breach toward Berlin. In the south, Koniev managed a quick defeat of the German forces and was now driving northwest toward Berlin against sporadic resistance by *ad-hoc* formations. Heinrici did all he could do to ensure Berlin was emptied of combat troops by ordering all remaining formations in the city to the Oder Front after 'Clausewitz' was declared. Heinrici now expected Weidling to move south into the northern wing

Towed 8.8cm Flak 36/37 AA destroyed or overrun by advancing Soviet columns during the retreat toward Berlin.
Photo courtesy of Wydawnictwo Militaria

Panther 312, presumably from *Kampfgruppe* Kather, which was sent into action against Koniev's forces. The Swastika was placed on
the panzer by the crew, but it was purposely highlighted on the photograph by the Soviet photographer.
Photo courtesy of Wydawnictwo Militaria

of the *9.Armee* and avoid any combat in Berlin. Heinrici's main concern was to prevent the *9.Armee* from being encircled by a combination of forces from both the 1st Byelorussian, and 1st Ukrainian Fronts. Berlin was left to its own defenses and Heinrici hoped that the city would either be declared 'Free' or that resistance would be minimal and quickly overcome by the Soviets to prevent significant destruction and suffering of the population. Heinrici, however, didn't realize the polarized forces now at work to shape Berlin's final fate. The *German High Command* was determined to defend Berlin by any means in a final climatic battle for the survival of Hitler's National Socialist State. Whether Berlin was declared 'Free' or defended mattered little to the Soviets. Conquering Berlin was not simply an act of military necessity to the Soviets but a *divine* right—the Soviets were going to assault Berlin and plant their flag on the burned-out roof the Reichstag.

Notes to Chapter 5

1   S. I. Golbov interview, (RC: 72/1).
2   Moscow Time.
3   Le Tissier, *Zhukov on the Oder*, pp. 15–9.
4   Oder and Berlin Russian Participants interviews, (RC: 73/7).
5   Ibid.
6   Ibid.
7   Le Tissier, *With Our Backs to Berlin*, pp. 100-101.
8   Le Tissier, *Zhukov on the Oder*, pp. 171–2.
9   Chuikov, p. 146.
10 Ibid, p. 147.
11 Le Tissier, *With Our Backs to Berlin*, p. 92.
12 N. N. Popiel unpublished account, pp. 4-5. (RC: 74/12)
13 Le Tissier, *With Our Backs to Berlin*, p. 101.
14 Chukov, pp. 150-151.
15 H. Jansen interview, (RC: 69/11)
16 Le Tissier, *Zhukov on the Oder*, p. 169.
17 Le Tissier, *With Our Backs to Berlin*, p. 40.
18 Yedenskii, p. 41.
19 Ibid.
20 Popiel, p. 9.
21 Ibid.
22 Yedenskii, pp. 41–2.
23 Ibid, p. 41.
24 Popiel, p. 7.
25 Ibid, p. 8.
26 Ibid, pp. 6-7.
27 T-311: 169/7221761 "Tagesmeldung"
28 T-311: 169/7221747, Weidling interrogation report, and Le Tissier, *Zhukov on the Oder*, p. 206.
29 Ryan outline notes, (RC: 75/1).
30 Weidling Interrogation Report.
31 Le Tissier, *With Our Backs to Berlin*, p. 102.
32 Ibid., p. 103.
33 Ibid., p. 104, and Le Tissier, *Zhukov on the Oder*, p. 202.
34 Popiel, p. 10.
35 Le Tissier, *With Our Backs to Berlin*, p. 115.
36 Stimpel, p. 86.
37 Ibid., p. 99.
38 Ibid., p. 100.
39 Le Tissier, *With Our Backs to Berlin*, p. 44.
40 Bötteler interview.
41 T-311: 169/7221763.
42 Weidling Interrogation Report.
43 Ibid.

44 T-311: 169/7221761.
45 Stimpel, p. 106.
46 Henseler interview.
47 Hillblad, p. 60.
48 Dufving interview and Weidling interrogation report.
49 Weidling interrogation report.
50 H.P. Scholles interview, (RC: 69/24).
51 Le Tissier, *With Our Backs to Berlin*, p. 107.
52 Le Tissier, *Zhukov on the Oder*, p. 217.
53 Illum interview.
54 Ibid., p. 4.
55 Le Tissier, *Zhukov on the Oder*, p. 225.
56 Ibid., p. 221.
57 Schultz-Naumann, pp. 159.
58 Böttcher interview.
59 Ibid.
60 Scholles interview.
61 N. Skorodumov, "Maneuvers of the 12th Guards Tank Corps in the Berlin Operation," p. 1.
62 Illum interview.
63 Schneider, p. 300.
64 Sharp, *Soviet Armor Tactics in World War II*, p. 92.
65 Schneider, p. 301, Fey, p. 314.
66 Ibid.
67 Scholles, p. 4.
68 Skorodumov, p. 5.
69 Chuikov, p. 157.
70 A. L. Getman, *Tanks are Heading to Berlin*, p. 337.
71 Army Group Weichsel War Diary, Apr 20–9, pp. 18–19 (RC: 64/3).
72 Chuikoiv, pp. 157–8.
73 Ibid.
74 Le Tissier, *Race for the Reichstag*, p. 29.
75 Ibid., pp. 36-37.
76 A. Lampe interview, (RC: 67/10).
77 J. Fest, *Hitler's Bunker*, p. 45.
78 Le Tissier, *Race for the Reichstag*, p. 37, and Fest, pp. 45–6.
79 Quoted in Fest, p. 47.
80 Army Group Weichsel War Diary, Apr 20-29, pp. 32 (RC: 68/4). This was never distributed to his formations.
81 Army Group Weichsel War Diary, Apr 20-29, pp. 14–17 (RC: 64/3).
82 Le Tissier, *Race for the Reichstag*, p. 39.

83 Army Group Weichsel War Diary, Apr 20–9, p. 29 (RC: 68/4).
84 Ibid.
85 Army Group Weichsel War Diary, Apr 20–9, p. 28 (RC: 68/4).
86 Heinrici memoir, (RC: 68:3).
87 Skorodumov, p. 3.
88 Ibid, p. 1.
89 Ibid, p. 3.
90 W. Timm interview (RC: 69/25), and Haas interview.
91 Illum and Scholles interview.
92 Scholles and Illum interview.
93 Roman Burghart interview (RC: 69/16).
94 Stimpel, pp. 108, and Jansen interview.
95 Le Tissier, *With Our Backs to Berlin*, p. 46.
96 Ibid., p. 117.
97 Weidling interrogation report.
98 Army Group Weichsel War Diary, Apr 20–9, p. 18 (RC: 64/3).
99 Ibid.
100 Weidling Interrogation Report.
101 Army Group Weichsel War Diary, Apr 20–9, p. 28 (RC: 64/3).
102 Weidling Interrogation Report.
103 W. Venghaus, *Berlin 1945: Die Zeit vom 16. April bis 2. Mai: Eine Dokumentation in Berichten, Bildern und Bemerkungen*, p. 160.
104 Koniev unpublished memoir, p. 71.
105 Ibid, p. 66.
106 Ibid.
107 Le Tissier, *Zhukov on the Oder*, pp. 6-7.
108 Ibid, pp. 81–2.
109 Ibid. pp. 86–7, and Le Tissier, *Slaughter at Halbe: The Destruction of Hitler's 9th Army, April 1945*, p. 18.
110 Koniev interview.
111 Koniev unpublished memoir, p. 89.
112 Army Group Weichsel War Diary, Apr 20–9, p. 17 (RC: 64/3)
113 Ibid, pp. 18–9.
114 Schultz-Naumann, p. 160.
115 Le Tissier, *Race for the Reichstag*, pp. 34–5.
116 Ibid.
117 K. Münch, *The Combat History of the German Heavy Anti-Tank Unit 653 in World War II*, pp. 226–7.

6

ASSAULT ON BERLIN

21 APRIL
SATURDAY

ARMY GROUP VISTULA

Not until morning did Heinrici fully grasp the scope of the Soviet breakthrough across Busse's front and confirm that the objective was in fact Berlin. He knew communication was lost with Weidling's *LVI Pz. Korps* since 2000 hours the night before and that fighting was ongoing across Busse's sector. Intelligence reports filtered in from various commanders with a continuous theme of disintegrating units and retreats. Heinrici now ordered *CBDA* at 0930 to send all available *Volkssturm* to the Oder Front in support of the *9.Armee* under his authority as commander of *AGV*, in which Berlin was placed after the start of 'Clausewitz.' He ordered Reymann "to pull out everyone and to defend Berlin, if possible, far away from Berlin."[1] With the Oder Front wide open Heinrici now vowed to draw forces from the Reich's capital to avoid undue destruction and suffering in the city. This was not his first call for troops as operational maps show twelve *Volkssturm* battalions from Levy I, the remnants of the *Wachregiment Großdeutschland*, elements of two *SS Polizei Bataillons*, and a new *Kampfgruppe* known as *Regiment Solar en route* to the Oder Front as early as 19 April.[2] On 20 April it was reported that at least nine *Volkssturm* battalions were sent into the *9.Armee* area of operations alone to act as a blocking force at various locations.[3] Goebbels became concerned about the forces being pulled out of Berlin and asked Hitler to authorize the replacement of Reymann as *CBDA* in the early afternoon. Hitler obliged and *General* Kuntze was appointed *CBDA* later in the day. Kuntze was the head of the *National Socialistische Führungs Offiizer (NSFO)* organization.[4] It was believed that Kuntze was an ardent Nazi with the correct level of ideological support for the regime. Reymann, in turn, was then placed in charge of *Armee Detachment Spree* located in and around Potsdam.[5] Heinrici's efforts offered little respite for the beleaguered *9.Armee*. As Berlin was emptied of forces they ran smack into the vanguard of a fast-moving Soviet juggernaut that had little taste for pitched battles after the horrendous losses it had suffered over the last four days. Many of the *Volkssturm* units were caught in the open while on the move and quickly defeated in the face of withering firepower and determined Soviet armored forces. Fixed German strongpoints found themselves quickly bypassed and surrounded.[6]

1st BYELORUSSIAN FRONT

The fall of Müncheberg brought operational freedom for the 1st Byelorussian Front. Zhukov now directed his forces to surround Berlin from the north and south. The 2nd Guards Tank Army soon crossed the autobahn ring on the northeast side of Berlin while in the south the 8th Guards and 1st Guards Tank Armies received orders to swing southwest and approach the city from that direction in order to isolate Berlin from German forces outside the city. Zhukov grew concerned with the inactivity of the *9.Armee* to his south as he was not sure what Busse's intentions were. He pulled the 69th Army from deployment on the Oder and dispatched it with the 3rd Army to seal off the *9.Armee* from the north. Unknown to Zhukov, elements of Koniev's 28th Army were driving north along Busse's western shoulder.

The 12th Guards Tank Corps successfully captured Alt Landsberg in the morning after an evening of fierce fighting that cost it a number of tanks. This tank unit in the vanguard of the Soviet advance was now poised to drive directly into Berlin. The previously day's drive by the 12th Guard Tank Corps cut the avenues of retreat behind the *LVI Pz. Korps* forcing German stragglers southwest. The Soviet tankers cut a path into the German defense over the last several days that allowed the 26th Guards Rifle Corps of the 5th Shock Army to advance 23 kilometers from Straussberg to the eastern districts of Berlin one day. The infantry continued to clear pockets of German resistance left behind as it closed up the gap with the armor forces. After resting for the better part of the day and allowing the corps' infantry to catch up, new movement orders were issued. The 48th Guards Tank Brigade was given the orders to take the village of Menow from the rear then continue to Ahrensfelde. The 49th Guards Tank Brigade received orders to take up position south of Hoenow to hold the flank of the 48th Guards Tank Brigade then prepare to assault into Kaulsdorf and Marzhan. The 34th Guards Motorized Rifle Brigade was to push south at Kaulsdorf and take Lichtenberg.[7] The 66th Guards Tank Brigade was to take the town of Eiche then move into corps reserve. This plan was unrealistically ambitious. The 12th Guards Tank Corps indeed had advanced farthest into Greater Berlin than any other Soviet unit at that point, but where it took the entire corps to capture the town of Alt Landsberg after nearly a day of fighting, the corps commander decided to split his forces and spread them out in a 7 kilometer arc driving his tank units uncoordinated into a difficult and unknown urban environment. This plan was presumably approved by Zhukov. By 2000 hours an unknown German unit of battalion strength and with 12 Panzers struck the corps south of Hoenow. The only known German unit operating in this location with Panzers was the *Wachregiment Großdeutschland*. The soldiers of *Großdeutschland* were either advancing toward the Oder Front or pulling back into Berlin. After fighting off the German counterattack the Soviet Corps Commander, General Schevtschenko, instructed his senior

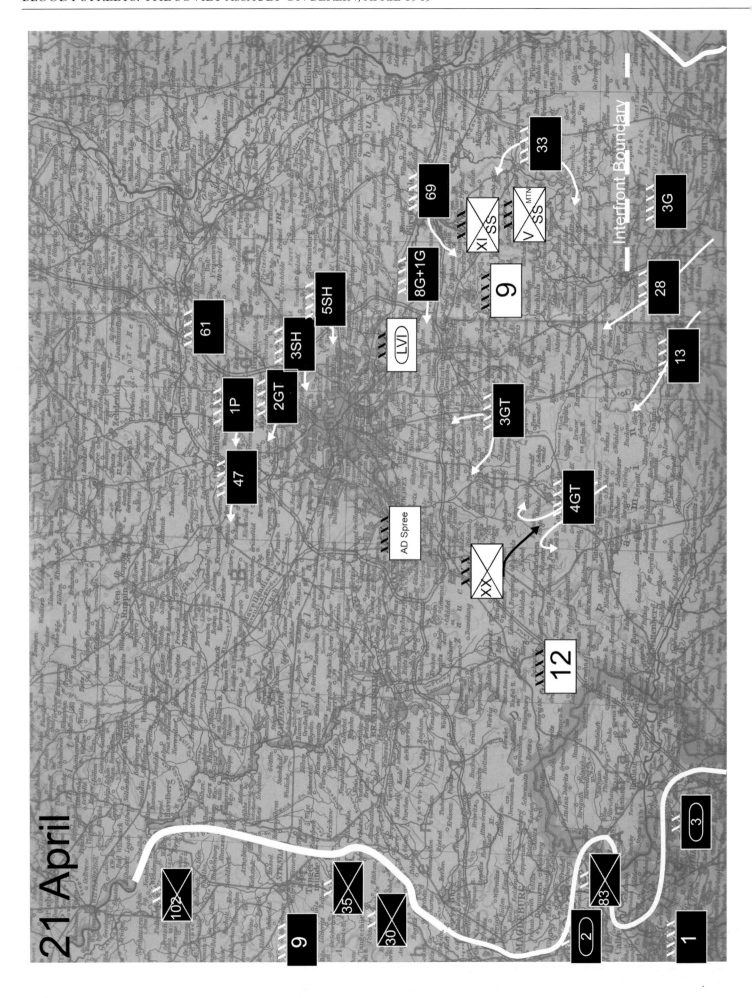

21 April

Polish troops move on Berlin from the north. They are using a lend-lease American truck to tow their 76-mm ZIS-3 gun. Photo courtesy of the Bulgarian Ministry of Defence.

commissar to bolster his troop's morale. Schevtschenko had driven his tankmen non-stop since 16 April and they suffered significant losses in both men and material over several sharp engagements. They must have been on the verge of physical collapse, and certainly his subordinate commanders were probably questioning their future orders. In addition, the luxuries encountered by Soviet soldiers in the middle class German homes caused looting that combined with the ever-present raping of German women served to undercut discipline.[8] According to the Soviet account, Schevtschenko now instructed Commissar Colonel A. A. Vitruk to make his rounds of all the battalions that night in order to ensure his troops were mentally prepared for the next assault into a city of "millions of inhabitants."[9]

FÜHRERBUNKER

Berlin made the transition from a distant target to the front line overnight. By mid-afternoon the predictable aerial bombings were replaced by ferocious Soviet ground artillery. Soviet long-barreled guns now fired shells into Alexanderplatz and the Tiergarten indiscriminately.[10] The artillery was more horrific than the aerial bombing raids. Artillery shells landed without warning sending shrapnel in a wide arc. The immediate Soviet threat finally spurred Berlin officials to shut down factories as the city's fuel stocks at the power stations were almost depleted. Soon the use of utilities was curtailed with electricity and gas usage forbidden except for hospitals, and other key facilities. Public transportation was also limited to essential movement by officers.[11] Berliners now faced the impending horrors of urban ground combat.

In the *Führerbunker* Hitler had an afternoon conference where he received a continuous stream of alarming news about the advance of Soviet armored forces all around Berlin. Among the key issues was the location of the *LVI Pz. Korps*, the potential for the *CI Korps* to

"Berlin Remains German!" Slogans such as this greeted the advancing Soviets as they reached the outskirts of Berlin. Here a Soviet ISU-152 passes a JS-2 as it advances down a residential street in the suburbs of Berlin. Courtesy of the US National Archives.

launch a spoiling attack into the flank of Zhukov's forces, and the possible pull back of the *9.Armee* to shorten the front. By 1600 *AGV* reported that there was a "Complete gap between Finow-Kanal and the northern end of the *LVI Pz. Korps*. The troops near Bernau has dissolved, enemy can simply walk into Berlin. In the back of the *9.Armee,* northern bottleneck already half-closed [by Soviets]."[12] The supply situation now became acute for Busse's forces. A different report by *AGV* diverted a train with fuel and supplies destined for southern Germany to the *9.Armee*. It was made clear though, that Busse's force had to fall back south of Berlin to obtain ammunition.[13] Hitler's decision was clear. No pullback of any unit of the *9.Armee* was forthcoming. Instead they would hold in place. In addition he ordered an immediate attack into Zhukov's right flank from Eberswalde with Steiner's *III (germ.) SS-Pz. Korps* now renamed *Armeegruppe Steiner* and Weidling's *LVI Pz. Korps*. Hitler's order stated:

> It is the exclusive task of *Armeegruppe Steiner* to restore by attack with *4.SS Polizei Division* and if possible, with strong forces of the *5.Jaeger Division* and the *25.Panzergrenadier Division* which have to be released by the *3rd Marine Division*, then link with the units of the *LVI Panzer Korps (SS-Panzergrenadier Division 'Nordland'), 18.Panzergrenadier Division, 20.Panzergrenadier Division, Panzer Division Müncheberg,* and part of the *9.Fallschirmjäger Division* and to defend the link up by all means.
> It is expressly forbidden to fall back to the west.
> Officers who do not comply unconditionally with this order are to be arrested and shot right away.
> You (Steiner) are answerable with your head for the execution of this order.
> The fate of the Reich's capital depends upon the success of your mission.[14]

Steiner's order came straight to him bypassing normal command channels. This order marked a transition in authority regarding military operations around Berlin from Heinrici to the *Führerbunker*.

Hitler's micro-management is typical of how operations were conducted during the later stages of the war. Heinrici had already endured the loss of key Panzer divisions by Hitler in March, and Hitler interfered with the planned deployment of the *18.Pz.Gren.Div.* that caused its deployment to be virtually useless in the defense of the Oder Front. His new order upset both Steiner and Heinrici. Steiner had no forces that could launch this offensive immediately.[15] Steiner reported to Krebs through *AGV* that "because of the overall situation the order cannot be carried out. Won't even have the time to do it. The Divisions [required for the offensive] have already taken up positions in a broad front, defending themselves." Krebs reply was an adamant re-statement that the offensive must take place.[16] Heinrici was appalled and told Krebs that the situation with the *9.Armee* was critical now that the Soviets almost completed their encirclement and that there was no value in launching Steiner's attack. The only option was to pull the *9.Armee* out of its positions along the Oder River to prevent Soviet encirclement. Heinrici backed his report by telling Krebs that if Hitler didn't reconsider his plans then he would relinquish command of *AGV*.[17] This attitude caused Krebs to replace Heinrici's Chief of Staff General Eberhart Kinzel with General Ivo-Thilo von Trotha. Krebs believed von Trotha to be an ardent Nazi and that he would monitor Heinrici's decisions. In fact von Trotha had served under Heinrici before and was not sympathetic to Krebs.[18] The stage was now set for the *Führerbunker* to take over complete command of the operations around Berlin the coming days. As evening approached, the soldiers of the *LVI Pz. Korps* engaged in fierce rearguard actions as they continued their retreat to the southwest.[19]

LVI PZ. KORPS

The intact formations of the *LVI Pz. Korps* withdrew back toward Berlin during the night of 20/21 April. They were without communication to higher headquarters, and constantly on the defensive as they fought fierce rearguard battles to prevent encirclement by the pursuing Soviet armor columns that finally gained freedom of movement after four harsh days of combat. All manner of German vehicles flooded toward the city along clogged roads, particularly Reichsbahn 1, which served as the main east-west artery to Berlin.[20] Under Weidling's direction the majority of units in his command maneuvered southwest in an attempt to reach the *9.Armee*. Lead elements of the *20.Pz.Gren.Div.* reached Köpenick by morning while the rest of the division was strung out over a 9-kilometers column. In this quiet southeast suburb of Berlin they were greeted by incredulous looks from the inhabitants who now realized that the slogans painted on the local town centre walls that read "Berlin Remains German!" and "*Panzerfausts* and soldiers are stronger than Soviet Tanks!" now meant something.[21] Averdieck looked around from his SPW and noted the lack of Berlin's defenses. It appeared to him that there was no single force or command in charge. Everything he saw gave a feeling of inevitable defeat.[22] *Müncheberg* reached the suburb of Rüdersdorf, 13.5 kilometers to the east of the *20.Pz.Gren.Div.* after forty-eight hours of non-stop movement from the town of Müncheberg. Arriving between the two formations was the intact *18.Pz.Gren.Div.* that maintained good order during the retreat. Farther north *Nordland* was in disarray and retreating directly into Berlin due to the continued Soviet pressure the divisional elements found themselves under.

Elements of *Nordland* retreated west-southwest in a 13 kilometer arc between Friedrichshain and Köpenick. The main elements of *SS-Pz.Gren.Rgt.24 Danmark* moved west in four large columns down Reichsbahn 1 into Berlin.[23] As *Nordland* reached Berlin, soldiers of the unit encountered frequent checkpoints manned by *Hitlerjugend, Feldgendarmerie,* or *SS*. If you didn't have the correct movement orders you were quickly placed into *ad-hoc* formations or *Alarm Units* and sent back to the front. Everything was in a state of confusion as Soviet artillery and aircraft continued to interrupt the retreating units and everywhere soldiers reported Soviet tanks, most of which were nothing more than hallucinations caused by lack of sleep and stress. One German veteran of *Nordland*, Heinz Genzow, reached Alexanderplatz with elements of *SS-Flak-Abt.11* when he was confronted by officials to determine if he had the correct movement orders. Genzow's memory still recalled years that his first impression of Berlin was that the city was a 'witch's cauldron' where you had no idea where the enemy was at any given time.[24]

Other units broke down under the pressure that fighting over the last several days inflicted. Motivation and morale were key problems. The divisional commander of the *Berlin Division* brought the remnants of his soldiers together and ordered the men to "'Make sure that you get home safe and sound. There is no sense in this anymore'"[25] Voigtsberger, the divisional commander, continued to serve Weidling as a liaison officer after he disbanded the remnants of his division.

Notes to Chapter 6: Assault on Berlin, 21st April Saturday

1   Army Group Weichsel War Diary, Apr
    20–9, pp. 80, 81 (RC: 64/3).
2   Ibid, p. 19.
3   Army Group Weichsel War Diary, Apr
    20–9, p. 35 (RC: 68/4).
4   The *NSFO* was established on 22
    December 1943 to increase ideological
    indoctrination of the *Wehrmacht* based on
    Hitler's belief that the German Army was
    not capable of continuing an ideological
    struggle. The *NSFOs* were based on the
    Soviet Commissar model and the
    organization's influence increased after the
    failed assassination plot to kill Hitler on
    20 July 1944. See Bracher, *The German
    Dictatorship*, (Praeger: New York) p. 462,
    T-77: 852/5597556 and "XVI. Die
    Mitwirkung der Partei on der politischer
    Aktivierung der Wehrmacht," T-77:
    852/5597604.
5   Army Group Weichsel War Diary, Apr
    20–9, pp. 63, 64, 80, 81, 93, 94 (RC:
    64/3).
6   Ibid, p. 118.
7   Skorodumov, p. 3.
8   *After the Reich*, pp. 95–102. A different
    view comes from Zhukov himself who
    viewed the rapes as a product of his
    soldier's demoralization after years of
    combat instead of a cause of
    demoralization. See Zhukov, p. 202.
9   Skorodumov, p. 3.
10 Army Group Weichsel War Diary, Apr
    20–9, p. 98 (RC: 68/4).
11 Le Tissier, *Race for the Reichstag*, p. 21.
12 Army Group Weichsel War Diary, Apr
    20–9, p. 101 (RC: 68/4).
13 Army Group Weichsel War Diary, Apr
    20–9, pp. 132/133 (RC: 64/3).
14 Source is Ryan AGV 77/78 message to
    OKH. Army Group Weichsel War Diary,
    Apr 20–9, p. 74 (RC: 68/4).
15 Schultz-Naumann, p. 161.
16 Army Group Weichsel War Diary, Apr
    20–9, p. 111 (RC: 68/4).
17 Ibid, p. 76.
18 Ibid, pp. 93-94.
19 Schultz-Naumann, p. 166, and Ibid, p. 110.
20 Le Tissier, *With Our Backs to Berlin*, p. 47.
21 Bensch Interview, p4.
22 Le Tissier, *With Our Backs to Berlin*,
    pp. 117–18.
23 Scholles interview.
24 Venghaus, p. 160.
25 Le Tissier, *With Our Backs to Berlin*,
    pp. 48.

6

ASSAULT ON BERLIN

22 APRIL
SUNDAY

FÜHRERBUNKER

In Berlin the last issue of the newspaper *Das Reich* was published with an editorial by Goebbels entitled "Resistance at any price." The article ominously called for the sacrifice of every man, woman, and child in the defense of Berlin. Goebbels wrote: "The hour of the last triumph is awaiting us. It will be bought with blood and tears but it will justify all the sacrifices that we have made."[1] There was, however, no clear-cut plan for a decisive blow against the Soviets. In the *Führerbunker* moods of depression and excitement swung like a pendulum throughout the day as it became obvious that Steiner was not going to launch the attack as ordered. Hitler held his daily conference at 1500 with Bormann, Keitel, Jodl and Krebs in attendance. He declared his intention to stay in Berlin and see out the fighting while sending Generals Keitel, Jodl, as well as Bormann to southern Germany to continue directing the war from there. Hitler was later swayed from this order and convinced that Berlin could be relieved and the Soviets defeated by a pincer movement combining Steiner's forces from the north with an advance on the city by the 9.*Armee* in the southeast and the new 12.*Armee* in the west. U.S. forces had stopped at the Elbe and made no serious attempt to cross the demarcation line outlined in 'Eclipse'. This signaled to the German General Staff that 'Eclipse' was valid and that the 12.*Armee* under *General* Walter Wenck could turn east toward Berlin without any interference by the Western Allies. Keitel, Jodl, and Krebs were the architects of this plan and not Hitler. It does not appear that Hitler could have developed this plan in his deteriorating mental state especially when toward the end of the day he reportedly told his Generals rather despondently "Do whatever you want. I'm not giving orders anymore."[2] Later in the day he directed a message broadcast a message stating to Berliners that he would remain the city to the end.[3] *OKW* and *OKH* staffs were now combined into a single operations staff and sent to Plön where it would serve both Dönitz and Hitler. Calls went out across Germany for all military assistance to be sent to Berlin. Immediate support arrived at 2300 as 600 *SS* soldiers sent by Himmler from his personal bodyguard battalion arrived. These forces were immediately incorporated into the Zitadel garrison and dispersed through the Government Quarter.

Goebbels decided to exert his influence by removing the *CBDA* and *AGV* from the responsibility of defending Berlin. He grew concerned at the movement of the *Volkssturm* battalions out of the city and perhaps suspected some complicity between Reymann and Heinrici. Now that it was decided to make Berlin the focal point of one last decisive battle, Goebbels wanted to ensure that no one subverted the final plan. He demoted *Leutnant General* Kaether back to the rank of *Oberst* and removed him from his position as head of the *CBDA*. *AGV* was removed from any responsibility over the defense of Berlin. Under Goebbels influence, Hitler now took personal command for the defense of Berlin.[4] Orders went out from the *Führerbunker* to send all *Volkssturm* battalions back to Berlin. These units were to be replaced by thirty 'March' battalions that consisted of *Kriegsmarine* and *Luftwaffe* recruits currently being raised in Döberitz.[5] Incredibly, though not surprisingly, the orders showed the complete loss of reality about the dire situation facing *AGV*. There was no way that the *Wehrkreis* could arm these new battalions. Instead the order specified that "Since the armament has to be done with the arms of the relieved *Volkssturm* battalions, the relief must be limited to those *Volkssturm* battalions whose tactical situation permits to do so."[6] No records show this actual change of forces ever taking place.

Generalmajor Walter Wenck, with Knights Cross, 12.*Armee* commander. In the coming days, the name "Wenck" would mean salvation for many German defenders in and around Berlin.
Courtesy of the Bundesarchiv.

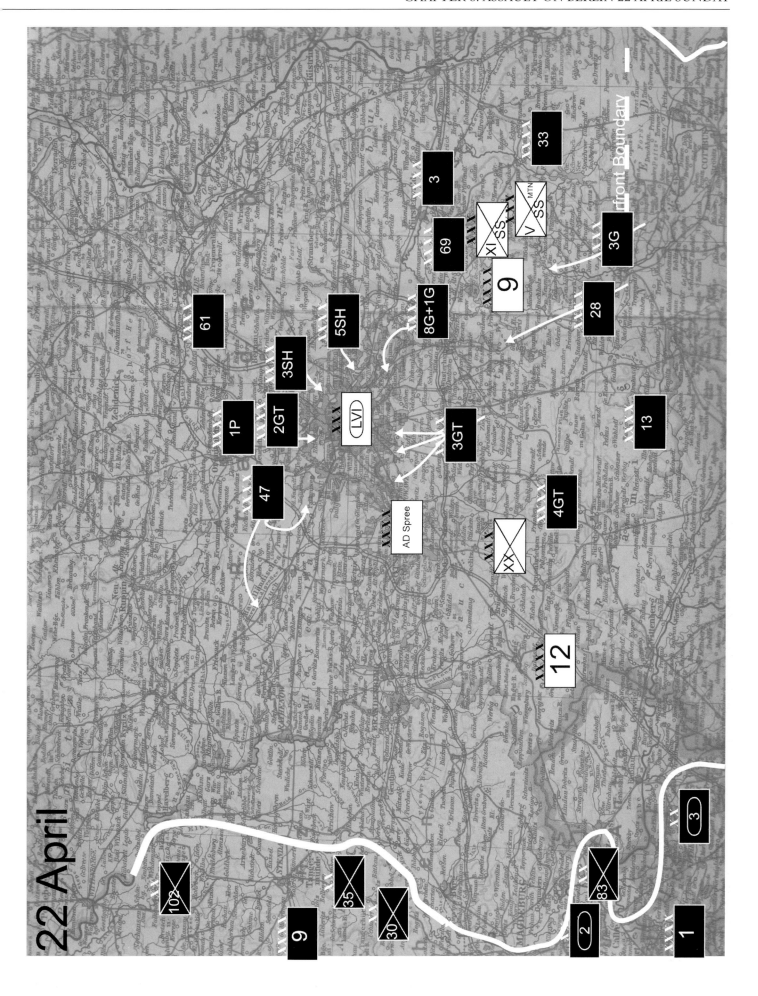

22 April

ARMY GROUP VISTULA

Heinrici received orders for the redistribution of his forces for the upcoming pincer movement toward Berlin by phone from Krebs. He then passed them on to the *9.Armee*. Busse read the orders with a sense of incredulousness as they stated that his forces were attack "the deep flank of the enemy advancing in northern direction toward the Reich's capital and to cooperate with the southern wing of the *12.Armee* attacking from the west in the direction of Jueterborg."[7] In addition, Heinrici continued to order Steiner's counterattack to begin as pressure mounted from Krebs. Heinrici and Krebs argued over the deployment of the *9.Armee* most of the afternoon. The *9.Armee* was now running low on fuel, ammunition, and had no reserves available to meet the penetrations of Soviet armor occurring along its southern and southeastern front. Cottbus, Busse's southeastern anchor, was lost to Koniev's forces during the day.[8] The loss of this city threatened the German garrison still on the eastern bank of the Oder in the 'fortress' Frankfurt-an-der-Oder. Heinrici told Krebs that given the situation the only option was to allow those forces to move back across the Oder so that Busse could shorten his lines in preparation for the planed attack. Krebs took this argument to Hitler, who agreed with the redeployment, believing that the withdrawal of forces might help the in the final decisive battle for Berlin. At 0100 on 23 April the order was given to shorten the *9.Armee's* lines.[9] In reality Heinrici planed to use the order to allow Busse free reign to withdraw his forces west and breakout toward Wenck's *12.Armee*. One topic that arose in many of the phone conversations between Heinrici's headquarters and the *Führerbunker* was the location of the *LVI Pz. Korps*. It appears that Krebs finally located Weidling in Köpenick by late evening and communicated this to Heinrici.[10]

LVI PZ. Korps

Weidling's staff exerted themselves in their attempt to maintain control of the various units in retreat while at the same time trying to reach either *AGV* or *9.Armee* HQ for orders as they were still out of communications. Not all his subordinates were happy with the tactical or operational situation and were taking matters into their own hands. Henseler was ordered to report to a small house in Münchehofe. When he arrived his papers were thoroughly checked by a tight cordon of *Nordland* guards. When he entered the building he was greeted by representatives from all of *Nordland's* pioneer companies. What Henseler heard next was incredible. Zeigler made the decision to move *Nordland* south of Berlin then west to the Western Allies and avoid fighting in Berlin—without any orders or permission from Weidling. The pioneers were ordered to race ahead and secure necessary bridge crossings over the Havel River so that the division could pass over them. The officer in-charge of the gathering, presumably *SS-Sturmbanführer* Voss, who commanded *SS-Pioneer-Abteilung 11*, stated "It will be your job to secure the Havel bridges, take care of any guards who may be there, and insure the possibility of getting the Division across the Havel by bridges or if necessary by boats."[11] Then each pioneer company commander was given orders to secure specific targets and told that this had to be kept secret.[12] This order certainly was in character for Zeigler who was playing a dangerous game since his division ran out of fuel and was unable to deploy to the correct area Weidling ordered on 18 April.[13] Zeigler's disdain for serving under a *Wehrmacht* officer combined with his desire to avoid Soviet captivity and reach the West apparently drove him into this significant act of late war treachery.

1st BYELORUSSIAN FRONT

Promising reports reached Zhukov's headquarters in a small quaint village in the eastern approaches to Berlin. His forces were finally moving, particularly in the north and southwest. Along the eastern approaches his units made mixed progress against sporadic but fierce resistance. As his forces began to enter Berlin's suburbs they naturally slowed the pace of advance. Zhukov at last reached the outskirts of Berlin and sliced completely through the *3.Panzer Armee* and *9.Armee* boundaries.

His northern wing, consisting of the 9th Guards Tank Corps, and the 125th Rifle Corps, continued their advance west keeping to the southern bank of the Finow canal. Zhukov was concerned that the Germans would defend the Havel River crossings north of Spandau, perhaps trapping his forces as the northern wing of his encirclements began to take the shape of a long outstretched finger. In fact Steiner's forces were tasked to launch an attack south toward Spandau while blocking forces were ordered to quickly reinforce the area. *Kampfgruppe Müller* from the Döberitz training grounds, consisting of *Panzerjäger Brigade Krampnitz*, *Pioneer Abteilung 968*, and *Machine-gun Abteilung 116*, was sent to hold the Havel against Zhukov's forces.[14] Given the fluidity of battle it is not clear if *Kampfgruppe Müller* reached its intended blocking positions, but it was forced to retreat into Spandau during the Soviet encirclement of Berlin. What is clear is that Zhukov's forces found the Havel crossings intact and undefended.[15] Zhukov's fears were alleviated when his tanks crossed the bridge at Henningsdorf and gained freedom of movement west of Berlin. The 7th Guard Cavalry Corps quickly followed the lead units across the Havel and fanned out to scout and screen Berlin's northern and western approaches.[16]

The 3rd and 5th Shock Armies slowed their advance considerably once they entered the northern and eastern districts of Berlin. A combination of continued operations over the last six days along with considerable losses in men and equipment caused an operational pause for these units to regroup. Soviet scouts continued on in small infiltration groups around suspected German positions into the city. It was the responsibility of the main elements to reduce staunchly defended points, especially around major factories, and raised S-Bahn stations that marked the outer edge of the inner defensive ring. The towns of Bucholz, Biesdorf, Pankow, Weißensee, and Lichtenberg now found themselves in the front line of the Eastern Front. The *CBDA* attempted to pull forces together and defend the Inner Defense Ring of Berlin. A defense line running from Königswusterhausen-Märkish-Bucholz-Lübben-Burg was ordered but lack of fuel prevented the movement of troops from various defensive sectors into the threatened areas. In addition, most of the *Volkssturm* were now outside Berlin and orders were forthcoming to pull them back into the city.[17]

The lead elements of Berzarin's 5th Shock Army closed up the gap created by the 12th Guards Tank Corps and ran into organized resistance at Hellersdorf. The small Berlin town was occupied by local German defenders. The German forces consisted of one of the few well-organized formations still in Berlin. *Major* Funk's *57.Fortress Regiment* moved up from Berlin during the prior evening. Funk's unit consisted of the *3./115 Siemenstadt Volkssturm Abteilung* in the center; on the left was a *Wehrmacht Abteilung,* and on the right was the

Warnholz Polizei Abteilung. All units were deployed in a defense perimeter behind tank barricades. The Soviets formed up in the morning and launched their attack. The Germans sent up some StuG IIIs, presumably from *Nordland*, and reserve infantry from the *3./121 Volkssturm Abteilung*. This combined force stopped the Russians in front of the town. The Soviets did not want to be tied up in the reduction of this fixed position and decided to move around the German defenders forcing the *3./115* to withdraw by 1300 hours. As the *3./115* pulled back, the other battalions in the regiment became exposed and were left with no choice but to retreat as well.[18]

It is not clear if the 12th Guards Tank Corps launched its attack as planned. If it did, it ran into significant problems in coordinating the attack and suffered additional losses, or the soldiers of the unit simply showed signs of disobedience. In either case, Berzarin decided that he didn't want this unit operating in his area and ordered Schevtschenko to move his corps north, than west, into the 3rd Shock Army's boundary and prepare for an assault into Berlin from Reinickendorf.[19] This movement took several days. It soon became clear that the unit was exhausted and that Schevtschenko was simply not up to the task of command anymore. By 26 April he was replaced by General of Tanks M.F. Salminov and sent back to a deputy position in the 9th Guards Tank Corps. The 12th Guards Tank Corps primary role in the assault on Berlin was over.[20]

Nordland's SS-Aufk.Abt.11 continued to be pressed by the near reckless advance of the Soviet armored forces. Relief only came when the *SS* veterans passed through the positions of younger *Hitlerjugend* waiting for an opportunity to prove themselves, equally as recklessly, in battle.[21] In one encounter, the members of *SS-Aufk.Abt.11* watched *Hitlerjugend* tank hunters stop a Soviet armored assault with *Panzerfausts*. This was seen repeated over and over in the upcoming street battles in Berlin.

> In the foxholes over there, three small human beings lay crouching, with their hands clenched hard around their Panzerfäuste, with thumping hearts listening to the ever louder thunder from the tank engines. Man against machine! Now the whole ground over there was trembling from the enormous weight of the giants. Rigid with excitement we stared out. There could not be 50 meters between them. They had no nerves, those three. The tanks maintained very small distances between each other, 10–15 meters perhaps, as they rolled forward. They had seen our infantry retreating and hardly thought that death could be waiting for them in the abandoned positions. Soon they were quite close to the foxholes. My cigarette burned, unnoticed, between my fingers that were shaking with excitements.
>
> For God's sake get up, now before it is too late! The tanks had driven into a perfect position for the three comrades in the holes. The small gap between them became their destruction. When the first tank had come to a distance of 10 meters, three heads and Panzerfäuste came up like lightning, three short bangs, fire shot out of the Panzerfäuste and three tanks were hit. Two of them were burning. One of them exploded almost immediately. The third rotated round and round on it damaged tracks. The heads disappeared quickly with the empty tubes and came up again with three new Panzerfäuste. Before it had time to withdraw from the Panzerfäuste's short range of fire, the rotating tank received its deathblow and at the same time the two remaining were penetrated by annihilating tank mines.
>
> Five heavy tanks were burning out in the field, destroyed by three unknown infantry soldiers who now rushed up from the holes and in a zigzag ran back over the field to get away from the advancing Russian infantry.[22]

The *Panzerfaust* continued to prove the dominating weapon of the battlefield during the Soviet assault into Berlin causing serious losses in Soviet armor.

A significant battle was waged for the Friedrichsfelde S-Bahn station highlighting the difficult defensive positions the raised stations presented to the Soviets. The solid buildings offered good protection from direct and indirect fire. Their height offered the Germans excellent observation points. Illum's company along with a pioneer platoon from *Nordland*, and stragglers from other units took up position on the north side of the railway embankment. After clearing Marzhan in the morning, the Soviet 11th Tank Corps moved southwest and approached the Friedrichsfelde S-Bahn station. The 11th Tank Corps, operating independently as all Soviet corps did during the Berlin operation, split into two separate battle groups just like the 12th Guard Tank Corps did several days earlier. The Right Squadron under command of Major General Yushchuk consisted of the 65th Tank Brigade with the 50th Heavy Tank Regiment, 12th Motorized Rifle Brigade, 243rd Mortar Regiment, 1493rd Self-Propelled Gun Regiment, the 1461st Self-Propelled Gun Regiment and the 1071st Light Artillery Regiment with two battalions of M–13 Rocket Launchers and two anti-aircraft battalions. The Left Squadron under the command of Major General of Tank Troops Gritsenko consisted of the 20th and 36th Tank Brigades.[23] This form of task organization demonstrated one of the few examples of operational and tactical maturity in the Soviet Army born out of the necessity.

As the Soviet reconnaissance forces of the Left Squadron approached the rail embankment they immediately came under heavy fire from elements of the *SS-Pz.Gren.Rgt.24 Danmark* where Illum's assault company was positioned in the defense. Other units of the 5th Shock Army advanced westward down Reichsbahn 1, just to the south of Illum's position effectively cutting off any rapid withdrawal in that direction. It was decided by the Germans to hold the position in order to allow other units time to withdraw ahead of the Soviets. Soviet Senior Lieutenant Gevorgyen received the order to hold the railroad embankment until the main force arrived of Gritsenko's Left Squadron. The fighting was ferocious according to the Soviet account where they claim the Germans launched five successive counterattacks. Illum's account does not suggest this level of aggressiveness; although neighboring units certainly would have launched their own counterattacks without coordinating with Illum's force. Illum was able to obtain support from several StuG IIIs from *SS-Pz.Abt.11 Hermannn von Salza* located nearby. *SS-Untersturmführer* Walter Timm of *Hermann von Salza* had three StuG IIIs under his command south of the rail embankment and was ordered to move forward and assist in holding the barricades around the S-Bahn station. His small armored force moved forward and found that directly ahead was a tank barricade blocking the street. The barricade was made up of empty trolley cars. This was the typical form of barricade found in and around Berlin. Timm issued orders to his assault guns to counterattack the Russians opposite the barricade. The small armored force moved down the street with Timm's assault gun bearing around the right side of the trolley and the other assault guns bearing around the left side. The assault guns on the left were commanded by *SS-Untersturmführers* Muhs and Gutzeit. Suddenly Timm heard a deafening explosion and was told by radio that Muhs' assault gun was destroyed by Soviet fire. Gutzeit quickly withdrew behind the barricade while Timm's assault gun crawled forward to see if he might be in firing position. Suddenly he watched the dark green muzzlebrake of a Soviet tank poke from behind the barricade accompanied by a very long gun tube. At first he though it was a Soviet ISU–152 assault gun but soon realized it was a massive JS–2 tank. It is apparent that the 11th Tank Corps split up the JS–2s from the 50th Heavy Tank Brigade and provided them to both Squadrons. Timm wisely threw his assault gun in reverse

A column of T-34/85s accompanied by SMG infantry pause along Landsberger Allee between Lichtenberg and Horst Wessel. Smoke billows from the center of Berlin obscuring visibility. Photo courtesy of the Bundesarchiv.

and withdrew back behind the barricade. Both StuGs maintained their positions for an hour until an amazing shot by the gunner of the JS–2 passed through the broken windows of the trolley barricade striking and destroying Gutzeit's assault gun. Timm radioed his regiment who immediately sent a King Tiger from *s.SS-Pz.Abt.503* to relieve him. Once the King Tiger arrived Timm was ordered to tow the second assault gun to Spandau where the battalion established a repair facility. After towing the second assault gun across the Spree he found he could not continue towing it due to mechanical difficulty and left it along the road while he went on to Spandau alone. When he arrived at the repair facility Timm finally had a few minutes of peace after the frantic last few days and now felt depressed and nervous over the loss of his comrades and the developments occurring around him. Timm's only recourse was to get drunk, as many German and Soviet soldiers were doing to relieve their misery.[24]

A Soviet T–34/85 commanded by Lieutenant N.D. Lyashchenko carrying sub-machine gun infantry advanced to an area of buildings that the Germans just occupied in a counterattack (presumably north of the barricade and S-Bahn station). Suddenly from point blank range a *Panzerfaust* was fired from a second story window and pierced the turret, mortally wounding Lyashchenko, but leaving the tank intact. The Soviet infantry threw grenades at the window and poured a volley of fire at the building in order to prevent the Germans from firing any more *Panzerfausts* while they retreated. Here the tankers of the 11th Tank Corps began to get a taste of the warfare they would need to endure in Berlin.[25] Fighting went on throughout the day between the Soviets and the defending German contingent in the S-Bahn station. By late afternoon the Germans finally retreated, allowing the station to fall to the Soviets. Illum held onto the embankment until evening as he probably was not informed of the German withdrawal from the station. This was typical of the defensive action during the retreat from the Seelow Heights. Mixed German units were often found fighting together without a single commander or organized defensive plan. Units often withdrew without informing surrounding units due to the confusion and lack of unified command structure. Soviet infantry soon began to infiltrate past Illum's soldiers. Illum quickly ordered his company to withdraw south along with the *8./SS-Pz.Gren.Rgt. Danmark* that arrived in the sector as reinforcement. Zhukov now ordered the 11th Tank Corps to come under the command of the 5th Shock Army instead of the 8th Guards Army since the tank corps was operating so far north of Chuikov's forces. The 11th Tank Corps spent the next two days reorganizing in preparation for the final assault into the Berlin.[26]

The combined elements of the 1st Guard Tank and 8th Guards Armies continued to face off against the *LVI Pz. Korps* as Chuikov worked his way through the difficult lake country southeast of Berlin. The 8th Guards Army's 269th Rifle Regiment of the 88th Guards Rifle Division crossed two rivers on 22 April. First they swam across the Spree to reach the peninsula between Müggelsee and the Dahme in the morning, and then they found boats at Wendenschloss, south of Köpenick, which they used to cross the Dahme River under cover of darkness and establish themselves in Grünau and Falkenberg before dawn on 23 April.

In Köpenick elements of Chuikov's combined armies operating on his northern wing followed *Müncheberg* and engaged the Germans in heavy fighting for the suburb's S-Bahn station. *Müncheberg's* Panzers and Panzergrenadiers were primarily responsible for the defense in this area while other units of the *LVI Pz. Korps* continued to retreat behind *Müncheberg's* defensive screen. During the early part of the day 20–30 JS–2 tanks, presumably from the 1st Guards Tank Brigade, attacked through the district throwing the Germans into panic.[27] Many Germans began to retreat north toward Neukölln. King Tigers of *s.SS-Pz.Abt.503* were already in Neukölln covering on Sonnenallee towards the bridge. They had arrived there recently after retreating through Köpenick earlier in the day. They soon received orders to head southwest back into Köpenick and participate in a counterattack along with Panzergrenadiers from *Müncheberg* to retake the S-Bahn station that was just lost to the Soviets.[28] Overhead Soviet PO–2 biplanes flew low concentric circles over the battlefield looking for German troop formations. Differing accounts suggest they either marked the German targets for the fighter bombers, or even took advantage of their quiet approach to surprise and attack the Germans themselves from a low altitude. Fierce street fighting raged in Köpenick during the entire day as the Soviets tried to push through the district and across the Spree into the south of Berlin. By the end of the day the Germans were able to hold the Soviets back and temporarily retake the S-Bahn station.[29] This allowed the main force of the *20.Pz.Gren.Div.* to continue its withdrawal west reaching Neukölln by nightfall.[30]

1st UKRANIAN FRONT

Koniev's forces, unknown to Zhukov, continued to make fast progress from the southwest into Berlin. On his left flank, the 4th Guards Tank Army's 5th Guards Mechanized Corps formed a protective screen toward Beelitz. Their advance was virtually unopposed except at Luckenwalde where local German forces put up stiff resistance. The soldiers of the 5th Guards Mechanized Corps also took a POW camp at Treuenbritzen, liberating 1,600 British, American and Norwegian soldiers including the former commander of the Norwegian Army, General Otto Ruge.[31] In addition to POW camps, Koniev's forces also began to liberate workers' camps that held Russians used as forced labor in the various industries in and around Berlin. In both cases, any Russians found inside were given a submachine gun or rifle and thrown into the combat units and sent forward to fill in the manpower gaps caused by four years of continuous fighting. Koniev's forces were short on manpower just like Zhukov and they adopted the practice of incorporating released Soviet POWs and workers directly into their front ranks to maintain as consistent a level of force as possible. In just one example, a former Soviet veteran that participated in Koniev's drive north stated after the war how his entire battalion was made up of former Soviet POWs liberated from German concentration camps during the advance on Berlin.[32]

The 6th Guards Mechanized Corps reached Beelitz that evening and rested prior to pushing north. On the right flank the 10th Guards Tank Corps swept through Saarmund and Schenkenhorst to seal off the approaches to Potsdam by evening. Both the 6th Guards Mechanized Corps and the 10th Guards Tank Corps pushed further to the northwest around Berlin and were soon in position to link up with the vanguard of Zhukov's 47th Army to complete the encirclement of Berlin.[33] The success of the 4th Guards Tank Army was mirrored by the 3rd Guards Tank Army on the right. They were given the prestigious task of leading Koniev's main effort into Berlin.

The 3rd Guards Tank Army fought through the previous night, forcing the Notte Canal near Zossen. Once over the canal, there was no other natural obstacle between Koniev's forces and the outlying Berlin suburbs. These forces advanced into Berlin on abroad front. By evening the leading elements of the 7th and 6th Guards Tank Corps reached the Teltow Canal at Stahnsdorf and Teltow respectively, while on the right the 9th Mechanized Corps crossed the autobahn at 1100 and was well into the suburbs of Lichtenrade, Marienfelde and Lankwitz by nightfall.[34] The soldiers of the 4th Guards Tank Army were not able to cross the Teltow Canal. Increased German resistance from the north bank of the canal forced a pause.[35]

The drive north was not without incident. One Soviet tank sub-machine gunner, Lieutenant Evgeni Bessonov, whose brigade was part of the 4th Guards Tank Army recorded after the war that on their 450 kilometer advance into Germany in 9 days "the roads were covered with mines, blocked with barricades and heaps of rubbish, especially in built-up areas and in front of them, as well as under railway and road bridges, which had high embankments. They used up *Panzerfausts* against our tanks. Battles raged during day and night without any break and this was seriously exhausting."[36]

The *Skorning Kampfgruppe*, formed from the *2./Fortress Regiment 60* contained a *Volkssturm Company*, an artillery battery and other minor units under the command of *Oberstleutnant* Wolfgang Skorning. This unit was deployed along the southern defense sector between Marienfelde and Bucow and encountered the lead elements of Koniev's forces in the southern suburbs. Tank barricades made up of moveable trolley cars were set up along major highways. Another German unit, the *Krause Abteilung*, failed to close one of the anti-tank barriers allowing lead Soviet tanks to pass through into Marienfelde. Elements of *Skorning's Kampfgruppe* hunted them down and destroyed them on the street known as Alt Mariendorf, 3 kilometers to their rear. It is apparent that the uncoordinated use of Soviet tanks was not limited to Zhukov's formations as Koniev's forces were now making the same mistakes.[37]

In many of the southern districts *SS* went door-to-door drafting young boys into military service while generally looking for stragglers. Günther Pienkny enlisted in the *Kriegsmarine* in 1944 at the age of 16 but went AWOL in Berlin when he was home visiting his mother. He was soon discovered by the *SS* who were recruiting for the *Hitlerjugend* and given the option to join *SS* forces being raised to fight the Soviets advancing on Berlin or be shot. He chose the former option, but his friend was able to transfer him into *Hitlerjugend Gruppe 200* under the command of a 32 year old *SS-Bannführer* Heinz Buttermann. Buttermann was a former *Leutnant* that held the Iron Cross First Class and also one the leaders of the Berlin *Werewolf*. Under Bormann's direction, the Werewolf was organized to conduct partisan-style raids against the Russians in Berlin.[38] Buttermann had at least one safe house, known as the 'Villa' that was to be used by the boys in his formation in case their district was overrun by the Soviets. Pienkny's group of 15–17 year old boys were now sent to the Teltow Canal to prepare defensive positions opposite Koniev's forces.[39]

The increased resistance experienced by Rybalko's forces caused Koniev to assign additional assets to his main effort in Berlin. Koniev assigned the 10th Breakthrough Artillery Corps, 25th Breakthrough Artillery Division, and the 23rd Anti Aircraft Artillery Division for additional support. Koniev also ordered the 2nd Fighter Aircraft Corps to be transferred to Rybalko's operational command.[40] Koniev commanded Rybalko to hold on the Teltow Canal and prepare for an assault across on the morning of 24 April. This pause was needed to give the men of the 3rd Guards Tank Army rest after their non-stop six day drive to Berlin. Koniev also required time to allow the assigned artillery assets to move into position. To the east, the 28th Army continued to advance along the left flank of the *9.Armee* drawing nearer to Zhukov's 8th Guard Army moving southwest.

Koniev officially beat Zhukov into Berlin. Zhukov clearly did not know this yet. Zhukov's success in Berlin was sealed by Koniev's deployment into the city as his forces were now in position to blunt the drives of both the *12.Armee* and *9.Armee*.[41] Stalin was still playing both commanders against each other and had no intention to coordinate their future efforts. Stalin decided to wait a few more days to see which general made the most progress into the heart of Berlin before Stavka was ordered to draw a fixed inter-front boundary between the opposing Front Commanders.

Notes on Chapter 6: Assault on Berlin, 22nd April Sunday

1   Ryan outline for 22 April (RC: 75/1).
2   Quoted in Fest, p. 65.
3   Le Tissier, *Race for the Reichstag*, p. 58 and Schultz-Naumann, pp. 163–4.
4   Fest, p. 59, Le Tissier, *Race for the Reichstag*, p. 62, and Army Group Weichsel War Diary, Apr 20–9, p. 137 (RC: 68/4).
5   Army Group Weichsel War Diary, Apr 20–9, p. 134 (RC: 64/3).
6   Ibid, p. 144.
7   Army Group Weichsel War Diary, Apr 20–9, p. 136 (RC: 68/4).
8   Army Group Weichsel War Diary, Apr 20–9, pp. 146–7 (RC: 64/3).
9   AGV Army Group Weichsel War Diary, Apr 20–9, pp. 180 (RC: 68/4).
10   Ibid, pp. 178, 179 (RC: 68/4).
11   Henseler interview.
12   Ibid.
13   This assessment of Zeigler comes from a very careful review of a number of first hand accounts. It differs dramatically with other historian's accounts that attempt to "white wash" Zeigler's actions. For example, in Wilhelm Tieke's authoritative account of *Nordland* in *Tragedy of the Faithful*, p. 296, he states that Weidling, not Zeigler, summoned all commanders of the *LVI Panzer Korps* to Biesdorf to a meeting where it was decided that the entire corps would fall back to the west and away from Berlin. It was decided that *Nordland* would take the vanguard and hold the Spree bridges at Ober Schöneweide to secure the crossings. It may be that Tieke confused Zeigler's meeting with the earlier discussion about what to do about Berlin. Weidling certainly did not want to fight in Berlin, but he was certainly not going to abandon his chain-of-command.
14   Army Group Weichsel War Diary, Apr 20–9, pp. 74–5 (RC: 68/4)
15   Schultz-Naumann, p. 166.
16   Le Tissier, *Race for the Reichstag*, p. 50.
17   Ibid, pp. 54, 51, and Army Group Weichsel War Diary, Apr 20–9, pp. 127–8 (RC: 68/4).
18   Le Tissier, *Race for the Reichstag*, p. 91.
19   Skorodumov, p4.
20   Ibid.
21   Hillblad, p. 83.
22   Ibid, p. 81.
23   Platonov, pp. 14-15.
24   Timm interview.
25   Platonov, p. 17.
26   Ibid, p. 15.
27   H. J. Eilhardt, *Frühjahr 1945: Kampf um Berlin Flucht in den Westen*, p. 52.
28   Schneider, p. 301.
29   Army Group Weichsel War Diary, Apr 20–9, p146 (RC: 68/4).
30   Le Tissier, *With Our Backs to Berlin*, pp. 118.
31   Koniev unpublished memoir, pp. 11–12.
32   E. Bessonov, *Tank Rider: Into the Reich with the Red Army*, p. 230.
33   Koniev unpublished memoir, pp. 111–12.
34   Ibid.
35   Ibid, p. 114.
36   E. Bessonov, *Tank Rider: Into the Reich with the Red Army*, p. 198.
37   Le Tissier, *Race for the Reichstag*, pp. 56–7, and Venghaus, pp. 337–8.
38   The *Werewolf* organization was created to conduct guerilla warfare in an occupied Germany. It was given much propaganda press during the final months of the war. There were post-war instances of sabotage, black marketeering, and related acts of political violence that appear traceable to this organization. In general, it never materialized as a viable post-war movement.
39   Pienkny interview.
40   Koniev unpublished memoir p. 108.
41   Koniev's role in ensuring Zhukov's operationally success has gone largely unstated in postwar histories that tend to rely on dated, counter-factual accounts put out by Chuikov and Zhukov in the 1960s and 1970s. It is very clear to this author that without Koniev's insertion into Zhukov's battle-space, Zhukov's forces would have had an even more difficult time maintaining the operational momentum to take Berlin. The German *9th* and *12th Armees* would have had a free hand in reinforcing Berlin without Koniev's direct involvement.

6

ASSAULT ON BERLIN

23 APRIL
MONDAY

LVI PZ. KORPS

The *LVI Pz. Korps* HQ moved across the Spree and the southern branch of the Teltow Canal during the night of 22/23 April and established itself in the suburb of Rudow. Communication with the *9.Armee* was finally established after more than 30 hours of silence. *Generalleutnant* Hölz, Busse's Chief of Staff, immediately gave a specific order to Weidling to secure the northern flank of the *9.Armee*. This relieved Weidling's staff that expected to be ordered into Berlin.

Böttcher, the operation's officer for the *18.Pz.Gren.Div.*, completed his rounds supervising the withdrawal of his troops south of Berlin when he arrived at his command post in the early morning hours and received the incredible news that he might be shot on orders of Hitler. The division's Personnel Officer approached Böttcher in the dark waving a flashlight and excitedly exclaimed "Listen, Böttcher, the Führer has been told that the Korps and the *18.Panzergrenadier Division* refuse to defend Berlin. There is a great danger that *General* Weidling, his Chief of Staff and, yourself [sic] will be arrested and put against the wall."[1] Böttcher laughed at this notion but the officer was insistent stating that *General* Weidling was on his way to see Hitler and that Böttcher should be prepared to meet him to discuss this further. Böttcher proceeded to division HQ and immediately made his report to Rauch on the state of the withdrawal. *General* Rauch listened to his report patiently then burst out "Böttcher, what the hell is happening? Two gentlemen from the *Führerbunker* came here with orders to arrest you. Would you mind telling me what this is all about?"[2] Böttcher explained to *General* Rauch the conversation with Weidling and the other Operations Officers that took place several nights ago. He then told Rauch that based on a call from HQ, Weidling was already on his way to see Hitler in Berlin.

Once contact was reestablished with Busse and higher HQs, Weidling sent *General* Voigtsberger (former commander of the destroyed *Berlin Division*) to OKH as liaison. Voigtsberger returned with news that Hitler ordered him and Böttcher arrested and shot for moving to Döberitz and evacuating the front. This decision was formed in part, on orders of the *9.Armee's* commander, combined with general confusion over orders issued by Weidling that sent the corps' *Hiwis* and *Hitlerjugend* to Döberitz.[3] In reality Weidling's troops were fighting to hold the front at the same time they were attempting to join with the *9.Armee*. Weidling was upset at the accusations and immediately left for the *Führerbunker* to clear up the issue and left von Dufving in command. His final order was to link up with the *9.Armee*, avoiding Berlin.[4] As far as Weidling was concerned the soldiers of his unit would follow Heinrici's wishes and avoid combat in the Reich's capital.

Weidling arrived at the *Führerbunker* around 1800. He immediately demanded an explanation of the order that he be shot. After several hours of discussion he convinced *Generals* Krebs and Burgdorf that he spent the last several days fighting the Russians and that his headquarters was only 1–2 kilometers behind the front. It was clear from Krebs perspective that Weidling's forces were exactly what was need to hold Berlin while the relief forces from the *12.Armee* and *9.Armee* advanced toward the city. Most of Weidling's forces were already fighting along the outskirts of Berlin. It was not a hard choice to order Weidling to move the *LVI Pz. Korps* into Berlin. Krebs informed Weidling of his new orders and that Hitler would be notified immediately.[5] Weidling asked his Operations Officer, *Major* Siegfried Knapp, to report the possible change of orders to von Dufving. After reaching the corps by phone, Knapp advised Weidling that von Dufving received a teletype from the *9.Armee* stating Weidling was relieved and a *General* Burmeister was now in charge. Weidling, now fuming, expressed his outrage to Krebs and Burgdorf and asked for his leave so that his successor could take over. Krebs then calmed him down and informed Weidling that Hitler wanted to see him immediately.[6]

Weidling now met Hitler for the second time in his career.[7] Weidling's meeting with Hitler shocked him. He commented that Hitler's face resembled a smiling mask and when he sat down his left leg kept moving, swinging like a pendulum but only faster. Weidling explained his current unit dispositions then answered Hitler's inquiries to the fighting qualities of his troops. Hitler went into an explanation of the new plan for the defense of Berlin designed to stop the Russians in a decisive final battle using the *12.Armee*, *9.Armee,* and a thrust from the new *Armeegruppe Steiner* positioned around Oranienburg. Finally, Weidling was ordered by Hitler to move his corps into Berlin to bolster the city's defenses and to take over command of Berlin, responsible directly to Hitler.[8] Weidling was then given a map of Berlin with a description of the various defense sectors that existed.[9] Weidling tried to push the point that it was madness to defend Berlin and that it should be declared an open city. Krebs responded, somewhat condescendingly, that Hitler had spoken and that the fall of Berlin meant the end of the war and Germany.

Weidling left the *Führerbunker* then called von Dufving and gave his final order to turn his divisions 180 degrees around and deploy them into Berlin. The conversation between Weidling and von Dufving was emotional. Von Dufving argued that turning the divisions around would cause a serious loss to the remaining *LVI Pz. Korps* forces due to the problems inherent with disengaging from an ongoing

23 April

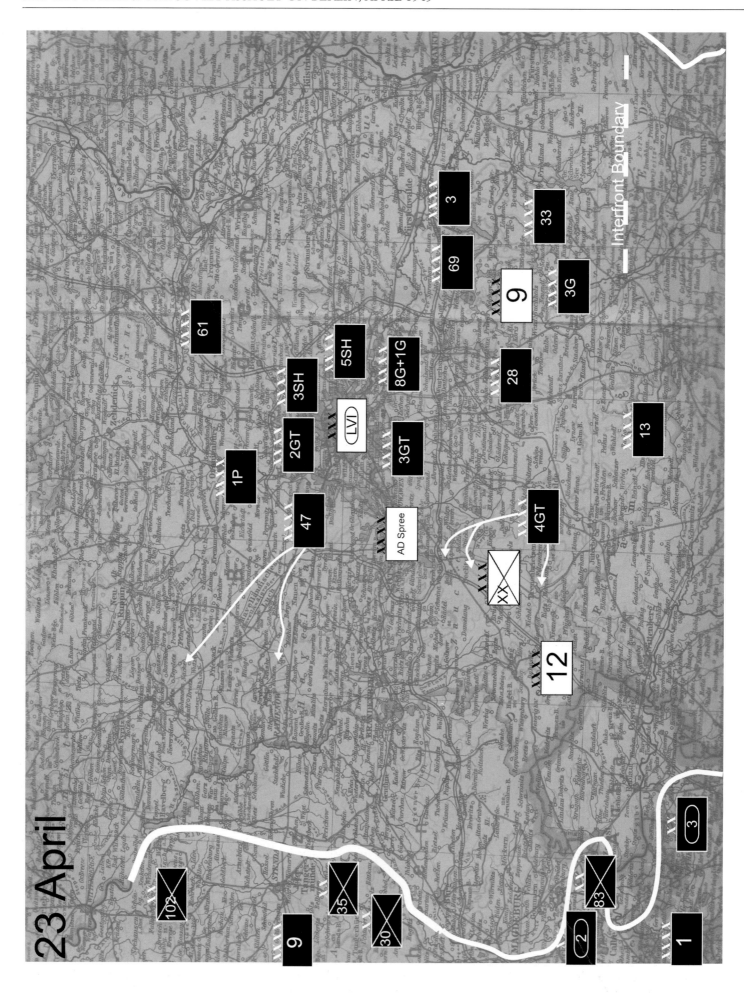

battle. "I don't see how I can do that. A counter-order means disorder. We can't carry out this new maneuver because if we do, to turn around the corps at this point will mean the loss of 60% of the effectiveness of the corps, because there will be complete confusion and disorder" von Dufving argued. Weidling's reply was simple: "You know what will happen to me if the corps doesn't carry out this order."[10] Weidling later confided in von Dufving, after returning to his HQ, that "the end was near anyway and if I have to die I want to do it honorably."[11] Weidling's sense of military duty bound him to follow Hitler's orders, thwarting the bold and careful planning by Guderian and Heinrici to avoid any combat in the city. The combat-tested soldiers of his corps now became the defensive backbone of a dying regime bent on dragging the war out to the bitter end. The order to the soldiers of the *LVI Pz. Korps* was clear: 'Defend Berlin!'

ARMY GROUP VISTULA

Heinrici slowly lost operational control of the *9.Armee*. The pace of Soviet operations, battlefield chaos, and multiple overlapping orders to his subordinate commands from the *Führerbunker* eroded his ability to shape the battlefield around Berlin. The forces of Rokossovsky's 2nd Byelorussian Front strengthened their attacks at several locations along the western bank of the Oder River in the *3.Panzer Armee* sector. By day's end, Manteuffel reported to Heinrici that his front was still stable despite 'deep inroads' made by Soviet forces. Defensive fighting raged for the towns of Tantow and Kolbitzow. German counterattacks were launched against Pritzlow and Kreuzbruch. Heinrici received orders that Steiner's forces were to pull back from the Eberswalde bridgehead. This helped prevent the isolation of *Regiment Solar* and an assault gun brigade holding the line there. Steiner's forces, despite being a critical component of the *3.Panzer Armee's* southern flank, were simply no longer under the command influence of Manteuffel or Heinrici.

Steiner was ordered by the *Führerbunker* to shift his forces to the west near Oranienburg and launch a relief attack on Berlin from that direction. Oranienburg was already under attack by Zhukov's forces. The *1.Marine Division*, without sufficient anti-tank weapons, was engaged in a fierce defensive battle for that town's train station.[12] In preparation for the attack *OKH* and Steiner called for additional forces, like the *25.Panzergrenadier* and *7.Panzer Divisions* that were currently engaged in critical defensive tasks under Manteuffel's command.[13] In response to the request for these key divisions, Manteuffel asked Heinrici to order the withdrawal of his forces to the secondary positions along the Wotan line the following day to help consolidate the front and prevent his forces from fracturing under the difficult circumstances. He made it clear that he didn't believe he could hold the Oder River line for more than 24 hours. As if the threat of Rokossovsky's forces to the army's front wasn't enough to worry about, behind the *3.Panzer Armee* there was still a threat that elements of Zhukov's 2nd Guards Tank Army might wheel right and drive north behind the *3.Panzer Armee's* front cutting off any chance of withdrawal.[14] As Heinrici tried to plan out his next steps for Manteuffel's forces based on what Zhukov's next moves were, the *9.Armee* to the south was already in a critical situation.

Busse's forces were about to be surrounded. Koniev's 28th Army continued its advance north creating a screen along the western edge of Busse's forces as it neared Zhukov's forces closing in from the northeast. Farther west Koniev's main tank forces were already on the Teltow Canal in Berlin and preparing for the assault crossing into the city. This double envelopment effectively cut off the *9.Armee* from the west. By the afternoon wireless radio communications occurred for the first time between elements of Koniev's forces and General Katukov's 1st Guards Tank Army driving southwest around city.[15] Due to the short range of Soviet wireless communications at that time, this could only mean that the two conversing forces were very close and that the *9.Armee* no longer had a front with the *LVI Pz. Korps* to the northwest.

Ammunition, fuel, and equipment now became scarce as the Soviet pincers closed around the *9.Armee*. Under the guise of preparing his forces for the planned attack toward Baruth, Busse was able to withdraw the majority of his forces on the east bank of the Oder to the west along with most of their heavy equipment.[16] Without the ability to receive motorized or rail supply in his sector, however, Busse now relied on aerial drops to obtain supplies.[17] The date for the 'attack' was set for 25 April.[18] Heinrici knew that the *9.Armee* was in mortal danger. Heinrici began to develop a solution under the guise of the Berlin relief plans generated out of the *Führerbunker* to save the *9.Armee*.

12.ARMEE

General-Feldmarschall Keitel arrived at the small forestry house known as 'Old Hell' that served as HQ of the *12.Armee* at 0100 to personally announce to the commander that he was given the historic task of relieving Berlin.[19] Wenck was in uniform dozing off and on in a large easy chair. After being woken by his aide, Wenck still groggy from sleep, met with Keitel. Keitel acted excited despite an obvious tension in the air. After listening to Wenck's report about the state of the *12.Armee*, Keitel "gravely, but also in a kind of matter-of-fact way" stated "Hitler has broken down and you have to turn around your troops and drive toward Berlin, together with the *9.Armee* of *General Busse*."[20] Wenck was surprised at the order and his first concern was the American threat to his rear. Keitel told him he did not need to worry about the Americans. It is clear that at the time Wenck was not informed about 'Eclipse'. Keitel presumably explained that 'Eclipse' represented a demarcation line that assured *OKW* that the Western Allies were not going to cross the Elbe River.[21] The second concern he had was the planned attack route that took him through the difficult lake districts south of Berlin. Instead, Wenck argued "I would rather free Berlin from the north, north of the lakes by way of Nauen and Spandau. But I would need at least two more days to mount the attacks."[22] Keitel replied as expected: "We can't wait two more days." Wenck conceded that this was probably true and agreed that the attack by his army would be carried out. After Keitel left, Wenck paced the floor of the room while he discussed his own plans. Wenck informed his aide that "We will drive as close to Berlin as we can, but we will not give up our positions along the Elbe—it would be pure nonsense to drive towards Berlin and then get ourselves encircled by the Russians. We will try to get out the civilians and troops from Berlin, but that's all we can do."[23] In the upcoming days, Wenck's Army would be assigned yet another difficult task, the rescue of the *9.Armee*.

Heinrici was briefed by Krebs late in the afternoon about the planned relief attempt of Berlin by Wenck. Heinrici had no way to know the strength of this 'new' army operating behind Berlin but believed that it was in a position to assist *AGV*. Heinrici reached Wenck by phone at around 2315 in the evening. He asked Wenck to move whatever available forces he had to the area between Brandenburg and Nauen in order to prevent the expected Soviet drive northwest around Berlin. He also asked Wenck to attack east from Treuenbrietzen.

The 1920s built Shellhaus at the corner of Bendler Strasse and Tirpitz Strasse on the Landwehr Canal. Weidling initially set up his defense HQ across the street. The area was defended by a contingent of the *Wachregiment Grossdeutschland*. The bridge over the Landwehr Canal was blown during the battle. This picture suggests that this area saw extensive fighting as the damage to the building's façade appears to have been done by Soviet armor firing over open sights. Author's collection.

The latter directive was designed to reach the *9.Armee*. As Heinrici stated over the phone "Busse must be gotten out of that mess. This must be done by Wenck, his old friend." Confronted with a directive to relieve Berlin, while shifting forces well to the northeast of their current deployment and relieving the *9.Armee*, Wenck replied to Heinrici that all the units everyone thinks he has only existed on paper. They are, as Wenck called them, 'Santa Clauses!' or non-existent.[24] Heinrici repeated his orders and soon called Busse and informed him "Can you believe it? Wenck is going to attack tomorrow with 3 formations via Treuenbrietzen. He is sending you his regards, and will do everything to get his friend out of this."[25] Heinrici clearly exaggerated the truth in order to give Busse some hope. Heinrici, who was in command of a force encircled by the Soviets in 1944, knew that hope was a key emotion to maintain a soldier's motivation in war. If Busse thought there was no hope then the *9.Armee* was doomed.

FÜHRERBUNKER

Hitler knew that if Berlin fell that it was the end for him, the Nazi Party, and Germany. The Propaganda Ministry broadcast his final intentions earlier that day:

> The Führer is, as reported by the Ministry for Enlightenment and Propaganda, in Berlin …. The leading personalities [of the Nazi Party] are determined to remain Berlin and to defend the Reich Capital to the last.[26]

Hitler's immediate senior commanders, Jodl, Keitel, and Krebs worked to draw up plans for a final concentric attack from *Armeegruppe Steiner*, Wenck's *12.Armee* and Busse's *9.Armee*, now that he had declared his intention. From the *Führerbunker* came the calls for final victory by holding Berlin and defeating the surrounding Soviet forces. The expectation was that all three German forces would link their efforts in a drive into Berlin destroying the lead Soviet formations in the process and buttressing Berlin's defenses against any Soviet incursion. The reality could not be farther from the expectations set by the *German High Command*. Under Heinrici's guidance, Busse was not preparing for an attack toward Berlin but rather to breakout to the west. Wenck was also not going to relieve Berlin. Instead he prepared a plan to rescue as many soldiers and civilians alike from Berlin, while attacking east to provide Busse's forces an avenue of escape. At the same time he ordered his staff to maintain a presence along the Elbe to ensure an escape route to the Western Allies. Steiner, torn between duty and his desire to avoid capitulation to the Soviets, continued to stall Hitler's calls for an offensive toward Berlin, although he reached a point where he had no choice but to launch some form of an attack with his meager forces. As the *3.Panzer*

Armee commander, Manteuffel fought the redeployment of his forces to Steiner's ordered offensive, so that he could hold off the Soviet attacks on his front and flanks. All three 'relief' efforts were now set in motion as Weidling's forces began their deployment into Berlin to hold off the Soviets while waiting for their arrival. Military events around Berlin now unfolded in a paradox of orders fostered in competition, confusion, desperation, and a near-euphoric believe that victory, or at least some form of relief, was possible.

EASTERN DISTRICTS

Tanks and assault guns of the 5th Shock Army began moving down Landsberger Allee from the Lichtenberg district in the early morning hours when they suddenly came under massive fire that destroyed the lead tanks and sent the rest of the column looking for cover. This murderous fire was not generated by *Panzerfausts* or artillery, but from the 12.8cm guns of the Friedrichshain Flak Tower that now engaged Soviet ground targets for the first time.[27] All three Flak Towers had the coordinates of every major building and installation throughout the city in their fire control system. Forward Observers were posted throughout the city to report on enemy troop and tank concentrations to the tower gunners who then engaged the targets with deadly accuracy. It was even possible for all three Flak Towers to combine their firepower on certain targets. These fortresses were centers of resistance that offered refuge to soldiers and civilians alike. The Soviets altered their initial advance into the city in an attempt to avoid their deadly 12.8cm guns.[28] It was also on 23 April that the flak gunners of the *1.Flak Division* relegated to the anti-tank role started to engage Soviet ground targets as they neared the S-Bahn train stations that marked the outer edge of the inner defensive belt. Their 8.8cm guns fired over open sights down the long alleys and boulevards, quickly halting Soviet armor columns in their tracks.

Nordland was bearing the brunt of the Soviet assault into the eastern defense sectors of Berlin. Zeigler, who ironically wanted to avoid combat in Berlin, found that he and his men could not stem the irresistible pressures the Soviet offensive placed on the movements of his combat formations. Just to the east of Karlshorst elements of *SS-Aufk.Abt.11* came across a force of *Volkssturm* manning local barricades accompanied by *Hitlerjugend* combat teams. The *Hitlerjugend* continued to make a significant impression on the *SS* veterans. As one veteran recalled:

> Added to the confidence in battle of these warlike children, came a rancorous frenzy and a boundless contempt of death, which we grown-ups could not muster. With the agility of weasels they climbed and struggled their way into completely impossible positions, to knock out a Russian tank with a *Panzerfaust* or to finish off one or several advancing Red Army soldiers with a hand-grenade. There were quite a number of Russian tanks put out of action by small boys in their early teens during the battle of Berlin.[29]

The *SS* veterans along with the *ad-hoc* assortment of *Volkssturm* and *Hitlerjugend* held a defensive perimeter along the edge of the race track. The Russians continued their practice of flanking maneuvers combined with a quick assault of the German positions and drove the Germans back. Here the 9th Rifle Corps of the 5th Shock Army was tasked with taking Karlshorst. The German defenders could hardly hold a position for more than an hour before they were forced to retreat again. Only at the power station was there significant defensive fighting. The 301st Rifle Division sustained heavy losses in taking the large concrete building.[30] As the mix of German forces slowed the Soviets, *Nordland's* pioneers continued with their orders to find and secure bridges for the passage of the division's forces out of Berlin.

Henseler found *Nordland's* HQ in the morning before it moved into Berlin. Here he was given orders to secure the Treskov Bridge between Oberschöneweide and Niederschöneweide. Upon reaching the bridge he set up a security perimeter and placed his HQ in the Marktplatz. He was soon confronted by terrified civilians who were fleeing the advancing Soviets and begged him to take them with him when he began moving again. They experienced no enemy activity that afternoon and evening pulled over the Spree to the Späth Tree Nurseries in Niederschöneweide where his Battalion HQ was located. When they arrived they came across stragglers of *SS-Art.Rgt.11*. Everyone was drinking and Henseler was surprised that the artillerymen knew of Zeigler's plans to escape Berlin. It was no secret anymore as everyone seemed incredulous at their orders to defend the doomed city.[31] Just to the north of where Henseler crossed the Spree his comrade found the going much tougher.

Illum and his men found themselves in Oberschöneweide looking for a crossing point over the Spree after his retreat from the Friedrichsfelde S-Bahn station. They were at the junction of Sectors B and C as they proceeded on their last known orders to move south around Berlin. Here the men of Illum's company were mixed in with a group of *Wehrmacht* soldiers resting along the steps and doorways along a small street. The men soon heard the unmistakable sounds of Russian armor approaching. Without orders being issued, these men quickly withdrew into the houses and awaited the tanks. After a week of non-stop combat the soldiers went into automatic repeat, relying on tactics that brought them past success and survival. Illum's company allowed the Soviets armor to maneuver past their position. It was apparent that these tanks, probably from the 11th Tank Corps, were operating independently without infantry support on orders to find a crossing over the Spree at any cost. Without warning, and in quick succession, the first and last tanks in the column were hit by *Panzerfausts* and destroyed. This immobilized the remaining six tanks in the narrow street while each in turn was destroyed by a *Panzerfaust*. The Soviet crews that attempted to escape were shot down.[32] Illum's company was now down to 10 men as the defense of the previous day took its toll. Soviet aircraft soon hit the surrounding buildings forcing Illum and his men to pull out of the area and head west toward the Spree. They soon came upon a *Wehrmacht* supply column that was caught in the air raid and partially destroyed. Their drivers had apparently taken to nearby shelter during the attack and were not around. Illum and his men quickly commandeered a nearby radio truck that was still operational and drove across the Spree into Niederschöneweide. On the other side of the Spree they noticed a complete lack of any soldiers. With the help of a local Military Police checkpoint, Illum and his men found the *SS-Pz.Gren.Rgt.24 Danmark* HQ at a brewery near the Görlitzer railway station in Sector C by early evening. His company soon received orders that they were now to hold Berlin and Illum's men were tasked to defend a bridge over the Schiffahrt Canal.[33] The 4th Guards Rifle Corps closed up on Oberschöneweide and reached the Spree by evening south of the remaining bridges after sharp street battles with the remaining German stragglers on the eastern bank of the Spree. The Dnepr Flotilla arrived by truck that evening with a variety of boats that helped the Soviets cross.

Combat stress started to affect even the well-trained and motivated soldiers of *Nordland*. Haas recalled how a group of SS soldiers began to retreat after the Russians launched an attack from across a gully. The soldiers' commander, an officer of unknown rank named Spoerle, tried to verbally order his men back to their defensive positions. The soldiers refused to listen to Spoerle's orders so he shot one.

Grudgingly, the rest of the soldiers returned to their positions. During the next Soviet attack across the gully, a member of the battle group apparently took matters into his own hand and shot Spoerle through the head.[34] Some German soldiers began to rebel against their commanders, who often became despondent or violent under the stresses they found themselves faced with during the fighting for Berlin. In another instance, Timm was ordered by his battalion commander to send two StuG IIIs to the Jannowitz Bridge. When Timm arrived he was confronted by a *Wehrmacht Leutnant* who informed him that he was crazy as he was supposed to blow the bridge at the first sight of Russians. Timm ordered his assault guns back to their original positions when he ran into his commander *Obersturmbannführer* Kausch. Timm's commander became infuriated that he did not follow orders and started screaming at his subordinate. The Battalion Commander soon caught himself and according to Timm, realized that "all this makes no more sense." He then ordered Timm to Saarlandstraße in direction of Hallesches Tor. What this highlights is the utter level of exhaustion and frustration that the soldiers of the *LVI Pz. Korps* felt after seven days of non-stop combat without any pause. Meanwhile, Haas's company was now reduced to seven men as the rest had disappeared (fled) or been killed. They retreated across the Spree into Treptow where they spent the night in a hastily constructed trench. Scholles' company found themselves to be among the last of Nordland's unit crossing over the Spree through the battered streets and bridges of Oberschöneweide. By evening all bridges across the Spree between Oberschöneweide and Niederschöneweide were blown with only partial success in destroying them.[35]

As *Nordland* retreated over the Spree into the southern districts of the city they began to encounter hostility from some Berliners. Most of the eastern and southern districts were working class. It was also in these districts where much of the Communist movement during the turbulent Weimar years was rooted. Many of the civilians here were tired of combat and resented the *SS* soldiers for what they represented politically as well as for the fact that their presence could only prolong the inevitable. Much of the hostility was centered on jeers and verbal assaults, but it some cases open fighting broke out as Berlin Communists exchanged fire with the retreating *Nordland* soldiers.[36]

SOUTHERN DISRICTS

The combined force of the 8th Guards Army and 1st Guards Tank Army continued to drive southeast in order to encircle Berlin from that direction. The numerous lakes and rivers they encountered continued to impede their progress. Detachments were created and ordered to advance ahead of the main body to identify and capture useful crossing points. Chuikov's combined force split as it drove around both the north and southern shores of the Müggelsee. The 29th Guards Rifle Corps took intact the railway bridge leading south across the Spree at Dammvorstadt. The 39th Rifle Division cleared Köpenick after bitter rearguard actions by the retreating Germans taking its bridges across the Spree and the Dahme rivers intact. Körner's King Tiger was in Köpenick when the Soviet advance began again that day. His crew quickly knocked out a JS–2 but didn't see a second one before it fired. The second JS–2's shell caused a freak accident inside the gun tube that tore the loader to pieces.[37] Körner's King Tiger was then ordered to the last known location of the maintenance company in Spandau. By evening the 28th Guards Rifle Corps closed on the area below the southern spur of the Teltow Canal in Grünow. The local defense commander of Defense Sector C received additional reinforcements in the form of *Hauptmann* Überschär's *Hitlerjugend* commandos to deal with the developing Soviet threat in this sector. Armed with *Panzerfausts*, Kübelwagen and private automobiles they drove around the city launching attacks against Soviet armor then made a quick retreat to ambush the Soviets again.[38] More new recruits were drawn up and sent to Defense Sectors C and D in the wake of Chuikov's and Koniev's uncoordinated advance into Berlin.

Soldiers filtered in from the east, some reinforcement moved in from the west, and collection points were created at key spots within the city like the Olympic Stadium, Reich Sports Field, and Ruhleben Barracks. Besides stragglers, the 2nd Levy of the *Volkssturm* was also called up. These men had received no training in the proceeding months and had no weapons. They were often assigned to a senior *Wehrmacht* Sergeant and typically treated as 'second class' soldiers even by the 1st Levy *Volkssturm*. One particular group of 2nd Levy recruits received orders to move to the Teltow Canal after their initial assembly. Men in this unit disappeared daily. After moving around for several days and not being given any assignment by the various commands, this group found an abandoned store and sat out the fighting without firing a shot.[39]

Koniev's forces continued to consolidate along the Teltow Canal in preparation for the crossing scheduled for the morning of 24 April. The 3rd Guards Tank Army spent the rest of the day regrouping. During the day elements of the 128th Rifle Corps from the 28th Army arrived but the 152nd Rifle Division was caught up fighting elements of the *9.Armee* and did not join its parent corps for several days. Koniev viewed the crossing of the canal as a major obstacle and the last step before he could enter the heart of Berlin. While he clearly exaggerates for his readers, the following passage illuminates his thinking about the problem. Koniev wrote:

> Imagine this deep and wide moat, with high concrete-coated, steeply descending banks, filled with water. Even in the twenty-kilometer section at which Rybalko's tankmen had arrived, on the German side everything that the Germans had at hand, 15,000 men, had been massed. This density – 1200 men per kilometer, in conditions of street battle – I must say was very high. And also there were more then 250 guns and mortars, 130 tanks and armored personnel carriers, and more than 500 machine guns. And there was such a large quantity of *Panzerfausts*, that, in essence, they could be considered as unlimited.[40]

Koniev exaggerates the German's strength, but he articulates the key problem—crossing the canal under fire. His infantry could swim but tanks and artillery needed to use the remaining bridges or attempt to build pontoons across the high-walled canal. It was at this time that the orders for blowing the city's bridges were issued by Weidling as Berlin's new military commander. Not all the bridges were destroyed immediately, some being retained, such as the Frey Bridge on the Heerstraße and the Mussehl Bridge over the Teltow Canal. Koniev decided to launch his attack on a wide front using all three corps of the 3rd Guards Tank Army simultaneously. He was very concerned about ensuring superiority of firepower at the crossing points and consequently assembled 3,000 pieces of artillery, mortars, and self-propelled guns along a breakthrough section of 4.5 kilometers. According to Koniev: "Six hundred and fifty barrels per kilometer of front! Perhaps this was the only case of such a density of artillery fire in all my practice during the war."[41] As Koniev's preparations moved forward, German forces on both sides of the Teltow Canal were moving into new positions without any knowledge of Koniev's future assault into Berlin.

Soviet motorcycle scouts take a break in a residential district of Berlin. Note the wrecked store front on the left suggesting that some fighting recently occurred here. Photo courtesy of RGAKFD Moscow.

Skorning moved his force north of the Teltow Canal and set up a defense line in buildings opposite key crossing points.[42] To the west, Pienkny's unit dug in opposite of Giesensdorfstraße where it crosses the Teltow Canal. While they were waiting a Tiger I rolled up from the direction where the Russians were supposed to be and approached two *SS* soldiers posted out in front of the *Hitlerjugend Gruppe 200* as lookouts. It was assumed that the Tiger I was a straggler from the German forces retreating into Berlin. One of the Panzer crew leaned out of the turret and asked the *SS* soldiers if they had ammunition for his.08 pistol that he presented to the *SS* lookouts. When the one of the *SS* soldiers reached into his pocket the Panzer crewman pulled out an MP44 and sprayed both *SS* soldiers with bullets killing them on the spot. The Panzer crewman slammed the hatch shut and the Tiger I quickly turned back around and headed in the direction it came. The *Hitlerjugend* were stunned and eventually fired *Panzerfausts* at the retreating Tiger I, but in their excitement they missed. What occurred was an apparent infiltration by Seydlitz soldiers operating in the vanguard of Koniev's forces and helping him to secure crossing points over the Teltow Canal.[43] In the evening Pienkny's force were replaced by a *Volkssturm* unit and withdrew to Oskerlange Bridge. While in their positions they tried to enter one of the nearby buildings but the civilians refused them entry exclaiming they wanted no soldiers with weapons in their homes. As the boys went back out into the nearby park to set up their position they received sniper fire from the surrounding buildings as this area contained strong Communist sympathizers.[44]

WESTERN DISTRICTS

Soviets forces continued their rapid crossing of the Havel during the night of 22/23 April. The 47th Army, 9th Guard Tank Corps of the 2nd Guards Tank Army, and 7th Guard Cavalry Corps led the vanguard. The 9th Guard Tank Corps broke up into brigades that were leant out to the units of the 47th Army. The 125th Rifle Corps, supported by the 50th Guards Tank and 33rd Guards Mechanized Brigade, closed upon the defenses of Spandau and Gatow airfield with the design to quickly capture those sectors of the city. As the Soviets moved into position, they made no attempt to penetrate the town of Spandau. The 77th Rifle Corps, and 38th Rifle Division, supported by the 65th Guards Tank Brigade headed south. The 7th Guards Cavalry Corps fanned out to secure the countryside as far as the Elbe River.

Spandau was defended by a variety of German formations. There were several *Volkssturm Battalions, Hitlerjugend, Galician Luftwaffe Cadets,* and elements of a *Wehrmacht RAD* (*Reichsarbeitsdienst*) unit mobilized and based in the Ruhleben barracks. One German defender, a young soldier named Helmuth Altner saw the chaos begin to take shape within this sector of the city:

> Time passes relentlessly as it comes to the final hours. A group of women appear from the South. Men rush along the streets looking furtively around them. SS patrols in cars are driving along the streets, stopping a man here and picking one up there, their engines humming. *Volkssturm,* here mainly in SS uniform, close the anti-tank barriers behind them, while Hitler Youth go about proudly carrying *Panzerfausts*.[45]

Soviet troops move into the suburbs of Berlin. Note the horse drawn 76mm ZIS-3 guns.
Photo courtesy of the Bulgarian Ministry of Defence.

Particularly disturbing to Altner was the frequency of the *Waffen-SS* and *Volkssturm* patrols that continued to comb every building for able-bodied men to fight. Anyone thought to be a deserter was summarily shot, hung, and labeled as a traitor with a sign.[46]

Berlin's population was now being forcibly mobilized and sent into battle.

NORTHERN DISTRICTS

Few German defenders existed in the districts north of the S-Bahn ring marking the Inner Defensive belt. Several *Volkssturm* and *Polizei Battalions* were scattered across the north. The expectation was that the main Soviet attack would come from the east and south so there was little need for forces here. Reports showed the 2nd Guards Tank Army heading east and north not south. German intelligence had not determined the exact location and direction of attack for the 3rd Shock Army and was unaware of Colonel General V.I. Kutznetsov operational intentions. The 1st Mechanized Corps cleared the area as far down as Tegel Airport against light resistance. The remnants of the 12th Guard Tank Corps pushed its way through the undefended suburb community of Reinickendorf with the 79th Rifle Corps on its left in Niederschönhausen. Tactics of the 3rd Shock Army's Corps demonstrated the same basic principles executed by other armies under Zhukov's command. All units demonstrated rapid and uncoordinated movement. German defensive positions were bypassed. Those that could not be bypassed or areas of suspected German forces were immediately blasted with area artillery and Katushya Rockets followed by armor moving up to be employed as mobile artillery in the direct fire role. Then Soviet infantry would move forward to assault what remained of the German positions.[47]

As the Soviets settled down in the northern residential district for the night, German reinforcements began to arrive. The remnants of the *Wachregiment Großdeutschland* filtered back from the Oder Front. Seemingly independent of orders, it moved into Moabit, Wedding, and Pankow to take up defensive positions behind the S-Bahn ring. This area was very familiar to the soldiers of *Großdeutschland*, as they were the only combat unit stationed in Berlin during the war, with their headquarters and barracks located in Moabit.[48] These soldiers were well armed, trained, and had their own assigned assault guns.

Notes to Chapter 6: Assault on Berlin, 23rd April Monday

1   Böttcher interview.
2   Ibid.
3   von Dufving interview.
4   Ibid.
5   Ibid.
6   Weidling Interrogation Report.
7   The first was when Hitler awarded him the Oakleaves to the Iron Cross on 13 April 1944.
8   Weidling Interrogation Report. In his justifications for going along he stated that he didn't know the strength of the *12th Armee* or Steiner's forces. He simply believed that there was enough strength in the remaining German divisions outside of Berlin to mount an effective offensive to relieve Berlin.
9   Ibid.
10 von Dufving interview.
11 Ibid.
12 Army Group Weichsel War Diary, Apr 20–9, p. 236 (RC: 64/3)
13 Ibid, p. 211 (RC: 64/3), and Army Group Weichsel War Diary, Apr 20–9 pp. 237–8 (RC: 68/4).
14 Army Group Weichsel War Diary, Apr 20–9, pp. 241–2 (RC: 68/4).
15 Koniev unpublished memoir, p. 119.
16 Army Group Weichsel War Diary, Apr 20–9, p. 230, 246 (RC: 68/4).
17 M. Bauer, *MS #R-79 Ninth Army's Last Attack and Surrender Apr 21 – May 7, 1945*, p. 14. (RC: 62/2).
18 Ibid., p. 9.
19 Schultz-Naumann, p. 17.
20 W. Wenck interview (RC: 67/24), and H. W. Ritter, *"Factual Report of Interviews with General A.D. Walter Wenck,"* (RC: 67/24).
21 *Summary of Final Battles between the Order and Elbe in Apr/May 1945 (Especially the Battles of 12th Army*, p. 7. (RC: 67/24)
22 Wenck interview.
23 Ibid.
24 Army Group Weichsel War Diary, Apr 20–9, p. 245 (RC: 68/4).
25 Ibid, p. 246 (RC: 68/4).
26 Ibid, p. 202 (RC: 68/4).
27 L. von Zabeltitz interview (RC: 69/8), and Army Group Weichsel War Diary, Apr 20–9, pp. 227–8 (RC: 68/4).
28 Zabeltitz interview.
29 Hillblad, p. 91.
30 Ibid.
31 Henseler interview.
32 Illum interview.
33 Ibid.
34 Haas interview.
35 Scholles interview.
36 Burghart interview.
37 Schneider, p. 301.
38 Venghaus, p. 228.
39 H. Hellriegel interview (RC: 69/33).
40 Koniev unpublished memoir, p. 116.
41 Ibid, p. 118.
42 Venghaus pp. 337–8.
43 Some may find this incredulous, but this is not the first or the last account where a German Panzer was taken over by Seydlitz or even Russian forces and ambushed German soldiers. This Tiger I was probably abandoned at the Kummersdorf training grounds south of Berlin when it was overrun by Koniev several days earlier.
44 Pienkny interview.
45 Altner, p. 82.
46 Le Tissier, *Race for the Reichstag*, p. 86.
47 Ibid, p. 80.
48 Spaeter vol. 3 pp. 501–2.

6

ASSAULT ON BERLIN

24 APRIL
TUESDAY

Gradually we lost all human appearance. Our eyes burned and our faces were lined and stained with the dust that surrounded us. We no longer saw blue sky; everywhere buildings were burning, ruins falling, and the smoke billowing back and forth in the streets.

The Silence that followed each bombardment was merely the prelude to the roar of engines and clank of tracks heralding a new tank attack.

Recollection of a German veteran of Berlin[1]

Notice! He who approves or encourages measures which weaken our resistance is a traitor! He is to be hanged or shot at once! This includes such measures that are supposedly ordered in the name of Goebbels or the Führer himself!

Hitler proclamation issued in the last issue of Berlin *Der Völkische Beobachter*[2]

The first announcement to the world that the Soviet Union launched an attack on Berlin came in the form of an article published in the London edition of *Pravda*. The article read: "The Germans had made a thorough, skillful job of their defenses. All the way from one line to the next, the attacking troops were under flanking fire. All the fields were criss-crossed with ditches, many of them flooded. Camouflaged anti-tank guns lurked in the orchards. I have never seen anything to equal the density of the German trench system on the Berlin approaches."[3] The release of the news story came with official confirmation that Berlin was surrounded and cut off from the rest of the world. The German Propaganda Ministry likewise issued *Der Panzerbär* ['The Panzer Bear'].[4] This four-page newspaper subtitled 'Combat Paper for the Defenders of Greater Berlin' provided a daily summary of the prior day's action and let Berliners know they were now *the* front and *last* line of defense for Nazi Germany.

Berlin was now virtually sealed off by land. Somewhere between 0600 and 1030 Koniev's 71st Mechanized Brigade met elements of Chuikov's combined 8th Guards and 1st Guards Tank Armies at Schönefeld Airfield southwest of Berlin.[5] This meeting completed the encirclement of the *9.Armee*. The 61st Guards Rifle Division and elements of the 9th Mechanized Corps met with other forces of Chuikov in Mariendorf by evening, completing the encirclement of Berlin from the south.[6] Koniev's 6th Guard Mechanized Corps of Lelyushenko's 4th Guards Tank Army reached Brandenburg and the Havel River late in the day. While Koniev's soldiers did not link up with soldiers of the 47th Army, Zhukov's 77th and 129th Rifle Corps continued their advance south to a position only five kilometers north of Koniev's forward position.[7] Farther west, Koniev's 5th Guards and 13th Army reached the Elbe.[8] Koniev was now in an extended position with his forces operating far from their logistic base and spread thin between two desperate German armies poised to attack his flanks.

12.ARMEE

In the early morning hours Wenck issued orders to his divisions in preparation for their movement and attack toward the east. Under Wenck's command were *XXXIX Panzer Korps*, *XXXXI Panzer Korps*, the *XXXXVIII Panzer Korps,* and the *XX Korps*. All were engaged in a wide area that spanned from the Baltic in the north, to Wittenberg in the south along the east-west bend of the Elbe. He immediately ordered the *XXXXI Panzer Korps* to leave a small security force along the Elbe then to move east and form a defensive line east of Brandenburg-Potsdam, but west of Nauen, and to hold the rear of *AGV*. The only force he could immediately deploy for the attack east was *Generalleutnant* Carl-Erik Koehler's newly formed *XX Korps* that was deployed along the Elbe to defend against any U.S. Army crossings. The *XX Korps* was now assigned several new divisions for the upcoming attack. The *Theodor Körner Division* was immediately ordered from the Elbe to the Belzig area and subordinated to *XX Korps*. Its mission was to conduct security and reconnaissance in force to the northeast, and southeast; secure its right flank with the *Ulrich von Hutten Division*; and to push east and determine if a corridor to Busse's *9.Armee* was possible. Along with the *Körner Division* came the *Sturmgeschütz Brigade 243*. The *Ulrich von Hutten Division* was ordered to leave its positions along the Elbe, disengage with U.S. forces, and deploy to the area of Wittenberg to defend against any future Soviet attack. The *Ferdinand von Schill Division* was ordered to complete its mobilization and prepare for a march on 25 April to the area of Niemegk. Once it deployed the division would fall under the command of *XX Korps*. In addition *Sturmgeschütz Brigade 1170* was prepared for movement with *Schill* east to participate in the coming offensive.[9] The *Scharnhorst Division* was ordered to remain its positions to defend against any possible U.S. attack across the Elbe.[10]

These divisions were *Reichsarbeitsdienst* or *(RAD)* under the *Type 45* division model. This meant the divisions were pulled from the existing labor force in Germany and that they were reduced in the number of battalions in each regiment.[11] They consisted of thousands of new recruits, pulled together from the *Hitlerjugend*, and Officer Cadet Schools. The divisions numbered no more than 7,500–9,000 men each (this was a fairly high allotment of soldiers for late in the war).[12] There were senior officer and NCOs assigned to these units. The divisions were surprisingly well equipped, trained, and motivated by all accounts. In the case of *Schill*, this division consisted of two grenadier regiments of three battalions each as well as an assault gun brigade from *Großdeutschland*. In addition it may also have had a self-propelled Sturmartilleriebrigade.[13] It is also not clear if they were equipped with motorized transport, although in the case of *Körner*, they used civilian buses to deploy to their new assembly area.

Koehler's men executed their difficult movement orders successfully. They conducted an amazing night march and by mid-morning were in their assigned positions. The divisions' movement was aided by the complete cessation of all Western Allied air activity over the *12.Armee* lines starting on 23 April,[14] and by the use of several autobahns that ran east-west from the Elbe toward Berlin. These high-speed roads explain how these divisions managed their difficult task with apparent ease.

The *Hutten Division* immediately ran into elements of Koniev's 13th Army to the east and northeast of Wittenberg after completing its night march. The Soviets were easily repulsed as *Hutten* launched an attack into the Soviet flank looking for a link up with *Körner* to the north. The Soviets did not expect any German resistance to their front and quickly withdrew to assess the situation after the initial contact with German forces. The presence of the Soviets presumably surprised Koehler as well. He immediately requested the redeployment of the *Scharnhorst Division* from the Elbe River to the area north of Wittenberg to seal left flank of *Körner*.[15] *Körner* meanwhile launched its attack as ordered pushing out 12 kilometers from Niemegk to Treuenbrietzen, as well as southwest to forge a link-up with *Hutten*. The 13th Army's vanguard in this area was quickly repulsed. In the town of Treuenbrietzen *Körner* fought elements of the 5th Mechanized Corps's 10th Guards Mechanized Brigade in an all-day see-saw battle for the town.[16]

Koniev initially had no knowledge of a German *12.Armee* west of Berlin. He was particularly alarmed when his forces screening between the 4th Guards Tank and 13th Armies ran straight into disciplined and well-organized German troops. Koniev quickly rerouted the 5th Guards Mechanized Corps and part of his air fleet to deal with the German attack from the east.[17] Koniev downplays his surprise at finding German formations operating on his left flank in his memoir but he does discuss the lack of forces available to confront the various operational problems caused by his over-extended lines:

> I was also concerned with the fact that on the Beelitz-Treuenbritzen Front, we should have additional forces on hand. It was necessary to find them. I had already taken one division from Pukhov and sent it to Potsdam in order to hold everything that Lelyushenko would capture there [meaning *Armeegruppe Spree*]. Now we had to withdraw one of Pukhov's corps to the second echelon of the army, to the Jüterbog region, where this corps could be used in two ways, depending on the situation: either it could reinforce the inner line, at Berlin, or reinforce the outer line, the westerly direction, in the vicinity of Beelitz-Treuenbritzen, where the 5th Mechanized Corps … was already operating.
>
> This especially concerned me, because already on 23 April a number of signs had appeared that some sort of regrouping was beginning among the Germans in the west and [that] they [were] obviously preparing to hit us from the west.[18]

As Wenck's forces redeployed, his name and the *12.Armee* became synonymous with 'rescue' for the civilians and soldiers trapped in Berlin and the *9.Armee* pocket.

Wenck's advance was capitalized on by the Propaganda Ministry, much to the shock of Wenck. At 1900 and again at 2045 the following message was broadcast via Berlin radio:

> … Fuhrer gave an order of historical importance. German troops leave the west to participate in the battle for Berlin. Involved are the best divisions which stood ready for special assignments at the west front. They are already engaged in the battle for Berlin. The first units are already in the outskirts of the city. By this action the Reich manifests its determination to defend Berlin at all costs and to prevent an overflowing by the Asiatic Storm. There can be no doubt that the coming days, even hours, will bring the decisive turn in the fight.[19]

In addition, yellow pamphlets were produced and apparently dropped among the German lines that read:

> Order of the Führer of the 23 of April 1945: Soldiers of the *Armee Wenck*! An order of great importance called you from your positions against our western enemy and orders you towards the east. Your order is clear: Berlin remains German. The ordered objectives have to be reached on all accounts, because from other sides operations are also going on with the aim of inflicting upon the Bolshevists the decisive defeat in the battle for the German capital and with that a change in the German situation completely. Berlin does not capitulate to Bolshevism. The defenders of the German capital have taken new courage after the news of your rapid concentration, and fight with defiance and doggedness in the hope to hear soon the thundering of your arms. The Führer has called you. Like in the old times of victory you have lined up for the start. Berlin is waiting for you. Berlin is longing for you with its whole heart.[20]

Wenck was enraged by the radio broadcast and the printed pamphlets. He ordered all the pamphlets found among his units burned. These communications caused two problems for Wenck. First, they provided false hope to all Berliners that he had plans to rescue them by direct attack. Second, his forces lost all operational surprise with these unplanned activities.[21]

Wenck's advance had significant psychological effects on the German forces in Berlin. Amazingly, the Western Allies decided not to interdict Wenck's forces at all.[22] His advance toward Berlin coupled with the inactivity of the Western Allies created the illusion of a potential split between the Western Allies and the Soviets. Everyone was in high spirits with the idea that the Western Allies would help the Germans. The rumors about peace with the Western Allies now grew rampant and caused worry in the minds of the German High Command who viewed these rumors as undermining the German soldier's will to fight. A radio message was released to all German Army Groups signed by Krebs. The radio message stated that "Criminal rumors spread by the enemy speak of a truce with America and similar things which are fit to paralyze the fighting spirit. We must vigorously challenge these rumors and its circulation. Our fighting will be continued until victory ....."[23] The reality is that many Germans drew strength from the belief that a truce was made with the Western Allies and that they might join the fight against 'Bolshevism'. This belief was only reinforced by a complete lack of Western Allied military response when Wenck's *12.Armee* turned away from the Elbe and began its drive toward Berlin.

ARMY GROUP VISTULA

Significant activity continued in *AGV* as Wenck's forces turned east. Steiner spent the day organizing his meager forces for the offensive he did not want to launch. The *III (germ.) SS-Pz. Korps* was the backbone of *Armeegruppe Steiner* and consisted of *Fortress Regiment 62, Kampfgruppe Harzer* (including *Kriegsmarine Rgt. 9, SS-Panzergrenadier Regiment 8,* and *SS-Panzerjäger Bataillon 23*), *Kampfgruppe Schirmer, Kampfgruppe Kresin,* and *Kampfgruppe von Wolf*.[24] Steiner's forces were *Wehrmacht, SS, Kriegsmarine, Luftwaffe,* and *Volkssturm* personnel all mixed together. Steiner again delayed his attack against the flank of the 61st Army moving west along the Finow Canal. He was critical of his task when he spoke to Heinrici, and explained that even if he launched the planned counterattack he "won't be able to make a deep thrust ...."[25] Despite his protests the *25.Panzergrenadier Division*, with a battalion from the *1.Marine Division* and sixty tanks prepared to launch a counterattack against the 1st Polish Army now fighting around Oranienburg.[26] Farther south, Busse's situation continued to grow critical. Aerial supply was now organized by air-landing and aerial drops after the *9.Armee* was cut off from all land supply.[27] Busse continued to consolidate and organize his forces for a thrust west toward Wenck, while still fighting off attacks by Soviet forces from the south and north. The *3.Panzer Armee* continued to be placed in a precarious position, and repositioned its forces to prepare local counterattacks in order to forestall any Soviet breakthroughs. Heinrici now ordered that the remaining German units in Stettin be withdrawn back across the Oder to prevent their isolation.[28]

The *Luftwaffe* launched one last, if not one of the largest sorties, during the final months of the war to assist the defenders of Berlin. A total of 252 aircraft took part in the attack that included 158 fighters, and 83 ground attack aircraft. The aircraft over the skies of Berlin include some of the *Luftwaffe's* most advanced jet aircraft in service. Soviet ground forces were jammed along restrictive roads in and around the city and made rich targets for the German aircraft. The final *Luftwaffe* sortie claimed the destruction of 11 Soviet tanks and 243 motorized vehicles.[29] The number of *Luftwaffe* aircraft lost was not reported but was probably high.

LVI PZ. KORPS

Weidling reviewed the defense sector maps and operational situation with his staff in a makeshift HQ located within the Tempelhof Airport's administrative buildings. He subsequently issued new movement orders to his formations. Weidling's plan was to appoint his commanders and deploy his divisions in each of the Defensive Zones based on four factors: current combat power of his remaining divisions; importance of the defensive sector; level of threat to the sector; and relative combat experience of the current sector commander. Based on these factors his deployment orders sent the *20.Pz.Gren.Div* to sector E in order to maintain a defensive zone between Berlin and Potsdam; *Nordland* to Defense Sector C where the bulk of the division was already engaged against the advancing Russians; *Müncheberg* to Defense Sector B; the *9.Fallschirmjäger* to Defense Sector A; *18.Pz.Gren.Div.* into a reserve position northwest of Tempelhof airport; and the remainder of the *408.Volksart.Korps* to the Tiergarten.[30] This initial deployment reflected the belief that the Soviets were going to attack from the east and south and not from all directions at once. His deployment also suggests that he had no knowledge that Koniev's forces were already operating in Berlin along his southern front.

Weidling and his staff began to visit the various Defense Sectors to ascertain the current combat readiness and composition of local forces after he completed his initial deployment plans. His findings were less than favorable. Upon the completion of his inspection he noticed few anti-tank weapons except *Panzerfausts*, and about 300 anti-aircraft artillery (primarily 8.8s) scattered around and used in the anti-tank role. The ground forces he encountered were mainly *Volkssturm* mingled with units of all kinds.[31] No single, stable regular army unit was found, and the artillery assets in the city were primarily batteries of captured guns spread throughout the various sectors.[32] The German High Command's war diary recorded that these forces " ... were not organically integrated units, but ... a hodgepodge of remnants and splinter groups thrown together without formal organization. With varying degrees of training, armament and equipment, their combat value was accordingly low."[33] Weidling made his HQ along the Hohenzollendorf. He returned there to check on the movement of his troops into Berlin. At 1100 he received a phone call from Krebs asking him to see him immediately at the *Führerbunker*. When Weidling arrived Krebs announced that he made a favorable impression on Hitler the day before and that he was now officially appointed Commander of Berlin. Weidling replied "I would have preferred your order to shoot me. Then fate would have spared me."[34]

As the *LVI Pz. Korps* executed its movement orders it became apparent that both the situation in the city and the assaulting Soviet forces were preventing operational movement. Each sector commander treated their area as a fiefdom and any soldiers moving through them were typically rounded up and placed into *Alarm Units*. Weidling asked that his soldiers be given *carte blanche* movement and not be restricted. In practice this worked if the soldiers had their pay books or other documents stating their unit. Not all soldiers still had official documentation after the chaotic withdrawal from the Oder River. Stragglers of the *LVI Pz. Korps* certainly found themselves pressed into local *Alarm Units*.[35] A memorandum was passed down from the *Führerbunker* to all the Defense Sectors listing the units assigned to Weidling's command and granting them free access to move around the city.

Weidling and his staff took stock of their forces now that their units began to settle into various Defense Sectors in Berlin. Von Dufving stated that the Panzer Korps was now down to 40 Panzers and 80 SPWs.[36] This meant that they had lost nearly 80% of their Panzers during combat operations over the last nine days. Weidling estimated that he brought about 13,000–15,000 troops into the city but based on all available research and first person accounts that number probably did not exceed 13,000.[37] Weidling lost about 43% of his manpower. Since the Soviet assault began on 16 April Weidling was loosing approximately 18 Panzers, and 1,065 Panzergrenadiers and Fallschirmjägers per day. He received no reinforcements. *Müncheberg*, as von Dufving predicted, was not able to completely disengage from the Soviets. Only one-third of its armor and infantry were able to move into Berlin after a breakout from a pocket around Waltersdorf in the south of Berlin that took place at 0300. The rest of the division was either destroyed by the Soviets or broke out into the

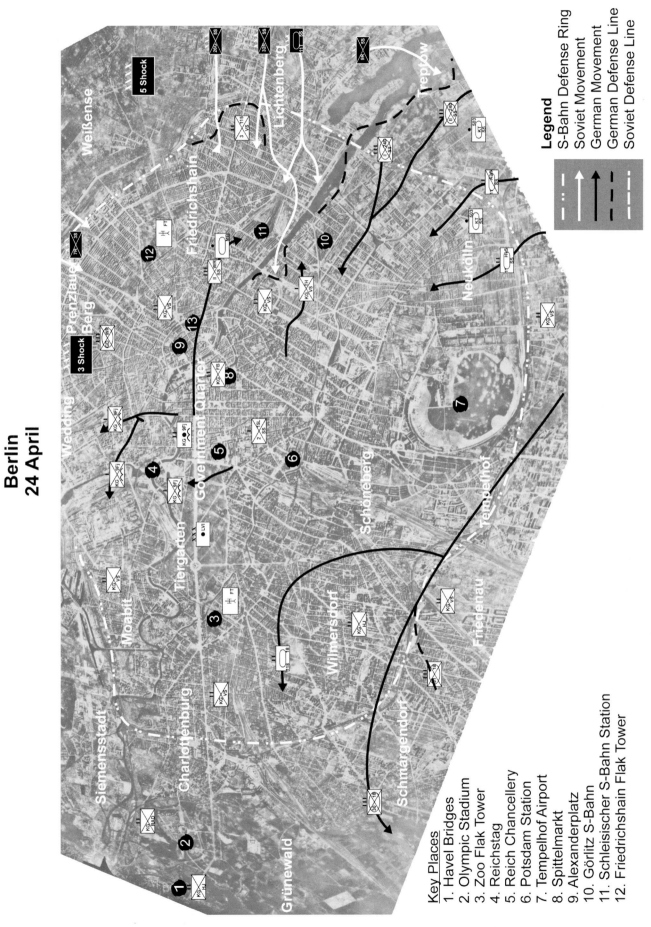

**Berlin
24 April**

Key Places
1. Havel Bridges
2. Olympic Stadium
3. Zoo Flak Tower
4. Reichstag
5. Reich Chancellery
6. Potsdam Station
7. Tempelhof Airport
8. Spittelmarkt
9. Alexanderplatz
10. Görlitz S-Bahn
11. Schleisischer S-Bahn Station
12. Friedrichshain Flak Tower

Legend
S-Bahn Defense Ring
Soviet Movement
German Movement
German Defense Line
Soviet Defense Line

Oberstleutnant Erich Bärenfänger, commander of Defense Sector A was a staunch supporter of Hitler, and would be field promoted to *Generalmajor* by Goebbels during the battle. Photo courtesy of C. Habisohn.

northern wing of the *9.Armee*. The *20.Pz.Gren.Div.* moved west without strong leadership. Its commander became despondent during the withdrawal from the Seelow Heights. Unknown to most of his command staff, the division's commander became suicidal as well. The *20.Pz.Gren.Div.* was strung out along the Teltow Canal when it ran directly into Koniev's assault resulting in additional losses and disruption. *Nordland* was also in poor shape. The division fractured during their deployment along the Seelow Heights. There was no leadership from Zeigler who apparently lost interest in command. His forces were in disarray fighting toward the west under constant pressure of the Soviets. Elements of the division were scattered in a wide arc from Alexanderplatz to Neukölln. Other elements were still traveling west as ordered to find and secure crossing points across the Havel River for the division's escape west. *Nordland's* cohesion as a division ceased to exist. The *9.Fallschirmjäger* was down to a regiment in size and Weidling didn't expect much from them. The *18.Pz.Gren.Div.* remained the strongest of all his divisions and he kept them for a mobile reserve that could strike east or south against the area believed to be the main line of Soviet advance into the city.[38] Among his orders of the day was the destruction of the remaining bridges across the Teltow Canal as it became apparent later in the day that Soviet forces were poised to cross over.[39] The artillery from the *408.Volksartillerie Korps* had practically no ammunition and was only able to bring about two-thirds of their guns into the city. They were equipped with 4 7.5cm cannon, 4 field howitzers, 5 15.2cm Russian field howitzers, and 4 21cm mortars.[40]

Weidling faced dual problems of command and supply in addition to the problems associated with combat power. Shortages of ammunition were common to all the field units, supply being a matter of chance, or the ingenuity of the unit commander. There were in fact ample supplies of standard German ammunition within the city, but obtaining access to them was often difficult. Defense Sector Commanders hoarded ammunition and supply for their own uses. This often led to conflict between Defense Sector Commanders and those appointed by Weidling. In Defense Sector A for example, *Oberstleutnant* Bärenfänger and *Generalmajor* Mummert of *Müncheberg* were in open conflict over who commanded the forces in the sector.[41]

EASTERN DISTRICTS

The eastern approaches to Berlin came under heavy attack by the 5th Shock Army and elements of the 3rd Shock Army to the north. The 7th Rifle Corps advanced through Prenzlauer Berg District, and down the two main roads toward Alexanderplatz. The corps penetrated the inner defense ring across the Prenzlauer Allee and Weissensee S-Bahn stations without any serious resistance.[42] The 26th Guards and 32nd Rifle Corps of the 5th Shock Army strongly supported by independent armor elements from the 11th Guards and 67th Tank Brigades advanced astride Frankfurter Allee just inside the inner defense ring and to the west of Frankfurter Allee S-Bahn station. Among the solid stone factory buildings the Russians encountered two companies of the *115 Siemenstadt Volkssturm Bataillon* in the early morning. These *Volkssturm* companies were almost surrounded but did not retreat. They put up stiff resistance against the advancing Russians. The Soviets used direct fire from their assault guns and mortars to force the defenders from the factory and nearby rail complex buildings. German Forward Observers were dispatched from the Friedrichshain Flak Tower by the early afternoon to coordinate fire from the Flak Tower's 12.8cm guns. The Forward Observers took up positions nearby and radioed the Soviet's locations to the Flak Tower. As fire from the 12.8cm guns hit the Soviet positions their offensive ground to a halt. General Berzarin was upset with the lack of progress. He knew he could not destroy the Flak Tower so he decided to decimate the *Volkssturm* defenders resisting in their positions. Berzarin ordered every building in the area marked for destruction by Soviet artillery. He gave orders not to spare any of the ammunition for his 2,000 guns.[43] The use of mass firepower in urban terrain proved more of a hindrance for Berzarin's forces. The resulting rubble often blocked the few avenues of approach through the main avenues and side streets. German survivors were often able to survive the indirect fire and quickly repositioned forces to new makeshift defensive points created by the Soviet artillery fire.

Defense Sectors A and B were generally better equipped with 8.8cm anti-tank guns and barricades for a defense than other sectors due to the belief that the Soviet's main axis of advance into Berlin was the eastern approaches. The defense force located in this sector had the benefit of fire support from Friedrichshain Flak Tower as noted above. Another direct benefit was the concentric road network that

Soviet super-heavy 203mm howitzers in Berlin. Photo courtesy of RGAKFD Moscow

Another photograph of a Soviet super-heavy 203-mm howitzer in action. These massive howitzers caused considerable damage and could take out a building. Photo courtesy of the Bulgarian Ministry of Defence.

A wing of Soviet Ilyushin Il-2 Shturmoviks flying over central Berlin. The Soviets did not dominate the airspace over Berlin as the *Luftwaffe* managed to put up fierce resistance over the city. In addition to German fighters, the three Flak Towers presented dangerous opponents. The Soviet aircraft often could not tell friend from foe in the dense tangle of rubble strewn streets and thick smoke. Significant incidents of friendly fire occurred by Soviet aircraft that routinely attacked their own force concentrations in the city. Photo courtesy of the Bundesarchiv.

A battalion size unit of Soviet T-34/85s pauses along a broad Berlin avenue. Early Soviet employment of tanks in Berlin did not follow any urban tactical dispositions making them easy targets for German infantry armed with *Panzerfausts* lurking in the ruins. Note the apparent lack of any infantry support to protect the tanks. Photo courtesy of the Cornelius Ryan Collection, Mahn Center, Alden Library, Ohio University, Athens, OH.

A column of six ISU-152 tank destroyers rests during their advance into Berlin. Again, note the lack of any defensive tactical disposition or infantry support. The lead ISU-152 shows its wear as both the right and left side fender have been ripped off. Dense smoke obscures visibility to the rear of the column. Courtesy of the US National Archives.

Postwar photo of Tempelhof. This was Chuikov's goal. His forces met considerable resistance from the *Luftwaffe* Flak Battery stationed on the airfield that was supported by Panzers from *Müncheberg*. Author's collection.

Eastern Districts
24 April

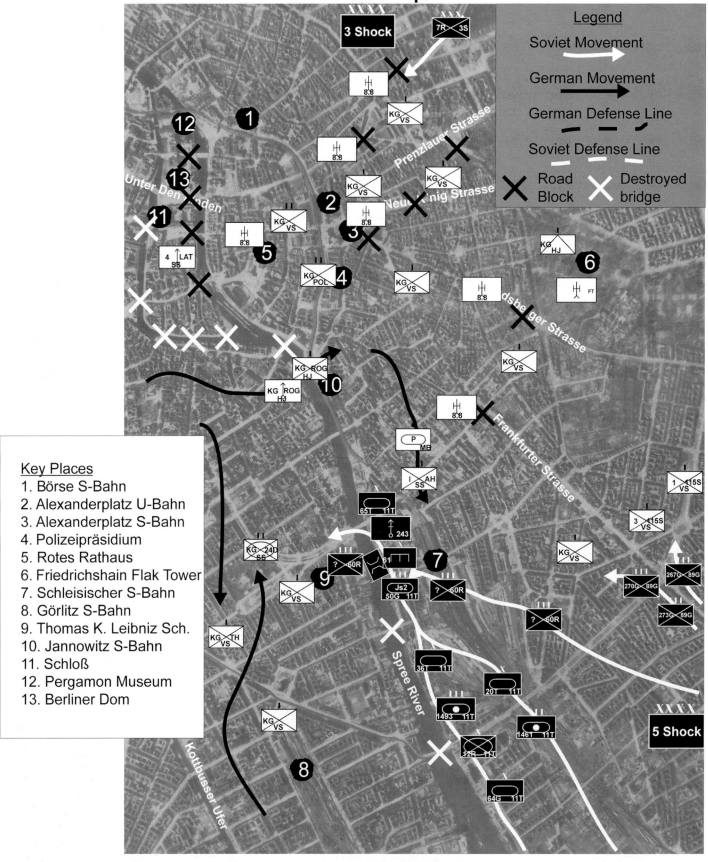

Legend
Soviet Movement
German Movement
German Defense Line
Soviet Defense Line
Road Block
Destroyed bridge

3 Shock

5 Shock

Key Places
1. Börse S-Bahn
2. Alexanderplatz U-Bahn
3. Alexanderplatz S-Bahn
4. Polizeipräsidium
5. Rotes Rathaus
6. Friedrichshain Flak Tower
7. Schleisischer S-Bahn
8. Görlitz S-Bahn
9. Thomas K. Leibniz Sch.
10. Jannowitz S-Bahn
11. Schloß
12. Pergamon Museum
13. Berliner Dom

A column of Soviet infantry makes its way along a Berlin street. Note the anti-tank rifle carried by the soldier near bottom right of the photo. (RGAKFD Moscow)

A Soviet officer leads a squad of heavily laden infantry up a ladder and onto a bridge crossing the Teltow Canal. Movement through the rubble of Berlin was arduous even when not under German defensive fire. Photo courtesy of the Cornelius Ryan Collection, Mahn Center, Alden Library, Ohio University, Athens, OH.

focused on Alexanderplatz. All major east-west avenues into the center of Berlin converged on the Alexanderplatz U-Bahn and S-Bahn stations. This allowed the defenders to use interior lines and U-Bahn tunnels to maximize their defensive power. The U-Bahn station was itself an underground fortress that went down several levels and protected German civilian and soldier alike. To the south was the *Polizeipräsidium* (Police HQ), a commanding building with two-meter thick walls. In essence it was an above-ground fortress that dominated the advance down Frankfurter Allee. Berzarin was forced to move his forces south and approach Alexanderplatz from that direction in order to avoid much of the main German defense and the 12.8cm Flak Tower guns. This indirect movement toward Alexanderplatz, and eventually the Spree River cost the Soviets significant time, and ultimately left much of Defense Sectors A and B in German hands until 2 May.

Reinforcements to the eastern Defense Sectors were dispatched by Seifert from Defense Sector Z that included *I./LSSAH Wachregiment* under the command of *SS-Hauptsturmführer* Mrgulla, and several Panthers from *Müncheberg*. A mortar section was also dispatched that consisted of *Hitlerjugend* and *Volkssturm* under command of *SS-Hauptscharführer* Willi Rogmann from the *LSSAH Ausbildungs-und Ersatz Bataillon*. Many stragglers from the Oder Front were also coming through here and being fed back into the front line as *Alarm Units*.

Among the stragglers now formed into *Alarm Units* were members of the *15. Waffen-Grenadier-Division der SS (lettische Nr. 1)* that consisted of Latvian volunteers in the *Waffen-SS*. These soldiers recently fought in Pomerania then escaped the Soviets and crossed the Oder River where they reformed into *SS-Fusilier Battaillon 15*. This unit was ordered by Heinrici to move into reserve and hand over much of their automatic and heavy weapons to the German units moving toward the front. The division was now down to approximately 2,000 men and under independent command of *SS-Standartenführer* Janumus. Janumus planned on a retreat to the Elbe and to surrender his force to the Western Allies. He believed that the war was lost and knew that any surrender to the Soviets meant instant execution. The plan was to try and go through Berlin into order to reach the Elbe. It appears that the rumors of a demarcation line along the Elbe reached down to the soldiers in the field. The division split into several battalion-sized units in order to increase their chances to reach the west.

On the morning of 20 April the soldiers of *SS-Fusilier Battaillon 15* left for Berlin under the command of *SS-Hauptsturmführer* Wally. At day's end they arrived in Berlin's eastern suburb of Erkner and occupied positions on the east bank of the Erkner Canal. The battalion went to Berlin organized in the following way: 1st Company (130 men) commanded by German *SS-Untersturmführer* Donath and platoon commander cadets Melderis and Sils; 2nd Company (105 men) commanded by German *SS-Untersturmführer* Schmidt with platoon commanders *SS-Untersturmführer* Stauers, *SS-Untersturmführer* Tîtmanis and *SS-Sturmscharführer* Laivioð; 3rd Company (80 men) with *SS-Untersturmführer* Rutkis, *SS-Sturmscharführer* Kamps and *SS-Obersturmführer* Neilands; and 4th Heavy Weapons Company (55 men), which really was only a platoon and one mortar (without ammunition), commanded by German *SS-Untersturmführer* Kilp with platoon commanders *SS-Untersturmführer* Liepnieks and Cadet Krûmioð. The Battalion Commander *SS-Hauptsturmführer* Wally drove in a separate vehicle and became separated from the rest of his men during the chaotic withdrawal across the *LVI Pz. Korps* front. He eventually reported to *SS-Standartenführer* Janumus without his battalion. The soldiers of *Fusilier Bataillon 15* were unable to link up with Janumus, but the Latvian officers had information that Janumus intended to break to the west. *SS-Fusilier Bataillon 15s* three company commanders were German, but using the circumstances that the battalion commander was in Berlin, the Latvian officers decided to act independently and try to make it to the Elbe. They knew that Janumus would try to make his way west through Potsdam, so they made that their initial objective.

On the night of 22 April, when the Soviets began artillery preparation for their next attack, the Latvian companies left their Erkner positions and began looking independently for withdrawal routes. This was not easy. In the area near the front every intersection was controlled by German military police posts. These halted units retreated without permission, but sent separate soldiers to *Frontleitstelle*. In this situation the *2./Fusilier Bataillon 15* was luckiest. Together with a platoon from 3rd Company, they succeeded in reaching the center of Berlin by hitching a ride with a withdrawing German unit, presumably *Nordland*. Once they reached Berlin they were soon found by collection officials who ordered the 2nd Company to assemble along a narrow street between Wilhelm and Friedrichsstraße near the Reich Chancellery. Here the battalion commander would arrive and take command of the unit.[44]

The situation in withdrawing from the Erkner Canal developed somewhat differently for the *4./Fusilier Bataillon 15*, which together with its heavy mortar was in the second line of entrenchments. As Russian tanks approached, the Germans from the forward positions withdrew, and the Latvians with them, since it was not their task to engage in close combat under such circumstances. There were no officers, and command was taken by *SS-Scharführer* Uldis Dukurs. Dukurs was an experienced soldier who first saw combat in December 1943 near Velikaja River in Pskov district, Russia. During heavy fighting in Pomerania he had taken the place of wounded company commanders several times, until being wounded himself and returning to his battalion shortly before its departure for Berlin. Withdrawing from the Erkner canal, the 4th Heavy Weapons Company was forced to abandon its 120mm mortar due to lack of any transport. Dukurs understood that the first military checkpoint would stop them and send them to combat as ordinary infantry. To avoid having his men embroiled in close combat, the experienced commander 'acquired' an abandoned German cart with two 81mm mortars and was able to convince the outlying military police checkpoints he was trying to reach his unit in Berlin. In the area of Karlshorst, Dukurs was suddenly stopped by two cars, and a familiar voice asked "*Scharführer* Dukurs, how many men do you have?" Unexpectedly, the 'lost' Battalion Commander Wally had been found driving with officers of Defense Sector B. Dukurs' 24 men from the heavy weapons company along with his two mortars were immediately ordered to Defense Sector B reserve, and nicknamed the *Lettische Funfzehnte* (Latvian fifteenth). The group was deployed to the Reichsbank building, located immediately behind the Berlin Schloss near the Spree canal (called *Kupfergraben*). They were soon located near a SS platoon of Spanish volunteers that made it into Berlin under slightly different circumstances that are explained later in the text. Bärenfänger attempted to involve Dukurs' group in close fighting by placing them against the 5th Shock Army units in Alexanderplatz. Dukurs argued against the employment as combat infantry citing his mortars. Bärenfänger agreed with Dukurs that the mortars were more useful than a few more men with rifles and the Latvians stayed in reserve.[45]

Along with the Latvians all types of German soldiers filtered into Berlin from the battlefields to the east looking for their units, orders, or escape. Many soldiers simply attached themselves to the nearest unit. Tillery, who was a member of the shattered *Berlin Division*, crossed over the Frankfurter Allee and asked for a ride on one of two Hetzers that belonged to *Pz.Rgt.118 Schlesien*. As Tillery observed, "There were soldiers wandering around all over the place, but no kind of order. There were hardly any proper units left, just stragglers everywhere and no leadership."[46] The crew agreed to let Tillery on board and soon the assault gun commander, *Leutnant* Lorenz, asked him to join his unit as a Panzergrenadier. The two Hetzers then drove off looking for their Regimental HQ. After finding it they were tasked with defending a few streets, but no Russian attack materialized that day.

The 9th Rifle and 11th Tank Corps of the 5th Shock Army launched successive independent attacks against the German defenders on the eastern bank of the Spree between Defense Sectors B and C cutting into *Nordland's* forces positioned in defense. *Danmark's* two battalions were strung out along both the west and east banks of the Spree running from north of Treptow Park south to Niederschöneweide where *SS-Pz.Gren.Rgt.24 Danmark* was located. The *III./SS-Pz.Gren.Rgt.24 Danmark* held the left flank while the *II./SS-Pz.Gren.Rgt.24 Danmark* held the right. *Danmark* was awaiting relief by combat engineers of the *SS-Pi.Abt.54* from *Nordland* allowing the battalion to pull back over the Spree and occupy positions on the west bank.[47] While they were waiting for relief, the Soviet's 9th Rifle Corps launched an attack to cross the river. They first tried to gain the partially-destroyed bridge (either Stuben or Treskow) by assault during the early hours of morning from the eastern bank. The *Volkssturm* security posts on the east bank were quickly wiped out, but the Danes using *Panzerfausts* fought off the Soviet attempts to storm the bridges and reach the west bank.[48] After several hours, the Russians brought up the 1st Brigade of the Deneper Flotilla and used assault boats to begin crossing to the north and south of *II./SS-Pz.Gren.Rgt.24 Danmark's* position. In the north the Russians crossed the Spree taking Treptower Park where *III./SS-Pz.Gren.Rgt.24 Danmark* was located. Elements of 3rd Motorized Rifle Regiment fought off a local counterattack by ferrying across five T–34/85s from the 220th Tank Brigade. Lieutenant A.N. Azarov was crucial in the defense of the Soviet bridgehead and he was awarded Hero of the Soviet Union for holding off the Germans. *Danmark's* Regimental Commander now gave the order to withdraw across the Landwehr Canal in the north to avoid encirclement. The regiment was ordered "to act according to their [own] judgment" now that they were split from the rest of the division.

During 24 April the 11th Tank Corps headed west out of Friedrichsfelde, pushed through Lichtenberg, and reached the banks of the Spree without significant resistance. The entire tank corps then wheeled right and drove northwest up the eastern bank of the Spree until it reached a point just a few blocks west of the Schlesischer S-Bahn station. Captain A.V. Yudin of the 3rd Tank Battalion, 65th Tank Brigade of the 11th Tank Corps, waved his hand across the horizon and uttered "So this is Berlin!" "It was perfectly plain to see the buildings had been broken to pieces, to look at the skeletons of blocks of buildings and at factories; numerous churches raised above them once high but now shattered spires and in certain places the sun glintered [sic] on a narrow strip of the River Spree …. Columns of black smoke rose up into the air and covered the whole of the city with a huge black cloud."[49]

Soviet units began to cross into each other's area of operation as Berlin's street layout forced the units to be channeled into the centre of the city. The 65th Tank Brigade came across a lead regiment of the 60th Rifle Division from the 32nd Rifle Corps that had swung far out to the left flank of the corps after breaching the S-Bahn defensive line. The 60th Rifle division was operating together with support of the 243rd Mortar Regiment in an attempt to cross the Spree. Soviet engineers from the 61st Engineer Brigade began building pontoon bridges across the river while they checked the partially-destroyed bridge leading from Andreasstraße. While the engineers conducted their work, Soviet artillery pounded the buildings on the western bank to keep any German defenders from interfering in the crossing. The 243rd Mortar Regiment took up positions in the Andreas Kirke and used a three-storey house 50 meters from the bank as an observation point to support the crossing. One battalion of the 60th Rifle Division forded the river with little opposition and occupied a building on the opposite bank. The fact that an entire battalion occupied one building demonstrates the lack of manpower the Soviet corps operated with in Berlin. These Soviet soldiers were now closer to the city center than any other known Soviet combat unit. The Soviets tried to expand their bridgehead but ran into stiff opposition from the solidly-built stone Thoma K. Leibniz elementary school across Köpenickerstraße. Local *Volkssturm*, *Hitlerjugend*, and presumably elements of *III./SS-Pz.Gren.Rgt.24 Danmark* armed with assault rifles and *Panzerfausts* prevented the Soviet bridgehead from expanding.[50]

The Soviet Regiment and Battalion Commanders went to the observation point of the Mortar Regiment and were able to directly shell the school forcing the German defenders out of the building. By evening the 50th Guards Heavy Tank Regiment maneuvered to the east side and began to use direct fire against the buildings on the far bank. The 122mm guns of the JS–2s were capable of blowing holes through concrete walls of average thickness and proved deadly in the direct fire role against German infantry. The Soviet engineers finally repaired the damaged bridge during the night as Soviet armor prepared to cross the bridge in support of the beleaguered infantry battalion on the far side.[51]

Kampfgruppe Thiemer soon arrived to the west as reinforcements. *Kampfgruppe Thiemer* was formed at the Reich Sports Field on 23 April. The unit's leader, *SS-Oberscharführer* Thiemer, commanded 75 soldiers, including 40–50 *Hitlerjugend*, a *Polizei* mortar team, members of the *LSSAH Wachregiment*, and *Volkssturm*. One of the *Hitlerjugend* members was Aribert Schulz who was also a trained member of the *12.SS-Panzer Division Hitlerjugend*. These different groups were typically placed together to bolster their fighting power. After ammunition was handed out they marched on foot to Heinrichplatz in Kreuzberg where they took up positions.[52] Here they had a commanding position on the east-west boulevard that ran several blocks north of the Görlitzer Bahnhof. Toward the evening Soviets tanks appeared, presumably from the 220th Independent Tank Brigade operating in the vanguard of the 9th Rifle Corps, forcing the group back to Oranienplatz. Soviet shelling caused the first casualties of the unit as they again moved back only to be stopped at a tank barricade located in front of the Jerusalemer Church manned by SS. The *Kampfgruppe* now received orders to take up positions at the Spittelmarkt where Schulz and the rest of the *Kampfgruppe* set up HQ at the Kolonnaden Cinema. Schulz and other members of his unit were ordered to move north and take up a defensive position in the cellar of a house on Leipziger Straße right next to the Leiser Shoe store. A large tank barricade formed of moving vans and armed with Teller Mines blocked the main east-west road into the Government District.[53]

SOUTHERN DISRICTS

At 0400 Henseler's engineer battalion received the order to relieve the *SS-Pz.Gren.Rgt.24 Danmark* in its current positions and link up with a *Wehrmacht* reconnaissance unit on the right flank. As his unit moved out they soon discovered that the 9th Rifle Corps had already crossed the Spree and his men could not locate either battalion of *SS Pz.Gren.Rgt.24 Danmark* as they were already in retreat north. The pioneers then took up positions along the S-Bahn line just west of Berliner Straße. While setting up a defense perimeter, one of Henseler's patrols located the *Wehrmacht* unit on its right flank but it was 1.5 kilometers away, far too long a distance for his understrength company to maintain any links with. His unit also located a 5cm anti-tank gun that he set to guard one of the underpasses along the S-Bahn line. This weapon system was now incorporated into his unit's defense. By daybreak the lead elements of the Soviet's 9th Rifle Corps that crossed the Spree launched a massive infantry assault across Berliner Straße toward the S-Bahn line. The SS pioneers returned heavy fire inflicting losses on the Russians and forcing them to withdraw. The Soviets then renewed their attack with armor from the 220th Independent Tank Brigade ferried across the Spree. Henseler was unable to move the 5cm anti-tank gun and reposition it to meet the new threat. The Soviets breached the line to the north and south of his company and Henseler was forced to withdraw. Henseler moved through the gardens of Dauerwald where he met civilians from nearby residences that informed him the Soviets were already in Johannisthal to the south—these were Koniev's forces. He was given directions to the city center and Henseler led his company west into Britz then north into Tempelhof over the Teltow Canal via the Borgmann Bridge.[54]

Defending the bridge was a local Nazi Party Leader and his *Volkssturm* unit. They had orders to blow the bridge at the first sign of Soviets on the southern bank of the Teltow Canal. Henseler and his men were asked to assist in the local defense. As Henseler's men crossed over the bridge local women on the near bank scolded the soldiers for leaving them to the mercy of the approaching Russians.[55] Henseler and his men waited at the bridge until 1100 when Russian infantry began their approach through the gardens on the south side of the bridge. The Nazi Party leader hesitated to blow the bridge, but finally initiated demolition when Henseler gave him written permission to do so. When the detonation went off, a small hole in the middle of the bridge was the only result as the explosives were not enough to drop the entire span. The Nazi Party leader then took off to get more explosives leaving Henseler's men and the *Volkssturm* behind. As Henseler waited, he noted that the *Volkssturm* quietly left their positions heading north. Henseler decided to move on as well. He ordered his men east and came across the Britzer Bridge that was occupied by local *Polizei* with orders to blow the bridge, but they too were confused about what to do next. Henseler had the impression that no one was in charge of the defense of Berlin. He believed that the confusion was the result of the disintegration of the chain of command, and he was essentially correct. What Henseler did not know was that Weidling had already issued orders for the destruction of the Teltow Canal bridges, but that those orders were questioned by every local official that thought they had complete control of their various sectors. Henseler and his men continued east and turned right on Buschkrugallee. Henseler always led from the front, as most German officers were trained to do. His men were equally well trained and knew that when he stopped they were to take up immediate concealed defensive positions. Constant combat honed his unit's skills. As he moved down the street he heard someone yell out "Where are you going?" As Henseler stopped he saw he was confronted by a *Wehrmacht Major* wearing a *Ritterkreuz* (Knights Cross) and about eight other heavily-armed men.[56] He replied that he was looking for his unit's headquarters but the *Major* didn't believe him retorting "That's what they all say! The enemy is over there" as he pointed to the direction Henseler just came. The grim faces on the *Major's* men concerned Henseler but his *SS-Oberscharführer*, a Romanian of German descent, saw what was happening and had the company out in the street with their assault rifles pointed at the *Major's* men. The *Major* had not seen Henseler's company concealed in the rubble and their grim, ghost-like appearance from the surrounding ruins immediately changed the situation. The *Major* was immediately conciliatory and stated that he had trouble keeping order in this sector and offered his assistance to Henseler and his combat pioneers. Henseler thanked the *Major* but continued to look for his headquarters as Soviet artillery fire raked the area. The *Führerbunker* order that granted free passage through the city for Weidling's units simply did not make it down to local unit commanders operating in each sector due to an inadequate command-and-control system. After a few more hours Henseler and his men finally found the *SS-Pi.Abt.11* HQ. He soon learned that the other two pioneer companies had suffered significant casualties during the last few days.

Meanwhile, Scholles' *II./SS-Pz.Gren.Rgt.24 Danmark* was having difficulty keeping ahead of the advancing Russians. They crossed the Teltow Canal blowing the bridge behind them but that slowed the Russians down little. The Russians continued to cross the canal and forced *II./SS-Pz.Gren.Rgt.24 Danmark* back again. Scholles' company was now down to 30–40 men and he could not hold off the dual pressure from both the south and now the east in Treptow Park where the *III./SS-Pz.Gren.Rgt.24 Danmark* already withdrew. The Germans pulled back beyond the Baumschulenweg S-Bahn Station and set up a defensive perimeter. The Russians infiltrated to the left and right heading toward Neukölln. Next, the Soviets shelled the area with mortar fire to keep the Danes pinned while Soviet snipers were sent forward to take up positions along the raised S-Bahn tracks. Patrols from the *II./SS-Pz.Gren.Rgt.24 Danmark* managed to link with the *III* Bataillon briefly on the left. Runners from *Nordland* HQ brought a message that a counterattack was being prepared by units of *SS-Pz.Abt.11 Hermann von Salza* and *SS-Aufk.Abt.11*.[57] In preparation for the counterattack the Regimental Commander of *Danmark*, *SS-Sturmbannführer* Sørensen, took up an exposed position to survey the Russian troop movement. As Sørensen brought his field glasses to his eyes to check the Soviet positions an enemy sniper opened fire from the surrounding ruins. The Soviet bullet entered the back of Sørensen's head and exited through his upper chest killing him instantly.[58] This was *SS-Pz.Gren.Rgt.24 Danmark's* last Regimental Commander. Once his death became known by Division HQ, *SS-Pz.Gren.Rgt.24 Danmark* was split into several *Kampfgruppe* that came under the command of *SS-Aufk.Abt.11* for the rest of the battle.[59] *SS-Pz.Gren.Rgt.24 Danmark* ceased to exist.

SS-Aufk.Abt.11 moved into Britz by noon but the planned counterattack never materialized due to the pace of Soviet operations. A general retreat started north across the Teltow Canal as the Russians continued to push forward. The German forces tried to get to Neukölln over the Teltow Canal but there was only a narrow bridge across the Chausserstraße forcing movement to be slowed.[60] Suddenly several JS–2s broke through the German perimeter set up around the crossing site and advanced on the SS infantry. According to one SS eyewitness "Hundreds of SS men, who for years had faced death innumerable times without loosing their heads, were caught by wild panic."[61] A SPW lurched forward across the bridge in order to avoid direct fire from the JS–2s even while the fuse to blow the bridge was lit. The SPWs on the bridge made it across before it blew, but many German soldiers were still caught on the bridge or on the south bank. On Hermannstraße an 8.8cm crew tried to ready their gun to engage the Soviet armor but a salvo from a Stalin Organ hit the gun and killed the crew. Germans jumped into the water and tried to swim across in their panic.[62] As the remaining forces of *SS-Aufk.Abt.11* drove toward the city center through Neukölln they saw painted slogans on the sides of buildings that read "SS Traitors and extenders of war!" German Communists with red armbands started to fire on the SS soldiers from rooftops using stolen *Volkssturm* weapons.[63] Death lurked behind every corner in Berlin.

Chuikov advanced his forces forward against German resistance that was uneven and without direction. The Soviet infantry and tanks quickly bypassed German strong points and crossed over into Neukölln where a major battle developed at the former *Nordland's* HQ located in the Labor Office by late afternoon.[64] 8.8cm Flak guns and Sturmgeschütz from *Hermann von Salza* engaged the Soviet tanks and assault guns.[65] The Germans launched a series of local counterattacks that kept the uncoordinated Soviet units off balance.

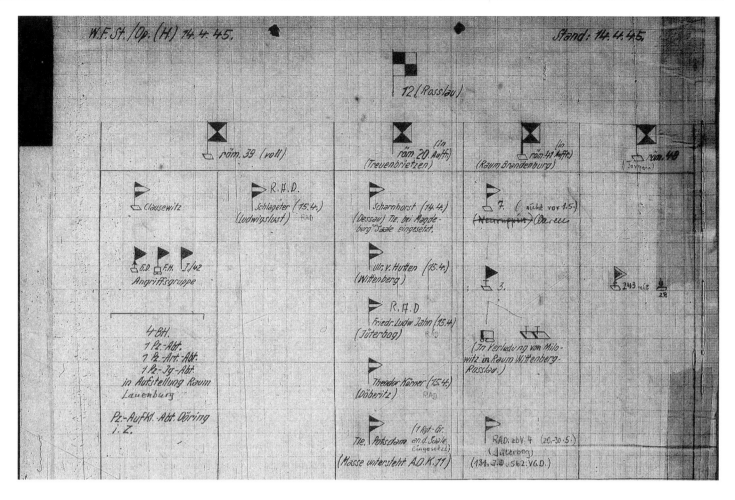

Image of the *12.Armee* order of battle. Courtesy of the US National Archives.

German Nebelwerfer and King Tigers of *s.SS-Pz.Abt.503* shifted from one threatened street to the next. One King Tiger, under the command of *SS-Untersturmführer* Gast, knocked out an ISU–122 assault gun that attempted to cross the Teltow Canal.[66] After a column of T–34s were shot up by German Panzers and Panzergrenadiers the Russians pulled back. The Russians continued to infiltrate German positions all night in preparation for a morning advance.[67] Chuikov's immediate goal was to take Tempelhof airport and he drove his subordinate commanders to reach this objective without concern for combat losses.

Koniev's U.S.-built Packard staff car raced to the Teltow Canal through the rubble of the southern suburbs of Berlin order to reach Rybalko's headquarters before the assault across the canal began. Driven by a rivalry with Zhukov, Koniev risked his armor forces in an unprecedented drive into the southern districts of Berlin with the aim of reaching the Reichstag first. The drive north was aided by meticulous German roads that Koniev admitted in his memoir did not exist in Russia or Eastern Europe during the war. Koniev wrote how the idea of a rapid advance through the German forested mastiff west of the Spree seemed to daunt him during his map planning. In reality the roads to Berlin " … were good, and the superhighways from Breslau to Berlin turned out to be especially useful. It became, as it were, the basic axis of traffic in the 1st Ukrainian Front's sector."[68] Koniev's gamble paid off and he reached Berlin a full 24 hours before Zhukov. His units were now crossing the Teltow Canal and entering the heart of Berlin ahead of his rival. Koniev arrived at the Teltow Canal at the end of the massive artillery preparation. Koniev massed 600 guns per kilometer of front for the offensive and was raking the buildings on the far bank, then followed up with a heavy smoke screen. Even before the artillery stopped, small assault groups crossed the canal in order to capture a foothold on the far bank. Koniev meanwhile took up an observation point in an eight-storey building along with Rybalko, and senior artillery and air corps commanders to better coordinate the assault.

The assault was made by the three tank corps of the 3rd Tank Army. On the left was the 7th Tank Corps that launched its attack opposite Stahsdorf, the 6th Guard Tank Corps in the center opposite Teltow, and the 9th Mechanized Corps to the far right opposite Stieglitz. The 9th Mechanized Corps crossed the canal using pontoons and several partially-destroyed bridges. Once the Soviet vanguard reached the far bank it was immediately engaged by German defenders. It was difficult to get any armor across as all the bridges were blown and the few pontoon bridges were not able to move tanks across the canal fast enough to support the Soviet soldiers hanging onto the small enclaves carved out of the ruins. This area was defended by the *Skorning Kampfgruppe, Bataillon Krause,* and presumably supported by *Pz.Gren.Rgt.51* that was *en-route* to its new sector of assignment. The Germans probably did not realize that the Soviet forces were not Zhukov's but Koniev's crossing the canal.

The 7th Guard Tank Corps crossed over the Teltow and immediately ran into elements of the *20.Pz.Gren.Div.* as well as local defense units. The 7th Guard Tank Corps proved unable to expand their bridgehead during the course of the day's fighting. Only in the center, where the 6th Guards Tank Corps crossed, was there success in establishing a bridgehead.[69] Here the 22nd Guards Motorized Rifle Brigade led the assault crossing in wooden boats and the partial remains of blown bridges. This assault occurred while the Soviet artillery was still pounding the far bank. The division's armor was situated along the southern bank to provide direct fire support. They established themselves on the opposite embankment and were joined by the rest of the brigade at 0500 hours. The 48th Guards Rifle Division followed and enlarged the bridgehead by storming building after building along the northern bank. By 1100 hours the engineers had their first pontoon bridge to move guns and tanks across. By late afternoon the success of the 6th Guards Tank Corps drew the 9th Mechanized and the 7th Guards Tank Corps to reroute their forces to the 6th Guards Tank Corps bridgehead. The 9th Mechanized and 7th Guards Corps crossed over the Teltow Canal in this sector and then began moving to the left and right of the north side of the canal. This was no small feat of maneuver and demonstrates a higher level of coordination among Koniev's corps not seen in Zhukov's Front. By evening the forces of Koniev 3rd Tank Army were across the Teltow Canal and had advanced at least 0.5 kilometers into the city.[70] As Koniev's forces spread out they began to run into the mixed assortment of *Hitlerjugend* and *Volkssturm* units that were drafted and thrown piecemeal into the path of advancing Soviet forces.

Pienkny's *Hitlerjugend Gruppe 200* was headquartered in Lichterfelde at a former school. After Koniev's crossing of the Teltow Canal, Pienkny's unit received orders to attack into Zehlendorf and reach the Telefunken factory on Goerz Allee. Orders were issued that if the group was split up they would meet at a safe house well stocked with food and weapons where they were to stay during the day then leave at night to hunt down Russians. By around 2100 hours the *Hitlerjugend Gruppe 200* was moving down Ringstraße when they spotted two stationary T–34/85s at Friedrich Platz circle with another T–34/85 advancing from the nearby graveyard. These tanks belonged to the 6th Guard Tank Corps that was in the process of consolidating its position on the north side of the Teltow Canal. The boys moved silently down both sides of the streets with strict orders not to fire unless Buttermann, their commander, gave the order. Pienkny and two other boys, Rainer and Muhler, took up positions behind an advertising pillar where they stacked four *Panzerfausts*. They waited in silence as the T–34/85 moved toward them. As soon as the T–34/85 was 10 meters away, Rainer grabbed a *Panzerfaust*, ran into the middle of the street, and fired point blank destroying the tank. At this close range the concussion of the explosion cracked the advertising pillar and presumably knocked Rainer to the street. Rainer got up then ran back and grabbed a second *Panzerfaust* destroying a second T–34 standing to the left of the square. The tank on the right now began to move forward slowly not knowing exactly what destroyed the lead two tanks. Rainer then picked up a third *Panzerfaust* and waited until the tank was in range and fired, blowing up the third tank as it drew near. After the three tanks were destroyed everything became quiet and the group continued its advance toward Zehlendorf along the darkened streets. Soon they approached the Dahlemer Weg that crossed over the S-Bahn tracks and Schubertstraße. Here Buttermann took the lead and led the group up the stairs to the top of the bridge. As they neared top of the stairs the Russians unleashed an ambush on the *Hitlerjugend*. Murderous machine-gun fire opened up from the top of the bridge, the S-Bahn tracks, and the street below. Fifteen boys fell dead on the spot and another twenty on the street bolted in all directions. The boys on the stairs and around Buttermann held fast. Buttermann then charged up the stairs to the top of the bridge when two Russians leaned over the bridge and opened fire, shooting Buttermann in the stomach. The Russian patrol then quickly withdrew. When the boys reached Buttermann they opened up his jacket and saw blood everywhere. Buttermann whispered with his last breath "Try to get through to the villa." Then he reached into a pocket, took out a cyanide capsule, and bit it killing himself. His body was carried back down the steps by the light of several small fires that were started in the surrounding houses due to tracer bullets.[71] The majority of the *Hitlerjugend Gruppe 200* then disbanded with a core group making their way back to their HQ at the School on Albrecht-Achilles-Straße.

At 2400 hours units of the 1st Guards Tank Army reached the Teltow Canal and met units of the 3rd Guards Tank Army. They quickly learned that Koniev's forces were across the Teltow Canal and fighting in the inner city. According to Koniev, the inter-front boundary was modified by Stavka on the morning of 23 April owing to the fast advance of Koniev forces into Berlin. This new boundary passed to the left of the Anhalt S-Bahn station and still left Koniev the ability to strike toward the Reichstag.[72] Zhukov wasn't notified of this boundary change, and he was certainly not aware of Koniev's presence this far into the city until his own forces and those of Koniev linked up at the Teltow Canal. This news was passed on to Zhukov, who was incredulous and questioned the reliability of the report. Then he followed up with an order: "Members of the Military Soviet will personally go to the forward attachments and ascertain who, in fact, actually first reached the line of the Teltow Canal."[73] Instead of tasking his staff to coordinate future actions with Koniev, he demonstrated only concern with who reached the canal first and what Koniev's future objectives were.

Zhukov quickly ordered Chuikov's forces to wheel northwest and advance across Koniev's front. This order created conditions for both converging Russian forces to run directly into each other in their drive for the Reichstag. Zhukov's decision was militarily unsound and presumably based on jealously and his appetite for glory. The 28th and 29th Guards Rifle Corps wheeled right through Rudow into Mariendorf and closed up on the Teltow Canal, while the 4th Guards Rifle Corps crossed the Spree to clear part of Johannisthal 'Island' before taking up position in Britz that evening. Everything was prepared for Chuikov's attack across the canal.[74]

WESTERN DISTRICTS

Zhukov's 47th Army now prepared for an assault on Spandau and the Gatow Airfield along the western bank of the Havel. The Soviets allotted the 125th Rifle Corps, 50th Guard Tank Brigade, and 33rd Guard Mechanized Brigade to this mission. These units slowly closed in on Spandau but did not attack on 23 April.[75] This last minute decision to attack Spandau and Gatow airfield highlights the lack of focused planning and coordination that plagued Soviet operations. Spandau was part of defense Sector F under the command of *Oberstleutnant* Eder. *SS-Gruppenführer* Heissmeyer was in charge of the main combat forces in Spandau. His forces consisted primarily of the *Hitlerjugend Gruppe Heissmeyer* as well as Galician boys in the *Luftwaffe*, *Wehrmacht Ersatz* troops, and assorted *Volkssturm* units. As it became obvious that the Soviets were planning to attack Spandau the local depots began to equip whatever soldiers were available with *Panzerfausts* and World War I vintage machine guns. On 24 April the local *Polizei* were also armed and sent into defensive positions around the town.[76] Sometime after the first Soviet attack, Heissmeyer left the city and escaped to the Alps leaving his soldiers and staff alone in the city.[77]

In the early morning of the 24 April the Soviet 76th and 60th Rifle Divisions of the Soviet 47th Army attacked Spandau simultaneously from north and west. The Soviet attack pattern was not unique. An early morning artillery preparation hit potential key defensive targets followed by an advance of armor with little or no infantry support. The Soviets encountered stiff resistance in the streets and were not prepared to push the attack. After trying to pierce the outer defense of Spandau all day the Soviets pulled back for the night. The 47th Army called in air support to help reduce German positions in Spandau.

Father south the 175th Rifle Division attacked Gatow Airfield but was likewise repulsed. Gatow was defended by a mix of *Luftwaffe* cadets, *Volkssturm* and construction battalion troops supported by an artillery battery on the east bank of the Havel and the 12.8cm twin-cannon of the Zoo Flak Tower. Despite the initial success of the German defenders the *Volkssturm* abandon their posts. The airfield, however, stayed in German hands.

SS-Brigadeführer Gustav Krukenberg was not a professional soldier by training. During World War I he did serve as a *Hauptmann* of the German General Staff but he quit in 1920. He had been the director of an English Chemical Company and held several semi-diplomatic posts before Hitler came to power. In September 1939 he was ordered back to active duty and placed on the General Staff in the rank of Oberst. He rose through the ranks and by 1944 was transferred into the *Waffen-SS*. Due to his political connections, and fluency in French he was given command of the *33. Waffen-SS Grenadier-Division der Charlemagne (französische Nr. 1)*. This division was made up of a composite of various French soldiers, whose motivations and loyalties varied. His division was part of the *3. Panzer Armee* and saw extensive fighting in Pomerania and the Stettin area. In the early morning hours of 24 April he received notice by telephone to report to the Reich Chancellery immediately for a new assignment. Although he didn't know it at that time, Krukenberg was to replace the despondent Zeigler in charge of *Nordland*.[78] Krukenberg left for Berlin at about 0830 in several staff cars and between 9–15 trucks. Along with him came nearly 500 French Soldiers known as *Sturmbataillon Charlemagne* that were made up of *SS-Bataillon 57* and one company of *SS-Bataillon* 58. The majority of the men were heavily armed with the Sturmgewehr assault rifles, MG 42s and *Panzerfausts*.[79]

Krukenberg's drive into Berlin was surreal. Along the way the convoy of Frenchmen passed countless German soldiers moving west. They even ran into a signal detachment of *Nordland* whose commander said they had orders to move to Holstein (this unit was still following orders to retreat west and reach the Western Allies).[80] They also encountered Soviet soldiers who were still maneuvering to seal off Berlin, but they were able to bypass them and finally enter Berlin across the Havel River. As they drove into Berlin's western suburbs they were greeted with cheers from many German civilians who thought they were the vanguard of Wenck's *12. Armee* arriving in the city. Surprisingly, he saw no soldiers in defensive positions along the Charlottenburger Chausse except for 3 *Hitlerjugend* on bicycles carrying *Panzerfausts*. As he stated after the war "I honestly wondered who was defending Berlin."[81] They arrived at the Olympic Stadium at 2200 hours where he left the Frenchman for the night. Then Krukenberg continued to wind through the rubble to the Reich Chancellery arriving shortly before midnight. Krukenberg and his aid, *SS-Hauptsturmführer* Pachur, were shocked by the desolation at the Chancellery. They were met by no guards and they entered without anyone checking for identification. They wound their way down to the bunker where they asked for *SS-Obergruppenführer* Hermann Fegelein, who was the *SS* liaison at the Chancellery. Fegelein took note of their arrival and escorted them to the ante-room and instructed them to wait for Krebs. By 0300 Krebs arrived with Burgdorf and briefed them on the strategic situation telling them that "a move by the Americans into Berlin is being negotiated and it will only be a question of holding the Russians back for a week."[82] This was clearly a false report, and against orders, but was probably used to bolster Krukenberg's morale as even Krebs realized the effect of this revelation. Without a belief in rescue from Wenck or the Western Allies there was no reason to defend Berlin. After this astonishing news, they were told to report to Weidling, the new *CBDA*. Krukenberg and his aid headed back to the Olympic Stadium where the Frenchmen were camping for the night.

NORTHERN DISTRICTS

The 2nd Guards Tank Army did not swing behind the *3. Panzer Armee* as Heinrici feared. In fact the 2nd Guards Tank Army, like the 1st Guards Tank Army to the south, was so battered during the assault on the Seelow Heights and following breakthrough battles that it no longer operated as an independent army. The 9th Guards Tank Corps was subordinated to the 47th Army and operating on the west side of the Havel. The 1st Mechanized and 12th Guards Tank Corps were subordinated to the 5th Shock Army, but now it was decided that they were needed in the northern districts where Zhukov was short of manpower and available units. The 12th Guards Tank Corps was subordinated to the 3rd Shock Army and operated in combination with the 79th Corps. Only the 1st Mechanized Corps operated independently. Now it was ordered to redeploy between the Havel and the 3rd Shock Army to fill in the gap. It appears that this unit, along with the 12th Guards Tank Corps, accomplished the re-deployment in as a little as one day, although this seems optimistic given the challenges of terrain, coordination, and enemy activity that both units faced.[83]

The 1st Mechanized Corps advanced south from its new position, crossing the village of Jungfernheide to close up to the Hohenzollern Canal by the evening. During the night the corps conducted a crossing operation and landed a number of combat groups on the other side at the edge of the modern industrial Siemenstadt suburb founded by the Siemens Company.[84] It now prepared pontoon bridges to move its armor across the canal.

The 79th Rifle Corps of the 3rd Shock Army came through the southern part of Reinickendorf and swung as far west as the deserted *Luftwaffe* Hermann Göring Barracks before turning south and hitting strong resistance from the Westhafen warehouse and Plötzensee prison—presumably from local police and factory protection units. Elements of the 12th Guards Tank Corps were now filtering into the area and were presumably parceled out to support the various subordinate rifle corps in their operations.

The 12th Guards Rifle Corps worked its way down through the working class district of Wedding where the urban terrain featured large tenement block complexes. Strong Communist sympathy was presumably present from the local population as the Soviet advance was uneventful. There were few German forces in the area as Soviet shooting lasted only about thirty minutes then the soldiers went house-to-house, searching the cellars. It does not appear that the Soviets employed massed artillery strikes in this area. As Soviet soldiers of this corps came up to the inner defense ring at the Wedding S-Bahn station they were met by determined defenders that put up fierce resistance. Strong artillery fire was called in to defeat the position, presumably defended by *Volkssturm*. On the 12th Guards Rifle Corps left flank left was the Humboldt Flak Tower protected by deep railway cuttings that acted as a moat. Even if the Soviets wanted to take the position, fire from the 12.8cm guns on the roof kept the Soviets to the far side of the park. The Soviets simply could not invest the position and bypassed it instead.[85]

As the vanguard of the 3rd Shock Army advanced into Defense Sectors G and H, Weidling assigned several of his most competent formations available to bolster the local defense forces in those areas. Among the first to arrive were the remnants of the *Wachregiment Großdeutschland* that now fell under Weidling's authority after retreating back into Berlin. The *Großdeutschland* soldiers were motivated, well-trained, equipped, and had their own SPW and Panzers, presumably Sturmgeschütz IIIs or Hetzers. Soon the remnants of *Fj. Rgt. 27*

A knocked out German 3.7cm Flak Gun typical of what *Fj.Art.Rgt.9* brought into the city. Photo courtesy of ASKM.

with their few remaining Hetzers from the *9.Pz.Jg.Abt.* arrived to take up positions near the Humboldt Flak Tower. The local defense units consisted of small anti-tank squads organized by the Humboldt Flak Tower as well as local *Volkssturm*, *Hitlerjugend*, and *Polizei* units. This area was intensely bombed by the Western Allies primarily due to the various warehouses, fuel storage facilities, factories, and interconnected waterways. This turned the area into a sea of burnt-out ruins and rubble-strewn streets that impeded any swift Soviet advance.

The 500 soldiers of the *9.Fallschirmjäger* were now under the command of *Oberst* Harry Hermannn. His forces were split into two battle groups. He set up his headquarters in the Schönhauser Allee Brewery and based his operations in the area around the Humboldt Flak Tower along with the *Fj.Rgt.27*.[86] Elements of both the *Fj.Art.Rgt.9* and *Kompanie Blumenthal* numbering 80 men worked their way into Berlin and were allocated to Defense Sector Z. The remnants of *Fj.Art.Rgt 9* managed to bring 12 8.8cm anti-aircraft guns into the city that were employed in the ground defense as well as 20–25 Quad 2cm and nine 3.7cm guns that were very effective in the anti-personnel role.[87] The confusion of the retreat and new orders shifting troops from the southern to northern districts took their toll on the soldiers who were in non-stop combat for over a week. Dr. Hans Rhein was assigned to defend an area near the Humboldt Flak Tower with other members of *Fj.Art.Rgt.9* now being employed as infantry. He understood that the overall defense of a city like Berlin was impossible with the forces available. He stated after the war that "any coordination of orders between different units and *Kampfgruppe* was impossible, for the orders not only lacked any deeper knowledge of the overall situation, but very often were completely void of all basic conception of what was possible or impossible."[88] Hans Werner Arnold of the *5./Fs.Art.Rgt.9* entered Berlin from the south through Köpenick and became fed up with the lack of information passed down to the soldiers.[89] He made his way was through Treptower Park then on to the Platz-der-Republik where he set up opposite the Moltke Bridge with a Quad 2cm gun to cover newly-formed tank hunter squads being sent across the Spree River to engage Soviet armor now expected to advance from the north.[90]

CENTRAL DISTRICTS

In Defense Sector Z an organized defense began to take shape around the key Government Quarter buildings that housed the remaining Nazi Political leadership and Adolf Hitler. The two battalions of the *SS-Regiment Anhalt* were organized with the *II./SS-Rgt. Anhalt's* right wing boundary at Belle-Alliance-Platz where it followed the Landwehr Canal to the Tiergarten, then cut across the Tiergarten to the Spree River. It then followed the Spree through the Diplomatic Quarter as far as the Kronprinzen Bridge where it linked with the *I./SS-Rgt. Anhalt*. The *I./SS-Rgt. Anhalt* under the command of *SS-Hauptsturmführer* Thomas Mrgulla continued east through Königsplatz, the Reichstag, along the south bank of the Spree than south into the Government District. The area around Königsplatz and the Reichstag came under the subordinate command of *SS-Obersturmführer* Babick.[91] The command situation in Defense Sector Z remained confused and tense through the battle as Seifert was in charge of the entire Defense Sector, but Mohnke remained in command of the *SS* in the four square block area around the Reich Chancellery. *Oberst* Seifert made his HQ in the Reich Air Ministry and Mohnke's command post was on Hermannn Göring Straße. The defensive positions held within the Tiergarten were porous as the defenders only managed a two-man foxhole every fifty meters. The Panzers of *SS-Pz.Abt.11 Hermann von Salza* under command of *SS-Obersturmbannführer* Kausch were also positioned here as a reserve.[92] The Tiergarten became the congregation point for all the various artillery pieces that made their way back into Berlin. The trees offered some concealment from Soviet aircraft, and the soft ground allowed the quick building of defensive positions for artillery and tanks alike.

Notes to Chapter 6: Assault on Berlin, 24th April Tuesday

1   Le Tissier, *Race for the Reichstag*, p. 76.
2   Ryan outline for 24 April.
3   Soviet War News, The Press Department of the Soviet Embassy in London, 24 April (Ryan Collection).
4   Berlin's symbol is a Bear.
5   Chuikov, p. 168, and Koniev unpublished memoir, p. 140. The discrepancy comes from the differing accounts of the meeting.
6   Koniev unpublished memoir, p. 140.
7   Ibid, p. 142, and Le Tissier, *Race for the Reichstag*, p. 78.
8   Koniev unpublished memoir, p. 127.
9   K. Voss, and P. Kehlenbeck, *Letzte Divisionen 1945: Die Panzerdivision Clausewitz and Die Infanteriedivision Schill*, pp. 289, 293 and G. Reichhelm, *MS #B-606 The Last Rally: Battles Fought by the German 12th Army in the Heart of Germany, between East and West (13 April – 7 May 1945*, pp. 21–2 (RC: 67/23).
10 *MS #B-606*, pp. 21–2.
11 The *Reichsarbeitsdienst* or *(RAD)* division was created in 1934 as part of Nazi Germany's Labor Service and supported the Wehrmacht as an auxiliary combat formation.
12 These *RAD* divisions were formed in the middle of April. (T-77: 1430/205-206).
13 Voss, and Kehlenbeck, pp. 280-281.
14 *MS #B-606*, p. 17. The cessation of Western Allied air raids was due to the fear that direct aerial combat might occur between U.S. and Soviet fighter planes.
15 Ibid, p. 22.
16 Le Tissier, *Slaughter at Halbe*, p. 72.
17 Koniev unpublished memoir, p. 143.
18 Ibid, p. 128.
19 Army Group Weichsel War Diary, Apr 20–9, p. 200 (RC: 68/4)
20 Ritter, p. 13.
21 Wenck interview.
22 Haaf interview.
23 Army Group Weichsel War Diary, Apr 20–9, p. 266 (RC: 64/3).
24 "Organization of *III SS Panzer Korps*, Apr 23, 1945" (RC: 61/5).
25 Army Group Weichsel War Diary, Apr 20–9, p. 298 (RC: 68/4). It should be noted that contemporary accounts record 24 April as being the date of Steiner's counterattack, however, this is incorrect.

The confusion is based on the account found in *The Last Thirty Days*, pp. 168–9. The telephonic records of *AGW* are clear, no attack by Steiner occurred on 24 April. See also Le Tissier, *Race for the Reichstag*, p. 84.
26 Army Group Weichsel War Diary, Apr 20–9, p. 298 (RC: 68/4).
27 Army Group Weichsel War Diary, Apr 20–9, p. 230 (RC: 64/3).
28 Ibid, p. 299 (RC: 68/4).
29 Army Group Weichsel War Diary, Apr 20–9, p. 387 (RC: 64/3).
30 Weidling Interrogation Report.
31 Ibid.
32 Ibid.
33 Schultz-Naumann, p. 172.
34 Weidling Interrogation Report.
35 Jansen interview.
36 von Dufving interview.
37 Weidling Interrogation Report.
38 Ibid.
39 Ibid.
40 Army Group Weichsel War Diary, Apr 20–9 pp. 258–9 (RC: 68/4).
41 Schultz-Naumann, pp. 170–1.
42 Le Tissier, *Race for the Reichstag*, p. 91.
43 Ibid.
44 Pçtersons, pp. 68–73.
45 Ibid, p. 104.
46 Le Tissier, *With our Backs to Berlin*, p. 48.
47 Scholles interview.
48 Ibid.
49 Platonov, p. 18.
50 Ibid.
51 Ibid, p. 19.
52 A. Schulz interview (RC: 70/11)
53 Ibid.
54 Henseler interview.
55 Fear of rape was rampant, and these women's fears were realized as Henseler's men later reported heard their screams. Why the women simply did not cross the canal with the soldiers is a mystery.
56 Ibid.
57 Scholles interview.
58 Ibid, and Illum interview.
59 R. Michaelis, *Die 11.SS-freiwilligen-Panzer-Grenadier-Division "Nordland,"* p. 109.
60 Hillblad, p. 96.
61 Ibid, p. 97.
62 Ibid.

63 Ibid, p. 98.
64 W. Tieke, *Tragedy of the Faithful: A History of the III. (germanisches) SS-Panzer Korps*, p. 298.
65 Scholles interview.
66 W. Fey, *Armor Battles of the Waffen-SS 1943–45*, p. 374.
67 Hillblad, p. 23.
68 Koniev unpublished memoir, p. 136. In the early days of April, German jet fighters, presumably ME 262s, often made strafing runs against Soviet supply columns on the autobahn between Breslau and Berlin in order to interrupt Koniev's buildup. After the offensive began on 16 April the German jets made no more appearances.
69 Ibid, pp. 139–41.
70 Ibid, p. 142.
71 Pienkny interview.
72 Koniev unpublished memoir, p. 115, and Le Tissier, *Race for the Reichstag*, p. 95.
73 Popiel, p. 16.
74 Le Tissier, *Race for the Reichstag*, p. 95.
75 Altner, p. 106.
76 Ibid, p. 93.
77 Ibid, p. 107.
78 Krukenberg interview.
79 R. Forbes, *Pour L'Europe: The French Volunteers of the Waffen-SS*, p. 263.
80 Ibid, p. 264.
81 Krukenberg interview.
82 Ibid.
83 Le Tissier shows the 12th Guards Tank Corps on his map on pp. 52–3 of *Race for the Reichstag* as having been ordered on the 22nd/23rd to move and completing the redeployment on 24th April. This seems unrealistic given the logistics necessary to manage a complicated movement across another army's boundary and still deploy in time to attack.
84 Ibid, p. 87.
85 Ibid, p. 87–90.
86 Venghaus, p. 180.
87 H. Rein interview (RC: 69/12).
88 Ibid.
89 Werner interview.
90 Ibid.
91 Le Tissier, *Race for the Reichstag*, p. 153.
92 Ibid.

6

ASSAULT ON BERLIN

25 APRIL
WEDNESDAY

In the south the Soviets reached the line Neubabelsberg-Zehlendorf-Neukölln. In the eastern and northern parts of the city the fights are still going on. West of the city Soviet spearheads reached the area of Nauen and Ketzin. At Oranienburg the northern bank of the Stettin Canal was successfully defended despite strong attacks. Repeated attacks on Eberswalde had led to penetrations into the southern part of the city.[1]

OKW **Radio Announcement**

Zhukov's assault ran into stiff resistance as his soldiers reached the S-Bahn ring that marked the city's inner defense line. Situated around the S-Bahn ring were fixed positions, many in the S-Bahn stations themselves, as well as increased numbers of anti-tank guns. Weidling's efforts at implementing an organized defense contributed to the German's overall ability to counter Soviet attacks. Weidling, however, ordered several costly counterattacks that forced the Germans into the open where they became easy targets for devastating Soviet rocket and artillery fire. Operating on interior lines did allow the quick re-deployment of German forces to threatened Defense Sectors. As German troops drew back into the city experienced officers and NCOs became co-mingled with less experienced soldiers forming company sized *Kampfgruppe*. These units provided the nucleus to rally morale and offer organized resistance. The German infantry now began to form, fight, disperse, and then reform again conducting what in modern warfare terms is known as asymmetrical warfare. The hit-and-run tactics employed by the Germans were primarily a product of countering the Soviet's massive firepower that easily scattered German formations the size of a battalion or larger caught in the open. This was not a combat behavior that German commanders consciously employed by doctrine, but rather an adoption of new urban fighting tactics required for survival under the circumstances. It is true that the *Wehrmacht* did encounter similar tactics before, especially during the 1944 Warsaw Uprising, but these tactics were often considered 'partisan' or 'criminal' activities not suited for a field army, let alone the *Wehrmacht*. While the Germans became tough targets, often avoiding fixed combat, the Soviets contributed equally to their own operational difficulties. Zhukov's corps advanced and attacked German strongpoints independently, without the benefit of coordinating these assaults with neighboring units. Subordinate units simply overcame enemy resistance on their own using brute firepower. These units then became tangled among the ruined roads that led toward the city center or became disoriented in Berlin's streets when they struck out to locate new avenues of approach. Lack of effective communications between infantry and tank units continued to cause unnecessary Russian losses. Both sides' commanders routinely behaved as if they were fighting a mechanized engagement in open terrain.

1st BYLEORUSSIAN FRONT

Zhukov's forces began to falter in the face of the tactical situation they now faced in Berlin. The German defense proved layered and effective. At the local unit level German anti-tank guns, mobile armor, and *Panzerfaust*s caused havoc with each attempt by the Soviets to advance through the streets. Berlin's concentric avenues either ended at or ran perpendicular to staunchly defended raised S-Bahn stations, and numerous waterways added complexity in negotiating these key urban terrain features. Chuikov outlined these issues in his postwar memoir:

> Almost everywhere [on the 25th] the fighting had been of exceptional ferocity. Every house, every block of the defense area and sectors, was packed with fire points and nests of men wielding 'Faustpatronen' [*Panzerfaust*]; the latter had made good use of balconies and windows on upper floors, as points from which to launch their weapons from above against tanks and concentrations of men.
> There were many railway lines in Berlin, intersecting the city in various directions and forming very convenient defense positions. The approaches to stations, bridges and level crossings were all turned into powerful strong points; canals and the points at which they crossed became defense lines at which the enemy did his best to halt our advance. Death-dealing fire met our men from every point – from streets, alleys, basements and ruined buildings.[2]

Soviet commanders now realized that they had to change their tactics and adapt to the urban environment. Chuikov correctly articulated the problem and solution in his memoir when he stated that " … manoeuvre [sic] to surround a city is an operational art, the storming of a city is a matter of tactics carried out by small units." The key to their success in urban fighting was "the role of officers commanding small units, and the initiative in action … [that] become of prime importance in a city battle."[3] Chuikov, it appeared, gave

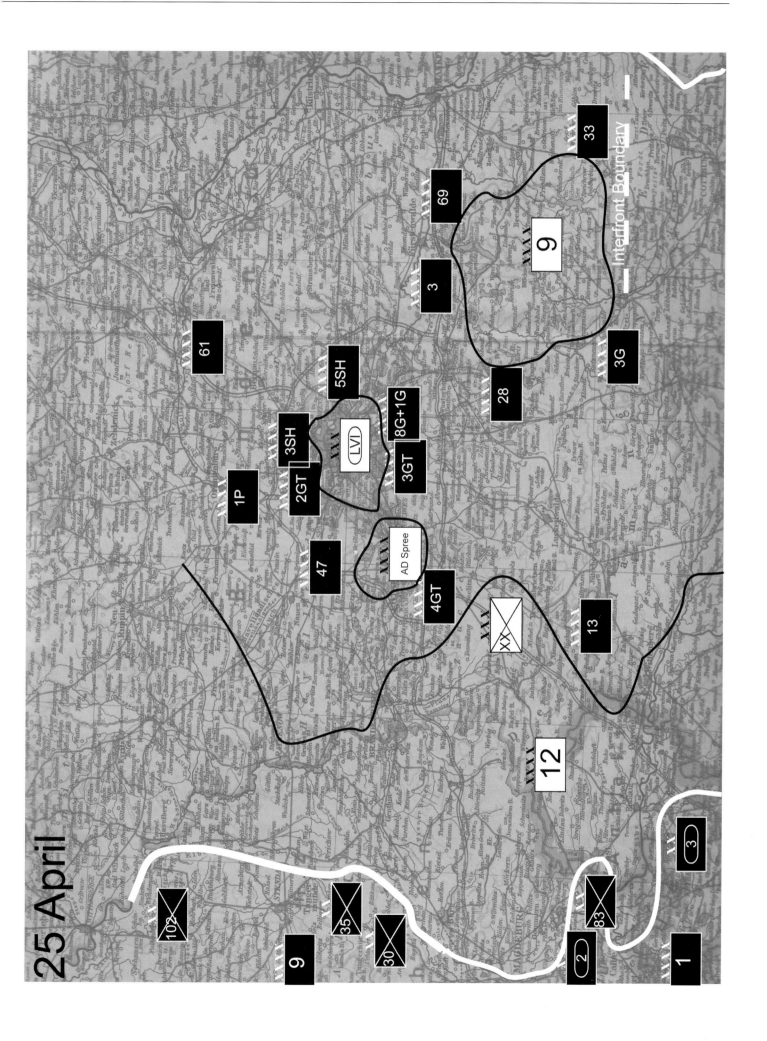

25 April

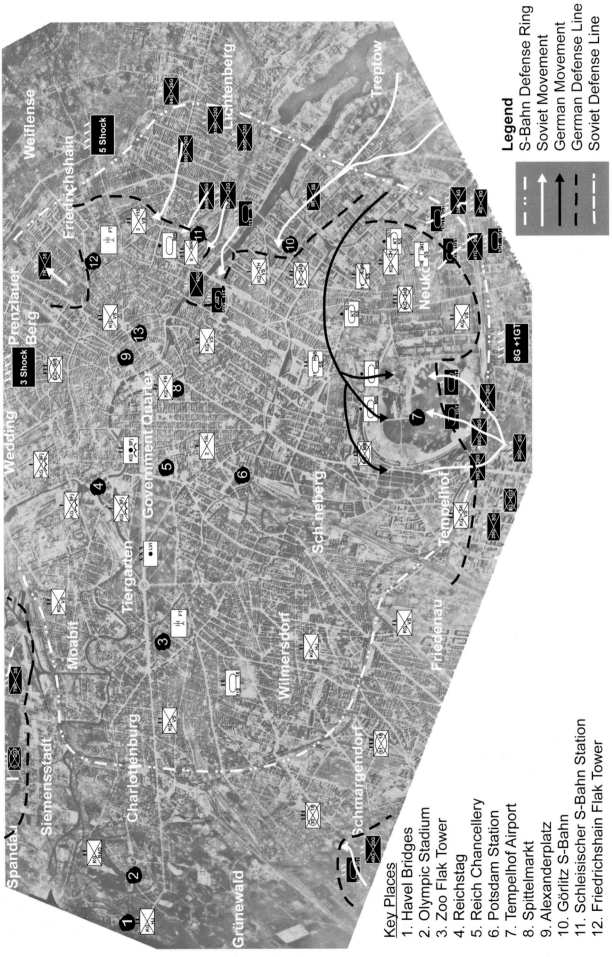

**Berlin
25 April**

Key Places
1. Havel Bridges
2. Olympic Stadium
3. Zoo Flak Tower
4. Reichstag
5. Reich Chancellery
6. Potsdam Station
7. Tempelhof Airport
8. Spittelmarkt
9. Alexanderplatz
10. Görlitz S-Bahn
11. Schlesischer S-Bahn Station
12. Friedrichshain Flak Tower

Legend
S-Bahn Defense Ring
Soviet Movement
German Movement
German Defense Line
Soviet Defense Line

greater credence to these tactics in words than he did in practice as there is little evidence to suggest that his army's soldiers adopted these principles broadly. The order of the day was typically to advance and attack no matter what the situation was like on the ground. It appears that any Soviet adoption of new tactics to overcome the adverse urban conditions found in Berlin was done on their own initiative and not by orders from higher command. By 25 April the fighting in Berlin turned into small independent unit actions.

Particular concern was raised at the increased rate of Soviet tank losses. Chuikov echoed the problems of armor operations encountered in Berlin with clarity:

> … armored troops with their grim and powerful machines were unable to produce the same effect in battle within a city as they did by massed blows in the field. In a city a tank regiment or battalion … is obliged to move in column along the street, and becomes a vulnerable target.
>
> Some commanders, however, evidently not desirous of loosing their independence of action and concerned for their prestige, did in spite of everything send their tanks in to the storm of Berlin column. They sent them in, and then saw the machines, stretched out in line along the streets, first become immobilized in traffic jams and then go up in flames, one after the other. The leading tank is set on fire—and there is nowhere for the others to go; just wait for a 'Faustpatronen' [*Panzerfaust*] to get you in the side, and be burnt ….[4]

Zhukov also commented unfavorably on the deployment of tanks in Berlin when he wrote the first public article of his experiences in 1965. He laments in the article that it was decided to commit three infantry and two armor armies (2nd Guards Tank, 3rd and 5th Shock, and 8th Guards, 1st Guards Tank) into Berlin at once to rapidly defeat the German forces in the city. It is interesting to note that in his article he makes no mention of Koniev's forces. Using a careful tone, Zhukov stated about the assault on Berlin that "It should be added that the space for maneuver and the specific missions which are appropriate for the maneuver capabilities of tank units didn't exist at that time."[5] In other words the decision—or rather *Zhukov's* decision—to order a heavily armored force into a city the size of Berlin was an operational mistake.

Zhukov continued to make poor operational judgments that often impeded his ability to quickly capture Berlin. After digesting the fact that his rival Koniev beat him into Berlin, Zhukov issued two orders that were in accordance with his jealous personality and brutal behavior. First, he ordered Chuikov's combined forces to advance across Koniev's front and cut off his route to the Reichstag. This action was deliberately done without any coordination between Chuikov and Koniev. With Koniev's advance blocked, Zhukov had to quickly defeat the remaining German defenders and reach the Reichstag. He ordered his airforce to conduct a major new operation designed to blast out the German defenders in his path—once again relying on massed firepower to overcome adverse operational conditions. In order to facilitate the further advance of his troops, the 16th and 18th Air Armies were ordered to launch a new Soviet air offensive against fixed and mobile German targets in the city. The goal was to weaken the German positions and assault through them toward the Reichstag as quickly as possible. The air operation was known as 'Salute' and was planned to last two days. It consisted of 1,368 aircraft to include over 500 bombers. According to Soviet sources the best pilots were chosen in order to avoid striking friendly troops on the ground.[6] Zhukov's two decisions solved no problems. They increased the destruction of the city blocking available avenues of approach and roving Soviet aircraft often hit friendly force concentrations. The dust, smoke, debris and proximity of German and Soviet soldiers prevented Soviet aircraft from effectively distinguishing between friend and foe.

1st UKRAINIAN FRONT

The massive uncoordinated air operations so close to Koniev's forces resulted in serious fratricide. Koniev readily describes this in his memoir, though he strives to downplay the scope, source, and impact that the air attacks had on his troops. He recorded that:

> During the street fighting in the city, in general, it was very difficult to orient precise attacks of the airforces on precisely those objects which at the given moment had to be subjected to attack. Everything was in ruins, everything wrapped in flame, smoke, and dust. From above, in general, it was difficult to make out where and what things were going on.
>
> From the reports received by me from Rybalko, I understood that he was suffering losses from the attacks of our airforces, sometimes here and sometimes there … [7]

This was a costly pattern that continued throughout the battle.

By midday the 6th Guards Mechanized Corps from Koniev's 4th Guards Tank Army met troops of the 328th Rifle Division and the 65th Guards Tank Brigade from Zhukov's 47th Army near Ketzin completing the encirclement of Berlin to the northwest. Ninety minutes later, at 1330, the 58th Guards Division met a reconnaissance element of the 69th U.S. Infantry Division near Strel, followed shortly after by the link up of the 173rd Guards Rifle Division and 69th U.S. Infantry Division near Torgau along the Elbe River. Berlin was encircled and Germany was split in two.[8] Despite Koniev's apparent successes he was not in an enviable position. The German 12.Armee was poised to strike into his weak right flank, while the 9.Armee struck his left.

Koniev's forces were operationally stretched thin. While he receives significant credit for his handling of the difficult situation, the fact remains that it was Koniev's rivalry with Zhukov that placed his soldiers in the midst of their military challenge. In the west the 6th Guards Mechanized Corps focused on its drive along the approaches to Potsdam where *Armeegruppe Spree* maintained a solid defensive perimeter among the lakes and canals that made Potsdam a virtual island.[9] The 5th Guards Mechanized Corps and the 13th Army maintained pressure on Wenck's extended lines with the aid of the 2nd Air Army's 1st Air Attack Corps. Koniev's forces struggled to maintain a defensive line as the German formations continued aggressive probing to the east. They were so short of manpower that the 1st Air Attack Corps launched successive waves of fighter-bombers that not only attacked the German formations directly but also dropped anti-tank mines along the key avenues of approach of Wenck's formations in order to slow them down.[10] His use of aircraft in this area suggests that he simply did not have enough ground forces to conduct a proper defensive screen against the German formations. In the east, he began to mass artillery against what he expected was the planned breakout of the 9.Armee.

The 28th Army was ordered to screen the western side of Busse's *9.Armee* all the way into Berlin's suburbs along the inter-front boundary with Chuikov. The responsibility of holding back the *9.Armee* was given to Colonel General V.N. Gordov's 3rd Guards Army that moved north after the fall of Cottbus. The 3rd Guards Army continually pushed on Busse's southern and southwestern flank. Koniev likely realized that the three corps of the 3rd Guards Army along with elements of the 28th Army was not enough to reduce the Germans trapped in the pocket. All he could do was hope to hold them back. Koniev demonstrated a key understanding about how the operational situation around Berlin was masterfully manipulated by Keitel and Jodl. Under the circumstances he did not fault the efforts of either Wenck or Busse.

> As a matter of fact, Keitel, who had at first participated in the organization of the advance of Wenck's army, succeeded in misinforming both sides, as they say. He did not disclose to Wenck entirely that tragic situation in which the surrounded *9.Armee* of the Germans had already found itself, as well as the position of the *3.[Panzer] Armee* north of Berlin, which was partially surrounded, thus inspiring vain hopes in him. But when he reported to Hitler, he apparently exaggerated the real capabilities of Wenck's army.
> As a result Hitler continued to believe in the reality of his plans—that the combined efforts of the *9.*, *12.*, and *3. [Panzer] Armees* still could save him, together with Berlin. Obviously, it was precisely with these hopes that his decision to remain Berlin was associated, to a considerable degree.[11]

Koniev did not really know what Wenck or Busse would do or what their true capabilities were at the time he fought them in April 1945. The radio broadcasts from the Propaganda Ministry certainly indicated that Koniev could expect a combined attack by both German armies toward Berlin through his overextended lines. Despite the ominous situation on his flanks, Koniev's main focus remained reaching the Reichstag before Zhukov.

3. PANZER ARMEE

Manteuffel's *3.Panzer Armee*'s defense was now desperate. His men fought successfully to hold off the Soviet bridgehead expansion, then retreated to the Wotan Line in order to consolidate their forces. Rokossovsky's 2nd Byelorussian Front continued to grind down the German defenses and finally broke into the Stettin Bridgehead. The Germans in and around Stettin lost their morale after the strenuous fighting. The *3.Panzer Armee* report for 25 April cited that "Our units in that area have no more fighting spirit and evidently no longer the will to continue further fighting ...."[12] Local counterattacks were not successful, although the *25.Pz.Gren.Div.* did launch an attack into the flank of the 1st Polish Army from the area of Oranienburg and Germendorf. The Panzergrenadiers penetrated to the main rail line at Germendorf, piercing the surprised Polish line.[13] It was noted by *AGV* that the *Luftwaffe* ground forces supplementing the front line combat troops began to retreat on their own as discipline broke down. Heinrici ordered the General of Military Police and twenty officers of the *Luftwaffe* to quickly restore order among the *Luftwaffe* troops.[14] Steiner continued to procrastinate in his attack south. By the end of the day he received the vanguard of *7.Pz.Div.*, and the entire *5.Marine Division* that finished its deployment in spite of heavy Soviet air interdiction. It was made clear by Jodl that Steiner needed to start moving. As added incentive Jodl explained to Steiner that he had to employ these forces in an attack or that he would lose them back to the *3.Panzer Armee*, and that Steiner would be subordinated to Holste's Panzer corps that was recently dispatched from the *12.Armee* screening to the west.[15]

9. ARMEE

AGV tried to coordinate supply airdrops for the *9.Armee* all night. Fifteen aircraft were organized for the attempt. These aircraft were large 'transport machines' and could certainly have been the giant cargo Me 323s. Three of the planes took off prior to the scheduled 2400 hour departure and never returned. Presumably they were unable to locate the landing strips that were to be lit only at 2400 and no sooner. Since the first three aircraft never returned to base, they were presumed shot down by the base commander. The *Luftwaffe* base commander decided to ground the rest of the aircraft and the airlift to the *9.Armee* was stopped.[16] The *9.Armee* meanwhile began its planned breakout to the west.

Busse's plan was to launch two *Kampfgruppe* toward Baruth to secure the roads west prior to the final drive toward Wenck's lines. Busse waited to launch the initial attack until the Frankfurt-an-der-Oder garrison finally reached his main forces three days after they pulled out of the east bank of the Oder River. He created *Kampfgruppe Pipkorn* led by *SS-Standartenführer* Rüdiger Pipkorn that consisted of the *35.SS-Polizei Grenadier Division* and the remaining elements of the *10.SS-Panzer Division Frundsberg*. These forces were cut off from *Armeegruppe Schröner* when Koniev drove through the inter-front boundary. In addition, Busse inherited *Oberst* Hans von Luck's *Panzer Grenadier Regiment 125* and remaining Panthers of the *Panzer Regiment 22* of the *21.Panzer Division* also caught in the *9.Armee* pocket. Von Luck's forces made up the second *Kampfgruppe*. The offensive was planned to start at 2000 that evening.[17] The Soviets had other plans and renewed attacks by the 28th Army screening from the west threw off the timetable and split the two *Kampfgruppe*. *Kampfgruppe Luck* was still fighting off Soviet attacks along its planned line of advance by 2230 and was not expected to launch its attack until 2400. *Kampfgruppe Pipkorn* did launch its attack toward Baruth on time and met with initial success south of Krausnick.[18]

12. ARMEE

Hutten's attack northeast the day before penetrated the flank of the 27th Rifle Corps between Cobbelsdorf and Zahna. This attack helped relieve further Soviet pressure toward the west and allowed the final redeployment of the *XLVIII Pz. Korps* over the Elbe River from the south. *Scharnhorst* continued its deployment east uninterrupted, while *Schill* finished its deployment equally without incident.[19] Fighting continued to rage in Treuenbrietzen with additional attacks by *Körner*. The *12.Armee* detached the *XLI Pz. Korps* under the command of

Three T-34/76 Model 1943s that appear to be either knocked out or abandoned in the street. The reserve fuel drum on the left hand tank was knocked off and is lying on the ground. Two Soviet soldiers with shoulder weapons are hugging the ruined wall to the right. By 1945 the T-34/76 was outclassed and under armored. It stood little chance of survival in the open against the German medium and heavy Panzers. In an urban environment like Berlin, *Panzerfausts* fired from upper stories easily penetrated the thin top armor of the tank's turret or the engine deck, quickly immobilizing the tanks or killing the crew. Courtesy of the US National Archives.

A knocked out Panzer IV/L from *Pz.Div. Müncheberg* in a Berlin suburb. Photo courtesy of ASKM.

General Holste to block the Soviet advance via Rathenow behind the *3.Panzer Armee* lines. These forces were pulled from the Elbe front against the Western Allies.[20]

Wenck and his staff weighed their strategic situation and their options. The Russians had encircled Berlin. *Armee Detachment Spree* was also surrounded in Potsdam. By the afternoon Koniev's forces began infiltrating in between the *Hutten* and *Körner Divisions*. In the midst of his operational area were 10,000 refugees from the eastern provinces that wanted protection from the Soviets. It soon became obvious that an attempt to relieve Berlin from the planned attack route east would fail even if they joined up with Busse's forces. Wenck's staff decided the best course of action, contrary to Krebs' orders from 23 April, was to launch a coordinated attack to the northwest of Berlin linking up with a similar southeast thrust from *AGV*, destroy elements of the 47th Army operating in that area, then keep a corridor from Berlin open. Wenck quickly briefed this plan to *OKW* and was told that he had no other option but to continue his plans to launch an attack east, link up with the *9.Armee*, then attack northeast toward Berlin.[21]

LVI PZ. KORPS

Weidling wasted no time in visiting the various sectors and arranging his forces accordingly after he was officially appointed *CBDA*. Among his first tasks was to visit the Zoo Flak Tower and determine its suitability as a headquarters. Upon reaching the tower he met with *1.Berlin Flak Division* commander, *Generalmajor* Otto Sydow. Sydow gave him a tour of the massive bunker. While there the Soviets launched an air attack on the Flak Tower as part of their new air offensive 'Salute' causing a significant explosion outside in the Zoological Garden. Weidling commented that "From one bomb which burst quite near the bunker the whole lofty

Brigadeführer Gustav Krukenberg took command of the *33. Waffen-SS Grenadier-Division der Charlemagne* in September 1944. He brought several hundred members of this unit into Berlin. Once in Berlin he was made commander of the *11. SS-Freiwillige-Panzergrenadier-Division Nordland*. German propaganda photo courtesy of the Cornelius Ryan Collection, Mahn Center, Alden Library, Ohio University, Athens, OH.

tower seemed to tremble. That was an absolutely exceptional feeling!" Based on the over-crowdedness of the Flak Bunker, and the target it represented to the Soviets, Weidling decided to move his HQ in the Bendlerblock area opposite the Shell Haus within Defense Sector Z. Here he was close to the Reich Chancellery and the location was more discrete.[22]

Weidling left the Flak Tower to see *General* Bärenfänger at Alexanderplatz where the immediate threat to the city was perceived. Weidling's staff car advanced slowly along Potsdamer Platz and Leipziger Straße due to the heavy bombardment caused by Soviet artillery fire. He recounted later that "dust of bricks and stones hung in the air like mist." He parked his car on the west side of the Spree on Schloß Straße and walked the long route to Alexanderplatz. The entire area was devastated, and Russian mortars were going off everywhere. Weidling and his staff moved in leaps and bounds to the U-Bahn entrance. Upon entering they found the platforms and tunnels crammed with German refuges in the first two floors of the U-Bahn station. Bärenfänger's HQ was on Platform E. *General* Bärenfänger was a former *Hitlerjugend* commander and a true believer in the Nazi cause. He was well liked by Goebbels. Bärenfänger requested more ammunition and armor support from Weidling as the Soviets were driving hard toward Alexanderplatz. The majority of Bärenfänger's weapons were old German bolt-action and captured Italian rifles. Fortunately there were plenty of *Panzerfausts* available and the main avenues were dotted with dug-in 8.8s. During the visit, Weidling saw the large number of Soviet tanks that were destroyed by his meager forces of *Volkssturm* and *Hitlerjugend* all around the approaches to the U-Bahn station.[23] Weidling made no promises about support and left to visit other units in the city. He recalled during his interrogation:

> I myself went to the *11. SS-Freiwilligen-Pz.Gren.Div. Nordland,* whose command post was now to be found in Kempenicker Straße. On the way there I saw a large number of soldiers from this division who were seeking about for some sort of cover in the western part of Berlin. In reply to my question one of them said, "We were told to come here."
>
> The *SS-Pz.Gren.Div. Nordland* had been conducting extremely difficult defensive operations. Powerful enemy forces had been ferried across the River Spree and from the north they had smashed into the flank of the division. I once again was obliged to express my opinion to *SS-Brigadeführer* Zeigler. Zeigler was always able to find objective reasons for the explanation for all of his failures. When he reported about the extremely small numbers of men who were to be found in his division (each one of the regiments of the [division] consisted really of a weakened company), on the great lack of arms and on the losses of nearly all of his officers and non-commissioned officers, I demanded of him that he should collect all his people who were milling around with nothing to do in the western parts of Berlin and with all decisiveness get them back into the front line. My opinion was therefore the more strengthened that for Zeigler all means were good means which enabled him to get the hell as fast as possible out of Berlin. After that visit I petitioned for the removal of Zeigler from the post of divisional commander, and this was done. *SS-Brigadeführer* Krukenberg replaced Zeigler.
>
> From the *SS-Pz.Gren.Div. Nordland* I went to the *18.Pz.Gren.Div.* which had just taken up a new defensive sector. Powerful elements of the enemy were attacking towards Dahlem and towards Zehlendorf [these were Koniev's forces]. Of all the divisions of the *LVI Panzer. Korps* the *18.Pz.Gren.Div.* was the one which had fought the best and which possessed the greatest combat capability. The commander of the division, *Generalmajor* Rauch, had a great understanding of his business and with great calmness conducted the operations of his forces. On the way I was once again able to check how the orders were being carried out for blowing up of the bridges across the Teltow Canal.

Very few preparations had been made for the demolition of the Berlin bridges. In Berlin itself there were almost no explosives. *Oberst* Reifor explained that everything which had to do with demolition of bridges, was in fact not located with the command of the defensive districts, but with *Reichsminister* Speer and his institutions, as across the bridges ran the electric and telephone cables and that blowing them up could be a serious economic loss.[24]

When his rounds were complete Weidling finished preparations for a briefing with the *Führer* on the current situation that included a reordering of his combat formations.

Weidling appointed new Defense Sector commanders by the afternoon. The new deployments and commanders were:

Sectors A & B (East): *Generalmajor* Mummert, now the nominal *LVI Pz. Korps* commander, since Weidling became the Commander of Berlin, was placed in charge over Bärenfänger. *Müncheberg* was tasked organized in support of Defense Sector's A and B.

Sector C (Southeast): First *Brigadeführer* Ziegler then Krukenberg, of *Nordland* was placed in command along with the remnants of his division and additional task organized elements of *Müncheberg* assigned to defend Tempelhof Airport.

Sector D (astride Tempelhof): *Oberst* Wöhlermann, the *LVI Pz. Korps* Artillery Commander was placed in charge. He replaced the 62 year old *Luftwaffe Generalmajor* Schreder. His forces were those local to the Defense Sector.

Sector E (Southwest and the Grunewald Forest) *Generalmajor* Georg Scholze took over command along with his *20.Pz.Gren.Div.* The main elements of the *20.Pz.Gren.Div.* already moved far to the west of Berlin, presumably on orders of Scholze.

Sector F (Spandau and Charlottenburg): *Oberstleutnant* Eder was left in command. The forces arrayed here consisted of a variety of locally raised *RAD*, *Hitlerjugend* and *Volkssturm* units as well as stragglers formed from various units that retreated west through Berlin from the Oder Front.

Sectors G and H (North): *Oberst* Harry Herrmann took over command along with the remnants of the *9.Fallschirmjäger* and *Wachregiment Großdeutschland*.

Sector Z: *Oberstleutnant* Seifert was in command. All *SS*, however, were under the command of Mohnke who was given responsibility of the Government Quarter. This arrangement held particular confusion for soldiers and units that passed through the area. Mohnke did not consider himself or his troops as part of Weidling's command. His position highlighted the near-hostile attitude between *Wehrmacht* and *SS* command relationships during the battle for Berlin.[25]

Soviet mortar team sets up along a broad Berlin boulevard to conduct indirect fire support missions against German positions.
Photo courtesy of the Bundesarchiv.

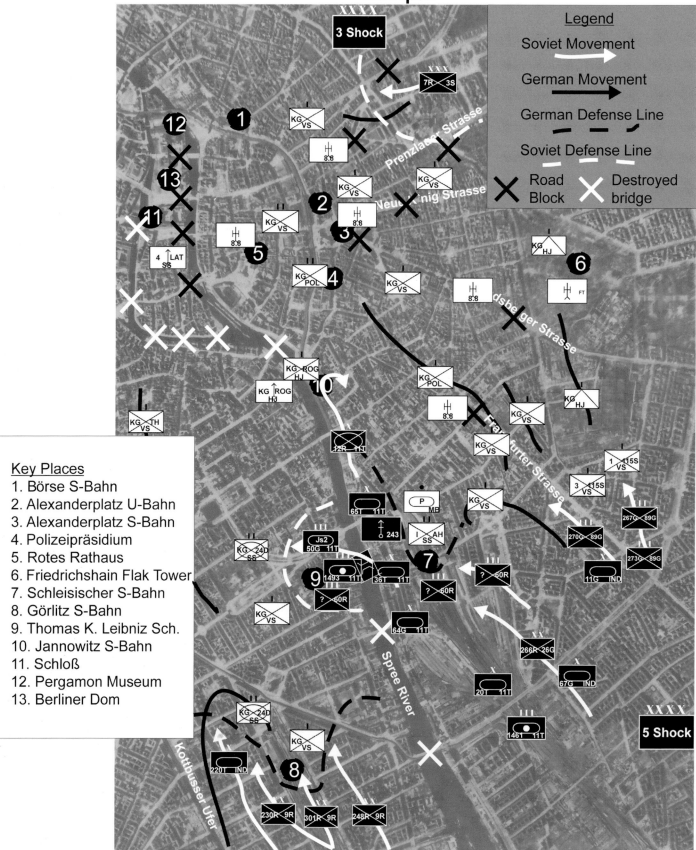

Eastern Districts
25 April

Key Places
1. Börse S-Bahn
2. Alexanderplatz U-Bahn
3. Alexanderplatz S-Bahn
4. Polizeipräsidium
5. Rotes Rathaus
6. Friedrichshain Flak Tower
7. Schleisischer S-Bahn
8. Görlitz S-Bahn
9. Thomas K. Leibniz Sch.
10. Jannowitz S-Bahn
11. Schloß
12. Pergamon Museum
13. Berliner Dom

Legend
Soviet Movement
German Movement
German Defense Line
Soviet Defense Line
Road Block
Destroyed bridge

Weidling began to realize that the forces at his disposal were not enough to defend the city of Berlin for any period of time. He immediately ordered his staff to begin developing a new breakout plan for Adolf Hitler and the remainder of the garrison.[26]

FÜHRERBUNKER

Weidling noted a change in the mood at the *Führerbunker* when he arrived at 2200. Hitler already had an earlier briefing with Goebbels and Krebs. Krebs continued providing Hitler with false reports about the status of Wenck's attack from the west, and the prospects of the other relief attempts being coordinated. His optimistic assessments created a false sense of hope that continued throughout the day. Hitler's mood was reinforced by the arrival of Ritter von Greim and Hanna Reitsch, who landed on the east-west axis that now constituted a makeshift runway between the Brandenburger Tor (known also as the Brandenburg Gate) and the Siegessäule (known also as the Victory Column) on order of Hitler. Von Greim, who was wounded on landing due to the Soviet shelling, was notified of Göring's dismissal and his own appointment to *Reich Marshal of the Luftwaffe*. A brief ceremony was held for the appointment, and Hitler informed his guests that Berlin's situation was better than it appeared.[27] According to the *OKW* diary, Hitler recovered from his near collapse of 22 April and now believed that victory in the war might be achieved in the successful defense of Berlin. This change in his belief was clearly reinforced by his senior Generals who convinced him that relief attacks underway would succeed.[28]

The reality was far worse than anyone wanted to admit. U.S. and Soviet forces met at Torgau on the Elbe, splitting Germany in half. There were no signs of any immediate fallout between the Western Allies and the Soviets. Supply for Berlin's garrison was now difficult, and relief operations by air drop were organized for the evening. *Großadmiral* Dönitz was subsequently ordered to supply Berlin with troops by any means necessary.[29] These were troops that Weidling could desperately use, even though he was already thinking of a way to breakout. Hanna Reitsch offered to fly Hitler out but he flatly refused. In a situation briefing with Krebs and Goebbels earlier in the day, Hitler reaffirmed his decision to stay in Berlin and die there. During the briefing Goebbels argued to Hitler about the relevance of Berlin by insisting that a moral victory could be achieved on a global scale.[30] Hitler's response was clear. He felt that he could not justify the harsh measures he imposed on his troops if he left Berlin. Not only would it appear that he was running away, but there was no viable plan to operate the Nazi Government from southern Germany. He was unsure of the best course of action at the start of his conversation but finally settled on a decision to stay and fight in Berlin until his death—he would loose or win the war based on what happened in and around Berlin.[31] These words were echoed to Weidling after his situational briefing. As Hitler began to speak, all his words focused on a single train of thought, according to Weidling's recollection: "If Berlin falls, there is no doubt that Germany will be defeated."[32] The briefing ended at 0200 on 26 April and as Weidling made his way back to his new headquarters he increasingly became aware of the precarious position that he placed the soldiers of the *LVI Pz. Korps* by deciding to move them into Berlin.

EASTERN DISTRICTS

The 5th Guards Shock Army renewed its assault toward Alexanderplatz and the areas to the southwest where its units already crossed the Spree. Soviet forces continued to struggle through a tangle of dense rubble and roadblocks toward the vital road junction. On the right flank, the 89th Guards Rifle Division slowly worked it way through the dense housing on either side of Frankfurter Allee toward the Friedrichshain Flak Tower. They moved slowly as the 12.8cm Flak guns were constantly looking for ground targets.[33] Recent experience showed that they were under observation by forward German spotters assigned to the Flak Tower, so they had to adopt a more cautious approach in this area. In addition the German defenders continued a stiff resistance among the ruined factories forcing the Soviets into prolonged combat. The employment of massive artillery fire among the German positions failed to dislodge the defenders. The two companies of the *115 Siemenstadt Volkssturm Bataillon* were the main German units in the area. The battalion was armed with fifty K98s and two light machine-guns, and they were joined by other miscellaneous *Polizei* and *Wehrmacht* stragglers from the Alexanderplatz area as well as *Luftwaffe* cadet tank hunters from the Flak Tower. They held a defensive perimeter along the west side of Richthofenstraße with their back to the St. George cemetery.[34] Farther south the 266th Rifle Division of the 26th Guards Rifle Corps and several regiments of the 60th Guards Rifle Division of the 32nd Rifle Corps became involved in serious fighting around the Schlesischer S-Bahn Station. The railway station was defended by *SS-Hauptsturmführer* Mrugalla's *I./SS Anhalt* that was dispatched to bolster the defense along with two Panthers of *Müncheberg*. These forces arrived in response of Bärenfänger's earlier request for reinforcements. This force was supplemented by Rogmann who placed six 8cm mortars on the elevated S-Bahn tracks east of Jannowitzbrücke S-Bahn station.[35] Later in the day Soviet infantry, presumably from the 11th Tank Corps' 12th Motorized Rifle Brigade, advanced down the street toward the German position. Rogmann's mortars opened fire and ripped apart the Soviet infantry on the open road. Mortar shells usually make a hole about two hands wide in soft dirt, but they shatter on impact when they hit a hard surface like concrete. This makes them very dangerous in an urban battlefield. Their explosions showered deadly metal splinters on a near-horizontal plane wounding many Soviets in the legs and abdomen. Soviet counter-battery fire in this area was decisive and Rogmann's position was quickly zeroed and fire returned. Four of Rogmann's mortars were destroyed in the counter-battery fire and all but four *Hitlerjugend* were wounded or killed. Rogmann retreated and later in the day used improvised rocket launchers to fire Nebelwerfer rockets over open sights, destroying several Soviet tanks approaching along Holzmarktstraße toward the Jannowitz Bridge.[36] This ended the 11th Tank Corps attempt to find a crossing farther north than their present location.

The 11th Tank Corps continued to consolidate its positions on the west bank of the Spree during the day, citing the difficult nature of urban operations in their official history. The 50th Guards Heavy Tank Regiment was ferried over as well as additional infantry forces in preparation for the next assault. The Soviet Official History records that "The intensity of the fighting increased. There was a struggle for each house and each storey of each house …. It is difficult to conduct operations in the streets of a large city and that was especially true of Berlin where each house and each cellar spat fire … "[37] The 11th Tank Corps could no longer advance into Berlin on its own and required additional infantry assistance from the 5th Shock Army. Acting independently, the tankers of this corps drove long and hard against the Germans since the 16 April and were one of the corps that led the drive into Berlin from the east. Now, these tankers found themselves bogged down in urban terrain, measuring their progress in blocks and not kilometers.

Soviet Katushya rocket launchers are loaded and readied for firing. The Katushya rockets were inaccurate but had an immense psychological effect against enemy troops. Photo courtesy of the Bundesarchiv.

The 9th Rifle Corps advanced northwest behind the 220th Tank Brigade and became involved in heavy fighting around Görlitzer S-Bahn Station that dominated the center of the front. These Soviet units had just forced the Landwehr Canal to the south behind retreating Nordland forces. Here remnants of *SS-Pz.Gren.Rgt.24 Danmark* and local *Volkssturm* maintained a strong cordon to the northeast of the main *Nordland* defense in Neukölln. The German defense at Görlitz S-Bahn station helped protect *Müncheberg's* flank as the division's remnants were strung out through Neukölln in a race north before they were caught in the flank by the 8th Guards Army.

The Panzers and Panzergrenadiers of *Müncheberg* were moving northwest from Köpenick through this area to their ordered deployment in Sectors A, B, and C. In the morning the division's remnants successfully disengaged from a large Soviet attack in Köpenick that included up to thirty JS–2s. After the disengagement *Müncheberg* received orders to reinforce Alexanderplatz and was *en-route* when the order was canceled at 0900 due to Chuikov's attack across the Teltow Canal. By mid-morning, however, the division was organized with some elements heading to Alexanderplatz and others heading to Tempelhof Airport.[38]

SOUTHERN DISRICTS

Krukenberg met with Weidling who told him that he lost confidence in Zeigler's ability to command. Krukenberg was now in charge of *Nordland* and needed to assume command immediately. Krukenberg asked for written orders because he was concerned he could not effect a transition without written authorization. Weidling grabbed a piece of scrap paper and wrote the order down handing it over to Krukenberg and told him this would have to do under the circumstances.[39] It did not take long for Krukenberg to find *Nordland's* headquarters in Neukölln as the division staff parked all their vehicles in a very unmilitary way in front of the Labor Office. Russian aircraft from 'Salute' easily spotted the group of military vehicles from the air and attacked, causing significant confusion and wreckage. BMW trucks made their way down Hasenheide stopping at the entrance of the block where *Nordland's* HQ was located. French *SS* armed with assault rifles jumped out and quickly sealed off both ends of the block as Krukenberg exited his staff car and walked into Zeigler's headquarters quickly taking command. "*'Nordland's'* HQ was in an utter state of confusion. No one knew exactly where the regiments were located or where their new defense positions were located" Krukenberg stated after meeting Nordland's staff. According to Krukenberg " … the entire division was scattered all over the place. Many of the men had just simply moved off. The division seemed to have lost its unity …. No information was available on the situation in the area." After assuming command, Krukenberg walked over to the local mayor's office to find out what he knew of the situation and while he was waiting in the mayor's office " … I looked out of the window and in the distance I saw Russian tanks."[40] *SS-Rottenführer* Burghart, a veteran of Nordland, recalled the change of command distinctly:

> Outside, facing the entrance were two or three trucks with soldiers, their automatic guns aimed at the door. To Burghart it looked like they were going to fire any second …. While he stood there, some more trucks with *SS* troops drove up. About 30 men jumped out, and started to bar the street. They prevented all soldiers from entering the

A Panzerstellung with a MK IV turret sits abandoned as a column of Soviet SU-76s rolls by this position. Panzerstellung's were employed throughout the city, and some had Panther turrets as well. German Panzers that ran out of petrol towards the end of the fighting were placed in hull down positions and employed in a similar manner. Photo courtesy of the Bundesarchiv.

headquarters …. A few minutes later Zeigler came up from the cellar together with Emert, his driver. He looked at Burghart and said: "Take all your stuff out of the car. I will no longer need neither you nor the food rations."[41]

Burghart then watched Zeigler escorted away in one of the trucks. Several SPWs arrived immediately after Zeigler's departure carrying wounded *Nordland* soldiers looking for a hospital or first-aid station. The French *SS*, still guarding the area called for the SPWs to halt, but the drivers, thinking these men were Seydlitz troops, ignored their orders. One Frenchman fired his Sturmgewehr at the lead SPW, which promptly returned fire with a MG 42 wounding several Frenchmen in the process. The confusion, fear, uncertainty and unfamiliar faces played havoc on everyone's nerves.[42] Shortly after Zeigler was removed, *Nordland*'s HQs was ordered to the State Opera House north of the Landwehr Canal. Burghart and twelve men were ordered to the Leineweber Department Store on the Spittelmarkt where Soviets forces were advancing from the east and southeast. He was now under the authority of Seifert as the Spittelmarkt was part of Sector Z. Burghart, along with thirty men set up a defensive position and held here against the Soviets until 1 May.[43]

Krukenberg met with Weidling in the afternoon to explain the situation with *Nordland*. He informed Weidling that the division now numbered 1,500 men and six Sturmgeschütz assault guns spread out throughout the city. The divisional artillery was in the Tiergarten, while the supply and support elements were in the Pichelsberg-Spandau area.[44] Weidling then ordered him to pull *Nordland* out of Neukölln and into Sector Z to avoid being cut off by the advancing Soviets. Krukenberg came under the command of Seifert and he ordered his men to fill in defensive positions to the east and south of the government district.[45] Krukenberg issued the orders then left to meet with Seifert who was not happy about receiving another command staff. He welcomed *Nordland*'s troops but stated that he would rather have his own commanders lead the soldiers of *Nordland*. This attitude concerned Krukenberg. Also disconcerting was the fact that his subordinate commanders reported that there were no pre-existing defensive positions as described by Weidling after they completed their initial reconnaissance. Krukenberg settled in for the night at the State Opera House realizing that Berlin had no real defense and no clear command organization. He planned on visiting with Fegelein the morning to address his concerns while his forces remained in their positions south of the Landwehr Canal. During the rest of the day *Nordland* elements fought a series of fierce small unit actions throughout Neukölln as Chuikov's forces started their offensive across the Teltow Canal from the south.

The *18.Pz.Gren.Div.'s, 1./Artillerie Batterie Schlesien* and *2./Artillerie Batterie Holstein* started the morning around 0100 with word that the Russians were infiltrating through the rubble between their artillery batteries. The main regiments of the division were already over the canal to the northwest in the center of Berlin, but due to the fluid operations the artillery batteries trailed behind south of the Teltow Canal. The Russian infiltration was Chuikov's forces preparing for their morning assault. The Germans quickly realized the precariousness of their position and pulled over the Teltow Canal and into Neukölln where they met elements of *Nordland*'s HQ at City Hall. They rested until about 1000 then were ordered to move to the Tiergarten and Flak Tower where almost all remaining German artillery was positioned.[46] While approaching the Flak Tower they took up positions in the Berlin Zoo during a Soviet artillery barrage. A

Soviet artillery shell struck a pond with Pelicans, raining both water and dead birds all around the soldiers. In a nearby cage a badly wounded brown bear roared loudly with pain. This depressing sight caused the soldiers to continue to move away from the Zoo.

Chuikov's forces launched a two-pronged attack across the Teltow Canal in their effort to carry out their orders to take Tempelhof Airport and drive northwest across Koniev's front to prevent him from any further advance toward the Reichstag. On the left flank the 29th and 28th Guards Rifle Corps supported by the 8th Guards Mechanized Corps crossed the Teltow Canal in the sector between the Tempelhoferdam and the S-Bahn tracks marking the inter-front boundary. Chuikov suggested that this was done without much support from either artillery or aircraft.[47] This is in stark contrast to the crossing of his neighbor Koniev from the prior day. Chuikov's lack of support suggests either that he truly was under pressure to outflank Koniev and could not spend time preparing an assault or it could mean that Koniev's offensive drew much of the German defenders west away from Chuikov's line of advance. On the right flank the 4th Guards Rifle Corps supported by the 11th Guards Tank Corps crossed into Neukölln where it ran into the elements of *Nordland* still in defensive positions in that area.

The soldiers of *Pz.Gren.Rgt.24 Danmark* were hit hard by the death of their charismatic commander Sørensen the day before. With his death, the remnants of his regiment were ordered absorbed by the *Pz.Aufkl.Abt.11* under command of *SS-Sturmbannführer* Saalbach.[48] Before the regiment was completely disbanded there was one thing left to do. Illum drove out to a cemetery west of Pichelsberg where he found the director still in his office. Illum requested a burial plot for his commander, but the director required the proper forms, including a death certificate, and the 300 Marks to pay for the plot. Illum was in no mood for bureaucratic bickering while fighting was ongoing and responded to the cemetery director by telling him " … this man gave his life for your city, and now you even want money in order to give him a descent burial!" The Cemetery Director decided it was not in his best interest to argue with a distraught, well-armed combat soldier, and acquiesced. A nearby female Berliner watching the events offered to pay the Cemetery Director's fee but Illum refused and gave the grave-diggers some cigarettes instead. He then drove back to Division HQ to collect the body and brought it back to the cemetery with a Regimental Honor Guard.[49] During the burial *SS-Sturmbanführer* Hermannn, a German who had been with the Regiment since 1944, gave a speech. The only written account of it ever published is described below:

> I stand here beside your open grave, and I must not only bid farewell to a courageous comrade I have known for so long as an exemplary leader and officer of this regiment; I must also say to you at this moment a word of thanks from my people. My people, to whom you and so many from your country have sworn loyalty and comradeship-in-arms in the fight against Bolshevism, an oath which you and so many have paid for with your lives!
>
> Now it burns deep in my heart that you should have had to loose your life in this way. I have also been deeply shaken in these last days, since I know how courageous you and your Danes have fought in this inferno, whereas so many German units have moved out to the west or are lying around inactively. May you find rest here in the heart of our bleeding city![50]

After the speech the Regimental Honor Guard provided a gun salute followed by a *Seig Heil* and the singing of the old German Soldiers' song 'I had a Comrade.'[51] Illum and the rest of the group left for Neukölln.

In Neukölln the remnants of *Nordland* continued to hold defensive positions while their operations staffs planned for the move north across the Landwehr Canal. *Kampfgruppe Pz.Gren.Rgt.24 Danmark, 16.(Pi)/Pz.Gren.Rgt 24 Danmark* under *SS-Untersturmführer* Christensen, as well as the *Sturmbataillon Charlemagne*, and assorted *Volkssturm* units were strung out across the sector.[52] *Pz.Gren.Rgt.23 Norge* had suffered so many losses in the past few days that it ceased to exist as a regiment and its members were distributed in smaller *Kampfgruppe* where required in Neukölln and the Central Districts. *SS-Aufk.Abt.11* was still intact and near the center of Neukölln. Three King Tiger of *s.SS-Pz.Abt.503* were also in the area providing roving support as needed. All these units fell under Krukenberg's new command but he had no way of effectively coordinating their operations, especially as he was setting up his new HQ well to the north at the time.

Henseler's company was ordered to take up position on Richardplatz in Neukölln with his Battalion HQ. As he and his men moved through the rubble the entire area was on fire and dense, black smoke filled the sky. He soon received word of Krukenberg's appointment as commander of the division. One of Krukenberg's first orders was that no subordinate command posts could shift or move unless they submitted written orders to Division HQ. Henseler's battalion staff viewed this as useless in the chaotic fighting that *Nordland's* soldiers found themselves in Berlin.[53] Krukenberg's order clearly demonstrated his concern over *Nordland's* lack of cohesion and apparent independent actions allowed under Zeigler. At the same time they reflect his lack of understanding regarding the current nature of combat operations.

The Soviet 35th and 47th Guards Rifle Divisions along with armor from the 40th and 45th Guards Tank Brigades began to infiltrate the side streets around Henseler's Battalion HQ all morning forcing the battalion to withdraw by noon. Henseler and his company moved north along Richardstraße to the main Post Office in Neukölln, in the vicinity of Berliner Straße. Here they noticed a dug-in Panther buried up to its turret on the side of the street commanding the intersection. The Panther was not a *Panzerstellung*, but rather a Panzer, probably from *Müncheberg*, that ran out of fuel and was ordered to dig-in. Henseler and his men approached the tank with the expectation to occupy it and turn the nearby building into a strong-point. When he approached the Panther's crew came running out of the nearby building, where they were obviously drinking, and proclaimed the tank theirs. Henseler then moved his force up the other side of the street where they could both support the Panther's crew and fire south down the avenue against any approaching Russians.

Chuikov's forces consolidated their gains across the Teltow Canal and prepared for a quick push through Neukölln up the east side of Tempelhof. The Germans soon realized that the Soviets were going to push aggressively throughout the day. By mid-afternoon the Soviets launched their expected attack up the broad street to cross Berg and Berliner Straße. The Soviet assault began, as usual, with an advance by unsupported T–34/85s from the tank regiments. The Panther's crew, either unaffected or emboldened by their inebriation, managed to knock off seven attacking Soviet tanks before their turret was hit by enemy fire and the crew bailed out. Nearby *SS-Unterscharführer* Bender's King Tiger from *s.SS-Pz.Abt.503* was at the intersection near the U-Bahn station at Hermannstraße where it also successfully defended the area from advancing Soviet tanks.[54] Another King Tiger, defending near the Post Office, was knocked out by enemy fire and abandoned. The third King Tiger counterattacked with *Danmark* troops from Hasenheide, knocking out several additional enemy tanks in the process. As now practiced by the Soviets, their assault was halted and they then launched a heavy artillery and mortar attack on the area in preparation for a second attack. The barrage destroyed the Post Office and other buildings in the vicinity. The Russians counterattacked by late afternoon, finally piercing the German resistance established in the rubble and crossing over Richardstraße forcing the King Tigers, and Henseler's Danes back toward Hermannnplatz.[55]

After successfully defending against Koniev's 9th Mechanized Corps assault across the Teltow, *Kampfgruppe Skorning* moved east along the canal where they saw Soviet tanks ready to cross from Chuikov's 8th Army near Tempelhof. They moved into Tempelhof, southwest of the airport when they where hit with accurate artillery fire and suffered accordingly.[56] Chuikov was determined to take Tempelhof that day and ordered an immediate attack on the airfield. The Soviet attack on the airfield was conducted by the 28th Guards Rifle Corps supported by two brigades of the 1st Guards Tank Army. The corps attack was organized with the 39th Guards Rifle Division on the left, the 79th Guards Rifle Division on the right, and the 88th Guards Rifle Division moving up the center. Soviet artillery was tasked to keep the runways clear of escaping aircraft. A special task force of tanks and soldiers had the explicit duty to prevent any aircraft from escaping—in case Hitler or other high-ranking Nazis tried to leave the city. The Soviets managed to reach the airfield but the main German defense by *Müncheberg* elements held. The remaining company of Tiger Is was positioned along the north end of the airport where their 8.8s easily dominated the open area to the south. Panzergrenadiers positioned themselves in key buildings along both sides of the airport. At dusk, more Soviet tanks with infantry arrived on the airfield but due to concentrated German fire failed to take the hangars or administrative buildings. *Leutnant* Kroemer of Müncheberg recalled:

> 10 A.M.: Russian drive on the airport becomes irresistible. New defense line in the center of town. Heavy street fighting—many civilian casualties. Dying animals. Women are fleeing from cellar to cellar. We are pushed northwest. New order to go north, as before. But the command situation is in obviously complete disorder, the Führer[bunker] must have false information, the positions we are supposed to take over are already in the hands of the Russians. We retreat again, under heavy Russian air attacks. Inscriptions on the house walls: 'The hour before sunrise in the darkest', and 'we retreat but we are winning'. Deserters hanged or shot. What we see on this march is unforgettable ....The first skirmishes in the subway tunnels, through which the Russians are trying to get back of our lines. The tunnels are packed with civilians.[57]

Kroemer's account highlights the confusion of command, and the chaos in the streets. It also provides one of the few glimpses of the civilian plight. Four million civilians remained in Berlin during the assault and it is easy to forget that they continued to survive under severe conditions of combat and reprisals by both sides. By evening, Chuikov's forces stopped their advance for that day. They had moved far into the city and his divisions were strung out along narrow corridors on either side of Tempelhof Airport. German forces were still fixed in many key positions despite the violent attacks by artillery and Soviet aircraft. Chuikov needed to capture the airport and continue his drive northwest. To the west, Koniev continued his aggressive drive northeast toward the Reichstag.

The 18.Pz.Gren.Div. managed to remain largely intact and combat effective during the retreat from the Oder Front. They still had plenty of fuel and ammunition, and there was no real opportunity for the division to expend any during the withdrawal operations from the Oder. Now the Panzergrenadiers and Panzers moved into a reserve position in the vicinity of Wilmersdorf—Steglitz while the divisional operations section under Böttcher set up a small command post in the Zoo Flak Bunker. Rausch, the division commander, was ordered to stay at the *Führerbunker*. The operation staff of the 18.Pz.Gren.Div. enjoyed the best possible communications of any of the units, as they had access to both landline phones and wireless radios. The division's regiments received all tasking directly from the Zoo Flak Tower during the remaining days of the battle.[58] Once the Panzergrenadiers took up position they were ordered to scout ahead of their positions to locate the 20.Pz.Gren.Div. on their flank where it was supposed to be holding the line south of Grunewald. Soon the scouts realized that Koniev's forces had crossed the Teltow Canal in force and were quickly moving northeast. The 20.Pz.Gren.Div.was nowhere to be found.

The commander of the 20.Pz.Gren.Div. became despondent during the retreat from the Seelow Heights. His forces bore the brunt of Chuikov's initial assault in the Oderbruch and in the town of Seelow. It is probable that Scholze ordered his forces west without permission, as he had lost his wife and four children in an air raid several weeks earlier. The recent experiences of sustained combat coupled with the loss of his wife and children wore down Scholze's remaining will. On this day Scholze committed suicide and left his division to continue their retreat through Berlin. When Koniev struck on 24 April a portion of the 20.Pz.Gren.Div. was caught on Wannsee Island while the rest managed to slip between the closing Russian pincers west of the city and ended up in Ketzin. The majority of Pz.Gren.Rgt.90, the divisional supply and Panzer battalions were reformed into *Panzer Brigade 20* and re-organized outside Friesack on 25 April with two infantry battalions, two artillery detachments, an armored company with eight assault guns, one anti-aircraft and one infantry mortar company—all fully motorized. The problem was that many of the new 'combat soldiers' were drawn from the divisional supply troops who were deserting daily, and it was clear not much could be expected from those that remained.[59] The division was now assigned to Hölste's corps to the north, but it was obvious to all the soldiers that based on the amount of smoke coming from the surrounding villages as well as the Soviet gun fire that the way north was not an option. The Soviets also knew where this formation was as their 'Lame Duck' biplanes continually tracked the German formation by dropping flares on the column. By 27 April the Brigade Commander *Major* Rostock, and his aide *Hauptmann* Kern abandoned the remnants of the division in order to make it home on their own. The soldiers of *Pz.Brig.20* continued west and ultimately their remaining officers brought them over to the U.S. forces along the Elbe where they surrendered.[60] None of this was known to Weidling, who now ordered the 18.Pz.Gren.Div. to launch an immediate counterattack through Koniev's lines and re-establish contact with the missing 20.Pz.Gren.Div.

Even after making contact with Chuikov's forces there was no coordination between the two Soviet Fronts as they continued to strike towards the Government Quarter. Rybalko's forces were reinforced by the 28th Army's 20th and 128th Rifle Corps that reached the Teltow Canal between Lankwitz and Mariendorf. His main armor forces continued their drive to the north and northeast. The 9th Mechanized Corps supported by the 61st Rifle Division passed through Steglitz *en-route* to Schöneberg and presumably ran into elements of Chuikov's forces screening to the east. In the center the 6th Guards Tank Corps supported by the 48th Guards Rifle Division disposed of a German flak battery opposite the Botanical Gardens in Königin-Luise-Platz and reached the outskirts of Schmargendorf in the centre. On the left flank the 7th Guards Tank Corps supported by the 20th Rifle Division headed up through Dahlem taking the *Luftwaffe's Luftgaukommando III* complex on the way. The goal of securing the heavily-wooded Grunewald to the Havel went to Colonel David Dragunsky's 55th Guards Tank Brigade that was 1,500 strong and had to use tank crews that lost their tanks as infantry due to the

Spandau
25 April

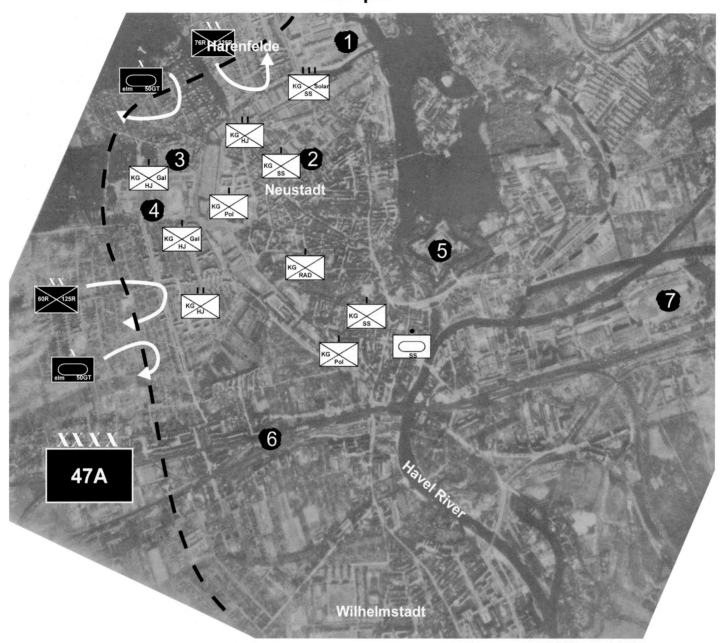

Key Places
1. Hackenfelde Aircraft Instrument
Factory
2. Military Supply Depot
3. Napola School
4. Polizei School
5. Zitadel
6. Spandau West Station
7. Ruhleben Racecourse

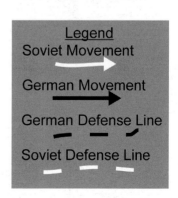

Legend

Soviet Movement

German Movement

German Defense Line

Soviet Defense Line

Soviet artillery was employed over open sight to knock out German strongpoints. Photo courtesy of RGAKFD Moscow.

This is the Spittelmarkt commercial center looking west down Leipziger Straße from the corner of Seydelstraße. The Spittelmarkt was the junction of seven major roads connecting the eastern and southeast districts of the city to the main avenue of approach to the Government Quarter. This area was heavily defended by the Germans and under daily Soviet attack. The Soviets never completely captured the Spittelmarkt and it was utterly destroyed during the bitter fighting as all the new buildings attest to their postwar construction. Author's collection.

191

This is the old Gertraudenstraße Bridge leading from Fisherman's Island to the Spittelmarkt. This area was defended in part by Spanish members of the *Waffen-SS*. The bridge is now in disuse to commercial traffic. Author's collection.

shortage of manpower experienced by all Soviet formations. Dragunsky's formation was later augmented by two additional infantry companies from the 23rd Guards Mechanized Rifle Brigade.[61]

Koniev's forces fighting in Berlin now began to operationally suffer from the combination of improper armor employment in urban terrain and friendly fire. As almost all Soviet formations experienced, the continued employment of armor without infantry support cost severely. As Rybalko's forces drove further into Steglitz they found that they had to alter their employment of armor. Losses were mounting and Koniev was concerned. In his memoir he records that Rybalko's tankmen " ... had to take [Berlin] inch by inch, and in conditions when the defenders of the city were abundantly armed with such a dangerous weapon to tanks as the *Panzerfaust*."[62] After suffering significant losses in tanks during the day, his armored forces organized around a platoon to company of infantry. Around this nucleus of infantry, that numbered no more than 10–25 men, there were three to four tanks, two to three self-propelled guns, several large caliber guns up to 203mm, two to three 'Stalin Organ' rocket launchers, a group of combat engineers with explosives, and several artillery pieces for direct support.[63] This again highlights that Soviet commanders had no operational concept for the urban terrain that Berlin presented or how to manage the infantry and armor coordination. Koniev's field commanders receive credit for adapting to the challenges that terrain and *Panzerfausts* presented. Due to the pace of operations, Koniev readily admits that his infantry " ... when assisting the tanks, they suffered serious losses, we had to bear this." Koniev, had no intention of slackening his drive toward the Reichstag, but now was keenly aware that "With all the courage of their crews, the tanks themselves were in no position to achieve decisive success in street fighting."[64] As Koniev's tankmen task organized to overcome these challenges, he also received disturbing reports that his men were being attacked by neighboring Soviet formations.

Two Soviet Fronts assaulted the largest urban complex on mainland without their efforts or objectives coordinated. Koniev's memoir states that "The farther the troops of both fronts advanced toward the center of Berlin, the more difficulties arose, especially in the application and direction of airforces."[65] Operation 'Salute' aside, soldiers of both fronts now began to encounter each other in the street and often exchanged fire. A series of clashes began in the morning that cost them an unknown number of Russian lives. Not much has been written about the street fighting between the two Soviet Fronts other than what is stated by a few veterans and Koniev himself, who is the only senior officer of the battle to offer insight into its effects:

> When at the front, as a consequence of some negligence or other suddenly you attack your own men, and even more so if you inflict losses, this is always perceived very sharply and dramatically. This was perceived especially sharply during the battle for Berlin, all the more so in that reports of such a type came in one after another during the entire day of the 25th, and apparently not only to me, but also to Zhukov.[66]

These clashes forced both commanders to complain to Headquarters of the Supreme-Commander-in-Chief about the future direction of fighting between the fronts in the city. Neither commander wanted to voluntarily give up their right to reach the Reichstag first. The result was a distinctive shift to the west of the inter-front boundary that left Rybalko's 9th Mechanized Corps east of the new line.

While this shift was communicated to Zhukov, it appears not to have been communicated directly or promptly to Koniev. Koniev's forces continued to operate in the area until the end of the battle.

Hitlerjugend Gruppe 200 disbanded after the death of Buttermann the night before. Still shocked at the death of his leader, Pienkny followed Buttermann's last orders and made his way to the Villa that was prepared for Werewolf operations. He arrived at the safe house and met three other boys from his unit. In the damp basement of the safe house he found mattress, some equipment, and enough food to last six months. Pienkny and another boy decided not to wait at the Villa and 'play Werewolf' as they preferred to join another combat unit. They made their way to the Schöneberg Town Hall where the two boys received orders to make their way to Yorckstraße where the two main southern S-Bahn lines converged in the Anhalter Freight Yard. Their goal was to keep look out and report on any Soviet tanks that penetrated into the area. As the boys made their way there they came upon a group of civilians talking excitedly in the street. When Pienkny asked the group what was going on they explained that there was a thirty-five car freight train the rail yard loaded with Danish butter and bacon, but it was guarded by two *SS* men that refused to allow anyone to approach. The civilians explained that they had had no food for days and were starting to starve. The *SS* guards were shooting anyone on sight that approached the train. The two boys decided to approach the train and see what was happening for themselves. As they approached they noticed dead *Volkssturm* and civilian bodies lying on or near the tracks, many with head shot wounds. As they reached Platform 2 they saw about four *SS* Guards who yelled that if the boys were looking for food they would be shot as no one was allowed to plunder the train. Pienkny and his comrade Pusenjack decided that they were going to kill the *SS* guards. The two boys took up position under a neighboring train and shot one of the guards in the leg. When he collapsed, his comrades came over to help and both boys opened up with automatic weapons fire and killed the remaining *SS* guards. Both boys boarded the train and stuffed their pockets with food, then proceeded to tell the civilians that they could now board the train and take what they wanted. As the civilians converged on the train, Soviet artillery began to hit the freight yard and destroyed it with a direct hit. The two boys quickly took shelter under the Yorckstraße S-Bahn overpass until the shelling stopped then they made their way west toward Bülowstraße.

Pienkny and Pusenjack were now confronted by a *Luftwaffe Oberfeldwebel* who commanded a small battle group armed with a 2cm anti-aircraft gun. The *Oberfeldwebel* yelled out "Cowards, why are you going back?" Pienkny instinctively knew that the situation he now found himself in was grave, so thinking fast he put his arm around Pusenjack and stated that he was bringing back his wounded friend. The *Oberfeldwebel* yelled "There is no going back!" and ordered his crew to open fire with the 2cm gun. The crew probably shot wide seeing that these were just two boys. Pienkny and his comrade jumped behind an advertising pillar, and quickly made their escape under cover from Russian mortars that started to hit nearby as they zeroed in on the sound of the 2cm gun firing.[67]

WESTERN DISTRICTS

The Soviet 47th Army launched a second attack into Spandau and Gatow. The 125th Rifle Corps finally succeeded in isolating the Spandau defense but failed to capture the town. The Soviet force was not large enough for the task and relied on airpower and artillery to force the German defenders out of their defensive positions. The Zoo Flak Tower continued to support the defenders at Gatow that expected a variety of incoming flights during the day.[68] Calls for reinforcements continually went out across the radio waves and *OKW* command channels now that Hitler decided to make the final stand for Nazi Germany in the streets of Berlin. One of those reinforcements was an eighteen year old *Kriegsmarine* recruit trained in radar operation named Heinz Kratschmar who was stationed in Stralsund on the Baltic Coast. During 24 April Heinz and other cadets were called to formation and issued food and weapons. Heinz received two *Panzerfausts*, two hand grenades, one case of MG ammunition and a German KAR98 rifle. Then he and the other cadets were loaded onto trucks and driven to the airfield at Güstrow. There everyone was sent into the air raid shelter where they spent a fitful night while Soviet aircraft bombed and strafed the airfield every thirty minutes.

At 0300 a senior NCO woke up the recruits and ordered them out of the shelter. Everyone moved across the pock-marked airfield silently toward an old Focke-Wulf transport aircraft waiting with the engines running. The seats were torn out to make room for the twenty-two men and their equipment. As the plane began to taxi, another air raid occurred and explosions landed to either side of the aircraft as it throttled down the broken runway and took off into the dark of the morning of 25 April. During the flight Heinz and the others were told their destination—Berlin. These men were part of a contingent of *Kriegsmarine* recruits Dönitz promised Hitler as reinforcements for the capital. In all, 300 naval recruits from various training schools were mustered and sent to Berlin. Only about three planes reached their destination, bringing in nearly seventy men.

The Fokke-Wolf flew at treetop-level to avoid Soviet fighter aircraft and German anti-aircraft fire as there was no way to coordinate this flight with any friendly ground forces. The night was bright and moonlit and Heinz and the others could see the destruction and burning villages all the way to Berlin. The pilot miraculously landed at Gatow airfield on the western outskirts of the city. Heinz and the others rushed out of the aircraft and into a nearby ravine where they met other naval recruits that landed earlier. The Russians were already in the woods on the opposite side of the airfield and firing at the sailors-now-turned-infantrymen. This motivated the new arrivals to make their way east toward Berlin. By 0800 they reached the town of Gatow on the Havel where several trucks brought them into the city. Along the way they experienced intermittent artillery fire and saw 13–14 years old boys everywhere digging trenches and armed with *Panzerfausts*. They were finally ordered into the Ministry of Foreign Affairs as reinforcements for Defense Sector Z while their future deployment in the city was discussed.[69]

NORTHERN DISTRICTS

The 1st Mechanized Corps fought local battles to clear the modern industrial suburb of Siemenstadt where the scarcity of supporting infantry led to heavy tank losses. The factories in this area armed their own *Factory Protection Units* that appeared to be well equipped with *Panzerfausts* and machine-guns. The attack into the built-up area was launched at 1430 hours and continued for the next three days before the Soviets closed up to the Spree on the 28 April. Colonel General S.I. Bogdanov's requests to Zhukov for more forces were finally answered during the evening of 25 April with the arrival of the 2nd Polish Heavy Artillery Brigade and the 6th Polish Pontoon Bridging Battalion.[70]

The 3rd Shock Army's 79th Rifle Corps crossed the Hohenzollern Canal at the Plötzensee locks at dawn on 25 April under cover of a heavy artillery barrage. They cleared the area up to the bank of Westhafen Canal but found they could go no further. The bridge was blown and so strewn with debris that only five men could attempt to cross at any time. The opposite bank was covered with machine-gun positions and the S-Bahn station was turned into a bunker complex. A Panzer IV *Panzerstellung* was placed near the tracks covering the bridge. The burnt-out factories were also fortified positions. The initial Soviet attempt to cross the bridge failed so they prepared for an early morning crossing with additional artillery and engineer support.[71]

The 12th Guards Rifle Corps crossed into Moabit by the Fenn Bridge at Nordhafen, securing the crossing against possible counterattacks from that direction but making no attempt to outflank the Westhafen position. Hampered by the Humboldt Flak Tower in the center of their lines, they spent the next few days caught up in house-to-house fighting among the factories and densely-packed tenement blocks north of Invalidenstraße.[72] Reinforced by the remnants of the *27./Fj.Div.9* and *Wachregiment Großdeutschland*, the defense proved tenacious and aggressive. Many German civilians in this area were early supporters of the Communists and had less than favorable feelings for the Nazis. In expectation of their 'liberation' they often hung white flags out of their windows. Unfortunately, these acts were often done prematurely. The fluid combat situation in the rubble ensured that key blocks and intersection often changed hands several times. In those cases the local *SS* and *Polizei* units took reprisals into their own hands. These civilians were considered 'traitors' and dragged out of their homes and hanged at the nearest lamp-post. In addition, any soldiers walking around without proper papers or orders were also hung.[73] One German veteran of the battle, Fritz Wrede, who was assigned as part of *Kampfgruppe Rossbach*, was based out of the Schultheiss Brewery along with 140 other men led by an *Unteroffizier*. Based on the corner of Schönhauserallee and Franseckistraße, they were regularly sent out in the role of *Feldgendarmerie* to maintain order. As a member of the unit, Wrede witnessed many of the reprisal attacks against civilian and soldiers alike. He believed that it only served to reduce morale among those German soldiers fighting in Berlin.[74]

On the extreme left flank of the 3rd Shock Army was the 7th Rifle Corps that fought their way down to the edge of Alexanderplatz on 25 April. The 7th Rifle Corps, proved unable to continue the offensive on their own and simply waited out the rest of the battle. Their operational area soon came under the responsibility of the 5th Shock Army. The area between the 7th Rifle Corps and the S-Bahn station remained German until the end of the fighting.

CENTRAL DISTRICTS

The Soviet 9th Rifle Corps wheeled north after their attack across the Teltow Canal into Neukölln. The Soviets then launched an attack over the Landwehr Canal where they encountered stiff resistance at the Görlitz S-Bahn Station in the southeast corner of Defense Sector Z. Just to the northwest was a network of streets and boulevards that converged on a key area known as the Spittelmarkt. The Spittelmarkt was a large open area with a traffic circle where many German department stores and business existed. This concentric road junction marked the beginning of Leipziger Straße, the wide boulevard that ran west straight into the Government Quarter. It dominated a number of crossing points onto the southern end of Schloss Island as well as the main avenues of approach across the Spree a little further east. The Spittelmarkt now took on significant tactical importance as the Soviets required this junction to facilitate both their north-south and east-west movements into Defense Sector Z. The Germans also realized this and quickly sent reinforcements into the area in the form of small *Kampfgruppe* of the *Danmark* and *Norge* regiments from *Nordland* and mixed *Volkssturm/Hitlerjugend* units. A new *Volkssturm* unit received orders to occupy the Spittelmarkt U-Bahn Station in the morning. When the unit reached the station they found it housed the local Nazi party leadership and was also being used as a makeshift hospital. It was suspected that Russian tanks were to the east preparing for a reconnaissance up Wallstraße toward the Spittelmarkt where *Kampfgruppe Thiemer* was positioned in defense the day before. Aribert Schulz was nearby and he watched the following events unfold. From Schulz's position in the cellar they could see right down Wallstraße. Soon three T–34/85s were seen maneuvering toward the *Volkssturm* positions from the expected direction. A group of *Nordland* soldiers came up and deployed toward the approaching Soviet tanks. Hiding in the rubble they fired *Panzerfausts* at the lead tank destroying it in the middle of the street. The two other Soviet T–34/85s, apparently following at some distance, quickly went into reverse and backed down the street. Soon the Soviets launched a heavy artillery strike all along the Spittelmarkt in retaliation and preparation for their next attack.[75]

Following the artillery barrage Schulz was sent with a message to his HQ at the Kolonnaden Cinema. When he arrived at the cinema a *Feldwebel,* whose decorations included several Tank Destroyer badges, was brought in for wearing civilian trousers. After being questioned, he was turned over to a lanky red-haired 19 year old *SS* soldier who was armed with a scope-mounted K98. The red-haired boy led the *Feldwebel* out into the street, gave him a shove to the ground and fired a round into his back killing him on the spot in a summary court-martial. Schulz was shocked by the act. He witnessed his first, and unfortunately not his last, example of the flying court-martials that occurred all over central Berlin during the last days of the battle in an effort to 'stiffen' resistance. When Schulz returned to his men in the evening he was joined by a four-man wireless radio team from *Pz.Gren.Rgt.23 Norge*, presumably in order to provide on the spot reporting back to Mohnke at the *Führerbunker* about the progress of the Soviets in this area. The added benefit of having the Norwegian wireless operators was that Schulz and the other boys began to hear messages from the *Führerbunker* that spoke about the coming of Wenck's relief army. This news helped everyone's morale and justified their efforts against the Russians in the rubble of Berlin.[76]

The Zoo Flak Tower soon received word that the Soviets were closing in around the other two Flak Towers. Supply convoys were sent to each remaining Flak Tower during the evening to obtain all available ammunition stocks and bring them back to the Zoo, as it was thought that they might fall into Soviet hands in the near future. This was an enormous undertaking given the tactical circumstances.[77] Expecting that the Soviets might soon enter the area, *Oberst* Trost now organized twenty-man tank hunting squads of *Luftwaffe Cadets* and *Hitlerjugend* stationed in the Zoo Flak Tower. He armed them with carbines and *Panzerfausts* then positioned the squads around the Zoological Gardens. A local HQ was set up in the Aquarium.[78]

The 11th Tank Corps launched several separate attacks into the Spittelmarkt from Wallstraße. The old narrow streets made maneuvering for the Soviets difficult. The presence of a U-Bahn station also held surprises for the Soviets as German soldiers often launched quick assaults into the rear or flank of Soviet armor columns only to retreat back into the U-Bahn tunnels and make good their escape. Author's collection.

Hermannplatz and the Karlstadt Department store were heavily defended by members of *Nordland* and the *Charlemagne*. A Soviet armor column that attempted to breach the German defense of the area was ambushed nearby and destroyed by German Panzers. Author's collection.

The Zoo Aquarium housed a HQ detachment sent by the Zoo Flak Bunker that coordinated the anti-tank missions of *Hitlerjugend* volunteers. Tank hunting missions were dispatched directly from the Aquarium into the nearby streets. Author's collection.

Notes to Chapter 6: Assault on Berlin, 25th April Wednesday

1   OKW File, Last Announcements of OKW, 25 April (RC: 62:8).
2   Chuikov, p. 186.
3   Ibid, pp. 183–4.
4   Ibid.
5   G. Zhukov, "Taking Berlin," (RC: 73:11).
6   A. A. Novikov, "The Air Forces in the Berlin Operation."
7   Koniev unpublished memoir, p. 158.
8   Ibid, pp. 154, 157.
9   Ibid.
10 Ibid, p. 156.
11 Ibid, p. 155.
12 Army Group Weichsel War Diary, Apr 20–9, p. 303 (RC: 64/3).
13 Ibid, p. 303, and M. Bauer, *MS #R-69 The End of Army Group Weichsel and Twelfth Army, Apr 27 – May 7, 1945,* p. 14 (RC: 62/3).
14 Army Group Weichsel War Diary, Apr 20–9, p. 308 (RC: 64/3).
15 Army Group Weichsel War Diary, Apr 20–9, p. 367 (RC: 68/4).
16 Ibid, p. 363.
17 Le Tissier, *Slaughter at Halbe,* pp. 84–5.
18 M. Bauer, *MS #R-79 Ninth Army's Last Attack and Surrender,* p. 26 (RC: 67/17).
19 Joachim Schiefer, *Historischer Atlas zum Kriegsende 1945,* p. 39.
20 Schultz-Naumann, p. 168.
21 *MS #B-606,* p. 25.
22 Weidling Interrogation Report.
23 Ibid.
24 Ibid.
25 Ibid, and Le Tissier, *Race for the Reichstag,* p. 106.
26 Ibid.
27 Fest, p. 87.
28 Schultz-Naumann, p. 24.
29 Ibid.
30 Heiber and Glantz, p. 721.
31 Ibid, pp. 723, 725.
32 Weidling interrogation report.
33 Le Tissier, *Race for the Reichstag,* p. 107.
34 Ibid.
35 Ibid.
36 Ibid, p. 109, and Le Tissier, *With Our Backs to Berlin,* p. 161.
37 Platonov, p. 17.
38 Schultz-Naumann, pp. 175–6, and Venghaus, p. 230.
39 Krukenberg interview.
40 Ibid.
41 Burghart interview.
42 Michaelis, p. 110.
43 Burghart interview.
44 Scholles interview.
45 Krukenberg interview.
46 Venghaus, p. 256.
47 Chuikov, pp. 186–7.
48 Scholles interview.
49 Illum interview.
50 Ibid.
51 The woman cared for the grave years after the end of the war.
52 R. Landwehr and H. T. Nielsen, *Nordic Warriors: SS-Panzergrenadier-Regiment 24 Danmark, Eastern Front, 1943–45,* p. 152.
53 Henseler interview.
54 Schneider, p. 302.
55 Fey, pp. 315–16, and Venghaus, pp. 115–16.
56 Venghaus, pp. 337–8.
57 Thorwald, pp. 230–1.
58 Böttcher, pp. 7–8.
59 Le Tissier, *With Our Backs to Berlin,* p. 120.
60 Ibid, p. 121.
61 Le Tissier, *Race for the Reichstag,* pp. 114–15, and Koniev unpublished memoir, p. 157.
62 Koniev unpublished memoir, p. 154.
63 Ibid.
64 Ibid.
65 Ibid, p. 158.
66 Ibid.
67 Pienkny interview.
68 Le Tissier, *Race for the Reichstag,* p. 105.
69 H. Kratschmar interview (RC: 66/1).
70 Le Tissier, *Race for the Reichstag,* p. 106
71 Ibid, p. 107.
72 Ibid.
73 F. Wrede interview (RC: 69/36).
74 Wrede interview.
75 Schulz interview.
76 Ibid.
77 von Zabeltitz interview.
78 Ibid.

6

ASSAULT ON BERLIN

26 APRIL
THURSDAY

Yesterday, in the battle for Berlin, which is decisive for the future of the Third Reich and the life of Europe, both sides threw reserves into the battle. In the southern part of the Reich Capital heavy street fighting is raging in Zehlendorf, Steglitz and on the southern border of the Tempelhofer F[i]eld. In the east and north are troops, bravely supported by units of the *Hitlerjugend*, The Party and the [*Volkssturm*] offer fierce resistance at the Schlesien Bahnhof and Görlitz Bahnhof and between Tegel and Siemenstadt. In Charlottenburg, too, fighting flared up. Numerous [tanks] of the Soviets were destroyed in these fights. Soviet tanks advancing from Ketzin entered Brandenburg. The enemy advancing against Rathenow was stopped by counter-attacks when he was still before the city. Assaults at Fehrbellin brought no success for the enemy. South of the city some villages were retaken by our troops.[1]

OKW **Radio Announcement**

26 April brought a cloudless blue sky over Berlin. The soldiers in the streets hardly noticed as the smoke from hundreds of burning buildings masked both sun and sky. Most soldiers did not know what day it was, let alone the time. While fighting continued in the streets, significant battles raged outside Berlin.

ARMY GROUP VISTULA

The *3.Panzer Armee* managed to hold the front against the 2nd Byelorussian Front for one more day but the soldiers under Manteuffel's command had reached their breaking point. Russian armor broke through the Wotan defensive lines east of Prenzlau but was thrown back by a counterattack. The *CI Korps* held the line along the Hohenzollern Canal against Soviet assaults all day. The *25.Pz.Gren.Div.* failed to enlarge its bridgehead created the previous day as the Poles moved blocking forces into the area. Several Polish counterattacks were repulsed by the Panzergrenadiers, but they proved to be in a precarious position. At Eberswalde the Russians crossed the Finow Canal to the north of the German positions. The *1.Marine Division* was pulled out of the front line and back to the Wotan position as it began to show signs of disintegration. The *3.Marine Division* was not able to halt the Soviet advance into Sachsenhausen and Steiner's forces continued to drag out preparations for their ordered offensive. According to *3.Panzer Armee* reports, their ability to hold of the Soviets during 26 April was due largely to their artillery that continued to hammer the Soviet infantry assaults. *AGV* reports confirmed that "Our artillery, partly in close combat, was instrumental in avoiding a full breakthrough of enemy infantry."[2] In addition to artillery, there was a large-scale use of the remaining *Luftwaffe* assets. As most of the Soviet combat aircraft were tied up in operations closer to Berlin, the *Luftwaffe* was able to gain local superiority above the *3.Panzer Armee's* front. According to German reports the *Luftwaffe* shot down 18 Soviet aircraft, and destroyed 20 tanks on the ground.[3] *Regiment Solar* proved combat effective despite being a newly formed unit. This unit stopped enemy spearheads west of Grünow then moved into the area of Prenzlau to assist in blocking the Soviets. It was clear that Heinrici needed additional mobile forces to be ready to meet the inevitable Soviet breakthrough. The only place he could obtain them was from Steiner who was still under orders by *OKW* to launch his attack south toward Berlin. At 1145 Heinrici called the *Führerbunker* and requested from Krebs that Steiner's attack be cancelled. He articulated his need to redeploy those forces in order to parry the Soviets attack on the right wing of the *3.Panzer Armee*. Krebs took the request to Hitler who refused and continued to insist on Steiner's attack.[4] It was only a matter of time before the *3.Panzer Armee* front collapsed.

FÜHRERBUNKER

Hitler issued a coordinating order for the relief of Berlin at 1900 hours on 25 April. That order did not reach *OKW* until 0025 hours on 26 April. The order read:

> Hard and determined, without giving thought to the flanks and the neighboring sectors, the individual attack group, each tightly knit together; will have to force their breakthroughs; only then will it be possible to reestablish the connection between *9.Armee* and Berlin and to destroy strong elements of the enemy. …

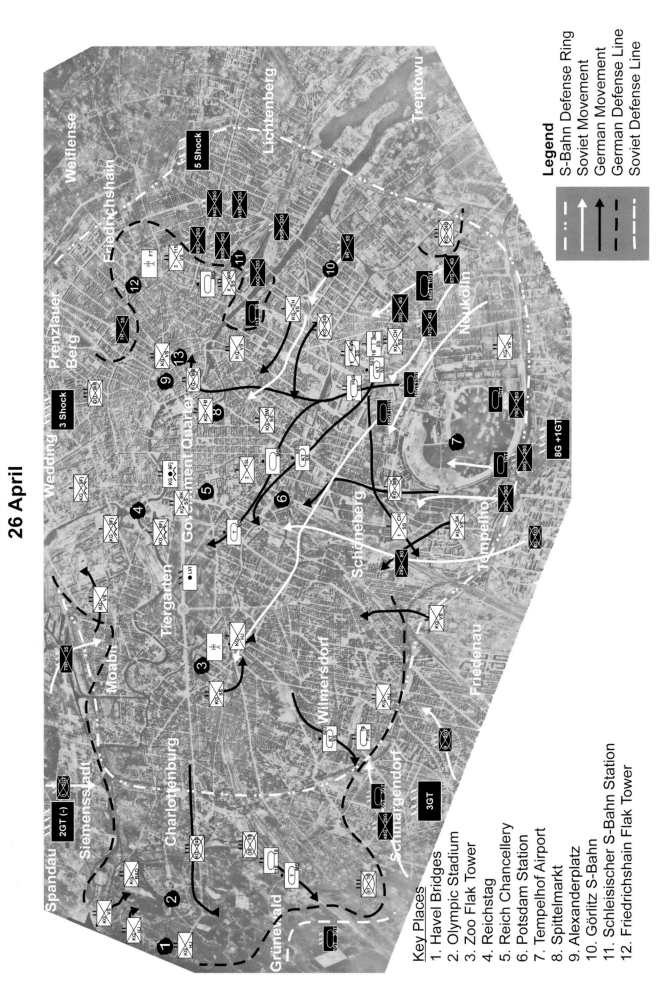

Berlin
26 April

Legend
S-Bahn Defense Ring
Soviet Movement
German Movement
German Defense Line
Soviet Defense Line

Key Places
1. Havel Bridges
2. Olympic Stadium
3. Zoo Flak Tower
4. Reichstag
5. Reich Chancellery
6. Potsdam Station
7. Tempelhof Airport
8. Spittelmarkt
9. Alexanderplatz
10. Görlitz S-Bahn
11. Schlesisischer S-Bahn Station
12. Friedrichshain Flak Tower

9.Armee will hold on to its present eastern front between the Spreewald and Fürstenwalde and will attack on the shortest route toward [sic] west and establish contact with *12.Armee*.

12.Armee's southern group will leave screening forces in the sector Wittenberg and launch an attack from the area of Belzig along the axis Beelitz—Ferch to cut off the rear communications of the 4th Soviet Tank Army advancing in the direction of Brandenburg, and will immediately continue its attack toward [sic] east until it will have established contact with *9.Armee*.

Once the two armies have joined it will be important to wheel north and to destroy the enemy units in the southern part of Berlin and thus to establish a broad connection with Berlin.[5]

Jodl issued a reply at 0815 hours on 26 April that sounded encouraging, citing that both armies were advancing and making progress toward their goals. Jodl's report back to Hitler was not truthful and had little basis in what was really happening on the ground. It is not clear why Hitler's senior generals fed Hitler a steady stream of false reports. No reasonable explanation for this behavior exists to justify their actions. This is simply one of the many enigmas of the war.

9. ARMEE

Kampfgruppe Pipkorn and *Kampfgruppe von Luck* reached Baruth in the early morning hours of the 26 April. A major battle developed with Koniev's forces who anticipated the attack west from this direction. The *Kampfgruppe* were unable to make headway and abandoned the attacks in the morning. Von Luck disbanded his formations and told his men to breakout west, while he and his immediate staff drove east back into the pocket where they were captured on 27 April.[6] In the pocket, Busse now tried to develop a new plan. On his north front he had the *XI SS Panzer Korps*, to the east was the *V SS Mountain Korps*, and in the south was the *V Korps*. He had a total of 200 operational armored vehicles including at least 100 Panzers. The total amount of soldiers in the pocket numbered about 150,000 not including tens of thousands of civilians. The key problem for Busse was his need for supply. Aerial resupply, however, became a challenge as authorities in Berlin continued to override Heinrici's orders. According to *AGV* daily reports, ammunition and fuel for the *9.Armee* were "precarious." Several tons of ammunition did make it into the pocket either by aerial drop or landing but the priority for aerial resupply continued to be Berlin.[7] Heinrici reached Jodl at 2240 hours by phone to discuss supply priorities for that evening:

Heinrici: Air supply for the *9.Armee* was curtailed once more. Am angry and unhappy about it. People by the thousands are being left in the lurch. We can't justify this to our comrades in arms.

Jodl: The need in Berlin is even greater than in the *9.Armee*. If Berlin is not held through today, I won't need any attack anyway; everything is considered.

Heinrici: But not correctly considered.

Jodl: I have to consider the importance. With Berlin we lose everything.

Heinrici: But Busse must get out fast, then we'll have a chance to help Berlin.

Jodl: The ammunition depot in Krampnitz was blown up ahead of time. Otherwise the supply situation in Berlin would not be so desperate. People there are hysterical. We can't leave the people and [Hitler] in the lurch.

Heinrici: I did not say that. Please don't twist my words around.

Jodl: It seems to me that an army should have better resources than the poor population of Berlin. Tonight it will probably be the last time that we can fly into Berlin; afterwards everything will be available for those on the outside.

Heinrici: Please remember in your deliberations that the *9.Armee* has many thousands who must be give help, after they were put into such a situation.[8]

The air resupply for Berlin that night amounted to only a few canisters of salvaged ammunition.[9] Busse continued to prepare his forces for the breakout west.

12. ARMEE

Wenck's XX Korps continued to exert strong pressure against Koniev's forces. *Hutten* and *Körner* put up an aggressive defense against the Soviets, and now *Scharnhorst* began to move into positions northwest of *Körner* and ran into prepared resistance by Koniev's alerted forces. The Führer's order issued earlier in the day through *OKW* now called for a split attack both east toward the *9.Armee* against increasing Soviet resistance, and north-east toward Ferch to cut off Soviet elements operating west of Potsdam. While it is not clear that Jodl ever passed those orders on to Wenck or Busse, Wenck began to realize he had to make his own operational decisions based on the stiff resistance his forces faced directly east against alerted enemy forces. In addition he had to consider his western flank along the Elbe. If he put all his combat formations east, he ran the risk of allowing his forces to become encircled like the *9.Armee*. Options raced through Wenck's mind as he considered the need to redeploy the majority of his divisions a second time and prepare a large offensive northeast toward Potsdam while screening directly east against increasing Soviet pressure. Wenck continued to review operational maps and options with his Chief of Staff *Oberst* Günther Reichelm throughout the day.

LVI PANZER KORPS

Weidling's staff was greeted at their Bendlerstraße HQ by a contingent from *Wachregiment Großdeutschland*. A young *Leutnant* responded to *OKH's* request for volunteers in Berlin and came to assist in the defense. His name was Thater, a member of *Pz.Gren.Div. Großdeutschland*. Upon arrival he was given command of 76 soldiers from the *Wachregiment*. This small *Kampfgruppe* took up positions around Bendlerstraße, including the Bendler-Block, Shell-Haus, and Ministry of Tourism, to protect Weidling's new HQ. MG 42s were positioned to command the main avenues of approach across the Landwehr Canal.[10]

A solid picture of the Soviet forces arrayed around Berlin's inner defense ring now emerged after Weidling spent three days locating sector commanders, reviewing the tactical situation, and coordinating unit movements. During this time the tactical situation changed every minute as the Soviets continued offensive operations into the city and various *Kampfgruppe* formed, fought, dissolved, and reformed. At least his main combat forces were now embedded within the various Defensive Sectors. Weidling reviewed his situational maps and perceived three key threats. First, the Soviet advance into Neukölln was a dangerous thrust toward the Government District that could easily cut off Germans forces in Defense Sectors A and B if allowed to reach the Landwehr Canal. It also directly threatened Tempelhof Airport that Chuikov's forces had reached the day before. Second, the apparent absence of the *20.Pz.Gren.Div.* from its positions along the Teltow Canal and southeastern parts of Berlin threatened the German forces in Spandau all the way east toward Tempelhof. Finally, positions needed to be held along the Havel in order to allow Wenck access into Berlin or as a means of escape for Weidling's soldiers. He immediately ordered a series of counterattacks and reinforcements. In the south, he ordered a counterattack consisting of the combined *SS-Pz.Aufkl.Abt.11* and *SS-Pz.Gren.Rgt.24 Danmark* along with the *Sturmbataillon Charlemagne* to clear the Soviets from Neukölln. King Tigers from *s.SS-Pz.Abt.503* and Sturmgeschütz IIIs from *Pz.Abt.11 Hermann von Salza* were ordered in for support. In the west, the *18.Pz.Gren.Div.* received orders to counterattack Koniev's forces and link up with the *20.Pz.Gren.Div.* Tiger Is from *Müncheberg* were ordered to lead the assault. Weidling also ordered a newly formed *Hitlerjugend Bataillon* consisting of 500 boys commanded by *Oberbannführer* Dr. Ernst Schlünder along with a few experienced officers and NCOs to take up positions along the Havel and hold the two southernmost bridges opposite Spandau for Wenck's approaching forces.[11] Schlünder, a decorated World War I veteran, posted 300 of his boys on the western side of the Havel with the remainder on the eastern side. He maintained communication with the Reichssportfield by runners.

Weidling's staff finalized a breakout plan that Weidling planned to present to Krebs and Hitler at the evening conference. This breakout plan was as follows:

> First Echelon: On the right two-thirds of the *9.Fallschirmjäger Division* with *Kampfgruppe Eder* from Defense Sector F. On the left flank, south of Heerstraße, was the *18.Panzergrenadier Division*. The majority of all available tanks and assault guns were placed into the First Echelon.

> Second Echelon: *Kampfgruppe Mohnke* consisting of the two available *SS Regiments* plus the *Kriegsmarine* reinforcements brought in by air. Hitler and other Nazi government members were part of this group.

Third Echelon: Remainder of the *Müncheberg Panzer Division*, *Kampfgruppe Barenfänger*, remaining *Kampfgruppe of Nordland* and the last one-third of the *9.Fallschirmjäger Division*.[12]

Weidling and Reifor took the final breakout plan and drove from his HQ to the Reich Chancellery. This was the last night that Weidling was able to drive through the rubble as Soviet artillery and rocket fire increased significantly throughout Defense Sector Z. The Soviets were closing in on the Government Quarter. At the corner of Tiergartenstraße and Hermannn-Göring-Straße shells began to burst along the road. Weidling's driver accelerated the car to get out of the kill zone and drove straight into a downed power line or telephone cable that ripped the hood off the car and struck Reifor in the neck, nearly decapitating him.[13]

A Soviet T-34/85 crew takes a pause in operations to pose for a Soviet propaganda photographer. Note the still burning rubble in the background. Photo courtesy of the Cornelius Ryan Collection, Mahn Center, Alden Library, Ohio University, Athens, OH.

At the evening conference Krebs accepted Weidling's logic that the Berlin garrison needed to be readied for a breakout before ammunition ran out or if Wenck was only able to reach Berlin's outskirts and not penetrate through the Soviet cordon into the city. Krebs then agreed to allow Weidling to brief the plan to Hitler. Weidling conducted the brief as usual. He focused on the situation of the troops, then the supply situation and the medical situation in the city. Of particular note was the state of the supplies and ammunition. Once that was given, Weidling briefed his breakout plan to Hitler. Before Hitler and Krebs could comment, Dr. Goebbels attacked Weidling's plan in strong language. It was obvious that Goebbels had no intention of leaving or surrendering Berlin. Hitler, however, gave the plan some thought. According to Weidling, Hitler finally replied "Even if the breakout should succeed, we would tumble from one 'pocket' into another. We would then have to live in the open air or in a farmhouse and wait for the end." Hitler than decided that the best course of action for him was to remain in the Reich Chancellery. According to Weidling, "Therefore, the Führer rejected a plan of a breakout."[14] Weidling returned to his command disappointed and informed the unit commanders of the decision that they would have to fight until the end.[15]

Weidling's frustration with the situation he found himself in was aggravated by a phone call from Goebbels requesting that Bärenfänger call him within an hour. Weidling agreed and when he received the next call it was *General* Burgdorf who declared that Bärenfänger was given a field promotion to *SS-Brigadeführer* and given control of sector's A and B instead of Mummert. Bärenfänger, a *SS* officer, was upset that he lost control of the two key defense sectors to a *Wehrmacht* commander. Being a close friend of Goebbels, he requested assistance and Goebbels was able to obtain a field promotion from Hitler that day. *Generalmajor* Mummert, who was the sector commander at the time, was relieved and went back to Tempelhof to take command of the *Müncheberg* once again. This heightened Weidling's mistrust of the *SS* and eroded his command authority in Berlin even further.[16]

EASTERN DISTRICTS

Another T-34/85 tank crew eats breakfast, presumably before the start of the day's operations. Photo courtesy of the Cornelius Ryan Collection, Mahn Center, Alden Library, Ohio University, Athens, OH.

The whole area from Friedrichshain to Alexanderplatz came under local German counterattack during the day. The official history of the Soviet 11th Tank Corps records the events of this day in dramatic and fluid terms. The unit's tenuous toehold across the Spree was in jeopardy as the 5th Shock Army struggled to clear the German defenders out of a wide area in the eastern sectors. In one recorded counterattack, the Soviet 243rd Mortar Regiment fired 282 mortar rounds at a group of Germans as they counterattacked in order to cut off their forces now on the western side of the Spree.[17] The counterattack was launched from the area of the Schlesischer S-Bahn Station and suggests that the Germans consisted of a combination of *SS-Rgt.Anhalt* and the usual *Volkssturm*. House-to-house fighting raged in the cellars and upper storeys of buildings as the Germans attempted to push the Soviets back. The Soviets managed to bring up JS-2s, T-34/85s and self-propelled guns that were employed to fire over open sights point blank at German positions, often exposing themselves to *Panzerfaust* fire. By the afternoon, small groups of German infantry managed to infiltrate through Russian lines, probably not knowing exactly where the Russians were. INSERT IMAGE 6.19 NEAR HERE

Extreme close-quarter combat now occurred between the reconnaissance troops of the 2nd Battery of the 11th Tank Corps and the Germans. The Soviet history records the events as follows:

> The mortar crews fired at them with mortars, with [assault rifles] and rifles. The reconnaissance man of the 2nd Battalion, V.M. Vasilev, allowed the Hitlerites to approach to 30 or 40 meters and began to shoot them down at point blank range with a German [*Panzerfaust*]. The commander of the reconnaissance section of the 2nd Battalion, Sgt. V.I. Senkin, finding himself in the forward observation position of the 6th Battalion and being at that time cut off from his own forces, ordered fire to be directed at him. As a result the Hitlerites lost 15 men killed. To the fire position of the 5th Battery of the 2nd Battalion there moved up a group of Hitlerites. Junior Sgt. G.P. Stepaov was the first to come to grips with them and shot them down. Three soldiers and three officers were taken prisoner by the Soviet troops. The counter-attack was beaten off.[18]

What this Soviet account highlights is that there was no infantry left for counter-attacks. The 11th Tank Corps had one infantry brigade assigned but it appeared not many were still left at this point to screen the advancing armor let alone the combat support units like the mortar section. They relied on Soviet armor to be employed directly against enemy infantry in a fluid situation. This was extremely problematic as the tankers could never really know where the Germans were and they were clearly at the mercy of a well-placed *Panzerfaust* shot.

The 11th Tank Corps had to get moving again but blocked roads and barricades prevented easy passage toward the city center. Reconnaissance squads were now sent out to determine the nature of German defenses and ways around the multitude of barricades. These missions were perhaps the most dangerous undertaken by Soviet scouts in Berlin. They had no idea where they were going or where the enemy was. They crawled over shattered ruins of jagged rock, glass, and steel girders. More often than not they could not return the same way they came because the Germans became alerted to their presence. Returning back to their own lines was made even more difficult due to the fact that

Eastern Districts
26 April

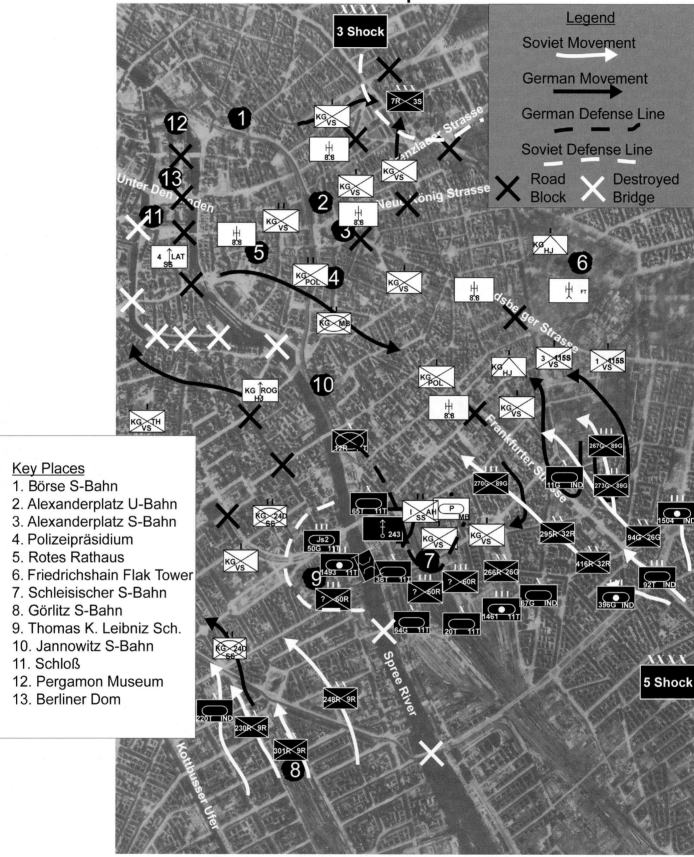

Key Places
1. Börse S-Bahn
2. Alexanderplatz U-Bahn
3. Alexanderplatz S-Bahn
4. Polizeipräsidium
5. Rotes Rathaus
6. Friedrichshain Flak Tower
7. Schleisischer S-Bahn
8. Görlitz S-Bahn
9. Thomas K. Leibniz Sch.
10. Jannowitz S-Bahn
11. Schloß
12. Pergamon Museum
13. Berliner Dom

Colonel General N. E. Berzarin, 5th Shock Army commander and
Commandant of Berlin.
Photo courtesy of the Bulgarian Ministry of Defence

they might be mistaken as Germans and shot by their own comrades.[19] The 11th Tank Corps took a full day to recon, destroy road blocks, and in one case demolish several buildings in order to make a passable route for their next offensive along the west side of the Spree. As they waited in the rubble, German counterattacks continued.

Berzarin, commander of the 5th Shock Army, was made the Governor of Berlin by Zhukov. He began a systematic program of reinstating service to Berlin's residents as well as providing food and water in the already conquered eastern districts. This was a necessary tactic to help prevent the German population from outright hostility given the open contempt and near barbaric behavior generally shown by Soviet soldiers. There was a practical reason as well. Now that the Soviets moved from conquerors to occupiers in the eastern districts it was clearly in their interest to keep out disease by restoring basic water and sanitation services. There were also intangible benefits that the Soviets received by helping the civilians, especially out in the open streets. Genzow was operating in the area and noted how the Russian practice of giving out food and water to the population prevented the Germans from firing on the Russians because they were surrounded by civilians.[20] By late afternoon the situation in Defense Sectors A and B was not changed. Some German units like the *115 Siemenstadt Volkssturm Bataillon* retreated back to the Friedrichshain Flak Tower after the local counterattacks were launched. This unit reached the Landsberger Allee and Friedenstraße undetected but exhausted after their defensive fighting against the Soviets. This unit received orders on 27 April to return to their former positions. These orders were simply unrealistic, like so many orders issued by German commanders during the assault. The *115 Siemenstadt Volkssturm Bataillon* continued to fight near the Flak Tower until the end of the battle.[21]

Due to the loss of Tempelhof in Defense Sector C (see below), *Müncheberg* was ordered to the area of Alexanderplatz. No sooner had the main body of Panzergrenadiers arrived when Soviet Katushya rockets struck the area forty-six times.[22] Bärenfänger decided to demonstrate his new command authority and issued arriving officers of *Müncheberg Panzerfausts* and ordered them out into the streets to hunt down Soviet armor. Meanwhile *SS* and *Feldgendarmerie* started combing through cellars looking for stragglers or German soldiers putting on civilian clothes.

Across the Spree the lone 9th Rifle Corps continued operations that included assaulting the Görlitzer S-Bahn station and driving northwest up the wide boulevard of Oranienstraße. After an early morning assault the German defenders finally pulled out of the S-Bahn station as Soviet penetrations to the northeast and Chuikov's assault on Tempelhof Airport changed the situation. The 1050th Rifle Regiment of the 301st Rifle Division cleared the Görlitzer S-Bahn Station by 0700 hours and the troops continued to push forward. Tank elements of the 220th Tank Brigade were already exploring routes north through the lightly defended area.[23]

A Battery of "Stalin's Organs" stands at the ready. Soviet rockets were area based weapons and could not be employed with any accuracy in Berlin. Their effect was typically psychological, though well placed barrages could bring down buildings on their German defenders. This photo appears to be taken after the war due to the large number of German civilians milling about and the lack of any Soviet security. Photo courtesy of RGAKFD Moscow.

A Soviet machine-gun team takes an overwatch position in a Berlin apartment. The sheer scale of Berlin's urban landscape was immense. Photo courtesy of the Cornelius Ryan Collection, Mahn Center, Alden Library, Ohio University, Athens, OH.

A *Volkssturm* unit is emplaced and ready to engage Soviet tanks with *Panzerfausts*. No weapon dominated the fighting for Berlin more than the *Panzerfaust*. This weapon revolutionized urban warfare by destroying the majority of all Soviet tanks during the assault. Photo courtesy of the Cornelius Ryan Collection, Mahn Center, Alden Library, Ohio University, Athens, OH.

A Soviet infantry squad uses the rooftop to stage their next assault. Late in the fighting some Soviet units adapted to the urban landscape and began moving across rooftops then worked their way down the buildings, flushing the German defenders out. While this tactic showed ingenuity, it was not always successful as the Soviets quickly become pinned down themselves by crossfire from neighboring buildings. Vertical fighting in already weakened structures often caused the whole building to collapse on attacker and defender alike. Photo courtesy of the Bundesarchiv.

SOUTHERN DISTRICTS

Weidling's counterattack to eliminate the threat from Chuikov's forces in Neukölln now began. The attack was planned for a 0500 start. On the right flank were Panzergrenadiers and tanks of *Müncheberg* who were given the responsibility to attack south down the east side of Tempelhof airport. In the lead were 2 Tiger Is, 5-8 Panthers Gs that were still operational, and several SPWs.[24] Having already suffered losses during the last 10 days of battle, the number of *Müncheberg* soldiers probably numbered no more than 200-400 Panzergrenadiers broken up into several *Kampfgruppe*. In the center, near the Town Hall, the newly arrived *Sturmbataillon Charlemagne* organized into four companies for the early morning attack. They planned to advance down Berliner Straße supported by *Kampfgruppe* from *Nordland* advancing down the left flank along the Landwehr Canal. A King Tiger from *s.SS-Pz.Abt.503*, two Panther Gs from *Müncheberg*, located at the intersection of Donau and Fuldastraße, and several Sturmgeschütz IIIs from *Hermann von Salza* provided direct fire support for the French.[25] As the French made their way to the jump-off positions they passed the German tankers who were smoking and joking in the early morning hours before the attack.[26] Fenet decided to attack with the *3.* and *2./Sturmbataillon Charlemagne*. The *1./Sturmbataillon Charlemagne* went to Defense Sector D on the west side of Tempelhof, while he decided to keep the *4./Sturmbataillon Charlemagne* in reserve. Fenet established the Battalion HQ at the ruined Town Hall.

Chuikov started the day with a massive artillery barrage across his planned area of advance. Unknown to the Germans, Chuikov planned his own resumption of the assault on Tempelhof Airport that included a second massive assault through Neukölln. Soon after the barrage stopped the *4./Sturmbataillon Charlemagne* assembled in the open while its commander, Jean Olliver, gave orders out to his *Leutnants*. Suddenly a nearby Sturmgeschütz III of *Nordland* opened fire on the assembled Frenchmen killing 15. Other members of the platoon quickly opened fire with their *Panzerfausts* and destroyed the German assault gun. It was believed that the German assault gun was captured by the Russians, although it was more likely crewed by Seydlitz troops operating in the vanguard of the Soviet formations.[27]

The order for the German attack came shortly before 0600. *Müncheberg* advanced south of Hasenheide Volkspark along Oderstraße. There were probably Russian snipers, scouts and anti-tank guns throughout this area as they were left behind from the previous day's attempt to take the airport by Chuikov. By 0700 with the Tiger Is in the lead, the Panzergrenadiers attacked across the still-intact bridge over the S-Bahn tracks to reach Emmaus Cemetery at the corner of Tempelhofer and Mariendorf Damm before they were halted by Chuikov's forces preparing for their own assault north.

The two main French companies conducting the assault moved forward in parallel with the *3./Sturmbataillon Charlemagne* advancing down Braunauer Straße and the *2./Sturmbataillon Charlemagne* advancing down Berliner Straße, then Richardstraße. The *3./Sturmbataillon Charlemagne* under the command of *SS-Unterführer* Pierre Rostaing had a King Tiger in support. The King Tiger advanced only a short

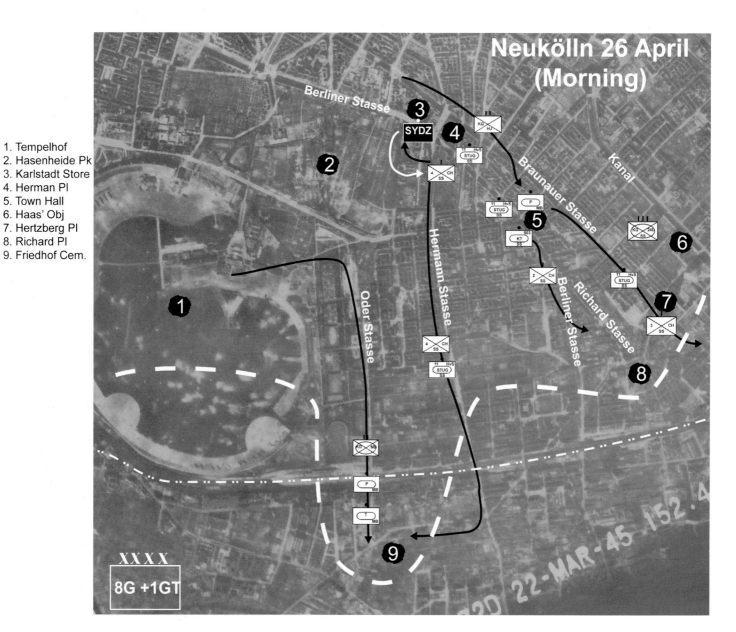

1. Tempelhof
2. Hasenheide Pk
3. Karlstadt Store
4. Herman Pl
5. Town Hall
6. Haas' Obj
7. Hertzberg Pl
8. Richard Pl
9. Friedhof Cem.

distance then it halted for lack of fuel. It provided support to the French from its position where it knocked out several T-34/85s spotted down the wide boulevard. The noise of Soviet artillery fire increased to the point that the men could barely hear shots being fired by the enemy. Soviet machine gun fire almost immediately killed Rostaing's adjutant, and his *1st Platoon* leader needed to be replaced as he refused orders to advance out of fear.[28] The French reached a former German barricade now occupied by the Soviets that they attacked and captured. Rostaing noticed a T-34 located down a side street and immediately knocked it out with a *Panzerfaust*. He was so close that when the tank exploded, not only was he wounded but the Frenchman that handed him the *Panzerfaust* was decapitated by shrapnel. He turned and noticed that twelve of his men were also dead on the other side of the barricade without any explanation. Rostaing looked left, then right, before he finally noticed a Maxim crew-served machine-gun poke out from a doorway. He opened fire killing the Russian crew. In the noise of battle no one heard the machine-gun bursts that killed the Frenchmen huddled behind the barricade waiting for the T-34 to be knocked out. It was now almost 0700 and the *3./Sturmbataillon Charlemagne* already lost 25% of its strength. That was one soldier killed every 5 minutes due to Russian fire. Russian snipers were also picking off or wounding the French as they continued to move down the wide boulevard. They soon reached Hertzbergplatz that was defended by a Soviet anti-tank gun. A StuG III was ordered forward and the German assault gun opened fire and destroyed the Soviet gun allowing the French to advance onto the square where they engaged and killed another Soviet machine-gun crew.[29] They decided to continue their advance to the S-Bahn line running along the Teltow Canal.

The *2./Sturmbataillon Charlemagne* advance down Berliner Straße was not as successful. They almost immediately were confronted with significant Russian fire.[30] The Russians were in this area in force preparing for their own morning advance through the district. Fenet now received orders from a runner from *Nordland* HQ that brought confusion. The order read "If the attack has not already begun, stop and come and get new orders; if it has, then do your best!"[31] After he sent a runner back to HQ to ascertain the situation he found that the Soviets began their own advance on the flanks and the French now formed a salient in their lines.

At noon, Fenet ordered a reserve platoon of French and a StuG III to advance from Hermannplatz south down Hermannstraße.[32] These soldiers soon arrived at positions reached by those of *Müncheberg* earlier in the day. Supported by the two Tiger Is, the combined force kept the Soviets at bay until the Tiger Is were pulled back. It was around this time that *Müncheberg's* Panzergrenadiers were ordered to head to Alexanderplatz (see Eastern Districts activity above). Fenet decided to recall the French companies and establish a defensive position in the Town Hall. Reinforcements in the form of 200 *Hitlerjugend* armed with K98s and *Panzerfaust* arrived to bolster the increasingly isolated French.[33]

Haas was supplying forces with ammunition when he was commandeered by the sector commander and sent to Neukölln. He arrived at the Town Hall where he was ordered to lead a counterattack to take a bridge back from the Russians at Sonnenallee as part of a general counterattack in the area. According to Haas, he was given the orders by a General, presumably Krukenberg, who was surrounded by other foreign officers, presumably French. According to Haas, the General told him to give his boys something to drink beforehand and offered them some Cognac. Haas found it very odd he and his men would be liquored up, but this was certainly not uncommon at this point in the fighting. The stress and availability of alcohol in Berlin led to its wide use by Soviet and German soldiers alike. Haas received a StuG III for support, but when he found the assault gun around the corner the commander refused to drive any closer to the bridge. Haas was too drunk to argue and continued to advance toward his objective. As he approached the bridge a German tenant from a nearby building approached Haas and informed him that Russians were in the area in force. In his inebriated state Haas didn't seem to care. As he approached the bridge the small group of soldiers noticed a Russian ammo carrier that Haas engaged with a *Panzerfaust* and destroyed. It was now dark and by the light of the flames he noticed 10-15 Soviet tanks lined up on his side of the canal. He realized he could not defeat the force with the 100 men under his command so he retreated to a nearby restaurant and sent word back to HQ that he could not destroy the tanks. The Russian attack through Neukölln soon isolated Haas and his men who spent several days in the restaurant sending runners back and forth with HQ until he received no more orders and realized the staff left without informing him.[34]

In the morning Henseler and his engineers were ordered to hold the corner of Innstraße and Weserstraße to the southeast of the Town Hall during the planned counterattack. The *Danes* occupied the first floors of buildings on either side of the street and were able to hold off the Soviets all morning. The Soviets, however, continued to find ways around the *Danes* and infiltrated the upper floors from a neighboring building. Henseler ordered smoke grenades thrown into the street and he and his men dashed to the building on the other side of Weserstraße. He noticed that two Russians had taken up positions on the second floor balcony from the building he just left. Henseler quickly grabbed a *Panzerfaust* and quietly opened a first floor window drawing no notice from the Soviets. Once opened, he charged the weapon, aimed, and fired. The hollow shaped charge struck the balcony dead on destroying it and killing the two Russians perched there only a few moments ago. The Russians now infiltrated this side of the street along the rooftops and at ground level. Henseler, unsupported and without heavy weapons, did not want to engage in close quarter combat now that he and his men were surrounded by Russians. Several civilians then came out of the basement of the building to find out what was happening. After a brief conversation the civilians showed Henseler and his men a way out through several backyard gardens. The *Danes* quickly pulled out of the building and headed northwest under constant Soviet attack until they reached Hermannplatz. In the large open square they ran into other German soldiers, presumably *Müncheberg, Volkssturm* and *Hitlerjugend* located around the ruins of the now burnt-out Karlstadt Department store. By evening they moved north again and set up a screening line along Schönleinstraße.[35]

Weidling's counterattack apparently delayed, but did not stop Chuikov's offensive planned for 26 April. Late morning brought the planned offensive by Chuikov to clear Neukölln, take Tempelhof Airport, and reach the Landwehr Canal opposite the Potsdamer and Anhalt S-Bahn Stations. Chuikov ordered his men to keep moving and bypass all resistance and allow follow-on forces to deal with the German defenders. Soon after the German counterattack, Chuikov's artillery blasted Tempelhof and Neukölln, followed by a general offensive. *Müncheberg's* elements defending the airport now retreated north back across the airfield as Chuikov's forces renewed their attack from positions along the west and south end of the airport. Vladimir Abyzov was a Soviet soldier who participated in the assault for Berlin and Tempelhof. His account of that day, and his combat in general, demonstrated clearly the reckless pace of advance set by Chuikov in his sector. Abyzov recalled after the war:

> Fighting went on continuously around the clock . . . The artillery roared and thundered. The mortars barked with rage. And the submachine gunners fired without interruption from the right, left and somewhere from the top.
> The whole city was in flames. Dense foul smoke curled over the roofs and hung heavily over the injured land. It seeped into the houses and basements through every crack and slot. There was no air to breathe. Despite this, we ran

falling to the ground between the road blocks and then rising again to run further through the yards, along and across the streets, hurling hand grenades into the empty eye sockets of the windows.

Our Guards Regiment had been engaged in street fighting for more than five days now and this kind of fighting was very different from our lessons at school. There was no clear-cut frontline, nor was there a rear or any carefully worked out combat mission. If you are on the first floor, it is your frontline, the ground floor being your rear. But that was five or ten minutes ago, now everything seemed to be in utter confusion. For some reason the Germans appeared on the ground floor, the second floor was a sea of fire. Where was the front, where was the rear from the standpoint of the Infantry Field Manual?

When street fighting had just begun, we tried to observe the requirements of camouflage, to fall to the ground when necessary and even to dig foxholes with our entrenching shovels. But then we had no time for digging in. Forge ahead! Forge ahead! Once though we did remember our entrenching shovels. That was when we were fighting for Tempelhof airfield. We were on one side of the runway and German tanks were dug into the ground on the other. The Nazi tanks were firing armour-piercing shells. They would flop down in front of and behind us with a hollow sound, like fat quails in autumn, falling on mown grass. We used knives and our hands to dig into the ground. Why on earth had we thrown away our entrenching shovels?

Bursting into a five-storey building, we threw hand grenades into the doorway as a preventative measure. We then 'swept' through the rooms. We had taken the first, second and third floors. Half of the house was in our hands and half in the hands of the Germans. It was divided by a very thick wall.. . .Junior Lieutenant Sorokin, Hero of the Soviet Union,. . .called out to Medvedev:

"Burst the wall with your faustpatron [*Panzerfaust*]!"

Standing in the doorway Medvedev leveled his weapon at the wall. A flame accompanied by a blast produced a lot of dust and smoke. We could see nothing. We felt our way to the wall where we expected to find a big hole. But there was no hole, only a dent. [36]

Abyzov and his men ran back into the street and received orders to take the next building bypassing the Germans. The mission was clear: get moving as fast as possible. The attack on the airfield ran into opposition by dug-in armor that could have been from any unit. The fact that he believes they were dug-in suggests that these were tanks that probably ran out of fuel. According to Chuikov's memoir, the 39th Guards Rifle Division renewed its offensive up the west side of the airport followed by the 79th Guards Division assaulting up the east side through Neukölln.[37] An interesting aspect of Abyzov's account is the clear asymmetrical nature of the fighting in Berlin. He specifically noted that the combat experience in Berlin proved different than any training he received before the battle and that the enemy was everywhere and nowhere all at once. No front line existed, and combat missions were not organized effectively.

Fenet and his men setup a defensive perimeter in the Town Hall and fought off all Russian attempts to take the building by storm. The *3./Sturmbataillon Charlemagne* was soon recalled under protest from Hertzbergplatz. The 40th Guards Tank Brigade continued to fight their way through Neukölln during the day. The commander, Lieutenant Colonel M.A. Smirnov struggled to maintain forward movement toward the Landwehr Canal and Potsdamer S-Bahn Station. He sent his armor into two fast-moving columns through the side streets in the hope of finding ways to avoid the roadblocks. One column of T-34/85s approached right up Berliner Straße in rapid single file.[38] Several tanks were knocked out with *Panzerfaust* but the others rolled on as they had no infantry support and clearly did not want to be caught in the open. A second King Tiger was notified of the advancing Russian armor and the German crew placed their Panzer along Jägerstraße, a side street north of Berliner-Richardstraße.[39] As soon as the first T-34/85 was spotted the 8.8cm gun of the King Tiger opened up and knocked the lead tank out forcing the other Soviet armor to find another route. Presumably, the second King Tiger destroyed a number of other Russian tanks on Berliner Straße as both King Tigers ran out of ammunition. Both Panzers were ordered back to Hermannnplatz where one of the crew was wounded by a Russian sniper after dismounting from his Panzer. The King Tigers were ordered back to Potsdamer Platz for maintenance during the evening.[40]

By 1700 Fenet's *Sturmbataillon Charlemagne* was now without any Panzer support and isolated in the Town Hall. After beating back countless Soviet attacks, Chuikov ordered heavy artillery to open up across Neukölln. The heavy fire broke the morale of a number of German soldiers who now left their positions and started to head north toward the Landwehr Canal. What happened next is typical of the stress and chaos in battle. A Frenchman decided to halt the fleeing soldiers and establish order:

Suddenly, *Oberjunker* Douroux saw about one hundred men appear from roads near to the town hall. They were in flight. They were throwing away their weapons. Pistol in hand, Douroux rushed among them. He knew that he had to check their stampede or else they would spread panic before them. But a gigantic blond German beat him to it. Standing in the middle of the road, legs apart, firing on the enemy with a MG 42 help at hip level, he too saw them in flight. He turned around and fired a long burst just over their heads. When this had no effect he did not hesitate to fire lower and shorter. This stopped them dead. He then went back to firing on the enemy along Berliner Straße. Douroux rounded them up and pushed them forward.[41]

At around 1900 reports reached Fenet that Soviet tanks had reached Hermannnplatz, 900 meters north of their position. The French had no choice left but to pull out of their positions. Fenet organized his Frenchmen and *Hitlerjugend* into squads then retreated back toward Hermannnplatz reaching it by dark in good order. One of Smirnov's tank columns did locate a clear way through to Yorckstraße and Blücher Straße. The column probably advanced up either Oderstraße, where *Müncheberg* advanced south earlier in the day, or by advancing up side streets parallel to Hermannstraße. It is possible that this column of Soviet tanks wheeled left through Hasenheide Park appearing on Hasenstraße. The corps commander quickly ordered a repositioning of forces and sent the 45th Guards Tank Brigade to the new route to accelerate the offensive.[42] Unfortunately for the Soviets, the Germans were alerted to their movement. Metal tank tracks are very noisy on paved roads and the Soviet preparations prior to their tank operations often gave away the direction and size of the tank forces to the German defenders. As Soviet tanks appeared outside Hermannnplatz approaching from Weser or Braunauerstraße , they were picked off by at least one if not two Sturmgeschütz III from *Nordland*. According to accounts, at least forty Soviet tanks, advancing unsupported, were knocked out with many of their crews killed by the waiting German forces in the rubble.[43]

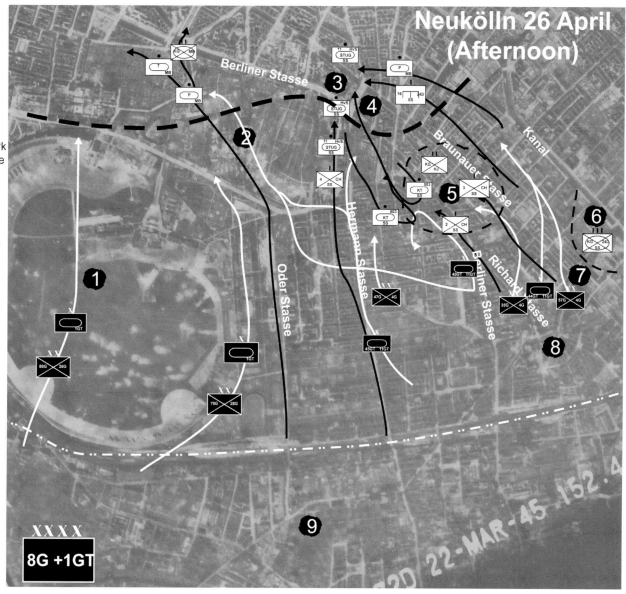

Neukölln 26 April (Afternoon)

Legend
1. Tempelhof
2. Hasenheide Pk
3. Karlstadt Store
4. Herman Pl
5. Town Hall
6. Haas' Obj
7. Hertzberg Pl
8. Richard Pl
9. Friedhof Cem.

Two JS-2 were destroyed through catastrophic explosions caused by near simultaneous hits presumably from the Zoo Bunker's 3.7cm Flak Guns. The larger 12.8cm guns could not depress low enough to hit these two tanks so close to the bunker.
Photo courtesy of RGAKFD Moscow

Soviet infantry look cautiously down one of Berlin's wide boulevards that was the scene of recent fighting. Note the billowing smoke in the right background. In the center above the cap of the Soviet rifleman appears to be a knocked out German Panther or King Tiger with a depressed barrel. Photo courtesy of RGAKFD Moscow.

The combined force of the 8th Guards Army and 1st Guards Tank Army were not only dealing with Neukölln but also the district of Tempelhof in the attempt to finish their encirclement and capture the airport. The Soviets advanced north throughout the day without serious resistance as only local German defense forces were located throughout this district. Chuikov also directed his forces to drive northwest through Schöneberg toward the Berlin Zoo. This was obviously due to Zhukov's order to cut off Koniev from the city's center. It appeared that Tempelhof did not fall until the evening after the withdrawal of German troops instead of a direct assault. The French *1./Sturmbataillon Charlemagne* was kept in reserve by Wöhlermann who was the Defense Sector D commander at the time. Not until late afternoon was the *1./Sturmbataillon Charlemagne* ordered to deploy between the airfield and a cemetery to the west, possibly, the one off Kolonnenstraße. It is clear from the French account that Tempelhof airfield was still not taken by the Russians, but under heavy direct artillery fire confirmed by Chuikov in his account.[44] By evening Soviet infantry advanced past *1./Sturmbataillon Charlemagne* to occupy a series of buildings to the northeast that gave them a distinct tactical advantage over the defenders left on the airfield. The Russians finally assaulted the Frenchmen in the cemetery when they realized that the French position would cause problems for any further advance. Close-quarter combat occurred in the macabre setting of broken tombstones. The French soon extracted themselves and made their way to Hermannnplatz where they joined Fenet and the rest of *Sturmbataillon Charlemagne* late in the evening. Near midnight the French and *Nordland* forces began a general retreat over the Landwehr Canal. The French made their way to the Thomas Keller brewery opposite the Anhalt S-Bahn Station, the *Kampschule*, and the State Opera House.[45]

Chuikov's forces continued their offensive without pause through the night. Abyzov recounts how his unit took a factory, presumably north of Yorckstraße near the Landwehr Canal. He states:

Late in the night we took part of a factory. There were rows of machine tools and crates with finished components. The windows were closed with blackout screens. . .

Lieutenant Ionov, the company commander, appeared before us with a tight belt around his waist. "The company shall rest!" he said.

Outside the factory there was a large yard; on the opposite side—a low and long stone building. There the 3rd Battalion was beating off an enemy assault. And we were given a respite.[46]

The respite did not last long. Abyzov's comrades woke him up. The Germans had taken the low building across the square in a counterattack and the 3rd Battalion had been forced to occupy the same building as Abyzov's unit. Now they were preparing a counterattack. The Russians broke the windows, charged through the open square and took the low building back but with adrenaline pumping the Russians pushed their assault too far:

We recovered the low long building, which turned out to be the machine repair section of the factory. In the heat of the assault we rushed out the wide-open gate. But the Germans poured long bursts of tracer bullets at us and we were forced to withdraw to the machine repair shop.

There were about seven or eight casualties—either killed or wounded. As they were being carried out several shots were fired from somewhere above and two of our volunteer medical orderlies lay on the asphalt. That was a sniper job.[47]

The Russians quickly set up a defensive perimeter and settled in for the rest of the night as they tried to avoid the bursts of machine-gun and sniper fire directed at the windows of the Repair Shop. Further west, tanks of the 34th Heavy Tank Regiment drove across Kolonnenstraße, over both the Potsdamer and Anhalt rail lines, and finally northwest where they penetrated to the Kaiser Wilhelm Memorial Church on Kurfürstenstraße. According to Chuikov, well-armed *Gestapo* used *Panzerfaust* to knock out the lead tanks that became immobile after running over mines. One Soviet tanker named Hermann Shashkov remained with his immobile tank, despite it being hit several times by *Panzerfausts*, and set on fire twice. The other members of the tank crew were killed and when Russian soldiers finally reached the tank, they found Shashkov armed with only a knife still alive in the crew compartment.[48]

The approach of Soviet tanks so close to the Zoo Bunker caused the call for volunteers to head out into the local streets and hunt down Russian armor. Harry Schweizer was a *Luftwaffe* flak gunner who took up the call. Schweizer was one of four soldiers that formed a tank destroyer team. These boys left the Zoo Flak Tower armed with a *Panzerfaust*, a glass bottle containing a milky fluid that when mixed with oxygen in the air would cause the tank engine to stop, and two escorts with Sturmgewehr assault rifles to shoot the tank's crew once they bailed out. A new command post was set up in the Aquarium and tank barriers erected at the Zoo S-Bahn station. Not long after this patrol hit the streets they located a Russian T-34/85 at the corner of Wichmannstraße and Keithstraße, one block south of the Landwehr Canal. This tank's gunfire dominated the street. Schweizer recalls the attack on the Russian tank:

We crept through ruins and cellars until we could see the tank from a cellar window each. The tank stood across the street from us and was firing steadily down Keithstraße. A Russian with a slung sub-machine gun was standing in a doorway near the tank watching it fire. We debated whether we should shoot the soldier or the tank first, deciding upon the tank since the tank crew would be alert. Comrade Hitzinger fired at the tank with a *Panzerfaust* from his cellar window and hit it, but at the same time cried out with pain, as he had not taken the back blast into account and was burning all over. The Russian in the doorway had vanished. We attended to our comrade and put out the flames with our jackets, and then took him back to the hospital in the bunker.[49]

During the evening they returned back to the Aquarium and were told to report to a *Gestapo* unit fighting along Budapester Straße near the Kaiser Wilhelm Memorial Church, presumably the same unit that engaged Chuikov's tanks earlier in the evening. Once there they fired at a Russian machine-gun post dug-in on the corner. One of the boys with Schweizer was shot by the Russians and wounded. He was then detailed to bring eight elderly *Volkssturm* to the *Gestapo* unit. He did this but two of the elderly men were wounded in the process, causing Schweizer to loose his stomach for street fighting. Schweizer had enough and returned back to the Zoo Bunker. He was then sent to wait in the Tiergarten with a *Panzerfaust* for Russian tanks but none came across the Landwehr Canal that evening.[50] Soviet snipers and scouts infiltrated the area around the Zoo Bunker complex, taking refuge in the dense vegetation. They rapidly covered the smaller L Tower with accurate fire and stopped anyone from walking out onto the roof.[51] The westward penetration by Chuikov put him well west

Spandau
26 April

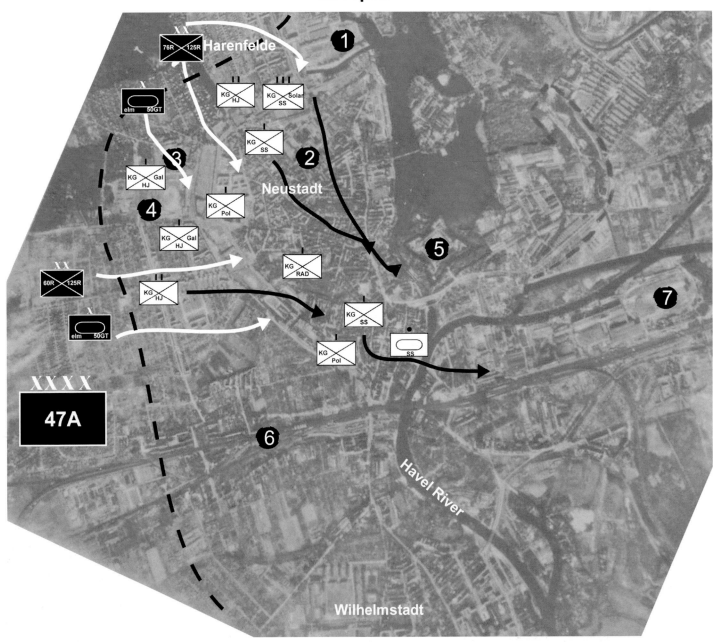

Key Places
1. Hackenfelde Aircraft Instrument Factory
2. Military Supply Depot
3. Napola School
4. Polizei School
5. Zitadel
6. Spandau West Station
7. Ruhleben Racecourse

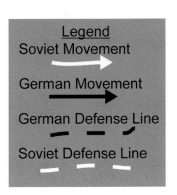

Legend
Soviet Movement
German Movement
German Defense Line
Soviet Defense Line

of the new established inter-front boundary. The 3rd Guards Tank Army approaching from the southwest was unaware that Chuikov's forces had already worked their way across the 1st Ukrainian's front. In fact, in all probability, advance units of Koniev were already operating in the area. No coordination between the two Soviet commands occurred.

Hauptman Kurt Ache was in charge of the *Nachrichten Abteilung 18* equipped with 200 men and a dozen Funk (radio) Panzers. After retreating into Berlin, Ache was ordered to set up his HQ at the Zoo Bunker. On 22 April Ache received orders to dismantle four wireless sets and send them to the *Führerbunker*, along with radio Panzer units into Karlhorst, Britz, Tempelhof, Schöneberg, Friedenau, Wilmersdorf, Grunewald, Charlottenburg, and Hallensee. Central wireless communication was then established inside the Zoo Bunker, which already had the best landline communications in the city. This disposition of units helped alleviate some of the command and control issues, but not to a high degree. According to Ache, "Thus in these areas at least, it was possible for the leaders more or less to have a picture of the situation, and to send reinforcements—as far as they were available—into especially endangered areas. Otherwise, even the smallest unit operated according to its own judgment. Due to the sudden chaos it was impossible to conduct a unified defense of the city."[52] On 25 April his unit located in Rüdesheimer Platz came under attack by Koniev's 6th Guards Tank and 9th Mechanized Corps. Ache's account suggests that Koniev was not in the area in force, but clearly he was focused on reaching the Reichstag and pushing forward toward Berlin's Central Districts. Koniev's forces continued to advance northwest and on 26 April they reached Schmargendorf S-Bahn Station, where Ache's troops were asked to relocate and defend as there were apparently no other forces available. *Untersturmführer* Feige's King Tiger was assigned to assist in the defense and during the day they knocked out six Russian tanks. By the afternoon, according to Ache, he turned the defense of the S-Bahn Station over to an unidentified *SS* unit.[53]

The planned counterattack by elements of the *18.Pz.Gren.Div.* began in the early morning. The intent of the attack was to reestablish a connection with the *20.Pz.Gren.Div.* It is also likely that Weidling had an eye toward Wenck's relief forces, and a possible breakout in the direction of southwest Berlin as he made this counterattack force unusually strong. According to Arno Pentzien, an artilleryman in *Art.Reg.18*, the attack plan was briefed at 0700. The attacking forces consisted of the *I.* and *II./Pz.Gren.Rgt.30*, six Panzers, and fifteen SPWs. Although it is suggested by at least one historian that the Panzers were all Tigers, this is in fact not accurate. The majority of the King Tigers were already committed to other sectors along with at least half of the available *Müncheberg* Tiger Is. It is entirely possible that at least one to two Tiger Is of *Müncheberg* were present. The other tanks were probably Panthers, also from *Müncheberg*, as well as Jagdpanzer IVs from *Pz.Rgt.118 Schlesien*. As the German forces assembled for the attack, Koniev's forces detected the German preparations as they prepared for their own morning assault through the district. Soviet artillery and rockets struck the German assembly area. The Germans received some losses, quickly recovered, and then launched their planned attack down Avus toward Zehlendorf and Dahlem. The Panzer force made good progress initially then ran into anti-tank guns and armor of the 7th Guards Tank Corps located in the area. Communications with the *Schlesien* and *Holstein* artillery battery located in the Tiergarten was not working and the Germans were unable to call on indirect fire to assist in the attack. By 1000 hours the attack was called off. The Russians immediately went on the counterattack bypassing the Germans along their flanks and forcing them to displace and retreat back northeast across Hagenstraße. By 1400 Russian infantry were working their way through the area and picking off any German soldiers they could see. Pentzien noticed a pattern. The Russians were calling out to the German civilians in order to get them to leave the area before they launched their next attack.[54] This enabled the Germans to move out ahead of the Russians.

Pz.Gren.Rgt.51 was forced back to the line of Schildhornstraße between Breitenscheidplatz and the Schloßstraße in Steglitz after taking the brunt of the attack from the 6th Guards Tank Corps.[55] Koniev's memoir is silent on the events of 26 April, although he focuses attention on the difficulty of the fighting in Berlin. This suggests that he may not have seen the gains he was expecting, as he does not even mention the German counterattack. By evening it became apparent that the connection with the *20.Pz.Gren.Div.* was no longer possible. Weidling requested that Krebs officially move the *20.Pz.Gren.Div.* under the command of *Armeegruppe Spree* suggesting he still didn't realize the extent that the *20.Pz.Gren.Div.* had left Berlin.[56]

A reconnaissance element of the 6th Tank Corps consisting of a platoon of tanks with mounted infantry approached up Kaiserallee toward the S-Bahn ring. The Germans positioned a small patrol of *Hitlerjugend* under command of a *Fallschirmjäger* NCO along this key street. The first T-34 approached, followed by the second with mounted infantry about 50 meters behind. Behind that tank others were heard in the distance. A German machine-gun positioned in a forth floor room opened up and scattered the Soviet infantry on the second tank while several members of the *Hitlerjugend* move out into the street. Using nearby bushes of Haisen Platz they stalked the first Soviet tank. The second tank opened fire with its main gun into the nearby bushes after becoming alerted to the approach of the *Hitlerjugend*. Suddenly a whoosh was heard as the tracks and side of the first tank were struck by a *Panzerfaust* knocking it out. The second tank now opened up with machine-gun fire but the *Hitlerjugend* made it back to their positions with only one comrade wounded. The other boys of the ad-hoc unit proceeded to knock out the other tanks forcing the Soviets to pull back and regroup. Based on the German description of the battle, the Soviets were operating without any indirect fire support. This suggests that this armor force was the vanguard of a Soviet corps pushing hard to advance as far as it could while its artillery assets were being repositioned.[57]

After Sorensen's burial, Illum's *Kampfgruppe* was ordered to the Grunewald area in response to the reported progress of Koniev's attack from the south. By evening the Soviet infantry and armor pushed into Illum's positions, probably without knowing that Illum's forces were there. Skirmishes now broke out in the dark. The enemy could only be discerned by the locations of muzzle flashes from their automatic weapons and tank fire. Illum and his men realized that the Soviets were pushing on their flanks and they had no choice but to retreat or be surrounded. Once they disengaged from the fighting, Illum and his men quickly located a truck, loaded onboard, and drove north toward Spandau.[58]

WESTERN DISTRICTS

The 47th Army regrouped over the previous day. The first assault into Spandau failed due to the lack of Soviet forces, poor coordination, and strong resistance from the miscellaneous groups of German defenders. The second assault into Spandau forced the Soviets to adopt a more methodical approach that typified Soviet operations in Berlin. Strong artillery fire struck suspected German positions, followed by tanks and self-propelled guns that pushed through while blasting German defenders still remaining. Finally, an infantry assault usually preceded by mortar fire was launched along the flanks to surround or dislodge the defenders so that they might be easily cut down in

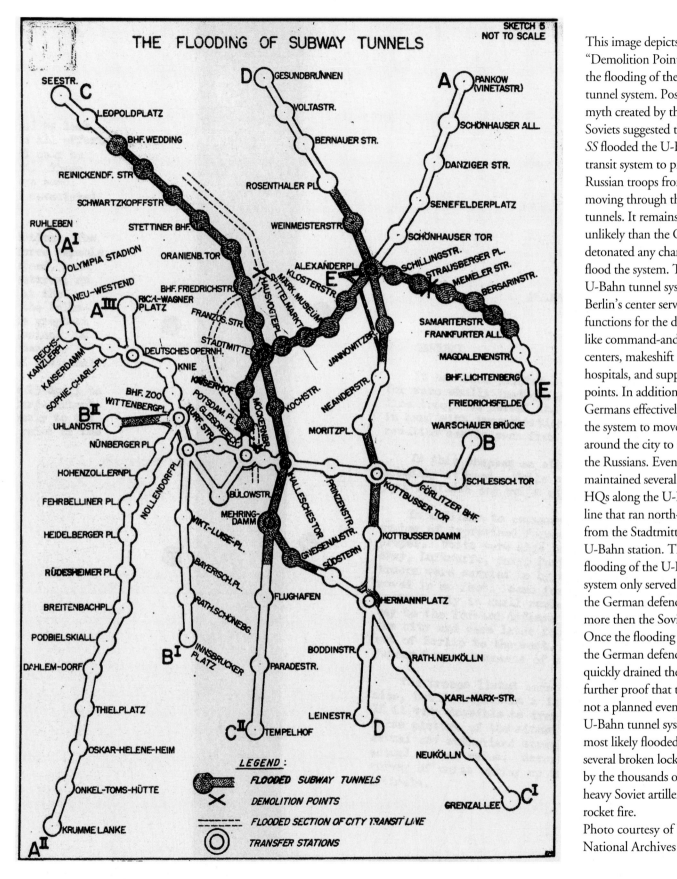

THE FLOODING OF SUBWAY TUNNELS

SKETCH 5
NOT TO SCALE

LEGEND:

FLOODED SUBWAY TUNNELS

DEMOLITION POINTS

FLOODED SECTION OF CITY TRANSIT LINE

TRANSFER STATIONS

This image depicts the "Demolition Points" for the flooding of the U-Bahn tunnel system. Postwar myth created by the Soviets suggested that the *SS* flooded the U-Bahn transit system to prevent Russian troops from moving through the tunnels. It remains highly unlikely than the Germans detonated any charges to flood the system. The U-Bahn tunnel system in Berlin's center served key functions for the defenders like command-and-control centers, makeshift hospitals, and supply points. In addition, the Germans effectively used the system to move quickly around the city to attack the Russians. Even the *SS* maintained several combat HQs along the U-Bahn line that ran north-south from the Stadtmitte U-Bahn station. The flooding of the U-Bahn system only served to hurt the German defenders more then the Soviets. Once the flooding began, the German defenders quickly drained the system, further proof that this was not a planned event. The U-Bahn tunnel system most likely flooded due to several broken locks caused by the thousands of tons of heavy Soviet artillery and rocket fire.
Photo courtesy of US National Archives

Spittelmarkt
26 April

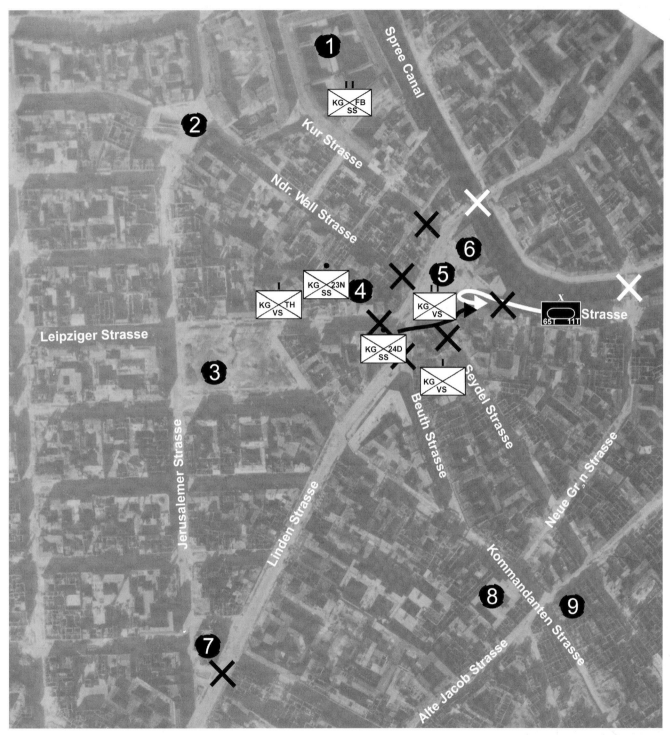

Key Places
1. Reichsbank
2. Hausvogtei Platz
3. Donhoff Platz
4. St. Joseph II Hospital
5. Spittelmarkt Platz
6. Foreign Exchange
7. Jerusalemer Church
8. Reich Stationery Office
9. Theatre

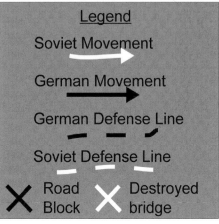

Legend

Soviet Movement

German Movement

German Defense Line

Soviet Defense Line

✕ Road Block ✕ Destroyed bridge

crossfire once exposed. In Spandau, as in most of Berlin, many German defenders were simply melting away into the population exchanging their uniforms for civilian clothes. The fact that many of the soldiers were local boys didn't help the situation. German commanders now began to exert different pressures to force their soldiers to stay and fight. Helmut Altner retreated back to Berlin from the Oder Front several days earlier after the *156.Infantrie Division* collapsed during the Soviet assault. There were only 58 *Hitlerjugend* survivors from his unit of 150.[59] Back in Berlin, Altner and the other boys were reformed, rearmed, and sent into Spandau to bolster the defense. Altner's commander was ordered by a *Waffen-SS* officer in the area to remove his soldier's paybooks. The reason was because it was rumored that the Soviets shot any German prisoner out of hand if they did not have one, thinking the soldier was a member of the *Waffen-SS*.[60] By removing their paybooks the boys might remain with their unit and fight instead of going home to wait out the assault.

Altner's company engaged the Soviets among the quiet residential streets of northern Spandau in an uneven struggle. His unit held a multi-storey row of apartment buildings as the Soviets advanced down the block. A Soviet T-34/85 slipped past the defenders and began to advance alongside the gardens at the rear of the row houses. As it advanced down the block it began to fire at each of the houses in turn after seeing German soldiers in the windows. No one had a *Panzerfaust* and Altner and his men rushed out of the buildings into the street to avoid the fire. Their *Leutnant* quickly ordered them back into the houses. As Altner and his comrades reached the front doors they found that the home's residents locked them in the hopes that the German soldiers could not enter again and draw Soviet fire. Altner and his squad broke the door in and moved back into the buildings. In his memoir Altner reflected on the paradox of this situation as he not only had to fight the enemy but also his countrymen in the meaningless defense.[61]

A second Russian attack occurred in the evening across the whole of Spandau and finally reduced the German defenders who retreated back across the Havel River. The only defenders left in Spandau were *Hitlerjugend* and elements of the *Rgt.30 Januar* sent to hold the Havel crossings north of Spandau. They were swept into Berlin by the 47th Army several days earlier.[62] As night descended on the defenders, the sky was marked by endless tracer fire from the Zoo Flak Tower that Altner described as a constant silver stream across the night sky.[63] This was the twin-barreled 12.8cm cannon from the Zoo Bunker firing into Spandau to assist in keeping the Soviets back. Altner and his men made their way back to the Havel looking for a crossing to the east bank of the river.

To the south of Spandau, Gatow airfield continued to hang on against the odds. The airfield's defense was assisted by a flak battery of 8.8s positioned on the east bank of the Havel that provided direct support against any Soviet armor or infantry attacks from the nearby woods. Weidling realized the importance of keeping this airfield open and ordered *Luftwaffe Generalmajor* Aribert Müller to take charge of the defense.

NORTHERN DISTRICTS

In the north the 1st Mechanized Corps of the 2nd Guards Tank Army continued to close up to the Spree River through Siemenstadt opposite Charlottenburg. The Polish Engineers were given orders to prepare for the crossing of the canal, presumably during the evening. Toward the east the 3rd Shock Army continued to make good progress.

The 79th Rifle Corps renewed its offensive at dawn to get across the Westhafen Canal. The 3rd Battalion of the 756th Rifle regiment tried to cross the ruined Königsdamm Bridge under cover of a massive artillery barrage but failed. Then they launched another attack with divisional artillery in support and a small number of Soviet soldiers reached the other side but were forced back after a German counterattack. The German positions on the opposite side consisted of several entrenched machine-guns in the warehouse to the east that dotted the wharfs, the multi-storey brick Beusselstraße S-Bahn station directly across from the bridge, and a dug-in *Panzerstellung*.[64] The defenders were local *Volkssturm*. The Soviets launched a third attack sending chemical engineers forward who made it to the other side of the canal and created a smokescreen that allowed other soviet soldiers to cross and expand the bridgehead. The Soviets tried bringing up direct support artillery but the horse-drawn carriages lost their horses in German crossfire that still raked the bridge. This forced the Soviet infantry to drag the guns across the canal by hand. After being held up most of the day, the Soviet infantry finally bypassed, then dislodged the German defenders. The bridgehead was quickly consolidated and the Soviets prepared for their assault through Moabit. By the afternoon Soviet units pushed forward against virtually no resistance until they reached the Moabit prison.[65]

The majority of Moabit was undefended because Weidling did not realize the extent of the Soviet encirclement or where the majority of the Soviet forces were located outside of Berlin. German civilians and retreating soldiers quickly brought word that the Soviets were in these northern districts and advancing on the city center. Unfortunately there was little the German defenders could do about stemming these assaults without additional units to deploy into blocking positions.

Hermannn's *Fallschirmjäger* settled into their defensive positions to the east of Moabit. Approximately 500 *Fallschirmjäger* took up positions near the Humboldthain Flak Tower and surrounding city blocks. Hermannn and the division staff initially set up their command post within the Flak Tower. To the east of the *Fallschirmjäger* was the *Wachregiment Großdeutschland*. This unit knew Berlin better than any other unit in the city, especially the northern districts as they were based in Moabit. Several hundred of the soldiers, along with armored halftrack and approximately six Hetzers took up a strong positions running east of Gesundbrunnen S-Bahn Station along the raised S-Bahn tracks, the Schönhauser Allee S-Bahn Station, and finally the Prenzlauer Allee S-Bahn Station.[66] Elements of the 12th Guards Rifle Corps pushed between Schönhauser Allee and Gesundbrunnen S-Bahn Stations. The Russians were able to temporarily cross the defense line and hold the north side of Kopenhagener Straße while the south side was still in German hands.[67] It was in this area that *Unteroffizier* Franke of *Großdeutschland* distinguished himself by destroying seven T-34s that tried to pierce the German defense line during the day. This feat, done single-handedly using *Panzerfausts*, earned him a trip to the *Führerbunker* where he met Hitler and was awarded the Knights Cross for his exploits.[68]

CENTRAL DISTRICTS

Krukenberg went to the Reich Chancellery where he met Fegelein face-to-face. During the conversation Krukenberg expressed concern over the fact that his men were placed under Seifert (a non-*SS* commander) and that *Nordland* was broken up into small combat groups and sent out to reinforce various sectors of the city (like Illum's unit). Weidling, who was already at the bunker, overheard their conversation and joined in arguing the need to split the already fractured *Nordland* into small *Kampfgruppe*. After Weidling left for a meeting,

Colonel General V. I. Kuznetsov (in the middle), 3rd Shock Army commander, and his staff.
Photo courtesy of the Bulgarian Ministry of Defence

Fegelein suggested that Krukenberg report directly to *Brigadeführer* Mohnke, who was in command of all *SS* forces for the defense of the Government Quarter within Defense Sector Z.[69] Mohnke gave Krukenberg his support after a brief conversation and ordered *Nordland's* remaining soldiers position his force east and southeast of the Government district. He was told to make his command post at the Stadt Mitte U-Bahn station. Krukenberg stated after the war:

> I was an idealist, I thought that some sort of a defense had been set up for the center of Berlin. I found absolutely nothing. In the subway for example, where my command post was to be, and which I thought had already been setup, I found that there were no lights, no telephone, there was a single wagon standing in the subway station and that was all. I now had to install all the necessary items that a command post needed. I didn't have the faintest idea of what was going on because nobody had even supplied me with maps and I never did get correct maps showing the situation as it developed.[70]

Krukenberg was not alone in feeling disconnected and ill-informed regarding the pace of operations in the city. Weidling later heard about Krukenberg's new orders and it confirmed his mistrust of all *SS*.

No German commander in Berlin clearly understood the situation at any given time. The best that was accomplished was an understanding of the immediate two or three block radius around a given unit. Wireless communication, with only a few notable exceptions, was non-existent. Lack of communications was so bad that Krebs had to pick out random numbers from the phone book and dial them in hopes to reach someone who knew what the current tactical situation was in the phoned area. The process of eroding command-and-control continued for Weidling who not only struggled with the lack of ability to issue orders to his own forces, but also fighting competing command structures like Bärenfänger in the east and now Krukenberg and Mohnke in the Government Quarter. Lack of communication and growing mistrust hampered his ability to affect a rationale and cohesive defense of Berlin. The failure of his ordered counterattacks showed how quickly the Soviets could bring firepower to bear on any large assembled force of Germans. Not until 1 May when the breakouts began did the German formations under Weidling again form battalion-size units to conduct operations within the city. German formations now formed small unnamed tactical level *Kampfgruppe* of *Wehrmacht*, *SS*, *Volkssturm*, and *Hitlerjugend* striking the Soviets only to retreat back into the rubble. As these tactical units were dispersed due to terrain or reduced during combat actions, the survivors simply reformed with other stragglers into a new tactical units and the process started all over again. German soldiers inside Berlin increasingly adopted asymmetrical warfare principles in order to avoid massive Soviet firepower.

The late afternoon and early evening saw a number of German *Kampfgruppe* and stragglers cross over the Landwehr Canal into Defense Sector Z in the wake of Chuikov's rapid advance through Neukölln. A *Kampfgruppe* of *Müncheberg* situated at the northern end of Tempelhof retreated northwest across the Landwehr Canal to the Anhalt S-Bahn station under a near continuous artillery barrage. Below the S-Bahn station were a variety of U-Bahn tunnels that crisscrossed the S-Bahn complex. The soldiers of *Müncheberg* moved below for security. One member of the unit recounted the following in his diary:

> The station looks like an armed camp. Women and children huddling in niches and corners and listening for the sounds of battle. Shells hit the roofs, cement is crumbling from the ceiling. Powder smell and smoke in the tunnels. Suddenly water splashes into our command post. Screams, cries, curses in the tunnel. People are fighting around the ladders that run through the air shafts up to the streets. Water comes rushing through the tunnels. The crowds get panicky, stumble and fall over rails and ties. Children and wounded are deserted, people are trampled to death.[71]

Post-war accounts attribute the flooding of several U-Bahn tunnels as the work of the *SS* under orders from Hitler. This may have been possible as reports that the U-Bahn tunnels were being used by the Russians certainly reached the *Führerbunker*, but a more plausible reason exists. Many German units in Defense Sector Z, including Mohnke, had their command posts in the bunker like U-Bahn stations that were also used extensively by the Germans to maneuver around the Soviets without being hit by artillery or mortars. It is highly improbable that Mohnke, who was in command of the *SS* in the Government Quarter and exerted command influence over most of the

SS in Defense Sector Z, would have allowed the indiscriminate flooding of the U-Bahn tunnels. The most likely scenario was that one of thousands of large caliber Soviet artillery shells lobbed indiscriminately into Berlin's center struck and broke one of the locks along the Landwehr Canal causing the tunnels to flood.

SS-Pz.Gren.Rgt.24 Danmark's supply and maintenance elements moved into the Tiergarten from Spandau as the Russian attacked that district during the day. *SS-Scharführer* Scholles was one of *Danmark* soldiers that reached the Tiergarten just before dawn as the Soviets started the day with the usual artillery barrage that hit the Zoo and surrounding park. Other *Nordland* stragglers filtered back into the Tiergarten from the fighting in the southern districts. Presumably Weidling (as Krukenberg had not spoken to Fegelein yet) ordered that the baggage train of *Danmark* was joined with the division's stragglers to form a new *Kampfgruppe*. The *Kampfgruppe* was formed under the leadership of *S-Untersturmführer* Bachmann who was commander of the signal company from *II./Pz.Gren.Rgt.24 Danmark*. The *Kampfgruppe* consisted of about 100 soldiers, only half of whom were armed. They were ordered to march to the Hallesches Tor and take up a semi-circle defense facing south. As so many German units, this *Kampfgruppe* had no communication to any units on the left or right. Bachmann only knew his immediate task to defend against any Soviet attacks that came from the southern bank of the Landwehr Canal. Soon Soviet artillery began to rake the ruins where the small *Kampfgruppe* was located. Sitting in the ruins during the artillery barrage, Scholles had time to reflect on his unit's current situation and he began to feel "completely alone" according to his postwar account.[72] Mental fatigue certainly took its toll after ten days of constant combat without rest.

Rhein's *Fj.Art.Rgt.9* moved up to Friedrichstraße Station and setup their HQ. The roving death squads were very active in Defense Sector Z, as Rhein noted two corpses hanging under the Friedrichshain S-Bahn Bridge. One body was that of an officer and another sergeant. A sign hanging above them read "I was hanged because I failed to keep my self-propelled gun battle ready, as the Führer had ordered it." [*Ich wurde gehängt weil ich mein Sturmgeschütz nicht einsatzbereit hielt wie es der Führer befehl*].[73] The remaining 80 *Fallschirmjäger* of the regiment were now ordered to move to Königsplatz as infantry reinforcements. Kuntze was one of *Fallschirmjäger* that fell in under Rhein. Kuntze's battalion staff also centered itself in reserve at Friedrichstraße. Kuntze and the remaining *Fallschirmjäger* now took up defensive positions in the Ministry of the Interior, Kroll Opera House, and north of the Spree around the Lehrter S-Bahn station and adjoining Reichs Sport Field. They took orders from *SS-Obersturmführer* Babick who had his command post in the cellar of the Reichstag building and had command over the buildings located in Königsplatz.[74]

Timm and the rest of the StuG IIIs of *Nordland* retreated north from Neukölln and soon relocated to a reserve position in front of the Gestapo HQ building on Prinz-Albrechtstraße under the command of *SS-Sturmbanführer* Saalbach. Their defensive line ran along an anti-tank barricade in front of Wilhelmstraße facing Zimmerstraße. According to Timm he stayed there for the next 3-4 days without ever again being ordered to attack the Soviets. Although he received artillery and mortar fire from the Russians daily, no direct combat occurred. Other assault guns from his unit were ordered into combat on several occasions over the next several days. These assault guns remained in operational reserve until the breakout was ordered during the evening of 1 May.[75] While Timm seemed to have located an island in the storm, fierce battles began at the eastern end of Defense Sector Z.

Forward elements of the 11th Tank Corps continued to assault the vital Spittelmarkt road junction on the eastern edge of Sector Z. The *Hitlerjugend* holding positions there received their rations by running back to the Reich Chancellery where members of *LSSAH Wachbataillon* dished out food from a hot kettle as well as 'iron rations.' Schultz received his unit's rations then ran back to his positions where their senior NCO, a veteran from the Eastern Front, cautioned the boys about eating too much because it would make any stomach wounds worse. The Soviets again prepared for their ground assault on the Spittelmarkt with a heavy artillery barrage. Once the barrage was complete Schulz and the other boys picked up their weapons and headed out to the barricade to await the expected Soviet assault. Soon Soviet infantry were seen moving into the Spittelmarkt from Wallstraße but before they reached the tank barricade the Norwegians from *Kampfgruppe Norge* that took up positions in the Weinitschke Typewriter factory the day before opened fire. Their automatic weapons caught the Soviet infantry in the open and they soon pulled back down Wallstraße past the burnt-out hulk of the T-34/85 destroyed the day before. A truck with a loud speaker now approached the Spittelmarkt broadcasting a message in German from the Seydlitz Troops asking all German defenders to surrender in four hours or face destruction. The morale of Schulz and the other boys was still high so the broadcast message had little effect on the *Hitlerjugend*. Their morale was bolstered by the general fear that the Soviets didn't take prisoners.[76] The Soviet's use of psychological operations was not new but appeared to be increasing in frequency now that they reached the inner island fortress of Defense Sector Z. Zhukov's patience was at an end as May Day was fast approaching. Presumably he ordered the use of all means to get the Germans to surrender and quickly stop fighting.

Notes to Chapter 6: Assault on Berlin, 26th April Thursday

1 OKW File, Last Announcements of OKW, 26 April (RC: 62:8).
2 Army Group Weichsel War Diary, Apr 20–9, p. 379 (RC: 68/4).
3 Ibid, pp. 371,372, 379–81.
4 Schultz-Naumann, p. 29.
5 *MS #R-79*, p. 32.
6 Le Tissier, *Slaughter at Halbe*, p. 88.
7 Army Group Weichsel War Diary, Apr 20–9, p. 382 (RC: 68/4).
8 Ibid, p. 383.
9 Schultz-Naumann, p. 157.
10 Spaeter, vol III, p. 502.
11 Weidling Interrogation Report, and Holzträger, p. 71.
12 Weidling Interrogation Report.
13 Ibid.
14 Ibid.
15 Ibid.
16 Ibid.
17 Platonov, p. 19.
18 Ibid, p. 20.
19 Ibid, pp. 21–3.
20 Genzow interview.
21 Le Tissier, *Race for the Reichstag*, p. 123.
22 Eilhardt, p. 52.
23 Le Tissier, *Race for the Reichstag*, p. 123.
24 Venghaus, pp. 437–8, Tieke, *Tragedy of the Faithful*, p. 307.
25 Forbes, p. 274.
26 Ibid.
27 R. Landwehr, *French Volunteers of the Waffen SS*, p. 59. Forbes, states that the 4th Platoon was in the cemetery (Berliner and Hermannstrasse) to the north, p 274. See also footnote on p. 277.
28 Forbes, p. 275.
29 Ibid, p. 276.
30 Ibid, p. 278.
31 Ibid.
32 Ibid.
33 Landwehr, *French Volunteers of the Waffen SS*, p. 60.
34 Haas interview, pp. 5–6.
35 Henseler interview, pp. 9–10.
36 Abyzov, pp. 49–50.
37 Chuikov, p. 190.
38 Forbes, p. 280.
39 Schneider, p. 302, and Forbes, p. 280.
40 Schneider, p. 302.
41 Forbes, p. 281.
42 A. L. Getman, *Tanks are Heading to Berlin*, p. 366.
43 Forbes, p. 281.
44 Ibid, p. 282, and Chuikov, pp. 190.
45 Forbes, p. 283.
46 Abyzov, p. 54.
47 Ibid.
48 Chuikov, p. 191.
49 Le Tissier, *With Our Backs to Berlin*, pp. 126–8.
50 Ibid.
51 von Zabeltitz interview.
52 K. Ache interview (RC: 70/7).
53 Ache interview.
54 Venghaus, p. 260.
55 J. Engelmann, *Die 18. Infanterie und Panzergrenadier Division 1934–1945*, pp. 151, 153.
56 Weidling Interrogation Report.
57 H. Bonath interview (RC: 70/11)
58 Illum interview.
59 Altner, p. 83.
60 Ibid, p. 118.
61 Ibid, p. 116.
62 Ibid, p. 121.
63 Ibid.
64 P. Slowe and R. Woods, *Battlefield Berlin: Siege, Surrender & Occupation, 1945*, p. 134.
65 Le Tissier, *Race for the Reichstag*, p. 120.
66 Spaeter, vol III, p. 502.
67 Wrede interview.
68 Spaeter, vol III, p. 502.
69 Krukenberg interview.
70 Ibid.
71 Thorwald, p. 222, and Schultz-Naumann, pp. 175–6.
72 Scholles interview, and Michelis, p. 110.
73 Jansen interview. This crew belonged to an assault gun that was damaged. When a local *SS* commander asked them to integrate their assault gun into his defense the crew refused stating they were taking it to the Tiergarten for repairs. The *SS* commander, upset at what he perceived as cowardice, ordered his men to hang them from the S-Bahn bridge.
74 Venghaus, p. 207.
75 Timm interview.
76 Schulz interview.

ASSAULT ON BERLIN

27 APRIL
FRIDAY

The enemy penetrated into the inner defense ring from the north in Charlottenburg and from the south in Tempelhofer Field. The fight for the center of the city has started at the Hallesches Tor, the Schleisischer Bahnhof and at the Alexanderplatz. The east-west axis is under heavy fire.

… West of Berlin the area Brandenburg-Rathenow-Kremmen was successfully defended against enemy attacks.[1]

OKW Radio Broadcast

The Soviet assault continued to grind through the rubble-strewn streets in uncoordinated acts of violence that did not resemble known military doctrine. Soviet units were on their own to figure out how best to carry out Zhukov's and Koniev's directives, while adopting new tactics to preserve diminishing combat power as they advanced. The Soviet assault Berlin came with a high human cost. Zhukov was loosing an average of 7,804 soldiers per day, and Koniev an average of 4,949 per day in the fighting taking place in and around Berlin.[2] North of Berlin, Zhukov's 2nd Byelorussian Front conducting operations against the *3.Panzer Armee* was loosing soldiers at a rate of 2,570 per day.[3] In total the Berlin Strategic Offensive Operation was resulting in losses of upwards of 16,000 men per day when one also takes into account the daily rate of 387 men per day that the Polish Army incurred fighting alongside the Russians. An average of 100 Soviet tanks and self-propelled guns were also being lost daily in the street fighting and outside Berlin. These were the highest rate of losses since the German invasion of the Soviet Union in 1941, nearly four years earlier. Soviet commanders were hardly able to cope with the recovery and treatment of wounded as many simply died due to a lack of medical attention. Recovery of knocked tanks was also difficult and many repairable tanks were simply left to block routes of advance until the fighting was over. Not all the losses were among ground forces as Soviet aircraft were being lost at a rate of 40 per day due to both the viciously contested airspace by remaining *Luftwaffe* fighters and the actions by *Luftwaffe* Flak personnel.

The number of German wounded brought into Berlin's hospitals was reported to Hitler as approximately 9,000 since 22 April. The daily average of wounded Germans reached approximately 1,500, though this number appears low.[4] This statistic does not take into account the number of mounting civilian and military deaths outside the city.

ARMY GROUP VISTULA

The *3.Panzer Armee* reached breaking point. The Soviets finally pierced the front at Prenzlau with 40 tanks driving west toward Klinkow. The *SS-Rgt. Solar* engaged in heavy defensive fighting in Prenzlau but was not able to hold off the Soviets. The flak battery located on the outskirts of the town began to fall back under the pressure.[5] The *3.Marine Division* ceased to exist as it was caught piecemeal by the Soviets during the German retreat in the area. As the Soviet breakout continued in the center, in the north the Soviets crushed a *Polizei Division* defending the autobahn south of Stettin and began to advance past the port city.[6] All during the day Heinrici fought to cancel the orders to relieve Berlin using the *7.Pz.Div.* and *25.Pz.Gren.Div.* and employ them instead to defeat the Soviet breakthroughs to the north. This fight raged all day over the telephone and ultimately ended with Steiner loosing control of the *25.Pz.Gren.Div.* He also lost the responsibility for the assault south toward Berlin as this 'burden' was not placed on the shoulders of Holste. Krebs sent a signed order to *AGV* at 1320 stating:

> Führer has decided that the group attacking west of Oranienburg is being removed from the command of *SS-Obergruppenführer* Steiner and, under the command of *General* Burmeister, Commander of the *25.Pz.Gren.Div.*, and by concentration of all forces, continues its attack on a broader front to the south. It is necessary that the commanding *General* of the XXXXI Pz. Korps assumes command over attack group as soon as possible.[7]

Heinrici prudently requested that Holste be placed under his command in order that these forces could still be used to prevent a Russian breakthrough opposite the *3.Panzer Armee* lines, but by the end of the day the operational situation deteriorated well beyond the point of saving.

The constant fighting between *AGV* and the *German High Command* negated any impact that that the *7.Pz.Div.* and *25.Pz.Gren.Div.* might have made in the relief of Berlin or as operational reserves behind the *3.Panzer Armee* front lines. Nevertheless it should be noted that the *25.Pz.Gren.Div.* did successfully fight off all attempts by the Russians to breach its defensive line east of

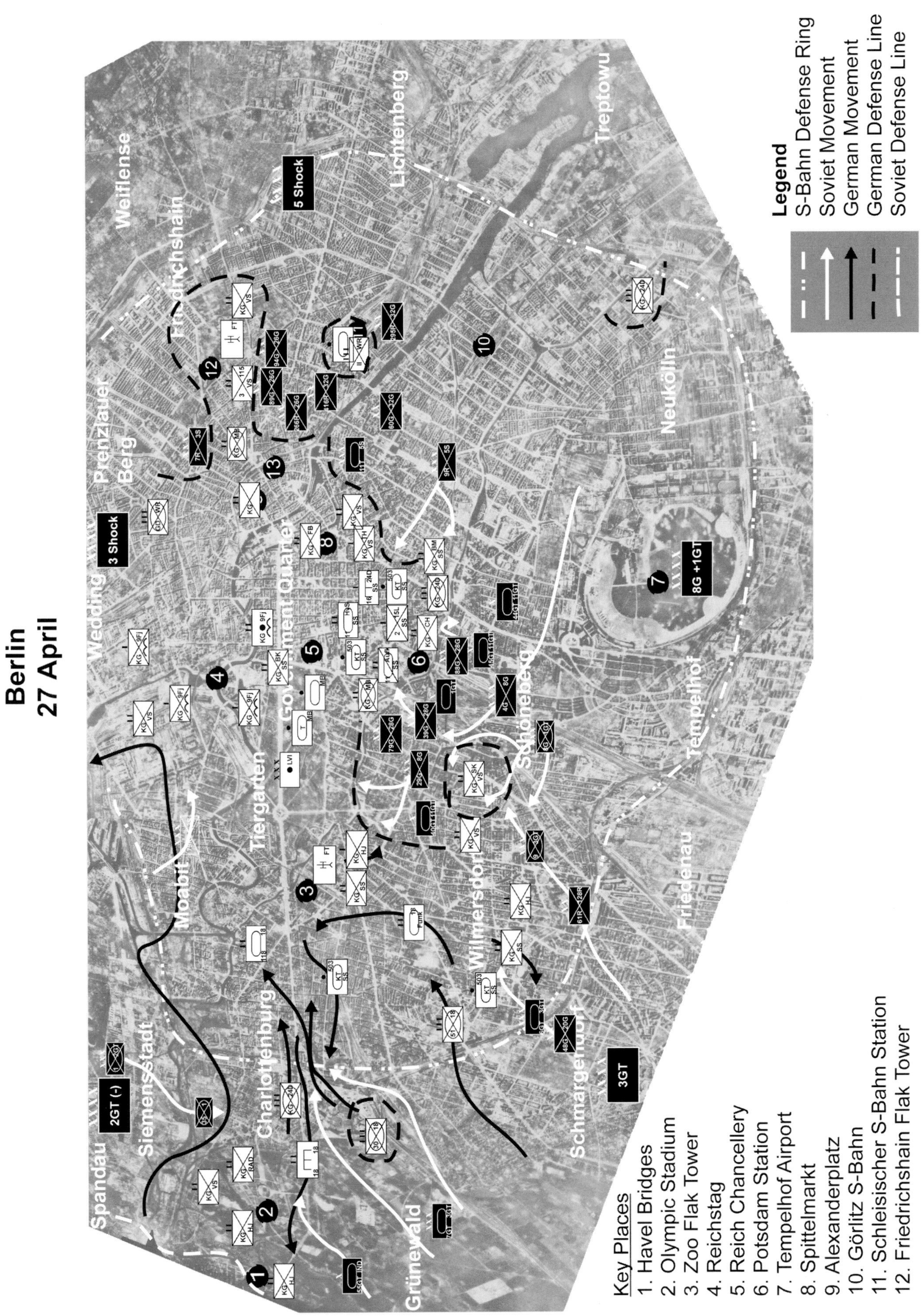

Berlin
27 April

Legend
S-Bahn Defense Ring
Soviet Movement
German Movement
German Defense Line
Soviet Defense Line

Weißensee
Friedrichshain
Lichtenberg
Treptow
5 Shock
Prenzlauer Berg
Wedding
3 Shock
Neukölln
Tiergarten
Government Quarter
Tempelhof
Schöneberg
Moabit
Schmargendorf
Friedenau
Wilmersdorf
Charlottenburg
Grünewald
Siemensstadt
Spandau
3GT
2GT (-)

Key Places
1. Havel Bridges
2. Olympic Stadium
3. Zoo Flak Tower
4. Reichstag
5. Reich Chancellery
6. Potsdam Station
7. Tempelhof Airport
8. Spittelmarkt
9. Alexanderplatz
10. Görlitz S-Bahn
11. Schleisischer S-Bahn Station
12. Friedrichshain Flak Tower

Oranienburg. After numerous phone conversations Heinrici finally received the release of these two divisions. However, this order came too late as they had almost no operational petrol. They had a total of 190 tons left with the expectation that another 100 tons were on their way, although no one knew when the resupply might arrive.[8] The release of the *7.Pz.Div.'s* 82 Panzers represented a significant waste of rare combat resources.[9] Manteuffel also weighed in on the use of both divisions and believed that it was now too late to save the situation.[10] Now all that could be hoped for was that both of these divisions could avoid being surrounded and destroyed by the advancing Soviets. By 2300 that night the entire *3.Panzer Armee* was in retreat west along with most of the local German population. Manteuffel called up Heinrici's headquarters and reported "I just returned from *General* Garais. He reports—and I saw it myself—complete disintegration."[11] The following units were ordered to be taken off the *3.Panzer Armee's* rosters: *1.Polizei Jäger Brigade, SS-Langemarck, SS-Wallonien, 1.Marine Division*, and almost all the flak artillery units.[12] The report concluded: "Now the battle [is] for the self-preservation of the Army, moving everybody to the west. The columns of refuges contain the most valuable human cargo. They should have stayed at home. We don't have time anymore, the political leadership must act, the soldier has spoken. 100,000 human beings are fleeing."[13]

9. ARMEE

Busse's *9.Armee* pocket continued to shrink as he readied for the final breakout. Some German units already began to head out west on their own, and a thrust by Zhukov's 3rd Army pierced the northwest edge of the pocket forming a smaller pocket of Germans known only as the Prieros pocket. In sharp fighting, the Germans prevented the loss of the important road junction located in the village of Märkisch Buchholz, but the key villages at the center of the breakout sector, Halbe and Treupitz, were lost to the Soviets.[14] The deteriorating situation became known to *OKW* throughout the day as reports filtered in to Keitel. The *9.Armee's* situation was summoned up as "being, unfortunately bad."[15] Calls for assistance from the *12.Armee* were communicated by Heinrici. Keitel continued to believe rather optimistically that Busse would attack northwest and join forces with Wenck to attack Berlin.[16]

12. ARMEE

The *XX Korps* maintained an active defense in the east. *Scharnhorst* pushed the Soviets back from the gap that formed between *Körner* and *Hutten* eliminating the Soviet presence on the 4 kilometer stretch of autobahn between Treuenbrietzen and Niemegk. In Treuenbrietzen fighting continued as the Soviets began to move in additional units to deal with *Körner*. Wenck had to make a decision during the early morning hours of 27 April. For several days the three key divisions of the *XX Korps* pushed east against the Soviets but had to hold due to immediate counterattacks. Wenck exclaimed to his staff that "We will drive as close to Berlin as we can, but we will not give up our positions along the Elbe—it would be pure nonsense to drive towards Berlin and then get ourselves encircled by the Russians. We will try to get out the civilians and troops from Berlin, but that's all we can do."[17] In conversation with his Chief of Staff, the question of Busse's *9.Armee* must have been mentioned because Wenck appears to restructure his plan with three goals: attack northeast and provide a corridor for *Armeegruppe Spree* around Potsdam to be rescued and possibly over a way for the Berlin garrison to escape; hold a corridor for Busse's *9.Armee* to escape Soviet encirclement north of Treuenbrietzen; and finally provide the protection and passage to the Elbe for hundreds of thousands of refugees and wounded soldiers. Wenck turned to his chief-of-staff and stated "If we are able to do this we will retreat to the Elbe and surrender our arms to the Americans. That is our last task."[18] Wenck finally abandoned Keitel and Krebs' direction to attack east and link up with the *9.Armee*. Instead he ordered a night movement for *Hutten* and *Scharnhorst* to position them on the left flank of *Körner* and along with *Schill* drive northeast toward Potsdam. Wittenberg was abandoned during the evening in order to save the civilian population further horrors of combat, and to shorten Wenck's lines.[19] In support of the new offensive the *Sturmgeschütz Brigade 1170* was placed in the vanguard of the new assault.[20]

Once again the young soldiers of the final mobilized divisions of the *Wehrmacht* had to disengage from the enemy, move to new assembly areas at night, and then prepare for a pre-dawn attack. By all accounts these orders were not issued until the last possible moment of 27 April. This was done presumably for operational security reasons as Wenck did not want another surprise radio broadcast from *OKW* telling the world about his new attack plan.

1st UKRAINIAN FRONT

Koniev's forces outside of Berlin proved unable to deal with the three challenges directly confronting the 1st Ukrainian Front. Wenck's *12.Armee* was sufficiently blocked from advancing directly east, but Koniev did not have the available manpower to hold the *XX Korps* in place through direct attacks. Wenck, deciding on the path of least resistance, now began to secretly withdraw forces directly opposite Koniev to position for an attack northeast toward Potsdam. In the east, Busse's *9.Armee* began its full breakout west toward the *12Armee* lines. The 1st Byelorussian Front committed the 3rd, 69th, and 33rd Armies to block and assist in the reduction of the pocket from the north and east. Blocking the breakout was the 1st Ukrainian Front's 28th and 3rd Guards Armies. As the breakout got underway additional forces from Koniev's Front were dispatched to stop the actual German forces that managed to breakthrough Halbe. The 24th Shock Corps, from the south was dispatched toward the German Proving Grounds at Kummersdorf, followed by infantry divisions from the 13th Army that was currently engaged with defending against the advance of the Wenck's *XX Korps*. Even several armored brigades from the 6th Guards Mechanized Corps, engaged with blocking the area southwest of Potsdam, opposite the future advance of Wenck's forces, were also dispatched southeast to block Busse. Further south, and often neglected in histories regarding the battle of Berlin, the *4.Panzer Armee* launched a counterattack north into the flank of the 5th Guards Army that was responsible for screening a wide area running from the 13th Army just south of Wittenberg all the way back to Breslau in Silesia. Although Koniev does not mention this attack in his memoirs, the *4.Panzer Armee* continued their offensive for five days pushing the Soviets back on a wide front starting from Radeburg, just north of Dresden, to the outskirts or Ortrand, nearly 18 kilometers to the north. In addition, the 1st Guards Cavalry Corps launched an attack south toward the German town of Nossen, east of Dresden that formed a wedge between *Armeegruppe G* and the *4.Panzer Army*.

Due to the lack of any U.S. Army activity against *Armeegruppe G,* German forces quickly launched a counterattack cutting off the Soviet salient and pushing them back to their start lines.

With three major counterattacks against his forces underway, Koniev's main focus became preventing the *9.Armee's* escape. In his memoir, Koniev gave unusual praise to Busse. He drops the typical Communist rhetoric of the time and wrote " … the *9.Armee,* breaking out of their encirclement, acted courageously and stubbornly, and fought to the death. And it was precisely by such a decisive nature of their actions that they gave us quite a few unpleasant surprises and difficulties in these last days of the war."[21] What is important to stress is that the better part of six Soviet Armies were now engaged in stopping Busse. That is almost the same amount of Soviet armies engaged in the reduction of Berlin. By comparison Busse had at least four times as many soldiers and tanks as were in Berlin under Weidling's command. The breakout of the *9.Armee* highlights the acute manpower shortage faced by the Soviets in the final stages of war and the impact that Weidling's small force fighting asymmetrically made to the defense of Berlin.

FÜHRERBUNKER

Weidling heard that the company-sized elements of a *Kriegsmarine Bataillon* had arrived at Gatow the day before as *Grossadmiral* Dönitz promised Hitler. These sailors were ordered by Hitler to deploy under Mohnke in the Government District within Defense Sector Z and not be deployed under Weidling into the other Defensive Zones.[22] This upset Weidling who raised the question of their deployment to Hitler during his situation brief in the evening. Hitler's response was that no single General was to have control over all the defense forces in Berlin. Hitler pointed out that he trusted Mohnke—meaning the *SS.* Hitler believed that if he gave control of all the forces to any single commander there would simply be no forces left.[23] What Hitler was referring to was Reymann's order to send out twenty *Volkssturm Bataillons* to the front lines leaving Berlin without a main defense force. The irony that the main defense was now coming from the *LVI Pz. Korps,* through pure operational circumstances, was not lost to Hitler.[24] This conversation only served to widen the command gaps in Berlin's defense and diffuse the remaining combat power available to Weidling.

Hitler's main concern was bringing in high quality German troops from any branch of service into Berlin for the defense. In his concluding remarks for the daily brief with Weidling, Hitler ran down the list of potential reinforcements he expected to arrive by air. Then he stated that if he wanted to defend Berlin to the end he needed the best available troops and not the worst. The fact that Berlin was being defended by many groups of foreigners instead of pure Germans disturbed Hitler who specifically pointed out that it was wrong in his mind for 300 Frenchmen to have to defend the city.[25] The *Führerbunker* received daily reports on the exploits of Danes, Norwegians, Latvians, Spaniards, Galacians, and especially the French in their defense of Berlin. In the end, Hitler may not only have juxtaposed the fact that Berlin was being defended by accident after it's main defense force was sent out of the city, but also the fact that its staunchest defenders were non-German.

EASTERN DISTRICTS

Irregular fighting continued on 27 April throughout Defense Sectors A and B as Berzarin consolidated his forces for the final push into the center of Berlin. Alexanderplatz remained in German hands as small anti-tank teams continued their patrols down the side streets. The remaining anti-tank guns and barriers along key avenues to the north and east remained intact as burnt-out Soviet armor bore testament to their effectiveness. Outside of Alexanderplatz the Soviet zone of operations was fragmented. Isolated pockets of German resistance continued as the 26th Guards and 32nd Rifle Corps pushed their assault. The *SS* and *Volkssturm* defenders in the Schlesischer S-Bahn station were now surrounded as the main Soviet forces passed them to the north. The German position was formidable and while Berzarin wanted it reduced, he did not want his forces stalled any longer.

Genzow's unit continued to fight in the area of Prenzlauer Straße. His unit, depleted through attrition, was replenished with new soldiers conscripted into his *Kampfgruppe.* His unit now consisted of 16 men and 6 *Hitlerjugend* from the *Luftwaffe* (presumably from the Flak Tower). The *Hitlerjugend* had no rifles but did have four *Panzerfausts.* Only the 16 soldiers were armed with old rifles and an average of seventeen rounds of ammunition. Their patrol settled into an area of buildings off the main avenue when at 1000 the Soviets started infiltrating around Genzow's positions and almost encircled his small force. He also had a few Nazi Party Officials assigned to him that soon fled by noon after he extracted his small unit from the Russian encirclement. This area of Berlin was named Horst-Wessel after the young Nazi activist who was shot in the face by a local communist and later died. Many Communist sympathizers still lived in the area and they took the opportunity to shoot at Genzow's *Kampfgruppe* from rooftops during their retreat back toward Alexanderplatz. After several sharp battles he had only four men left in his unit when he reached Friedrichshain Park.[26]

The Friedrichshain Flak Tower and surrounding park continued to remain free of Soviet troops. During the afternoon briefing to Hitler, Krebs remarked that the eastern districts of Berlin were holding despite Berzarin's continued offensive. He singled out the commander of the Friedrichshain Flak Tower for particular praise due to his direct fire support of the German ground troops throughout the district.[27] Only southeast of Alexanderplatz was significant progress made by the 5th Shock Army.

The 11th Tank Corps continued to exploit its bridgehead over the Spree while the 9th Rifle Corps advanced northwest after the fall of the Görlitz S-Bahn station. Other Soviet elements made their way toward the Spree south of Alexanderplatz in the area between Alexanderstraße and Königstraße. The 11th Tank Corps received engineer support from the 5th Shock Army in the early morning hours. Soviet commanders realized that this was now one of the few units operating on the west bank of the Spree and was pivotal in helping them tie down German forces from moving east into Defense Sectors A and B where the 5th Shock's other two corps continued to struggle. According to one German *Volkssturm,* the Soviets moved engineer and assault troops up into the area of Spittelmarkt armed with flame-throwers. Soviet infantry assaults against the Spittelmarkt now began as the engineers attempted to smoke out the Germans who held tenaciously to every piece of rubble in the area.[28]

As the Soviet pressure mounted, Schulz was ordered by his commander to remove all *SS* insignia. Removing the collar tabs and shoulder patch was easy enough, but he had to scratch the '*SS*' runes off his helmet and this left obvious marks. Schulz was alone at the barricades during the night when a single T–34/85 drove down Kürassierstraße toward him. He ran back to the cellar where his comrades

Eastern Districts
27 April

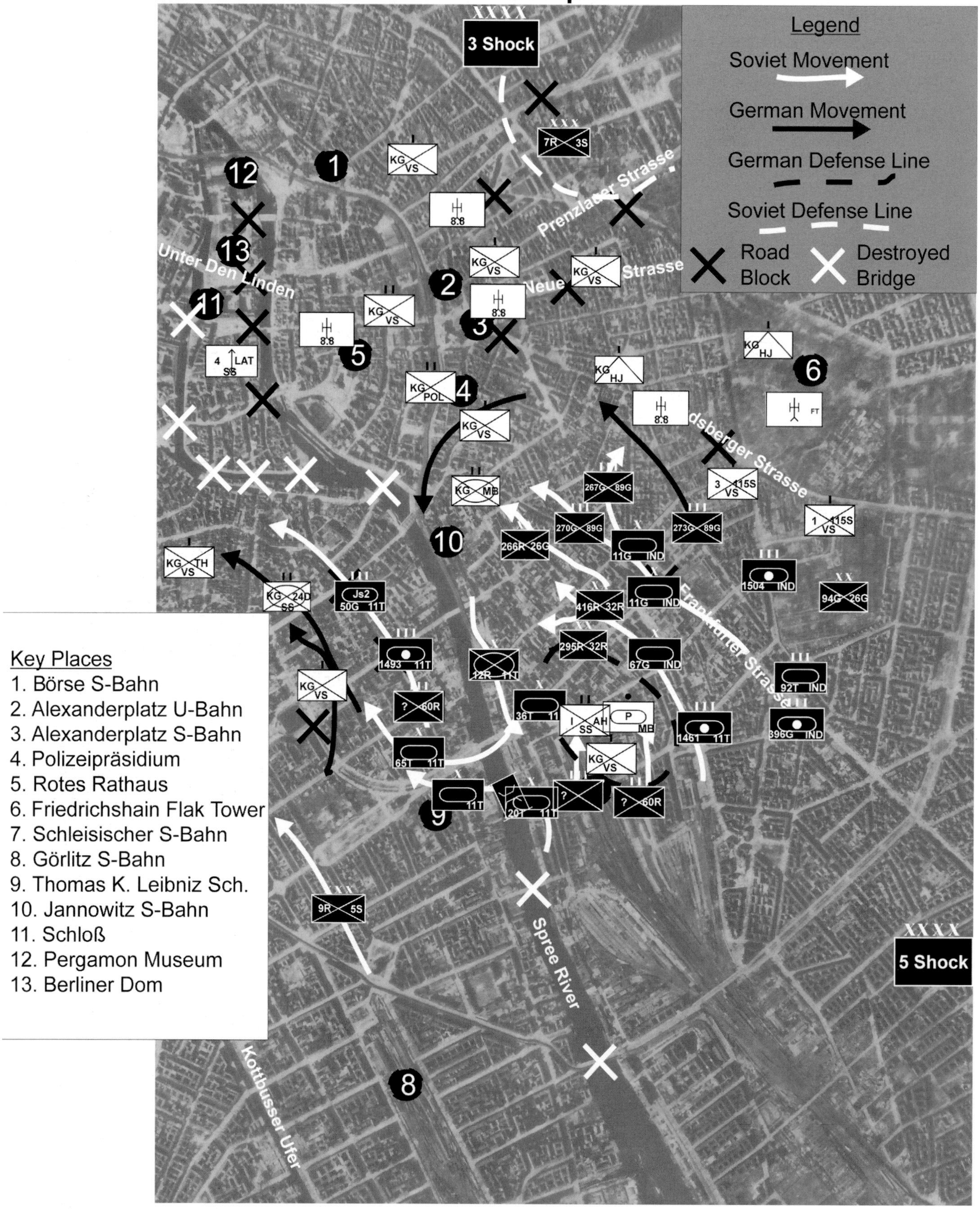

3 Shock

Legend

Soviet Movement

German Movement

German Defense Line

Soviet Defense Line

Road Block — Destroyed Bridge

5 Shock

Key Places
1. Börse S-Bahn
2. Alexanderplatz U-Bahn
3. Alexanderplatz S-Bahn
4. Polizeipräsidium
5. Rotes Rathaus
6. Friedrichshain Flak Tower
7. Schleisischer S-Bahn
8. Görlitz S-Bahn
9. Thomas K. Leibniz Sch.
10. Jannowitz S-Bahn
11. Schloß
12. Pergamon Museum
13. Berliner Dom

Prenzlauer Strasse

Neue Strasse

Unter Den Linden

Landsberger Strasse

Frankfurter Strasse

Spree River

Kottbusser Ufer

Spittelmarkt
27 April

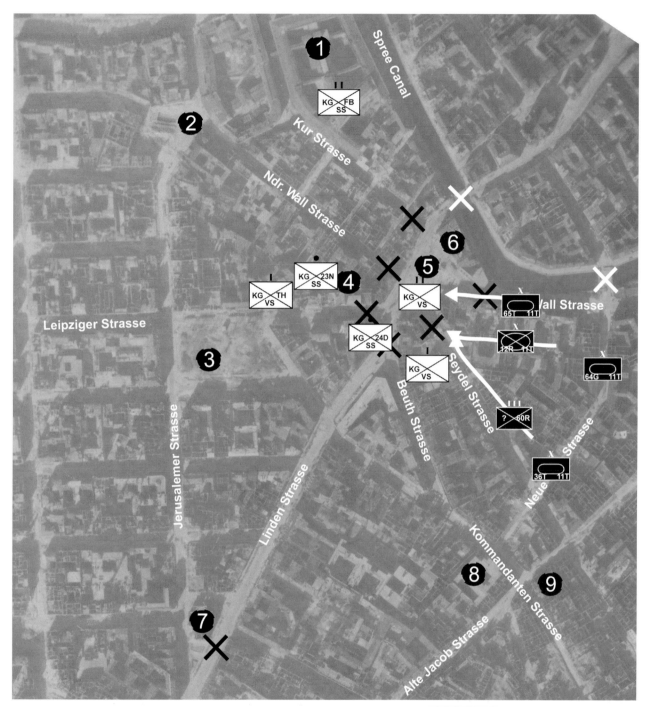

Key Places
1. Reichsbank
2. Hausvogtei Platz
3. Donhoff Platz
4. St. Joseph II Hospital
5. Spittelmarkt Platz
6. Foreign Exchange
7. Jerusalemer Church
8. Reich Stationery Office
9. Theatre

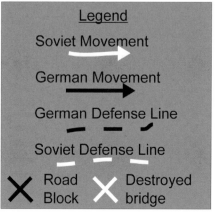

Legend

Soviet Movement

German Movement

German Defense Line

Soviet Defense Line

Road Block

Destroyed bridge

A rare photo indeed! Here we see a lend-lease Sherman Firefly being employed by an unidentified Soviet unit in Berlin.
Photo courtesy of RGAKFD Moscow.

The barrel of a Soviet T-34/76 tank points at buildings along a Berlin street. Judging by the civilians in the background, and vehicles parked along the road, this was most likely taken after the ending of the fighting.
Photo courtesy of RGAKFD Moscow.

A Soviet Officer pauses for a photo at a knocked out Panther Panzerstellung positioned at a key road junction containing a U-Bahn entrance and a raised S-Bahn track. This area was clearly fiercely contested.
Photo courtesy of RGAKFD Moscow.

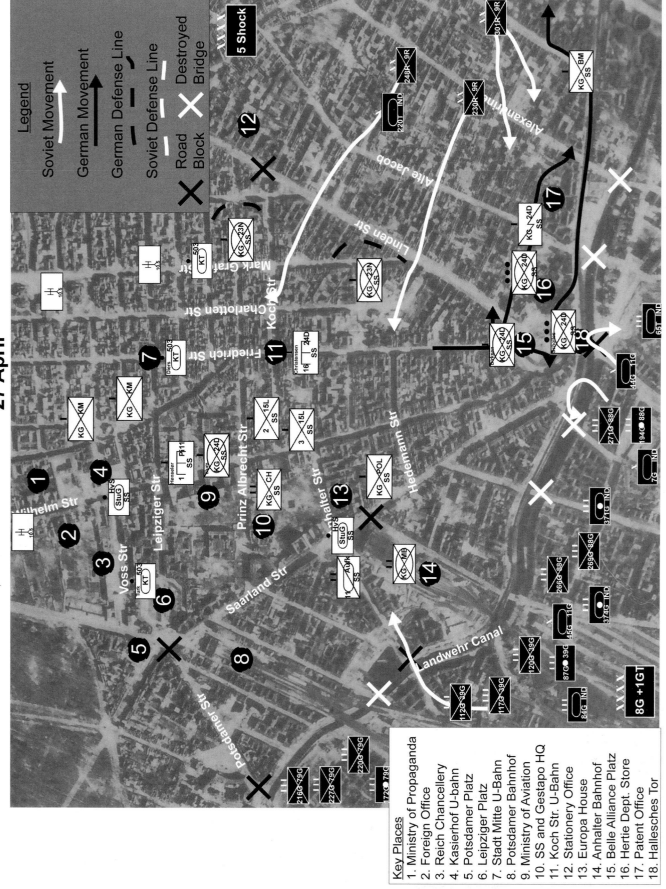

Central District
27 April

Legend
Soviet Movement
German Movement
German Defense Line
Soviet Defense Line
Road Block
Destroyed Bridge

Key Places
1. Ministry of Propaganda
2. Foreign Office
3. Reich Chancellery
4. Kasierhof U-bahn
5. Potsdamer Platz
6. Leipziger Platz
7. Stadt Mitte U-Bahn
8. Potsdamer Bahnhof
9. Ministry of Aviation
10. SS and Gestapo HQ
11. Koch Str. U-Bahn
12. Stationery Office
13. Europa House
14. Anhalter Bahnhof
15. Belle Alliance Platz
16. Hertie Dept. Store
17. Patent Office
18. Hallesches Tor

were in order to get someone with a *Panzerfaust*, as Schulz only had a bolt-action rifle. Several boys ran out of the cellar. One 14 year old *Hitlerjugend* grabbed a *Panzerfaust* before racing up the stairs into the darkened street. The T–34/85's turret began a slow turn toward the barricade with the intent to blow it up when suddenly the tank exploded from a side shot by a *Panzerfaust*. As the tank was burning the commander's hatch creaked open and a single Soviet tanker made his way out and surrendered. He was quickly brought to the cellar where his leather pants were taken by a *Fallschirmjäger* and Schulz took his leather jacket, which was a bit oversized. The Soviet tanker was searched and found to have photos of key Berlin locations like Alexanderplatz and the Radio Tower. The prisoner was then taken back to the cinema where Schulz's HQ was still located. Here he was interrogated for two hours then taken outside and let go. The Soviet tanker walked a few paces back toward his lines thinking he was being released when he was shot in the back by the same red-haired *SS* boy that shot the German deserter the day before. In his innocence, Schulz was shocked by this act. He later understood that no Soviet prisoners were being taken and held during the battle. There was no place to hold them under the circumstances so they were immediately shot after interrogation.[29]

CENTRAL DISTRICTS

Neukölln was a burning wasteland after both sides launched attack and counter-attack through the district. It was an uneven contest that Chuikov's soldiers won. German forces evacuated during the night as units retreated back across the Landwehr Canal into Defense Sector Z. Some unit elements unfortunately found themselves surrounded by Soviets in Neukölln as they were either not notified of the general pull-out or were simply caught as Soviets bypassed them in their advance through the rubble. One platoon of French *SS*, caught behind the lines tried to escape north. One of their members pretended to act like a French Foreign Laborer and walked out into the street. The Soviets questioned him and then let him go on his way.[30] There were so many foreign slave laborers in Berlin that many of the foreign fighters quickly blended into the local population. The Soviets, who were primarily concerned if you were German, often let foreign speaking inhabitants alone. This was especially true if foreign fighters took the extra precaution of shedding their military uniform and donning civilian attire. Many German soldiers who spoke Dutch, Lithuanian, or Polish easily escaped Berlin this way after capitulation. Chuikov's forces now closed on the Landwehr Canal as they started to evaluate potential crossing sites.

Defense Sector Z became the main focal point for attack as Chuikov's rapid advance into Tempelhof and Neukölln drove a wedge into the southern defense of the city forcing the defenders back across the Landwehr Canal. Repositioning of German forces continued throughout the area. It also appeared the Weidling was able to win the argument over *Nordland's* deployment with Krukenberg as the Danes and Norwegians were parceled out throughout the sector. The newly-formed *Kampfgruppe Bachmann* received orders to move east to the area of Kottbusser Tor on Skalitzerstrasse where the 9th Rifle Corps started to advance. The remainder of the *SS-Pz.Aufkl.Abt.11*, and two StuG IIIs were ordered to occupy the Anhalter Bahnhof currently defended by a variety of local forces and a *Kampfgruppe* from *Müncheberg*.[31] *Danmark's* remaining soldiers, operating under the command of *SS-Pz.Aufkl.Abt.11*, were now pushed out from Anhalt S-Bahn station along the Landwehr Canal to Belle-Alliance-Platz. The remnants of *Norge* deployed in a variety of *Kampfgruppe* along the line Lindenstraße -Spittelmarkt-Fischerinsel (Fischerinsel is also known as Fishermann's Island or Museum Island). *Nordland's* pioneers,

Victoria Park is the highest elevation in Berlin. It also has a natural spring in the center of the park. Once Chuikov took Tempelhof airport, he ordered 155mm howitzers placed at the top of the hill and commenced firing indiscriminately at the city center and at both the Potsdamer and Anhalt S-Bahn stations. Author's collection.

Apparently a German sniper was active along this already Soviet occupied street (see the three Soviet PAK guns on either side of the street). A Soviet SU-76 assault gun returns the favor by opening fire on the suspected position. The open top SU-76s proved extremely vulnerable to both *Panzerfaust* and sniper fire. Photo courtesy of the Bundesarchiv.

artillery and other support units were also parceled out, primarily in Defense Sector Z. The combat effectiveness of this German unit and others began to significantly drop by 27 April due to ammunition shortages, lack of heavy weapons, and non-existent artillery and mortar support.

As *Kampfgruppe Bachmann* moved east, a company-sized *Kampfgruppe* from *SS-Pz.Gren.Rgt. Danmark* was dispatched to take the unit's place at the Hallesches Tor. Scholles' men were among a squad from *Kampfgruppe Bachmann* that presumably remained at the Tor to coordinate the positioning of the arriving unit. An assault group from the former *II./SS-Pz.Gren.Rgt. Danmark's* signal company was formed and placed in reserve behind the main defense line. Diers' King Tiger took up position at the Stadtmitte U-Bahn station orientated toward Belle-Alliance-Platz, also in reserve.[32]

Mummert made his HQ in the Anhalter Bahnhof after Bärenfänger was field promoted to an equivalent rank and given command of Defense Sectors A and B. Next to the Anhalter Bahnhof were Potsdamer Platz and the Potsdamer Bahnhof. Both the Anhalter and Potsdamer Bahnhof were the main rail transportation hubs that serviced southern Germany. The whole area was targeted extensively for aerial attack by the Western Allies and was essentially in ruins, though the Germans managed to keep some rail traffic moving in and out of the stations before the Soviet assault. This area now became a target for Chuikov who moved 105mm howitzers onto the slopes of Victoria Park to fire over open sights at the two Bahnhof stations. Victoria Park, just two blocks north of Tempelhof, is the highest elevation in Berlin with a commanding view of the city, a fact that Chuikov quickly took to his advantage as his guns could rake a wide stretch of the city.

The retreat over the Landwehr Canal ushered in a sense of desperation among many Germans who began to exhibit signs of defeatism under the continued pressure of non-stop combat. Flying court-martials increased with frequency in Defense Sector Z as a result. Mummert detested the fact that other soldiers, many of whom were young and without combat experience, were judging the lives of his experienced combat troops. He quickly ordered that no flying court-martials would occur in his area and that anyone trying to implement a summary execution behind his lines would be shot.[33] *Müncheberg's* remaining Panthers and Tiger Is moved back to the Tiergarten where the central tank repair facility was set up after the fall of Spandau. Many of his Panthers slowly ran out of fuel and were subsequently set up as fixed anti-tank positions. It appears that by the evening of 1 May no Panthers or Tiger Is were operational due to lack of fuel or mechanical difficulties. This judgment is based on the lack of any mention of either vehicle types by any of the participants in the various breakouts.

Henseler's men retreated along Urbanstraße all night, fighting the Soviets until they reached the Hallesches Tor and Landwehr Canal in the early morning hours. As Henseler and his men tried to cross the Belle Alliance Bridge they were stopped by a one-armed *Hitlerjugend* leader who refused to let them pass, possibly suspecting that Henseler's force were Seydlitz Troops. Henseler persuaded the man not to fire on his men and eventually he was allowed to move across the bridge and pass the tank barricade positioned on the opposite

A Soviet soldier makes a call over a field phone during the battle. This was probably a staged photograph due to the dramatic backdrop.
Photo courtesy of the Bundesarchiv.

side. Henseler's men moved up to Belle-Alliance-Platz where they ran into a runner from *Nordland* HQ who ordered his company to the Air Ministry on Wilhelmstraße. In the western part of Berlin, Illum's assault company along with the engineer platoon he was assigned also received orders to leave their positions near Spandau and report back to their respective HQs in the city center.[34]

Henseler and his men worked their way up Wilhelmstraße with difficulty. No Soviet artillery was falling at the moment but the intense bombardments of the preceding days showed its effect. Burning buildings, smoke, ruins, downed electrical lines, all made the journey cautious and time consuming. The Air Ministry was intact and swarming with officers and soldiers from every type of unit without any sense of purpose. Henseler took his men upstairs where there was less confusion and for the first time in days they rested and had some cooked ham. After a short rest Henseler set out to find his Battalion HQ located in the cellar of the building. After traversing the long hallways he found his commander and staff in a room drunk. *SS-Sturmbannführer* Voss had a bottle of liquor in one hand and a *Luftwaffe* Secretary on his knee. Henseler was astonished at Voss' behavior and what he said next. Voss said loudly, "Glad to see you made it, old man! Come on, pour yourself a glass of booze, in 24 hours it will all be over—let's drink while we have the time!"[35] Henseler obliged his commander as he settled down with the staff and took the scene into perspective. Apparently all the various pioneer platoon leaders sent out on their mission to secure crossings over the Havel were now recalled back by their commander, presumably on orders from Krukenberg. Soon other company commanders from *SS-Pi.Abt.11* arrived. One of the commanders, Gildish, told Henseler how he reached the Spandau bridges and held them until he was informed that the breakout plan was now off with the replacement of Zeigler. He then took his men back to the city center.[36]

Despair hung in the air of the *Nordland's* Pioneer Battalion's staff. Everyone discussed how they would all commit suicide rather than be taken prisoner by the Soviets once the city fell. While Henseler didn't initially plan on suicide, he was now caught up in the dark mood fostered by his drunkenness and he agreed to kill himself when the time came. In his stupor he began to wander the basement halls of the Air Ministry and found that the entire cellar was full of people having one last romantic encounter before the end came. "Unlimited supplies of liquor were on hand and everyone was drinking furiously. In one room soldiers were standing on tables and singing old marching songs, in another a phonograph was playing a scratchy record of jazz music. Here and there couples were thrashing on sofas or in odd corners, completely ignoring the other people around them."[37] At around 1900 a *Luftwaffe Hauptmann* from the communications section ran down the hall waving a piece of paper exclaiming that "The Wenck Army is on its way to Berlin! We just have to hold out for 24 hours! The Wenck Army is here!"[38] This electrified everyone, who only moments before were acting out of drunken instincts. Now orders were being shouted, "Combat commands report to your posts!" As the activity continued, Henseler stumbled back upstairs and slept the night with his men.[39]

At dawn, Chuikov's artillery opened up at a number of key crossings along the Landwehr Canal. Chuikov's artillery targeted the Belle Allianz Bridge and suspected German positions in the Hallesches Tor beyond in preparation for an assault by the 29th Guards Corps currently waiting in positions along Barutherstraße. At 1100 just to the east of Scholles' position, along the Prinzenstraße crossing, a flood of soldiers in panic crossed the bridge. *Volkssturm, Wehrmacht, Luftwaffe*, officers up to the rank of major and higher officers from staff HQs were seen escaping out of Neukölln and Tempelhof with the renewed Soviet artillery barrage. These were the last remnants of the defenders from the day before that managed to stay hidden in the ruins until they could make a break for the northern bank of the Landwehr Canal. Scholles noted how these soldiers seemed defeated and in despair as they were either throwing their weapons away or handing them to the *Nordland* troops they passed. Presumably many of these men were from *Müncheberg* as *Generalmajor* Mummert appeared and calmed the soldiers around the bridge. Due to the proximity of Chuikov's forces moving along the southern bank of the Landwehr Canal, Scholles' unit weakened their position at the Hallesches Tor and moved a smaller *Kampfgruppe* that included the assault reserve signal company to bolster the area of Prinzenstraße.[40]

Soviet artillery dominated the fighting for Berlin. The Soviets set up their guns wherever ground conditions allowed. They opened up their day's offensive with artillery and continued to use it until nightfall. Photo courtesy of the Bundesarchiv.

As Chuikov's artillery raked the north bank of the Landwehr Canal, scouts from the 9th Rifle Corps infiltrated between the Norwegians and Danish positions through Orainienstraße and by 1200 they reached Charlottenstraße. The Russian scouts maneuvered around *Danmark's* outposts–behind their primary defensive line along the Landwehr Canal. There were apparently no strong German units between the Spittelmarkt and the Hallesches Tor, although *Kampfgruppe Bachmann* was dispatched to presumably seal this gap. The Soviets also tried to push through to the Reich Chancellery. They attempted this maneuver through an intrepid battlefield ruse often used by both sides during the war. The Soviets took two captured Czech-made Panzer 38Ts and placed them in the vanguard of an armor column of T–34/85s all flying Swastikas from their turrets. The goal was to pass the column off as German and presumably breach any manned German defenses without direct combat. As the Soviet column passed into German lines, the Germans quickly realized the trick and all enemy tanks were quickly knocked out by *Nordland's* Sturmgeschütz III assault guns positioned in reserve. At least one Soviet tank crew was captured.[41] The appearance of Soviets so close to the Reich Chancellery and in the center of Defense Sector Z caused serious concern in the *Führerbunker*. Mohnke heard the reports and quickly ordered the bridges blown across the Landwehr Canal. Mohnke also ordered 10.5cm light artillery pieces brought from the Tiergarten and placed in the Gendarmenmarkt to cover Belle-Alliance-Platz, in Pariser Platz to cover Unter-Den-Linden-Palace, and in Leipziger Straße aimed at the critical road junction of the Spittelmarkt. There were only twelve rounds per gun and when they were done firing, the men were ordered to deploy as infantry.[42] By the afternoon Russian assault groups from the 9th Rifle Corps began an advance along Charlottenstraße following the reports of their scouts. The movement of the 5th Shock Army's 9th Rifle Corps was unknown and uncoordinated with Chuikov's forces operating blocks away along the south bank of the Landwehr Canal.

The bridge to the right of Hallesches Tor was immediately blown and rendered impassable. *SS-Pioneers* sent by Mohnke moved to the Hallesches Tor and began wiring that bridge for demolition. Scholles' unit was now ordered back to Belle-Alliance-Platz from their positions. Their mission was to hold this vital road junction with only a few machine-guns, no anti-tank guns, or Panzers for support. The *SS-Pioneers* managed to blow the bridge only partially. After the dust from the explosion settled enough of the bridge was left intact that Soviet tanks could still cross. The rest of the remnants of *SS-Pz.Gren.Rgt.24 Danmark* not already assigned to a defensive position arrived at the Hallesches Tor under command of *SS-Untersturmführer* Dirksen who was the former commander of *11./SS-Pz.Gren.Rgt.24*. Dirksen immediately called for volunteers to move to the areas on the left and right of the Belle Alliance Bridge along Gitschinerstraße. The Soviets became alarmed at the rapid explosions and rushed to the crossings in an attempt to get their tanks across before any more bridges were blown. T–34/85s quickly moved up to the Landwehr Canal and began blasting the German positions on the opposite side of the bridge killing or wounding *Nordland* soldiers holding their positions. By 1430 the first Soviet tanks, presumably from Chuikov's 44th Guards Tank Brigade, crossed the Landwehr Canal into the Hallesches Tor.

Dirksen launched a counterattack from the ruins and destroyed a T–34/85 with a *Panzerfaust* temporarily blocking any further moves across the bridge by Soviet armor. Soviet infantry from the 9th Rifle Corps advanced west from Charlottenstraße and occupied several city blocks directly behind the *Norge* and *Danmark* defenders forcing them to abandon their defensive positions at Belle-Allianz-Platz. Scholles' unit moved through the U-Bahn tunnels north in the hope to avoid any firefight with the Soviets, while other German forces were forced west to the Anhalter Bahnhof. Soviet artillery and aerial bombs tore huge holes in the street, exposing the U-Bahn tunnels. Soviet soldiers infiltrated into the U-Bahn system and prepared ambushes in the tunnels for Scholles and other German

Soviet ISU-152s take a break from the fighting.
Photo courtesy of the Cornelius Ryan Collection, Mahn Center, Alden Library, Ohio University, Athens, OH.

units. By dusk a number of vicious, close-quarter skirmishes with grenades and automatic weapons took place in the U-Bahn tunnels. Scholles' men found it difficult to hold the U-Bahn line from Belle Alliance to Kochstraße with only 30 men. Reports of the desperate situation were sent by runners back to Krukenberg at Division HQ in the Stadtmitte U-Bahn station. These reports caused Krukenberg to reorganize the defense of the area. *SS-Untersturmführer* Christensen was immediately appointed battle commander of Friedrichstraße. He quickly established his HQ at the Kochstraße U-Bahn station and prepared to defend the area against any more advances by the 9th Rifle Corps.[43]

The combined 8th Guards and 1st Guards Tank Armies now occupied a wide stretch of territory along the south bank of the Landwehr Canal running from Neukölln in the east, to the Zoo Bunker in the west. Each of Chuikov's corps were assigned their independent missions and moved to consolidate their positions. The 39th Guards Rifle Division fought all night to maintain control of a series of factories near the Landwehr Canal. In the morning the division realized they were almost opposite the Anhlater Bahnhof and quickly moved northwest toward the Schöneberger Bridge in an early attempt to seize a crossing point across the canal.[44] Chuikov's soldiers moved well west of the inter-front boundary between the 1st Byelorussian and 1st Ukrainian Fronts in order to block Koniev's advance on the Reichstag. This dangerous maneuver during wartime urban operations resulted in dramatic friendly fire instances starting later in the day.

South of the 39th Guards Rifle Division's position German defenders were pouring heavy machine-gun fire onto Russian positions. The Germans were located throughout a multi-storeyed building opposite the Heinrich von Kleist Park. The heavy machine-gun fire dominated the freight yard that Chuikov's infantry passed through heading west. Chuikov decided that this position could no longer be tolerated and ordered the 41st Engineer Brigade equipped with flamethrowers to eliminate the German defenders.[45] The use of flamethrowers in an urban environment was often not enough to eliminate a position. In this case, the flamethrowers were used to start a fire in the building's basement to smoke the Germans out of the upper floors. The Engineers' efforts had little effect. It took storming the first floor followed by an assault into the basement using flamethrowers as direct fire weapons to flush the defenders into the streets where Soviet soldiers waited to gun down the building's former occupants. Further west Soviet tanks now broke into the area around the Zoo Flak Tower and fired directly at the bunker windows with little effect. The Zoo's Flak Tower guns could not depress low enough to fire down at the Soviet tanks so tank-hunting teams were called on to destroy the Soviet armor.

SOUTHERN DISTRICTS

Koniev's forces closed in on the S-Bahn inner defensive ring that ran from Westkreuz to Schöneberg S-Bahn Stations in the southwest of the city. Rybalko's forces received extra rifle divisions from Luchinskiy in testimony to the lack of manpower and intensity of the fighting.[46] *Pz.Gren.Rgt.51* continued a fighting withdrawal through Schmargendorf, then behind the S-Bahn inner defense line back to Berliner Straße in Wilhelmsdorf.[47] They were pushed back by the 6th Guards Tank Corps, while on the right, against little opposition, the 9th Mechanized Corps along with the 61st Rifle Division from the 28th Army's 128th Rifle Corps took Wilmersdorf, Innsbrucker Platz, and Schönberg S-Bahn stations advancing well into the Schöneberg district. The 7th Guards Tank Corps, along with the 28th Army's 20th Rifle Division now launched an attack up both sides of the Hohenzollerndamm and Avus where the *Pz.Gren.Rgt.30* had launched their counter-attack to reach the *20.Pz.Gren.Div.* the previous day. In this case, Koniev's forces decided to conduct a night infiltration without any heavy artillery fire first. It was a change in tactics, as the Russians struggled to identify more adaptive techniques to overcome the German defenders.

During the night Soviet infantry infiltrated and attacked the position of the *II./Pz.Gr.Rgt.30* and Arno's artillery battery causing alarm among the defenders. The initial infiltration was quickly eliminated but the Russian infantry continued to find new paths through the side streets and rubble that offered less resistance. By daybreak the Germans realized that they were surrounded by the Russians who cut their land cable back to the Zoo Bunker. Soon five T–34s began a drive up the Hohenzollerndamm but the German infantry destroyed three with *Panzerfausts* and temporarily halted the Soviets. Now surrounded, a breakout toward German lines near Hallensee S-Bahn station was planned for late afternoon. At 1700, 1,000 German soldiers, along with civilians trying to escape the advancing Russians, made their way north through the side streets. The Soviets soon realized what was happening and launched a series of attacks to stop Arno's group from reaching German lines. Near the Hallensee Lake two T–34s opened fire at the mass of soldiers and civilians causing panic. Several Panzergrenadiers move toward the tanks in the rubble and destroyed them with *Panzerfausts*. The Russians then moved up 76mm Pak guns to cover a direct assault launched by Soviet infantry yelling 'Hurrah.' The German rearguard managed to hold back the Russian infantry assault during close-quarter combat in the ruins allowing the bulk of the retreating soldiers and civilians to reach the Hallensee S-Bahn station several hours later. Körner and *SS-Untersturmführer* Schröder took up positions with their King Tigers at Kurfürstenstraße and at the Hallensee S-Bahn station opposite the advance of Koniev's 7th Guards Tank Corps.[48] They were ordered to the area after reports reached Defense Sector Z about the new Soviet assault from the southwest. The King Tigers provided needed cover to the retreating Germans and knocked out two T–34s in the process. The Panzergrenadiers that made it back to German lines now took up a defensive position behind the S-Bahn inner defense ring. Other Panzer reinforcements now moved out of Defense Sector Z toward Adolf-Hitler Platz to cover the northern flank of the *18.Pz.Gr.Div.'s* positions. Two 8.8cm Panzerjäger Tiger (P) Elefant self-propelled guns were dispatched to fight in the western sector by Mohnke.[49] These massive self-propelled anti-tank guns were from *s.PzJg.Kp.614*. This unit made its way into Berlin by way of Potsdam after Koniev's forces destroyed *Kampfgruppe Ritter* near Kummersdorf. They are the only known Elefants to fight in Berlin and very little is known of their tactical deployment.

A company of JS-2s carrying infantry support advance down a side street. It appears that a Soviet JS-2 was destroyed in the intersection up ahead, possibly causing the pause in operations. Smoke billows from the building to the right suggesting that combat recently occurred in this area.
Photo courtesy of the Cornelius Ryan Collection, Mahn Center, Alden Library, Ohio University, Athens, OH.

WESTERN DISTRICTS

The 55th Guards Tank Brigade under the command of Colonel David Dragunsky launched an independent offensive through the western district of Berlin. This unit was reinforced by the 7th Guards Tank Corps reserves of a battalion of motorized infantry, a rocket-launcher battalion, ten JS-2s, a company of ISU–152s self-propelled guns, plus two artillery brigades. This was intended as an independent force whose goal was to clear the Grunewald forest district to the Havel and advance to the banks of the Spree River at Ruhleben where it was expected to locate the troops of the 1st Byelorussian Front. As the reinforced brigade set out on its advance it immediately came across the German Flak Battery firing in support of the Gatow airfield. Dragunsky called in Soviet aircraft to knock it out as they knew the power of the 8.8s against armor and they did not want to directly engage the German guns. His force continued their cautious advance through the woods after the Flak Battery was knocked out. They reached the northern end of the forested district, just south of the Pichelsdorf Bridges by evening.[50] Their presence became known to the Germans who quickly dispatched forces to strengthen the defense. This area was under the defense of the *Reichsarbeitsdienst* commanded by *General Reichsarbeitsdienst* Decker. His forces put up significant resistance noted in the daily situation brief to Hitler that day.[51] *Pi.Abt.18* from the *18.Pz.Gren.Div.* was quickly dispatched to reinforce the *Hitlerjugend* holding the Pichelsdorf Bridge site. Now that the southeastern access across the Havel via Wannsee was closed to the Germans, it became of the utmost importance to hold the only bridge access over the Havel remain open in case Wenck did reach Berlin or the defenders wanted to breakout.[52]

Gatow and Spandau finally fell to the Soviet's 47th Army by the end of the day. The airfield's fall came not long after the 55th Guards Tank Brigade eliminated the Flak Battery on the eastern bank of the Havel. The remnants of the airfield's German defenders made their way north to the final crossings across the Havel intermingled with other stragglers leaving Spandau.

The reduction of Spandau continued as German stragglers found their way to the Havel crossings throughout the night. Altner's *Kampfgruppe* of *Hitlerjugend* moved through streets aglow from burning fires. The pavement was covered with the burnt corpses of

Spandau
27 April

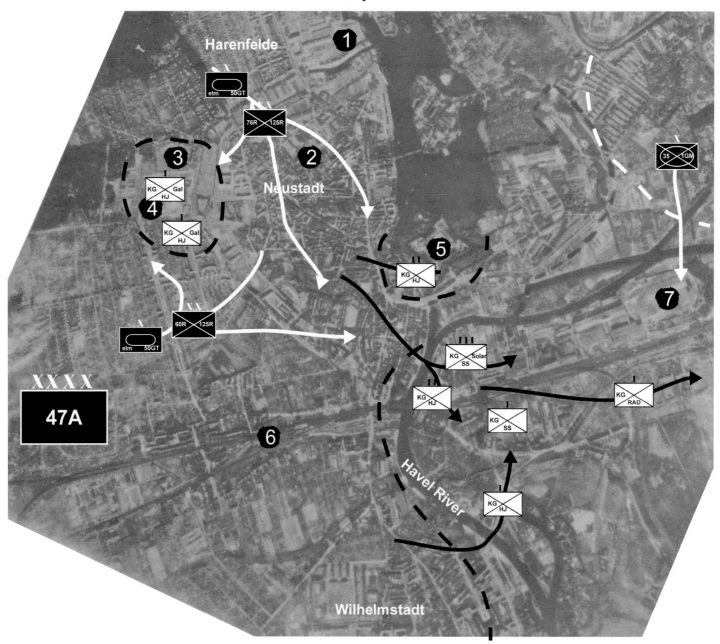

Key Places
1. Hackenfelde Aircraft Instrument Factory
2. Military Supply Depot
3. Napola School
4. Polizei School
5. Zitadel
6. Spandau West Station
7. Ruhleben

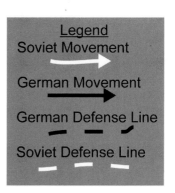

Legend
Soviet Movement
German Movement
German Defense Line
Soviet Defense Line

soldiers, women, and children. It was a haunting experience to the young defenders. In one of many instances of fratricide in Berlin's streets, Altner witnessed a German machine-gun team open fire on a group of suspected enemy soldiers followed by the whoosh of flame from a flamethrower-equipped Panzer that lit up the surrounding buildings. Cries of pain now echoed into the street. The machine-gun team and *Flammpanzer*, however, did not torch advancing Russian soldiers but retreating Germans. Trying to find German lines in the dark was a delicate affair as most troops were now fighting well beyond their physical and mental limits. In the dark any moving shape might be the enemy so they were shot.[53]

Several pockets of Germans continued to hold out within Spandau. The *Luftwaffe's* Galician boys continued to resist at the Napola School and Polizei compound for an unknown period of time. It is likely that they simply fought to the death as their capture by the Soviets would result in immediate execution as traitors to the Motherland. An unknown number of *Hitlerjugend* retreated into the Zitadel and continued to resist until the end of the fighting. The Soviet 47th Army halted its advance into Berlin this day. It now focused on consolidating control over Berlin's districts along the west bank of the Havel. There was just not enough manpower to attempt to breach the east bank of the river where the *Hitlerjugend* were defending in force along the southern crossings. Just across the Havel, the 35th Mechanized Brigade of the 1st Guards Mechanized Corps made the first crossing of the Spree River in the north with the assistance of Polish Engineers. They reached the Ruhleben racecourse just across from Alexander Kasserne without significant resistance.[54]

NORTHERN DISTRICTS

The 3rd Shock Army's 79th Rifle Corps continued advancing its way through Moabit. The 79th Rifle Corps was on a direct advance toward the Spree River and the Reichstag. It advanced unsupported and without any communications with neighboring units. The 79th Rifle Corps had unknowingly located the least-defended sector of Berlin and was heading straight for the prize that drove every Soviet commander during the fighting for Berlin—the Reichstag. The rest of the 3rd Shock Army's corps continued to perform poorly in the street fighting. The 12th Guards Rifle Corps was not able to breach the inner defensive perimeter marked by the raised S-Bahn tracks supported by direct fire from the Humboldt Flak Tower. Further east the 7th Rifle Corps was effectively halted and no longer advanced into Berlin.[55]

Notes to Chapter 6: Assault on Berlin, 27th April Friday

1 OKW File, Last Announcements of OKW, 27 April (RC: 62:8).
2 Krivosheev, p. 158.
3 Ibid.
4 Heiber and Glantz, p. 731. Goebbels reported this number to Hitler during a daily conferece meeting. It has no empirically basis that be crossed checked.
5 Army Group Weichsel War Diary, Apr 20–9, pp. 424 (RC: 68/4)
6 Ibid, p. 428.
7 Schultz-Naumann, p. 31.
8 Army Group Weichsel War Diary, Apr 20–9 pp. 433, 437 (RC: 68/4)
9 Ibid, p. 428.
10 Ibid, p. 434.
11 Ibid, p. 438.
12 Ibid.
13 Ibid, p. 439.
14 Le Tissier, *Slaughter at Halbe*, p. 105.
15 *MS #R-79*, p. 44.
16 Ibid, p. 45.
17 Wenck interview.
18 Ritter, p. 19.
19 MS #B-606, p. 26.
20 Klaus, and Kehlenbeck, pp. 293. See also *12th Armee* operational maps in the Ryan Collection.
21 Koniev unpublished memoir, p. 170.
22 Weidling Interrogation Report, and Weidling, *The Final Battle in Berlin* (RC: 69/2).
23 Heiber, and Glantz, p. 736.
24 Ibid.
25 Ibid, p. 738.
26 Venghaus, p. 161.
27 Ibid, p. 734.
28 Winge interview.
29 Schulz interview.
30 Forbes, pp. 283–4.
31 Michelis, p. 111, Tieke, p. 309, and Landwehr, *Nordic Warriors* p. 153.
32 Schneider, p. 302.
33 Le Tissier, *Race for the Reichstag*, p. 136.
34 Illum interview.
35 Henseler interview.
36 Ibid.
37 Ibid.
38 Ibid. While the author believes this incident probably took place on 28 April, it was left in the original account as described by Henseler.
39 Ibid.
40 Scholles interview.
41 Heiber, and Glantz, p. 731.
42 Ibid.
43 Scholles interview.
44 Abyzov, p. 56.
45 Chuikov, p. 192. In his book Chuikov laments the use of this weapon as a last resort; however, the Soviets were expending so much artillery and rocket shells indiscriminately that a flamethrower's use could hardly be considered inhumane.
   Koniev unpublished interview, p. 172.
46 Engelmann, p. 151.
47 Schneider, p. 302.
48 Heiber, and Glantz, p. 731.
49 Le Tissier, *Race for the Reichstag*, p. 131. Le Tissier suggests that this advance went much further, but no evidence exists to confirm this statement.
50 Heiber, and Glantz, p. 734.
51 Engelmann, pp. 151, 153, and Heiber, and Glantz, p. 734.
52 Altner, p. 125.
53 Ibid, pp. 142, 150.
54 Le Tissier, *Race for the Reichstag*, pp. 132–3.

6

ASSAULT ON BERLIN

28 APRIL
SATURDAY

In the center of the fighting yesterday was the battle in the Berlin area. Shoulder to shoulder with all able-bodied men our troops led a heroic fight against the Bolshevist mass attacks, defended every house and by counter-attack threw the enemy out of the inner defense ring of the city. Through attacks from the area south of Fürstenwalde our units [*9.Armee*] penetrated deeply into the flank of the Bolshevists who operated in the south from Berlin and pierced the main supply lines on the road Baruth-Zossen. Our young divisions full of enthusiasm attacking from the west [*12.Armee*] reached the wooded area of Beelitz and are engaged there in heavy combat.

Attacks from Brandenburg and Rathenow were repulsed with losses. On both sides of Oranienburg attempts of the Bolshevists to cross the Rhein and Hohenzollern Canal collapsed with losses for the enemy. However, southwest of Stettin the Soviets were able to advance towards Prenzlau.[1]

OKW **Radio Broadcast**

Resistance inside Berlin continued as the German defenders were compressed into a banana-shaped pocket. The main centers of resistance continued to be around the Friedrichshain Flak Tower, Alexanderplatz with the Polizeipräsidium in Defense Sectors A and B, the Spittelmarkt, Ministry of Aviation and Leipziger Platz in Defense Sector Z. While the Birkbuschriegel held in Steglitz, Koniev's forces were now in Unter den Eichen in Zehlendorf and at Wilden Eber in Dahlem. The Stössensee Bridge and area around the Radio Tower along the road to Ruhleben continued to remain contested.[2]

A second aerial reinforcement of Berlin occurred in the early morning hours. The *III./SS-Polizei* consisting of 400 *SS* armed for combat were stationed along the Oder Front and subsequently cut off from Berlin by the Soviet offensive. They retreated to Rechlin Airfield where the soldiers were assembled and loaded onto twenty-seven JU–52s for the flight into Berlin as reinforcements. The planes took off one by one and headed to Berlin with the expectation that they land on the east-west access as both Tempelhof and Gatow Airfields had already fallen to the Soviets. On the last flight was Wilhelm Leopold. According to Leopold only his JU–52 landed safely, debarking Leopold and 40 other *SS* soldiers at the Siegessäule. The aircraft was then loaded with wounded, and took off out of Berlin. Leopold and the other *SS-Polizei* marched through the Tiergarten to the Reich Chancellery where they reported and were assigned to the Anhalt S-Bahn station that evening along with members of the *Kriegsmarine*. Once they arrived they took up positions across from the street from the S-Bahn station.[3] It did not appear that any of the other twenty-six aircraft made it into Berlin, as they either landed at Gatow and captured, or they were shot down during the flight. These were the last reinforcements that made it into Berlin from the outside. Outside the city *AGV* was deteriorating.

ARMY GROUP VISTULA

The *3.Panzer Armee* front collapsed. The 2nd Byelorussian Front pierced the Wotan Line in several places cutting off Stettin and driving straight through the gap made in the vicinity of Prenzlau the day before. Reports filtered in at 0400 that upwards of 800 Soviet tanks broke through the German front west of Fürstenwerder along a 25 kilometer wide gap.[4] Throughout the day Heinrici attempted in good faith to seal off the gaps where he could but he purposely avoided sacrificing his troops in wasteful counterattacks constantly being ordered by the *Führerbunker*. He now had to deal with continued emergencies caused by desertions and retreats. This time it was the foreign elements of the *Waffen-SS*. Now that the Soviets broke through the front lines, many of the foreign volunteers began to fear capture by the Soviets and quickly headed west toward the Western Allies. In one telephone conversation he ordered the placement of an intercepting line near Waren to block non-German "SS-men from *Div. Wallonien, Langemarck, Nordland* who by the thousands are on the move from Neubrandenburg toward the west, they are hordes, riding on motor vehicles, even in columns. Terrible disaster is underway. Do everything you can; tomorrow morning no SS man may ride on motor vehicles toward the west!"[5] Heinrici, Manteuffel, and his subordinate commanders, except Steiner, were all in agreement that *AGV* must retreat to the west and avoid being surrounded at all costs. This drove the decision to keep the *7.Pz. Division* away from deploying in Steiner's sector and became the focus of Keitel's rage and dismissal of Heinrici.

Keitel no longer trusted the information he received by radio or telephone from *AGV*. He left his HQ and went out to meet Steiner and find out why his attack never materialized. Keitel learned that the *7.Pz. Division* was not where it was reported the night before by *AGV*. Heinrici had ordered both the *7.Pz.* and *25.Pz.Gren. Divisions* to deploy all available formations to Neustrelitz and confront the

Berlin
28 April

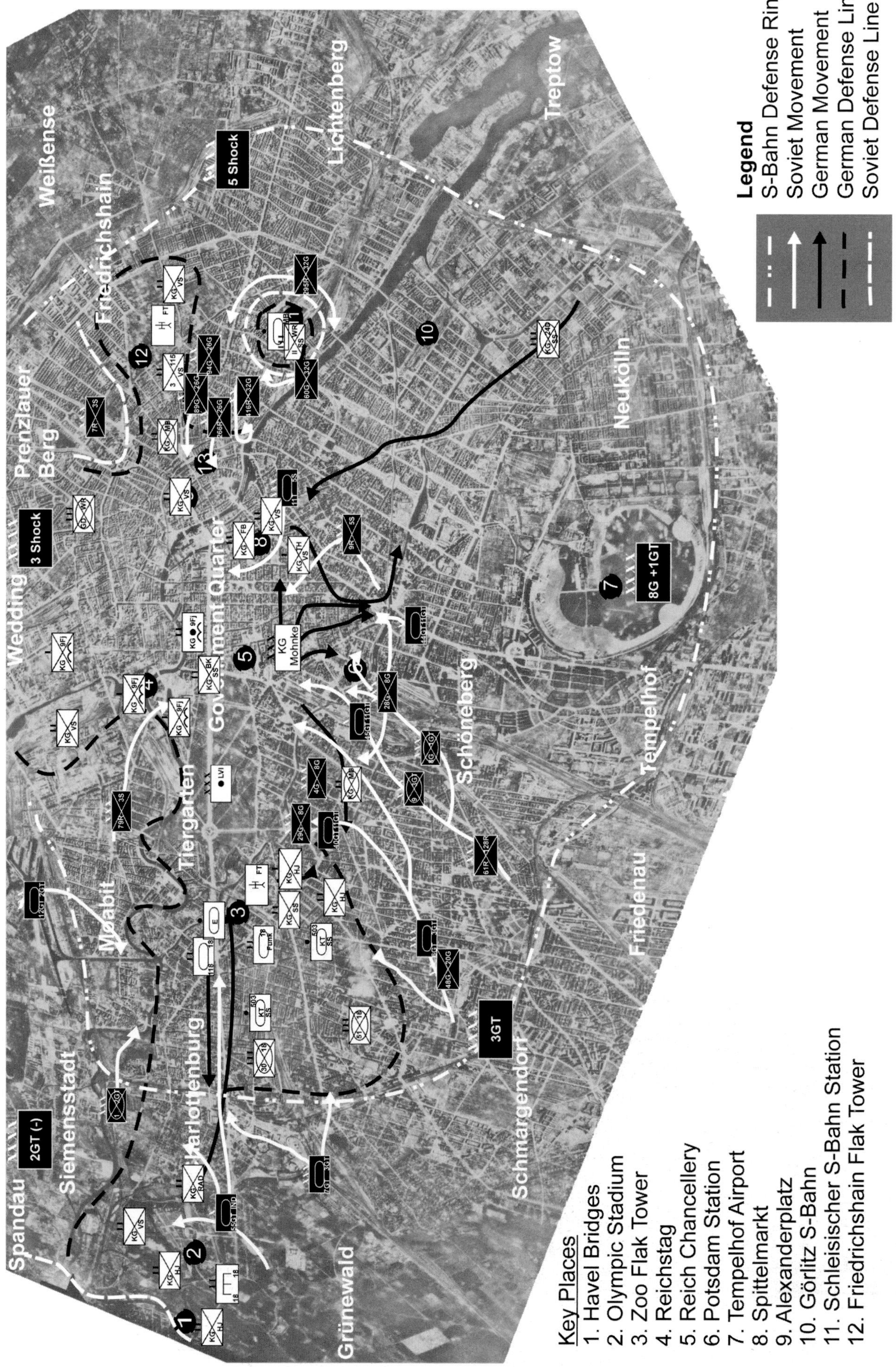

Legend
S-Bahn Defense Ring
Soviet Movement
German Movement
German Defense Line
Soviet Defense Line
Key Places
1. Havel Bridges
2. Olympic Stadium
3. Zoo Flak Tower
4. Reichstag
5. Reich Chancellery
6. Potsdam Station
7. Tempelhof Airport
8. Spittelmarkt
9. Alexanderplatz
10. Görlitz S-Bahn
11. Schleisischer S-Bahn Station
12. Friedrichshain Flak Tower
Weißense
Friedrichshain
Lichtenberg
Treptow
Prenzlauer Berg
Wedding
Government Quarter
Tiergarten
Moabit
Spandau
Siemensstadt
Charlottenburg
Grünewald
Schmargendorf
Friedenau
Schöneberg
Tempelhof
Neukölln
5 Shock
3 Shock
2GT (-)
3GT
8G +1GT
KG Mohnke

Soviet breakthrough along the flank in order to save the rest of the army group. In giving this order Heinrici overrode the *Führerbunker's* order to employ these forces in the relief attack on Berlin.[6] Keitel flew into a rage and immediately asked to meet with Heinrici and Manteuffel.[7] Unknown to Keitel, Heinrici and his subordinate commanders decided to withdraw the army group to the west. Heinrici had no intention of letting Hitler cause yet another pocket like the *9.Armee*.[8] Heinrici met with Keitel and Manteuffel in the afternoon at a predetermined crossroads where Keitel blasted Heinrici's handling of the operational situation along the *3.Panzer Armee's* front line. Manteuffel expected that Keitel might attempt to arrest Heinrici so he ensured that the crossroads were surrounded by his own men in ambush. The meeting occurred without incident although harsh words were exchanged between Keitel and Heinrici. After the meeting Keitel and Heinrici had a phone conversation in the early morning hours of 29 April. Keitel had a chance to meet with Jodl after his discussion with Heinrici and discussed the operational situation. During the phone conversation both Keitel and Heinrici exchanged accusations of interference and lack of judgment. In the end Keitel concluded the conversation with "I am relieving you herewith of your command, transfer your duties onto Gen. von Manteuffel and move to Plön, putting yourself at the disposal of the Army Reserve."[9] *AGV* Chief of Staff von Trotha was also relieved. Manteuffel refused the command and *Generaloberst* Kurt Student was asked to take over the last days of *AGV*.[10]

AGV's participation in the battle of Berlin was over. Heinrici had set into motion a plan to defend the Oder River line, preserve his troops, keep the Soviets out of Berlin, and if he was successful, force the Western Allies over the Elbe to capture the territory that planned to be given the Soviet Union as part of 'Eclipse'. Under the circumstances he directed his forces as best as he could despite disastrous orders from Hitler and the *German High Command*. Berlin was now under direct assault, the *9.Armee* was encircled but moving west and the *3rd Panzer Armee* avoided the trappings of being surrounded. Manteuffel now focused on bringing his soldiers west across the Elbe—the demarcation line that many Germans and non-Germans sought.

12. ARMEE

For the second time in a week the three main divisions of the *XX Korps* redeployed for an attack. The new attack was toward Potsdam and Berlin to the northeast. This feat was carried out with significant precision under less than favorable circumstances. First, *Hutten* disengaged the Soviets outside of Wittenberg, then deployed to an assembly area northwest of Belzig. *Scharnhorst* deployed to an assembly area to the left of *Hutten* just east of Belzig. Both divisions accomplished this feat quickly thanks to the newly-recovered stretch of autobahn that *Scharnhorst* took back from the Soviets during the counterattack the day before. *Körner* meanwhile began to pull back from Treuenbrietzen and moved out to the flanks in order to screen the territory vacated by *Scharnhorst* to the south. *Körner* also began preparations for their own assault to the northeast to protect the right flank of the offensive. Once their deployment was complete, *Hutten*, *Scharnhorst*, and *Körner* launched their attack in the evening of 28 April with great success. North of Belzig was *Schill* and *Sturmgeschütz Brig. 1170*. This combined unit completed their mobilization and moved out directly north on *Hutten's* left flank.[11] The 6th Guards Mechanized Corps was already stretched in its assigned task to bottle up the Germans in Potsdam. The surprise German counterattack through the evening caught it completely off-guard, forcing it to pull back.

Wenck's advance met little Russian resistance at first, although it increased the closer to Potsdam and Berlin they advanced. During the evening, radio contact was established with Reymann's *Armeegruppe Spree*. Reymann immediately energized his troops and started them east along the lakes to reach Wenck's lines. His men, fearing final surrender to the Soviets, looked to Wenck as their savior.

Some sources place the start of Wenck's offensive toward Berlin on 26 April. This confusion is drawn from the lack of empirical sources and the overuse of Wenck's confused postwar account where he claims that his offensive was launched on 26 April and drove 18 kilometers to reach Beelitz.[12] The problem is that none of the units in the *XX Korps* were in a position to reach Beelitz in anything less than 25 kilometers. In addition, the two key divisions, *Scharnhorst* and *Hutten*, were still well to the south. *Hutten* was over 40 kilometers away at Wittenberg.[13] The reality is that Wenck launched an attack east as originally ordered with *Körner* that was effectively blocked by

A destroyed 8.8cm Flak 37 AA gun and vehicles (inc. Praga RV truck with a Flak 38) from the *Ferdinand von Schill Infanterie Division* of the *12.Armee*.
Photo courtesy of ASKM.

Eastern Districts
28 April

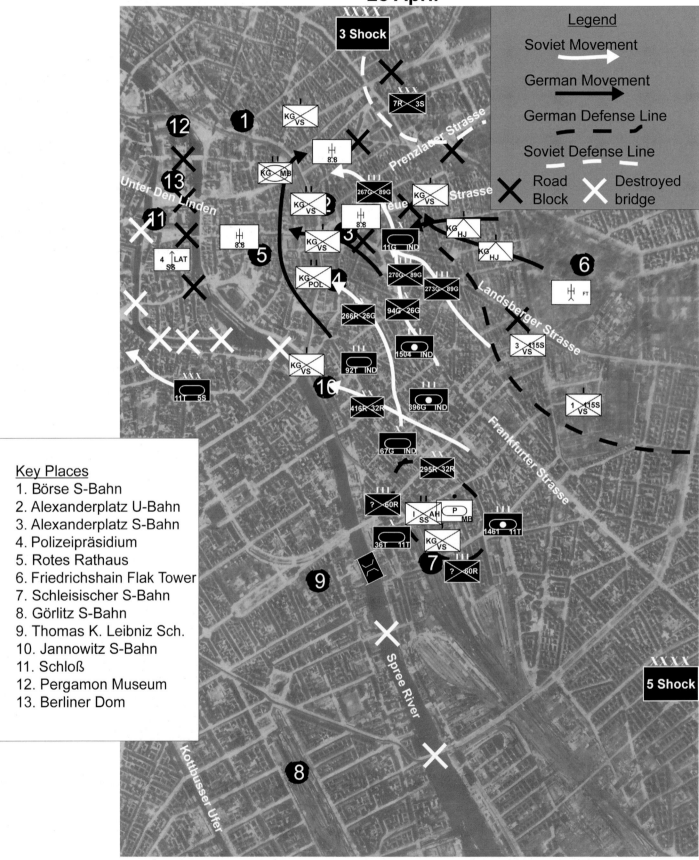

Legend

Soviet Movement

German Movement

German Defense Line

Soviet Defense Line

Road Block

Destroyed bridge

Key Places
1. Börse S-Bahn
2. Alexanderplatz U-Bahn
3. Alexanderplatz S-Bahn
4. Polizeipräsidium
5. Rotes Rathaus
6. Friedrichshain Flak Tower
7. Schleisischer S-Bahn
8. Görlitz S-Bahn
9. Thomas K. Leibniz Sch.
10. Jannowitz S-Bahn
11. Schloß
12. Pergamon Museum
13. Berliner Dom

A rare photograph of a destroyed experimental 8.8cm Pak 43/3 Waffenträger SP AT gun from the *3./Panzerjäger Abteilung* from the *Ullrich von Hutten Infanterie Division* of the 12.Armee. This vehicle was probably dispatched from the German Proving Grounds at Kummersdorf. Photo courtesy of ASKM.

Koniev's forces. He then decided on his own to rescue the garrison and Potsdam through an attack northeast after a surprise redeployment of his forces. He also hoped to be able to hold his line long enough for Busse to reach him as well.

FÜHRERBUNKER

Within the *Führerbunker* Hitler continued to inquire about the status of the various relief attacks. According to the *OKW* War Diary Krebs stated in a conversation with Keitel that Hitler believed all was lost in Berlin if no relief was forthcoming in 48 hours. This statement foreshadowed Hitler's suicide on 30 April. Telephone (landline) communications with the Reich Chancellery and the outside world were finally cut by the Soviets at 1238 hours. Only wireless communications were possible through the Radio Tower or relayed by runner.[14] By 2100 hours news of Himmler's peace talks with Count Bernadotte of Sweden was intercepted by the Propaganda Ministry. This revelation sent Hitler into a depressed mood as he now felt abandoned by not only Göring, but also Himmler, who he considered among his closest supporters. In the evening Hitler married Eva Braun. At 0130 hours on 29 April the marriage ceremony was completed. A bewildered *Volkssturm* soldier, Gauamtsleiter Walter Wagner, was brought in to perform the marriage ceremony. Shortly afterward Hitler dictated his last will and testimony to one of his secretaries, naming Dönitz his successor.[15]

The Jannowitz S-Bahn station on the east bank of the Spree River where German defenders under the command of Rogmann halted the initial Soviets attempt to cross the river. Author's collection.

Kottbusser Tor where *Kampfgruppe Bachmann* was sent to hold the crossing over the Landwehr Canal and the eastern approaches to the Government Quarter. Note the dominating presence of the raised S-Bahn tracks. Author's collection.

EASTERN DISTRICTS

Fierce fighting continued to rage all along the east bank of the Spree to the Friedrichshain Flak Tower. Berzarin's 5th Shock Army could not afford to bypass the pockets of German defenders any longer. If Berzarin thought about rerouting his troops through the 11th Tank Corps or 9th Rifle Corps crossing points to the south he must have realized that the difficulty in doing so might prove disastrous while the Germans held key defensive points in his rear area. He was now the appointed Governor of Berlin and pacification of his own operational area was paramount. He subsequently issued the following orders:

> According to an order of the High Command of the Red Army, I am in charge of all administrative and political power!
>
> 1. Dissolution of the NSDAP (National Socialist German Workers Party) and all organizations connected with it
>
> 2. Registration of high-personnel of all government and party offices within 48 hours
>
> 3. Resumption of work in all public operations
>
> 4. Introduction of occupation money
>
> 5. Temporary stoppage of all financing business of banks and sealing-up of safe[s]
>
> 6. Handing over to the district commanders, within 72 hours of all weapons, munitions, radio receivers, radio transmitters, cameras, automobiles, gasoline and oil
>
> 7. Sealing up of all printing plants
>
> Curfew from 10 p.m. to 8 a.m. Black-out to be continued. Religious services in churches and entertainment and restaurant service authorized until 9 p.m.[16]

Berzarin worked his difficult situation by using psychological operations. Bright yellowish-white notes requesting unconditional surrender were dropped by biplane throughout his sector and Soviet trucks now worked their way up and down the side streets blaring requests to surrender, according to one *Müncheberg* veteran.[17] Failing the use of psychological operations, Berzarin was not shy to employ direct combat.

The 26th Guard Rifle Corps' 94th Guards Rifle Division was detailed to support the 89th Guards Rifle Division assigned the task of attacking Alexanderplatz from the east and northeast. They were ordered to break through the German defensive line outside of Alexanderplatz and drive into the area where the 7th Rifle Corps should have been operating. Behind their lines Günzel's force continued to launch sorties against the Russians from the Friedrichshain Flak Tower across Palisaderstraße.[18] According to the 29 April issue of *Der Panzerbär*, the Soviets broke through the area with 26 T–34/85s—these were probably the remaining tanks of the 11th Independent Tank Brigade. A force numbering 150 soldiers conducted a sortie out of the Flak Tower and destroyed 10 of the Soviet tanks, forcing the rest back.[19]

Outside Alexanderplatz was the Polizeipräsidium. This was a fortress-like building that stood on the eastern side of the square dominating the approaches from Neue Königstraße to the northeast, Landsberger Straße to the east, and Alexanderstraße to the southeast. The Polizeipräsidium was the main Polizei HQ in Berlin and housed offices for the Counter Intelligence Division, Gestapo, and Polizei Signal Communications. Next to the Polizeipräsidium was a smaller building that also held the Gestapo Main Offices for Berlin. German heavy machine-gun, *Panzerfaust*, and small arms fire raked the main avenues of approach to this building defended by the now usual mix of *SS*, *Polizei*, *Hitlerjugend*, and *Volkssturm* found in Defense Sector A and B. It is conceivable that the building's height and communications

A Soviet infantry squad with a JS-2 in support advance into the ruins. Soviet infantry and armor never worked effectively together during the battle. The result was grievous tank losses. Photo courtesy of the Cornelius Ryan Collection, Mahn Center, Alden Library, Ohio University, Athens, OH.

A Soviet T-34/85 rolls over a German barricade. This is a still from the Soviet post war film *The Fall of Berlin*. It illustrates the blinding effects of smoke caused by burning buildings, dust and petrol, generated during the battle by moving armor. Visibility was often measured by meters.

Soviet infantry unit advances down a Berlin street. Movement had to be quick if in the open, otherwise you became an easy sniper target. The longer the battle took the more anxious Soviet commanders were to keep their forces moving toward the Reichstag. Photo courtesy of the Cornelius Ryan Collection, Mahn Center, Alden Library, Ohio University, Athens, OH.

Central District
28 April

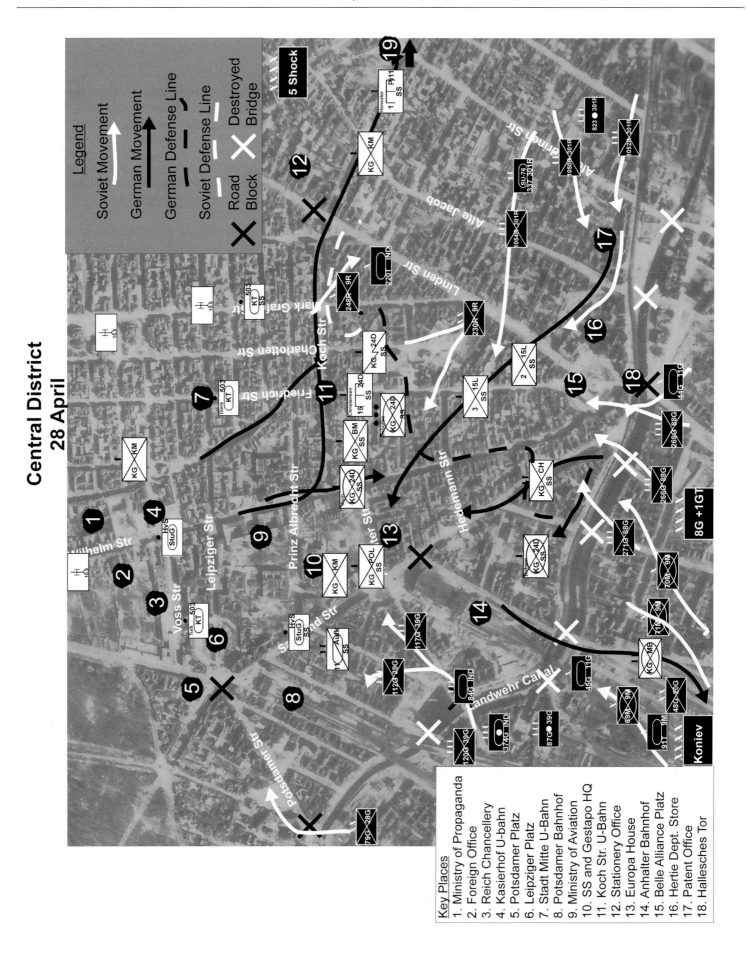

Legend

Soviet Movement

German Movement

German Defense Line

Soviet Defense Line

✕ Road Block

✕ Destroyed Bridge

Key Places
1. Ministry of Propaganda
2. Foreign Office
3. Reich Chancellery
4. Kasierhof U-bahn
5. Potsdamer Platz
6. Leipziger Platz
7. Stadt Mitte U-Bahn
8. Potsdamer Bahnhof
9. Ministry of Aviation
10. SS and Gestapo HQ
11. Koch Str. U-Bahn
12. Stationery Office
13. Europa House
14. Anhalter Bahnhof
15. Belle Alliance Platz
16. Hertie Dept. Store
17. Patent Office
18. Hallesches Tor

A German Panther Panzerstellung that suffered a catastrophic explosion. Note that the gun mantle has separated from the breechblock and both hatches were blown clear of the turret. Photo courtesy of ASKM.

A Soviet ML-20 152mm gun-howitzer artillery battery positioned in support. Note the use of foliage for cover and concealment. This was applied in an almost robotic way to any vehicle that was stationary.
Photo courtesy of RGAKFD Moscow.

Soviet infantry unit advances down a Berlin street. Movement had to be quick if in the open, otherwise the soldier became an easy sniper target. The longer the battle took the more anxious Soviet commanders were to keep their forces moving toward the Reichstag.
Photo courtesy of Cornelius Ryan collection, Mahn Center, Alden Library, Ohio University, Athens, OH.

Soviet support section sets up in the ruins. Photo courtesy of the Bundesarchiv.

Smoke pours out of ruins on the far side of the Spree. The Soviets were confronted with numerous water obstacles in Berlin that were difficult to overcome. The Germans tried to destroy as many bridges as they could. Lack of central control, few explosive devices, and a simple unwillingness by some commanders to destroy critical infrastructure allowed many of the spans to remain intact and passable. Photo courtesy of the Bundesarchiv.

Spittelmarkt
28 April

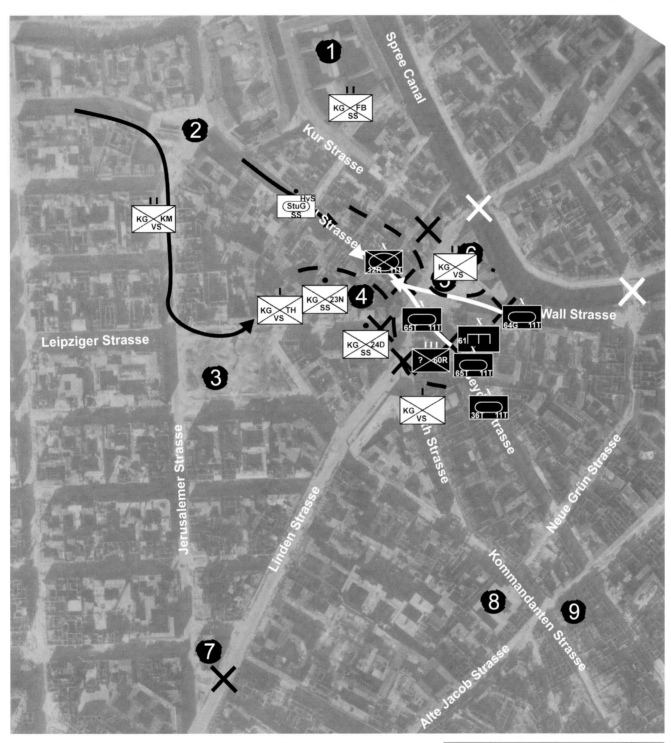

Key Places
1. Reichsbank
2. Hausvogtei Platz
3. Donhoff Platz
4. St. Joseph II Hospital
5. Spittelmarkt Platz
6. Foreign Exchange
7. Jerusalemer Church
8. Reich Stationery Office
9. Theatre

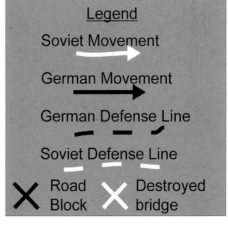

Legend

Soviet Movement ⟶

German Movement ⟶

German Defense Line - - -

Soviet Defense Line - - -

✗ Road Block   ✗ Destroyed bridge

Grossbeeren-Brücke across the Landwehr Canal. This bridge was blown and impassible to Chuikov's forces, though they were able to cross the canal farther west. The 5th Shock Army's advance from the east made any attempt by Chuikov to cross the canal pointless and dangerous due to the possibility of fratricide. Photo courtesy of the Bundesarchiv.

section allowed German Forward Observers from the Friedrichshain Flak Tower to call down 12.8cm fire on nearby Soviet positions. This building and surrounding complex now became a primary goal to control Alexanderplatz. This task was given to the entire 266th Rifle Division with direct support from the 322nd Independent Heavy Artillery Battalion. This close assault battle against Berlin's main Police complex raged for the next twenty-four hours and there were probably few if any German survivors.[20] The fact that a reinforced division was used to assault a single building highlights the lack of manpower available to the Soviets and the problems associated with reducing strongpoints in an urban environment.

To the southeast the Schlesischer S-Bahn station continued to hold out against all Soviet attacks. Fixed 8.8cm guns, German Panther Gs (presumably still deployed here) and the mixed German forces continued to resist the entire 32nd Rifle Corps. The 416th Rifle Division worked its way to Holzmarktstraße on the north bank of the Spree where it was halted by a German position at the elevated Jannowitzbrücke S-Bahn Station.[21] *Volkssturm* from Alexanderplatz had taken this position over from Rogmann and were maintaining a strong defense at this Spree crossing.

CENTRAL DISTRICTS

All units of the 11th Tank Corps were now operating on the west side of the Spree with the exception of the 36th Tank Brigade that was participating in the reduction of the Schlesischer S-Bahn station. The soldiers and tankers of the 11th Tank Corps prepared to continue their drive toward the Reichstag after taking several days to consolidate their forces and conduct reconnaissance. Their earlier probes of the Spittelmarkt by tank and assault engineers demonstrated that they needed to take this critical road junction or find a way to bypass the German defenders. The 11th Tank Corps was no different from any other Soviet unit fighting in Berlin that they experienced significant infantry losses in house-to-house fighting and significant tank losses during operations in the narrow, rubble-strewn streets. Poor coordination between infantry and armor continued to be a key problem and while in some cases the two forces worked excellently together in many others they did not. Major General I.I. Fushuk now issued orders to create 'light storm groups' to better organize and execute armored urban operations in Berlin.[22] In the case of the 11th Tank Corps, a light storm group equaled a section of medium T–34/85 tanks, one or two heavy JS–2 tanks, a platoon of submachine-gun infantry, one or two anti-aircraft guns, one or two anti-tank guns, and a section of combat engineers. After several unsuccessful probing attacks of the Spittelmarkt, Fushuk now ordered the next attack to consist of the new storm groups.

The Soviet force gathered on Seydelstraße south of Spittelmarkt Square. The exit from this street into the square was barricaded and manned by German troops. It was impossible for the Soviet armor to proceed without removing the barricades. During the early morning hours Soviet engineers crept up to the barricade, planted charges and blew up the structure. Soviet tanks were waiting down the street with their engines running. After the explosion they quickly advanced into the square under the command of Senior Lieutenant Berdyshev. As the tanks took up positions within the Spittelmarkt, they quickly brought fire down on known and suspected German positions while Russian infantry moved into the open square to take up any available defensive positions. Under cover of their tank fire, Soviet infantry quickly leaped across the square reaching Nieder Wallstraße on the north side. After securing the exit on Nieder Wallstraße Soviet armor and support elements quickly drove through the open square. The surprise and effectiveness of this coordinated attack apparently caught the Germans off guard, except for two alert Sturmgeschütz III crews that tried to engage the Soviets but were quickly knocked out.

The combined arms support allowed the Soviets to quickly break through and clear the square. The official Soviet History of the 11th Tank Corps states that "In the street fighting in Berlin, the German anti-tank methods of close-in fighting, especially with the [*Panzerfaust*] and grenades, inflicted significant losses on our attacking tanks."[23] Tankers now began to devise screens and attach them to the turret and body at a distance of 15–20 centimeters on welded brackets, sheets of metal 1–25 millimeter thickness or wire nets of 3 millimeter mesh. The screens proved very effective against the *Panzerfausts*, but these experiments were not institutionalized. Instead, they were left to individual units to devise on their own. The 11th Tank Corps actions continued to underscore a lack of Soviet training in urban combat, lack of coordination, but at the same time small unit ingenuity that served the tactical needs well.[24]

Soviet tanks and infantry continued toward Hausvogteiplatz in a northwest direction after the breakthrough of the Spittelmarkt. This underscored how important the Reichstag loomed in the minds of all Soviets engaged in Berlin fighting. It also highlights the lack of coordination between Soviet corps as the 11th Tank Corps might have moved a few blocks further west and utilized the 9th Rifle Corps' avenue of advance behind the Spittelmarkt to drive straight down Leipziger Straße where there were few German defenders. The 11th Tank Corps was operating a mere eight city blocks from the Reich Chancellery, the *Führerbunker,* and Adolf Hitler. A combine force of the 9th Rifle and 11th Tank Corps might easily have reached the heart of the Government Quarter.

The Soviets left infantry elements and presumably some armor in reserve around the northern approaches of the Spittelmarkt after they smashed through the northern barricades. Small groups of snipers infiltrate the ruins around the Spittelmarkt during the rest of the day making it a very deadly place.[25] Schultz left his cellar in the morning and immediately received rifle fire from a nearby building where Soviet snipers infiltrated during the night. He was ordered to head out with five other boys to clear out the house. Forty-five minutes later only two *Hitlerjugend* returned and reported that the others were killed. It was impossible to get near the Russian positions due to the firing.[26] Schultz quickly became desensitized to the death in the streets. He forced the image of the dead Russian tanker from the previous day out of his mind as well as those of the boys he witnessed killed trying to reach the Russian snipers. His only reaction was to realize he was out of cigarettes. He and a few other boys located a truck and caught a ride to a cigar store in Kürassierstraße in between the explosions of Soviet artillery shells, and returned like heroes after looting the store of its wares. Everyone settled in for a smoke in between the fighting.

Word made it back to Seifert that the Spittelmarkt was breached. He ordered *Hauptmann* Albert Lieselang to take an assault group to the Spittelmarkt area that consisted of *Volkssturm* and some of *Fregattenkapitän* Kuhlmann's sailors to bolster the defense. This force was caught by a Soviet artillery barrage in the open that wounded Lieselang and stopped the rest of the small force.[27]

The 9th Rifle Corps operated in a wide gap with the approaches to the Spittelmarkt on its right flank and Gitschiner Straße on its left. In the center of its line it reached Charlottenstraße, several blocks east of the Reich Chancellery. This Soviet corps found itself struggling through a maze of side streets trying to move forward quickly, usually bypassing German positions that often launched counterattacks in the corps' rear. The Soviet proximity to the Government Quarter caused continued alarm at the *Führerbunker* and either Seifert or Mohnke ordered an immediate counterattack.

Henseler and his men were ordered out of the Air Ministry building and sent to attack toward Moritzplatz and push the 9th Rifle Corps back. His men loaded up available ammunition and *Panzerfausts* then moved down Kochstraße to the Jerusalem Church where they launched their attack down Orainienstraße. The rumors of relief from Wenck's approach had given his men new hope and they set about their assault with new-found strength. As Henseler recalled "It was almost like in the old days, the sudden counterattack caught the Russians completely by surprise."[28] Henseler and his men quickly overcame Russian positions one-by-one. In one case they jumped over the large shield of a Soviet anti-tank gun positioned on a side street where they caught and killed three startled Russians calmly eating their morning soup out of a can. The surrounding Russians quickly retreated back toward Moritzplatz taking up positions behind a former German anti-tank barricade. Henseler quickly sent a runner back to HQ to inquire for new orders. Soon after, 30 *Kriegsmarine* soldiers arrived as additional reinforcements. Henseler noted how the *Kriegsmarine* soldiers had one peculiarity about them. Keeping to German Naval custom, the *Kriegsmarine* repeated every order issued to them by their commander, causing most of the *SS* to chuckle at this useless 'formality.'

The Soviets regrouped and launched their own counterattack back up Orainienstraße forcing Henseler and his men north up Kommandantenstraße then east one block to Stallschreiberstraße. Here Henseler found a military hospital located at a church full of wounded soldiers with no one to attend to them. Henseler ordered his company medic to remain behind and help the wounded the best he could. Then Henseler began to withdraw before he caused Soviet artillery fire to rain down on the hospital. The medic burst into tears at being left behind knowing he would simply have to go into Russian captivity—a traumatic event for most Germans and especially for foreign volunteers of the *Waffen-SS*. Henseler calmed the man down, told him to put on his Red Cross armband and surrender the place quietly when the Russians arrived. One of Henseler's men than ran up excitedly and informed him that a German-speaking Russian had now engaged in conversation with a German soldier in the street. Across the span of 25 meters a Russian, who had motioned to a German that they both remove their helmets as a sign of good faith, called on the Germans to surrender. The Russian asked "War is kaput, why fight longer?" The Germans refused to surrender and both men headed back to their positions and fighting flared up again. Henseler then took his men north to Neue Grünstraße and Beuthstraße near the Spittelmarkt, where they settled in defensive positions for the night. During the retreat Henseler's *SS-Oberscharführer* and good friend was killed.[29] While the 9th Rifle Corps pulled back on their right flank of their line after Henseler's counterattack, they did advance elsewhere.

During the course of the day the 1050th and 1052nd Rifle Regiments of the 301st Rifle Division took the Reich Patent Office on the Landwehr Canal, claiming to have killed 80 defenders and taken 146 prisoners at this strongpoint.[30] The *Latvian SS* were directed by Mohnke to take up positions in the area during the morning. According to their account fierce resistance was put up by the *Latvian SS* directly opposite the bridge at Hallesches Tor where Russian patrols tried to cross during the day. The *3./Latvian SS Fusilier Bataillon* defended the Reich Patent Office on Gitschiner Straße while the *2./Latvian SS Fusilier Bataillon* took up a reserve position in Belle-Alliance-Platz. Here the Latvians fought their heaviest battles. Eduards Stauers, commander of the *2./Latvian SS Fusilier Bataillon* was wounded in combat and replaced by Voldemârs Laiviðð, who led the Latvians until the end of the battle.[31] By the late afternoon, the Latvians pulled back as *Nordland Kampfgruppe* moved in to launch counterattacks.

Two days after the fall of Neukölln, Haas and his men were still holding out at their location on Weichselstraße. Hass' force was now its own *Kampfgruppe* waiting patiently for a runner to bring orders. When none came, he sent a runner to find the HQ. The runner soon returned and stated that the bunker that previously housed the Battalion HQ was empty. Either the Battalion HQ left without letting Haas know, or they sent a runner that was killed trying to reach him. The Russians had bypassed his position the previous day *en-route* to the Landwehr Canal. There were simply not enough Russians to search or garrison every corner of the city allowing Haas and his men to remain undetected. The sounds of battle grew louder all around Haas and his men as Chuikov's forces launched their assault across the Landwehr Canal further northwest. Haas made the decision to lead his men north through Soviet lines to Defense Sector Z. He was now down to approximately 60–70 men after the rest deserted on their own over the past several days. *Kampfgruppe Haas* slowly made their way out of the building moving through nearby burnt out structures northwest toward Pannierstraße. A keen Soviet sniper singled out Haas as the leader of the group and fired a single shot striking him in the leg and sending the rest of his men to ground.[32]

Kampfgruppe Haas quickly turned south toward Weserstraße where they soon found an operating German ambulance in a nearby street that was taking wounded to a Convent on Nansenstraße that was converted into an emergency hospital. Haas hitched a ride in the ambulance while his men made their way to the Convent. The Mother Superior came out when the ambulance arrived and notified the soldiers that if they wanted help they would have to remove their uniforms. This was a typical request by most clergy in Berlin to avoid any reprisals from Soviet soldiers. This was a particular concern now that the makeshift hospital was behind German lines. A wounded German soldier with Haas yelled back to the Mother Superior: "I am a German soldier, and I am not going to take my uniform off." This made Haas mad, as he was tired of all the fighting and thought he could wait out the battle at the Convent. The ambulance now decided to take its human cargo to the main hospital at the Zoo Bunker, presumably, because the soldiers appeared hostile to following the Mother Superior's instruction. The ambulance made a miraculous journey through Berlin to the Zoo Bunker behind Soviet lines. The most direct route was up Kottbuserdamm to Oranienstraße, then to Leipziger Straße through the Tiergarten to the Zoo Bunker. This route, as one might expect, should have seen significant Russian activity. Yet the ambulance driver made it through both German and Russian front lines several times to reach the Zoo Bunker—an amazing feat while artillery and rocket rounds fell all around. This demonstrates how porous the Soviet front line actually was within the city.[33]

In the Zoo Bunker hospital sheer horror met Haas' eyes. "The hospital looked like a slaughter house, wounded men were lying in pools of blood, the bodies of dead children were on the floor. The doctors seemed to do nothing else but saw and chop off arms and legs. Some of the cut off legs were still lying around, some of them with boots still on. Haas saw a woman, both legs torn off, who was holding a small child in her arms." This was the most terrifying thing he had seen in all his years of combat. During the next two days Haas slept amidst the carnage—the only place he was able to find any sanctuary from the endless combat of the last twelve days.[34]

Chuikov planed to cross the Landwehr Canal in force on 29 April. The attack was planned across a broad front using small 'storm groups' supported by the maximum use of firepower in both artillery and rockets. In several locations his men already crossed the canal and were trying to expand their small bridgeheads. In his account he remarks that this action had to be carefully coordinated since Soviet soldiers to the north were only 2,200 meters away across the Tiergarten. Chuikov's account does not mention either the proximity of the 5th Shock Army's 9th Rifle Corps operating several blocks to the northeast or any coordination with Koniev forces that were preparing their own offensive *through* Chuikov's lines with the objective of reaching the Landwehr Canal. Koniev and Chuikov should have known of each other's proximity. It is likely that their forces engaged each other in skirmishes the day before in Schöneberg without knowing. It is highly likely that Chuikov's attack across the canal on 28 April was stopped by Koniev's forces that slammed into his formations from the south causing losses and confusion among his men (this is discussed below). Both Zhukov and Koniev exchanged accusations that went to Stalin and Stavka for final resolution once the mistake was realized. Who had authority to operate in Berlin was now a very important question that required Stalin to answer.

Getting his men across the canal in force was difficult for Chuikov as the only bridge between Friedrich Wilhelmstraße and Halleschu Tor still intact was the Potsdam Bridge that had two aerial mines suspended from it. The whole expanse of the bridge was swept by machine-gun and *Panzerfaust* fire. The planned offensive was to take place between points opposite Bendlerstraße in the west to Belle-Alliance-Platz in the east, an area about 2,000 meters wide. Soviet reconnaissance activity started the day before and continued throughout the day with scouts looking at the tunnels leading under the Landwehr Canal—the S-Bahn tunnel leading from the Yorckstraße marshaling yard and the U-Bahn tunnel leading from the Belle-Alliance-Straße into Friedrichstraße. They reported that they were not practical to use, but Chuikov ordered that they move through them to harass the Germans from the rear with small groups and tie down German forces that might defend against the crossing. Chuikov paid particular attention to the political reinforcement of his units with Commissars as command-and-control was hard in the urban street fighting and it was important that orders were passed down and followed. This was also an example of how bad the morale situation was getting for the Soviets as many of their soldiers were in constant combat for two weeks straight and did not want to be the last to die in Berlin.[35] Chuikov wrote in his memoir that his soldiers only conducted probes during the day, but German veterans' accounts suggest that he did launch an attack in force but was stopped. The offensive failed due to the stiff resistance of German troops and by an assault by Koniev's men into Chuikov's flank and rear.

Chuikov's forces placed pontoon bridges across the Landwehr Canal near the Halleschu Tor in the early morning hours and sent over a large number of tanks. The French *SS* in the area quickly organized two anti-tank commando teams and sent them south of Belle-Alliance-Platz. *Nordland* troops quickly arrived to secure the French left flank and block any Russian progress at Belle-Alliance-Platz. *Sturmbataillon Charlemagne* broke up a series of Soviet attacks or probes destroying as many as a half dozen Soviet tanks. By the afternoon the French were cut off by Soviet patrols coming from the 9th Rifle Corps to the north. They decided to reconnoiter the area north of their positions and re-establish contact with the Reich Chancellery. A German NCO named Puechlong volunteered to lead the patrol because he knew Berlin. As he moved around a corner a Soviet anti-tank gun opened fired killing 6 of the 8 men in the patrol and seriously wounding 2 more.[36]

Later in the day the French managed to extract themselves and took up positions along Hedemannstraße. On their left flank along Friedrichstraße were troops of *Nordland* and on their right flank was the Anhalt S-Bahn station. They now blocked the three main roads leading from Belle-Alliance-Platz. The French took an almost romantic view in their ability to knock out Soviet tanks. Weber, who led the reserve *Kampfschule* unit during the fighting in Neukölln several days earlier, remarked to Fenet "Is it not beautiful?"[37] He was referring to a Soviet tank he just single-handedly knocked out.

Across the street the French noticed Russians occupying a building in strength, possibly in preparation for an assault across Hedemannstraße. A Frenchman named Roberto led a patrol through a sewer entrance into a series of interconnecting passageways that led them into the basement of the building being occupied by the Russians. They then set fire to it and retreated to an ambush position where they trained their Sturmgewehr on the exit. Soon the building caught fire and as the Russians emerged, they were cut down. Anyone left in the building were chased out with grenades then soon killed. This is not unlike Russians techniques described by their veterans to eliminate German defensive positions. It appeared to be a tactic developed during the street fighting to flush out opponents then kill them in the open from a concealed position instead of storming the building outright. Some fifty Soviet corpses lay in the streets. These bodies were soon crushed by the tracks of Soviet tanks that rolled over them to attack the French positions.[38]

Illum's assault company and the engineer platoon arrived at *Nordland* division HQ located in the Französische Straße U-Bahn Station on Friedrichstraße. Down on the dimly-lit platform were thousands of soldiers and civilians, primarily women and children, aimlessly milling about. Illum located the command train on the tracks and approached. He found out for the first time that Zeigler was replaced as commander of the division by Krukenberg. There were a number of high-ranking *Waffen-SS* officers here including *SS-Obergruppenführer* Hans Jüttner, Chief of the *Waffen-SS*. It appears that this meeting of so many high-ranking *SS* and *Waffen-SS* leaders indicated early planning for a future *SS* breakout of the city.[39]

To the south at Koch U-Bahn station *Kampfgruppe Bachmann* received orders by noon to advance south to Hallesches Tor and clear out the Russians that had crossed over the Landwehr Canal. Apparently *Kampfgruppe Bachmann* was ordered back from its mission to hold Kottbusser Tor the previous day. At 1300 the one hundred soldiers under Bachmann's command began their advance. After 100 meters aimed Soviet mortar fire rained down, inflicting 15 wounded and 4 killed. Among the wounded was *SS-Untersturmführer* Bachmann. This effectively ended their assault. Now leaderless, the *Kampfgruppe* moved into the Herold Insurance Building at the corner of Friedrichstraße and Puttkamerstraße. The Herold Insurance Building was already badly damaged. All that was left was the ground floor and the first floor. The building was home to approximately 40–50 soldiers from Scholles' *Kampfgruppe*, *Volkssturm*, *Gestapo*, and *Wehrmacht*. The survivors of *Kampfgruppe Bachmann* were now added to these forces.

Scholles and his men set up a defensive perimeter around the ruined building. Across the street on his right flank were members of *Sturmbataillon Charlemagne*. On Scholles' left flank were other members of *Nordland* under the command of an unknown *Feldwebel*. Presumably, these were the remnants of the assault group sent out for security along Prinzen Straße the previously day. Scholles and the survivors of *Kampfgruppe Bachmann* received word from Division HQ by runner that a counterattack was planned for tomorrow with new forces being assembled to the north. Russian scouts and assault groups now infiltrated so close to the Herold Insurance building during the day that heavy weapons such as mortars could not be used against them due to the Soviets' proximity to the defending Germans.[40]

Illum and the *16.(pi)/SS-Pz.Gren.Rgt.24 Danmark's* commander, Christiansen, were now ordered to prepare a joint counterattack for 29 April to push back the Soviet forces located in the vicinity of Belle-Allianz-Platz. The Christiansen's pioneers were ordered to clear Wilhelmstraße and Illum's assault force had the responsibility to eliminate any Russians located from Friedrichstraße down to the Hallesches Tor. Illum and Christensen made their way out of the U-Bahn station with their orders and proceeded to their units to issue warning orders for the next day's action. Illum's men waited nearby where civilians were lining up at *Nordland's* Regimental Field Kitchen. Here a Danish cook and his two *hiwis*, Ivan and Peter, gave out food. Even at this late date, many German units, particularly *Waffen-SS*, kept *hiwis* as extra labor to complete support tasks for their units. After issuing a warning order, Illum began to scout out his positions for the attack when he located two Sturmgeschütz IIIs and a heavily armored scout car that he wanted to use for support. The assault guns belonged to Timm, but all armored commanders refused to participate. This refusal may or may not have been a direct order to preserve forces for the expected *SS* breakout being planned, or it may have just been an act of self-preservation.

The German assault forces completed assembly by the afternoon. Both Illum and Christiansen mustered approximately 100 men for their respective *Kampfgruppe*. Manpower was extremely scarce despite the thousands of soldiers that could be found lingering in many offices and U-Bahn stations all around the Government Quarter. Illum organized his assault group into five combat teams each with a machine-gun for support. Only 12 veterans existed from Illum's original company that started the battle for Berlin back on 16 April. The rest of his manpower came from various division sections. In one case a legal officer from the division was pressed into service as a combat team leader in charge of two Hungarians named Zlucki and Adamek and two Transylvanians named Zipfel and Hänger. As Illum and his men loaded on to three trucks to be driven to their launching-off point, he noticed their old Regimental Banner hanging from the lead truck. The Regimental Banner was made in a club back in Denmark and sent to the old *Frei Korps* back in 1941. It was thought lost, but now was waving from the truck. The combination of the Regimental Banner and preparations for an attack lifted the flagging spirits of the motley group of soldiers preparing for tomorrow's assault as they drove to their starting point south of Französischestraße. Soon the men broke out into an old German drinking song 'In Junker's Tavern' and an old Boer song 'Now begins the bloody combat ….'"[41]

Illum's small combat group reached their start point and reconnaissance patrols were sent out to find the enemy. The returning patrols noted that Russian infantry and scouts advanced far up both Wilhelmstraße and Friedrichstraße. These were primarily infantry of the 9th Rifle Corps, though it is possible that Chuikov's forces were among the ruins. Illum's men settled down for the night along the deserted ruins of a side street.[42] Propaganda leaflets continued reports that the Americans were on their way or that Wenck and Busse would relieve Berlin continued to keep hope alive in the battle-weary German soldiers. Now came the rumors that Himmler had brokered an alliance with the West. As one veteran of Nordland fighting at the Potsdamer S-Bahn Station reported:

> The rumors that woke us up from our mechanical, trance-like, defensive fighting, and gave us new hope, and new spirit, said that *Reichsführer-SS* Himmler had contacted the supreme commander of the western allies, Eisenhower. It was said that he, after having heard Himmler's narration of the 'Red Danger', had realized the equally great effect on the British and Americans of this danger. It was a danger to the whole West. They now had supposedly agreed about a common struggle against Bolshevism, before the Red Army reached Berlin.[43]

The 39th Guards Rifle Division made preparations to attack across the Landwehr Canal toward the Anhalt S-Bahn station in the morning. Germans, presumably a *Kampfgruppe* of *Müncheberg*, emerged out of the underground U-Bahn station at the corner of Luckenwalder Straße and Schönebergerstraße in an attempt to throw back the Soviets. The men of Abyzov's battalion opened fire with submachine guns and pushed the Germans back toward the U-Bahn entrance. One of the men in his unit was heard yelling coordinates on a landline to their mortar battery "Twenty-seven! Twenty-Seven! Fire a few mortar shells at the underground railway station! Quick!"[44] The Germans were also aware of Abyzov's position and their mortars hit the mark first, killing and wounding a number of Soviets. The Germans emerged again from the U-Bahn station and again were forced back. Finally Soviet mortar rounds landed at the entrance of the U-Bahn entrance forcing the Germans to pull back under the Landwehr Canal toward Potsdamer Platz.

The Russians remained under fire all day and waited until dusk to make their way across the bridge and assault the ruins of the Anhalter Bahnhof stating that they took it in the early evening. The Soviets then crossed over one block northeast toward Dessauerstraße and consolidated their positions.[45] Across the street were several companies of *SS-Fusilier Bataillon 15* that settled into defensive positions here after their defeat at the Patent Office earlier in the day. Their positions were along the block between Prinz Albrecht and Anhalt Straße.[46] The Latvians poured machine-gun fire at the Russian positions and the crossing point between the Anhalt S-Bahn Station and the new Russians positions across the street. As Abyzov recalled "The little street behind the building of the terminal was streaked with enemy tracer bullets which flew like green, red and white bumble-bees."[47] This made resupply of the Russian battalion dangerous as the ammunition cans weighed 24 kilograms, a bit too heavy for one man to carry quickly across a street covered with enemy fire. The solution was simple. The Russians tied a long rope around the can and threw the other end across the street where it was dragged safely across. In addition to the Latvians were the members of Leopold's *SS Polizei* and the *Kriegsmarine Kampfgruppe* that arrived in the evening as reinforcements. According to Leopold, the Russians managed to bring several tanks across the Landwehr Canal by early evening. The Soviets quickly launched another attack northwest with the tanks in the vanguard but these were quickly destroyed by *Panzerfausts*. Across the street from Leopold's positions was a multi-storeyed local post office that had scaffold all along the front, presumably for repairs to damage done during the many Allied bombing raids of Berlin. The Russians took over the building and placed snipers all along the scaffolds. These well-trained men covered the entire area, making it very difficult for the Germans to maneuver.[48]

The soldiers of *Müncheberg* at the Potsdamer S-Bahn station were now under heavy enemy artillery fire. The Germans were low on fresh food and water was brought from the Spree and boiled. Nervous breakdowns caused by stress occurred within the unit. In the early morning hours the Soviets began to infiltrate through the U-Bahn tunnels under the Landwehr Canal and advanced toward Potsdamer Platz. *Müncheberg* soldiers were ordered into the adjoining U-Bahn tunnels to head south back under the Landwehr Canal toward Nollendorfplatz.[49] This maneuver was presumably done in on orders and in preparation for a future breakout west as this *Kampfgruppe* from *Müncheberg* clearly abandoned their positions guarding the Government District.

Two knocked out ISU-152s. It appears that the second ISU-152 might have tried to use the first one for cover before it was knocked out, presumably by a Panzerfaust. It is not clear if the T-34/85 to the right is knocked out as well, but given the lack of any Soviet soldiers or crew in the photo it is very likely. Photo courtesy of the Tank Museum.

This photograph highlights how dangerous operating a tank in Berlin was for the Soviets. Note the JS-2 below in the street (it has the painted white recognition stripes), then count how many windows might conceal a single German with a Panzerfaust. Photo courtesy of the Bulgarian Ministry of Defence.

Dense smoke clouds the street ahead of this Katushya. Note the surrendered German officer on the left and wounded German soldier on the right being escorted to the rear.
Photo courtesy of RGAKFD Moscow.

A JS-2 in the streets of Berlin. This tank's crew has added a significant amount of side and rear stowage not typical during regular operations. This suggests that the crew presumably needed to operate for a longer period without resupply. Photo courtesy of RGAKFD Moscow.

SOUTHERN DISRICTS

Koniev's 3rd Guards Tank Army began preparations for a morning assault. During the night of 27 April through the early morning hours of 28 April, Koniev's soldiers readied themselves for an offensive that would put them across the Landwehr Canal in force by evening. On the right flank the 9th Mechanized Corps supported by the 61st Rifle Division planned to launch an attack through Heinrich von Kleist Park toward the Landwehr Canal opposite the Anhalt and Potsdamer S-Bahn Stations. The 6th Guards Tank Corps, with the 48th Guard Rifle Division was to advance along the same line toward Nollendorfplatz on the right of the 9th Mechanized Corps. To the left, the 7th Guards Tank Corps and 20th Rifle Division planned an advance toward the Tiergarten to capture the Berlin Zoo.[50] Further to the west the 55th Guards Tank Brigade now planned to advance out of the Grunewald and east through Charlottenburg toward Defense Sector Z.

Koniev's main force was only 2 kilometers south of Chuikov's positions. His main avenue of approach to the Landwehr Canal went straight through Chuikov's flank. In many cases Chuikov's forces already occupied former German positions targeted by Koniev's artillery. As Chuikov's attack across the Landwehr Canal began, heavy artillery fire rained down on his men.

Koniev's artillery opened fire in the morning and raked the city blocks in front of his corps' positions all the way to the Landwehr Canal. His preparatory artillery fire rolled across the 8th Guards and 1st Guards Tank Army's flank. Chuikov probably tried to figure out what was going on as calls from his subordinate commanders rang in yelling about the massive unknown German artillery hitting their positions—of a volume and caliber that they did not realize the Germans still had in the city. Soon after the artillery barrage stopped, tanks and infantry of the 3rd Guards Tank Army advanced through the ruined streets of Berlin toward the Landwehr Canal. What happened next was an avoidable situation created by Zhukov's jealously and lack of sound military judgment. In the confusion there can be no doubt that Soviet soldier engaged Soviet soldier in open street fighting. Fratricide occurred easily enough, but now Soviet soldiers were assaulting one another from the ruins without knowing who the other actually was. It was not uncommon for Germans to capture Soviet tanks and use them, so it was probably no surprise when a Soviet tank of the 3rd Guards Tank Army opened fire on a tank or infantry position in Chuikov's sector. His men would have assumed it was captured by the Germans and destroyed the tank. It appears that this confusion was significant and lasted for hours, because Koniev is clear that the majority of the 9th Mechanized Corps did reach the Landwehr Canal. Koniev stated that " … I ordered Rybalko, *after his arrival at the Landwehr Canal*, [author's emphasis] to turn his units that had advanced farthest to the west, and later continue the advance in a new theatre of operations of the 1st Ukrainian Front, established at that time."[51] If Koniev's forces indeed reached the Landwehr Canal, this could only have been accomplished by assaulting through Chuikov's positions. The extent of fratricide between Koniev and Chuikov's forces became known in the West with the release of a little-known 1994 video documentary titled *Berlin: At All Costs!* In the documentary, filmed in the Russian State Archives, documents were revealed that recorded how Soviet soldiers of the two Fronts engaged in running battles against each other in the corridor from Innsbrucker Platz S-Bahn station straight to the Anhalt S-Bahn Station. The Soviet Staff Officers in the film noted that indeed Koniev's forces reached the Anhalt S-Bahn Station before Chuikov, suggesting that his men actually reached the other side of the Landwehr Canal. As tantalizing as this is, no other Soviet sources reviewed during this book's research offer insight into these events other than Koniev's unpublished memoir.[52]

Both Zhukov and Koniev exchanged harsh words once Koniev found out his forces attacked through Chuikov's positions to reach the Landwehr Canal. Stavka quickly ordered a new inter-front boundary to the west, ending Koniev's advance on the Reichstag, but still leaving him a clean-up mission within the western districts of the city. Koniev's conversation with the commander he ordered to reach Berlin and the Reichstag was "quite unpleasant." It must be hard to imagine the psychological blow that came to Rybalko's men after driving so hard, beating Zhukov into Berlin, then finding out that they had engaged their own countrymen in battle for half a day before being ordered out of the city. Koniev admits that he agreed with, and understood Rybalko's anger, but he had no other option but to leave Berlin. Koniev did not down play the day's events in his memoir but he also did not go into detail:

> As for my own considerations, I think that it was necessary to establish a precise boundary line between the two fronts at this period. We should exclude any possibility of confusion, losses from our own fire and other unpleasant things which are associated with the mixing of troops, and especially in conditions of street fighting ….
>
> The preservation of battlefield friendship and comradeship between the fronts in any situation, and under any circumstances, is much more important than any sort of personal vanity. I think that even at that psychologically difficult moment, in spite of all his feelings, Rybalko also understood this.[53]

By day's end the 9th Mechanized Corps along with elements of the 6th Guards Tank Corps started their withdrawal from the city leaving the 7th Guard Mechanized Corps and other elements to complete the assigned task of clearing the southwest districts. This repositioning, however, was not an end to Koniev's involvement in the battle.

Koniev's attack did impact the German defense in the area. The 6th Guards Tank Corps attacked the flank of the *Pz.Gren.Rgt.51* pushing them back to the line running along Hohenzollerndamm Straße to Hohenzollernplatz. The Germans did keep their control of the Hohenzollerndamm S-Bahn station that anchored their defense.[54] There was fierce resistance in the area as it took the entire day for the soldiers of the 6th Guards Tank Corps to capture most of Wilmersdorf. The remnants of Arno's *Kampfgruppe* that made it back to German lines went in position at Fehrbelliner Platz where it was to take the Soviets another day to break through. The Soviets in this sector employed a slightly more conservative approach to urban tank warfare. They began to use snipers and scouts to infiltrate forward of their armor and take up positions in the upper storeys of buildings to look for Germans armed with *Panzerfaust* before advancing with their tanks.

Soviet scouts took up position along Brandenburgisches Straße looking across Sigmaringer Straße and the German barricade positioned across the road leading north. A *Hitlerjugend* patrol that received reports of Soviet tank activity in the area approached through the U-Bahn tunnels and arrived at Fehrbelliner Platz U-Bahn station without incident. Upon exiting the U-Bahn tunnel they were immediately taken under fire by Soviet sharpshooters. The Germans opened up at the suspected Soviet positions with sub-machine-gun fire at a significant distance to keep the Soviets down. They then advanced toward the barricade using the ruins as cover. As the German patrol drew near, they fired several *Panzerfausts* over the barricade to scare off any tanks on the other side. The Soviets, already alerted by the scouts and wary of the *Panzerfausts*, actually withdrew their armor back only to strike the area with indirect fire loosing no tanks in the process.[55]

Soviet Assault on the Reichstag
28 April

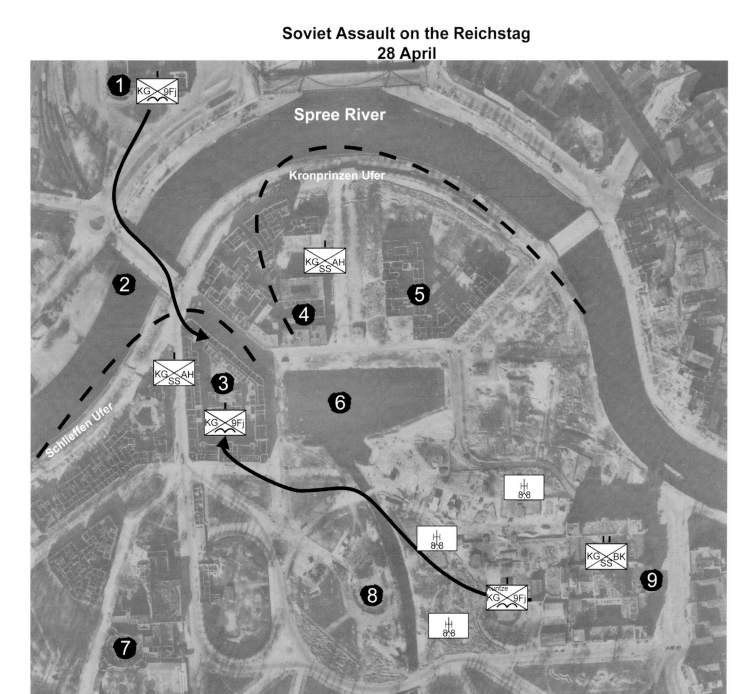

Spree River

Kronprinzen Ufer

Schlieffen Ufer

Key Places
1. Lehrter Bahnhof
2. Moltke Bridge
3. Ministry of the Interior
   "Himmler's House"
4. Swiss Consulate
5. Diplomatic Quarter
6. Speer's U-Bahn
   Construction Site and
   Flooded Tunnel
7. Kroll Opera House
8. Königsplatz
9. Reichstag

Legend

Soviet Movement

German Movement

German Defense Line

Soviet Defense Line

X Road
  Block

X Destroyed
  bridge

This is Moltke Bridge looking north-west across the Spree River in the direction that Soviet infantry and tanks advanced to capture the Reichstag. In 1945 both sides of the bridge were barricaded, and barbed wire and mines were strewn across the span. Sixty years later a mother and her daughter take a leisurely stroll. The Lehrter S-Bahn station can be seen to the right. Author's collection.

The same bridge looking south-east. The Reichstag's dome can be seen in the background. In 1945 only glimpses of the building were visible through the dense smoke that hung throughout the city. A row of buildings running southeast would have blocked the front of the Reichstag and to the right there would have been the immense Ministry of Interior or "Himmler's House." Author's collection.

Another view of the Moltke Bridge showing the length of the span. This photo is looking north toward the Soviet lines. Soviet soldiers and tanks crossing this span had to run the gauntlet of fire from the 12.8cm guns of the Zoo Flak Tower that raked the expanse of the span. Author's collection.

To the west around Hallensee S-Bahn station on Kurfürstendamm Straße, the 7th Guards Tank Corps struggled forward against determined resistance. One *Hitlerjugend* tank-hunting squad led by Willy Feldheim, who was 16 years old, went into action against the Soviets in this area. Feldheim was born in Berlin and in 1944 was given a choice to join the *Wehrmacht* or the *Volkssturm*. He joined the latter and was sent to form one of the three *Hitlerjugend* anti-tank brigades operating behind the *LVI Pz. Korps* line along the Seelow Heights. Feldheim retreated back to Berlin after the Soviet breakthrough and was assigned to a local tank-hunting unit that engaged the Soviets during the day and early evening. He returned to his barracks at night to replenish ammunition. In the early morning dark, Feldheim and nine other boys were ordered to the bridge running over the Westkpeuz S-Bahn tracks as the Soviets advanced in their direction. At the bridge they met a *Wehrmacht* officer who knew they were coming as reinforcements and ordered them to man the tank barricade across the bridge. Feldheim and another team member took up their positions and waited. The barricade was made of concrete, reinforced with iron and steel bars and was seven feet high. The barricade ran almost 6.5 meters wide and had a width of 3.5 meters.[56] After waiting 20 minutes the boys heard the "grinding clatter" of tank tracks. Soon they could see a Soviet self-propelled gun turning the corner and heading toward them. The Soviets used their self-propelled guns differently in the urban fighting depending on the unit. In this case, the Soviets sent one forward to breach the barricade. The self-propelled gun was probably a heavy ISU–152 as the 122 version's long barrel made it particularly vulnerable in the tight streets of Berlin. It does not appear that any Soviet infantry support was allocated as there is no mention of the Russians using suppressing fire to keep any Germans at the barricade down. Feldheim's partner whispered "Don't shoot, let him get close." "Let me get in the first shot now, wait, don't loose your nerve, let me get it." Feldheim's friend, whose first name was Heinz, clearly had experience in close-quarter tank fighting that the other boys respected. The ISU–152 drew closer. When it was approximately 45 meters away Heinz fired. "The shell hit the front of the vehicle. There was a violent explosion. The boys jumped up on the barricade and began to cheer."[57] The vehicle burst into flames as the ammunition cooked off exploding furiously. In the violence and confusion of combat, there are often unpredictable consequences. The Russian tankers had a shell chambered in the barrel and the heat of the burning self-propelled gun caused the shell to fire. The shell screamed into the barricade and exploded, tearing a hole and throwing the boys off. After collecting themselves they realized no one was hurt. Shocked, they initially thought there was as second self-propelled gun nearby until they realized what happened.

The *Wehrmacht* officer was elated at the performance of the boys and walked over to Heinz, handing him an Iron Cross that the officer was wearing on his uniform. The boys were ordered to head to the Hallensee S-Bahn station where Soviet tanks were reported

This wartime photo shows the Moltke Bridge looking toward the Soviet side. A JS-2 tank battalion is crossing. Notice the demolished tank barricade to the right and the series of knocked out Soviet armor strewn across the bottom of the photo. These tanks were either knocked out on the bridge or in fighting along the south bank toward the Reichstag. Several of the tanks have the triangle recognition symbol that was applied specifically to tell the difference between Soviet and Western Allied tanks.
Photo courtesy of the Cornelius Ryan Collection, Mahn Center, Alden Library, Ohio University, Athens, OH.

moving. They headed down Bornstedter Straße in single file passing a burned-out Russian tank. Soon they were fired on from an upper storey window by Russian soldiers. Feldheim ordered the boys to stay down and get to shelter fast. The boys quickly crawled into the ruins of a nearby building, except for Heinz and another boy. Feldheim yelled to them to get back but Heinz yelled "Don't worry." These were his last words as two Soviets leaned out of a nearby window and "flayed the two boys with their submachine guns." Feldheim was in a state of shock at the death of his friend. The other boys couldn't return fire from their location except one who was armed with a *Panzerfaust*. He fired the anti-tank rocket into the window where the Soviets were. As the explosion rocked the front of the building, Feldheim got up and ran into the street forgetting about protection and threw grenades into the windows where the Soviets were a few seconds ago. There was no immediate return fire and the boys assumed they killed the Russians. The war seemed to hit home for Feldheim and he lost his appetite for tank hunting that day. He ordered the boys back the way they came and led them past the barricade to their barracks further east on the Kurfürstendamm Straße.[58]

Pz.Gren.Rgt.30 held onto its positions along the S-Bahn line from Hallensee north to Bismarck Straße despite the best attempts of the 7th Guards Tank Corps to breach the line.[59] *Pz.Rgt.118* was subsequently ordered to move back to the Olympic Stadium to support the *Hitlerjugend* forming there and defend against incursions from the north where the 1st Mechanized Corps recently crossed the canal.[60] What was not realized was that the main threat was coming from the west not the north.

To the southwest of Koniev's extended front, the 10th Guards Tank Corps supported by the 350th Rifle Division launched their own attack across the Teltow Canal to establish a small defense perimeter on Wansee Island without approval from Koniev. The remnants of the *20.Pz.Gren.Div.* that did not make it to Döberitz defended fiercely against the attack blowing up the Glienicker Bridge in the process. In addition the 9th Mechanized Corps started an attack on Potsdam with the plan to destroy *Armeegruppe Spree* that was now moving to link up with Wenck's forces advancing from Beelitz.

Koniev's ambitions to reach the Reichstag were dashed as Stavka issued a new boundary between the two fronts at midnight Moscow time. In his conversation with Stalin, he was asked an all too familiar question "What do you think, who will take Prague?"[61] Koniev knew that *Armeegruppe Schörner* to the south was still a significant threat, and that U.S. forces were already on the move toward Pilsen, a mere 50 kilometers from Prague—the next tempting prize for Stalin now that it appeared Berlin would soon fall. Koniev now started planning for his new deployment. The majority of the 3rd Guards Tank Army began to pull back from the Landwehr Canal, leaving the 55th Guards Tank Brigade and elements of the 7th Tank Corps in the city to maintain control of the south west districts.

WESTERN DISTRICTS

The 55th Guards Tank Brigade launched a two-pronged attack out of the Grunewald in the early morning. The main attack drove north past the *Hitlerjugend* guarding the Havel bridges and the *Reichsarbeitsdienst* troops covering the Olympic Stadium. They overran a mixed flak and field artillery position in the grounds of the Reich Sport Academy sharing the same hilltop as the Olympic Stadium and pushed on down the back of the hill over the Ruhleben ranges toward the Charlottenburger Chaussee.[62] The early morning Soviet attack surprised the Germans as recorded by Altner:

> The night has woken up to frightening activity. The thundering of guns and exploding shells, with the roaring of collapsing walls, splintering of windowpanes and the hammering of machine gun fire, has become one single noise that paralyses the senses and makes one's eardrums vibrate. The din has become a constant thunder, above which it is almost impossible to distinguish the individual gunshots and explosions. It penetrates and consumes one like an inevitable disaster. The earth shakes until one expects it to open up at any moment and swallow everything up in the darkness.[63]

The Russians consolidated their positions around the Ruhleben Barracks after taking the Reichs Sports Field. Tank fire continued as Russian infantry moved into supporting positions. Throughout the night the Germans defending the barracks kept up a continuous stream of fire that held the Russians at bay. The non-stop combat and proximity of the Russians caused war-weary German soldiers to leap out of the surrounding trenches and make a run for the Russian lines across the street at the Olympic Stadium. In the morning a Russians T–34 advanced toward the German lines flying a white flag. The hatch opened and in German a Russian exclaimed "Comrades, give yourselves up!" He explained the war was lost and asked the Germans to throw down their weapons and head over to the Reich Sports Field to surrender. The hatch slammed shut and the T–34 backed up to the Russian lines. Germans by the dozen started to throw down their weapons and run over to the Russian lines. German officers and NCOs quickly ordered the deserters shot. Germans began to shoot Germans who were only a few minutes ago their comrades.[64]

The Russians finally launched their attack against the barracks but the remaining German defenders stopped the assault with machine-gun fire and *Panzerfausts*. *Hitlerjugend* reinforcements soon arrived. Orders were now issued to retake the Reich Sports Field by 1000. The Russian infantry were simply too few to hold back the thousands of Germans assembled for the counterattack. Exactly at 1000 the attack was launched up over the hill and into the Reich Sports Field pushing the Russians back across Heerstraße. The *Hitlerjugend* suffered 80% casualties by the time the fighting was over.[65] The second attack by the 55th Guards Tank Brigade also did not fare well.

Joachim Wetzki was born in Berlin. At fifteen years old he was mobilized in February 1945 as a *Hitlerjugend*. By 28 April, he had already experienced combat and his unit was positioned near the Reichs Sport Field when the 55th Guards Tank Brigade launched its attack. A dozen Soviet tanks drove across Heer Straße, the main east-west communications artery between the garrisons defending the Spandau Bridges, the Radio Tower, and the Zoo Bunker to the east. The Soviet armor headed north between Reichsportsfeldstraße and Ragniterstraße. The boys launched a counterattack with *Panzerfausts* that temporarily halted the Soviet advance and drove the remaining tanks back across Heerstraße.[66] Wetzki's counterattack might have helped Altner's defense of the Ruhleben Barracks by preventing Russian forces from outflanking those positions. The boys were then ordered to make their way across the Olympic Stadium to the east to reach the Ruhleben Barracks on Königin Elizabeth Straße, presumably to act as reinforcements. When the boys reached Adolf Hitler U-Bahn station they received orders that if any of the boys had not received military training at this point they could go home. This meant little now as the Soviets occupied much of the residential districts of Berlin. Many, however, took the offer and left leaving only 20 boys in the unit.[67]

Wetzki's unit was now divided into several groups and ordered to make their way into the city center. They found their way was blocked by 2 T–34/85s sitting on the raised S-Bahn Bridge over the Kaiserdamm U-Bahn Station. A 6 man team was selected to destroy the tanks. The group leader asked the boys to wait while he went ahead to reconnoiter. The group leader never returned and the boys went back to their barracks. By the evening the entire group came under the command of a *Leutnant* who now ordered them to head north and setup a perimeter near the Siemenstadt factory recently occupied by elements of the 1st Guards Mechanized Corps. Their *Leutnant* set up his command post slightly to the rear and told the boys to wait until relieved. When no relief came, it was discovered that the *Leutnant* had changed into civilian clothes and disappeared. The boys then pulled out of the perimeter and started heading back down Fürstenbrunner Weg.

The 55th Guards Tank Brigade consolidated in the afternoon after their defeat against the Ruhleben Barracks and drove east toward the city center. On a side street leading to Bismarckstraße, a small patrol of *Hitlerjugend* set up a defensive position. While positioned in a second storey corner window, their machine-gun fire kept small Russian patrols at bay.[68]

It was now apparent that the 55th Guards Tank Brigade was operating in close proximity to the elements of the 2nd Guards Tank Army. In direct response to the fratricide that occurred between Chuikov and Koniev's forces along the Landwehr Canal, agreements were presumably reached to avoid any direct conflict between the two Russian Fronts in this area. The 1st Mechanized Corps abandoned the Ruhleben district to the 1st Ukrainian Front and consolidated their weak forces. The 1st Mechanized Corps now concentrated on the bend in the Spree due north of the Schloss Charlottenburg Gardens, where the Spree Locks provided a potential crossing point for infantry. The subordinate 219th Tank Brigade conducted an assault across the adjacent Jungfernheide S-Bahn station strong point, where the S-Bahn embankment provided the only gaps screening the western part of Moabit. The 12th Guards Tank Corps crossed by the 79th Rifle Corps route over the Westhafen Canal into Moabit and began advancing toward the Spree and the mouth of the Landwehr Canal. By afternoon the 55th Guards Tank Brigade renewed their advance toward the Kurfürstendamm though it is not clear how far they went as Chuikov's forces were operating nearby. What is clear is that their advance temporarily cut communications with Defense Sector Z and caused Altner and other Germans to advance in the same direction and re-establish contact.

Oberst Edner of Defense Sector F ordered a strong patrol from Ruhleben Barracks to re-establish contact with Defense Sector Z and the Zoo Bunker. Altner was among the 500 boys selected for the mission. They passed through the Westend where they saw all the destruction wrought by the 55th Guards Tank Brigade's passage through the area. The patrol split into two groups on Adolf-Hitler-Platz to follow the U-Bahn tunnels in the direction of the Zoo above and below ground. Additional *Kampfgruppe* were sent from the Reich Sports Field toward Heerstraße to clear Pichelsberg and into Ruhleben, north of S-Bahn line toward the Spree.

Altner's patrol immediately ran into trouble when it reached the Kaiserdamm U-Bahn station where the *Waffen-SS* and *Hitlerjugend* armed with *Panzerfaust* mistook his patrol for Russians. They opened fire, killing 4 Germans in Altner's patrol. After both sides stopped firing at each other the *Waffen-SS* explained that the Soviets had occupied the area around Richard-Wagner-Platz, and that the Westkreuz and Charlottenburg S-Bahn stations were also in Russian hands. Altner's patrol then split up into small teams that were sent forward in the hope of avoiding any Russian surprise attacks. As they advanced through the tunnel machine-gun fire and explosions erupted around the patrol. There was nothing but confusion as tracer fire and explosions shattered the dark. The roof the U-Bahn tunnel had collapsed due to heavy artillery or tank fire, and the Russians fired directly down at the German patrol from the street above. Russian soldiers even fired *Panzerfausts* down the ventilation shafts showering shrapnel all across the tunnel. The patrol's ranks began to thin as dead and wounded mounted. The patrol soon made it to Wittenbergplatz U-Bahn station. Sounds of combat were coming from Nollendorfplatz where elements of *Müncheberg* took up positions after retreating from Potsdamer Platz earlier in the day. Altner was told by the local German patrols that the Russians were driving toward the Zoo Bunker but they were kept back by the tank hunting patrols in the area. Altner's force advanced back to the Zoo Bunker, where they entered the massive fortress to wait for further orders. In the bunker they heard rumors of a breach between the Western Allies and the Russians; that a new secret weapon would be deployed soon; Hitler and Eva Braun were married in their bunker; as well as others wild rumor mixed with facts.[69]

Altner and his unit continued to rest until after midnight when they were ordered back to Ruhleben. It is apparent from Altner's patrol that the 55th Guards Tank Brigade was spread out over a large area and presumably halted their advance between Bismarckstraße and Kantstraße. The Elefants deployed to this area by Mohnke presumably served to bolster the German defense and block the 55th Guards Tank Brigade's advance. The Elefants' 8.8cm main guns and thick armor made them veritable moving fortresses. As the battle for the western approaches to Defense Sector Z died down, the battle for the Reichstag began to unfold along the Spree River to the northeast.

NORTHERN DISTRICTS

No single military act symbolizes the Allied victory over Nazi Germany more than the raising of the Soviet 'Hammer and Sickle' flag over the Reichstag on 1 May 1945. There are several well-published accounts of the storming of the Reichstag by the Soviets and virtually none by the Germans. The accounts written by survivors of the fighting are often contradictory, especially when the timing and nature of the combat are compared. What follows is the most accurate account of the fight for the Reichstag published to date.

The 79th Corps pushed through Moabit all morning from their crossing point over the Spree at Beusselstraße S-Bahn station until they reached Klein Tiergarten. Local *Volkssturm* units defended this area but they put up only occasional resistance. The biggest obstacle for the Soviets was negotiating the ruined streets in the burning smoke and haze. The Soviets had no real maps of the city and their compasses were all thrown off by the metallurgy in the surrounding buildings and factories. Once the Russians reached Klein Tiergarten elements of the 150th Rifle Division were dispatched south of the park where they seized the factory buildings with little effort.[70] By 1100 the Russians noticed the Moabit Prison at the corners of Alte Moabit and Rathenower Straße. The Moabit Prison is star-shaped, multi-storeyed, and looks much like a medieval stone fortress. A rumor was soon started that this prison was under the command of Goebbels himself! As the battle for Berlin drew to a close, Russian soldiers were not looking to be the last ones to give their life for 'Mother Russia.' It is possible that this rumor was created by the Political Commissars to generate the psychological state necessary to get Russian soldiers motivated to attack this very imposing structure.

The Russian assault on the prison began with an artillery salvo followed by an attack of two regiments of the 150th Rifle Division. The defenders of the prison were probably *Sicherdienst (SD)*(SS Security Police), and *Volkssturm* as no soldiers of the *LVI Pz. Korps* were known to be in this area. After several hours of fighting the prison fell. Dr. Goebbels was not found inside, much to the disappointment of the Russians. They did open up the prison and released many of the inmates that included Czechs, Poles, and Frenchmen. In particular were Russian POWs that were immediately ordered to join the front ranks of the Russian infantry regiments. This was a particularly despicable practice, as the Soviets believed that anyone who surrendered to the enemy was a traitor. Prolonged exposure to a non-Soviet style Government, even as a prisoner, meant you were no longer politically reliable and retraining was simply not an option. Instead they armed the men regardless of their mental and physical state and pushed them into the frontline to fight. If they died in combat at least they did so knowing that they were redeeming themselves from the 'disgrace' of capture.

The Soviets pushed on in a southeasterly direction toward the center of Berlin by mid-afternoon. The leading scouts of the 79th Rifle Corps caught their first glimpse of the Reichstag and reported this back to corps staff. This confirmed what the steady stream of German prisoners captured in the Moabit fighting told the Russians "The Reichstag is ahead, past the Spree." After several reassurances that the Reichstag was in fact nearby, General S.N. Perevertin apparently ordered an immediate crossing while he directed the 150th Rifle and 171st Rifle Divisions to move up to Spree without delay. This forced the Russians to bypass strongpoints of German resistance all around the area, especially at the OKW Officer School to the north and the Lehrter S-Bahn Station to the east, where elements of the *9.Fallschirmjäger* were defending the left flank of their positions in Wedding.[71] Perevertin made his command post in the tall Customs building at the end of the street overlooking the Moltke Bridge. The commander of the 150th Rifle Division proceeded to set up his headquarters in the Ministry of Finance building.[72]

The Spree was a formidable obstacle in the center of Berlin. It was 50 meters wide with walled embankments that rose 3 meters above the water on either side. The bridge was intact but was barricaded at either end with trolley cars and barbed wire. Along the entire span were mines. The bridge was also set for demolition. Among the buildings on the southern bank were elements of the *I./SS Anhalt* as well as members of the *Volkssturm*, and *9.Fallschirmjäger*. These men numbered no more than several hundred. There were a series of diplomatic buildings to the east side of the bridge where the Swiss Consulate was located. On the west side was the formidable Ministry of the Interior, known to the Russians as 'Himmler's House'. The Ministry of the Interior was commanded by a Police *Oberst* in a basement bunker. Machine-gun positions were placed on multiple levels on both sides of the street. There were several fixed 8.8cm gun positions in and around Königsplatz in the front of the Reichstag. Immediate indirect fire support was available from the Zoo Flak Tower and artillery remnants available within the Tiergarten. The whole area in front of the Reichstag was a massive construction site that was part of Albert Speer's U-Bahn tunnel that was never completed. Babick was in charge of the defense at the Reichstag and the surrounding area.[73] He had at his disposal approximately 500 men defending the immediate area of the Reichstag. These soldiers were from all branches of the *Wehrmacht*. The Reichstag itself was a fortress. The windows and doors were walled up since the 1933 fire. The basement had corridors leading east to other buildings where a field hospital was located north of the Brandenburg Tor.

The Soviets tried to quickly force the Moltke Bridge in the late afternoon and were stopped by German defensive fire. This alerted the Germans on the south bank to the immediate presence of the Russians, a fact that they probably didn't realize earlier. A better organized Russian attack began at 1800 by Soviet scouts under the command of Junior Sergeant Peter Pyatniskii from the I/756th Regiment. Pyatniskii and his men moved over the first barricade easily but were soon hit with German machine-gun fire and mortars from the far bank. The mortar fire came from the remaining tubes of Rogmann, who had set up a defensive position amongst the diplomatic buildings.[74] The Soviet airforce was called up to run simulated attacks against the Germans defenders in the hope that this would keep their heads down. The proximity of Russian soldiers prevented the Soviet fighters from actually opening fire to prevent any more fratricide. Soviet tanks were now brought up to assist in the crossing. Self-propelled guns cleared the barricade on the north side of the bridge then rolled south along the span to support the soviet soldiers already on the bridge. Fire from the Zoo Flak Tower raked the bridge as alert *Luftwaffe* gunners saw the Soviet armor out in the open (it is also very possible they were notified by a Forward Observer). The 12.8cm shells vaporized Soviet tanks and several were presumably knocked into the Spree as others burst into molten flames.[75] "They did not simply hit a tank, but blew it apart, especially when catching it in the flank as was the case here" Rogmann recalled after the war.[76] Rogmann gathered up a number of *SS* and *Volkssturm* and prepared a counterattack to clear the bridge of Russians as pioneers were ordered to blow the bridge. Green 'Very lights' were fired into the air to notify the Zoo Bunker of the proximity of German troops and the 12.8s stopped firing. Rogmann launched his counterattack reaching the southern barricades and forcing the Russians back across the bridge. On the north bank were *Fallschirmjäger* located in the Lehrter Bahnhof that realized they were cut off and in the middle of a Soviet marshaling area. Soviet aerial bombing destroyed the Admiral Scheer Bridge that led into Wedding and Soviet infantry already occupied the area to the north of the Bahnhof leaving the *Fallschirmjäger* few options. These men decided to make a run across the Moltke Bridge to the southern side of the Spree and rejoin German forces defending in Defense Sector Z. They surprised the Soviets on the north bank of the river, who did not realize that there were any Germans operating in their rear area, and successfully made it across the bridge while under fire.

Captain Neustroyev reported the latest failure to cross the Moltke Bridge to his Regimental Commander Colonel Zinchenko. He briefed a new plan that consisted of a night crossing after preparatory artillery fire. Zinchenko agreed and set the next assault at 2000.[77] During the ensuing lull in the battle, German pioneers rigged their explosives and blew the bridge. Their attempt was unsuccessful and only caused a large hole in the span. At 1900 the Soviet regimental artillery opened fired on the German positions. German reinforcements were now ordered to the area assuming that the Russians would try another attack.

Babick ordered Kuntze to take additional reinforcements from the Reichstag to the Ministry of the Interior. Kuntze left the Ministry of Interior and moved across Königsplatz that evening using torch lights. He walked over planks to cross the wide flooded U-Bahn tunnel construction trench while Soviet shells struck all around. They made their way into the Reichstag through a side access way. When they entered the building chaos immediately broke out as explosions were heard on the upper floors. Presumably a small band of Russian scouts entered the building from the west as hand grenades were being thrown around the upper floors near the library. Soon smoke could be smelled as a fire broke out. Kuntze met with Babick amidst the fighting and was assigned additional men and more weapons. At that moment a Seydlitz soldier in a medical uniform revealed himself to the defenders in an attempt to get the garrison to surrender. He was immediately captured and taken away as he yelled "Free Germany!" Presumably Seydlitz troops with knowledge of Berlin's streets were now leading small groups of Russians to key buildings like the Reichstag. This band could certainly have been from the 9th Rifle or 11th Tank Corps, as their soldiers were operating just southwest of Unter Den Linden. According to Kuntze, this direct infiltration spread fear through the Reichstag's defenders until singing was heard. *Oberleutanant* Franz started to sing 'Ho, Ho, Ho, we are the men from Navaho!' and brought some nerves back from the edge. Kuntze now took his men, Sturmgewehr 44, and *Panzerfaust*, and left out the south exit. He made his way back across Königsplatz to the Swiss Consulate, then across the street to the Ministry of Interior.[78]

After an hour of firing, the artillery lifted slightly, and the Russians attempted to cross again. Pyatniskii took the lead along with a section of Sergeant Peter Scherbin. They reached the southern barricade for a second time and were able to get over it quickly. They immediately headed to their left into the Diplomatic Buildings where hand-to-hand fighting began in the darkened hallways and rooms. The success of this attack brought confusion on the German side, causing a lull in the battle. Over the next several hours the rest of the 1st Battalion passed over the bridge and into the Diplomatic Buildings. The key building was the Swiss Embassy and especially bitter fighting occurred in the darkened stone corridors as the Russians flushed out the defenders with hand grenades. Soon the 2nd Battalion began making their way across the Spree and into the same building. The two Soviet battalions numbering 500–700 men crammed into one building and spent the night there.[79]

Casualties sustained in the fighting across Moabit were replaced by released POWs as the leading Soviet battalions were not up to full strength. A battalion had an established strength of 500 men and consisted of 3 rifle companies, a support weapon company and a battery of 45mm field guns. But for this operation each battalion was split into two assault groups to which was added a detachment of self-propelled artillery. In addition, the 79th Rifle Corps was assigned the 10th Independent Flame Thrower Battalion and the 23rd Tank Brigade for the operation. Other units to the east of the 3rd Shock Army continued to struggle against stiff resistance among Berlin's northern districts.

The 12th Guards Rifle Corps struck the German line between Schönhauser Allee and Gesundbrunnen S-Bahn station. They crossed the defensive line in several locations and for several days the Russians held the north side of Kopenhagener Straße while the Germans held the south side. By 28 April Russian soldiers infiltrated into the backyards of Gleimstraße. Like all Russian units, any Russian laborers or POWs located in Berlin were quickly incorporated into Soviet the front lines to supplement the lack of manpower. Russian slave laborers that worked at the AEG factory were housed in area located on Volta Straße right behind the Humboldthain Flak Tower. The Russians quickly consolidated control of the area and typically looked into windows and moved on to the next street. If they received fire from a residential home and they suspected it was harboring German soldiers, they would set the house on fire. They began forcing German civilians into their cellars along Gleimstraße while they set up medium size artillery pieces in the doorways of the homes allowing them to fire across Falk Park into the city center. An artillery duel erupted with German artillery in the Tiergarten and from the Flak Tower causing the destruction of many homes among the Russian positions. The Russians now decided to shift east and attempt to take the Schönhauser Allee S-Bahn station from behind but were held up by a combination of German infantry fire and a German King Tiger tank that moved up onto the raised S-Bahn tracks and opened fire at Soviet supporting armor.[80] Members of *Großdeutschland* defending the area in small *Kampfgruppe* typically put up stiff resistance.[81] A notable instance follows, describing the destruction of several Russian tanks moving unsupported without infantry in the nearby streets:

> The first tank pushed its way around the corner of the house and rotated its gun alarmingly toward the roadblock in front of it. It neared the anti-tank barricade slowly, too slowly. A second tank turned in, followed by a third and a fourth. We were in good cover 'They can't hurt us,' said a grenadier to the *Leutnant* lying next to him. The first tank was now within 50 meters of the barricade, the fifth monster turning around the corner, when a terrible explosion shook the air. The *Leutnant* raised his head for a moment and looked and shouted: 'The last one's burning, let's get them!' Cautiously, remaining in cover, the *Leutnant* and four grenadiers stalked into an opposite-lying ruin, armed with *Panzerfausts* and grenades. A second explosion followed and the *Leutnant* saw another explosion … the third tank was out of action. The *Leutnant* now went after the first tank with his *Panzerfaust*, a shot, and explosion … the tank fired no more. The crew bailed out, sought cover behind the second tank, and was placed under fire by the grenadiers. The *Leutnant* fired another *Panzerfaust* and the second was no more.[82]

The Russians advance into the northern districts was stopped for now.

Notes to Chapter 6: Assault on Berlin, 28th April Saturday

1   OKW File, Last Announcements of OKW, 28 April (RC: 62:8).
2   Schultz-Naumann, p. 177, and H. O. Wöhlermann (RC: 69/3).
3   Venghaus, pp. 213–14.
4   Army Group Weichsel War Diary, Apr 20–9, pp. 451, 454–5 (RC: 68/4)
5   Ibid, p. 466.
6   Schultz-Naumann, p. 37.
7   W. Gorlitz, *The Memoirs of Field Marshall Wilhelm Keitel: Chief of the German High Command, 1938–1945*, pp. 218–19.
8   From the Memoir's of General of the Army Heinrici, section XVI.
9   Army Group Weichsel War Diary, Apr 20–9, p. 469 (RC: 68/4).
10 Schultz-Naumann. p. 39.
11 MS #B-606, pp. 26–8, Schultz-Naumann, p. 179, and Voss, and Kehlenbeck, pp. 291–2.
12 Ritter, pp. 19-20, Wenck interview, and Le Tissier, *Slaughter at Halbe*, p. 95.
13 The best source available is Wenck's Chief of Staff's account found in MS #B-606.
14 Ibid, pp. 34–6.
15 Le Tissier, *Race for the Reichstag*, p. 153.
16 Ryan outline for 28 April (RC: 75/1).
17 Eilhardt, p. 54.
18 Venghaus, p. 162.
19 Der Panzerbär, 29 April 1945.
20 Le Tissier, *Race for the Reichstag*, p. 147.
21 Ibid.
22 Platonov, p. 26.
23 Ibid, p23
24 Ibid.
25 Winge interview.
26 Schulz interview.
27 Le Tissier, *Race for the Reichstag*, pp. 147.

28 Henseler interview.
29 Ibid, and Venghaus, pp. 171–2.
30 Le Tissier, *Race for the Reichstag*, p. 147.
31 Pçtersons, p. 79.
32 Haas interview.
33 Ibid.
34 Ibid.
35 Chuikov, pp. 196–8.
36 Forbes, p. 291.
37 Ibid, p. 294.
38 Ibid.
39 Illum interview.
40 Scholles interview, and Landwehr, *Nordic Warriors*, p. 153.
41 Illum interview.
42 Ibid.
43 Hillblad, p. 78.
44 Abyzov, p. 57.
45 Ibid, 58.
46 Pçtersons, p. 82.
47 Abyzov, p. 59.
48 Venghaus, p. 214.
49 Le Tissier, *Race for the Reichstag*, p. 150.
50 Koniev unpublished memoir, p. 172.
51 Ibid.
52 C. Barrand, K. Jan Hindiks, A. Uvarov, *Berlin: At All Cost!*, 1994.
53 Koniev unpublished memoir, p. 173.
54 Engelmann, p. 153.
55 H. Bonath interview (RC: 70:11).
56 In the area of Charlottenburg, as noted in Chapter 2, the building of barricades and defense organization in this district tended to be better than other parts of the city except the eastern districts.
57 W. Feldheim interview (RC: 70:11).
58 Ibid.
59 Engelmann, pp. 151, 153.

60 Ibid.
61 Koniev unpublished memoir, p. 175.
62 Le Tissier, *Race for the Reichstag*, p. 131.
63 Altner, p. 143.
64 Ibid, pp. 144–8.
65 Ibid.
66 H. Wetzki interview (RC: 70/16).
67 Ibid.
68 P. Claus, p. 20 (RC: 69/16).
69 Altner, pp. 151–60.
70 S. A. Neustroyev second interview. (RC: 72/8).
71 Ibid.
72 Ibid.
73 Babick remains an enigma. Based on all German first hand accounts, this *SS* officer existed and he played a dramatic part in the organization and defense of the Königsplatz area. Unfortunately no further information can be found about this individual, who he was, or what happened to him after the battle. It is reasonable to assume that he came from the ranks of the *SS* Administration, instead of the *Waffen-SS* and that he died during the breakout.
74 Le Tissier, *Race for the Reichstag*, p. 146.
75 Ibid, p. 178.
76 Le Tissier, *With Our Back to Berlin*, p. 178.
77 Neustroyev first interview.
78 Venghaus, p. 207.
79 Neustroyev first interview.
80 Wrede interview.
81 Spaeter vol. III, p. 504.
82 Ibid, p. 503.

6

ASSAULT ON BERLIN

29 APRIL
SUNDAY

Fanatical house-to-house fighting rages around the center of Berlin. In heavy fighting the brave garrison made a good defense against the Bolshevist masses which attacked incessantly. In spite of that, a further advance of the enemy in some parts of the city could not be avoided. Along Potsdamstraße and at the Belle-Alliance-Platz violent street fighting is going on. Coming from Plötzensee the enemy forced his way through to the Spree River.

   South of Berlin the Soviets lead new units against our attacking divisions. Fights with unpredictable outcome are underway. Beelitz was taken and east of Wreder the link with the defense area of Potsdam was restored. Attacks against the eastern flank and southwest of Treuenbrietzen.[1]

***OKW* Radio Broadcast**

29 April brought no good news for the Nazi leadership in Berlin or the defenders of the city. Food and ammunition shortages began to impact operations. During the evening of 28/29 April air supply was dropped that amounted to six tons of food and 15–20 crates of *Panzerfausts*, yet distribution of these commodities was uncoordinated. Panzer maintenance proved almost impossible as the remaining repair shops moved to the Tiergarten and were under constant Russian shelling.[2] The relief efforts broadcast daily by the Propaganda Ministry and printed in the *Panzerbär* now began to ring hollow as no soldiers from Wenck's *12.Armee* arrived. Weidling confronted Hitler with what should be done about the final defense of the city and the German soldiers still resisting. He pointed out that the ammunition would run out by the evening of 30 April at the latest. Hitler replied that the soldiers should break out of Berlin small groups when they ran out of ammunition or supplies and join the remaining German units fighting outside the city. On one point Hitler was clear: there would be no surrender of Berlin.[3] Hitler's permission to breakout started a new planning cycle with Weidling's staff and the staff of the Zoo Bunker where Weidling planned to launch the breakout. The mood in the *Führerbunker* reflected the dashed hopes of a miraculous recovery by outside forces that everyone hoped would arrive to relieve Berlin. The last *Panzerbär* issued read "Our duty is clear: we are holding out. The Führer is with us. And where the Führer is, there is victory."[4]

LVI PZ. KORPS

Weidling convened a conference of Defense Sector commanders and instructed them to plan a breakout at 2200 hours that night—29 April 1945. Mohnke and Krukenberg were not invited to attend the meeting. Weidling and his staff were concerned that the *SS* would react adversely to the breakout plan. Weidling stated that he would authorize a breakout under his own authority if necessary.[5] The lack of coordination with the *SS* reflected the mistrust that continued to split the senior command elements and prevent organized operational planning for the defense of Berlin and the breakout even at this late hour.[6]

12. ARMEE

The young German trainees of *Schill, Hutten, Scharnhorst,* and *Körner* divisions continued their drive northeast through the early morning. This was considered the rear area for the 6th Guards Mechanized Corps that was focused on containing *Armeegruppe Spree*. The speed and surprise of Wenck's attack simply overwhelmed the overstretched Soviets. *Schill* and *Hutten* advanced over 10 kilometers across the heavily forested ground between Golzow and Brück reaching the east-west autobahn line south of Ferch. In the process they captured numerous Soviet supply units and a tank repair shop.[7] On the right, *Scharnhorst* took Heilstätten and the town of Beelitz. In Heilstätten there was a *Wehrmacht* Field Hospital with 3,000 patients now liberated from the Russians. The Germans also liberated a train that allowed them to shuttle wounded, sick, and refugees 50 kilometers back to the Elbe.[8] *Körner* continued to hold a strong eastern flank. The *XX Korps* redeployment and attack progress was electric. In a matter of twenty-four hours three key divisions redeployed across 20 kilometers. Then overnight they launched a spectacular attack that surprised the Russians, advancing another 20–25 kilometers toward Potsdam. This advance brought the *XX Korps* within 20 kilometers of Berlin. By the afternoon the *XX Korps* reached its limit for the day and settled into an active defense.

   The news of Wenck's approach sparked incredible hope among the occupants of the *Führerbunker*. One German officer recorded the effect that Wenck's advance had on troops in Berlin: "Once more a ray of hope woke the apathetic souls. If Wenck had come as far as Potsdam he would also be able to advance to Berlin. And if Wenck would reach Berlin then the *9.Armee* of General Busse would not be far away."[9] Secretary of State Dr. Naumann, who was in the remnants of the Propaganda Ministry located across the street from the *Führerbunker*, quickly ordered the message spread about the advance of Wenck. Against all military sense it was thought that Wenck's proximity and location should be broadcast for all Berliners to hear.[10] Announcements were immediately broadcast. Wenck's orderly was listening to the reports from Berlin at around 0200 in the morning on 29 April when he heard an announcement that shocked him. "General, the Army Report!" Over the air waves came an utterly shocking broadcast:

> "The High Command of the Army announces: In the heroic battle for Berlin once again the fateful battle of the German population against Bolshevism is expressed. While troops are defending the capitol in History's greatest single fight, our troops on the Elbe turned their backs on the Americans to relieve from outside the attack on Berlin. The divisions sent into action from the west have thrown back the enemy in a bitter fight on a broad front and have reached Ferch."[11]

The blood drained from Wenck's face. He looked at Reichhelm and exclaimed "My God, they must have gone out of their minds. They must have gone crazy. When these damn fools tell the world where we are we won't move a foot tomorrow. The Russians will concentrate everything they have got on this one sector, my *12.Armee*."[12] Wenck now sent a wireless communication to the defenders of Berlin. Whether by choice or due to the current operation environment this message went unanswered: "To the battle commander of Berlin, *General* Weidling. Attack *12.Armee* stopped south of Potsdam. Troops occupied in heavy defense battle. Suggest breakthrough to us. Wenck."[13] Wenck's intention was to push toward Potsdam but no further. The *XX Korps* would wait and hold out as long as possible to save as many German and civilians that could reach their lines.

The *XX Korps* established temporary contact with Reymann's Potsdam garrison.[14] Once the soldiers of the *12.Armee* reached Ferch, Reymann's 20,000 soldiers and accompanying civilians started to fight their way south across the narrow isthmus at Alt Grabow. Others used rowing boats to cross the Schwielow Lake and arrived at *12.Armee* lines. Reymann's forces were immediately employed to fill in a serious gap on the northwestern flank of *Schill*.[15] Wenck informed Keitel by radio that he could not advance his forces any further toward Berlin. Keitel replied that he acknowledged the situation and gave Wenck a free hand to conduct operations as necessary. Wenck now ordered the soldiers of the *XX Korps* to hold on for Busse's *9.Armee* approaching his lines from the east.

FÜHRERBUNKER

Hitler understood that the battle for Berlin was now coming to an end. There was no hope for a final German military or political victory. During the early morning hours Hitler married Eva Braun. He named Dönitz his successor and prepared three copies of his will. One courier was ordered to reach Dönitz, another to Schörner, and the third for Nazi Party headquarters in Munich.[16] Hitler summoned Mohnke for a noonday conference. At this juncture he no longer felt the need to receive updates from Weidling. Mohnke informed Hitler that the Soviets were only 300–400 meters from the *Führerbunker* and that the remaining German forces could only hold out for 24 hours.[17] The mood in the bunker continued to spiral downward through the day. By 2230 in the evening it was reported that Mussolini was captured and killed. The mutilation of Mussolini and his wife's body confirmed one of Hitler's lasting fears that if we was captured he would be transported to Moscow and put on display like an animal in a Zoo.[18] At 2300 Hitler sent Jodl a final communiqué requesting answers to five, now famous, questions:

1. Where are Wenck's advance elements?
2. When will they continue to attack?
3. Where is the *9.Armee*?
4. In which direction will the *9.Armee* breakthrough?
5. Where are Holste's points?[19]

The reply came early the next morning on 30 April and arguably pushed Hitler into action on a decision for suicide that he already made on 24 April. There was no longer any hope for relief from the outside. In the evening Wenck officially signaled *OKW* and told them that he could not continue the attack.

EASTERN DISTRICTS

The 26th Guards Rifle Corps broke through the porous German lines and moved around to the northwest of Alexanderplatz to take up the general attack positions of the 7th Rifle Corps. The 26th Guards Rifle Corps' 94th Guards Rifle Division attacked toward the Börse (Stock exchange) S-Bahn Station through the narrow streets of the city center. Beyond the Börse S-Bahn Station was Museum Island, which presented the challenge of crossing the Spree and its tributary in short order before the Russians could reach the heart of Defense Sector Z. The 89th Guards Rifle Division continued to fight along the approaches north and east of Alexanderplatz. The 266th Rifle Division remained fully engaged within the Polizeiprässidium until 1500 hours. Postwar Allied damage assessments of Berlin show the west side of the building significantly damaged suggesting that this side was the main effort by the Soviets. Presumably they used direct fire artillery and self-propelled guns to weaken the structure's walls along Neue Friedrichstraße before assaulting into the building. After the fall of the Polizeiprässidium the men of the 266th Rifle Division were given no rest as they quickly closed up to the massive red brick city hall known as the Rotes Rathaus. Like the assault on the Polizeiprässidium, the Soviet attack had tank and self-propelled artillery support but no headway was made until the Soviets blew holes in the walls from adjoining buildings using *Panzerfausts* to get access. The German defenders forced the Soviets to fight for every room and they did not take full possession of the building until the morning of 30 April. The 32nd Rifle Corps' 416th Rifle Division took the Jannowitzbrücke S-Bahn Station and closed up to the Spree as far as the remains of the Kurfürsten Bridge and began preparations to cross.[20] Presumably the Schlesischer S-Bahn Station finally fell; however, there is no record of that event. If the station did fall to the Soviets, it opened up the way to move forces quickly to the Spree. The German survivors, if any, most likely tried to make their way back to friendly lines on the west bank of the Spree.

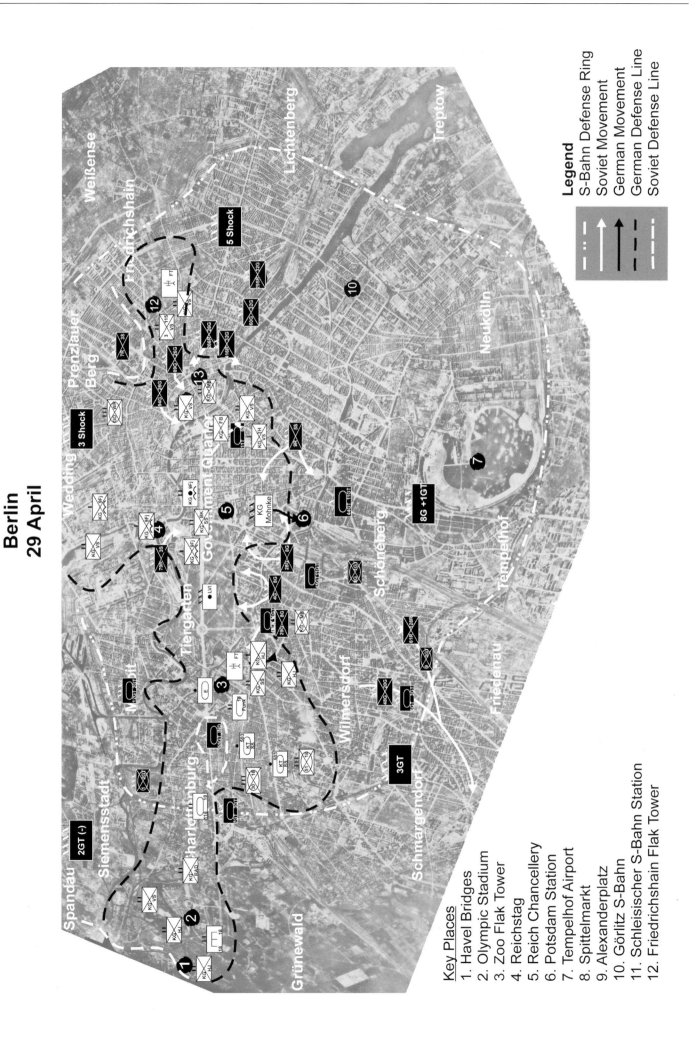

**Berlin
29 April**

Legend
S-Bahn Defense Ring
Soviet Movement
German Movement
German Defense Line
Soviet Defense Line

Key Places
1. Havel Bridges
2. Olympic Stadium
3. Zoo Flak Tower
4. Reichstag
5. Reich Chancellery
6. Potsdam Station
7. Tempelhof Airport
8. Spittelmarkt
9. Alexanderplatz
10. Görlitz S-Bahn
11. Schleisischer S-Bahn Station
12. Friedrichshain Flak Tower

Eastern Districts
29 April

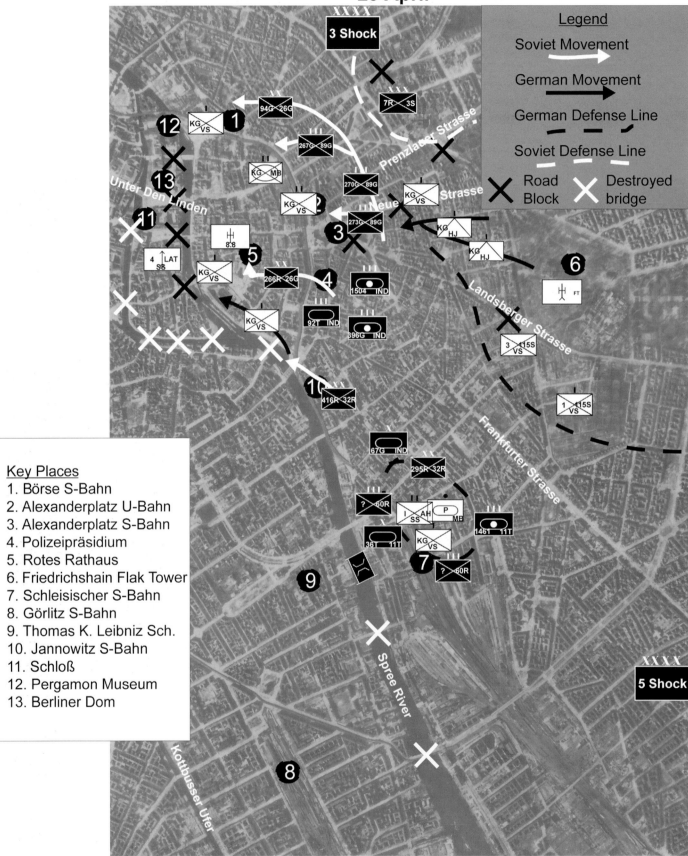

Legend

- Soviet Movement →
- German Movement →
- German Defense Line – – –
- Soviet Defense Line – – –
- Road Block ✖
- Destroyed bridge ✕

Key Places
1. Börse S-Bahn
2. Alexanderplatz U-Bahn
3. Alexanderplatz S-Bahn
4. Polizeipräsidium
5. Rotes Rathaus
6. Friedrichshain Flak Tower
7. Schleisischer S-Bahn
8. Görlitz S-Bahn
9. Thomas K. Leibniz Sch.
10. Jannowitz S-Bahn
11. Schloß
12. Pergamon Museum
13. Berliner Dom

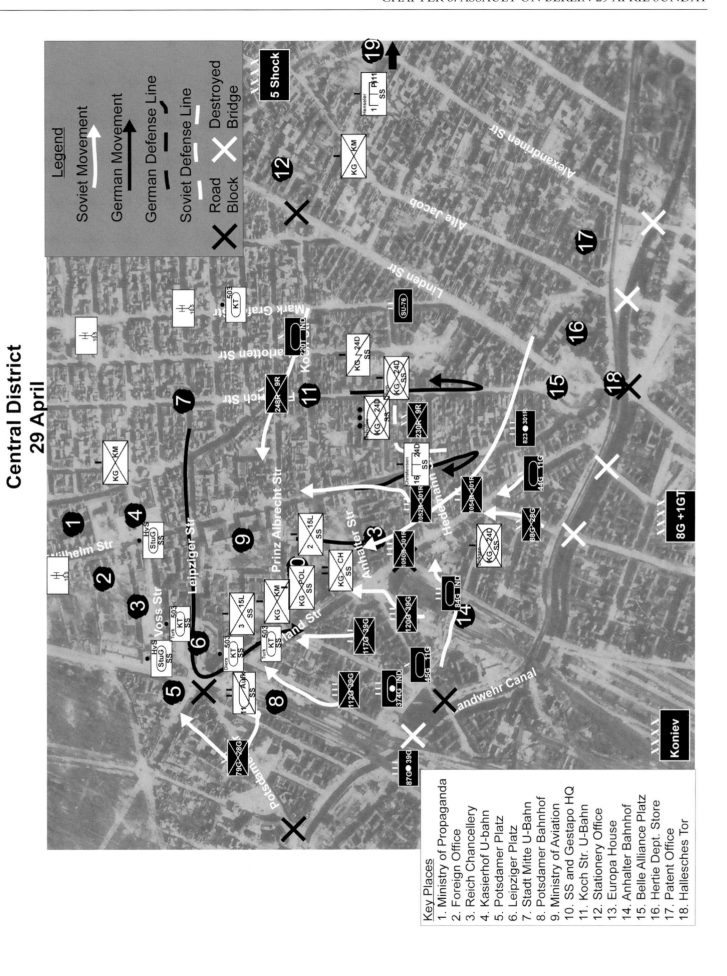

Central District
29 April

Legend
- Soviet Movement
- German Movement
- German Defense Line
- Soviet Defense Line
- ✕ Road Block
- ✕ Destroyed Bridge

Key Places
1. Ministry of Propaganda
2. Foreign Office
3. Reich Chancellery
4. Kasierhof U-bahn
5. Potsdamer Platz
6. Leipziger Platz
7. Stadt Mitte U-Bahn
8. Potsdamer Bahnhof
9. Ministry of Aviation
10. SS and Gestapo HQ
11. Koch Str. U-Bahn
12. Stationery Office
13. Europa House
14. Anhalter Bahnhof
15. Belle Alliance Platz
16. Hertie Dept. Store
17. Patent Office
18. Hallesches Tor

Spittelmarkt
29 April

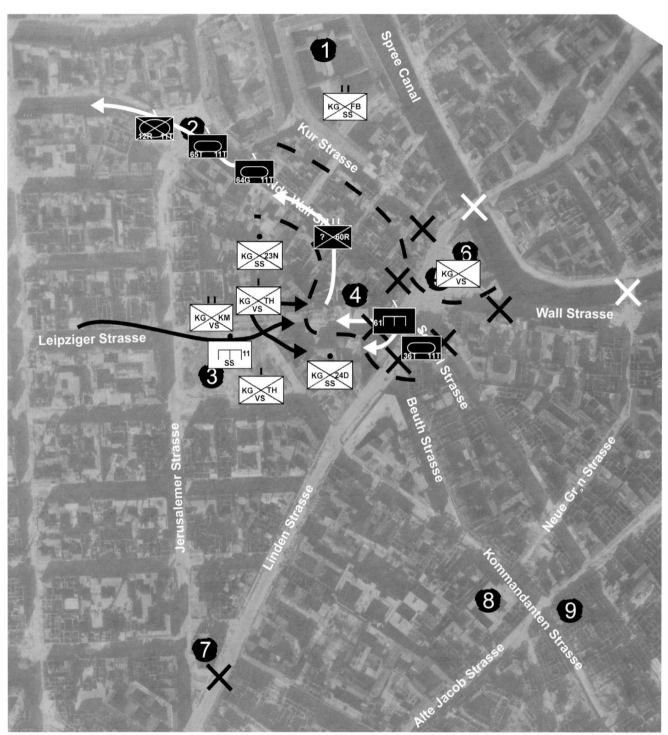

Key Places
1. Reichsbank
2. Hausvogtei Platz
3. Donhoff Platz
4. St. Joseph II Hospital
5. Spittelmarkt Platz
6. Foreign Exchange
7. Jerusalemer Church
8. Reich Stationery Office
9. Theatre

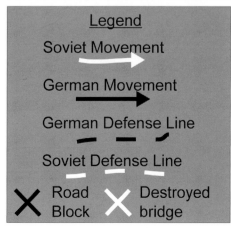

Legend

Soviet Movement

German Movement

German Defense Line

Soviet Defense Line

Road Block   Destroyed bridge

A Soviet artillery piece fires into Berlin's 'Zitadel' island. Note the billowing smoke in the sky and the captured German watch being worn by the Soviet soldier on the right leaning over a wounded comrade. Photo courtesy of RGAKFD Moscow.

CENTRAL DISTRICTS

Fighting in the Spittelmarkt appeared to die down on 29 April. The 11th Tank Corps passed through to the north, and the remaining Soviets made no attempt to take additional buildings. Schulz left his basement position and made his way to Leipziger Straße where he entered a civilian air raid shelter to retrieve water for the other *Hitlerjugend* in his squad. Schulz descended the steps and asked the fifty-year old air raid warden in the shelter for a pail of water. The warden gruffly replied: "for you, we have no water." Schulz, bewildered, went back to his basement and informed his commander who promptly sent Schulz back with another *Hitlerjugend* who pointed his MP44 at the warden and ordered a pail of water to be brought up. The warden promptly complied. Schulz now began to question the loyalty of the civilian population. This in turn, put him in a depressed mood about the fighting as he wondered if he would ever make it home.[21]

South of the Reich Chancellery, the early morning assaults planned by various *Kampfgruppe* of *Nordland* began. Illum's assault started off down Friedrichstraße and encountered the lead elements of the 230th Rifle Division advancing west. House-to-house fighting erupted as the Danes and Russians locked in fierce combat among the ruins. The counterattack caught the Russians unsupported. The Russian infantry gave way, retreating south. Soon the Danes reached Puttkamerstraße, then Hedemannstraße near Scholles' position. At 0900 Illum was directing the next phase of his attack when a T–34/85 moved up to support the Russian infantry. The tank fired several shots toward the Danes' positions. One shot smashed into the wall next to Illum and tore open one side of his face. His eye and leg were also badly wounded as the concussion threw Illum to the ground. He was soon picked up, given a makeshift dressing, and sent to the Hotel Adlon, which was now a large military field hospital.[22] Christensen's counterattack probably saw similar results in their advance but there are no accounts that provide details of this event.

Scholles and his men continued to defend the Herold Insurance building from elements of the 9th Rifle Corps now striking west and north of their positions. An additional 6 *Volkssturm* men arrived with Illum's counterattack to bolster the soldiers under Scholles' command. The Russians were close by and some of the German soldiers decided to fly a Swastika Flag out in the open that drew Russian fire and gave away their positions to returning German fire.[23] The Russians attacked Scholles and his men in the evening through direct assault. Both sides were now locked in hand-to-hand combat at the entranceway of the building.[24] By 2200 hours the 5th Shock Army's 9th Rifle Corps occupied all of Saarlandstraße and the southern part of Wilhelmstraße almost as far as the Reich Air Ministry.

Chuikov's forces renewed their attacks across the Landwehr Canal after sorting out the confusion caused by Koniev's attack from the day before. See-saw battles raged all along the Landwehr Canal with the Germans. During one of these attacks a Soviet soldier became the mythical image of the Soviet conquest of Berlin. Nikolai Masalov, a standard bearer of the 220th Rifle Regiment, of the 79th Guards Rifle Division presumably rescued a child from her dead mother's arms on the Potsdamer Bridge. This act of kindness became a rallying cry for Russian propaganda. A monument was built after the war commemorating this event.[25] Soviet armor tried frantically to get across the Landwehr Canal in force to support the infantry operating on the north bank. The Soviets sent engineers to remove land mines and defuse the two large aerial bombs suspended below the bridge. Next they attempted to rush the bridge several times and were forced back due to strong machine-gun fire from well protected and dug-in German positions among the ruins. The Soviets then tried to get tanks across but they were knocked out one-by-one by a dug-in Panzer, as well as by concealed infantry armed with *Panzerfausts*. Soon some Soviet

29 April issue of Der Panzerbär.
Author's collection.

infantry did manage to cross and secure a small foothold, but the tanks were still being knocked out. An ingenious Soviet tank crew decided to douse their tank with flammable oil and during the next attack they lit it on fire and rolled toward the bridge. The Germans thought the tank was knocked out and moving under its own inertia so they gave it no attention. After the T–34/85 rolled across the bridge the turret sprang to life and fired point blank into the German defensive positions dislodging the defenders and giving the Russians time to consolidate their forces and expand their bridgehead.[26]

The 39th Guards Rifle Division's 120th Guards Rifle Company now headed up Saarlandstraße to the Anhalt S-Bahn station but German strong points were encountered in the Christus Church, along the street, and in the Post Office building on Möckernstraße.[27]

Soviet armor now pushed out from the Anhalt S-Bahn station toward Potsdamer Platz, and east toward Saarland Straße. The *Sturmbataillon Charlemagne* broke up the initial cautious probes by the Soviet armor. Then the Soviets launched an all-out attack and fired point-blank into the buildings where the French were hiding. Walls collapsed and already half-destroyed buildings fell on the defenders. Arguments began to break out among the French regarding who would use the dwindling supply of *Panzerfaust*. Soon a sortie was arranged to the Reich Chancellery in order to replenish the stock.[28]

The Soviet attack pushed forward with the assumption that the French were buried alive in the rubble of the collapsed building. This misconception did not last long as the lead Soviet tanks went up in smoke from *Panzerfaust* fire at close range. After creating a diversion, the French retreated across to Hedemannstraße. Only 1 in 3 buildings remained standing in this area.[29] Close-quarter fighting occurred as the Soviets infiltrated through the ruins but were held back by the French. The Soviets recklessly tried a new tank attack that consisted of rolling up Saarlandstraße with as many tanks abreast as they could fit on the wide street. The attack by the 84th Guards Tank Regiment started north with as many as 8 tanks abreast, but this soon dropped to 2 because of their inability to navigate through the ruins in file. The French held their fire until the Soviets were down to two tanks abreast then attacked, destroying the lead two tanks. The Soviets retreated, but returned to tow away the knocked-out armor blocking Saarlandstraße.[30]

The Soviet pressure along Saarlandstraße drew the deployment of one of the remaining King Tigers of *s.SS-Pz.Abt.503* to the area. Diers' King Tiger rolled south from the Tiergarten to Potsdamer Platz, then south to the Anhalt S-Bahn station. Diers met up with Turk's King Tiger and both engaged the advancing Soviet armor, destroying at least 1 JS–2, 1 ISU–122 self-propelled gun, and several T–34/85s. The knocked-out Soviet tanks effectively blocked the Soviet advance up Saarlandstraße.[31]

The *SS-Fusilier Bataillon 15* HQ was moved to the Ministry of Aviation. What remained of the companies covered a sector from Prinz Albrecht to Wilhelmstraße. The *2./SS-Fusilier Bataillon 15* Company Commander, Laiviòð, placed his advance positions in the gardens along Prinz Albrecht and Anhalter Straße and set up his command post in the shelter of the Gestapo HQ building. Wilhelmstraße was covered by the machine guns of Leutnant Liepnieks' group. These positions were held by the Latvians until the end of the battle for central Berlin. On 29 April the Soviets began to bypass the Latvians from the west and in some places cross Saarlandstraße, directly threatening the Reich Chancellery. The Government District was the responsibility of *SS-Brigadeführer* Mohnke. He collected his last reserves—a half company from *Nordland's SS-Pi.Abt.54*, remnants of Laiviòð' *2./SS-Latvian Fusilier Bataillon 15*, and a group of Spanish volunteers who were members of *Bataillon Fantasma*. After the disbandment of the Spanish *Blue Division,* that served the Germans in Russia from 1941–1943, several hundred Spanish volunteers stayed on to fight for the Germans in the *Waffen-SS*. The political sensitivity of their continued involvement in the war on the side of the Germans caused the new unit to be named *Bataillon Fantasma* (Ghost Battalion). They came under the command of *SS-Hauptsturmführer* Wolfgang Graefe who was attached to the *Blue Division* in Russia. These Spaniards in Berlin made their way into the city before the battle with the desire to defend the city against the Soviets. Their exploits are less well known than other foreign volunteers, but they put of stiff resistance during the battle.[32]

At 1500 the Latvians counterattacked from the southwest corner of the block and forced the Soviets out of the ruins around the Europahaus. The counterattack's events were recalled by one of the Latvian veterans, Janis Pugulis:

> Our last counterattack was dramatic. Only after the war we found out that on the opposite (south) side of the small block on Anhalter Straße there were concentrated all three battalions of the Red Army 1050nd Rifle Regiment, and apparently they were not short of bullets. The counterattack succeeded and the Russians were pushed behind the Europahaus, and the Anhalt S-Bahn station, but it cost us dear. The lightly wounded withdrew themselves, we, the heavily wounded, withdrew later under heavy enemy fire. The Russian soldiers that lost the battle and been pushed

Two ISU 1-52s pause after moving through a German barricade. This photo was taken in an outlying suburb due to the lack of damage in the surrounding buildings. Photo courtesy of RGAKFD Moscow.

This is the Swiss Consulate's building on the north side of Königsplatz. This building and the Reichstag are the only two current buildings in Königsplatz that were standing in 1945 during the Soviet attack. The Swiss Consulate was part of a complex of multistory government buildings along the Spree where heavy hand-to-hand fighting took place. Author's collection.

Soviet infantry sprint down a contested street in Berlin. Note the signs of recent fighting along the right wall—machine gun bullet holes. Photo courtesy of RGAKFD Moscow.

Troops of Polish 1st Army attack in the Direction of Berlin. Note the 76mm ZIS-3 gun.
Photo courtesy of the Bulgarian Ministry of Defence.

over Anhalter Straße replenished ammunition, reloaded weapons and subsequently fired without remorse. One of our men was fatally wounded during our attack, fell against a wall and remained standing. The other side concentrated heavy fire on him. After each hit the fallen legionnaire jumped up like in a film, and it seemed that all the time he was trying to get to his feet to continue his heroic run against enemy bullets … waiting for help—the evening twilight, seeing the fallen legionnaires, slowly bleeding and losing consciousness, my heart hurt worse than my wound—we want to return home.[33]

The 301st Rifle Division continued attacking the Gestapo and SS Main Security Offices on Prinz-Albrecht-Straße —buildings desperately defended by those officers remaining and the *Latvian SS*.[34]

SOUTHERN DISRICTS

Koniev's 7th Guards Tank Corps continued attacks against the flank of *Pz.Gren.Rgt.51* that held the area along the Hohenzollerndamm in Wilmersdorf north of Kurfürstendamm. *Pz.Gren.Rgt.30* held the north side of the Hohenzollerndamm through Neue Kantstraße. Along the western boundary of their operational area was the Hallensee S-Bahn station that dominated the west-east approach from Koniev's operational area. Jagdpanzers of the *I.* and *II./Pz.Abt. Schlesien* were located here, along with two King Tigers of *s.SS-Pz.Abt.503*. The King Tigers, one commanded by *SS-Oberscharführer* Stolze and the other by *SS-Unterscharführer* Bender, along with the Elefants deployed earlier by Mohnke blocked any further advance of Koniev's forces.[35] This is certainly true for the case of the 55th Guards Tank Brigade whose forces would have run into *18.Pz.Abt.Schlesien* along their right flank. It appears that after making their initial advance towards the Zoo Bunker the 55th Guards Tank Brigade ceased operations in Berlin by either going to ground in the ruins or was simply defeated by the German forces concentrated in the area. Rauch's Panzergrenadiers continued to hold tenaciously to the inner defense ring. City blocks astride Westkreuz to the Hohenzollerndamm and from Kurfürstendamm as far as the Zoo

General Stanislav Poplavsky, 1st Polish Army commander. His forces were sent into Berlin to support Zukov's infantry starved armies. Photo courtesy of the Bulgarian Ministry of Defence.

Looking northwest from the roof of the Reichstag you can see the Moltke Bridge and where the Ministry of Interior stood to the left. Despite the fact that from the other side of the Spree to the Reichstag is no more than a brisk 5 minute walk, it took the Soviets three days of hard fighting to reach their goal. Author's collection.

Soviet Assault on the Reichstag
29 April

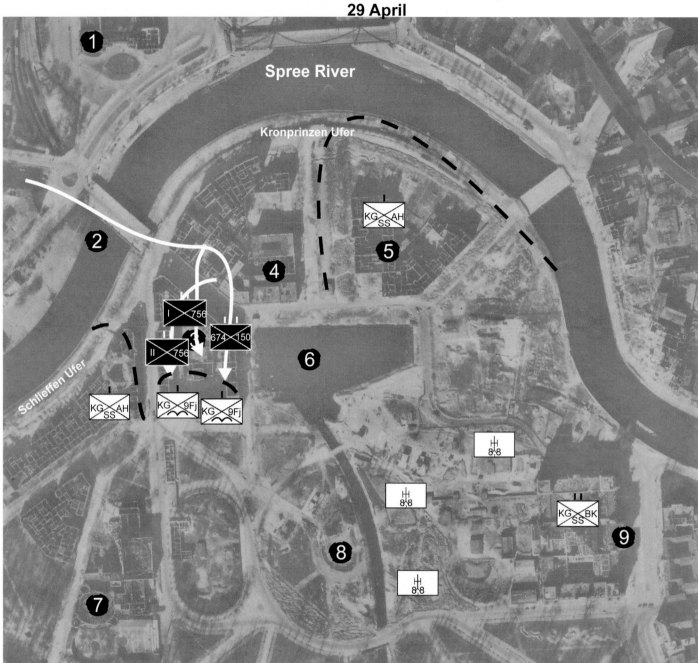

Spree River

Kronprinzen Ufer

Schlieffen Ufer

Key Places
1. Lehrter Bahnhof
2. Moltke Bridge
3. Ministry of the Interior
   "Himmler's House"
4. Swiss Consulate
5. Diplomatic Quarter
6. Speer's U-Bahn
   Construction Site and
   Flooded Tunnel
7. Kroll Opera House
8. Königsplatz
9. Reichstag

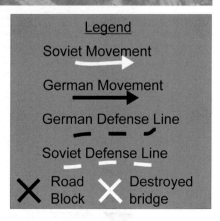

Legend

Soviet Movement

German Movement

German Defense Line

Soviet Defense Line

✕ Road
Block

✕ Destroyed
bridge

A view across Königsplatz from the steps of the Reichstag, looking northwest toward the Moltke Bridge. The distance the Soviets had to cross from "Himmler's House" to the Reichstag was over exposed terrain. Author's collection.

The Landwehr Canal looking east from the Zoo. Without pontoons, bridging equipment, or a usable bridge, Soviet armor was not able to cross these deep channels that criss-crossed Berlin. The Landwehr Canal protected the southern flank of the Tiergarten to the left where the remaining German artillery and Panzer repair workshops were kept. Author's collection.

A Soviet Katushya battery fires a salvo in the heart of Berlin.
Photo courtesy of the Bulgarian Ministry of Defence.

Bunker were solidly in German hands. Rauch's thoughts now turned from defense to offense as Weidling tapped the *18.Pz.Gren.Div.* to lead the breakout west. Rauch ordered his engineers to ensure that the Pichelsdorf Bridges (Stössensee and Frey) were up to a 30 ton capacity required for the Panzers.

At the Zoo Bunker a strange call came into Böttcher's office that served as the Operations Center of the *18.Pz.Gren.Div.* The officer on the other end was in the area of the Grunewald where he had arrested a man dressed in civilian clothes trying to get through his lines. The man stated he was given 'Top Secret' papers to get out of Berlin. Böttcher asked what the papers said and the officer on the other side began to read "I, Adolf Hitler," and continued to state that Dönitz was to be his successor, followed by other final testaments of the Führer. Böttcher did not know if this was real or if this was a novel attempt by someone to escape Berlin. He quickly called his commander *Generalleutnant* Rauch at the *Führerbunker* and asked him to confirm this report. Rauch told him he would get in touch with Bormann. A few minutes later Bormann called in a furious state and the following conversation reportedly occurred:

Bormann: This is Bormann (he yelled) into the phone. What's going on over there?

Böttcher: I have arrested someone here with documents that appear to be Hitler's Last Will and Testament.

Bormann: What the hell do you think you are doing? This is inconceivable! This man had orders to bring these papers out of Berlin. You have no right to arrest my people, nor to read Top Secret papers. You'll have to forget immediately what you have read or else. Are you aware that you have stopped this man from carrying out the Führer's order?

Böttcher: I had no idea about this. Nobody told me about this guy trying to get through my lines. The commander has done nothing but his duty. We have firm orders to arrest all deserters. Had I known, I would have been able to protect this man while he crossed my lines.

Bormann: I have sent out two more men with the same orders and the same papers. Take care that at least these two get through.[36]

At that exact moment, a second man was brought into the Zoo bunker carrying the same papers. The conversation continued:

Böttcher: A second man has been captured and is in my office right now. What am I supposed to do with these two?

Bormann: (now screaming) send them back to the Führerbunker![37]

Later, the third man was captured as well. Two of the men were *SS* in civilian clothes and were ordered to reach Wenck's lines at the southwestern edge of Potsdam. The third was a *Kriegsmarine* officer who was caught in a northwesterly direction trying to reach Dönitz. This event certainly began to generate rumors about Hitler's fate. As Bormann struggled with the best way to send out Hitler's Last Will and Testament the Soviet's continued their attacks across the Spree in the north.

NORTHERN DISTRICTS

The 1st Mechanized Corps repositioned itself to the east to avoid conflict with the 55th Guards Tank Brigade and fought their way through the gardens of the Schloss Charlottenburg and into the ruins of the building while the 219th Tank Brigade broke through the Jungfernheide S-Bahn Station position. A further push west from Charlottenburg Castle Gardens towards Heerstraße was stopped dead when a Forward Observer spotted a Soviet tank concentration and notified all three Flak Towers to open fire. The deadly 12.8cm fire stopped the Soviets tanks from advancing.[38] Sappers of the Polish 6th Pontoon Bridging Battalion built a pontoon bridge under fire for the Soviet infantry, and then repaired the damaged railway bridge to enable the tanks to join them. This presumably allowed tanks from the former 12th Guards Tank Corps (now parceled out to the rifle corps of the 3rd Shock Army) to cross the Spree. The problem was that none of the corps from the 2nd Guards Tank Army had any infantry left. Their tanks were operating on their own and being destroyed. The various unit commanders appealed up their chain-of-command to Colonel General S.I. Bogdanov who in turn went to Zhukov and relayed the desperate message that the elements of the 2nd Guards Tank Army operating in Berlin could not exploit their gains any further without additional infantry forces. Zhukov's had no infantry reserves left to hand over as the Soviets were simply running out of soldiers. Zhukov now turned to his Polish contingent and arranged for the Polish 1st Infantry Division to come to the aid of the 1st Mechanized Corps. It would take all of next day before the Polish troops arrived into the city as they had to move from the Oranienburg area by truck.[39]

During the night from 28/29 April the Soviets tried desperately to consolidate their position in the diplomatic buildings north of the Königsplatz. At 0700 Soviet artillery and rocket fire from the rail yards on the north bank blasted 'Himmler's House', and the Kroll Opera House to the southwest. Due to the proximity of the Russians soldiers to the target area the artillery fire had to be precise and was not as heavy as it might have been. The Germans, now aware of the Soviet presence opposite the Ministry of the Interior began firing out their windows across Moltkestraße at the Russians. The two battalions of Russians from the 756th Regiment fought back across the street all morning. The *SS* and *Fallschirmjäger* fired *Panzerfausts* at the opposite windows forcing the Russians to stay back in the inner corridors. Colonel Zinchenko, the Regimental commander, had come across the Moltke Bridge under cover of darkness and was now with his two battalions in the Diplomatic Buildings across the street. He ordered them to prepare for further combat operations as the Ministry of Interior had to be cleared before further offensive action could be taken toward the Reichstag. Captain Davydov's 2nd Battalion was chosen for the attack, giving the 1st Battalion some respite after leading the crossing of the Spree. Davydov's rifle companies made several attacks across the street during the morning, but the German fire kept them back. By 1300 his men were able to take several rooms on the first floor. They quickly consolidated in preparation for further action in the building.[40]

Kuntze was now ordered by Babick to find a King Tiger to support the German defense. He made his way from the Ministry of Interior to the Brandenburger Tor where he asked for a King Tiger as per his instructions. The King Tiger was promised as the message was presumably relayed back to the *Führerbunker*. In the meantime a Jagdpanzer IV(L) arrived. Kuntze acquired some food supplies and loaded them on the engine deck and rode back to the Ministry of Interior on the assault gun. He offloaded the food, which was quickly dispersed to his troops in the building then rode back with the assault gun without engaging in any combat with the Soviets. On the way back to the Brandenburger Tor Kuntze noticed that a Soviet flag was flying on the Quadriga. A group of Soviets, possibly from the 9th Rifle Corps or 11th Tank Corps, placed a Soviet flag at the top of the Brandenburger Tor. He notified the assault gun commander of the flag. The Panzer commander raised the main gun and fired a high-explosive shell at the Quadriga, removing the Soviet flag and damaging several houses as well, much to Kuntze's surprise.[41]

The fighting in the Ministry of Interior raged unabated throughout the day. As the 2nd Battalion fought along the northern side of the building's first floor, the 1st Battalion was ordered to move into the building and assist. Senior Lieutenant Pankratov led his men up a second storey landing where he was wounded in the leg, then in the head, during fierce hand-to-hand fighting. He had to be carried out and his Senior Sergeant Gusev took over. The Soviets and Germans continued to suffer casualties in the fighting. General Persevertkin, alarmed at the slow pace of operations, ordered a second regiment, the 674th across the Spree and into the Ministry of Interior. The German shelling of the Moltke Bridge from the Zoo Bunker was fierce during the course of the day. Few infantry reinforcements and Soviet tanks were able to move across the Spree until the Soviet engineers could effective clear the barricades on the south side. At 2100, almost twenty-four hours since the first Soviet regiment crossed, the 674th Regiment finally reached the southern bank of the Spree. In the words of the 1st Battalion commander:

> In the evening help came to us in the form of the battalion of Major Logvinenko from the 674th Rifle Regiment of the 150th Division. He managed to clean the enemy out from the south-western part of the house. Bitter, intensive fighting for the Ministry of [Interior] continued with unabated fury. We suffered heavy losses but we continued to press on. We continued to take rooms, corridors and landings on the staircases. Fires broke out in the building—furniture, fittings, papers all were burning. A thick smoke spread about which burnt and stung our eyes, and it made it impossible to breathe. Only in the depth of night did the roar and thunder in the first storeys begin to die away and then to pass up to the upper storeys. The uninterrupted fighting was now growing weaker, stage by stage, and on the morning of the 30 April the enemy resistance was completely broken.[42]

German defenders that made it out of the first floor retreated toward the Kroll Opera House directly to the southwest. Any Germans on the upper floors fought to the death or were simply killed by the weary and exhausted Russians if they tried to surrender.

Street fighting in Berlin proved more ferocious and deadly than the Soviets ever expected. Soviet officers drove their men non-stop to take the city. Here a Soviet squad appears to be running across a rubble strewn field in an attempt to reach the apartment complex on the opposite side. Once the Soviets ran the gauntlet of German sniper or machine-gun fire to cross the street, they often had to engage in fierce hand-to-hand combat in order to capture the target building. This type of combat was both physically and mentally exhausting.
Photo courtesy of the Cornelius Ryan Collection, Mahn Center, Alden Library, Ohio University, Athens, OH.

Notes to Chapter 6: Assault on Berlin, 29th April Sunday

1 OKW File, Last Announcements of OKW, 29 April (RC: 62:8).
2 Weidling Interrogation Report.
3 Le Tissier, *Race for the Reichstag*, pp. 156, 163.
4 *Der Panzerbär*, Ryan Outline notes.
5 Le Tissier, *Race for the Reichstag*, p. 165.
6 Weidling Interrogation Report.
7 MS #B-606, p. 28, and *12th Armee* operations maps.
8 Le Tissier, *Race for the Reichstag*, pp. 117–20.
9 Ritter interview.
10 Ibid.
11 Ibid, and Wenck interview.
12 Wenck interview.
13 Ritter interview.
14 Le Tissier, *Race for the Reichstag*, p. 155.
15 *MS #B-606*, p. 29.
16 Fest, p. 104.
17 Le Tissier, *Race for the Reichstag*, p. 164.
18 Ibid, p. 107.
19 Schultz-Naumann, pp. 41.
20 Le Tissier, *Race for the Reichstag*, pp. 160.
21 Schulz interview.
22 Illum interview.
23 Tieke, *Tragedy of the Faithful*, p. 318.
24 Scholles interview.
25 Chuikov, p. 161.
26 Ibid, pp. 160–2.
27 Le Tissier, *Race for the Reichstag*, p. 162.
28 Forbes, p. 295.
29 Ibid, p. 297.
30 Ibid, p. 296.
31 Fey, pp. 315–16, and Schneider, p. 374.
32 Bowen, "The Ghost Battalion."
33 Pçtersons, p. 83, and map p. 91.
34 Le Tissier, *Race for the Reichstag*, p. 160.
35 Schneider, p. 374.
36 Böttcher interview.
37 Ibid.
38 von Zabeltitz Interview.
39 Le Tissier, *Race for the Reichstag*, p. 158.
40 Neustroyev first interview.
41 Venghaus, p. 272.
42 Neustroyev first interview.

6

ASSAULT ON BERLIN

30 APRIL
MONDAY

The heroic fight for the central districts of the capital is going on with unabated fury. In fierce house and street fighting troops from all branches of the *Wehrmacht*, the *Hitlerjugend*, and the *Volkssturm* defend the central districts of the city—a shining symbol of German heroism. At the Anhalter Bahnhof, along the Potsdamer Straße, and in Schöneberg the enemy was stopped by our brave defenders.

Self-sacrificing *Luftwaffe* pilots dropped ammunition for the garrison of Berlin.

South of the city our relieving units are engaged in fighting the strong Bolshevist units which suffer heavy bloody losses.

Between Berlin and the Baltic Sea the front line runs now from Kremmen-Neustrelitz-Neubrandenburg-Anklan.[1]

OKW Radio Announcement

The mood in the bunker grew gloomier with each passing hour as reports from *AGV* echoed the lack of relief from outside of Berlin. Over the course of a week the *Führerbunker* functioned under the belief that the last formations of the German *3.Panzer, 9.Armee, 12.Armee* and *Armeegruppe Steiner* were making progress in their efforts to decisively destroy the Soviet forces outside of Berlin and relieve the garrison within the city. This belief was created by Keitel and Jodl, and given life through the false reporting of Krebs. Reality was very different. Outside Berlin, Manteuffel's *3.Panzer Armee* was in full retreat trying to desperately avoid encirclement. Busse's *9.Armee* was now split into several groups fighting with the desperation of doomed men to reach their savior Wenck. Holste, operating on his own, guarded the rear of *AGV* preventing the Russians from driving north behind German lines. Finally, the *12.Armee* halted their main offensive at Ferch while *Schill* launched one last attack and crossed the autobahn to reach the lakes to the north and hold a corridor open for Reymann's *Armeegruppe Spree*. Reymann's forces continued their withdrawal into Wenck's lines where they took up a defensive position west of Ferch in order to shore up the northern wing of the *XX Korps*. This was the farthest any of Wenck's division's advanced toward Berlin. Wenck's focus was to save as many soldiers and civilians he could by getting them back over the Elbe—the demarcation line between the Allies as mandated by 'Eclipse'. Despite the realization by *OKW* that the forces around Berlin were not going to reach the city, Jodl's radio message to the subordinate commands around Berlin continued to proclaim that "The fight must go on to gain time for political advantage."[2] His message rang hollow.

Hitler's view that a decisive victory in and around Berlin was possible materialized on 25 April after his near mental collapse three days earlier. This change was a direct response to his senior commanders and Goebbels' urging.[3] Goebbels, Hitler's closest confidant during the period, played a key role in reinforcing the belief that relief forces would arrive to save Berlin and bring final victory. For several brief days Wenck's advance east then northeast brought some reality to the fantasy that the Propaganda Ministry capitalized on through radio broadcasts and newspaper articles. The propaganda broadcasts only served to counteract the effects of Wenck's surprise and operational goals. Not long after midnight the replies to Hitler's questions from the previous day arrived. Keitel sent the following message from the new *OKW* HQ located south of Fürstenberg:

1. Wenck's forward elements are bogged down south of Lake Schwielow.
2. The army, therefore, cannot continue its attack on Berlin.
3. The bulk of the *9.Armee* has been encircled.
4. Holste's corps has been forced into the defensive.

Hitler now understood that there was no relief force coming to defeat the Soviets and save Berlin. His National Socialist state was at an end. Keitel's communication to the *Führerbunker* ended any rationalization to continue resistance in Berlin.

12. ARMEE

A radio communication went out from Wenck to Busse requesting him to hasten his forces' breakout toward the *12.Armee's* eastern flank.[4] Pockets of the *9.Armee* were at the western end of Kummersdorf regrouping for the next push toward Wenck. Ahead of these tired, desperate, forces were strong Soviet positions opposite the north-south rail line running between Trebbin and Luckenwalde. The final push toward Wenck and freedom was not going to be easy for Busse's forces.

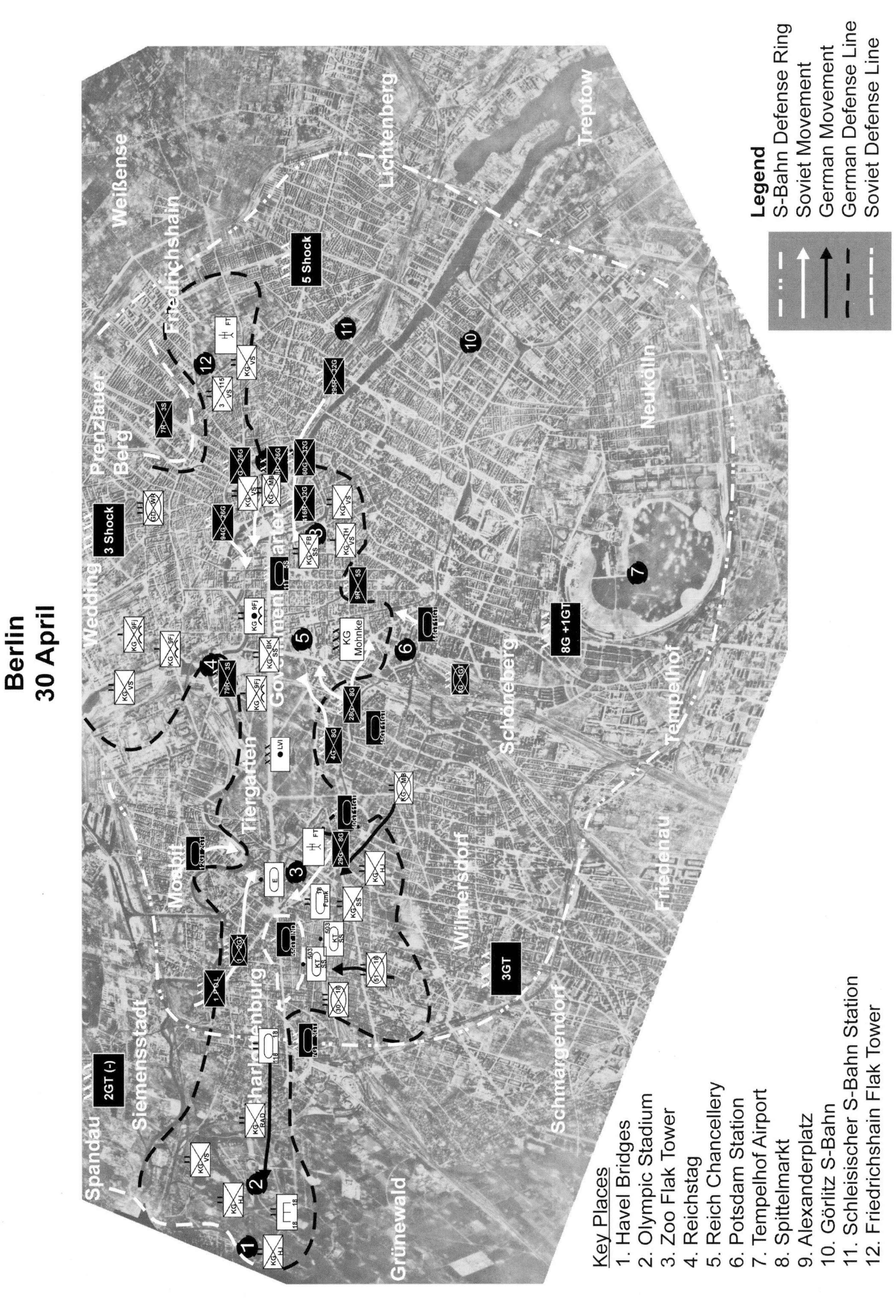

FÜHRERBUNKER

Hitler summoned Mohnke at 0600 hours. Intense Soviet shelling could be felt through the ferro-concrete walls of the bunker. He asked Mohnke where the Russians were. Mohnke replied that the Soviets were in the Adlon Hotel at the junction of Wilhelmstraße and Unter Der Linden, in the U-Bahn tunnel in Friedrichstraße, and just outside the Reich Chancellery beneath Vossstraße. He expected the Soviets to launch a massive frontal assault on the Reich Chancellery on 1 May to coordinate with the Communist holiday. Mohnke's assessment was essentially correct. The Russians were on Unter-den-Linden, but not in force. The Adlon Hotel was still in German hands. The Russians were in the U-Bahn tunnels, but not as far as the Stadtmitte U-Bahn station opposite Vossstraße. The Russians were going to launch an attack on 1 May, but on the Reichstag, not the Reich Chancellery. After Mohnke's update, Hitler gave him personal copies of his testament to take to Dönitz, after he was presumably told of Bormann's failure to get them out of the city the day before.[5] The war was over for Hitler. He made final preparations for suicide. By early afternoon Hitler and Eva Braun took their lives. Both bodies were subsequently burned and buried in a shallow grave outside the *Führerbunker* in the Reich Chancellery garden.

LVI PZ. KORPS

Weidling called a 1000 meeting of all sector commanders in his HQ. The Russians were only blocks away, so it was a feat to be able to bring everyone together so close to the Russian lines. Everyone arrived except for Bärenfänger who did not receive the radiogram until later. This may have been because Weidling did not want him in attendance because of his close relationship with Goebbels. Weidling briefed Hitler's verbal order of the previous day that a breakout of the city was approved if ammunition was low but no capitulation of Berlin was to take place. He then asked if a breakout of Berlin was now warranted, especially with Wenck so close to the city. All meeting members agreed to an immediate breakout. Weidling set the breakout time for 2200 that evening. The sector commanders left his headquarters at 1300 to prepare their forces.[6]

Shortly after everyone left Weidling was visited by a *SS-Sturmführer* who arrived with a letter from Hitler. Weidling, who was under some duress about how to inform Krebs of his decision to breakout, believed that he was going to be arrested. It turned out that the letter contained a confirmation from Hitler in writing that if ammunition was depleted Weidling could authorize a breakout of all remaining troops.[7] The caveat was that no capitulation of Berlin was allowed.[8] Weidling decided to go to the Reich Chancellery immediately and inform Krebs of his decision, now that he had confirmation from Hitler to take the action. Before he left, Weidling received a visit from another *SS* messenger. This time the letter was from Krebs, "General Weidling shall report immediately to the Chancellery, Gen. Krebs. All steps planned for 30 April are to be stopped without delay" signed by the aide-de-camp of *SS-Brigadeführer* Mohnke.[9] Mohnke presumably received a similar letter from Hitler, and notified Krebs, who in turn notified Goebbels. By evening Goebbels countermanded Hitler's authorization for a breakout, and all plans were placed on hold for 24 hours.[10]

Weidling arrived at the Bunker in the late afternoon. Upon meeting Krebs he was immediately informed of the following:

1. Today, April 30th, in the afternoon about 1530, the Führer had committed suicide.

2. His body had already been burned in the garden of the Chancellery in a shell crater.

3. The suicide of the Führer must be kept a deep secret.

4. Abroad, only Marshal Stalin was informed of the suicide of the Führer.

5. Sector Commander *Oberstleutnant* Seifert, under the command of *SS-Brigadeführer* Mohnke, has already received orders to contact the local Russian commands, asking them to take General Krebs to the Russian High Command.

6. General Krebs was to inform the Russian High Command as follows:
a. The Führer's suicide.
b. The contents of his Last Will, according to which a new German Government had been formed as follows:
   i. Reich President: *Großadmiral* Dönitz
   ii. Chancellor: Dr. Goebbels
   iii. Foreign Affairs: 'Reichsleiter' Bormann
   iv. Interior Minister: Seiss-Inquart
   v. Defense Department: *Generalfeldmarschall* Schörner
c. Ask for an armistice, before the new government would take over in Berlin.
d. The desire of the government to negotiate with Russia about the capitulation of Germany.[11]

Krebs explained that in order to negotiate a settlement with the Russians all plans for a breakout had to be stopped. Goebbels wanted to attempt a negotiation with the Soviets that might leave the Nazi Government in power to continue to fight, or negotiate a separate armistice with the west. Nazi political survival was the foremost concern on Goebbels' mind, not the welfare of Berliners or the soldiers fighting in the streets. Berlin no longer represented a focal point for a decisive military victory against the Soviets. Now Berlin became an object to use as barter. If Berlin was emptied of troops through a breakout, than Goebbels had no leverage in negotiations. Weidling even confronted Goebbels on this point stating "Sir, do you seriously believe that the Russians will negotiate with a government, with you as Chancellor?"[12] Preparations were now made to reach Soviet lines and bring the offer of negotiations. It was understood that Chuikov's forces were operating several blocks to the south. This is where the attempt to cross the frontline was made.

The news of Hitler's death and rumors of either a breakout or capitulation ran rampant through the German forces fighting in the city. Each commander and soldier was affected differently by the news and reacted accordingly. Most felt betrayed and many decided that it was time to take matters into their own hands. Leopold, who stayed with his *SS* men and held off the Soviets from advancing past the Anhalt S-Bahn Station learned of Hitler's death in the evening. He subsequently released his men from their duty stating "I said goodbye to them with the desire that each man must now make their own decision."[13] Further east, the commander of the Friedrichshain Flak

Eastern Districts
30 April

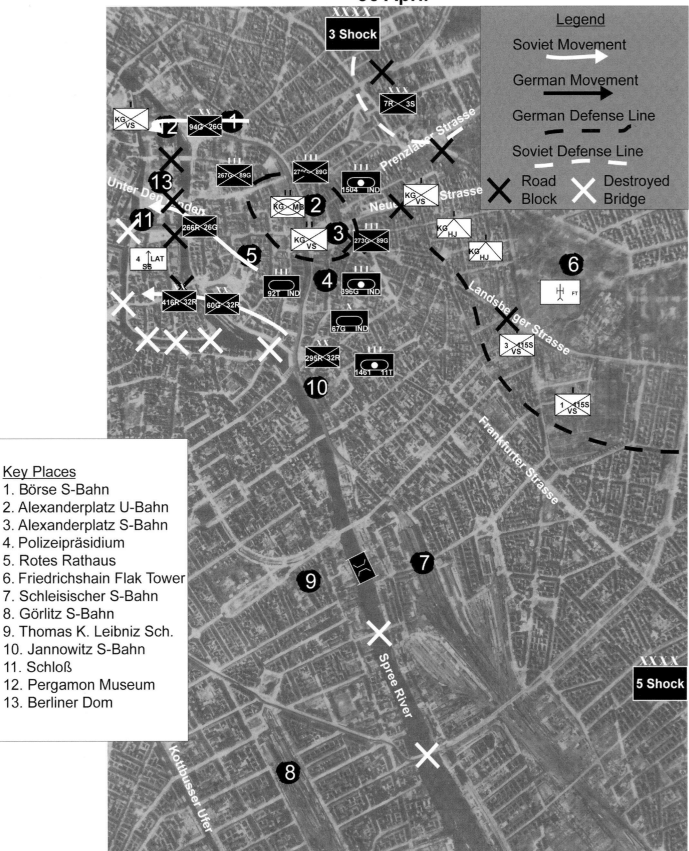

Key Places
1. Börse S-Bahn
2. Alexanderplatz U-Bahn
3. Alexanderplatz S-Bahn
4. Polizeipräsidium
5. Rotes Rathaus
6. Friedrichshain Flak Tower
7. Schleisischer S-Bahn
8. Görlitz S-Bahn
9. Thomas K. Leibniz Sch.
10. Jannowitz S-Bahn
11. Schloß
12. Pergamon Museum
13. Berliner Dom

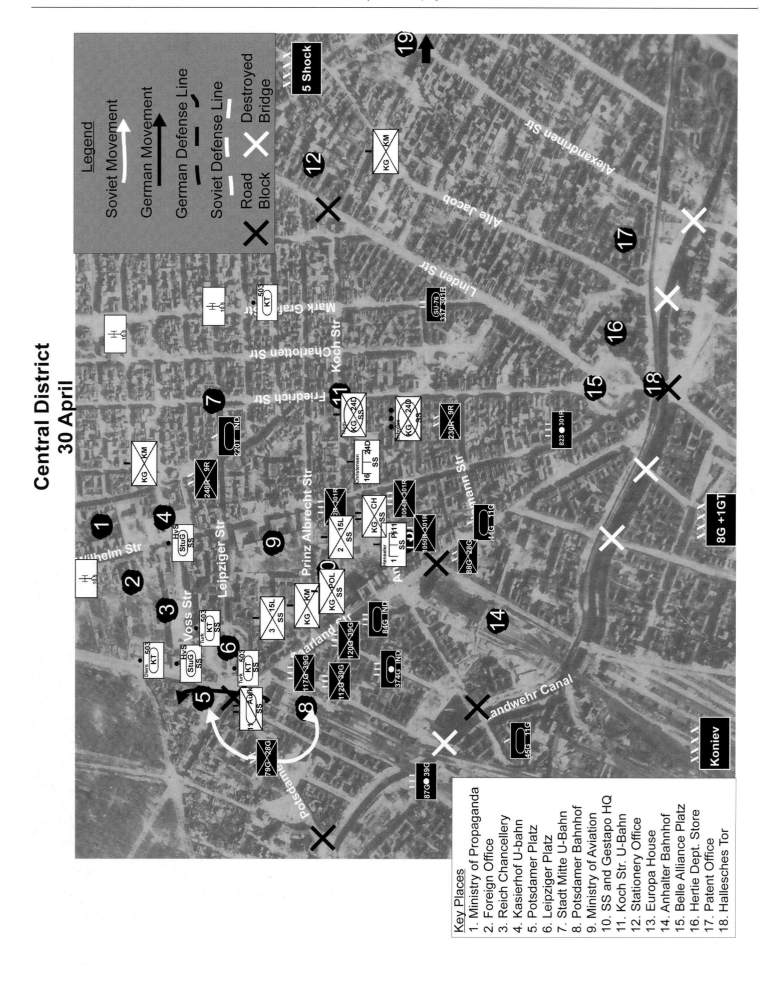

Central District
30 April

Legend

Soviet Movement

German Movement

German Defense Line

Soviet Defense Line

Road Block

Destroyed Bridge

Key Places

1. Ministry of Propaganda
2. Foreign Office
3. Reich Chancellery
4. Kasierhof U-bahn
5. Potsdamer Platz
6. Leipziger Platz
7. Stadt Mitte U-Bahn
8. Potsdamer Bahnhof
9. Ministry of Aviation
10. SS and Gestapo HQ
11. Koch Str. U-Bahn
12. Stationery Office
13. Europa House
14. Anhalter Bahnhof
15. Belle Alliance Platz
16. Hertie Dept. Store
17. Patent Office
18. Hallesches Tor

Tower now authorized a breakout for the remaining troops in the bunker. It is not clear if they knew about Weidling's breakout directive, but it is presumed they received word from the Zoo Bunker of Hitler's death. The remaining soldiers left in the dark and made their way west through the ruined streets toward Alexanderplatz but soon found the way blocked by Russian defensive positions. Inside the Flak Tower only medical staff and wounded remained so it was decided to surrender the Flak Tower to the Russians in the morning.[14]

EASTERN DISTRICTS

The 5th Shock Army finally began to impose military control through Defense Sectors A and B. The majority of Germans instinctively filtered back over the Spree onto Museum Island, heading west across Unter-den-Linden or northwest toward Prenzlau. Despite this, there is no evidence that Alexanderplatz fell to the Soviets, so presumably stiff fighting continued through the ruins in that area. What is known is that the 94th Guards Rifle Division continued with the reduction of the German defense of the Börse S-Bahn Station during the course of the day. The S-Bahn station fell in the afternoon as Soviet infantry infiltrated behind the German positions. Soviet engineers then destroyed a portion of the railroad embankment, which allowed Soviet tanks through, bypassing fixed German anti-tank positions located nearby. Leading elements pushed up Oranienburger Straße to contest the next German defensive position located in the Telegraph Office. By the evening the 94th Guards Rifle Division reached the Charite Hospital, while the 266th Rifle Division crossed the Spree under fire to take Museum Island with the Pergamon Museum and Dome Cathedral.[15]

The 32nd Rifle Corps launched their attack across the Spree on the southern part of Museum Island known as Fischerinsel where Schloss Berlin was located. Elements of the 60th Guards and 416th Rifle Divisions headed for the massive Reichsbank but received heavy fire from the Spaniards of *Bataillon Fantasma* located in buildings on the far side of the Kupfergraben Canal that formed the new German front line.[16]

CENTRAL DISTRICTS

An earlier issue of the *Panzerbär* made its way to Schulz and the other boys in their cellar at the Spittelmarkt. In this issue they read how Göring was replaced by von Greim and Himmler by Hanke due to their acts of treachery against Hitler. This caused some morning debate among the boys, especially about Himmler being replaced. The conversations came to an abrupt end as Russians forces launched another attack in an attempt to take the Spittelmarkt after the majority of the 11th Tank Corps passed north through the intersection. The Russians discovered that most basements in Berlin were interconnected and they began to break holes in basements and advance into German strongpoints from underneath the streets. The Russians apparently did this to get close to Schulz's unit as they stormed the first floor above the boys. The *Hitlerjugend* now launched a counterattack upstairs and a vicious firefight broke out between the Russians and *Hitlerjugend* defenders. The boys used their 'Volksgranaten' (grenades without their wood handles) to drive the Russians back out of the building. Finally a pioneer squad arrived from *Nordland* equipped with a flamethrower and torched the Russian's positions driving the survivors out.[17] Three Russians were captured, probably wounded, and sent back to Schulz's HQ where they were interrogated then immediately shot. Despite this setback, the Russians continued to push through the ruins moving along paths of least resistance. The Russians finally succeeded in taking the north side of Leipziger Straße and Dönhoffplatz on the south side by the afternoon. This left Schultz and the remaining German defenders in control of the south side of the Spittelmarkt. *Volkssturm*, *Hitlerjugend* and *SS* reinforcements made their way from the Government Quarter as evening drew near. Once they arrived immediate counterattacks were launched and as Schulz recalled, "in a wild fight they succeeded in recapturing the north side of the street." That evening the Propaganda Ministry conducted a radio broadcast that informed listeners that Wenck's army was close and that a ceasefire was concluded with the United States. Everyone in Berlin was to hold out for imminent rescue. This bolstered the spirits of Schulz and boys in the cellar who tried to hold onto any ray of hope.[18]

Just north of the Spittelmarkt was Kurstraße. Even at this stage in the battle efforts were made to continue building defensive works. One German officer brought 78 Dutch slave laborers and ordered them to build a tank barricade. The German officer and several others were to provide fire-support in case the workers were attacked. Members of

A view from the roof of the Berliner Dom Cathedral south along the Spree River. The Soviets didn't cross this part of the Spree until 30 April as the German defense of Alexanderplatz to the left of the photo was so tenacious. Author's collection.

the 11th Tank Corps presumably noticed this group and opened fire on them forcing the Dutch workers to find shelter in a partially-ruined factory building. The interior walls of the building were lined with tall metal closets. A Soviet mortar or artillery shell hit the building and the remnants collapsed on the group of laborers and German soldiers. One of the metal closets fell but was buttressed against a neighboring wall saving the German officer in command. Most of the others were not as lucky as they were buried in the rubble.[19]

Henseler and his men spent the night on a side street of Lindenstraße southwest of the Spittelmarkt. They stayed there until 1100 drinking liquor and eating food found in the Kepinski Restaurant nearby. The Russians launched a series of attacks that morning, but made little progress with their armor as a King Tiger was positioned nearby to block any advance. Before noon his men received notice to report to the Reich Air Ministry where Henseler received orders directly from Seifert to occupy and hold the Europahaus near Potsdamer Platz. Upon arrival, Henseler found the building already occupied by well over a hundred *Luftwaffe* personnel who eagerly put themselves under Henseler's command. They told him that the Russians were across the street and they thought they were trying to infiltrate into the Europahaus from the cellar. They also mentioned that they thought the Russians had infiltrated the upper storeys. Henseler and his men quickly barricaded the cellar doors and booby-trapped them with grenades. Then they conducted a cautious sweep of the upper floors and found no Russians.[20]

At the Herold Insurance building, Scholles and his men held out, while Christensen collected all available stragglers and continued to hold Friedrichstraße and Puttkamerstraße against Soviet attacks. The Russians tried hard to break through Puttkamerstraße in order to reach the Reich Chancellery and other Government Buildings. The men of *Nordland* continued to hear rumors about Wenck and how they would soon be rescued. These soldiers did not hear about any planned breakout presumably because they were needed to keep back the Russians from advancing any further.[21] Scholles wrote in his diary that day "We are fighting because we hope to get reinforcements from the West. Even though our position is slowly becoming hopeless, we continue to fight. It is the only thing we can do to avoid thinking about the darkness of tomorrow. I personally am completely absorbed by the fighting."[22]

The Soviets launched a series of attacks in an attempt to clear the Potsdam Bahnhof and the blocks that ran north from Anhalter to Vossstraße. Along Puttkamerstraße the French continued to resist against Soviet attacks. A Soviet POW taken prisoner revealed how Soviet tank crews were forced to mount offensives at gunpoint because they knew the crews in the lead tanks would not be coming back.[23] Russian tankers continued to suffer grievous losses, especially as the Germans were compressed into a smaller area giving them better coverage of key avenues of approach. Abyzov was witness to a Russian tank attack up Wilhelmstraße and his recollection of that event provides a unique Russian view of the violence that Soviet tankers endured during the street fighting.

> The long street receded somewhere into the darkness. Tanks and artillery were supporting us in the attack. As I pressed the trigger I felt the submachine gun leap into life. But I could not hear any shots for the roar of the artillery and the rumble of tanks.
>
> I saw the dark silhouette of a tank ahead of me. Where did it come from? Before I realized what had happened it started firing—a German tank. There it was, right in the middle of the street, firing at our tanks.
>
> It fired another round. Then I saw the fiery trail of a flying [*Panzerfaust*]. It set the German tank on fire. But our T–34 tank went up in flames too.
>
> We took the ground floor of a building on the corner. There was a strong smell of lavender and puddles on the floor together with a lot of broken glass. It was a barber shop. The battalion commander ordered us to consolidate the position ....
>
> A [*Panzerfaust*] exploded behind us on the floor. I was deafened by the din and could hear nothing ....
>
> Another tank—a Soviet tank—was set on fire. It was burning in a side street. We saw the tankmen open the hatch and escape through it to the pavement. One of them was in flames. Rolling on the ground he tried to extinguish the fire. One of our boys jumped out of the window to help the tankman.
>
> An enemy submachine gunner opened fire from the attic. Our boy fell down before he reached the tankman. The tankman was killed by the same burst.[24]

Nearby at the Potsdam S-Bahn Station, fierce fighting continued.

SS-Unterscharführer Karl-Heinz Turk was still in position with his King Tiger. He fought an hour-long battle against both Soviet tanks, and anti-tank guns that Chuikov's forces brought over the Landwehr Canal. By the end of the battle, a number of Soviet tanks lay burning in the street. One shot immobilized the right track of the Panzer. Turk quickly set off on foot to the Tiergarten to retrieve the only Bergepanther (Panzer recovery vehicle) in Berlin commanded by his friend. He made his way back down to Potsdamer Platz with the Bergepanther and recovered his King Tiger by bringing it back to the Reich Chancellery area for repairs. The King Tiger was fixed three hours later and Turk moved back down Saarlandstraße where he positioned the King Tiger behind a barricade at the Potsdamer U-Bahn Station. He received orders to hold the square as long as he could. Russian infantry tried to use the sewers to reach the King Tiger but the crew kept them back through the use of the Panzer's turret-mounted machine-gun.[25] All day Chuikov's phone rang. It was Zhukov, and he continued to ask if Berlin might fall before May Day. Chuikov's final reply that day was "I doubt it. Some German *SS* units are still fighting like tigers."[26]

In the Zoo Bunker the rumors of a breakout circulated among the remaining officers and staff. An *Oberleutnant* of the *18.Pz.Gren.Div.* approached Böttcher and stated "I and several other officers have discussed this planned breakout. We are not going to participate in it, for we are still bound to the Führer by our oath. We can not abandon our Führer in such a critical situation."[27] This idea of an oath resonated among many in the city during the last days. Böttcher was surprised to hear this and remarked after the war that he based it on two things: "Some of the officers would not break their oath out of religious consideration, while others were fanatic National Socialists and did not want to betray their political conceptions." Böttcher avoided any political debates at this stage and simply replied "You are free to remain Berlin, but I shall take up the question of the oath with my superiors and let you know about it."[28] Böttcher called *Generalmajor* Rauch at the Reich Chancellery and explained the situation. Rauch promised to discuss this with Weidling. He called back later in the evening and said "The question of the oath has been submitted to the Führer. The answer is 'I relieve all soldiers of their oath.'" If Rauch did speak to Weidling, Weidling may have simply responded based on his prior conversation with Hitler regarding a breakout if the ammunition and supplies ran out. Rauch, knowing that Hitler already killed himself, probably made up a story as he was

Spittelmarkt
30 April

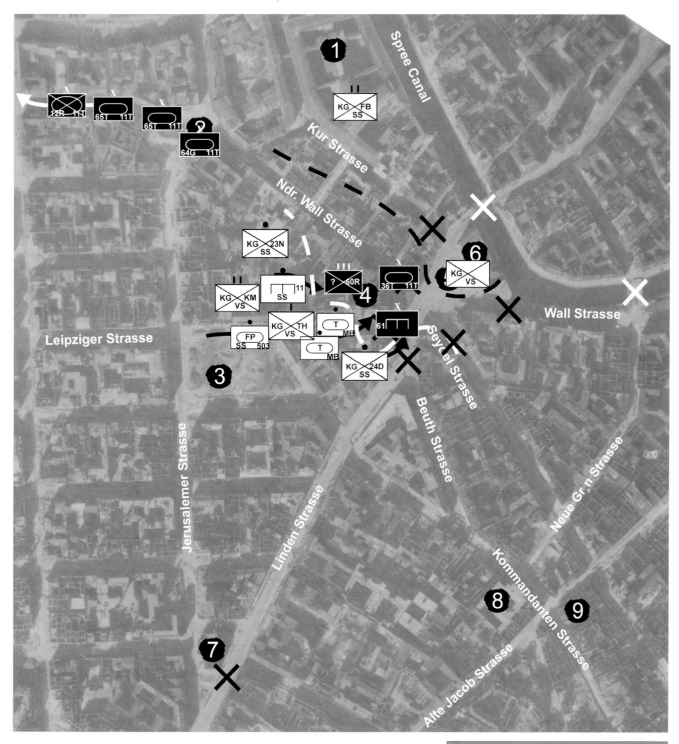

Key Places
1. Reichsbank
2. Hausvogtei Platz
3. Donhoff Platz
4. St. Joseph II Hospital
5. Spittelmarkt Platz
6. Foreign Exchange
7. Jerusalemer Church
8. Reich Stationery Office
9. Theatre

Legend

Soviet Movement

German Movement

German Defense Line

Soviet Defense Line

✖ Road Block   ✕ Destroyed bridge

This is a rare photo of Turk's King Tiger outside the Potsdam S-Bahn station. Note the tow hooks on the left side from when the King Tiger was initially towed to the area of the Reich Chancellery for repairs. Note the destroyed VW on the right riddled with bullet holes—a sign of the intensity of fighting in the area. Photo courtesy of ASKM.

Soviet gunners load a ZiS-3 76mm divisional gun sited on tram tracks during urban combat in Berlin. (RGAKFD Moscow)

Soviet submachine-gunners, who have taken a position in a destroyed church, fire on the enemy, Berlin, 1945. (RGAKFD Moscow)

still under a promise not to reveal Hitler's death. In either case it was lie of convenience to save his soldiers and get them out of the city and away from Russian captivity.[29]

SOUTHERN DISRICTS

The 3rd Guards Tank Army now maintained a limited force in the city despite losing their ability to drive on the Reichstag. The Ppanzergrenadiers of the *18.Pz.Gren.Div.* continued to resist Koniev's remaining forces. *Pz.Gren.Rgt.30* maintained a front along the S-Bahn line that marked the inner defense ring, while *Pz.Gren.Rgt.51* was pushed back toward Kurfürstendamm.[30] Stolze's King Tiger knocked out only one Soviet tank at Hallensee S-Bahn Station that day confirming the lack of forward operations in this area now that Koniev's main forces were withdrawing from Berlin.

WESTERN DISTRICTS

The 1st Mechanized Corps sent the remains of the 19th and 35th Mechanized Brigade down Schloßstraße to clear the areas north and south of Kantstraße respectively, heading toward the Zoo. The 35th Mechanized Brigade encountered strong German resistance on the line Kaiser Friedrichstraße and on the right flank near Charlottenburg Station and made slower progress. The 19th Mecha-nized Brigade reached the strongpoint on Karl-August-Platz that Dragunsky's troops had previously failed to overcome. Both flanks of the 19th Mechanized Brigade were now exposed. This brigade lost contact with the 37th Mechanized Brigade on the far side of Bismarckstraße where the latter was heavily engaged with the Ger-man defenses. The 19th Mechanized Brigade was also separated from

Soviet infantry attack through dense smoke caused by raging fires. Movement in the open was always risky. Photo courtesy of the Bulgarian Ministry of Defence

A view across Königsplatz near where the Ministry of Interior was located. In 1945 the land between here and the Reichstag was a tangled mess of construction equipment, trenches, 8.8cm anti-tank guns and a flooded channel. It took the Soviets several attempts to cross this expanse of terrain and reach the steps of the Reichstag. Author's collection.

Soviet Assault on the Reichstag
30 April (Morning)

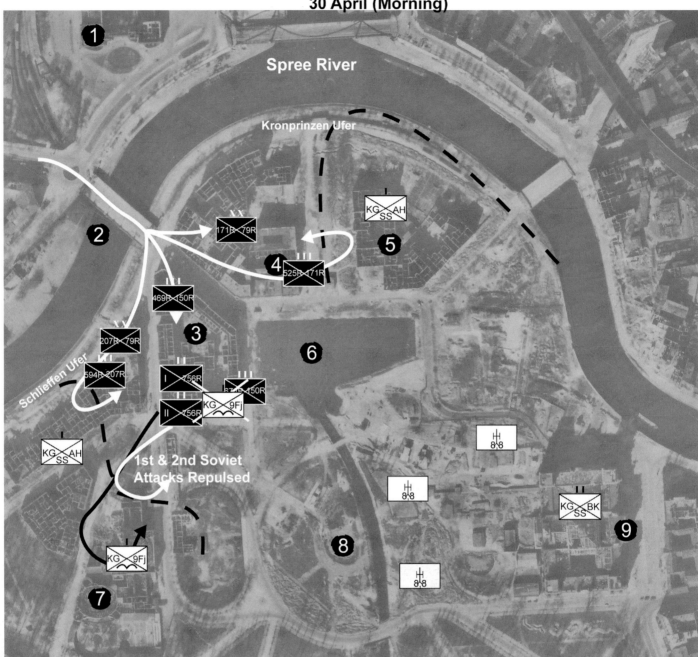

Spree River

Kronprinzen Ufer

Schlieffen Ufer

1st & 2nd Soviet
Attacks Repulsed

Key Places
1. Lehrter Bahnhof
2. Moltke Bridge
3. Ministry of the Interior
   "Himmler's House"
4. Swiss Consulate
5. Diplomatic Quarter
6. Speer's U-Bahn
   Construction Site and
   Flooded Tunnel
7. Kroll Opera House
8. Königsplatz
9. Reichstag

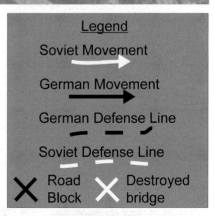

Legend
Soviet Movement
German Movement
German Defense Line
Soviet Defense Line
Road Block
Destroyed bridge

its northern neighbor, the 219th Tank Brigade, which was operating even further forward near Marchstraße north of Knie.

The 1st Polish Tadiuscz Kosciuszko Infantry Division arrived that evening. The Polish officers were horrified to learn that some of the infantry units in the 2nd Guards Tank Army suffered up to 95% casualties. The 3rd Polish Infantry Regiment was assigned to the 66th Guards Tank Brigade of the 12th Guards Tank Corps, which through lack of infantry support, had lost 82 tanks since the fighting began along the Seelow Heights on 16 April. The 1st Polish Regiment was subsequently split up into combat teams under the 19th and 35th Mechanized Brigade. The 2nd Polish Infantry Regiment was assigned to the 219th Tank Brigade and the entire 1st Mechanized Corps.

NORTHERN DISTRICTS

In the early morning of the 30 April the Russians were recuperating from the previous day's fighting in the Ministry of Interior. The pressure to continue the offensive and take the Reichstag overrode all human concerns of the Soviet leadership. A portable radio, one of the few available, was brought across the Moltke Bridge into the Ministry of the Interior during the night. Regimental Commander Zincenko needed to know what the status was of the attack. Neustroyev explained that he thought he was at the end of the building, but his orientation in the dark was off. The Regimental Commander then ordered him to start an attack on the Reichstag immediately. There would be no pause in operations for any reason. Neustroyev roused the battalion and launched a counterattack from the Ministry of Interior into the early morning darkness of Königsplatz. His men advanced in the dark, blinded by smoke and fire, and were immediately hit with machine-gun rounds, presumably from the Kroll Opera House. It is entire plausible that the first Russian attack toward the Reichstag occurred against the Kroll Opera House instead. No Russian in the battalion or even in 'Himmler's House' knew where the Reichstag actually was, especially in the dark. The 1st Battalion took their wounded and retreated back into the Ministry of Interior to wait out the night.[31] The only good news that Neustroyev received was the arrival of badly-needed reinforcements in the form of 78 men who were released from the Moabit prison. Not one of them had any combat experience but they were going into battle anyway.[32] Many soldiers who had just run the non-stop gauntlet of combat over the last several days fell asleep where they rested.

In the morning, through the mist and smoke that perpetually lingered in Königsplatz, the Russians finally began to see the area where they were fighting. Once again the call from the Regimental Commander went out to attack the Reichstag. Neustroyev looked out of the second storey window and saw a three-storeyed, grey building across an open expanse of ground. He had doubts that this was the Reichstag. His orders, however, were clear "If you believe this building to be the Reichstag, then attack!" For a second time Neustroyev's men jumped out of their positions and assaulted across the field toward the building they suspected was the Reichstag. Soviet artillery

This is an excellent aerial view depicting the difficult urban terrain in Berlin and the area around Königsplatz.
Courtesy of the US National Archives.

Soviet Assault on the Reichstag
30 April (Afternoon)

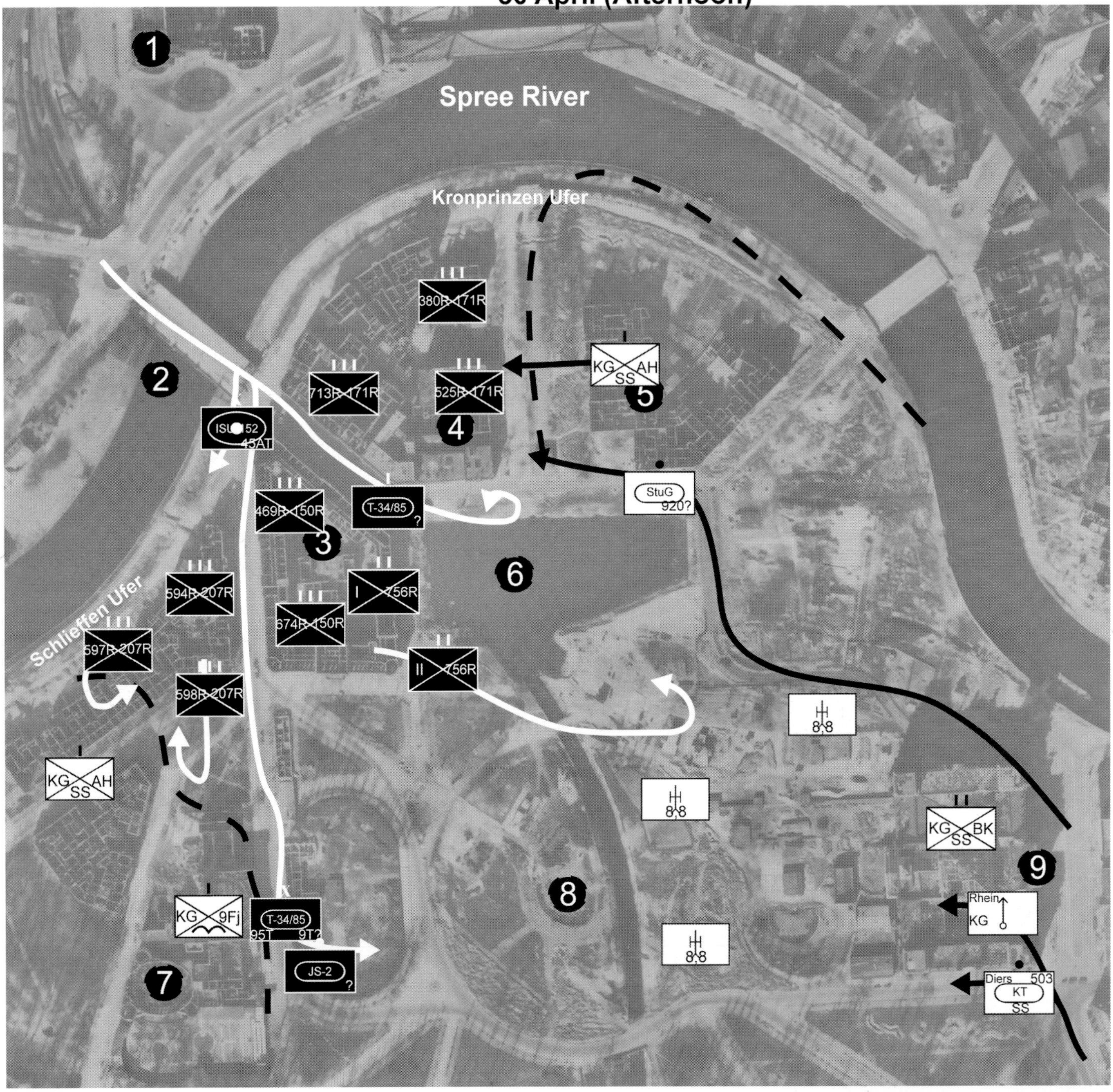

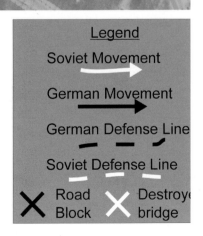

Spree River

Kronprinzen Ufer

380R-171R

713R-171R   525R-171R

KG × AH SS

ISU 52 45AT

469R-150R   T-34/85 ?

594R-207R   I × 756R

597R-207R   674R-150R

598R-207R   II × 756R

KG × AH SS

StuG 920?

8.8

8.8

KG × BK SS

Rhein KG

8.8

KG × 9Fj 95T   T-34/85 9T2

JS-2 ?

Diers 503 KT SS

Key Places
1. Lehrter Bahnhof
2. Moltke Bridge
3. Ministry of the Interior "Himmler's House"
4. Swiss Consulate
5. Diplomatic Quarter
6. Speer's U-Bahn Construction Site and Flooded Tunnel
7. Kroll Opera House
8. Königsplatz
9. Reichstag

Legend
Soviet Movement
German Movement
German Defense Line
Soviet Defense Line
× Road Block   × Destroyed bridge

Another view looking northwest over the Reichstag. The Ministry of Interior and Swiss Consulate are both clearly visible. This photo was taken on or about 2 May as you can see the Red Flag on the Reichstag dome and still smoking ruins all around the building. Photo courtesy of the Bundesarchiv.

from the north bank of the Spree opened fire and a 'Hurrah!' went up as the red flares were fired signaling the start of the Soviet assault. The Russians charged toward the building and after 50 meters a wall of steel from local mortars and, and anti-aircraft fire from the Zoo Flak Tower, rained down on the Russians. In addition, machine gun fire opened up and as Neustroyev stated "Our 'Hurrah!' sank with a crash."[33] The Russians retreated back into the Ministry of Interior. The Soviet attack was made not against the Reichstag but against the Kroll Opera House for a second time. If indeed they were attacking toward the Reichstag, then they clearly did not get far.

By mid-morning the Regimental Commander came across the Moltke Bridge and spent time trying to orient himself and the 1st Battalion. They knew the Reichstag was near but they could not be sure of the exact location. Soon Zinchenko oriented himself with a map and the surrounding buildings and noted the three storey gray building with a destroyed dome on the far side of Königsplatz. He then quickly declared that this was the Reichstag. As he headed off to radio the Division Commander, he ordered the 1st Battalion to prepare and launch a third attack in the direction of the building immediately across the open expanse of Königsplatz.

General Perevertkin soon ordered his remaining troops over to the southern bank to help reinforce the tired and somewhat depleted 150th Division. First he sent over the remaining Regiment of the 150th Rifle Division, the 469th. They headed into the Ministry of Interior. Next, he sent over the 171st Rifle Division to conduct operations across the north bank of the Spree and directly support the planned attack by the 150th. Finally, he ordered the 207th Rifle Division over the Spree to attack and secure the Kroll Opera House, thereby ending any threat to the flank of the main attack on the Reichstag.[34] Several of the artillery pieces brought across the Spree were now disassembled and hauled up to the second storey of 'Himmler's House' and placed in a position to support attacks on both the Kroll Opera House and the Reichstag. Shortly after the guns were in place Soviet artillery fire opened up on the Kroll Opera House.

The German defenders did not remain idle during the morning and launched several counterattacks. The first counterattack came from behind the Reichstag and hit the soldiers of the 525th Regiment who had moved into the open along Alsenstraße in an effort to take the buildings east of the Swiss Consulate. Soviet artillery from the north bank of the Spree forced the Germans back into the opposite buildings after a fierce fight developed. A second counterattack was launched by members of the *SS-Rgt.Anhalt* against the 594th Rifle Regiment along Schlieffenufer and was also beaten back. The Germans, however, retained the southern bank of the Spree along this street for the rest of the battle as the Russians did not have the manpower to clear the buildings. The Russians soon began to bring more armor across the Moltke Bridge.

The attack on the Kroll Opera House was undertaken in the afternoon by the 587th and 598th Regiments of the 207th Rifle Division by early afternoon. The attack was supported by tanks but immediately ran into fierce resistance from the German defensive positions inside the building. It is not clear if the Russians ever made it into the Kroll Opera House. What is clear is that they immediately dug in around the ruins and engaged the Germans in the building.

As the Soviet pressure mounted on the German defenders, Babick sent runners to the Reich Chancellery with requests for support. Rhein's forces were now ordered to the Reichstag. Rhein entered Babick's HQ located in a part of the former's President's Palace on Dorotheenstraße behind the Reichstag. He was then ordered to reinforce the Reichstag and help out Germans cut off in the Kroll Opera House. These reinforcements were led to the Reichstag through an underground tunnel.[35] Rhein took command of several Russian mortars from Babick after it was known that he had experience with the weapon. The mortars were set up in one of the inner courtyards of the Reichstag where they were well protected. Then he was given a portable radio and went to the roof and directed fire on Russian positions at the Kroll Opera House and across the Spree at the General Staff buildings located in the OKW complex north of Invalidenstraße. Russian tanks tried to reach the Reichstag via Rathenower Straße then by a direct route opposite the Kroll Opera House. Combined German shelling stopped their immediate advance according to Rhein. Soon the Russians started shelling the Reichstag with 21cm artillery. A JS–2 tank now rolled into view in front of the Kroll Opera House and opened fire on German positions in the Reichstag.[36] The appearance of Soviet tanks worried Babick who again asked for Panzer support by sending a runner to the Reich Chancellery for a second straight day.

In response to Babick's request Mohnke ordered Diers, commanding King Tiger 314, to head to the Reichstag and engage Soviet armor that had moved across Moltke Bridge. Diers had spent the last twenty-four hours with Turk defending the Saarlandstraße and Potsdamer S-Bahn stations from the advance of Chuikov's forces. Diers turned his Panzer around and advanced up Hermann-Göring-Straße where he came around the left side of the Reichstag and noticed nearly three dozen Russian tanks and other vehicles positioned in the open area between the Ministry of Interior and the Kroll Opera House. In one Russian account as many as 89 tanks, vehicles, and artillery pieces were pushed over the Spree in an attempt to get direct support to the forces advancing on the Reichstag.[37] Diers stayed at the Reichstag all day through 1 May. During the rest of the afternoon his Panzer claimed 30 kills against a variety of Soviet armor in the area of the Kroll Opera House. This included the JS–2 that Rhein stated was destroyed with one well-placed shot from Diers across the open expanse of Königsplatz.[38]

North of the Reichstag several StuG IIIs joined with another German counterattack that forced a wedge in between the 525th and II/380th Rifle Regiment. This wedge stalled the preparations for the next phase of the push on the Reichstag and forced the Russians to resort to hand-to-hand combat to beat back the Germans for a second time in this area.

The Soviet soldiers of the 2nd Battalion were operating beyond their human abilities. They had not received food, water or rest since taking the Ministry of the Interior and now there were asked to make yet a third attempt at the Reichstag in broad daylight. The third attack started off poorly as company commanders were unable to effectively coordinate their attack across the construction site. Construction debris and the flooded ditch caused the units to disintegrate into small groups of uncoordinated soldiers. It appeared that at least one group of Soviets made it to the entrance of the building but they were immediately forced back due to heavy enemy fire. As Neustroyev recorded:

> The situation was becoming serious. The enemy was laying down such a heavy fire on our positions that there seemed to be absolutely no safety from it. There was a whole circle of bursting shells and bombs. It was the time of full daylight but to us it seemed that the battle was taking place in the evening twilight. Somebody later said to me that on the 30th of April it was a sunny day in Berlin. But we never saw the sun. Not a glint of it could come down to us through the smoke.[39]

As the offensive bogged down, more tanks were pushed over the Moltke Bridge to support the offensive. The armor could either go straight down Moltkestraße and bear left at the flooded Königsplatz or travel around the Ministry of Interior and come out in front of the still-occupied Kroll Opera House. In either case the armor would be exposed and unprotected from enemy fire on several angles.

As the Soviet's began to take stock of the situation they realized that the assault on the Reichstag was still not immediately possible. The Kroll Opera House to the southwest was well fortified by the Germans and several large caliber guns were mounted in the second storey windows in well-concealed positions. The 207th Rifle Division was simply not able to reduce the German position there. To the northeast the rest of the Diplomatic Quarter stretched out along the bend of the Spree and the Germans had many defensive positions there. During the night only a few of the ISU–152 self-propelled guns from the 420th Anti-Tank Artillery Division made their way over Moltke Bridge along with some equally heavy artillery pieces. These few guns were placed in the area just at the entrance of Himmler's House where the southern end of the bridge was located. The Soviets were still receiving shell fire from in the Tiergarten as well as from the two Flak Towers located in Humboldt and the Zoo. While their gunners were not able to see directly into Königsplatz, they knew the direction and fired intermittently into the suspected Russian positions.[40]

The fact that Soviet soldiers made it to the Reichstag caused a false report to be sent to Zhukov that stated the Soviet Banner was flying from the roof. This report generated 'Secret Order No 6' to the Russian forces serving in the 1st Byelorussian Front. The order acknowledged that the Soviets had taken the Reichstag and raised the Red Banner on the top of the building at 1425 in the afternoon. This news shocked the officers and soldiers of the 150th Rifle Division who were at that moment struggling with how to reach and occupy the building. The corps and division staffs struggled with what this meant. Neustroyev in particular had to look at the Reichstag through binoculars to determine if he saw any flag on the building. He saw none and didn't believe anyone breached the building. At that moment the Division Commander radioed the Regimental Commander and stated "if there are no Soviet soldiers in the Reichstag and the Red Banner has not actually been raised, then take all measures to raise a flag, even if it is just on the outside column of the entrance. By any price!"[41] Zhukov had already lost the race to Berlin and was now about to fail in taking Berlin by May Day so the Reichstag—the very symbol of Nazism shared by all Russians—had to fall by 1 May no matter what the sacrifice.

The new offensive to take the Reichstag was set for 1800. The I/674th Regiment and I/380th Regiment received orders to begin the assault. Senior Sgt. I. Syanov who commanded a company from the 674th Regiment was given the assignment to lead the assault and break into the Reichstag. In addition, the 1st Battalion was ordered to scrape together those Russians that had been separated due to the sustained German fire and move them forward into the battle behind Syanov. This was one of the few signs of the disorganization that the first assault caused among the Russian formations.[42] Additional support was brought up by moving the 88th Heavy Tank Regiment over the Moltke Bridge to provide fire support toward the Reichstag by 1830 hours.[43] The Russians moved out across the Square by using walkways across the flooded tunnel, swimming, or moving around the north edge of Königsplatz. Soviet soldiers blew holes into the bricked-up doorway, presumably with captured *Panzerfausts*. The German defenders had positions on the upper floors but in general they were located in the basement. The Germans never expected the Soviets to make the Reichstag a main point of attack so the building and its small group of defenders were not set up for a protracted defense. According to Russian accounts, they reached the entrance way and threw grenades into the foyer then stormed into the Reichstag. It was not until 2300 that the Soviets stormed the building by force. The Russian attack gained them the main entrance foyer and the southern entrance of the building. Neustroyev was worried about when and where the German counterattack would come in the dark, so he decided to hold his companies together in a compact defense.[44] Soon Soviet banners representing the various companies and regiments were quickly hung in and around the entrance and out several first storey windows of the Reichstag. Neustroyev then began to let his men rest intermittently. He does state that no one made it to the roof the night of 30 April and there was no Red Banner No. 5 flying from the top of the Reichstag.

Outside, the Russians tried to send the 2nd Battalion of the 380th Regiment around the north side of the Reichstag in an attempt to break into the building from that direction. The battalion attacked and seized the remaining buildings on the Kronprinzenufer. Then they began their assault south across the open field toward the Reichstag. The Germans were positioned with several self-propelled guns, and perhaps a Panther tank along with additional infantry behind the Reichstag. These forces launched their own attack against the Russians and halted them. The Russians in turn brought up ISU–152s from the 185th Anti-Tank Battalion and managed to destroy the German armor and halt the German attack.[45]

Throughout Berlin there appeared a slackening of Soviet attacks. Soviet soldiers instinctively knew that the battle would soon be over. They did not want to be the last to die in the war. German morale started to ebb as no outside rescues appeared. German officers started to give out Iron Crosses and other medals freely to many soldiers in order to help keep up morale.[46]

Soviet Assault on the Reichstag
30 April (Evening)

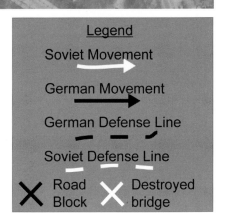

Spree River

Kronprinzen Ufer

Schlieffen Ufer

1

2

3

4

5

6

7

8

9

713R-171R

525R-171R

II 380R

469R-150R

ISU 52 45AT

I 380R

I ISU 52 45AT

594R-207R

II 756R

KG AH SS

597R-207R

598R-207R

II 574R

StuG 920?

H 8\8

KG AH SS

JS-2 88G?

JS-2 88G?

H 8\8

I 756R

KG BK SS

KG 9Ei

T-34/85 95T 9T?

I 574R

H 8\8

Rhein KG

JS-2 ?

Diers 503 KT SS

Key Places
1. Lehrter Bahnhof
2. Moltke Bridge
3. Ministry of the Interior "Himmler's House"
4. Swiss Consulate
5. Diplomatic Quarter
6. Speer's U-Bahn Construction Site and Flooded Tunnel
7. Kroll Opera House
8. Königsplatz
9. Reichstag

Legend
Soviet Movement

German Movement

German Defense Line

Soviet Defense Line

✕ Road Block   ✕ Destroyed bridge

Notes to Chapter 6: Assault on Berlin, 30th April Monday

1   OKW File, Last Announcements of OKW, 30 April (RC: 62:8).
2   Ibid, p. 44.
3   Schultz-Naumann, p. 24.
4   Le Tissier, *Slaughter at Halbe*, p. 177.
5   Le Tissier, *Race for the Reichstag*, p. 165.
6   Weidling interrogation report.
7   Schultz-Naumann, p. 180.
8   Weidling interrogation report.
9   Ibid.
10 von Zabeltitz interview, and Schultz-Naumann, p. 181.
11 Weidling Interrogation Report.
12 Ibid.
13 Venghaus, p. 214.
14 Ibid, p. 162.
15 Le Tissier, *Race for the Reichstag*, p. 166.
16 bid, p. 170.
17 Schulz interview.
18 Ibid.
19 Winge interview.
20 Henseler interview.
21 Scholles interview.
22 Ibid.
23 Forbes, p. 301.
24 Abyzov, pp. 63–4.
25 Fey, pp. 323–4.
26 J. P. O'Donnell, *The Bunker: The History of the Reich Chancellery Group*, p. 218.
27 Böttcher interview.
28 Ibid.
29 Ibid.
30 Engelmann, pp. 151, 153.
31 Neustroyev first interview.
32 Ibid.
33 Ibid.
34 Ibid.
35 H. Rhein interview (RC: 69/12).
36 Ibid.
37 Neustroyev first interview.
38 Rhein, interview. Rhein does not mention all the other Soviet tanks in the area.
39 Neustroyev first interview.
40 Ibid, and Le Tissier, *Race for the Reichstag*, p. 167.
41 Neustroyev first interview.
42 Ibid.
43 M. Baryatinskiy, *The IS Tanks*, p. 53.
44 Neustroyev first interview.
45 Neustroyev first interview.
46 Altner, p. 178.

6

ASSAULT ON BERLIN

1 MAY
TUESDAY

In the center of Berlin the brave garrison rallied around our Führer, and made a good defense on the narrowest area against Bolshevist superior forces. The heroic fight continues under heaviest enemy artillery fire and air raids in waves. South of the Reich capital units of our *9.Armee* made contact with the main forces [*12.Armee]* and form a line Niemegk-Beelitz-Wreder which they defend heroically against incessant attacks of the Soviets. Also between Rathenow and Fehrbellin our troops repulsed strong attacks of the enemy. In Mecklenburg the main thrust of the Bolshevists is directed against the area between Mueritz and Demmin. Here heavy fighting is going on. A part of the enemy forces wheeled to the northeast and tried in vain to cross the Peene-Enge, west of Anklam. In the northeast the stronghold of Wolgast repulsed all attacks. Bolshevist breakthrough attempts made from the east against Dievenow-Enge collapsed with heavy losses for the enemy.[1]

OKW **Radio Broadcast**

The battered, desperate, tired masses of the *9.Armee* began to reach the *12.Armee* lines between Treuenbrietzen and Beelitz. Perhaps 30,000–40,000 men of the original 168,000, along with over 100,000 refugees filtered through Wenck's front lines.[2] There was no time to celebrate the arrival of Busse's forces given the circumstances. According to Busse "The situation was so desperate, so serious that we had no time to discus anything. There was no great dramatic meeting, we simply had a glass of champagne [with Wenck] and then I went to bed for the first time in three days … "[3] The *12.Armee's XX Korps* had now held out 48 hours longer then expected and quickly prepared to move west toward the U.S. Army lines along the Elbe. The move west was not going to be easy, as Wenck stated:

> During the fierce rearguard actions without any supplies whatever, the *9.Armee* (roughly 25,000 to 30,000 men) [his estimate] had lost practically all heavy weapons and part of its small arms. The troops were so overtired and, further-more, so apathetic and exhausted as a result of the excessive mental strain that, in spite of strictest commands and threats, they could not be brought to move another step toward the West. The only way to ease the situation was by the Chief Army Quartermaster's active aid in supplying trucks, and by that of the *XX Korps* who, by means of the railway which had been rendered temporarily operable and some trucks organized the transport to the West. The *9.Armee* no longer represented any combat value, and therefore had to be moved on as speedily as possible and prepare to cross the Elbe as the first of the forces doing so.[4]

Wenck recalled what Busse looked like when he appeared at his HQ " … he was completely exhausted. He was dirty and filthy," as were the rest of his men.[5] The *12.Armee* fulfilled the second part of its self-assigned mission. Both *Armeegruppe Spree* and the *9.Armee* were rescued. Now the *12.Armee* had the goal of reaching the Elbe and surrendering to the U.S. forces on the other side. Despite the decision to head west, the name of 'Wenck' still offered hope to the beleaguered forces inside Berlin.

FÜHRERBUNKER

Inside Berlin, Goebbels strove to preserve National Socialism to the end as the city and its inhabitants were being reduced to rubble. His attempt at negotiations with the Soviets provides insight into how Hitler's political inner core, even after his death, continued to strive for his ideals. What follows is the factual account of the first round of negotiations between Krebs and Chuikov that started in the early morn-ing hours of 1 May and was recorded by a Soviet Intelligence Officer involved. [*Author's note:* the German ranks are italicized but left in their English translated form presented in the intelligence document. All spelling and grammatical mistakes are in the original.]

> Subject: Record of Conversations with *the Chief of the General Staff of the Land Forces of the German Army, General of Infantry* Hans Krebs, and the *Commander of the Defense of the City of Berlin, General of Artillery* Weidling, on the Capitulation of German Forces in Berlin.

> Source: Ministry of Defense Archives, Collection 1945.

> Compiled by the Chief of the Intelligence Staff of the 8th Guards Army, Lt. Col. Gladkii.

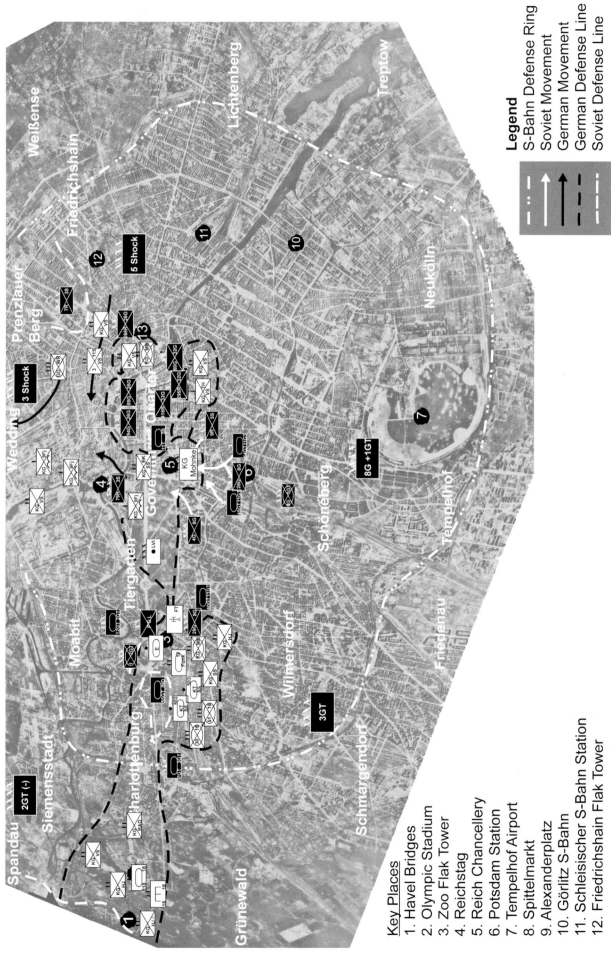

Berlin
1 May

Legend
S-Bahn Defense Ring
Soviet Movement
German Movement
German Defense Line
Soviet Defense Line

Key Places
1. Havel Bridges
2. Olympic Stadium
3. Zoo Flak Tower
4. Reichstag
5. Reich Chancellery
6. Potsdam Station
7. Tempelhof Airport
8. Spittelmarkt
9. Alexanderplatz
10. Görlitz S-Bahn
11. Schleisischer S-Bahn Station
12. Friedrichshain Flak Tower

I. The Course of Conversations with the *Chief of the General Staff of the Land Forces, General of Infantry* Hans Krebs, on the night of 1–5–1945.

At 2300 hours 30–4–1945 at the forward line of the combat sector of 102nd Guards Rifle Regiment of 35th Guards Rifle Division there arrived under a cover of a white flag a *Lt. Colonel* of the German Army with a packet which was addressed to the Commander of the Russian forces; the emissary asked that he should be passed without delay to a higher staff in order to communicate important information. Having arrived at the staff of 35th Guards Rifle Division, *Lt. Col.* Seifert handed over to the Commander of the Division, Guards Col. Smolin, and the Chief of Staff of 4th Guards Rifle Corps, Guards Col. Lebed, a written communication in Russian and in German, signed by the *Chief of the Chancellery of Hitler*, Martin Bormann. In this document it stated that *Lt. Col.* Seifert was empowered by the German Supreme Command to meet and talk with representatives of the Russian Command in order to fix a place and a time for the crossing of the line of the *Chief of the German General Staff, General of Infantry* Krebs, in order to pass on to the Russian military command extremely important information.

Col. Lebed quickly reported about the arrival of this emissary to Guards

Col. Gen. Chuikov who gave his agreement to receive and to listen to *General of Infantry* Krebs.

The decision of the Army Commander was quickly passed to *Lt. Col.* Seifert who replied that in about half an hour the *Chief of the General Staff of the Land Forces of the German Army* would cross the line of the front.

At 0300 hours General of Infantry Krebs, accompanied by the *Chief of Staff of LVI Panzer Korps, Col. of the General Staff* von Dufving, an interpreter, and one soldier crossed the line of the front in that sector where *Lt. Col.* Seifert had already crossed and were quickly conducted to the Staff of the 35th Guards Rifle Division. At the Staff of the Division awaiting them was the Deputy Commander of the Army, Guards Lt. Gen. Dukhanov, and the Chief of the Intelligence Staff of the Army, Guards Lt. Col. Gladkii (this is the Staff of the 8th Guards Army).

In reply to the question of Lt. Gen. Dukhanov about the object of his crossing the line, *Gen.* Krebs replied that he was empowered by Goebbels and by Bormann to place before the Russian Supreme Command some extremely important secret information. *Gen.* Krebs went on that he wished to communicate this information to the Commander of the Army, Col. Gen. Chuikov. At 0330 hours 1–5–1945 *Gen.* Krebs and *Col.* von Dufving arrived at the command point of the Army Commander, (at Chuikov's command point of 8th Guards Army). Having presented his documents, *Gen.* Krebs affirmed that he wished to pass on important secret information personally to Marshal Zhukov or to one of his plenipotentiaries. Col. Gen. Chuikov replied that he was empowered by the command to listen to *Gen.* Krebs and that awaiting them in his office were generals and officers who made up the Military Soviet of this front and senior officers of his staff before whom he, Krebs, could speak openly. In the office of the Commander of the 8th Guards Army there was to be found: the Deputy Commander of the Army, Lt. Gen. Dukhanov, the Commander of the 8th Guards Army Artillery, Lt. Gen. Pozharskii, member of the Military Soviet, Maj. Gen. Pronin, the Chief of the Operational Section of the Army Staff, Col. Tolkonyuk, the Chief of the Intelligence Staff of the 8th Guards Army, Lt. Col. Gladkii, and the Deputy Chief of the Intelligence Staff of the 8th Guards Army, Lt. Col. Matusov, and the military interpreter, Capt. Kelber.

Gen. Krebs put before Col. Gen. Chuikov three documents: one, an authorization in the name of the *Chief of the General Staff of the Land Forces, General or Infantry* Krebs, giving him the right to conduct conversations with the Russian Supreme Command and which bore the signature and the press of the *Chief of the Imperial Chancellery* Bormann; two, a communication of Goebbels and Bormann to Marshal Stalin, also bearing a signature and with the stamp of the Imperial Chancellery; three a list of the new imperial government and the Supreme Command of the Armed Forces of Germany which had been established according to the Will of Hitler. All documents were dated 30–4–1945.

In their communication Goebbels and Bormann stated that on 30–4–1945 at 1550 hours Berlin time Adolph Hitler had ended his life by suicide in Berlin. According to his posthumous Will (what that means there is according to Adolph Hitler's intention—the distinction between his intention and his Will which was laid down in his Will) the entire State power in the country was to pass into the hands of *Reichspresident* who was named *Gross-Admiral* Dönitz, the *Reichschancellor* in the person of Goebbels, and the *Chief of the Imperial Chancellery* Bormann.

Basing themselves on the posthumous intention of Hitler, *Reichschancellors* Goebbels and Bormann were now addressing themselves to the Soviet Supreme Command with a suggestion on a provisional breaking-off of military operations in Berlin itself in order to explore the possibility of setting up the basis for the conduct of peace talks between Germany and the Soviet Union, those people who had borne the greatest losses during the war.

In the list of the new members of government and of the Supreme Command of the Armed Forces of Germany which had been presented by *Gen.* Krebs and which had been composed according to the will of Hitler were to be found the following persons: *Reichspresident* Gross-Admiral Dönitz, *Reichschancellor* Goebbels, *Minister for Party Affairs* Bormann, the *Minister for Foreign Affairs* Seiss-Inquart, the *Minister for Internal Affairs* Hanke, the *Supreme Commander of the Land Forces General Field Marshal* Schörner, the *Chief of Staff of the Supreme Command of the German Armed Forces Col. Gen.* Jodl, *Chief of the General Staff of the Land Forces, General of Infantry* Krebs, the *Commander of the German Airforce, General-Field Marshal* von Greim, and the *Commander of the German Naval Forces, Gross-Admiral* Dönitz.

Having heard out *Gen.* Krebs, Col. Gen. Chuikov affirmed that he was in no way empowered to have any talks whatsoever with the German government; the matter under discussion must concern itself merely with the unconditional capitulation of the Berlin garrison. To this suggestion *Gen.* Krebs replied that Goebbels and Bormann could in no way undertake any act of capitulation, because in the first place the capitulation of Berlin would amount to more or less a self-liquidation of the new government which had been founded according to Hitler's intention, and secondly because they had no sanction for this from *Reichspresident* Dönitz, who was at the moment in Mecklenburg and with whom they had no communications whatsoever.

Krebs then went on to repeat that they were only asking for a provisional armistice as regards military operations in Berlin: that would give the possibility to set up communications with the remaining members of the new German government who at the moment were located outside Berlin, to inform them of the posthumous intentions of the Führer, and at the same time to inform the whole German people about the news of the death of Hitler and about the new government. Thus, the new German government would be able to gather its strength, would be able to establish itself on a legal basis and the Soviet government would have a legal partner in order to carry out the final talks for the conclusion of peace.

Col. Gen. Chuikov replied to this that concerning the request of the German government, he would submit this further on for the information of the Front Commander. Marshal Zhukov, having heard by telephone from Col. Gen. Chuikov about the request of the German government, put to Krebs by telephone the following questions: Where was Hitler's body?; Was the new German government simultaneously directing itself with a similar request to the Command of the Allied Forces, namely the Anglo-American troops?

Krebs replied that the body of Hitler had been burned at once, according to his Will (that is, Hitler's legal, written Will). Returning to the suggestion about peace talks with the Anglo-American Command, Goebbels and Bormann had not had the opportunity since they were at the moment surrounded by Russian forces and they were simply deprived of any means of communications.

At 0500 hours the Front Commander (Zhukov) confirmed the original statement about unconditional surrender and informed them that he had been in touch with Moscow in order to report to the government about the course of the conversations. On the receipt of the reply of the government, Col. Gen. Chuikov put the following questions to Krebs: Where at the moment was Himmler?; Where were Guderian and Goering?; What was the intention about the further resistance of the Berlin garrison?

Krebs replied that Himmler for some days before the death of Hitler had been excluded from the Party as a traitor because he had consciously not fulfilled the order of the Führer about the removal of all German troops from the Western Front for the defense of Berlin against the break-through operations of the Russian Army. Moreover, Himmler, without the agreement of Hitler, had begun conversations with the representatives of the governments of the United States and the United Kingdom about the capitulation of Germany. Moreover, Hitler simultaneously affirmed that Himmler was planning to replace Hitler and to install himself in power.

On the fate or Goering and Guderian, Krebs reported that Guderian had been seriously ill and already from the 15th of March, 1945, he had practically ceased to exercise the functions of the *Chief or the General Staff*. At that time

Soviet ISU-122s in a Berlin suburb, May 1945. (RGAKFD Moscow)

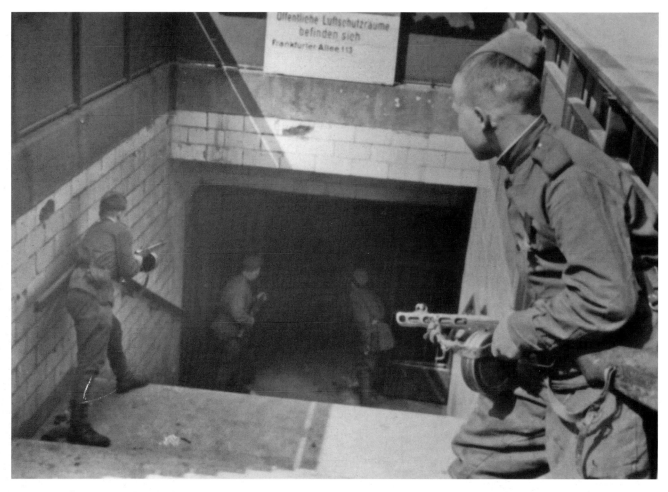

Soviet infantry armed with the ubiquitous PPsH submachine gun, cautiously explore the entrance to a U-Bahn station.
(RGAKFD Moscow)

the duties had fallen on Krebs himself as deputy to Guderian. From the 25th of April he, Krebs, had taken up, according to the order or the Führer, the duties of the *Chief of the General Staff of the Land Forces*. As for Goering, he also had been very ill and had been released from his duties and had in fact gone to Bavaria.

To the third question Krebs replied that they intended to defend the capitol [sic.] to the last soldier.

At 0800 hours in the morning there were sent to the Staff of the Front, that is, to Marshal Zhukov's Staff, all the documents which *Gen.* Krebs had brought with him.

In connection with the fact that the talks were now becoming somewhat extended, there had arrived in order to take part in them in his capacity as Deputy Commander of the First Belorussian Front, General of the Army Sokolovskii. He, that is Sokolovskii, suggested to Krebs that he, Krebs, should send the *Colonel* who was with him, Col. von Dufving, together with a representative of the Soviet Command, Lt. Col. Gladkii, to Goebbels in order to report on the course of the conversations and to lay before them the requirement of the Soviet Supreme Command on the capitulation of the Berlin garrison and to establish direct telephone communications with both sides across the front line.

At 0900 hours—9:00 a.m. in the morning—*Col.* von Dufving, accompanied by Lt. Col. Gladkii and the interpreter, Guards Sgt. Zhuravlev, went forward to the front line. While crossing the front line, they were fired on from the German side, after which the Army Commander (Chuikov) ordered Lt. Col Gladkii and the interpreter to return to their posts but *Col.* Dufving proceeded across the line to the German side. Shortly afterwards *Col.* Dufving returned to the same place in order to go about the business of laying down a telephone line across the line of the front which was in the process of being done.

Later in the day Henseler received word from the *Führerbunker* to keep Albrechtstraße free of any small arms fire for a set period of time. When the designated time came he called "cease fire." On the street he watched in amazement as a German communications soldier ran a field telephone cable mounted on his back to the Russian lines while carrying a white flag.[6] Gladkii report continues:

Having reported to Goebbels on the course of the conversation and on the Soviet conditions, *Col.* Dufving once again returned to our lines and by telephone from the command point of the 102nd Guards Rifle Regiment he reported to Gen. Krebs that Goebbels had demanded from him, that is, from Krebs, a personal report on the results of the conversation. Before he left, Krebs asked General of the Army Sokolovskii for a final formulation of the Soviet demands. They were formulated by Gen. Sokolovskii in the following manner; (1) The speedy and unconditional capitulation of the Berlin garrison; (2) The entire composition of the garrison would be guaranteed their life, they would be allowed to keep their medals and their personal possessions and the officers would be allowed to keep their cold [sic.] weapons and for the wounded there would be medical help. (3) In the case of the acceptance of this sugges-

Central District
1 May

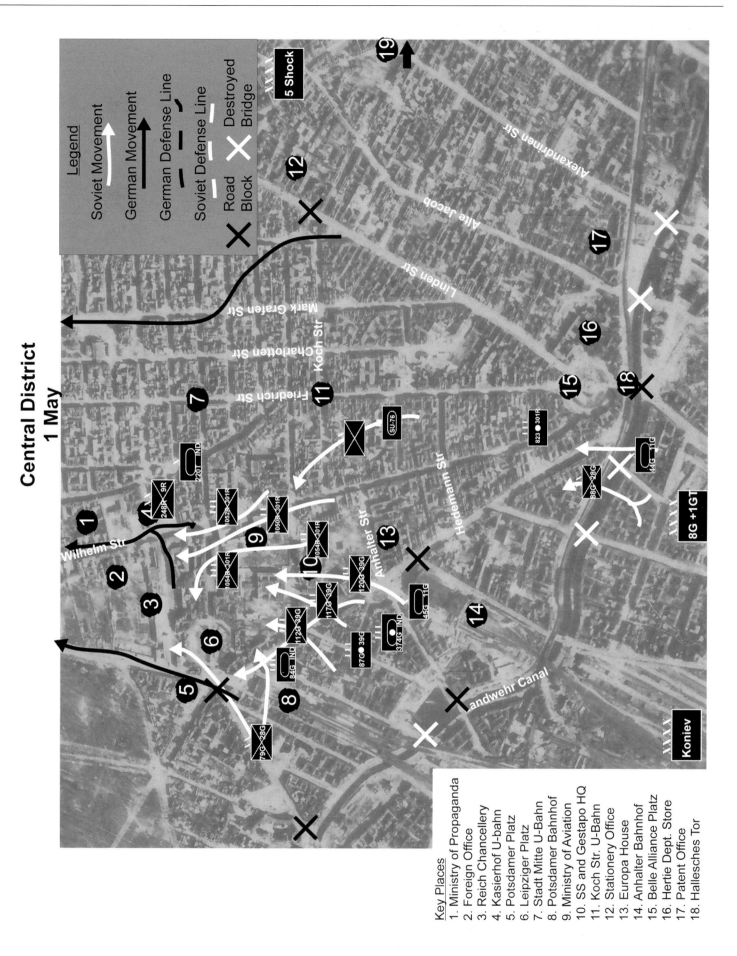

Legend

Soviet Movement

German Movement

German Defense Line

Soviet Defense Line

✕ Road Block

✕ Destroyed Bridge

Key Places
1. Ministry of Propaganda
2. Foreign Office
3. Reich Chancellery
4. Kasierhof U-bahn
5. Potsdamer Platz
6. Leipziger Platz
7. Stadt Mitte U-Bahn
8. Potsdamer Bahnhof
9. Ministry of Aviation
10. SS and Gestapo HQ
11. Koch Str. U-Bahn
12. Stationery Office
13. Europa House
14. Anhalter Bahnhof
15. Belle Alliance Platz
16. Hertie Dept. Store
17. Patent Office
18. Hallesches Tor

tion, the Soviet government would not regard as prisoners of war members of the new German Government or their chief advisors named according to the special list. (4) To the members of the government in Berlin there would be given by the Soviet Command the possibility of getting in contact with Dönitz in order that there should be a rapid approach to the governments of the three Allied Powers with the suggestion that there should be begun talks of peace. Nevertheless the Soviet Command could not guarantee that the governments of the U.S.S.R, Great Britain and the U.S.A would enter into any kind of talks at all with the German government.

At 1400 hours 1–5–1945 *General of Infantry* Krebs returned to the German lines. After the departure of Krebs the telephone link with the German side was maintained, military operations on this sector of the front were not renewed in the expectation of a final reply from Goebbels.

At 1800 hours there came across the front line a plenipotentiary of Goebbels a *Lt. Col.* of *SS* troops who handed the Army Commander Col. Gen. Chuikov a packet. In the packet under the signature of Krebs and Bormann was contained the reply of the German government to the Soviet suggestion in which it was clearly stated that the Soviet suggestion was not acceptable and that military operations would be renewed. The *SS Lt. Col.* was rapidly passed back to his lines, the telephone communication with the German side was cut and the assault on the surrounded Berlin garrison was renewed with great force.

End of Gladkii report.[7]

In the morning Krukenberg was called by Mohnke with urgent news. Mohnke reported that Krebs, von Dufving, and Seifert went through the Russians lines to negotiate with the Soviets and that they had not returned. Mohnke continued, "We suspect that they may lead the Russian into the center of Berlin and you are personally responsible that the Russians do not get into the middle by way of the subways or by other means."[8] This completely shocked Krukenberg who had no idea that a negotiation was even being attempted. The fact that Mohnke didn't trust the *Wehrmacht* officers responsible to conduct the negotiation demonstrated the clear rift between the *SS* and *Wehrmacht*. As Krukenberg recalled after the war, "the amount of distrust and suspicion which surrounded everybody at this time was fantastic."[9] Krukenberg went over to the Air Ministry, presumably to see if Seifert had returned. When he arrived he was shocked when he found several *Luftwaffe* officers and about one hundred soldiers who were making plans to surrender. This group refused to take any orders from Krukenberg. Krukenberg recalled what happened next:

> When I went over there, one incident took place which I shall never forget, perhaps because the *Luftwaffe* men did not want to be involved in the battle any longer. Whatever the reason, they apparently had heard of Hitler's death and they were getting ready to surrender. Seifert's aide, when he saw me, pulled out his pistol as though to fire. I was a little faster then he, and my bullet merely grazed. On hearing this shooting *General* Seifert suddenly appeared, I need hardly tell you I was quite angry, and I said: "That's no joke." Seifert calmed every body down and that was the end of the incident. However I could not get the *Luftwaffe* men to participate or even help in the defense so I had to leave.[10]

Friedrichstrasse as it approaches the S-Bahn station then crosses over the Spree River to the north. This was the location of the main breakout from the Government Quarter where the majority of *SS*, Nazi Politicians, and administrators attempted their breakout to join Steiner's forces to the north. Author's collection.

Now that the negation party returned from the Soviet, it is surprising that Mohnke was not informed. Krebs finally met with Goebbels and handed him a sheet of paper he received from Chuikov. It read:

1. Berlin surrenders.
2. All those surrendering must lay down their arms.
3. The lives of all soldiers and officers are to be spared.
4. The wounded will be cared for.
5. There will be an opportunity to negotiate with the Allies by Radio.

Goebbels was indignant at Chuikov's response. Goebbels believed in his own mind that *he* had delivered Berlin from the Communists during the 1920s and 30s and he was not about to hand it back over to them now.[11] Chuikov's reply ended any of Goebbels' hopes for a negotiation. He quickly prepared his own suicide and that of his entire family. By 2030 Goebbels and his wife shot themselves after killing their children through cyanide poisoning. Stalin was soon notified by Zhukov of the offer to negotiate and Chuikov's response. Stalin, suspecting that the German's will to resist was near its end, ordered a new offensive in the city to start at 1630.[12] The fact that Stalin had to order the attack is interesting as there is no record of any interference in the assault by Stalin prior to this directive. This suggests that Zhukov's forces may have taken the initial offer at negotiations as a premature surrender and stopped the majority of offensive actions in the city requiring Stalin to jump start combat operations. Perhaps Stalin wanted to re-emphasise that it would not be over until the city capitulated. In either case, Stalin's order was followed in spirit as Soviet soldiers increasingly avoided the need to launch costly offensives in the city, especially in the heavily-defended Government Quarter.

LVI PZ. KORPS

Weidling visited the *Führerbunker* again and noted everyone preparing to leave. Krebs informed Weidling that he had no more instructions for him or the soldiers fighting in Berlin. Weidling left immediately for his Benderblock HQ. At around 2100 he assembled his staff and explained that he was going to surrender Berlin to the Russians during the morning of 2 May but if any units wanted to pursue a breakout on their own they were welcome to try during the evening hours.[13] Weidling gave the city's defenders twenty-four hours to escape Berlin and Soviet captivity.

The secrecy around Hitler's death was lifted by Krebs, although many soldiers had already heard the rumors. News spread across Berlin that the Führer had died. Soon a radio announcement was also broadcast. With the war near its end, and Berlin on the verge of

Hitler's New Reich Chancellery along Vossstraße in July 1945. The Chancellery was never stormed by Soviet soldiers as Zhukov stated in his postwar account. Soviet soldiers stayed in positions across the street on 1 May, but did hit the building with artillery and mortar fire. On the following day Red Army soldiers walked across the street and into a virtually abandoned building as most of the occupants left during the night to try a breakout north. Courtesy of the US National Archives.

Vossstraße in 2005. An apartment complex now stands where Hitler's New Reich Chancellery did 60 years earlier. Behind the apartment complex is a children's play ground and parking lot that sit over the remains of the former *Führerbunker* and Chancellery Gardens. Author's collection.

A close up of the Hitler's balcony in July 1945. In April it served as a reinforced position with MG ports. Courtesy of the US National Archives.

capitulation, everyone had to make life or death choices. Some decided to breakout, others choose to stay in place and surrender. Yet many others decided that life without either Nazism or perhaps life under 'Bolshevik' rule was not an option and committed suicide.

CENTRAL DISTRICTS

Sporadic but diminished fighting continued throughout the various sectors in Berlin. Chuikov's forces continued to push into the Government Quarter but there was now a definite lack of effort by his troops, as few soldiers wanted to risk their lives so close to the end of the battle. One German veteran recounted Soviet tactics in the last days of the battle: "On 1 May there was artillery fire but no hand-to-hand combat. You know everybody talks about fighting around the Reich Chancellery and this area—there was, but mostly it was artillery fire and sniper fire. I at least was able to walk along the streets. It's my opinion the Russians were not too eager to fight—they wanted to live, too."[14] The lull was noticed by the German defenders who began to wonder if the war over as the sound of battle began to die down around them in the afternoon. The fighting even slackened in Potsdamer Platz where the Soviets fought viciously for the last day to breakthrough. Turk left his King Tiger still in position at the Potsdamer U-Bahn station and walked down into the U-Bahn tunnel to find some means to communicate to his battalion commander that his King Tiger was low on ammunition. When he descended the steps he encountered a large number of civilians who sheepishly asked this visitor from the world above if the war was over yet. Turk ran into a dispatch rider in the tunnel who notified Turk of Hitler's death. Turk also learned that elements of a *Nordland* pioneer platoon were nearby along with *Volkssturm* and *Hitlerjugend* reinforcements. Turk sent

Soviet Assault on the Reichstag
1 May

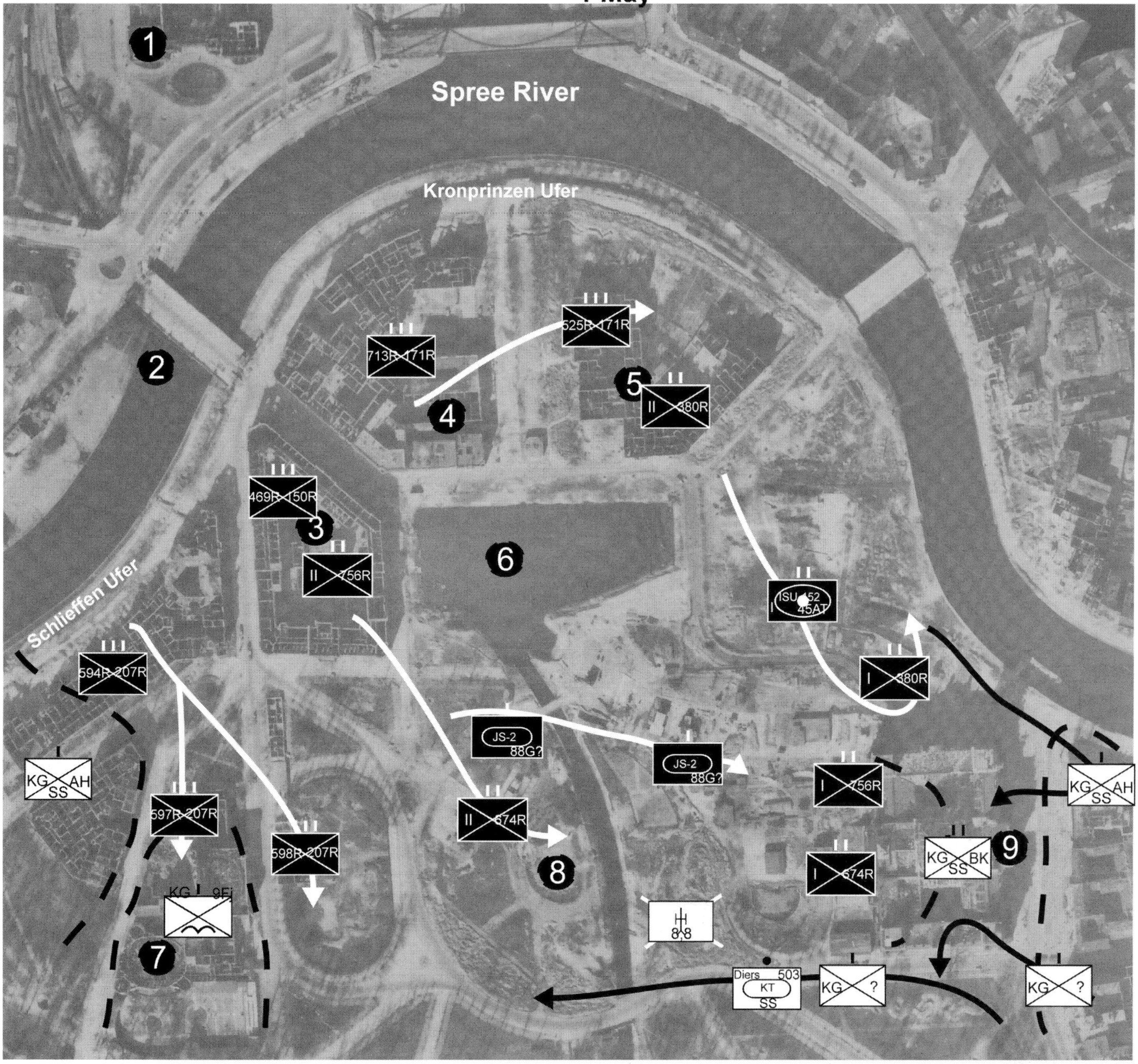

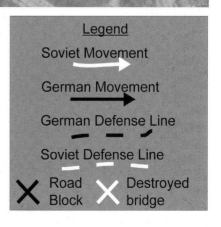

Spree River

Kronprinzen Ufer

Schlieffen Ufer

525R-171R

713R-171R

II 380R

469R-150R

II 756R

594R-207R

ISU-152
45AT

I 380R

JS-2
88G?

JS-2
88G?

KG AH
SS

597R-207R

598R-207R

KG 9Ei

II 574R

I 756R

KG BK
SS

KG AH
SS

I 574R

8\8

Diers 503
KT
SS

KG ?

KG ?

Key Places

1. Lehrter Bahnhof
2. Moltke Bridge
3. Ministry of the Interior
   "Himmler's House"
4. Swiss Consulate
5. Diplomatic Quarter
6. Speer's U-Bahn
   Construction Site and
   Flooded Tunnel
7. Kroll Opera House
8. Königsplatz
9. Reichstag

Legend

Soviet Movement

German Movement

German Defense Line

Soviet Defense Line

X Road Block X Destroyed bridge

word over to the *Nordland* commander, presumably Christensen, to send home the *Volkssturm* and *Hitlerjugend*. Christensen obliged the order then walked through the eerily quiet streets to Turk's position and informed Turk that a breakout was planned north over the Weidendammbrücke later that evening.[15]

Scholles and his men were still in the Herold Insurance Building where they spent a relatively quiet night as the Soviets were presumably under orders not to take offensive action while negotiations were ongoing between the German delegation and Chuikov during the evening hours from 30 April–1 May. By the afternoon of 1 May, as per Stalin's orders, the Russians did launch an attack on the building, despite the fact that in most other sectors fighting was dying down. The Russians reached the giant square building where hand-to-hand combat ensued both outside and on the ruined first floor. By evening the Russians held the entrance and the large Entrance Hall on the first floor while Scholles and his men held out on the rest of the first floor and several rooms on the ground floor. During the early evening the Russians brought up a machine-gun that they positioned at the entrance to fire at suspected German positions on the opposite side of the street. Scholles roused his men and ordered a night attack to throw the Russians out of the building. The fighting raged into the morning of 2 May. While the Germans retook the Entrance Hall, the Russians retained the entrance. Scholles was wounded and soon carried off to the Kochstraße U-Bahn Station.[16]

The 94th Guards and 266th Rifle Division were able to take the Zeughaus (Armory) and State Library on the north side of the Unter-den-Linden. The 416th and 295th Rifle Divisions took the State Opera building across the road and the Reichsbank.

The 301st and 248th Rifle Divisions of the 9th Rifle Corps managed to capture the Gestapo and Reich Main Security Office buildings on Prinz Albrechtstraße against stiff resistance from the Latvians. Overall, the day's progress still left the area on the eastern side of Friedrichstraße, the Gendarmenmarkt, Air Ministry and Potsdamer Platz in German Hands.[17] The 301st Rifle Division was now the closest Soviet unit to the Reich Chancellery. The Soviets were a mere 500 meters from where they believed Hitler was located based on German POW interviews conducted during their advance through the Government Quarter. In the rifle division was a Lieutenant Colonel Klimenke, who was given the task to lead a search-squad into the Reich Chancellery and find Hitler, if he was still there.[18]

To the east, more troops arrived in the Spittelmarkt for defense even at this late hour. *Kriegsmarine* troops, numbering about 76 sailors, marched over from Potsdamer Platz. They came under fire by the Russians near the Dönhoff Park, but they worked their way east until they found Schulz and the other *Hitlerjugend* boys in the basement of a nearby building. The arrival of these 'foreign'-looking troops sparked a belief that Wenck had finally arrived and was in the process of relieving Berlin. The final issue of *Der Panzerbär* also arrived, where it was noted that Hitler had died the day before. Hitler's death sparked no real sorrow among the troops although they were concerned about their next steps. At that point the group leader, Thiemer, called the boys to attention then holding his rifle horizontally said "We swear loyalty to your new commander and his government." The boys had to repeat this new oath of loyalty to Dönitz.[19] Soon after the brief ceremony the Soviets drove up a truck nearby that blared out a message for the Germans to surrender. This was being done by Seydlitz troops from the *Komitee Freie Deutschland*. The message was repeated that they wanted no more bloodshed and surrender was the only option. The group commander refused and Thiemer prepared for a final counterattack to push the Russians out of the Spittelmarkt even though the *Hitlerjugend* were down to 15–20 rounds each. Thiemer apparently requested forces directly from the

A July 1945 photo of the Reichstag still showing the vast amount of wreckage from the battle in April. In the foreground is one of the 1st Flak Division's 8.8cm guns. Photo courtesy of the Bundesarchiv.

Members of the 150th Rifle Division that participated in the storming of the Reichstag posing for the Red Army cameras as Heroes of the Soviet Union. Photo courtesy of the Cornelius Ryan Collection, Mahn Center, Alden Library, Ohio University, Athens, OH.

A rare photograph of the inside of the Reichstag in July 1945 showing the main meeting hall under the dome. Note what appears to be a *Panzerfaust* blast at the rear right. Soviets soldiers used captured *Panzerfausts* to breach obstacles and walls during the street fighting. Courtesy of the US National Archives.

Another rare shot of the balcony area inside of the Reichstag also taken in July 1945. Soviet soldiers fought their way up to the second story and crossed the balcony to reach the back steps that led to the roof where they raised Special Banner No. 5. Courtesy of the US National Archives.

Führerbunker because in the afternoon 2 operable Tiger Is from *Müncheberg* accompanied by a Flakpanzer IV Wirbelwind from *s.SS-Pz.Abt.503* and additional *Wehrmacht* soldiers arrived to support his attack. The total force numbered 200–300 men and their goal was to push the Soviets out of their positions along the southern edge of the Spittelmarkt and the first part of Kurstraße. The counterattack lasted all afternoon and into the evening as Thiemer drove his small force on with the desperation of a doomed man. The Germans pushed the Soviets back out of the Spittelmarkt, destroying 8–9 Russian tanks in the process. The cost was high as the German force lost half their men killed or wounded in the rubble of Spittelmarkt. There was no mention of German Panzer losses though the Germans probably lost several in the fighting. Among the wounded was Schulz's leader, Thiemer. Schulz's group was now taken over by *SS-Scharführer* Günther Schmitchen, presumably from the elements of the *Norge* Regiment defending the area. The Russians made no attempt to attack the Spittelmarkt any longer, as they realized the battle was nearing its end and the inclusion of additional German forces did not offer the Russians any more potential for success then they had in the proceeding days. By the evening the word was now passed to assemble in Spandau for a counterattack to join the U.S. forces along the Elbe.[20] Schultz and his men quietly left their basement in the evening and began to move west through the now eerily quiet, darkened streets. Their progress was lit by hundreds of fires. The flickering light from the burning ruins cast menacing shadows into the rubble strewn streets. Sporadic gun fire was heard here and there, but otherwise their progress went uninterrupted by the Soviets.

North of the Spittelmarkt, the 11th Tank Corps continued to fight its way northwest toward Unter-den-Linden and the Reichstag. The Germans continued to resist and the Soviet tankers had little respite from the fighting. Their losses in armor reduced their ability to conduct combat operations slowing their progress considerably after their dash through the Spittelmarkt several days earlier. In addition as the Soviets moved into the commercial districts, the multi-storeyed buildings offered the Germans an excellent advantage to shoot down on the Soviets tanks maneuvering through the narrow streets. When the German positions were uncovered, the tankers blasted the building until the roof collapsed on the defenders. This method was an expedient solution to the problem of the tanks not being able to raise their main guns high enough to fire at targets in upper storeys. The following example illustrates the continued difficulty the Soviet tankers faced. The Russians just finished reducing one German position when their lead tank received an anti-tank shot:

> One shot; a second shot. The lead tank has been [destroyed], but where is the gun? The commander of the Rifle Company, Lieutenant F.S. Strelkov, calls up a group of tommy-gunners. "Comrade Sergeyev, go forward on reconnaissance. Take 5 tommy-gunners. Task—to reconnoiter towards the right, in the direction of the enemy fire positions, and report at 1000 hours." "Order understood." replies the fearless Konsomol soldiers. The … raid lasts three hours. During this time the reconnaissance soldier N.I. Sergeyev personally destroys 5 enemy tommy-gunners and 3 enemy anti-tank weapons. The enemy shells fatally wound this daring young man, but the task was fulfilled and the enemy force reconnoitred. In the corner house there are up to a company of German tommy-gunners and a gun. The tanks open a withering fire but the gun continues to hold up the movement of the tanks. Lieutenant Stralkov calls up 3 more tommy-gunners and orders them to wipe out the gun and its crew. The group of tommy-gunners with Sgt. P.I. Davydenko with great care crawls up to the gun from the rear and begins to destroy it. The enemy resists stubbornly. Davydenko was severely wounded. But what has happened to the gun? Is it possible to leave an enemy gun which had been directing such heavy fire on our tanks? Enduring unbearable pain he crawls forward and with a [*Panzerfaust*], destroys the gun. Our tanks begin to move forward once again.[21]

It took time to clear the way for the tanks, and the Soviets realized only too late that tank operations and infantry operations were mutually required. In the above example, some four or more hours passed before the advance of the 11th Tank Corps resumed, illustrating the time-consuming nature of urban combat.

Zinchenko arrived at the Reichstag at midnight after crossing the ruined Königsplatz. He immediately asked about the location of the red banners. Neustroyev replied that the banners were all around, but Zinchenko was concerned only about Special Banner No 5. Neustroyev believed that he gave the banner to the Senior Sergeant in charge of the reconnaissance forces who accompanied the 1st

A Soviet photograph illustrating the destruction of street fighting in Berlin's center.
Photo courtesy of the Bulgarian Ministry of Defence.

Company into the Reichstag to make their way to the roof. After searching the units in the Reichstag, it turned out the banner was left in the basement of 'Himmler's House'. Zincenko called his staff at the Ministry of Interior over the landline that was now operating and immediately ordered the banner sent to the Reichstag—despite the shelling and small arms fire going on outside. Two intelligence officers offered to run the gauntlet back to 'Himmler's House' and retrieve the banner. After doing so, the order went out to hoist the banner on the roof and a small group of Soviets made their way into the dark only to return some minutes later without success. It was dark, they had no light and did not know where to go. Zincenko was enraged and turned to Neustroyev saying "The Supreme High Command of the Armed Forces of the Soviet Union on behalf of the Communist Party, our socialist native land and the entire Soviet People order you to erect the victory banner above Berlin. In this historical moment [your soldiers] could not find access to the roof!" His final words were "Battalion Commander, ensure the victory banner flies above the Reichstag!"[22] He then left to make his way back to the Ministry of the Interior. The intelligence officers and reconnaissance troops now headed into the unfamiliar darkened building to find the stairs going up to the roof. The Soviets waiting below in the foyer heard shouting, submachine gun bursts, and hand grenades then silence. As long as an hour later, the soldiers returned and stated that Special Banner No 5 was tied to the front of the building with their belts. The mission of raising Red Banner No. 5 over the Reichstag was accomplished at around 0130 on 1 May.

A large contingent of Germans remained in the basement launching forays up the steps against the Russians. The Russians were not immediately aware that a basement existed but they soon found an entranceway that led down a flight of stairs. A patrol went into the basement and upon reaching the bottom landing the Russians noticed a long concrete lined hallway. They proceeded to move down the corridor when the Germans fired a *Panzerfaust* and opened fire with automatic weapons immediately killing five Soviets and wounding a number of others who retreated back up the stairs. Neustroyev now located several German POWs in the building and asked for information on what was in the basement. He was informed that there were three floors with interconnecting passageways being defended. He was also told that there were large quantities of food supplies and ammunition below. This concerned the Russians, who had run out of grenades, were low on ammunition, and especially food and water. Many of the soldiers had not had a drink of water in twenty-four hours. The Regimental Commander informed the Russians in the Reichstag by field phone that supplies were on their way. The Germans, however, began to shell the Reichstag for several hours preventing anyone from getting to the building. In addition the defenders in the basement began raiding the main level at different locations, while outside German reinforcements launched counterattacks to push the Russians out. Under the mounting German pressure Neustroyev ordered an immediate attack into the basement in an attempt to force the garrison from launching any concerted attack into the upper level. The first assault into the basement failed and the Soviets took fifty casualties including twenty dead from one battalion alone.[23] The Soviets were simply not able to breach the stairwells and gain access to the underground corridors.

German cars destroyed by the fire of the Soviet Katushya rockets outside the Brandenburg Gate.
Photo courtesy of the Bulgarian Ministry of Defence.

The German shelling outside the building severed the communication line with Regimental HQ in the Ministry of Interior. Inside, the Russians felt increasingly isolated as they continued to maintain a tight perimeter on the first floor. Neustroyev expected another German counterattack as Russians on perimeter guard could see movement in the street around the building. By noon the expected counterattack from outside occurred and in three of the four places attacked the Germans breached the Reichstag and entered the building's main level. The Germans fired *Panzerfausts* point-blank at the Russians and both sides fought with an extreme ferocity. Small fires broke out that quickly grew, clouding the halls and rooms, choking defenders and attackers alike. None of the commanders inside the Reichstag had communication with each other anymore. Chaos ensued as both sides struggled to gain some advantage in hard hand-to-hand combat.[24] The Russians finally forced the Germans out of the main level that was now completely blackened from fire. As Neustroyev wrote: "But our situation was far from a good one. My men were at the limits of utter physical exhaustion. They made a very sorry sight. The majority of them were in rage. Most of them had burns [on their hand or faces]."[25] For the moment, the Russians in the building gained some breathing room.

The Germans launched several counterattacks in the surrounding area. One was launched toward the Kroll Opera House led by Diers in his King Tiger in order to relieve the German forces there. This also caused Soviet tank losses and kept them from reinforcing the Reichstag. The II/674th and entire 380th Rifle Regiment tried to reach the Reichstag and surrounding area from the north for a second time but their assault was stopped by German counterattacks launched from the area of the Presidential Palace.[26] Kuntze and his men moved during the night to the buildings behind the Reichstag where Babick's HQ was now located. He was informed by Babick that Hitler was dead. Kuntze now realized it was up to him to decide what to do. He went back to his men, informed them to prepare for a breakout north. He commandeered a Hetzer and a Volkswagen, loaded his remaining 20 men and prepared to head north across the Weidendammer Bridge.[27]

Sporadic fighting continued through the day. The Germans remaining in the Reichstag began to pull out of the building by the evening. Rhein and his men broke out, and then headed north. They initially crossed Friedrichstraße S-Bahn Station and moved into the ruins hours before the main breakout across the Spree. They ominously saw Russians crawling all over the streets.[28]

To the north, *Oberst* Rossbach issued orders for all remaining food supplies to be distributed to the local population. He then ordered that the rest of the *Volkssturm* in *Kampfgruppe Rossbach* to be ready to fight by early evening. All 140 members of the unit met at the Schultheiss Brewery that served as the unit's command post. Once assembled, they were read an order that authorized the unit to breakout northwest to reach Wenck. The idea that a rescue force was waiting for the defenders just outside the city continued to provide hope and motivation in order to continue the fight after weeks of some of the harshest combat seen in WWII. As Wrede recalled after the war how the story that Wenck's troops were waiting for them just outside of Berlin roused new hope in him and the rest of his comrades, who previously felt fatalistic about being completely isolated and cut off in Berlin.[29] *Oberst* Rossbach asked who was a Berliner. Out of the 140 only Wrede and another man stepped forward. They were asked to lead the rest of the company out of Berlin the morning via the Schönhauser Allee U-Bahn tracks that were elevated at this point. The men settled down and prepared for the morning's breakout.[30]

Boosted by the 1st Polish Infantry Division, the 1st Mechanized Corps made some progress. In fact, it appears that the Russians in this sector were simply exhausted and depleted on manpower. All of the advances in this area that occurred during the last days of fighting were done by the Poles. The Polish forces supported by the 1st Battery of the 1st Polish Field Artillery Regiment assembled on the line of Fritschestraße in support of the 19th and 35th Mechanized Brigades of the 1st Mechanized Corps. The first task of the 1st Battalion was to clear a defended barricade on Kaiser Friedrichstraße that blocked the entrance to Pestalozzistraße and had already cost the Soviets several tanks. This was achieved with the aid of both tank and artillery fire, while the infantry infiltrated the surrounding buildings.

The remaining tanks advanced to join up with the 19th Mechanized Brigade and its assigned 2nd and 3rd Battalions fighting at Karl-August-Platz at 1600 hours. For the next phase of operations three infantry assault groups were formed, one from each of the 2nd and 3rd Battalions, as well as of the surviving Soviet infantry. Each of the assault groups were supported by three tanks. Their goal was the area around the Trinity Church that formed the main defensive position. In the area remained the two Elefants of *s.PzJg.Kp.614*. There is no combat record of these two vehicles, but it can be assumed that they were responsible for knocking out Soviet armor in the area until they either ran out of fuel, ammunition or both.[31] The church itself was defended by a contingent of *SA* that were apparently looking for a way to avoid the fighting in Berlin and wait out the battle. They clearly put up some resistance, otherwise the Polish troops would probably have bypassed their position. The ensuing assault, conducted under cover of a dense smokescreen, succeeded, and by evening the church was in Polish hands.

The 2nd Polish Infantry Regiment, supported by the 2nd Battery, advanced through the 219th Tank Brigade's sector and occupied the wedge of ground bounded by the Landwehr Canal opposite the Technical High School. Meanwhile the 219th Tank Brigade was tied up in fighting for some positions along the Landwehr Canal. This put the Poles in a predicament, for the street they had to cross in order to assault the high school was deliberately widened by Albert Speer before the war to accommodate the reviewing stands for Hitler's parades along the East-West Axis. Attempts to cross without armored support at 0900, 1000, and 1430 hours were easily beaten back by machine-gun fire. Although some Soviet tanks did support the first two of these attacks with direct fire, they were not prepared to expose themselves to the *Panzerfausts* that the Germans were using. At 1500 hours the Soviet armor was ordered elsewhere, leaving the Poles unsupported.

The Polish regiment now had to rely on its own artillery support to make headway. The artillery guns were deployed at a range of only 500 meters, and two 76mm guns were dismantled and reassembled on the third floor of the surviving building next to the bridge. Scouts were then sent out to find alternative lines of approach, and eventually at 0140 hours on 2 May a flanking attack was carried out across the narrower Hardenbergstraße that proved successful, although 26 men were lost.[32]

The 3rd Polish Infantry Regiment, supported by the 3rd Battery, came to the aid of the 66th Guards Tank Brigade of the 12th Guards Tank Corps north of the Landwehr Canal. The brigade was down to only 15 tanks, and stuck on the line of Franklinstraße. The Poles broke through the German defenses and fought their way through a dense industrial area, reaching the line of Englische Straße, immediately north of the Charlottenburger Bridge by 2100 hours. The tanks found themselves exceedingly vulnerable to *Panzerfausts* in these conditions. The brigade was tasked with securing the bridge and taking the Tiergarten S-Bahn station. Scouts reported, however, that the station complex was strongly defended. It was decided to await daylight to enable a thorough reconnaissance. Meanwhile, attempts to cross the Charlottenburger Chaussee and secure the bridge proved futile until three JS–2s came forward to form a wall of steel across the road for the Polish infantry. The following morning the Poles managed to take the station by storm, opening the way into the Tiergarten. They quickly advanced east to the Siegessäule where they raised their national flag.

The Zoo Bunker busily prepared for a breakout. Staff burnt their papers and many changed into civilian clothes. Böttcher received a call from *General* Rauch who said "The Führer is dead. The breakout will take place on 2 May 2 at 0400."[33] By evening, the remnants of the *18.Pz.Gren.Div.* moved into the area around the Zoo Bunker without any immediate reaction from the Soviets who appeared to be waiting for hostilities to end and didn't want to take unnecessary losses. Everyone headed toward the Havel for the breakout above and below ground. Many walked through the U-Bahn tunnel until they reached the Reich Sports Field then headed to the bridges leading into Spandau.[34]

The Germans last main defensive bastion in the Zoo Garden began to be surrounded as Chuikov's forces conducted an initial heavy artillery and rocket bombardment then attacked with ground forces in the evening hours after watching the majority of German forces head west. His 29th Guards Rifle Corps crossed Budapester Straße and had knocked gaps in the perimeter of walls of the Zoological Garden where their tanks and artillery were now exchanging fire with the defense. They finally took the Kaiser Wilhelm Gedächtniskirche (Memorial Church) at the eastern end of the Kurfürstendamm. From here their artillery observers and snipers had a clear view of the Zoo Gardens. Elements of the 4th Guards Rifle Corps penetrated the Tiergarten residential sector just north of the Landwehr Canal. Soviet troops finally crossed into Siegesallee, and the 79th Guards Rifle Division of the 28th Guards Corps reported that they had taken Potsdamer S-Bahn station and were fighting for the Potsdamer Platz U-Bahn Station. The junction of Leipziger Straße and Wilhelmstraße were now in Soviet hands. Chuikov's advances were made possible in part by the fact that the German defenders had withdrawn in preparation for the breakout.

Remaining *Müncheberg* members continued to resist along Savignyplatz against the elements of Koniev's 7th Guards Tank Corps remaining in Berlin. Toward evening they slowly moved west joining *Pz.Gr.Rgt.51* now pulling back northwest. Civilians joined the soldiers as they moved west to reposition themselves for the breakout. Earlier in the day the ancient citadel on the Havel surrendered to the 47th Army. The Soviets turned their attention on this small military garrison that had taken its toll in Soviet tanks by launching forays with *Panzerfausts* into the surrounding city streets. The fall of the garrison now gave the Soviets control over the northern Havel crossings and good observation south where the Germans would soon be breaking out.

Notes to Chapter 6: Assault on Berlin, 1st May Tuesday

1   OKW File, Last Announcements of OKW, 1 May (RC: 62:8).
2   Le Tissier, *Slaughter at Halbe*, p. 201.
3   T. Busse interview (RC: 67/17).
4   *MS #B-606*, p. 32.
5   Wenck Interview.
6   Henseler interview.
7   Surrender of Berlin Garrison (RC: 69/1).
8   Krukenberg interview.
9   Ibid.
10 Ibid, and Weidling Interrogation Report.
11 Fest, p. 137.
12 Le Tissier, *Race for the Reichstag*, p. 179. There is a discrepancy of two hours between the Gladkii report and what Le Tissier records as the time of the actual renewal of offensive operations. The

reality is that fighting was still occurring. In Chuikov's sector, however, there was now a desire on the part of his troops to wait it out instead of risking their lives in the last moments of the war. Artillery and rocket fire clearly opened up on known German positions, but by all German accounts there was a significant lack of offensive Soviet tank and infantry movement in this area.
13 Weidling Interrogation Report.
14 A. Lampe interview (RC: 67/10).
15 Schneider, p. 324.
16 Scholles interview.
17 Le Tissier, *Race for the Reichstag*, p. 179.
18 "Chancellery Attack," Der Spiegel, Nr. 19, 5 May 1965, pp. 94–9. (RC: 66/30)

19 Schulz interview.
20 Ibid.
21 Platonov, pp. 27–9.
22 Neustroyev second interview.
23 Ibid.
24 Rhein interview.
25 Neustroyev second interview.
26 Ibid.
27 Venghaus, p. 272.
28 Rhein interview.
29 Werde interview.
30 Ibid.
31 Karlheinz, p. 227.
32 Le Tissier, *Race for the Reichstag*, pp. 179–81.
33 Böttcher interview.
34 Ache interview.

6

ASSAULT ON BERLIN

2 MAY
WEDNESDAY

At the head of the heroic defenders of the Reich Capital the Führer died in action. Actuated by the will of the people and Europe from the destruction by the Bolshevists he sacrificed his life. This pattern, faithful to the death, is binding for all soldiers. The remnants of the brave garrison of Berlin, split in various battle formations, continue their fight in the governmental section.[1]

OKW Radio Announcement

The troops of the 1st Byelorussian Front under the command of Soviet Marshal Zhukov with the support of the troops of the 1st Ukrainian Front after hard street fighting completed the defeat of the Berlin forces of the German troops and occupied today, 2 May, the capital city of Germany completely.

Stalin's Proclamation

At 0130 in the morning the 301st Division opened artillery fire on the upper floors of the Reich Chancellery. After the artillery barrage ended, Colonel Ivan Klimenke and his search-squad made their way to the Reich Chancellery building without encountering any opposition. What the Russians didn't know was that the *Führerbunker's* occupants, with only a few exceptions, left hours earlier to attempt a breakout to the north. The only people left in the massive complex were wounded, nurses, and a few remaining officers and soldiers who quickly gave themselves up. The Soviets soon located the entrance to the *Führerbunker*. Upon entering they were greeted by the bodies of officers who had recently committed suicide. There was an unbelievable stench of corpses and puddles of blood. Klimenke's men moved up the back staircases into the courtyard of the Reich Chancellery where they quickly located the bodies of Goebbels, his wife, and their children, but no Hitler.[2]

The main breakout was organized by *Luftwaffe Generalleutnant* Otto Sydow. Panzers and Panzergrenadiers from both the *18.Pz.Gr.Div.*, and *Müncheberg Pz.Div.* led by several King Tigers moved out in the evening of 1–2 May toward the Charlottenburger Bridge across the Havel that had been held by *Hitlerjugend* for over a week.[3] Only the Charlottenburger and Schulenburg Bridges survived over the Havel, and these had to be repeatedly fought over. The Frey Bridge farther south carrying the Heerstraße over the river had been destroyed the previous evening when a chance Soviet shell hit the prepared demolition chamber. *Major* Zobel led the first assault across the bridge in an armored carrier. They were soon followed by soldiers and civilians that used the U-Bahn tunnels to sneak under the Soviets opposite the Zoo Bunker through Charlottenburg reaching Kantstraße undetected. The bridge crossing was a massacre. German vehicles drove at high speed over the wounded, while Russian shells and machine-gun fire raked the open expanse of the bridge. *Hitlerjugend* charged across the bridge and were cut down. Panic and fear motivated people to attempt the deadly crossing.[4] The survivors continued west for several days shadowed by Soviet PO–2 biplanes that monitored the column from the air and reported the German positions to the surrounding Soviet units on the ground.[5] Most of the soldiers and civilians were surrounded by the Soviets although some did manage to make it to the Elbe River and cross over to the Western Allies. A member of *Müncheberg* recorded his trials during the breakout west. He wrote that by 3 May "The rear guards fall apart. They want to go west, they don't want to be killed at the last moment. The command crumbles. *General* Mummert is missing. Our losses are heavy. The wounded are left where they fall. More civilians join us."[6] By 4 May it was all over for *Müncheberg*. The diary continues: "Behind us, Berlin flames. Many other units must still be fighting. The *sky* is red, cut by bright flashes. Russian tanks all around us, and the incessant clatter of machine-guns. We make some headway in close combat ….We are at the end ourselves. Our ammunition is giving out. The unit breaks up. We try to go on in small groups. This was the end of one division in the Battle of Berlin."[7] Members of other units met the same fate.

The second major breakout occurred through the city's northern districts. This breakout consisted of primarily the *SS* that garrisoned the Government Quarter and was organized by Mohnke. The remaining King Tigers of *s.SS-Pz.Abt.503* and the Panzers from *Nordland* led the breakout attempt north. This breakout ran into significant trouble once it crossed the Weidendammbrücke although some of the armor continued on for some ways until the King Tigers ran out of fuel. The majority of the breakout group was simply massacred in the street on the opposite side of the bridge.

Several smaller groups initially led by Mohnke crossed the Spree to the west of Weidendammbrücke and tried to work their way north to join Steiner's forces near Oranienburg. Mohnke led the main group of *Führerbunker* members that eventually surrendered to the Soviets the following day.[8] Axmann and Bormann both led separate groups north across the Spree. Axmann eventually made it to the west, while Bormann committed suicide in the street near the Lehrter Bahnhof.[9]

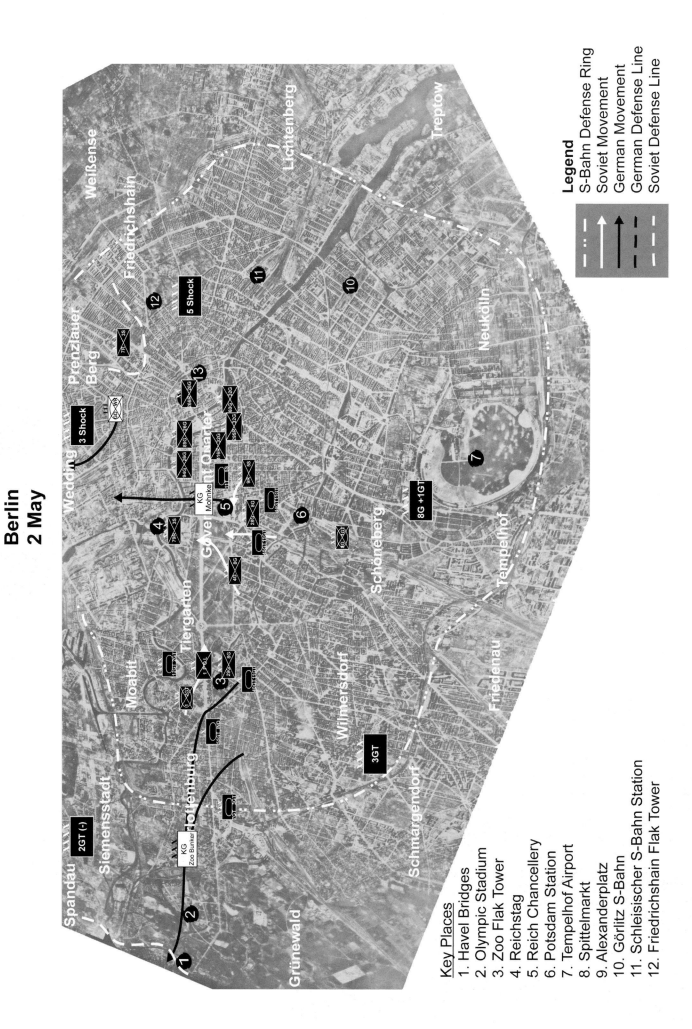

**Berlin
2 May**

Legend
S-Bahn Defense Ring
Soviet Movement
German Movement
German Defense Line
Soviet Defense Line

Key Places
1. Havel Bridges
2. Olympic Stadium
3. Zoo Flak Tower
4. Reichstag
5. Reich Chancellery
6. Potsdam Station
7. Tempelhof Airport
8. Spittelmarkt
9. Alexanderplatz
10. Görlitz S-Bahn
11. Schleisischer S-Bahn Station
12. Friedrichshain Flak Tower

A glimpse of the destruction that met the German breakout on the north side of the Spree River on the evening of 1-2 May. Destroyed German vehicles and dead bodies lie in the still burning street. In the chaos of the breakout, German Panzers crushed vehicles in their path as it appears might have happened to this Kübelwagen in the foreground.
Photo courtesy of the Cornelius Ryan Collection, Mahn Center, Alden Library, Ohio University, Athens, OH.

A *Nordland* SdKfz 250/1 from the *3.Kompanie* sits either abandoned or disabled on Chaussee Strasse along the route of the breakout north. German soldiers either riding in the vehicle or using it for cover were cut down by Soviet fire. This photo was taken just north of the previous one. (Note the three poles in the left background for a comparison.) Courtesy of the US National Archives.

This photo was taken on 4 May and shows the aftermath of the main breakout attempt north out of the Government Quarter from the south side of the Spree River heading north. Friedrichstrasse S-Bahn station is visible in the center of the photograph.
Courtesy of the US National Archives.

The German defenders in the area of the Humboldthain Flak Tower were in one of the better locations to breakout as the Soviet forces to the north were thin, especially after the movement of the 1st Polish Division into the city from the Oranienburg area. The *Fallschirmjäger* broke out in individual groups heading north, some with vehicles but most on foot. Some made it to the Western Allies. Nearby the *Wachregiment Großdeutschland* moved out with Hetzers and SPWs in an organized column that bypassed stiff Russian resistance. This group caused Zhukov to give chase.[10] While the vehicles were all lost, the majority of the *Großdeutschland* soldiers did make it to the *3.Panzer Armee* lines and eventually to the West.

At 0400 the Reichstag garrison located in the multi-storeyed basement surrendered after several attempts at negotiation. The number of Germans that gave up was at most 120. These soldiers were marched over to 'Himmler's House' where they were interrogated by SMERSH (forerunners to the KGB) then told to join groups of other prisoners marching east. The Russians in the Reichstag joked about Hitler being in the basement and searched the ruins. They found the tunnel leading underground but realized that it was so damaged by shelling that no one could have used it to escape during the Soviet assault. This was primarily why the garrison surrendered instead of retreating. Apparently a shell struck the street overhead during the fighting, collapsing the tunnel roof. The notion that thousands of Germans fought in the Reichstag was simply manufactured by Soviet commanders for both political and propaganda reasons after the war. The 674th and 756th Rifle Regiments of the 150th Rifle Division fought inside the Reichstag along with the 380th Rifle Regiment of the 171st Rifle Division that later reemerged to take the Brandenburger Tor, then reaching the Hotel Adlon. The other two Regiments, the 525th and 713th, secured the river bank and Siegesallee approaches respectively. The 207th Rifle Division closed up to the Charlottenburger Chaussee airstrip to await the 8th Guards Army from the south.

At 2240 Hours on 1 May Weidling broadcast his surrender to the Soviets. The 79th Guards, 39th Guards Rifle Division and 4th Guards Rifle Corps picked up the message.

> Hello, hello. *LVI Panzer Korps* speaking. We ask for a ceasefire. At 12.50 hours Berlin time we are sending truce negotiators to the Potsdam Bridge. Recognition sign—a white flag. Awaiting reply.

The transmission went out five times. The 79th Rifle Division replied:

> Understand you, understand you. Am transmitting your request to Chief of Superior Staff.

Weidling's staff replied:

> Russian radio station, am receiving you. You are reporting to Superior Staff.[11]

Weidling choose the middle of the day to start negotiations for final capitulation with the Soviets in order to allow anyone who wanted to breakout the opportunity. At the prescribed time *Oberst* von Dufving arrived with two majors from his staff. They were immediately brought to the commander of the 47th Guards Rifle Division. Colonel General Semchenko was handed a note from von Dufving that stated he had authority granted from Weidling to conduct capitulation discussions. Semchenko decided not to spend time sending the German delegation onto Zhukov. Instead, he decided to quickly pursue the surrender of the German garrison. He asked von Dufving how much time they needed to arrange for the surrender of the Berlin garrison. Von Dufving's reply was 3–4 hours and that they were prepared to conduct the surrender in the hours of dark as Goebbels stated that anyone caught surrendering would be shot. Von Dufving did not know that Goebbels and his family had already committed suicide that evening. By 0530 the 47th Guards Rifle Division's forward battalions reported that the German soldiers were assembling. At 1800 Weidling, his staff, and remaining German soldiers in his area walked over to the Russian lines and surrendered along with 1,200 soldiers.

Once in Soviet custody Weidling was immediately taken to Chuikov who confirmed his role as commander of the defense of Berlin. Once Chuikov was convinced of Weidling's authority he suggested that Weidling write up an order to be broadcast to the remainder of the garrison fighting. Weidling agreed and with Reifor wrote the following order:

> 30.4.45 the Führer ended his life by suicide and left us—sworn to be faithful to him—alone.
> According to the order of the Führer, you were to continue the fight for Berlin, in spite of the deficiencies in heavy weapons and ammunition, in spite of the whole situation, which made the struggle [for Berlin] plainly senseless. Each hour of the conflict increases the frightful sufferings of the civilian population of Berlin and of our wounded.
> Each, who falls in the struggle for Berlin, has been offered as a useless sacrifice.
> In agreement with the supreme command of Soviet troops I demand the immediate breaking off of the fighting.
> Weidling, General of Artillery,
> and Commander of the Defense of Berlin.

The 7th Section of the Political Section, of the 8th Army now took the message and began to transmit it across to the German lines in areas where resistance continued. In addition, the order was transmitted to the 3rd and 5th Shock Armies and broadcast out along those fronts as well. Before the arrival of Weidling to Chuikov's HQ, representatives of Deputy Minister of Propaganda Fritsche arrived and announced he was ready as the senior political representative of the Nazi Government to broadcast the order to the German garrison to surrender unconditionally. Chuikov assigned Lieutenant Colonel Vaigachev from the Political Affairs Division to head to the Ministry of Propaganda with the German representatives to broadcast the surrender. At the Ministry of Propaganda they found Fritsche who put the capitulation order into effect. Vaigachev asked the commander of the 74th Guards Rifle Division's 236th Guards Rifle Regiment to accompany him to the front lines as a precaution in case the Soviets tried to fire on them. When they reached the German lines, the Germans on the other side did in fact open fire on the small Russian party, which included a German flying a white flag. After it was known the Russians were looking to negotiate, the Germans held their fire. After reaching the Propaganda Ministry and meeting with Fritsche it was decided that in an act of good faith Fritsche should secure the surrender of the remaining *SS* in the city center. *SS-Sturmbannführer* Metz and a contingent of 4,000 soldiers spread throughout Defense Sector Z surrendered later in the day at Fritsche's request. Vaigachev then left the Ministry and reached the lines of the 1038th Rifle Regiment of the 295th Rifle Division of the 5th Shock Army. The regimental commander was subsequently ordered to take the Propaganda Ministry and seal it off to protect the archives and other documents. By the evening the remaining German soldiers left in Berlin surrendered.[12]

Soviet JS-2 tanks move toward the Reichstag past abandoned a German tracked vehicle from a Luftwaffe unit.
Photo courtesy of the Bulgarian Ministry of Defence.

A rare photograph showing a King Tiger and Wirbelwind from *s.SS-Pz.Abt. 503*and a Panther from *Pz.Div. Müncheberg* in the
background shortly after the German capitulation. Photo courtesy of ASKM.

Photograph of the Hotel Adlon's side entrance off Unter Den Linden taken on 4 May. The Adlon was used as a makeshift hospital for German wounded as the medical vehicles parked outside attest. German medical personnel often required that German soldiers discard their weapons before they would administer treatment so that they would not suffer reprisals from the Soviets if the hospital was overrun. Note the discarded German K98 and *Panzerfaust* near the passenger side door of the ambulance. Courtesy of the US National Archives.

The Altes Museum on the Lustgarten with the Berliner Dom to the right. The Altes Museum was still on fire on 4 May when this photograph was taken. The 5th Shock Army fought through this area only several days before on their way into the Government Quarter. Courtesy of the US National Archives.

Aftermath of battle. Area of the Brandenburg Gate at the entrance of Unter Den Linden taken after the battle. Courtesy of the US National Archives.

T-34/85 tank from the 55th Armoured Brigade 7th Guards Armoured Corps Third Guards Tank Army, Germany, April 1945

IS-2 tank from the 57th Independent Guards Heavy Tank Regiment 3rd Guards Tank Army, Germany, April 1945

PzKpfw V SdKfz 171 Ausf G Panther tank from Kampfgruppe "Käther", Berlin, April 22-23, 1945

PzKpfw VI SdKfz 181 Ausf E Tiger tank from Panzer Division Müncheberg, Berlin, April 1945

8.8 cm Pak 43/3 Waffenträger SP gun from 3rd Panzerjäger Abteilung Infantry Division Ulrich von Hütten, Berlin, April 1945

SdKfz 251/1 Ausf D APC armed with a 20mm gun from unidentified unit, Berlin, April 1945

PzKpfw V SdKfz 171 Panther Ausf G tank from 10th SS Panzer Regiment 10th SS Panzer Division Fründsberg, Germany, April 1945

StuG IV SdKfz 167 assault gun from Panzer Division Müncheberg, Berlin, April 1945

Jagdpanzer 38 (t) Hetzer SP gun from Infantry Division Scharnhorst, April 1945

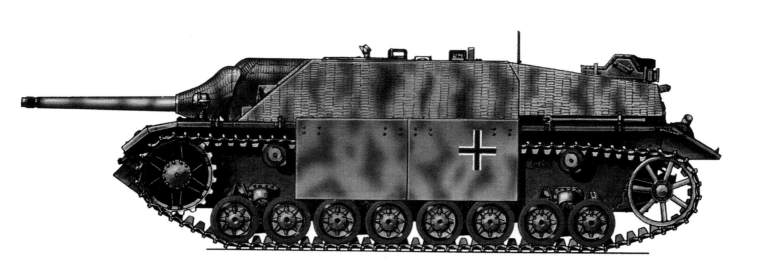

Jagdpanzer IV SdKfz 162 SP gun from Panzer Division Müncheberg, Berlin, April 1945

StuG III Ausf D SdKfz 142 assault gun from Infantry Division Ferdinand von Schill, 12 Army, west of Berlin, April 1945

SdKfz 222 (4x4) armoured car from Infantry Division "Scharnhorst", Berlin, May 1945

SdKfz 251/17 Ausf D APC from unidentified unit, Berlin, May 1945

Flakpanzer IV Wirbelwind from 503rd SS schwere Panzer Abteilung Berlin, May 1945

SU-100 SP gun from the 1977th SP Gun Artillery Regiment, Germany, April 1945

ISU-122 SP gun from the 385th Guards Heavy SP Gun Artillery Regiment, Germany, April 1945

Soviet soldiers gather at the Brandenburg Gate on 2 May to celebrate their costly victory over Berlin's defenders and Nazi Germany.
Two JS-2s are in the foreground and two more appear in the background near the barricade under the gate.
Photo courtesy of the Cornelius Ryan Collection, Mahn Center, Alden Library, Ohio University, Athens, OH.

Happy Soviet soldiers walk past a German 8.8cm flak gun south of the Reichstag on Hermann-Göring Strasse shortly after the capitulation of Berlin. It is not clear if this 8.8cm saw action as there is a lack of spent cartridges around the gun, though there are several cases of usable 8.8cm shells visible. Note the JS-2 in the woods to the left of the flak gun. Photo courtesy of the Bundesarchiv.

Surrendered Germans marching past the Soviet cameras. These soldiers appear to be mainly *Volkssturm* and *Hitlerjugend*—the primary defenders of Berlin.
Photo courtesy of the Cornelius Ryan Collection, Mahn Center, Alden Library, Ohio University, Athens, OH.

The destroyed Reichstag, 1945. In the foreground, note the 8.8 cm gun bearing what looks like a number of white circles around the barrel indicating 'kills'. This image gives an excellent impression of the ground the attacking Soviet forces had to contest. (RGAKFD Moscow)

General Bogdanov, the commander of the 2nd Guards Tank Army, inspects booty. (RGAKFD Moscow)

Soviet soldiers at the Reich Chancellery (*Reichskanzlei*), Berlin, May 1945. (RGAKFD Moscow)

Soviet troops in Berlin, 2 May 1945. (RGAKFD Moscow)

A female Soviet soldier from the Traffic Control Service. Photo courtesy of the Bulgarian Ministry of Defence.

Soviet soldiers celebrate their victory outside one the many official buildings in the Government Quarter of Berlin.
Photo courtesy of the Cornelius Ryan Collection, Mahn Center, Alden Library, Ohio University, Athens, OH.

Soviet JS-2 parked outside of the Brandenburg Gate. Note the camouflaged Soviet trucks and towed artillery in the background. Photo courtesy of the Cornelius Ryan Collection, Mahn Center, Alden Library, Ohio University, Athens, OH.

Another JS-2 takes a photo opportunity outside the Brandenburg Gate. Note the two female Soviet soldiers on the left. The female soldier in the left foreground dons both captured German binoculars and a German Officer's dagger.
Photo courtesy of the Cornelius Ryan Collection, Mahn Center, Alden Library, Ohio University, Athens, OH.

A Company of Soviet JS-2s kick up dust in the rubble of Berlin as they drive north up Hermann-Göring Strasse behind the Reichstag.
Photo courtesy of the Cornelius Ryan Collection, Mahn Center, Alden Library, Ohio University, Athens, OH.

German prisoners march east on Leipziger Strasse into captivity. Most of these old men and boys may never have fired a shot in anger during
the battle as the Soviets simply rounded every male up and marched them east. Few returned after nearly a decade of Soviet forced labor.
Photo courtesy of the Cornelius Ryan Collection, Mahn Center, Alden Library, Ohio University, Athens, OH.

Other soldiers in the city found themselves with few options in the morning of 2 May. The Latvians of the *SS-Latvian Fusiliers* changed into civilian clothes and passed themselves off as foreign workers in order to made their way West. The French *SS* woke the next morning and moved through the U-Bahn tunnels to the station opposite the Reich Chancellery where Fenet noticed the street crawling with Soviet soldiers and tanks. He then led the French back toward Potsdamer Platz where they ultimately all surrendered to the Soviets.[13]

Remnants of the *20.Pz.Gr.Div.* on Wannsee Island broke out on their own as Wenck's presence motivated them to try to reach German lines. This contingent of Germans numbered no more than 100 soldiers but they surprised Koniev's HQ as they tried to make their way to Beelitz. They caused considerable issues for Koniev who detailed nearby units to capture these forces.[14]

The Soviets quickly began rounding up everyone in Berlin who wore a military-like uniform. The Soviets didn't distinguish between a German's job or role. If a person looked official, they were marched off to Tempelhof. One veteran of the battle recounts what happened after the capitulation:

> At Tempelhof Airfield there must have been about 70,000–80,000 men in uniform. Here the Russians marched railway and street transport employees in uniform. Station masters with their bright red caps bordered in gold were taken by the Russians for generals. They had a hard time talking their way out of it and many of them had to march to Landsberg-on-Warthe Prisoner Camp along with the regular soldiers. They also had Berlin electricity employees in their mechanic uniforms and postal employees, just anyone caught running around in what looked like a uniform.[15]

The Soviets later claimed that they took 70,000 prisoners after Berlin's fall. Most of the German prisoners marshaled at Tempelhof were not soldiers by training and did not fire a shot in anger against the Soviets during the assault. Many were simply administrators, non-essential military personnel, or members of the military just hiding out and waiting for the Soviet assault to end. Most of the combat forces which the Soviets had engaged in Berlin since it was surrounded on 24 April left the city in one of a number of breakouts north, west, or southwest. Those forces captured outside of Berlin were marched off to different camps and not counted at Tempelhof. This makes Soviet official assessments of the number of actual German defenders in Berlin questionable.

The *12.Armee* retreated back to the Elbe finally reaching Tangermünde by 3 May. Negotiations with the U.S. 9th Army began quickly. On 4 May a U.S. delegation led by General Moore, General Keating, and Colonel Williams meet with the three German officers led by *General* von Edelsheim, a Knight's Cross, with Oak Leaves and Sword holder. *General* Edelsheim communicates Wenck's wishes:

1. To take over the wounded
2. To let the civilians, especially the women and children, over the Elbe onto the Western Shore
3. To let soldiers without weapons cross over to the western Elbe shores
4. After the end of the last combat of the army, which will be contained until the last cartridge is fired, to take over the orderly units and place them as honest soldiers at the disposal of the American High Command

Wenck, General of the Panzertruppen[16]

Soviet soldiers Egorov and Kantarya raise the red flag over the Reichstag. The Reichstag became a "tourist" stop for victorious Soviet soldiers who wanted to leave their name on the walls, and have their photograph taken while unfurling a Soviet flag on the roof.

Photo courtesy of the Bulgarian Ministry of Defence.

The response from General Moore was simple. He reconfirmed that the U.S. forces were still allied with the Soviets. The Germans would be allowed to cross at Storkau, Tangermünde, and Ferchland. The Germans soldiers would receive provisions for eight days and were expected to erect their own field hospitals. One final condition: "No civilians!" The German delegation spent the next half hour discussing this turn of events. The Americans, seeing the impasse, produced a recent edition of the *Stars and Stripes* that contained an article about the concentration camps recently liberated by the U.S. Army. The U.S. delegation informed the Germans that while they might argue that the Russians were barbarians, the Germans clearly were no better in their eyes. Faced with this view by the U.S. Delegation, the German reluctantly accepted the surrender terms.

The *12.Armee* set up a defensive perimeter and Wenck ordered that the civilians be placed in German uniforms and passed over the Elbe where they could. He was not going to leave the civilians behind after rescuing so many that arrived with the shattered *9.Armee*. The Russians soon launched a series of attacks that were repulsed under the watchful eyes of the U.S. GIs on the opposite bank. Soon the Russians started hitting the western shore indiscriminately with artillery fire and strafing from the air. The U.S. forces pulled back several kilometers in order to avoid casualties or potential conflict with the Soviets. The Germans than began to push civilians over the crossing points. Despite the resistance of the U.S. forces to allow civilians to cross the Elbe, Wenck managed to bring over 105,000 soldiers and civilians by 7 May. He averaged about 18,000 a day. His engineers quickly repaired a footbridge over the Elbe that facilitated the crossing.[17] By the evening of 7 May Wenck, his immediate staff, and several soldiers crossed the Elbe in a pneumatic boat while under machine-gun fire of the Russians.

Soviet Assault on the Reichstag
2 May

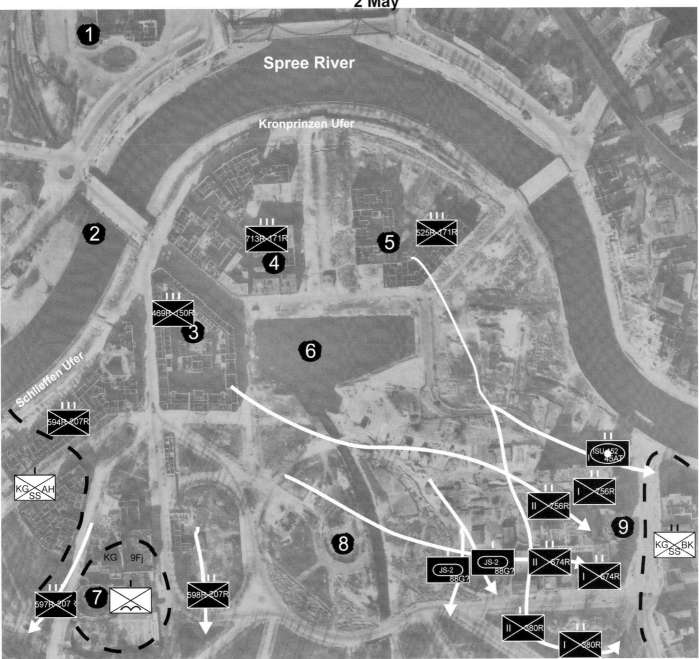

Key Places
1. Lehrter Bahnhof
2. Moltke Bridge
3. Ministry of the Interior
   "Himmler's House"
4. Swiss Consulate
5. Diplomatic Quarter
6. Speer's U-Bahn
   Construction Site and
   Flooded Tunnel
7. Kroll Opera House
8. Königsplatz
9. Reichstag

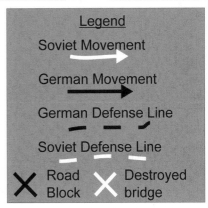

Legend
Soviet Movement
German Movement
German Defense Line
Soviet Defense Line
Road Block
Destroyed bridge

One of the most famous images of the Soviet assault on Berlin—the flying of the Hammer and Sickle off the back of the Reichstag on 2 May. Photo courtesy of the Cornelius Ryan Collection, Mahn Center, Alden Library, Ohio University, Athens, OH.

Remnants of Russian graffiti are still visible on the restored Reichstag in 2005. Here on the south side of the roof is the name of a Soviet soldier who came from Astrakhan, Russia. A city on the Caspian Sea south east of Stalingrad. Author's collection.

Photo of a destroyed JS-2 still visible in Königsplatz to the north of the Reichstag months after the battle ended. Courtesy of the US National Archives.

Two Soviet soldiers from the 150th Rifle Division pose outside the conquered Reichstag.
Photo courtesy of the Cornelius Ryan Collection, Mahn Center, Alden Library, Ohio University, Athens, OH.

Soviet soldiers leave their autographs on the Reichstag walls.
Photos courtesy of the Bulgarian Ministry of Defence.

A view of the Reichstag foyer. Every Soviet soldier that set foot in the Reichstag after the battle scrawled their names onto the building's walls. The restored Reichstag has preserved some of the Soviet graffiti today.
Photo courtesy of the Cornelius Ryan Collection, Mahn Center, Alden Library, Ohio University, Athens, OH.

Volkssturm that waited out the battle in the U-Bahn tunnels now discard their weapons and march off into captivity. Note the assortment of bolt action rifles, not well suited for urban combat where speed and volume of fire dominate during infantry engagements. Courtesy of the Budesarchiv.

It is possible that this platoon of tanks lined up outside the Victory Column is from the Polish contingent that fought in Berlin and reached this area on 1 May.
Photo courtesy of the Cornelius Ryan Collection, Mahn Center, Alden Library, Ohio University, Athens, OH.

Notes to Chapter 6: Assault on Berlin, 2nd May Wednesday

1   OKW File, Last Announcements of OKW, 2 May (RC: 62:8).
2   I. Klimenke, "Chancellery Attack."
3   Le Tissier, *With Our Backs to Berlin*, p. 129.
4   Hass interview.
5   Le Tissier, *With Our Backs to Berlin*, p. 55.
6   Thorwald, p. 258.
7   Ibid. Later that day this group surrendered to the Russians, marched back to Berlin, and then east into captivity.
8   *Wehrmacht* and *Waffen-SS* surrendered at the Schultheiss Brewery. Werde interview, and Le Tissier, *Race for the Reichstag,* p. 188.
9   Fest, p. 149.
10 Spaeter vol. III, p. 506.
11 "Surrender of Berlin Garrison 1st and 2nd May, 1945," p. 1 (RC: 69/1)
12 Ibid.
13 Forbes, pp. 309, 311.
14 Le Tissier, *Race for the Reichstag,* p. 193.
15 Lampe interview.
16 Ritter interview.
17 "Summary of Final Battles between the Order and Elbe in Apr/May 1945 (Especially the Battles of 12th Army)," p. 10, and Wenck interview.

6

ASSAULT ON BERLIN

3 MAY
THURSDAY AND BEYOND

In the capital of the Reich, the remnants of the brave garrison still keep up their heroic defense against the Bolsheviks in isolated blocks of houses and in the government quarter.

OKW **Radio Announcement**[1]

Klimenke spent 2–4 May conducting interrogations of the Germans captured in and around the Tiergarten to identify what happened to Hitler. He was leading a top secret Soviet investigation to confirm that indeed Hitler was dead. The investigation was known as Operation Myth.[2] A break came when he interviewed a former *SS* Body Guard of Hitler by the name of Harri Mengeshausen. Mengeshausen told Klimenke that while on patrol in the upper floor of the Reich Chancellery he stopped to peer out a window into the inner courtyard where he watched two other *SS* Body Guards, Günsche and Linge, carry out two bodies, soaked them with gasoline then lit them on fire. He stated that the gasoline burned but the bodies were not consumed by the flames. The bodies he saw were that of Adolf Hitler and Eva Braun. Klimenke then took Mengeshausen back to the Reich Chancellery to point out the crater, which he did. The crater was in fact a spot that the Soviets had located on their own. During the original search of the inner courtyard, some of Klimenke's men located a crater with a *Panzerfaust* lying on the bottom. For safety reasons the *Panzerfaust* was removed. In the process of removing the *Panzerfaust* a human leg was discovered protruding from the dirt. The Soviets quickly dug down and located the semi-burnt bodies of both a man and a woman. It was suspected that this was Hitler, but until they knew for sure the Soviet soldiers covered the bodies back up and marked the site. When Mengeshausen pointed out the same crater, this confirmed in Klimenke's mind that this marked Hitler's burial spot. He took Mengeshausen back to HQ where a full description of his recollections were written down and compared with a number of other interrogations provided by other occupants of the *Führerbunker*. Klimenke then ordered the bodies removed on the night of 4 May, and during the excavation they found two dogs buried below the corpses. One of the dogs was confirmed as Blondi based on the dog's collar inscription. The bodies of Adolf Hitler and Eva Braun were then wrapped in sheets, taken out of the *Führerbunker*, placed in wooden boxes and taken by truck to Klimenke's HQ.[3]

Hitler committed suicide in the *Führerbunker* on 30 April. The soldiers of the 150th Rifle Division hoisted Red Banner No. 5 on the roof the Reichstag in the early morning hours of 1 May. Berlin capitulated on 2 May after the majority of the combat soldiers left the city in a variety of breakout attempts. Hitler's burnt body was then located and removed on 4 May. By 12 May the newly formed government under Dönitz surrendered to the combined Western Allies and Soviet Union ending Germany's war in Europe.

The last radio announcement by OKW regarding Berlin was aired on 4 May.

> The fight for the Reich Capital has come to an end. In a unique heroic struggle, troops of all branches of the *Wehrmacht* and *Volkssturm*, faithful to their oath of allegiance, defended themselves to the last breath and gave an example of the best German military tradition.[4]

This offered little comfort to the German soldiers that endured the horrors of the German defense and Soviet assault on Berlin, many of whom now marched off into a decade of brutal captivity from which thousands would never return.

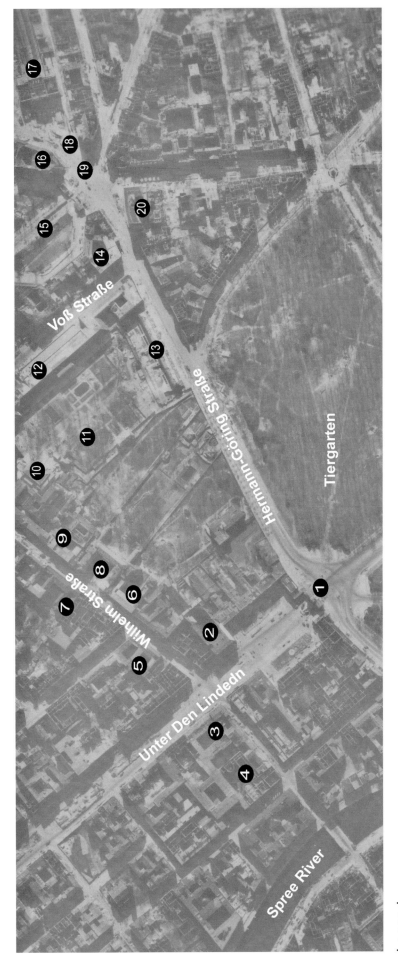

Wilhelm Straße and Hermann-Göring Straße
March 1945

Legend
1. Brandenberger Tor
2. Adlon Hotel
3. SS Ministry of the Interior Offices
4. Foreign Exchange
5. Ministry of Science, Education and National Training
6. Army Administration
7. Ministry of Justice
8. Former President's Office
9. Foreign Office
10. Führerbunker
11. Chancellery Gardens
12. Reich Chancellery
13. Leibstandarte SS Adolf Hitler Wachregiment Barracks
14. Gauleiter Berlin Office
15. Leipziger Platz
16. Post Office Branch Office
17. Potsdamer Bahnhof
18. Potsdamer U-Bahn
19. Potsdamer Platz
20. Columbus House

Voß Strasse, winter 1945. The Reich Chancellery is on the right side of the picture. Zhukov claimed in his memoir that the "battle" for Hitler's Reich Chancellery was among the toughest in Berlin. Note the absolute lack of small arms bullet holes on the façade of any building on the street. The Soviets did not attack this building; they walked into it after all combatants left during the breakout from 1-2 May.
Author's collection.

The Honor Courtyard entrance from Wilhelmstraße, winter 1945. The Soviets removed the giant bronze eagle designed by Kurt Schmid-Ehmen. The eagle's outline can be seen between the two middle pillars. This war trophy now lies in the Red Army Museum, Moscow. Also removed are the two Arno Becker designed statues that stood to the left and right of the stairs.
Author's collection.

The nearly 50 meter long Mosaic Hall just inside the entrance of the Honor Courtyard. All the red mosaic marble was removed by the Soviets. Another giant Kurt Schmid-Ehmen bronze eagle sat perched above the door in the center of the photo. That eagle was salvaged by a US Army Air Force Colonel in 1945 and now resides at the United States Air Force Museum in Dayton, Ohio.
Author's collection.

The long Marble Gallery accessed through the east entrance of the Mosaic Hall, winter 1945.
Again, note the lack of any bullet holes in the walls. Author's collection.

The Reception Room at the end of the Marble Gallery, winter 1945. The two giant chandeliers were smashed and the
contents of the entire room looted. Russian scrawl can be seen on the far wall. Author's collection.

German POWs in Berlin. Photo courtesy of the Bulgarian Ministry of Defence.

A German POW watches a column of JS-2 tanks roll past. Photo courtesy of the Bulgarian Ministry of Defence.

It's finally over. An old man and an abandoned artillery tractor.
Photo courtesy of the Bulgarian Ministry of Defence.

Berlin, May 1945 – a fallen German eagle.
Photo courtesy of the Bulgarian Ministry of Defence.

A Soviet soldier serves food to the population of Berlin in the
aftermath of the fighting.
Photo courtesy of the Bulgarian Ministry of Defence.

German POWs receive medical aid in front of the
Brandenburg Gate before being marched off to the east.
Photo courtesy of the Bulgarian Ministry of Defence.

A crew of a Soviet T-34-76 tank celebrates the victory.
Photo courtesy of the Bulgarian Ministry of Defence.

The battle for the Reich's capital may have ended, but the long
fight for survival in Soviet captivity had now begun.
Photo courtesy of the Bulgarian Ministry of Defence.

German women and children make their way down
Unter-den-Linden, presumably having emerged from a shelter.
Their faces are taught with the fear of an unknown future.
Photo courtesy of the Bulgarian Ministry of Defence.

The Reichstag with the Red Banner flying from the roof.
Photo courtesy of the Bulgarian Ministry of Defence.

Notes to Chapter 6: Assault on Berlin, 3rd May Thursday and Beyond

1   Schultz-Naumann, pp. 119–21.
2   Henrik Eberle and Matthias Uhl, eds. *The Hitler Book: The Secret Dossier Prepared for Stalin* (Public Affairs: New York), p. x.
3   Klimenke, "Chancellery Attack."
4   OKW File, Last Announcements of OKW, 4 May (RC: 62:8).

PART III: AFTERMATH

ESCAPE FROM BERLIN

Berlin's remaining garrison capitulated on 2 May to the Soviet Army. Germany surrendered unconditionally on 8 May to the combined Allied Powers and all hostilities in Europe ended on 12 May. The fighting for Berlin and Germany was over, but the fight for individual survival and freedom now began. Many soldiers that fought in German uniform changed into civilian clothes, buried weapons, burnt their papers, and made for the Western Allies sitting on the western bank of the Elbe River—the demarcation line outlined in 'Eclipse'.

There were four primary breakout attempts from Berlin during the evening of 1–2 May. There was the northern breakout across the Spree River by the *SS* and soldiers that fought in the Government Quarter; the western breakout across the Havel River by the majority of the *LVI Pz. Korps' Wehrmacht* contingent; the breakout north toward the *3.Panzer Armee* lines by the *Wachregiment Großdeutschland*; and the southeastern breakout from the Wannsee Island by the remnants of the *20.Pz.Gren.Div.* Many other smaller breakouts occurred through the porous Russian lines both inside and outside Berlin.

The following accounts were recorded after the Berlin Wall was built by the Soviets at the height of the Cold War in preparation for Ryan's book *The Last Battle*. They are derived directly from the interviews written down by the *Reader's Digest*-contracted interviewer or in the first person by the interviewee himself. They were among the first recollections these participants gave to a non-German person after the war and many of the topics were taboo then and still considered sensitive in Germany today.

These accounts stand independently. Clarifying remarks are interjected to keep consistency with the rest of the prepared text when appropriate.[1] There was no attempt to alter the text. All spelling mistakes were part of the original documents. Some of the accounts may contradict the known historical record currently accepted as fact regarding specific events or an individual's fate. The selected accounts represent a cross-section of events and are published here for the first time to illustrate the turmoil and confusion that existed in the aftermath of the final Soviet assault.

Peace did not descend across Berlin, Germany, or Europe quickly like red felt across a stage in the closing act of a play. Instead the curtain rose up, slowly at first, then abruptly. It was not made of cloth, but of steel, concrete, and barbed wire, that was completed in August 1961. For many of the participants in the Soviet assault, the struggle for survival in the final climatic battle that began along the Oder River on 16 April, and culminated in Berlin streets starting on 23 April continued for years behind the Iron Curtain.

The following accounts tell various stories of escape and surrender. They reveal a Germany in transition from conqueror and occupier to conquered and occupied. There are few redeeming aspects of these survivors' tales and some are unapologetic. Brutality, rape, indifference, death, disappointment, anger, occasional kindness, and survival all intertwine as common threads through each account. They provide a historical chronicle of what it was like in and around Berlin the days shortly after capitulation and the trials that individuals endured in the aftermath of Hitler's Third Reich.

Friedrich Böttcher[2]

18.Panzergrenadier Division

1 May

The news spread in the Zoo Flak Tower almost immediately. The doctors and nurses attending the wounded seemed relieved. They put on their Red Cross armbands and one doctor declared to Böttcher that immediately after the troops left the Flak Tower would be declared a hospital. It was either this news, or the news of the breakout that attracted great masses of civilians. They started to pour into the Flak Tower, jamming hallways and staircases, until it became almost impossible to move.

In the meantime the Russians had taken the Zoo and were shelling the Flak Tower directly. The staff of the *18.Pz.Gren.Div.* was supposed to break out of the Flak Tower with whatever troops were available. They were to meet the fighting troops of the Division near the intersection of two streets, at a telephone exchange between Charlottenburg Station and the Kaiserdamm (Böttcher does not remember the exact spot. It might have been at the telephone exchange Dernburgstrasse) to break out altogether.

Böttcher says that it was an act of courage to leave the security of the Flak Tower to get through the Russian lines of heavy shelling. All in all about 200 soldiers left the Flak Tower to go to the gathering point. They belonged for the most part to either the *18.Pz.Gren.Div.* or else to *General* Sydow's anti-aircraft units. Very few civilians were among them because for a civilian, the risk seemed hardly worth while. Böttcher had taken over command of the soldiers. The first part of their way was the worst. They ran a few yards, threw themselves to the ground, crawled, got down again and once more ran a few yards. Most of the streets leading directly to their meeting point were blocked off by the Russians and could not be passed. It was still dark outside when they left the Flak Tower, but by the time they reached the gathering point, 2 May started to dawn. They found no one at the rendezvous. Böttcher decided to wait, for he hoped that *General* Rauch, who had promised the day before that he would participate in the venture, would come. They waited for 45 minutes, but neither the general, nor the fighting troops of the Division showed up. Everything was calm around them. The bursting of shells could be heard from afar. Finally Böttcher decided that they could wait no longer if they still wanted to have a minimal chance of success.

The nearer they got to the Spandau Bridge, the more crowded were the streets. Soldiers, civilians, vehicles of all kinds formed a constant stream towards the West. It was impossible to keep in close touch with each other. Böttcher, the members of his staff, and the whole group who had left the Flak Tower were on foot. Their cars had been hit by Russian shells near the Flak Tower long ago. When Böttcher was only a few hundred meters in front of the bridge, he noticed that the human stream hardly moved at all, as if an invisible dam was stopping it. Böttcher and his adjutant, by the name of Salisch, fought their way ahead through thousands of civilians, mostly women carrying their belongings in suitcases or sometimes piled on prams, hand wagons or pushcarts. A few soldiers were among this mass of people and some children too. The last few meters before the bridge were deserted. People had crowded the doorways or against walls, for the Russians were firing at the bridge. On the bridge itself were burning vehicles and some corpses and wounded were sprawled around on the ground. Böttcher immediately saw that the firing was of small caliber guns coming from some light infantry weapons. While he tried to make out where the shots came from, an *Admiral* in full uniform came up to him. "Here, *Oberstleutnant*," he said "take my binoculars." Böttcher saw through the binoculars that the shots came out of the first house to the right. He could clearly see through an open window of the house where the Russians had set up a light machine gun on a table. Böttcher got hold of a four-barreled mounted AA gun which was among the crowd [Author's note: this was a Flakpanzer IV Wirbelwind that belonged to sch.*SS-Pz.Abt.503*], and gave its *SS* crew orders to fire into the building. After this the machine gun was silent and nothing moved inside the house. Böttcher then started to move across the bridge, along with the AA gun. The AA gun continued to spray the houses with bullets, and the fire was not returned. When they had reached the end of the bridge, Böttcher almost heard an audible sigh of relief coming from the thousands of people. The crowd had remained before the bridge, watching every movement of Böttcher and the gun, not daring to move during the few minutes of suspense that would decide whether they could continue their route towards freedom or not. When nothing happened, they all rushed forward at once. Böttcher stood for a second and watched this stream of people coming towards him. "Just like opening the gates of a dam, releasing an uncontrollable force," he thought. "Now I know what 'panic' means. This is it."

Although it was impossible for Böttcher to find his staff in this crowd, he nevertheless was determined to continue his route which was to push through in a southwesterly direction. All he could find in the chaos were an artillery commander of the *18.Pz.Gren.Div.*, *Oberleutnant* Koch of the field gendarmes and his adjutant Salisch. For protection he got hold of two [King Tigers] with an *SS* crew who were to accompany them. Behind the bridge and all through Spandau there was hardly any Russian firing, but shortly before Staaken they were caught up in heavy Russian fire. One of the [King Tigers] received a direct hit and burst into flames. The two men of the crew jumped out of the vehicle with their clothes burning and rolled themselves on the street. To Böttcher it was one of the most terrible sights he had ever seen.

It was impossible to cross through the town of Staaken, especially since Böttcher had so few men and no organized battle unit with trained reconnaissance men with him. They were forced to turn south towards Potsdam. In doing so, *Oberleutnant* was shot through the arm.

Until 9 May Böttcher and his group of about 20 men were roaming through the woods in the Potsdam area. They could not enter any village for fear of being taken prisoner by the Russians. They also had to be very careful of Russian mop-up troops who were carefully combing the woods. In the woods around Potsdam heavy fighting must have taken place, for traces of battle could be found all over: corpses and destroyed vehicles were littering the ground in many spots. It looked as if Wenck at one point had got this far.

Food and water were big problems during those days. There was very little to eat in the woods, and clear water was rare. Entering any village to ask for food was impossible. Once they found a pool containing filthy water full of green slime. The sun was already hot, and Böttcher was thirsty. In his field kit he found a piece of a compress which he used to filter the water with, to at least get rid of the disgusting green slime.

On 9 May Koch's condition worsened considerably. His arm was terribly swollen and he started to run a temperature. Through some stragglers Böttcher met in the woods they heard that emergency field hospital had been installed in the Parsonage of a nearby village. The remaining men immediately hunted up some civilian clothes for Koch and sent him off in the direction of this hospital. Böttcher and his men (by this time there were about 12 left) met some more stragglers somewhere in the woods. Each one of them had different bits of information: "The Americans are right near here," said one. "The way to the south is still open," said another. Or else "We should go West, it's the only possibility."

In the evening of 9 May they crawled into the undergrowth of a plantation of young trees which was an excellent protection. Soon a Russian mop-up unit was combing the woods all around them and slowly started closing in on Böttcher and his 11 companions. It was clear that the Russians did not know for a fact that German soldiers were hiding in these woods but was just on one of their routine patrols. The men in the tree nursery took cover as well as they could. The Russians fired a few shots into the nursery, but without aiming at anything. Finally they left again, to the great relief of Böttcher and his men who were unharmed. They slept all night.

Early the next morning they saw a young man in civilian clothes with a sack on his back approach their hideout. To their amazement he suddenly started to yell "Böttcher, Böttcher!" Böttcher crawled out of the plantation and went up to the young man to ask what he wanted and who he was. The young man said: "I was sent by *Oberleutnant* Koch, who is in the emergency hospital at the Parsonage. He has asked me to bring you civilian clothes." With this he put down the sack. "By the way, the war is over. The capitulation was signed 8 May." With this he departed.

Böttcher reported to his friends in the plantation. The news of the capitulation was depressing for all of them. All of a sudden everything changed. Up to now they were a military unit, they did what they were told to do and had still hoped to meet some German forces which would have permitted them to once more become a fighting unit. At this very moment they all realized it was over, the last open door had closed on them. They were no longer needed. They quietly put on the civilian clothing, and in doing so their entire mentality seemed to change. They were civilians again, with the problem of civilians. First they all wanted to go home. The whole conversation revolved around this. "Where do you live?" Boy, that's far. I hope you'll get through." "I wonder how things are at home—I haven't had any news in a long time." Böttcher encountered some difficulties in getting dressed. He had not taken off his boots in weeks, and his feet were swollen to such an extent that it was impossible to get them off. He had to put a pair of civilian trousers over his staff-officer pants and officer's boots, hoping nobody would notice. After everyone was dressed, they all got busy burying their uniforms and weapons. There was no reason for them to stay together any more so one after the other took leave. It was a sad moment, the end of an era. Each one went off with a "Good bye, maybe we'll meet again. Good luck, hope you'll make it home."

Böttcher took off with his adjutant Salisch. He wanted to go home to Silesia too, but first of all he wanted to know a little more about the capitulation. What were the conditions, if there were any? What future did he have? He decided to go into the village to see Koch.

The Parsonage was a very large house, and about 20 wounded men had been set up there. The minister's wife greeted Böttcher and Salisch like old friends. "*Oberleutnant* Koch has told me all about you. Thank God you're here safe and sound. Everything is over now." She immediately gave both men boiled potatoes and water sauce. To Böttcher, who had had no warm meal in many days, it was a feast. The living room where they ate was large and cozy. Besides the minister's wife, her daughter Eva and a younger son, the young man who had brought the civilian clothing out to the woods was present. The young man turned out to be a former "*Ordensjunker*" (a young man picked by the *SS* and trained in one of their schools to later become an *SS* leader and member of the "blood aristocracy") who had entered the German airforce later on. As a pilot he had lost one arm and he now wore a "Sauerbruch-Arm", (an artificial limb designed by the famous German surgeon Sauerbruch, the most modern in those times.)

Böttcher's adjutant Salisch had decided to go first to complete his partial civilian outfit. In the basement of the Parsonage the minister had stored a great number of odd pieces of civilian clothing from which the wounded could pick. While Böttcher was eating potatoes and Salisch was down in the cellar, all of the sudden the door flew open and a Russian NKVD officer [Author's note: it would have been SMERSH at this time] with two soldiers stood in the doorway. The officer took one look around the room, pointed at Böttcher and the *Ordensjunker* and shouted: "You soldier, and you soldier too." Böttcher was so surprised and scared he could not answer. He simply tapped with his index finger against his forehead, to tell the Russian that anyone accusing him of being a soldier must be crazy. The officer turned around and said to somebody behind him: "You soldier too." It was only then that Böttcher discovered Salisch, whom the Russians had rounded up in the cellar, green in the face and shaking all over. Salisch had never been very courageous, but at this moment he was frightened to such an extent he couldn't even talk. He started to stutter something in reply to the Russian, but it was incomprehensible. The *Ordensjunker*, on the other hand, seemed to have already had some experience with the Russians. He jumped up and shouted: "We soldiers? Can't you see that we're invalids?" To prove it he took off his jacket, rolled up his shirt sleeves and showed the Russians his artificial arm. He moved the fingers of the novel artificial limb. The Russians immediately came over, mouths agape in astonishment. They wanted to touch the arm, and after awhile the Russian officer motioned to the *Ordensjunker* to take off the arm so he could examine it better.

The Russians could not get over the fact that once the arm was taken off the fingers wouldn't move any more. The *Ordensjunker* had to put the arm on and take it off again about a dozen times in front of the goggle-eyed Russian who thought he was witnessing a miracle.

Böttcher in the meantime had been sitting on pins and needles. His civilian pants were too short for him, his German officer's boots showed too much as well as his staff officer's pants with their wide red staff officer stripe on the side. He pushed his legs under the table as far as they would go. The minister's daughter, Eva, who had been sitting next to him, whispered in his ear: "You are my fiancé and you have been working for the firm of Raspe." Böttcher thought that maybe this explanation was not sufficient to justify his presence at the Parsonage since he was not wounded. He also knew that as soon as the Russian officer got tired of the artificial arm it would be his turn. He looked around and discovered on the sideboard a little plate with some round white pills in it. He got up, picked up the plate and left the room. He went over to the wounded, going from bed to bed with these pills, whispering frantically: "Take one, but for God's sake don't swallow it! I don't know what it is." The Russian seemed to think Böttcher was a medic caring for the wounded and did not bother him. But he promised to be back in the evening, and said he wanted everyone to be there when he got back. During the afternoon the minister came back from an errand and greeted Böttcher and Salisch. "You have to leave right away," he said, "otherwise they'll arrest you." Böttcher explained to him that it was impossible, since the Russians were going to come back the same evening and would blame the minister if two men were missing. Eva once more helped Böttcher. She had been working for the firm of Raspe in Berlin and she knew the firm very well. She therefore typed a paper for Böttcher, stating that he had been working in the firm and had to be discharged because of the military and political situation. The paper also said that Böttcher's identity papers had been lost in an air raid. The paper was signed "Von Drage, Personnel Manager." Böttcher signed himself the name of "Von Drage" underneath. Eva also gave Böttcher a few more details about the firm of Raspe, the telephone number, where it was located and what it manufactured. A man by the name of von Drage was indeed the personnel manager of the firm.

Towards 2030 the Russian officer returned with two or three other Russians, all of them completely drunk. While roaming through the house they discovered the piano and immediately wanted to hear music. The minister started to play, hymns at first, then folk songs, and since the Russians still wanted more, he started on arias, pop songs and whatever came to his mind. For four hours he had to play. Whenever he repeated a tune the Russians got mad and shouted: "You played that before," and the minister had to stop and play something new. They finally left.

The next morning Böttcher and Salisch left the Parsonage on their way to Silesia. In the meantime, Böttcher had been able to take off his boots and he now wore a light summer suit and a pair of patent leather shoes. The shoes and suit belonged to the minister's brother-in-law who had committed suicide after he had witnessed the rape of his wife and daughters. The shoes were almost new and were really meant to go with tails on some gala occasion, for after a mile they hurt Böttcher's feet like hell.

While he and Salisch were walking along the road, always heading East, they suddenly found themselves within sight of a highway toll station. A number of Russians had taken the place of the toll taker and it was impossible for Böttcher and his adjutant to turn around and run away without being highly suspicious. They therefore marched on. The Russians dashed outside and arrested both of men, locking them into a large room behind the toll taker's booth where there already were about 20 people. Böttcher waited until the key had turned in the lock, crossed the room, opened the window and climbed out, with Salisch behind him. They continued their way through the fields for awhile, before going back to the main highway again. Their next stop was going to be Jüterbog where Böttcher had an aunt. About a day later they reached Jüterbog without any further incident.

Böttcher and Salisch immediately went to the aunt's house. By this time Böttcher's feet were killing him and he took off his patent leather shoes before even entering his aunt's apartment. They found that the aunt was not alone. The new mayor of the town as staying with her. He was a Communist, formerly a gardener in town of Muskau. The aunt was a hearty and uncomplicated person, who was very surprised to suddenly see her nephew, whom she knew as a career officer, wearing a light summer suit and no shoes. The new mayor was in the room next door and the walls were thin. Nevertheless she very loudly greeted her nephew and his companion. "My goodness, you're still alive. How did you manage to get out of Berlin? And what did you do with your officer's uniform?" Böttcher went white, his eyes on the door leading to the mayor's room: "For God's sake, don't shout so," he whispered. "You know that the Communist gardener is right next door. He might turn us in." "He?" said the aunt smilingly. "He's going to help us. I'm going to ask him to bring you some food." With this the aunt disappeared into the room next door. Shortly afterwards they saw the new mayor of Jüterbog crossing through the garden to go across the street into the town hall. Salisch and Böttcher, who in the meantime had found a pair of decent shoes, were ready to beat it. They expected that the mayor would immediately get in touch with the Russian authorities and have them arrested. While they were waiting, standing behind the door, they suddenly saw three or four Russian soldiers coming down the street. They were not very much alarmed for all of them were on roller skates, submachine guns slung over their backs, pushing each other for all they were worth. A little later they saw a town hall employee come towards them with two large paper bags full of food supplies. They stayed with Böttcher's aunt for the night, and the next morning they each received a pass to allow them to continue their trip.

They traveled for several more days, walking all day long, sleeping in barns or in the open, depending on which was more convenient. They had found out that the best way of protecting themselves against marauding Russians was to pretend that they were French laborers. Böttcher went to great pains teaching Salisch "Au Claire de la Lune" the French nursery rhyme, which was the only French song Böttcher knew. Whenever they spotted some Russians, they'd sing "Au Claire de la Lune," always the first verse, though, since Böttcher didn't know the others. The only trouble was that it was not a marching song, but a lullaby, and it was difficult to keep in step. Practically all the Russians believed the bluff. More often than not the Russians would come up to them, yelling "Comrade, comrade," and hug Böttcher and Salisch. Only once did they meet a Russian, who after having hugged them said: "Comrade, if you want to go home you have to turn around. You're marching towards the East. France is behind you—over there, to the West." Böttcher thanked him profusely, and for a full day they both had to march toward the West with the Russian, before they were able to escape and turn back again.

Böttcher safely brought Salisch back to his wife, who was overjoyed. Then he continued alone.

Towards the end of May Böttcher reached Waldenburg, where his parents lived. His wife had fled to Czechoslovakia and was still there. Böttcher decided it was too dangerous to remain Waldenburg since everybody there knew him and also knew that he was a career officer. He went to the estate of a friend of his, in Seitendorf, to become a farmer for the time being. One day after he got there his friend's estate was confiscated by the Russians and Böttcher found himself working the Red Army.

For a full year Böttcher remained in Seitendorf, and he got to know the Red Army and their routines very well. He was appalled by the corruption within Sokolowsky's troops. Böttcher did not get paid for his work, receiving only food in exchange. He also found to his amazement that the Russian field kitchens had four different menus every day: one for the general, one for his staff, one for high ranking officers and one for soldiers and noncoms.

Together with a Russian veterinarian, who was a major, and a sergeant, Böttcher soon started to sell cows, horses, hay and other things to the Poles in exchange for food and cigarettes; it was relatively easy with hay and cows, since they were rarely checked. The horses on the other hand had to be replaced. The veterinarian usually came up with some old broken-down horses he had stolen in exchange for a very good one that had been sold to the Poles.

The German population greatly profited from the fact that the Russians and Poles couldn't stand each other. Whenever a Russian plundered somewhere, the Germans would fetch the Polish police and when the Poles plundered they fetched the Russian police.

After about a year, Böttcher found the occasion he had waited for to go to the West. Some Russian marauders had shot a Pole, and the Polish police were madder than ever at the Russians. With the help of the Polish secret police, Böttcher managed to cross the Elbe and go the West. He was questioned by the British, but he never mentioned that he had been a staff officer. He was never in prison.

Hans Henseler[3]

11.SS-Freiwilligen Panzergrenadier Division Nordland

2 May

Henseler took his men to the assembly point and was ordered from there into the nearest U Bahn tunnel (this could have been either the Stadtmitte or Französische Strasse U-Bahn station). The tunnel was jammed full of all sorts of people, both military and civilian. There was no light except from occasional flashlights and matches. In order not to become separated, Henseler and his men had to hold onto each other by their belts. There was an enormous amount of confusion and they ended up waiting in the tunnel for approximately two hours, with no orders to advance any further.

They finally received an order to move forward through the tunnel, and go up on the street at the Friedrichstrasse railroad station and from there proceed northward to the Stettin railroad station. As they emerged out on the street at the Friedrichstrasse station, Henseler saw an immense crowd of soldiers from all sorts of units, civilians, including women with children, cars, trucks loaded with trunks—all swarming around the small area of the station. By now it was around 0100 but there seemed to be no firing of any sort. In the crowd, Henseler saw a group of soldiers go by, seemingly drunk and singing at the top of their voices in a language he could not understand. He asked who they were and someone told him: "Those are the French volunteers."

Despite the confusion, Henseler found Voss who gave him the following instructions "The breakout will be made in four waves. The first will consist of tanks, the second of self-propelled guns, and third of infantry and the fourth of whoever is still left over." Henseler was to be with the third wave.

They all gathered in a long column behind the big tank barricade on the north side of the Weidendamm Bridge. The first wave began to move forward and from the sound of it, the tanks got through without encountering too much fire. Since Henseler was toward the back with the infantry he could not see clearly what was happening up ahead. Then the second wave started through and the self-propelled guns also seemed to be able to get through without encountering too much resistance. Then the third wave started up Friedrichstrasse, but just as they began to move out, the second wave up ahead came under tank fire from the side streets. The self-propelled guns suddenly stopped and so did the column of infantry behind them. Meanwhile a German machine gun began firing over their heads from the tank barricade behind them, its bullets striking sparks from the houses on either side of the street. Many of those on the street either saw or thought they saw Russians firing on them from the roof tops and began to fire into the houses. Since these houses were already badly damaged, the fire immediately brought cascades of stones tumbling down on to the street from the upper stories.

Henseler says: "There was an infernal noise and confusion. We had to keep low because of the machine gun bullets cracking over our heads. There may not even have been Russians in the houses along the street, but the noise of the firing and the sparks made people think they were being fired on. The falling stones and masonry didn't help the matter".

Finally the first self-propelled guns, unable to go any further, abruptly wheeled around and drove back toward the barricade, directly into the group of infantry behind them. A number of soldiers were run down by their own guns because they were simply unable to get out of the way in time. Henseler and his men had to fight their way to the side and scramble up a huge rubble heap in order to get out of the way of the guns. Then the entire group flooded back behind the tank barricade.

The troops regrouped behind the tank barricade and then tried a second breakout in the same way, but this was also thrown back in confusion. After the second attempt had failed, Henseler suddenly ran into *Oberstleutnant* Seifert, who was dripping wet. Seifert told him he had jumped into the Spree and tried to swim to the right of the bridge in order to get through by one of the streets parallel to Friedrichstrasse. But he had been unable to get through and had now come back to his starting point.

Since it was by now clear that they could not go straight ahead or to the right, Seifert proposed they make a new attempt to the left of the bridge in the direction of the Reichstag building. A group of about 400 men, with a few self-propelled guns and a howitzer, grouped themselves under Seifert's command and began to move along the Spree toward the Reichstag. They had not gone far however, when they encountered a tank barricade which barred their path. It took them just 15 minutes to dismantle the tank barricade – the few iron rails which had been driven into the ground to form the backbone of the barricade were pulled out by one of the self-propelled guns. It was getting light by now and just before they reached the Reichstag building they came under fire from a Soviet tank. They spotted the tank however and the self-propelled gun was able to blow it up with a few shots.

They now turned toward the right again, moving in a northerly direction, and soon reached the railway embankment of the S-Bahn near Karlstrasse. They crossed the embankment and broke through into the grounds of the Charité Hospital. Here they abruptly discovered that the entire park of the hospital was covered with sleeping Russian soldiers. One of the Germans fired a machine gun into the crowd, there was a sudden wild scramble and all the Russians vanished. They moved up through the hospital ground to Robert-Koch-Platz and then across the Invalidenstrasse to the Gnadenkirche (Grace Church). Here they had to knock down a 6 foot iron fence to get by. They went around behind the church to Chausseestrasse and then followed this street up to the corner of Schwartzkopfstrasse.

Here they found an 8.8cm anti-aircraft gun standing in the street and not far away a water pump with a group of women standing in line with their pails. The women told the soldiers that the Russians were further up ahead but not back in the direction in which they had just come. This report was enough to make almost the entire group turn around and go back the other way. Seifert and Henseler tried to persuade them to keep going but finally there was no one left except Seifert, Henseler, and two others. From where they were standing they could see Russian troops moving some 300 to 400 meters away. They decided that it was senseless to attempt to move by daylight and took refuge on the third floor of a burned-out building directly opposite the Maikäfer barracks. By now Seifert was shivering: he was still soaked to the skin. They stayed in this building throughout the entire day.

(Henseler admits that he "lost a day somewhere in his narrative." Although he refers to the breakout as having taken place in the night from 30 April to 1 May, he admits it is more likely that it actually took place the following night from 1 May to 2 May [Authors Note: the interviewer was correct in this correction]. But he is unable to say where in the course of the narrative the missing day should be inserted. Assuming that the breakout did actually take place in the night of 1 May to 2 May, and this seems clear from all other sources—then the day the four men spent hiding in the building was 2 May).

From where they were, they could see the remainder of the group with which they had come streaming back up Chausseestrasse after they had run into severe [enemy] fire further back. But now they ran into new Soviet fire further up the street and for a time there was a great deal of running around and shooting in the area as the confused troops tried to break out singly. Finally the situation calmed down again, and a civilian or two actually came up out of the cellar of the house where they were hiding, but did not see them.

They hid until dark and then went through the Maikäfer barracks to a series of backyards on the other side of the street. They took some material from the seats of a shot-up car standing on the street and wrapped around their shoes in order to muffle the noise of their foot steps. Their one aim was still to try to get out of Berlin toward the north, but everywhere they encountered Russian troops. A little way up the Chausseestrasse they climbed into the Panke a small stream which flows through the area, and followed it along its banks under a row of houses. The small stream finally disappeared into a tunnel but as they themselves entered the tunnel, they discovered that it was blocked. What was immediately blocking their path was two other soldiers who had previously crawled into the tunnel and were also trying to get through. But since it was impossible to do so they returned and dodged into a ruin where they waited all day in the cellar. The other two soldiers remained behind somewhere near the tunnel.

During the night of 3–4 May they proceeded up through Wedding to Grenzstrasse where they climbed on to the S-Bahn railway embankment and followed it through the Humboldthain and Gesundbrunnen railway stations. They got off the embankment just before the Bornholmer Strasse station and went into some gardens. Here they discovered an old woman who gave them some food and hid them in a ruined cottage for the rest of the day.

At dusk on 4 May they went back to the railway embankment and resumed their march toward the north. As they were treading cautiously through the pitch-black night they suddenly saw the glow of a cigarette some 20 feet ahead of them: It was a Russian sentry who had just lit a cigarette. It was a stroke of sheer luck for them, for without that they would have run directly into him. They got off the embankment and went back through Pankow to Breite Strasse. Here they stumbled on a sort of farm and hid themselves in a barn. They found however they were not the only ones to have chosen this farm for quarters. The barn next door was occupied by Russians who shortly came into the barn where they were hiding. As they came in Seifert jumped out through a back window and vanished. Henseler never saw him again. Henseler himself dodged behind a chicken coop and thus avoided any notice from the Russians. A few hours later however the farmer entered and promptly saw what the Russians had overlooked: Henseler's feet were protruding quite visibly from beneath the chicken coop. Henseler came out and explained to the farmer what had happened, and the farmer let him stay there and brought him food.

On the evening of 5 May, when it began to get dark, the other three began to look for Seifert, whom they had last seen jumping through the window. They could find him nowhere in the area and set off once more toward the north to Schlosspark. Since they did not dare to walk along the main streets, they were compelled to continue through back yards and gardens. For this purpose they had found a ladder in order to help them climb the numerous fences. They crossed the park and once again began the wearying nocturnal trip through small gardens. Suddenly however, the miracle happened: They found themselves standing in front of a wide expanse of free fields, and realized they were finally out of the city. As the realization hit them there was a delirium of joy. They fell on their knees and gave prayers of thanks, the tears ran down their cheeks and they embraced each other and slapped each other on the back. Then suddenly they began running like children through the fields in their joy.

From here on Henseler made his way slowly and with many dangerous detours toward the Elbe. Over the course of the next week he parted company with his two original companions and with the help of civilians along the way he was able to dodge the numerous Russian patrols and approach the river separating him from the American occupation zone. Along the way he had joined up with a navy artillery man and the two of them finally came within sight of the river on the night of Pentacost Sunday, 13 May.

They had already picked the spot where they would try to swim across the river, and had carefully packed their few belongings in order to be able to carry them while swimming. The night was calm and dark and the river only some 15 feet away. They had been underway all day and Henseler wanted to take a moment's rest before starting the arduous swim. He saw what seemed to be a log on the ground ahead of him and went to sit down on it. To his stunned amazement the "log" suddenly stood up and pointed a machine pistol at him: it was a Soviet sentry who had been sleeping on the ground. His companion was in a foxhole next to him but for some reason he had chosen to sleep on the open field. The Russian was almost more frightened than Henseler and his companion, and since he had a machine pistol both of them quickly sat down and held their hands over their heads to show they meant no harm. Thus, after almost two weeks of an extraordinary escape journey, Henseler became a Russian prisoner of war within sight of his goal.

From the Elbe he was marched all the way back into Berlin and from there out to Fürstenwalde. But here once more his resourcefulness showed itself: He was able to dodge out of the column of prisoners being marched toward the east and flee back into Berlin. Here he managed to go underground in the sector which was later occupied by the British. After the British had arrived in the city [Authors note: the Western Allies arrived in Berlin August], he was able to make friends with a number of the Tommies, and eventually persuaded them to take him along in a truck to the western occupation zones. From here he made his way to his home in the Rhineland where he was eventually interned for two years before finally being released.

Dr. Hans Rein[4]

9.Fallschirmjäger Division

1 May

In the evening of 1 May, an order was given to the soldiers in the Reichstag to clear the building and try and break out towards the north by way of Friedrichstrasse station, and the Weidendamm Bridge. Both the station and the bridge were under heavy Russian shelling. Rein crossed the bridge with his 20 men and immediately dashed into a nearby ruin on Schiffbauerdamm, west of Friedrichstrasse. He thought the only chance of getting through to the north was by passing through the ruins and rubble of former occupants' homes during the night, since the streets were in Russian hands for the most part.

In one of the ruins Rein heard two men talking. One was an SS officer and the other a SS corporal. By listening to their conversation Rein discovered that the corporal knew this district very well and was supposed to guide the officer who obviously was not a Berliner. Rein immediately approached the SS officer and took up the subject with him: "Let's try to break out together – you, the corporal, and my men and myself. We are still 20 battle-experienced men, and we will be able to protect you." The SS Obergefreiter was very much against this plan. In his opinion the only way of getting through the Russian lines was to be either alone or maybe by twos. The chances of being unnoticed decreased with every additional man. The SS officer on the other hand seemed to fall for the idea, but he first wanted to see Rein's papers, to make sure he was in the right company [Authors note: the SS officer wanted to confirm that Rein was not a Seydlitz soldier].

Finally they got under way. The SS Obergefreiter was ahead, followed by the SS officer and Rein. Since it was a dark night, Rein had given exact orders to his men: "Proceed close behind me in Indian file. Never lose touch with the man in front of you." The last man was a particularly capable *Feldwebel* by the name of Geier.

Slowly the 23 men were making their way towards the north. They never dared walk upright – most of the way they had to crawl on all fours. Whenever they had to pass Russian positions they had to lie on the ground, inching themselves forward on their elbows. When they were able to pause for the first time, Rein noticed to his dismay that of his 20 men only seven or eight remained. *Feldwebel* Geier who had closed the way was not among them.

Somewhere along their painful route they saw a German Panther with an SS crew [Authors note: there were no known Panthers crewed by the *Waffen-SS* in Berlin. This was probably a Panther of the *Müncheberg Panzer Division* that was abandoned by their crew and commandeered by the *Waffen-SS*.]. They approached it and the SS officer seemed to know the commander of the Panzer, for he started what looked like a very cordial conversation. Rein grabbed the opportunity and asked the commander if he intended on breaking through towards the north. "Yes," was the reply. Rein then asked if he and his men could sit on the Panzer and the answer was "yes" again. Several soldiers, some SS men among them, were already sitting on the Panzer, and they all proceeded north.

On the way Rein heard how one SS man said to another: "Well, at least we are free now, and we can see how to get through, since the Führer is dead." It was the first time Rein had heard about Hitler's death and he was amazed. He very politely asked the SS man "When and under what circumstances did the Führer die?" The SS man knew the answer: "He shot himself, and his wife also committed suicide." Again Rein was amazed. "I didn't know the Führer was married," he said. "Who did he marry?" "Eva Braun. He married her a few days ago," was the SS man's reply. Rein did not know who Eva Braun was, nor was he particularly interested in knowing who she was or what happened to the Führer. He made no comment, partly because it had never been a habit of his to comment on other people's actions, partly because the subject was really closed, for all time.

When the crowded Panzer approached Schönhauser Allee, Russian shelling became heavier. The commander closed the turret, and finally stopped at Schönhauser Platz S-Bahn station. Rein gave orders to his soldiers to get off the Panzer, since it was too dangerous to remain seated there, and he intended to continue with his men on foot. As soon as they reached the nearby street leading from East to West (Probably Bornholmer Strasse) they discovered that it was impossible to cross the street without getting killed. The Russians were firing along this street from East to West. Rein and his seven men turned around and tried to continue by way of little side streets, and then by crossing through the houses or what remained of them. This was also impossible, for the houses had no windows facing north. The civilian population, on top of it all, was most unfriendly and chased the soldiers as soon as they came into sight.

In the morning (2 May) the situation was even worse than it had been during the night. It was impossible to cross any street without getting shot down like a rabbit. It was clear to Rein that for the moment they had to hide in one of the houses, if they wanted even the barest chance to stay alive. He wondered for a moment which would be a better hiding place: an attic or a cellar. He decided for the attic, for it seemed to be logical that the Russians would first search the cellar and the basement and then slowly proceed upwards, if they didn't get tired of the search beforehand.

Rein and his men managed to quietly reach the attic of the house that was still standing and settled there for the time being. They found a few pieces of civilian clothing up there, but since it was not enough for all the men, they did not touch it.

After a little while they heard steps on the stairway leading to the attic. Rein gave orders to release the safety catch on all weapons. The men turned out to be Germans. Their mission was clear: "The whole district was occupied by the Russians," they said. "You have already been reported to the Russians. Therefore we ask you to leave this building as soon as possible; otherwise the Russians will start shelling it."

Rein replied: "I fully understand the difficult position you are in but I must beg you to try and understand our position too. We are willing to leave the house, under the condition that you give us civilian clothing. If we leave the house in uniform we will get killed immediately." The two men hesitated for a moment, then one of them said: "We have to discuss this problem. You understand that one man alone cannot give you seven suits."

Rein: "Please, by all means, talk it over with the other inhabitants of the house." Even though he did not say so, he knew very well that it was not a question of the number of suits they needed. The two men visibly did not want to help.

A few minutes later they again heard footsteps coming towards them. This time two women appeared, who dashed into the attic, grabbed the few pieces of civilian clothing and left again with a very vicious" "Get out of here and be quick about it." Rein realized that their situation was really hopeless, but he did not say anything in reply.

Then a man came up: "The block commissariat instituted by the Russians is living in our house. He is willing to negotiate with you." Rein replied: "Send him up." The man then explained that the commissariat was not willing to come up to the attic, but that he would rather talk to Rein on the middle floor of the house.

Rein, who realized that the situation was becoming almost ridiculous, went with a corporal down to the third floor to meet this newly appointed commissary. The man gave the impression of being a decent guy. He started off by saying: "The Russians know you are here. You have two choices now: either you leave the building and give yourselves up or you'll get killed by the Russian shelling."

Rein immediately asked under what conditions they were to give themselves up and what their fate would be once they were in Russian hands. The commissary had an answer to this: "I can guarantee you that you will be treated as regular prisoners of war. You will be released as soon as the Germans have signed the capitulation."

Rein then asked to be given a few minutes to be able to discuss this with his men. It was the first time that instead of simply giving orders, he decided to "discuss" a decision with his soldiers. It was against all military tradition, but Rein knew that too much was at stake and that he did not have any right from a human standpoint to decide over life or death of his men.

His men all agreed on giving themselves up.

The commissary then told them how to proceed further: "You will leave the building with a white flag and go to a house I will show you."

Rein and his men did this. The house designated was full of Russian soldiers and a great number of German prisoners of war. Rein and his men were disarmed and put in a room with other prisoners. To his pleasant surprise he met *Feldwebel* Geier there, who told him that he had been taken prisoner during the night on their way through the ruins. He also had witnessed how a German civilian had come a few hours ago to report to the Russians that a number of German soldiers were hidden in the attic of his house. Throughout the day German soldiers were brought to this gathering place.

Towards evening all the soldiers were brought to staff headquarters of a Russian general. During the transfer Rein heard that Berlin had capitulated and he demanded to see the General. He seemed to be the only one ready to fight his fate. All the others looked resigned.

After some time Rein was brought before a staff officer who spoke excellent German. Rein immediately started negotiation: "We were assured that as soon as a capitulation was signed we would be released. This was the condition under which we agreed to give ourselves up to your troops without any resistance. A capitulation has been signed this morning and I request that my men and myself be released."

The Russian officer was polite but firm: "You fought until the moment you gave yourselves up. You are a fighter and so am I. Certain German troops are still fighting. If I let you go, I run the risk that you will once more continue fighting."

Rein bowed to the logic of the argument. He knew it meant being put in a Russian prisoner of war camp, but at least he was alive.

The very next day the prisoners started their march toward the East. They spent some time at Landsberg on the Warthe River, then they continued their daily marches until they reached Russia.

In Lansberg Rein learned during a conversation with *Hauptmann* Lange, who formerly commanded a self-propelled gun unit, and his adjutant *Oberleutnant* Sabel what had happened to the two soldiers he had seen strung up on Friedrichstrasse. Both men belonged to Lange's unit. One of them, the officer, was one of the bravest men Lange had ever commanded. He had received the German cross in gold for exceptional merits, and the Purple Heart [sic., Wound Badge]. He had been taken prisoner in France after the invasion, had managed to escape and to fight his way back to his unit. When the unit reached Berlin, the same officer was asked by his commander to take a self-propelled gun which was out of order and get it repaired. On his way, accompanied by a *Feldwebel*, the officer was stopped by an *SS-Obersturmbannführer* who ordered that he take the self-propelled gun to his positions nearby. The officer explained that the self-propelled gun was out of order and had to be repaired first. The *SS-Obersturmbannführer* then called several of his *SS* men and had both the officer and the sergeant hanged on the spot [Author's note: this is how the two bodies came to hang under the Friedrichstrasse S-Bahn bridge mentioned by several participants in the battle].

Rein spent four years in various Russian prisoner of war camps, and returned to Karlsruhe in 1949.

Fritz Wrede[5]

Kampfgruppe Rossbach (Mixed *Volkssturm* Unit)

1 May

During the night of 30 April—1 May, Wrede and the rest of the guard company received orders to distribute the remaining food supplies in the depot to the civilian population, and to prepare themselves to march and fight. The 140 men company reported to the command post at the Schultheiss brewery. There they were read an order that they were to break out of Berlin along the Schönhauser Allee with armored support in the direction of Mönchmühle (some 25 km north of Berlin) in order to make contact there with the Wenck army, which had reportedly formed a ring outside of the Russian forces [Author's note: Wenck was nowhere near the north side of Berlin but rumors ran wild among the soldiers of Berlin].

The story that Wenck's troops were waiting for them just outside of Berlin roused new hope in Wrede and his comrades, who had thought the troops in Berlin were now completely isolated and cut off. At the time it never occurred to them that Wenck's troops might not be there at all. When Wrede heard the order for the breakout, his first though was of his family: "Will we ever see each other again?" But he had been in the army too long to worry very much about such things—for him, orders were orders and the rest was a matter of luck.

Since a breakout could be successfully led only by people who were familiar with the city, *Oberst* Rossbach ordered all Berliners to step forward. Of the entire group, only 2 men stepped forward, Wrede and another man whose first name was also Fritz, and who lived on Straasburger Strasse. Since Wrede had grown up in the neighborhood and knew every street, *Oberst* Rossbach ordered him to take charge of the company and to lead them along the breakout route. Wrede, as a *Obergefreiter*, thus found himself in the peculiar position of leading a company of men, non-commissioned officers and even some officers.

At dawn the group started out toward the north along Schönhauser Allee, keeping under the shelter of the U-Bahn tracks which are elevated at this point. They could hear some isolated firing but there was no intense shelling in their area. When they reached the Schönhauser Allee U-Bahn Station however, they found an enormous pile up of army troops and could go no further since these troops blocked the street. Wrede told his men to stay where they were while he and Fritz went up further to see what the situation was. On the other side of the station a bomb had knocked down the elevated tracks, which now lay on the street and thus offered some shelter. As Wrede and Fritz crept up along the twisted steel girders to see if there was a chance of getting through, they suddenly saw 30 or 40 tanks and armored cars roar up along the street from the south. This was obviously the armored support with which they were supposed to make their breakthrough, but instead of stopping, the tanks kept going on top speed and vanished in the direction of Pankow. It was the last Wrede ever saw of his armored support. [Author's note: this armored column was very likely the *Wachregiment Großdeutschland* making their successful breakout north to the *3.Panzer Armee* lines].

It was now around 1000. Suddenly, a group of troops began to push forward past the station on the other side of Schönhauser Allee. Wrede noticed that many of them were from the *Großdeutschland* regiment and were heavily armed, but they were very young – about 16—18 years old and obviously inexperienced. The passage of the tanks had apparently alerted the Russians and now as the troops pushed forward a terrific barrage from Stalin Organ [rockets] hit the avenue. Wrede could not see where the guns were located – he only heard and saw the shell bursts around, and could only crouch in the shelter of the smashed railway girders. The boys from *Großdeutschland* however, ran directly into the murderous shell fire and there were heavy casualties among them. Wrede and his group could do little to help, since there were only armed with carbines and some pistols. Wrede had to watch helplessly as the inexperienced troops blundered into the Russian fire.

It now became clear that the Russian troops were preparing to counter-attack down the street toward the center of the city. Since Wrede knew it was hopeless to attempt a breakthrough under these conditions, he went back to his group, which was some 75 yards to the rear. Wrede told his men to go one at a time to the Paul Gerhard Foundation building, a large church building with a prayer room, to stack their rifles in the yard, throw away their ammunition and then go home. Wrede and Fritz then worked their way back down Schönhauser Allee to the Coliseum Cinema on the corner of Schönhauser Allee and Gleim Strasse. There they discovered four supply sergeants from the guard company sitting calmly on the movie steps and eating a breakfast of bread and sausages. (Wrede, like many other enlisted men, has an intense dislike of supply sergeants, with whom he has often been in trouble. He maintains they are lazy, bureaucratic, and constantly hoarding their supplies instead of distributing them to the troops).

Just as they reached the movie they could see the first Soviet heavy artillery pieces rolling over the Schönhauser Allee S-Bahn Bridge. The supply sergeants immediately jumped up and ordered Wrede and Fritz to get rifles and defend the area. Wrede however, was not going to be pushed around: he pointed out that he was the company commander and that they would have to obey him. One of the supply sergeants became furious and reached for his pistol but Wrede and Fritz were faster and leveled their weapons at the group. They made the four sergeants throw their pistols down the street and then they herded them down Schönhauser Allee to the corner of Gneist Strasse.

Here they suddenly saw several Russian officers walking calmly down the street in their long coats, but without any visible weapons. Realizing that much of the area was already in Russian hands, they dodged into the first house available, and knocked on the door of an apartment. A woman let them in and made coffee for all of them, saying: "Thank God you are German soldiers—now you'll clean the Russians out of here." The men didn't say anything to disillusion her.

After a while they ventured out onto the street again and saw that a Russian soldier was sitting on the sidewalk in an armchair which he had obviously taken from some apartment. Next to him was a large pile of army pistols. As they came up to him he asked them: "You pistol?" Wrede had been on the Russian front long enough to have some inkling of the Russian mentality. He simply replied: "No pistol, I go home to Mamma." The Russian nodded and waved him on; "Alright, you go."

Wrede and Fritz however, still wanted to know what had happened at the command post at the Schultheiss brewery, so they returned there. They found the huge building and the street in front of it swarming with army and *SS* troops, most of them still armed and apparently waiting for further orders. While there, Wrede saw an unarmed Soviet officer approach the building carrying a white flag and speak with some of the higher German officers. Shortly afterwards the word spread that the Russians had given the German troops 15 minutes to lay down their arms and surrender, after which an artillery barrage would destroy the brewery. The minutes went by, and finally the Soviet officer withdrew. Almost at the last minute the *SS* men began to throw down their weapons. Some of the army people also tried to get rid of their uniforms and to disappear along the back streets.

Now that an official surrender had taken place, Wrede and Fritz also wanted to go home, but first they decided to take along some of the large supplies of brandy and cigarettes which were stored in the brewery. They emptied their kit bags of the few items of spare clothing they had been carrying, and walked into one of the store rooms. But here Wrede again encountered his traditional enemy: a supply sergeant was sitting there at a large desk with a pistol in front of him, carefully taking a detailed inventory of all the stocks on hand. From their previous experiences the two soldiers knew there was no use, even at this time, in asking the man for permission to take some of the supplies. The only course left was that of direct action: while Wrede talked to him, Fritz went around behind the sergeant and smashed him over the head with a bottle of cognac. The two men then filled their bags with bottles of brandy and cartons of cigarettes and prepared to leave. Since the Russians they had seen so far had all told them they could go home, the two men shook hands, said goodbye and promised to see each other again soon when things were slightly more organized. Fritz then set off for his home on Strassburger Strasse and Wrede started back for Gleim Strasse, although he remembered uneasily that there had been firing there up to a brief time ago.

As he left the brewery to go up Schönhauser Allee, the streets were empty except for an occasional Russian artillery piece or tank driving past him. Here and there Wrede saw Russian guards posted at street corners who were taking weapons from stray German soldiers walking around, and then sending them on their way with the words: "War now kaput, you all go home." Wrede had only his uniform, his military belt and his small bag with him. Occasionally a face would peek out of a slightly opened doorway along the street, but otherwise everything was calm. As Wrede reached the corner of Schönhauser Allee and Cantian Strasse, five Russian soldiers armed with machine pistols emerged from a house doorway and called him to halt. As Wrede raised his hands and came over to them, one of the Russians asked him where he was going. Wrede pointed in the direction of Gleim Strasse and said: "I go there, home to mamma, two minutes from here." The Russian shook his head, replied: "No, no, over there is war. You come with us."

One of them marched him up Cantian Strasse to a ground floor apartment in a rear house on the corner of Gaudy Strasse and Sonnenburger Strasse, where there were 3 other Russian soldiers lying with their feet up on a bed. One of them, who spoke good German, asked him where he wanted to go. Wrede explained that he only wanted to go home and that he only lived diagonally across the Falk Platz. The Russian however smiled at him and said,: "You can't go through there. You are now right along the Soviet front line. You sit here and wait for further orders."

Wrede sat down on one of the chairs and reflected unhappily on the fact that he was only a few hundred yards away from his family. After a while he explained to the Russians that he had to go to the toilet and one of them lead him in to the bathroom. There he was astounded to discover that the Russians had carefully placed a piece of sausage and some butter under the water in the toilet bowl, apparently to keep them from spoiling in the warm spring weather. When he wanted to know where he was supposed to urinate, the Russian simply pointed to the bathtub. Wrede could only do as he was told.

Despite this somewhat unpleasant experience Wrede soon became very hungry and asked the Russians if he could have some food. Fortunately there was a bakery in the neighborhood which was still working, and one of the Russians gave him some fresh rolls and small box of lard. Wrede gulped this down and then sat waiting for what would happen next. After a while one of the Russians asked him: "Comrade, what time?" Wrede looked at his wrist watch – it was a large on which he had bought in Denmark—and told him: "A quarter to 7." The Russian smiled and said: "Come comrade, we trade watches." Wrede knew better than to argue: he took off his watch and gave it to the Russian, who pocketed it without bothering to give him anything in return for the "trade". He also had to give the Russians some of the cigarettes which he had in his bag.

A short while later, a soldier with Asian features entered the apartment and gestured to Wrede to follow him. As they went out on the street, he indicated that Wrede was to walk 5 paces behind him – apparently the traditional position for prisoners in his part of the world. Wrede was quite amused at this odd practice and even the people standing in the doorways of the houses along Sonnenburger Strasse shook their heads in disbelief as they saw them go by. The soldier lead him up Sonnenburger Strasse to the bridge which crosses the S-Bahn tracks toward Schönfliesser Strasse. There he let Wrede approach, gestured that Wrede should continue in the direction of Arnim Platz, and turned around and went back the way they had some.

It now occurred to Wrede that it would be a good idea to get rid of his uniform and to get some civilian clothes. But he was shocked to find that there was a deep animosity against the German soldiers on the part of some of the Berlin population. As he asked several people on the street whether they could not give him a jacket to put on, they told him: "Get out of here, you dirty war criminal!" These replies completely shattered Wrede, who realized for the first time the deep gulf which had been created between the civilians and the military. Dazed, tired and depressed, Wrede stumbled on toward Schönhauser Allee. There he saw many Russian soldiers on the street and one of them, a major, called out to him: "Comrade, where you go?" Wrede woke up out of his daze and answered: "Home." The major asked: "You Berliner?" Wrede said yes. The major called over a Russian soldier with a rifle and told him: "Take him to Kommandatura."

They went from Schönhauser Allee along Schivelbeiner Strasse, and turned left into Seelower Strasse where the Kommandatura had been set up in a house near the corner of Dänen Strasse. Here the Russian guard left him and Wrede went into the main door. In the hallway stood a German who asked him: "Do you want to go to the Kommandatura? Are you a Berliner?" When Wrede answered yes, he gave him a slip of paper which stated that the bearer of this pass was a Berliner who could move freely within the city limits and should be allowed to return home.

This pass however, had to be signed by the local commander. Wrede went into the office of the commander and handed him the slip. The officer glanced at it and was about to sign when the door burst open and a Russian soldier came in to report something. Wrede of course, could not understand what was being said, but the result was that the pass was promptly deposited in the waste basket and Wrede was pushed out of the door.

As Wrede walked out on to the street again, he was astounded to see standing before him a large part of the group of German soldiers which he had been ordered to lead out of Berlin earlier that day. He was immediately ordered by the Russians to take his place in the group and was promptly marched away with the others. Only later did he find out from other people in the group how bad his luck had really been. It seemed the Russians only marched away groups of 100 men, and he had been the 100th man they had collected.

As the column of prisoners marched northward through Prenzlauer Berg to Pankow, Wrede once again experienced the anger and animosity of parts of the population. As the soldiers trudged through the streets numerous people came up to them, spat in their faces and called them war criminals. To Wrede it seemed that all the local communists were taking their revenge and trying to humiliate these soldiers.

They spent that night in the Tivoli cinema on Berliner Strasse in Pankow. The next day they were marched through Weissensee, passed the little garden plot where Wrede used to plant flowers and vegetables on weekends, and on to Malchow. Along the way some civilians tried to give drinks of water to the thirsty soldiers. Wrede seized one such occasion to slip a note to a woman who was giving them water. The note, addressed to his wife, read: "Taken P.O.W. Figure to return in 2 years." He later learned that the note had actually reached his wife. From here they were taken to Alt Landsberg and eventually to Küstrin. Along the way they were given little food except some half-rotten meat and bread which was so full of chaff that it tasted as though it had been baked of straw.

At one point along the way a Russian sergeant came along the column and took whatever watches the men still possessed. He also took some watches however, from a group of German officers who promptly complained of the treatment to the Russian officers in charge. A Russian major appeared on the scene, made the sergeant return the stolen watches (the officers simply got the first watch that came to hand) and then shot the [Russian] sergeant on the spot [Author's note: some Soviet officers began to enforce strict discipline on their Russian soldiers. Discipline meant summary court-martial, which was common in the Soviet Army at this time and is an example of the brutal military climate that many Russian soldiers fought and died under].

After his return from imprisonment Wrede moved back to his old home in Prenzlauer Berg in East Berlin. He eventually fled from there to the Western sector a year and a half ago, [1960] just before the wall was erected.

Gunnar Illum[6]

11.SS-Freiwilligen Panzergrenadier Division Nordland

30 April

He was picked up and carried into the nearby Dresdner Bank, where old Hermann put a makeshift bandage on his head and face. From here he was carried to another first aid station, and then a medic team brought him to the emergency field hospital installed in the Hotel Adlon. Illum remembers mainly that the entire hotel was jammed full of wounded, who were lying on every available inch of floor space. He estimates there were several thousand wounded in the hotel, although he could of course not give any accurate figure. Here he was given a perfunctory examination by a doctor but because of his complicated eye wound he was transferred to the clinic on Ziegel Strasse, just over the Weidendamm Bridge.

Because of the heavy firing, he had to go down into the U-bahn tunnels to make the trip to the clinic, guided by a medic. His head now was fully bandaged and he could hardly see anything. As he got to the bottom of the ladder leading into the tunnel, he suddenly heard a voice say? "Is that you, *Oberscharführer*?" Illum recognized the voice at once: It was a man from his company named Knudsen, a simple farm boy. "What are you doing here, Knudsen?" He asked. "I don't know," the boy replied, "I'm standing guard."

Illum was finally brought into the clinic, which dealt only with eye injuries, where he was operated on. His pistol had already been taken away from him at the Adlon [Hotel], on strict orders that no weapons were allowed in hospitals. From there he was again moved to another military hospital installed in the Main Post Office building, where his leg was operated on by a Norwegian doctor.

Illum stayed at this hospital throughout 30 April and 1 May, lying together with the other patients on straw-filled sacks on the floor. After his operation he was moved down to the cellar where he lay near the door. Early on the morning of 1 May, the first Russians entered the hospital. Illum was terrified of what would happen to him because he was still wearing his *SS* uniform. One of the nurses threw a blanket over him however and he was able to take off his uniform, roll it up and hide it under the blanket.

The first Russians were met by doctors from the hospital staff. At once they began demanding watches and searched the entire place, even tearing bandages off some of the patients. This went on throughout the entire morning. Meanwhile, Illum heard the noise of battle lessening outside, and then silence except for a few isolated shots. All the women in the hospital had been hidden in a back room by the doctors before the Russians entered, but by the afternoon the Russians had discovered the hiding place. Now the rapes began, and continued throughout the entire afternoon, evening and night. To Illum it seemed that Russians kept coming through the hospital and raping women, and he could clearly hear the incessant screaming. It was a terrible ordeal for him to have to listen to those screams: "No one can imagine this who has not experienced it himself," he says.

Illum stayed in the hospital until 2 May, when the entire bunker had to be evacuated and he was transferred to the Charité [Hospital]. There he remained until mid-June, when all the wounded were abruptly transferred to the east. He was moved to a mental hospital in Herzberg and re-registered. Up to now he had successfully avoided detection as an *SS* man, since he had never had the blood group tattooed on his arm, and since he heard that all foreigners were to remain Germany rather than be deported to Russia, he claimed he was a Danish seaman [Author's note: members of the Waffen-SS had their blood group tattooed under their left armpit in order to facilitate battlefield triage when a soldier was injured.]

Next he was sent to Frankfurt-on-der-Oder with 60 other men in a closed cattle car. The trip took four days and eight of the patients died during that time. In Frankfurt he was placed in a huge hospital holding 20,000 men where he remained until the end of July. Around that time, when the eastern side of the city became Polish, Illum and 17 other patients were taken to the German side of the city and dumped on a hospital lawn there. After much difficulty and confusion, the hospital accepted them but Illum succeeded in escaping with faked papers (the official seal was made from bread) and getting to Berlin.

He reached Copenhagen again and rejoined his family on 19 December. On 21 December, he was arrested by the Danes, for in the meantime a law had been passed making membership in the *SS* a punishable offense. He was jailed and escaped again and fled to Sweden and subsequently to Switzerland.

Kurt Ache[7]

18.Panzergrenadier Division

30 April

On 30 April the Russians, coming from Tiergarten, stood in the afternoon only 200 meters away from the [Zoo] bunker. In the Jebensstrasse, in the house of the weapons office (Waffenamt), some Russian storm troops had settled. All around there raged a bitter hand-to-hand fighting. At dusk the bunker was lit up by the light of the fires raging from the burning houses.

At 2000 the following announcement sped through the bunker: 'The battle for Berlin is nearing its end. In view of the fact that the majority of occupants of the bunker is wounded and disabled soldiers and women and children it is not possible to consider the defense of the bunker anymore. Each civilian and soldier is free to choose either to stay in the bunker and await Russian occupation, which will come soon, or to try to reach the subway entrance Hardenbergstrasse/Zoo which is about 300 meters distant. In the latter instance, it is planned to proceed through the subway shaft to the Adolf Hitler Platz U-Bahn station to meet the troops waiting there. These troops are planning tonight to force a break-through through Spandau in the direction of Nauen, to break way for Wenck's army.'

Under great difficulties—heavy shelling—I succeeded in reaching the subway shaft with Hildegard, the children, part of my men and few other civilians. We left the bunker at about 2100. We went under the S-Bahn overpass, through the Jebensstrasse. I don't know how many people were in our group. It was a chaotic departure from the bunker. I took whoever happened to be coming along.

In the subway shaft reigned total chaos. A human mass of soldiers, women, children, old people, wounded, was already flowing from the station Wittenbergplatz in the direction of Adolf Hitler Platz. A few torches indicated where to go in the darkness. Above us on the street were the Russians and the intervening stations which we had to pass were the scenes of bitter fighting at the entrances to prevent the Russians from entering the shaft.

A hospital corpsman, a *Feldwebel* from my unit, carried little Püppi (Helga Panzer) on his shoulders. In the tumult we had lost sight of Wolfgang. At about 0100 on 1 May, we arrived at Reichskanzlerplatz, as the square is called today. There we found the remains of the troops which had gathered for the break-through. Among them the four radio cars of my unit. The battle group consisted of five Sturmgeschütz (self-propelled guns) four armored cars, about ten ordinary army trucks, and a couple of tanks. We proceeded through the Lindenstrasse to Ruhleben. The Russians stood back of Olympia Stadium. They didn't bother us though, they probably figured, why should they risk their lives and ammunition. Spandau was occupied anyway and no one would get through. And so even in the early morning hours it was quiet.

The crowd gathered in the gardens of the Laubenkolonien (these small gardening plots, each with its own little cottage or shack, are rented or bought by Berliners as week-end or hobby project they are found all over the city.) It was planned to start the break-through at 0600. At 0400 we heard the news on our radio that Hitler was dead, or rather, that he had fallen in battle. Fighting was supposed to have ceased. But in all the confusion and chaos around us, we didn't even react to this news.

From about 0200 until 0600 we (Hildegard, Helga, Lt. Helnerus and his fiancée Rita, Frl. Dreske with the Dutchman, Georg Kern and the hospital corpsman and myself), settled into one of the little huts and slept. When Wolfgang still hadn't shown up at 0400, I sent a couple of my men out to look for him. At about 0500 they found him. He was hanging around in the vicinity of the self-propelled guns with a couple of my men whom he knew well—he had become good friends with them in the last few weeks. Wolfgang was wearing his gym-training suit and embroidered on the left breast of this suit was the name 'Panzer'. He was very large for his nine years, gave the impression of being perhaps twelve or fourteen. He had a very full and round face. Since he had never had the opportunity to get together with soldiers, in spite of the strain and hardship of the last days, the whole thing was more of game to him. He was too young to recognize the seriousness of the situation. Therefore he didn't give it a thought when he was separated from us. Inasmuch as he had been with my soldiers, he believed that we had known all the time where he was. (we had lost sight of him for eight hours!).

At about 0600 we started out to break our way through Spandau. We knew that this district was occupied by the Russians. We were received by heavy infantry fire coming from the houses. It was getting too dangerous. At the outskirts of Spandau, I put the children into an armored radio car (Panzerfunkwagen). Hildegard was to have gotten into the car too but she stepped back in favor of a crippled woman. Otherwise there was no more room in the car; it was already occupied by slightly wounded soldiers and two other women.

The head of the procession was formed by the self-propelled guns and they started off slowly. Behind them were the radio cars and following these was a mass of soldiers and civilians. The Russians had settled in the houses on both sides of the street. Our men fought the street open by just shooting wildly into the houses. The main body of the procession came almost easily as far as the Havel. It looked as though we would make it. The Russians seemed weak and were offering little resistance. At the Havel bridge we met heavier resistance. While the motorized troops gathered at Brunsbütteler Damm, foot troops worked their way to the Spandau City Hall. Russian snipers were in the tower of the building. It was not possible to knock them out. When we went to join the motorized troops at Brunsbütteler Damm, they were still there. This was between 0800 and 0900 in the morning. The motorized troops were awaiting the arrival of those on foot in Brunsbütteler Damm. They had gathered along the left side of the street, protected by the houses. But here there was absolute silence.

One Panzer drove on ahead and returned with the news that the street was clear for the next three kilometers and that the bordering garden colonies on the left side of the street apparently were free of Russians too. Thereupon a self-propelled gun drove slowly up to where the garden colonies begin (Nauener Strasse). Those on foot followed and in the rear were the rest of the motorized troops. The procession was 1,000 to 1,500 meters long.

When we reached the garden colonies, the mass on foot left the street and proceeded parallel to the street through the gardens. Shortly before the bend in the road, at about the Magistrates Weg, came the first enemy attack. Solitary machine gun salvos came from ahead of us, slightly to the left (Hahneberg, probably). Then suddenly there was a dive bomber attack upon the lead tanks. The garden colonies were under constant fire from the plane guns. A Russian Pak and tank started [to fire at] the leading Panzer. It received a direct hit and suddenly stood sideways in the street. This stopped the entire procession.

Light artillery fire from Rahneberg was covering us too. We (that, is Hildegard, myself, Lt. Helnerus and Rita, Kern, my hospital corpsman and a couple other men of my troops) lay in the gardens about 30 meters away from the street. Not far in front of us was a barracks that was burning brightly. Opposite the barracks, on the other side of the street, there stood a brick house. About ten meters in front of it, on the street, was the radio car in which the children were sitting. The street was under constant shelling. Terrific losses among those on foot. I gave the order to try to reach that solitary brick house on the other side of the street. Hilde and myself and a few of my men succeeded in reaching the other side of the street and we took refuge in the entrance of the house, which was in the rear. Several wounded were lying there and Hildegard immediately started to help give first aid.

I myself crawled back to the front of the house, taking cover along the house wall. An artillery shell hit the street just five meters in front of the radio car. The car backed up several meters, stopped. The door opened. A woman sprang out and was hit immediately in the left foot. A few moments later the two children followed and then two of my soldiers. The street was under constant fire so that it was not possible for me to follow the children. One of my soldiers made a gesture to me which indicated that the children had arrived safely in the trench where he was. This trench was about 25 meters away from me, parallel to the street, on the left south side of the road. Lt. Helnerus, Rita, Kern, Frl. Dreske and the Dutchman were among those in that trench.

Meanwhile, the brick house was put under heavy shelling by the Russians. It was impossible to remain at the side of the street. We had to retreat behind the railroad tracks. Hildegard wanted to cross the street to get to the others. I prevented this, for it would have meant certain death for her. She could do nothing but retreat with us to the other side of the railroad tracks. I never ever mentioned to Hildegard that I had seen the children get out of the car. She learns it now for the fist time. I feared her reproaches. I was afraid she would say I should have let her cross the street. I was afraid that I would be held responsible that the children had been lost.

Now the Russians drove a wedge into the crowd from Hahneberg up the Brunsbütteler Damm. The Russians forced their way up Brunsbütteler Damm and split the crowd in two. The mass of civilians were on the south side. We were on the north side of Brunsbütteler Damm and were completely cut off from the others and there was no prospect of contact being reestablished. The Russian counterattack from the left flank advanced just to the edge of the street. Behind the railroad tracks all was quiet. Here were gathered the northern section of the crowd: about 500—600 men, soldiers almost exclusively. Among them was one *General* and several elderly staff officers and a chief-of-staff officer. These men were mostly old and had been reserve officers. They lost their nerves and could not take command. There was no one person in command of this group—it was a collective command on a very loose basis held by us lower officers.

Since there was no enemy action on this side of the tracks we decided to move in the direction of the West. About twenty advance troops went ahead armed with three machine guns. The crowd followed about 200 meters behind. Hildegard was one of the very few civilians. She had a typical layman's concept of the invincibility of weapons—of tanks and armored cars. Thus she wasn't worried about the children. I encouraged her in this belief and told her that the children would get through somehow. I really did think that they would get through—after all, they had reached the trench safely. Someone would take care of them from there.

As far as Falkensee we had no enemy action. We walked parallel to the railroad tracks (This is the S-Bahn line to Falkensee and at the same time the railway line to Hauen and Hamburg). At the village limits the advance troops met weak Russian resistance, which was broken easily. There were only a few Russians in Falkensee and these left the town hastily. They left behind an ambulance. This was a Ford type [Author's note: US Lend Lease provide this vehicle] and we were glad to have it. We put some of our wounded in it and took it along.

The people of Falkensee streamed out onto the streets and tearfully embraced us; they thought that we were the first of the legendary Army Wenck and were going to free them again from the barbarism of the Russians. We learned that in the village there was only a Russian bakery unit (hence the light resistance) but that the Russians who came through earlier had mishandled them terribly and raped almost all the women.

We circumvented the next town, Brieselang. On the streets were solitary Russian motor columns, otherwise no one was to be seen. As we approached a crossroads, we saw a group of Russian trucks, open trucks with canvas tops, passing the intersection. There were about six or eight of them traveling southward. We opened fire on them. I would have liked to capture them, for one of them was loaded with gasoline cans. We could have climbed into the Russians trucks, and thus disguised, gone on in safety! As we approached the intersection and then opened fire, the Russians fled, leaving their trucks behind them. I wanted to take the trucks now, but I was out-voted by other officers who felt it was too risky—those fleeing Russians might have alarmed reinforcements.

The fleeing Russians must have reported our position for shortly afterwards a slow Russian plane (Rata), or 'coffee grinder', as they often were called, began to circle over our heads. Whenever we had to move in the open, then it would be there, sometimes for more than an hour at a time. The Russians didn't bother to shoot at us; they figured they'd be capturing us anyway.

This was on 1 May. With hardly any enemy action, we marched through the night. On 2 May, we advanced only step by step. The heavy auto traffic and the few Russians that turned up here and there compelled us to be careful. Besides, we had to take into consideration that the Rata above us might have been reporting our position and we could be bumping into stronger resistance any moment. The ambulance we had left behind again—it had broken down. We were all on foot again. More and more of the soldiers had gone off on their own, so that on 3 May there were only about 100 of us left. Hildegard was the only woman and the only civilian. In a little forest just outside of Rauen the rest of the group divided into small groups of 10 to 15 men.

In another piece of woods outside Rauen we made a gruesome discovery. About thirty persons had hanged themselves high up in the trees. The majority of them were women and children; only two men, about 35 or 40 years old, were among them. They were obviously suicides, for they had hanged themselves in pairs: the middle of each rope was thrown over a limb and on each end dangled a body. (Hildegard only remembers seeing three women hanging somewhere in this area—branches had been rammed into their bodies and dangled between their legs.)

3 May was my father's birthday. Early in the morning, at about five, we were lying in the woods outside of Nauen and could observe the main road leading into town. Here there was a heavy traffic of Russian vehicles. All of a sudden light artillery fire started. The shells

flew over the forest and hit right and left in this main highway on which the Russian traffic moving. A last tiny ray of hope rose within us; in our desperation we suddenly believed in that phantom, the 'Army Wenck' again.

With one of my *Feldwebels* I crawled ahead to a little clearing, a fire-break through the woods. Suddenly we heard a call in German from the other side of the fire-break: 'Come on over, then you've made it!' I couldn't decide to advance any further and to follow this call. I was mistrustful of it. I returned to our little group to ask them what they thought of it. Meanwhile the light artillery fire on the road had just about stopped. Once in a while a shot was still fired.

Back with my group—they all lay exhausted on the ground, only the *Feldwebel* was standing erect—suddenly there was a rifle shot. The sergeant fell dead, shot through the heart. With another man I advanced to the break-through again. Looking through a field glass I saw several soldiers in field-grey uniforms about 100 meters away. They were approaching the clearing, moving upright and dashing from tree to tree for cover. The two of us were well hidden by two spindly pine trees and they didn't discover us. They were about twenty meters away from us and we heard them speaking with a very heavy Saxon dialect. Suddenly I saw on their uniforms the letters 'FD'. Now the mystery solved. They were members of the so-called Army of Liberation 'Free Germany' [Author's note: also known as Seydlitz Troops], which had been fighting under the Russians in the Berlin area.

Now it was clear to us that we had to separate in order to give each one a better chance to flee and to escape. We removed half the *Feldwebel's* dog tag (the Germans wore oval perforated dog tags—in case of death, the lower half was broken off as identification for official purposes and the upper half, bearing the same information, was left on the body.) We covered the body with leaves and pine twigs.

Now we divided into groups of twos and threes. General goal: the West. Since the Free Germany corpsmen came from a northerly direction, we headed now directly west to get around them. We had to cross a broad open field about three to four hundred meters wide in order to find cover again. Two men walked in front, at an even pace. After they had advanced about 100 meters, Hildegard and I started out. Hilde and I had progressed about 100 meters when I looked back. I glanced to the edge of the woods and saw a light Russian Pak (anti-tank gun) being shoved out of the woods by four Russians. The two men ahead of us didn't notice this, they didn't turn back. Hildegard and I lay down, facing the woods. After a short while the first shot whistled over our heads and landed in front of the two men ahead of us. They fell to the ground and then in spurts made their way forward. After a short pause, the second shot came. The Russians fired at us about ten times. Hilde and I sprinted in spurts between the shots to a deserted little farmhouse.

We crawled on farther. After we were sure that the Russians weren't following us anymore, we ran into a barn. There under the hay I had my field cap, my shoulder pieces. I removed my Panzer unit jacket and rolled it in a tent canvas. Hildegard was wearing two sweaters one on top of the other. I put on one of them now. It was a black turtle neck sweater and it more or less fit! My pistol I put in my pants pocket, army pass and pay book in my boots. I put on my grey-green officers raincoat again—it was so dirty that no one would have recognized it for what it was. I took the tent bundle over my shoulder and my briefcase in my left hand. That briefcase carried a generous supply of Schokacola (a cola and chocolate mixture in table form: three or four of the tablets which were the size of a nickel and about twice as thick were enough to satisfy one for several hours.) In addition we had some bacon, some army dried bread and about ten packages of cigarettes. My men had all gotten generous rations in the Zoo Bunker and so all of them were well provided for on the break-through, for all the rations were high energy concentrates. The same could not be said for other units though.

In a little forest we slept for about three hours. We were too tired to go on. Hilde's feet hurt terribly. She had wanted to rescue her favorite shoes (open-back blue suede cocktail shoes) and she had put them on when we left the bunker, wearing rubber boots over them.

As we walked along a field path in the direction of Nauen, a Russian soldier with a machine pistol came across the pasture towards us. He stopped us said: 'You soldier, you kaputt'. Hildegard had the presence of mind to start speaking to him in French and I told him in very broken German that I didn't understand him: "nix verstehen." He was satisfied with this and demanded "Papyrossi" – cigarettes. I gave him a pack and he went happily on his way.

At about 1600 (still 3 May) we were just outside of Nauen. On the road leading into the town stood a caravan of refugees, about twenty carts drawn by horses. There were only a few women to be seen. I had the feeling that it must be a German refugee group. Happy that we might find an opportunity to join, them, Hildegard and I crossed a pasture to go up to one of the wagons. A young woman wearing a quilted grey jacket and a bandana was sitting on the side of the wagon. I asked if we could join her. In broken German she answered that this was a Polish refugee caravan on its way home. Since early morning they had been standing here. The men of the caravan had been picked up by the Russians to help build an airfield and they wouldn't return until evening. On her wagon, among other things, there lay an old raincoat. I traded my officers' raincoat for this one, so as to appear still more like a civilian. The woman was delighted with the trade.

At this moment a Russian patrol team on bicycles stopped and wanted to take Hilde and me along. The young peasant woman spoke to the soldiers in Russian. She told us later that she had told them that we too were refugees' and that they should leave us alone. They demanded 'Uri, Uri' and when we shook our heads, they grabbed us by the wrists and tried to pull our watches from our wrists. We gave them to the soldiers then. The two soldiers mounted their bicycles again and rode off.

The young Polish woman advised us not to go into Nauen over night but rather recommended that we go to an out-of-the-way farm which she described to us. Shortly before dark we arrived at the farm [and met] the farmer and his wife and an elderly woman servant. After much hesitation they agreed to take us in for the night. They explained however that we were not all too safe with them, for from time to time Russian soldiers came by plundering and their farm was also subjected to these visits. Since both of us were young, it was not without danger for us.

They directed us to a room off the kitchen. There were Russian letters chalked on the door. The farmer explained to us that this room, as of tomorrow, was confiscated by the Russians as quarters. Probably we would be able to sleep here undisturbed because the plundering Russians would not attempt to break into a room locked from the inside. They gave us some bread and a glass of milk and then, at about 2000 we lay down exhausted on field cots.

The next morning, 4 May. It had just dawned when we were awakened by loud voice and a rifle butt was rammed against the door several times. We heard the old farmer's wife calling repeatedly: 'Kommandaturaa, Kommandatura'. Then the pounding at the door stopped. Our room lay on the ground floor and had a little veranda. I sat on the cot, pistol in hand, for I feared that now the Russians would probably try to get in through the veranda. They did pass through the garden in front of the veranda but let us alone.

The farmer couple brought us into the kitchen now, gave us milk and bread again and advised us to stay in the kitchen until the forenoon. At about 0800 a couple of drunken Russians came up the walk. Hilde quickly put on an old bandana so as to look older and then the two of us sat in the corner peeling potatoes and cleaning vegetables. The drunken Russians demanded something to eat. The farmer gave them bread and milk and they left again.

At about 1000 we left the farmhouse in the direction of Nauen. In ¾ hour were in the town. An elderly woman, in her late fifties, stopped us and took us along into her apartment. She had just come from the hospital where she was acting as a nurse's aide. On the way she advised us to be extremely careful and advised leaving Nauen as soon as possible, for the Russians were grabbing all able-bodied men and women for work and then taking them off. She told us too that in the previous night for the second time she had raped by Russians in the hospital.

When we entered her apartment we were met by a terrific mess. Broken dishes, clothing lay strewn around. Everywhere, excrement. We were refreshed somewhat by a cup of coffee. Hilde was given a pair of shoes and about 1500 we sneaked over the freight yards in the direction of Berlin. We had decided to return to Berlin as fast as possible. It was senseless to go on any farther. We couldn't escape the Russians anyway. The fact that we turned back to Berlin saved us from being taken prisoner by the Russians, for as we later heard, all those moving west fell right into Russian hands and were held. By moving eastward, no one bothered us, for the Russians knew they had us anyway. The fact that we were a couple allayed suspicion too.

We wandered along deserted field and forest paths. On the way I burned my wage book and other papers which could have endangered us. My pistol and all medals I had tossed into the outhouse at the farm that morning.

On the way back to Berlin were stopped repeatedly by Russian soldiers and patrols. Thanks to the fact that Hildegard spoke perfect French and that we conversed only French with one another, we were able to pass for French alien laborers. Besides we looked very tattered and I certainly no longer gave the impression of being a former German soldier—I hadn't shaved for two weeks.

On 6 May at about 1800 we arrived at the Hohenzollerndamm S-Bahn station. My first thought was to get to my official residence in the high command (AEG building) to get some civilian clothing. Since Russians and civilians were plundering there it was no problem to get into the building. In the cellar, under my apartment, I had furnished a guest room. This was now filled with furniture and household goods of all sorts. The door was ajar; in front of it lay my mother-in-law's fur coat, which I had stored there. The entire corridor was filled with parts of field grey uniforms, for the clothing depot lay next to my guest room. In my own quarters, as far as I could see nothing had been disturbed. My civilian pass lay in my bookcase. Hildegard and I took as many civilian things over our arms as we could carry (including the fur coat!). We filled pockets with jars of canned fruit and meat.

Our next goal was now the Schmargendorf station. There I had relatives, the aunt and uncle who had the big café and pastry shop in the corner house at the corner of Rudolstädter and Hecklenburgische streets. After about twenty minutes we reached the house, found nothing but rubble. We had to flee on at once, for a woman from the neighborhood saw me—she had been a Communist from way back and yelled: 'There he is that war criminal; Hang him!' Much later I learned why she had made this accusation. Back on the 26 April I had turned the defense of the area over to an *SS* unit, and they had set fire to the big corner house where my relatives had their café. The neighborhood though didn't know of this change in command and were holding me personally responsible for this arson!

And so Hilde and I fled on, this time to the Marcobrunnerstrasse 1, to her apartment. In less than twenty minutes we were there. The apartment door was ajar and the safety latch was on from the inside, for the door was damaged. We tried to force our way in. Then Hilde's brother-in-law, Herr Rader, the husband of Hans Panzer's sister, appeared at the door. When he recognized the two of us, he yelled: 'Get out of here you Flintenweib (camp follower). And you too, you army officer! You've got no business here anymore!'

We retreated, no knowing what else to do. Where to go now? We walked along the Laubacherstrasse and suddenly someone called: 'Kurt, Kurt!' It was the jeweler Otto Wiese from Laubacherstrasse 32. He took us in. He had had luck; his home was undamaged and had not been plundered. After a thorough wash and something to eat, we spent the night in the air raid bunker of the house.

The next morning, 7 May, Hildegard and I rode on two bicycles which Otto had provided for us, to Hilde's parents in Mahlow. We hoped to hear something of the children. I hoped that Frl. Dreske, who had been with the children, would have brought them to the grandparents. But this hope was in vain. Hilde's parents were dismayed when they heard our story. Towards noon we rode back to Berlin again.

Our next hope was the Zoo Bunker. Perhaps there would be some wounded soldier or civilian there who could tell us something. At the door of the Zoo Bunker stood two Russian sentries who wouldn't let us in. After we had waited for two hours, a lieutenant came out and took us and eight other civilians into the bunker to do clean-up work. The stairways were to be cleared and cleaned because at 1500 a delegation of English officers were expected to inspect the bunker.

On 30 April I had hidden a suitcase of Hilde's with children's things in it in the furnace room of the bunker. We weren't supposed to enter the cellar but we went down anyway. I knew my way around quite well and I had a flashlight. The suitcase was still there. It was open but some of the things were still in it.

I 'organized' two rucksacks. These were filled with bacon, army bread, cigarettes, coffee, tinned foods. Food supplies in huge quantities lay scattered around everywhere. Everywhere was an indescribable chaos. After three hours work we left the bunker with our booty.

W stayed overnight at Wiesen again. The next morning, 8 May, we pedaled out to Mahlow again to Hilde's parents. We spend the night there.

On 9 May all residents of Mahlow were to be registered. Hilde's father advised me to go back to Berlin as I had no legal residence in Mahlow and must face arrest. The afternoon of 9 May, I went back to Berlin to the Wieses. I decided to leave Berlin as soon as possible and make my way to my evacuated family in Seefled in Tirol, Innsbruck.

On the morning of 10 May, I went to the Gertrauden hospital in Wilmersdorf in the Paretzerstrasse, where I had heard that there was a German nurse who spoke and wrote Russian. I found her and had her write an attest for me:

> Kurt Ache is on his way from Berlin to Austrich-Seefeld in Tirol—per bicycle. Route is the Autobahn Berlin—Munich.
> signature and a Russian Stamp

On 11 May at about 1000 I started off on a lady's bicycle. After about 100 meters on the Avus (the start of the Autobahn and at the same time Berlin's auto racetrack) I had a flat tire. Laying briefcase and rucksack aside, I went to work repairing the damage. Suddenly a young Russian with a machine pistol stood in front of me. From my rucksack he took a pair of trousers and a pair of under shorts and few cigarettes. He looked at my certificate and said: 'Nix gutt, nix gutt' (no good). But he grinned and went on.

There wasn't much traffic on the Avus. A few pedestrians, and once in a while a Russian auto. At about Dreilinden (where the Soviet zonal control point is today) a bicyclist in civilian clothing caught up with me. He had a blue-white-red flag on his bike. He must have been a Frenchman then. We started to talk and he told me that the Russians had freed him from the Gestapo prison on Alexanderplatz. He had been an alien laborer in Berlin. He had received a pass and now he was on his way to Paris. He was terrifically hungry. I was well supplied with bacon, chocolate, cigarettes and I gave him something to eat. We decided to ride together to the American zone. This acquaintance was of tremendous importance to me. When the Russians made controls, he just showed his pass, which worked wonders. When the Russians pointed to me, then he gave them to understand that the document was valid for both of us. And so we were always permitted to pass undisturbed. The stamp on his pass was a large and impressive one and apparently none of the Russian patrols could read and so they couldn't check whether the pass really was valid for two or not. [Author's note. Many of the conscripts for the Soviet Army came from the vast Central Asian districts where the literacy rate was low.]

We had intended to cross the Elbe at Dessau—Rosslau just outside the city, all travelers were directed to gather in a large pasture. Foreigners separate. And so I stayed with my friend and pretended to be a Frenchman. We arrived here on 13 May at about 1500. At 1700 a Russian officer appeared and declared to us 'foreigners' that if we wanted to get into the American zone, then we would have to go to Wittenberg on the Elbe. There we would have the possibility to get to the west.

We started off at once and arrived in Wittenberg at about 2000 on the market place where stood a group of three men and two women who waved to us. They were French alien workers and had beckoned to us because they saw the French colors on my fiend's bike. They welcomed us heartily and took us along to the villa in which the Russians had quartered all the Frenchmen. They showed us mattresses upon which we should sleep and gave us a bit to eat. An hour later were joined by a former concentration camp prisoner and a ten year old boy. It was the first time I had ever seen or had a chance to speak to a concentration camp inmate.

The next morning we inspected the villa. On the top floor were office rooms. The villa was joined to the back side of a department store which could be reached through the offices on the top floor. The door was locked but a glance through the key hole showed us that the adjoining room was full of racks of dresses and men's suits. We wanted to take advantage of this chance to re-clothe ourselves. We improvised a pass key with which we pushed out the key which was in the lock from the other side and opened the door. In the middle of the room were several Russian women who were picking out clothing for themselves. We didn't notice them until they screamed: I quickly picked up the key, pulled the door shut again and locked it.

But as we arrived downstairs in the villa again, we were welcomed by two auxiliary policemen (Polish), who arrested us and marched us off to the city hall and delivered us to the Kommandatura on the third floor. One by one were led into a room. There sat a woman in uniform. She declared to each one that we were sentenced to death for attempted plunder. The concentration camp inmate was led in first, and then I came. It was about ten minutes then before the Frenchman friend of mine was taken in. In the meantime, the concentration camp inmate talked to the two sentries in Russian. He could speak some Russian as he had been in Russia as a laborer in 1932/33. Then he came to us and told us that as soon as the Frenchman had been 'sentenced' and came back out again, then the three of us should flee. He had made all arrangements with the sentries. They would go down the hall and while they were gone, we should flee.

No sooner said than done. We dashed back to the villa, grabbed our bicycles and off we went. A few days later I was with my family in Seefeld.

I didn't return to Berlin until September 1945. At that time I went with Hilde to Staaken to show her the exact route we had taken. We talked with many people. It was my assumption that the children must have been picked up and taken eastward.

In 1959 I had a private talk with Georg Kern, the last person to have seen the children alive. He told me that he assumes that Wolfgang died of blood poisoning. He had applied a tourniquet to the leg; put a label on it stating when it had to be reopened. If this was not done, then the boy very likely died of blood poisoning, even though the wound itself had not been very serious. I am certain that both children are dead ....

Hanns-Heinrich Lohmann[8]

49.SS-Panzergrenadier Regiment 'De Ruyter'

21 April

The morale among Lohmann's troops had always been good. Not because they still believed in final victory, but out of fatalism. The motto of these days was: "Enjoy the war as long as it lasts, for peace will be terrifying."

Around 21 April, when the Russians launched their big attack, things happened very fast. Frohnhöfer lost control over his troops very quickly. Lohmann realized after a few hours that his neighbors had disintegrated and that none of the *Volkssturm* and *Kriegsmarine* units they originally consisted of had remained close-knit formations. The *Kriegsmarine* had no idea how to behave in an attack and Lohmann particularly remembers a young man in the uniform of a seafaring captain who seemed to be fighting his machine gun. He called out to Lohmann in an exasperated voice: "How in the hell do you work this machine?"

On 24 April, Lohmann had to move his headquarters from Kasekow to Ratzebruch, which was on hilly terrain. They managed to hold on to their positions for two days, then they received the message that the Russians had broken through the lines of their Southern neighbor and that an attack towards their flank might be expected. This made their withdrawal necessary. They had no longer any connection with their Northern neighbors.

On 26 April, they retreated to the lake lands near Prenzlau. From there they retreated West everyday, since the HKL was moved towards the West continuously. Lohmann never forgot Steiner's advice, "don't experiment." His troops retreated, fighting but without ever attempting the slightest counter-attack.

28 or 29 April, they reached Lake Müritz. The Russians followed them on their heels and started to attack before they had even taken up position. Since the passageway leading towards the West between the two lakes was too narrow, Lohmann had to give orders for a

counter attack towards Mirow. They soon found out that the streets were jammed with refugees to such an extent, that it was impossible to get through with Panzers or self-propelled guns. The counter attack never took place.

Even though Lohmann and his troops were constantly fighting, Lohmann knew that this was nothing compared to the major impact of Russian forces as it was taking place to the south. It was clear to him that the Russian's major objective was Berlin, and that the attacks directed at him were meant to keep him busy and out of the Russian flank.

On 3 May, Lohmann reached Parchim. The troops managed to hold the town and the main road leading towards Ludwigslust until the evening, thus permitting a great number of German troops to continue their flight towards the West. While the fighting went on, an American jeep with four American soldiers in it appeared. They watched for a while, how Lohmann's Panzers were knocking off 10 or 12 Russian tanks, did not say a word and left again. One of Lohmann's officers wanted to know what to do—go after them and take them prisoners or not. Lohmann was horrified: "For God's sake – that's the last thing to do. Who knows, tomorrow they might be fighting alongside with us."

During the following night, 3–4 May, Lohmann managed to hold a bridgehead across Stör Canal which permitted some more German troops to get out to the West.

In the morning of 4 May, Lohmann sent his adjutant to discuss surrender with the American officers on the other side of the canal. The adjutant came back rather puzzled and reported the Americans had said they had no right to discuss surrender since Lohmann and his troops had never fought against them. It was up to the Russians to negotiate with them, they said. Lohmann received quite a shock in hearing this, but sent back his adjutant with the word that the required conditions could of course be fulfilled and he was ready to fight against the Americans. While the adjutant was delivering this message, Lohmann told his men they could go home. They were no longer bound to their units by their oath. "All I ask for is that my officers take leave of me so I know where I stand," he specified.

While his men were taking off, the adjutant returned saying the Americans were accepting to negotiate the surrender. Lohmann had still enough fuel in his car to drive for about 100 kilometers and he asked the Americans to be allowed to drive behind their lines, since he wished to take no chances of possibly being overrun by the Russians. The Americans refused. Lohmann was first sent to a camp at Wöbbelin, and then he was turned over to the English and remained in a camp near Bremervörder until 1948.

Lohmann learned later on that the only officer who got home without being caught was his adjutant, Scholz.

Walter Timm[9]

11.SS-Panzer Abteilung 'Hermann von Salza'

1 May

On 1 May, Salbach ordered Timm and his crew to go to Französische Strasse that evening in order to try to break out of Berlin toward the North through Pankow. Salbach mentioned only the self-propelled gun section in this connection, and did not say whether any other units would take part in the breakout. They assembled that night at the Französische Strasse U-Bahn station in Friedrichstrasse. The only people Timm knew there were from the armored weapons carrier section.

Gradually other troops and vehicles arrived and late that evening (it may have been around 2200) they were ordered to start moving up Friedrichstrasse toward the North. By now the street was crowded with a varied collection of Panzers, assault guns, trucks, cars and other vehicles, all streaming north. Soldiers of all ranks and units crowded the sidewalks walked between the vehicles or sat on them where there was room. It was a dense, confused mass of men and machines and it was almost impossible for a compact group to stay together. Even the vehicles of Timm's assault guns section were separated in the crowd. There was sporadic shell fire from the Russians but no sort of concentrated artillery barrage.

A while later Timm noticed that one of the *Feldwebels* of his group was missing, and went back to the U-Bahn station to see if he had not remained behind. Just at the entrance to the station he received a light shrapnel wound in the left upper arm. It bled freely but since it was only a flesh wound he simply tied a handkerchief around it and then forgot about it. He was unable to find the *Feldwebel*, returned to the assault guns (the vehicles were moving so slowly that he had no trouble catching up with it) and continued on up the street.

Around Unter den Linden Timm encountered a group of some 20 *Wehrmacht* infantry troops who begged him to let them ride on the assault guns. He let them climb on and drove ahead. There was still no concentrated Soviet fire except for an occasional shell. Around midnight they reached the Weidendamm Bridge where all the vehicles had piled up. Some of the buildings in the area were burning and there was complete chaos – troops and vehicles from all over crowded the area. Timm's assault gun was directly in front of the bridge but he could ride no further because of the traffic jam.

Timm climbed out of the assault guns, went around the back of it and found himself face to face with the *Nordland* division commander, *General* Ziegler. Timm had only seen him a few times before, in his role as division commander, but recognized him immediately. With Ziegler were one or two other officers, including a *Hauptsturmführer*.

Ziegler told Timm: "The Russians have infiltrated to both sides of the street here around the bridge and we must get through. Further on there is still a sort of no-man's land. I have to get in touch with Mohnke and must get into your assault gun here."

As they started around the right side of the assault gun in order to get in, someone (Timm has no idea who) fired a *Panzerfaust* at the self-propelled gun from the direction of Weidendamm. The projectile just missed the top of the assault guns but of the troops which had been sitting on it, nothing was left. Says Timm: "There was suddenly nothing more on my assault guns—it was as though they had all been swept away."

As Timm was still momentarily dazed, Ziegler said: "Hurry up, we must go!" Ziegler and the Hauptsturmführer climbed into the assault guns, but since there was not enough room for them and the crew, Ziegler told Timm to throw out the loader. The loader was a very young boy and Timm was reluctant to simply dunk him outside and abandon him. But Ziegler would brook no argument, he barked at Timm: "I am ordering you to get this man out of here!" Timm reluctantly told the loader to give up his place but told him to lie on the roof the assault gun just behind the turret where he would probably be safe.

When they were all in the assault guns, Timm spotted an SPW (Schützenpanzerwagen) belonging to his section and got him to tag along behind his assault guns. They moved cautiously up to the bridge and then Timm fired three explosive shells into the houses on both sides of the street on the other side of the bridge. Timm was furious at Ziegler for having thrown out the young loader and got a small revenge by leaving the ventilator closed as he fired the gun. As the fumes billowed back into the assault guns Ziegler began to cough violently and became quite agitated. Timm notice that on the whole, Ziegler seemed extremely nervous.

The assault gun then drove full speed ahead over the bridge followed by the SPW. On the other side of the bridge Timm reached up to close the hatch. As it was still slightly open, a hand grenade fell into the assault gun from above and exploded, showing Timm's face and neck with tiny bits of shrapnel. It burned very much and blackened on side of his head, but the tiny bits of shrapnel were mostly just under the skin and Timm was able to continue. They drove straight ahead in a general northerly direction for about 2 kilometers but Timm has no idea of the exact route they took. Here everything was quiet and the two vehicles found themselves quite alone. No foot soldiers of any sort were to be seen.

At this point, Ziegler said: "Stop here. I must get in touch with Mohnke. I will be coming right back. Wait for me." Ziegler got out of the assault gun and vanished down the street. Timm never saw him again. But as Timm got out of the assault gun he found the body of the young loader lying behind the turret, riddled with shrapnel. They carried the boy into one of the houses and laid him in the hallway.

They waited for about an hour and then Timm determined to push on without Ziegler although the area was still quiet. The *Hauptsturmführer* wanted to wait longer but Timm told him: "Waiting is out of the question—we must go on." They drove on for a little while and then Timm, who had opened the hatch to look up, suddenly saw that the motor was burning. Opening the hood he saw that the gas tank was on fire from the outside. He told the others: "There is no sense in going on, we can't extinguish it." They abandoned the assault guns and Timm, the two crewmen and the *Hauptsturmführer* climbed in and joined the three men already in the SPW.

From here they rolled on at random, with no specific idea of where they were. Just as it was getting light (probably around 0400) they reached Schönhauser Allee. They could see vehicles rolling along Schönhauser Allee toward the north but they didn't know what they were. Driving on a bit further to see, Timm found the vehicles belonged to the *5.Luftwaffe Field Division* [Author's note: Timm was mistaken. This might have been elements of the *9.Fallschirmjäger Division* but their was no *5.Luftwaffe Field Division* in Berlin]. They were now at the Schönhauser Allee U-Bahn station and the Luftwaffe men were driving up the street in all sorts of vehicles, assault guns and SPWs. Timm tried to get directions from them, but the situation was too confused to get any precise information. He walked a bit further up the road but the conditions were just as chaotic. Finally he spotted a *Luftwaffe* colonel, sitting on a stool in a burned out store front with his head in his hands. When Timm asked him for information, the colonel simply told him: "Go up to the next corner and you will know everything." Up ahead a bridge ran along the street, and as Timm came up, the saw that it was full of burning Panzers.

He returned to the SPW and held a council of war. They all agreed that it was useless to go on in the SPW, since they would be sure to be hit by the Soviet fire. From that moment on it was every man for himself.

Meanwhile a dense crowd of troops and vehicles had formed along the street, close, says Timm, that "it was like a Nazi-party rally at the Lustgarten." At this moment, heavy Soviet artillery fire smashed into the mass of people from the north. Timm thinks the fire came from 12.2cm guns. One shell exploded near the place he was standing and Timm was hit by a chunk of shrapnel in the left ankle. He managed to hobble under the U-Bahn tracks which are elevated at this point, and then clambered painfully on to a *Luftwaffe* assault gun which was heading back toward the center of town.

After a while however, he began to loose strength, got off the vehicle and asked two soldiers who were standing nearby to help bring him into a house. They carried him down into a cellar (Timm has no idea where this was) where a number of civilians were hiding. The soldiers wanted to lay him on the bed there but one of the women protested loudly: "My clean white linen!" So Timm sat down in a corner, put his leg up on a stool and lost consciousness. It was now around 0500.

He woke up again around noon on 2 May and found that the civilians had all left the cellar. A while later however, two men came into the cellar and brought in a glass of water. Timm asked them to help him out onto the street because he wanted to get to a hospital to have his wound treated. Just as they came out of the house, a Soviet truck rolled by on the street. Two Russian soldiers took him and heaved him onto the truck which was already full of other wounded German soldiers. He was brought to a nearby hospital where he was treated quite well: he got an anti-tetanus injection and his wound was cleaned and bandaged. This field hospital had been set up in a shop, with mattresses placed on the floor in the front room. Timm was the first to be laid on one of these mattresses. As he lay there a Russian soldier with Asiatic features whom he had not seen before came up and said to him: "Pistol." Timm gave him his pistol and as he did so his sleeve jacket fell open. The Russian immediately said: "Watch," and Timm gave him that too. The Russian then went out, got hold of two German civilians and told them to bring Timm to another hospital which had been set up in a school.

This second hospital was staffed by German civilian doctors. Here Timm was operated upon, without anesthetic, by a woman doctor who confessed to him that she was actually a specialist in skin and sexual disorders. One of the nurses also took off his tanker boots and burned all his identity papers [Author's note: this was because he was *Waffen-SS*]. Since he was wearing the green riding jacket and his trousers were fairly dirty by now, he almost looked like a civilian.

The next day Timm was moved on a horse-drawn cart to the Pankow hospital. Here the same nurses visited him almost every day and brought him food from the Russian officers' club where she worked. Timm tried for a while to pass a civilian but this did not work. One day a Soviet doctors' committee came to the hospital and a nurse there pointed out all the soldiers among the patients. He was then taken to a camp in Frankfurt-an-der Oder where he again met up with Kausch, his former regimental commander. Since neither one of them wanted to admit they had been in the SS, Timm said he was a *Wehrmacht Obergefreiter* and Kausch said he was a *Leutnant*. Many of the other inmates obviously knew the truth but no one denounced him.

Timm's leg wound developed complications, and the Russian doctors wanted to amputate his foot. He managed however to persuade them to refrain from amputating and the wound finally healed. He was in a number of hospitals and prisoner of war camps, but although he was still being considered as an *Wehrmacht Obergefreiter*, he knew that he could not go home to Schleswig-Holstein without being denounced by one of the neighbors. He finally confessed his *SS* membership and was interned until December 1947. When he was eventually released, he weighed only 112 pounds.

Wetzki Hans[10]

Hitlerjugend

1 May

At the railway station thing were still relatively quiet but there were a large number of troops on the streets in the station itself and in the bombed-out Atlas Hotel on Friedrichstrasse, on the other side of the Weiderdamm Bridge. In the railway station he also saw roughly two battalions of black-uniformed *SS* men, which he at that time took to be members of the *Leibstandarte Adolf Hitler*. (There is some doubt however, that the members of the *Leibstandarte* would have been wearing black uniforms—these *SS* men were more likely police and ministry officials.) Wetzki also saw two hospital trains standing in the station tunnel. These may be the ones which were flooded when the Landwehr canal was blown up the following day. Just north of the Weiderdamm Bridge was a massive tank barricade guarded by a quadruple mount of two-centimeter anti-aircraft guns.

Wetzki and his group were partly in the railway station and partly in the Atlas Hotel. Now a dispute arose about which group was to lead the breakout attempt in the direction of Oranienburg toward the north. The *Wehrmacht* soldiers said the *SS* should logically lead the attack. The *SS* however, pointed out that the *Hitlerjugend* groups were probably the freshest ones on hand and urged them to lead the breakout. While this wrangle was going on, a group of five armored vehicles suddenly came up from the direction of Unter den Linden. They consisted of one King Tiger tank, two Jagdpanzer IV (L) self-propelled guns, and two armored reconnaissance cars. It was finally decided that the armored cars would go first, followed by the *Hitlerjugend*, the *Wehrmacht* and the *SS* in that order.

The anti-aircraft gun was then withdrawn and the King Tiger tank drove slowly into the narrow slot of the tank barricade. Wetzki had heard that both Bermann and Weidling were in the tank. But the only person he saw was the tank commander, who looked out of the hatch for a moment and waited for orders to start rolling. Wetzki was standing behind the barricade; there was no fire coming from the north. Suddenly the King Tiger began to move forward out of its barricade and the *Hitlerjugend* group followed, going along the houses on both sides of the street. Some also clambered over the roofs in the same direction. The other Panzers and armored cars followed slowly behind. As they got to the corner of Johannis Strasse the entire group was suddenly caught in an incredibly intense fire from artillery machine guns, rifles and every other conceivable weapon, … [page cut off] … or hear anything, and could only crouch behind whatever shelter was available. They knew now that there was no possibility for a breakout. The Panzers however, continued up the street under the hail of fire and got as far as the corner of Elsasser Strasse. Wetzki later saw all five them standing on the street, blown up and completely burned out.

The boys began to withdraw cautiously back down Friedrichstrasse. At one point, they found themselves caught between the fires, since some of the *SS* troops had worked their way into the University Women's Clinic and were firing towards the north, while the Russians were shooting towards the south. The *Hitlerjugend* were shooting in all directions and trying desperately to get back across the bridge to the shelter of the railway station. By this time it was between 0400 and 0500.

They managed to get back into the station, where the *Wehrmacht* soldiers took over the leadership of the breakout attempt. Since it was obvious there was no possibility of making a breakthrough on the street level, they decided to try the subway tunnels. They were split into two groups; one would go through the S-Bahn tunnel toward Stettiner S-Bahn Station while the other would go through the U-Bahn Tunnel toward Oranienburger Tor. The *Hitlerjugend* group began to move slowly through the U-Bahn Tunnel. It was very quiet and a mass of other military people was thronging up the tunnel behind them. As they reached the Oranienburger Tor Station, with the rest of the group pushing behind them, Wetzki glanced up and suddenly saw a Maxim heavy machine gun set up on the overpass over the tracks and a Russian officer with a white flag standing beside it. The officer shouted at the group: "Comrades, Hitler is kaput, the war is over, give yourselves up!" The SS men immediately began to shout: "It's a dirty trick, Hitler is not dead, anyone who tries to surrender will be shot, we'll still be freed!" The *Feldwebel* told his group quietly: "Boys, throw away everything which can possibly be compromising to you." They all dropped their guns and most of them also threw away their identity cards, although Wetzki simply pushed them deep inside his boot. Meanwhile the German troops continued to mill around in the tunnel and argue about what their course of action should be. This remarkable dispute continued for almost an hour, with the Russians waiting impassively on the over-pass above the tracks with the machine gun ready. Finally the Soviet Officer told them "Comrades, our patience is at an end, you must surrender immediately." Although no one wanted to be the first to make the decisive move, they finally all slowly straggled up out the station and onto the street. Here they were lined up in columns of 60 men and led off. As Wetzki marched away down the street with his group of prisoners he saw a Soviet tank or artillery piece standing on practically every corner of the streets which he passed.

They were marched to the Bethanien Hospital on Adalbert Strasse, which was the assembly point for the POWs. From there, always guarded by armed Soviet troops wearing leather jackets, they were marched to the Schlesische S-Bahn Station, passed the Plaza variety theater, over Frankfurter Allee, Siegfried Strasse, the Mager slaughter houses, to a former forced laborer's camp where they arrived on the evening of 2 May. After four weeks of detention and three interrogations, Wetzki was released and could go home again.

Wetzki's war service was over but his story has a grim sequel. On 3 September, 1945 he and 18 other former *Hitlerjugend* members from Hoppegarten were arrested on charges of supporting fascism, incitement to armed revolt, and membership in a secret organization—the *Werewolf*. Three of them were sentenced to death and, as far as Wetzki knows, were executed. The others received varying prison sentences. Wetzki himself was sentenced to 10 years. He was first imprisoned in various camps in the Berlin area, but was finally sent to the Siberian concentration camp at Vorkuta. In 1950, after having served half his sentence, he was released and returned to Berlin. Here he quickly became involved with the 'Combat Group against Inhumanity' an organization which was originally designed to gather news of prisoners behind the Iron Curtin but which was rapidly taken over by Western intelligence services as a spy outfit. In 1952 Wetzki was lured by a double agent into East Berlin, and rearrested on charges of espionage. He was sentenced to 8 years imprisonment and released in 1960. Thus, between the ages of 15 and 30, he spent almost 14 years either in the *Hitlerjugend* or in various prison camps.

Roman Burghart[11]

11.SS-Freiwilligen Panzergrenadier Division Nordland

1 May

… heavy Russian shelling. On the bridge stood a German AA gun, whose tires were flat and the engine broken. It could not be moved any more. The Russians, who were on the other side of the Spree Canal, fired at anyone attempting to approach the bridge. Burghart asked his men and the BdM girls [Bund Deutscher Mädel, League of German Girls] to wait inside a building, that he was going to try and cross the bridge. "If I don't come back, go out and look for me," he said. Like many other soldiers, he soon realized that it was impossible to get across alive. He returned to his remaining two men and the girls and they went back into the subway shaft. At Friedrichstrasse station Burghart met *Sturmbannführer* Vollmer who looked depressed and tired. "What are we going to do now?" Burghart asked. Vollmer looked him up and down and said: "Burghart, everything is finished, over." Then he turned around and went upstairs to the street. Later Burghart learned that Vollmer had been killed on 2 May at the exit of Friedrichstrasse subway station.

Burghart, the men and the BdM girls were looking for a spot where they could lie down and sleep, since they had not slept properly for weeks. After a few hundred yards they found some space in the subway shaft, where they slept until the morning of 2 May. A voice shouting: "Get up, we will try to break through to the Zoo Bunker along the subway shaft", woke them up. Burghart, his two men and the girls followed the call and started once more to march along the subway tunnel. In some parts they walked in water up to their ankles. It was pitch dark, and soon Burghart noticed that he had lost one of his men and the BdM girls. After many hours of this dreary march they saw light. It was the subway station Oranienburger Tor.

The station was crowded with civilians. When they saw the soldiers, about 100 of them coming along the tunnel, they were greeted with hostile shouts: "What do you want here? Berlin has capitulated—throw away your weapons." "Hitler has committed suicide, Goebbels has taken poison. Give up!"

Burghart was maddened at such slack, unpatriotic spirit. "We did not listen to such stupid talk," he proudly recalls, "we simply continued towards the exit, to see what was going on outside." Some civilians warned them against leaving the station, since it was surrounded by Russian tanks. On

the steps leading up to the street they met civilians with red and white armbands. One of them said in faulty German: "Throw away your arms and give up. You are surrounded by Russians."

Burghart replied: "Send for a Russian officer." A few minutes later a Russian captain appeared with some Russian soldiers. He did not flinch, even though he saw that the German soldiers had their machine pistols ready. He spoke excellent German and asked the Germans to throwaway their weapons. "Berlin has capitulated, therefore you are capitulation prisoners. You will be released within two weeks." Burghart asked: "What will happen to soldiers of the *Waffen-SS*?"

The Russian replied: "They will be treated the same way as the *Wehrmacht* soldiers." Since the Germans did not move, nor throwaway their weapons, the Russian continued: "You will have 10 minutes to make up your minds. If you don't want to capitulate, we shall shoot you. One of you should come upstairs with me, to see for himself that any kind of resistance is useless. Nothing will happen to him." One soldier indeed went upstairs and came back saying that it was so, that any kind of resistance was sheer suicide.

After that they all threw their weapons away and went upstairs. First they were taken into the courtyard of a nearby house, where the Russians picked out the wounded and had them taken away by ambulance. They had to hand over their watches and any other valuables. Then life in Russian prison camp started for Burghart, until 1950, when he was released.

Burghart says: one could never believe and understand, and I still can't, that Germany would come to such a bitter end. I always believed that Dönitz would negotiate with the Western Allies to throw the Russians out of Germany. For a long time at the prison camp I was sure that the British and the Americans would fight against the Russians. Nobody ever told me that I was going to be a prisoner for five years. First they said we had to clear rubble in Posen and that we could go home then. After that were told we had to help with the harvest in the Ukraine and then we could go home. Finally I spent five years in Russia. Eleven years for nothing.

Albert Schulz[12]

Hitlerjugend

1 May

During the night from 1–2 May, the German troops were ordered to withdraw to the Reich Chancellery on Wilhelm Strasse by way of Dönhoff Platz. The general order was to gather at the Reich Chancellery and then break out together in the direction of Spandau in order to reach the American lines and be taken prisoner there. Passing Dönhoff Platz at around 0145, however, Schulz was wounded in the thigh by a burst from a machine pistol. His comrades carried him into a cellar on Jerusalemer Strasse, cut open his trousers and strapped his wounded leg onto a wooden board. In the same cellar was a *Volkssturm* man who had been shot in the stomach and an *SS* man with a shoulder wound. There were also three unwounded *Hitlerjugend*. Schulz begged the three of them not to leave the wounded alone, but suddenly all three of them vanished out of the cellar.

Schulz did not give up hope. He still had his rifle and was determined to shoot the first Russian soldier who might walk into the cellar. Suddenly, however, he remembered that there was a first aid station in the municipal counting house (Stadtkontor) in Kur Strasse. The *Volkssturm* man, in great pain from his stomach wound, said he would not be able to walk but Schulz urged him to try. He told the *SS* man to take off the board and bandages from his leg. He then stood up, leaning on his rifle, while the *SS* man supported him from the other side with his good shoulder. In this way they left the cellar and headed towards Kur Strasse. The *Volkssturm* man tried to follow but dragged himself only a few meters and then collapsed on the street. Schulz and the *SS* man made it with great difficulty to the first aid station but the effort tore Schulz's leg wound open again and just as the reached the station, he lost consciousness.

He was re-bandaged by an orderly there but after a short time lost consciousness again, and when he woke up, he saw that he was on an operating table. The doctor leaning over him: "Count slowly." Schulz began counting but suddenly he noticed brown-uniformed figures walking up and down in the background and realized that Russian soldiers had occupied the station. He drifted off again and when he work up he was lying in a hallway with his leather jacket spread over his legs.

It was not long before a Russian soldier came along and took the leather jacket, which Schulz had originally gotten from the Russian prisoner. This jacket also contained a number of photos of Schulz's comrades who had fallen during the fighting, as well as Schulz's pay book, but there was nothing Schulz could do to get them back. Feeling extremely unsafe in the open hallway, Schulz asked one of the nurses if she could not manage to put him into one of the side rooms. While he was still lying in the hallway, other Russian soldiers came through and offered German cigarettes to the patients lying there. Schulz also heard one of the Russian officers telling a doctor: "If any of the Soviet troops touches a woman here, he will be immediately shot."

Later that day Schulz was finally placed into a room with three others: a *Hauptmann* with both feet blown off, a Norwegian with a lung wound and the red-headed *SS* man, who had a head wound. Schulz and the *Hauptmann*, as the less seriously wounded, were both placed on the floor while the other two shared the only bed in the room. The red-haired *SS* man became delirious and screamed for hours in pain, and then died. Shortly there-after, the Norwegian also died.

On 3 May, Russians came through the hospital bringing food and cigarettes to the German patients. Along with them came an interpreter from Minsk who told the Germans that the war was now over and the Third Reich destroyed. Later that day the Russians also took away cases of Polish zlotys, which had been piled up against the walls of the counting house. When the cases were removed, a whole pile of weapons was found in the place behind where the cases had been. These were guns which had been thrown away by the various patients as the Russians entered the first aid station. The interpreter carefully packed all the weapons away into trunks and carried them away.

During 5–6 May all the patients in the station were registered and examined by Soviet doctors. They were also carefully interrogated as to their rank and unit. None of them obviously admitted to being members of the *SS*, least of all Schulz. He told the interrogators that he was only 16 and really had no idea of which unit he had been pulled into. The interpreter nodded understandingly and said: "Yes, you are only a child."

In a more precarious situation however, was a French member of the *33. SS Grenadier-Division der SS Charlemagne* whose acquaintance Schulz had made at the hospital. This man, Leon de Gaspari from Lyon, had a swastika tattooed on his leg. As the Russian interrogators came down the row of patients one of the nurses sent de Gaspari out to "get some medicine," and he was therefore able to escape the notice of the examiners. Since the *12. SS Panzer Division Hitlerjugend* had been formed just before the beginning of the battle, its members did not yet have their blood group tattooed inside their left arm, as was the case with most other *SS* men. This fact enabled Schulz to persuade the Russians that he was not a member of the *SS*. [Author's note: the *12. SS Panzer Division Hitlerjugend* was formed in 1943. Schulz was probably recruited into an Ersatz or replacement battalion for the division that was fighting in Hungary and Austria at the time.]

Schulz soon became good friends with de Gaspari. The French man was a real operator: he soon got beds for them (in the meantime Schulz had again been moved out into the hallway), and obtained supplies of canned food. He also quickly made friends with one of the nurses, and arranged that he could go and stay with her. He was naturally anxious to escape from the station and pointed out that this was quite possible since there were a large number of civilian clothes lying around.

On 8 May a Russian officer came into the hospital and made a speech to the patients, announcing that the war was finally over, the Third Reich had officially surrendered to the Allies and that everyone was now going home. The news of the surrender was generally a welcome relief for most of the troops, but some of them took it rather hard. The *Hauptmann* whose feet had been blown off was found a few hours later, dead from cyanide poisoning. The incident caused quite a stir in the hospital, and from then on guards were placed in the rooms to prevent any further suicides.

On the same day the first civilians began to trickle into the station to look for missing relatives. Those of the patients who were Berliners eagerly questioned the visitors about their friends who were still outside and the state of the various neighborhoods from which they came. Schulz was told that the house at Hoffmann Platz had been destroyed by German artillery fire which had been aimed at a Soviet artillery [position] in the neighborhood. Through one of the visitors however, Schulz was able to send a message to his home. A few days later his mother, a former member of the Communist Party, came to see him at the first aid station. Her political affiliations had no been of much help to her during the first hours of the occupation—she had already been raped three times. She told her son that she would find a way to get him out of the station, and he decided that if this worked, he would get out along with de Gaspari. [Author's note: the Russians had little sympathy for German communists. The war between Germany and Russia was a conflict of both ideology and race. It made no difference what political affiliation you claimed, if you were a German you were the enemy.]

This plan however was stalled when Schulz began to suffer from gangrene (Brand). The Russian doctor said he thought the leg would have to be amputated, but one of the German doctors opposed this prognosis and succeeded in saving his leg.

By now it was already mid-May and a persistent rumor swept through the station that all prisoners of war would be transported to Küstrin. The doors of the station were abruptly sealed off and nobody, not even some of the civilian visitors, were allowed to leave. His mother had been visiting him on that day and was also caught in the situation, but she went to see the hospital commander and was able to get out. On 21 May the transportation of prisoners had already begun. Schulz had almost lost hope of escaping imprisonment when one of the German doctors went to the hospital commander and argued that he was too young to be taken along. The commander finally gave his mother a slip allowing her to take Schulz out of the hospital and told her: "He is still only a child." His mother thereupon took Schulz home with her.

Four weeks later, as he was still recuperating at home, they received a sudden visit by two NKVD men. This time there was little that he could deny about his membership in the *SS*: the two men had the army pay book which was in the leather jacket that the Russian soldier had taken from Schulz on the first day at the station. The NKVD men told him to get these things and to come with them. At this point however, his mother protested violently, pulled out her old Communist Party membership card and demanded that her son be allowed to remain with her. The two investigators examined the card and listened to her emotional plea, then nodded quietly and let him go.

In September Schulz received an unexpected visit from de Gaspari, who told him that he had been released from a prison camp and was about to apply for repatriation as a former forced laborer.

Notes to Chapter 7

1 () refer to comments that were made by the original interviewer; [] represent comments made by this author.
2 Böttcher interview.
3 Henseler interview.
4 Rein interview.
5 Wrede interview.
6 Illum interview.
7 Ache interview.
8 Hanns-Heinrich Lohmann interview (RC 66:2). Lohmann's regiment did not fight in Berlin but fought just to the north of the city within the *3.Panzer Armee* lines. The inclusion of his account offers a unique view of the U.S. and Soviet relations along one part of the demarcation line. His account is corroborated in P. Pierik, *From Leningrad to Berlin: Dutch Volunteers in the Service of the Waffen-SS 1941–1945*, pp. 263–4.
9 Timm interview.
10 Hans interview.
11 Burghart interview.
12 Schulz interview.

8

ASSESSMENTS

Berlin's fall to the Soviet Union irrevocably altered Europe. Beyond the political-social shifts, the Soviet assault on Berlin foreshadowed what future conflicts in urban terrain might be like; the intensity, weapons, and brutal nature of modern urban warfare.

HUMAN COST OF THE BERLIN STRATEGIC OFFENSIVE OPERATION

The total human cost of the Berlin Strategic Offensive Operation is arguably over 700,000 soldiers and civilians killed or wounded. This equates to an average of nearly 44,000 killed or wounded each day of the Soviet assault. For the purposes of comparison, the U.S. Army (including U.S. Army Airforce) suffered 116,991 battle deaths and 469,637 wounded, captured or missing in the European Theatre of Operation from 1941–1945.[1] In sixteen days of combat the total German-Soviet casualties exceeded the total losses for the U.S. Army on mainland Europe for the entire war by almost 20%!

The Soviets suffered 361,367 military casualties alone. Soviet cemeteries in Treptower Park, Pankow, and the Tiergarten contain the bodies of over 20,000 Soviet dead. Over 1,000,000 Russian soldiers received the 'Soviet Medal for the Capture of Berlin.' This was awarded to both combat soldiers and rear area personnel that participated in the fighting in and around Berlin. Over 600 soldiers were awarded the 'Hero of the Soviet Union' with 13 receiving the rare second gold star. These numbers are an indication of how many Soviet soldiers participated directly or indirectly in the assault.

The combined German losses from the *3.Panzer Armee, 9.Armee*, and *12.Armee* are not known but probably exceed 200,000 killed, wounded, or captured.[2] Losses of German civilians both in Berlin and outside the city are impossible to calculate with any sense of accuracy. There are no official memorials and few cemeteries for the German dead. As one historian of the battle eloquently stated: "Throughout the Soviet Zone and Sector of Berlin, except in rare instances, the 'Fascist Wehrmacht' dead were accorded no honorable burial, being merely tumbled uncounted into mass graves or buried in the trenches they had defended."[3] The total number of German civilian deaths that occurred during the fighting in Berlin is not precisely known, though a current estimate is 125,000.[4] There is no estimate for the German civilian losses in the operational areas around Berlin. In all but one case the following individuals whose accounts are related in Chapter 7 were participants already introduced in the proceeding chapters.

Soviet grave located at the foot of the Soviet War Memorial at the Seelower Höhen museum. Author's collection.

The Soviet War Memorial at the Seelower Höhen museum. The Soviets built hundreds of cemeteries for their dead all along the Seelow Heights it what was East Germany. German dead were bulldozed into unmarked graves or buried under the earth where they lay. Their remains are often found during road construction or other public works projects.
Author's collection.

EISENHOWER AND BERLIN

Stephen Ambrose, a prolific historian of WWII, concluded in his *Eisenhower and Berlin, 1945: The Decision to Halt at the Elbe* that Eisenhower's decision to attack southern Germany instead of across the Elbe River toward Berlin caused Nazi Germany to surrender.[5] Ambrose's assessment lacks broader historical analysis of the strategic situation faced by both the Western Allies and the Soviet Union at the time of Eisenhower's decision. Eisenhower's drive into southern Germany and Czechoslovakia did little to accelerate the collapse of the Third Reich. The immediate collapse of the Eastern Front or the death of Adolf Hitler provided the only catalysts to bring hostilities to a quick end. In the beginning of April 1945, both these conditions might have been met with a Western Allied drive on Berlin.

The political and social ramifications of Stalin's capture of Berlin that resulted in the Communist stranglehold of Eastern Europe, the ensuing Cold War, and the many bloody insurgencies and revolutions that raged throughout Europe for the next forty years could not have been known to Eisenhower at the time he had to make the strategic decision to cross the Elbe River. So important was Berlin to the maintenance of freedom in Germany and Central Europe that Lieutenant General Lucius Clay, who commanded U.S military forces and the U.S. military government in Germany stated in 1948, just three short years after the end of the war, that "We've lost Czechoslovakia and we're in danger of losing [Finland]. If we intended to hold Europe against Communism, we dare not move from this position. I believe that the future of democracy demands that we stay [in Berlin]."[6] With this knowledge today, the question remains: What would have happened if Eisenhower ordered the Western Allies over the Elbe toward Berlin—the main European demarcation line between Democracy and freedom or Communism and subjugation?

Eisenhower was well within his military authority to help the Red Army by eliminating the *Wehrmacht* forces defending the Eastern Front and facilitating the collapse of the remaining forces in *Army Group Vistula* as prescribed in the SHEAF G–3 report dated 14 April discussed in Chapter 1. The advance over the Elbe would have quickly eliminated the possibility of Berlin being defended as staunchly as it was, alleviating significant losses for both the Soviets and Germans. The *12.Armee* only had a few strong divisions to defend the Elbe River and the *3.Panzer* and *9.Armees* would not have disengaged from the HKL opposite the Soviets to fight the Western Allies. In fact, a Western Allied move over the Elbe might have induced Heinrici to order his force to stop fighting the Soviets and surrender to the Western Allies once he believed Berlin was secure from a Soviet assault. Hitler and the *German High Command* had little authority left to direct German units to block the Western Allied forces in their drive on the capital. Heinrici's control of military units around the city ensured that Guderian's earlier directive to allow Western Allied forces into Berlin without a significant fight would be followed.

There were almost no Germans units along the western approach to Berlin to engage a quick drive by Eisenhower's forces. The majority of Berlin's *Volkssturm* were already on the move east toward the HKL and there were no sizable units, like the *LVI Panzer Korps*, deployable into the city as all major combat formations were already fighting the Soviets. Wenck's *XX Korps* was dispersed in a wide semi-circle along the *12.Armee's* southern front and there is no telling if it could have reformed or maneuvered to engage U.S. forces near Berlin, though it seems highly unlikely. When the Western Allies stopped at the Elbe they also stopped all air interdiction of German unit movements to the east. Air interdiction certainly would have adversely impacted the *12.Armee's* ability to maneuver forces rapidly against the Western Allies within the area east of the Elbe. It can also be presumed that Eisenhower's advance on Berlin would act as trigger for

Hitler's suicide, followed by the rapid collapse of the remaining Nazi political hierarchy in much the same way that those events occurred after the Soviet encirclement. Hitler, it must be remembered, already decided to remain Berlin and he had no intention of being captured alive. With the Soviets to the east and U.S. forces entering Berlin from the west, his available options were even fewer than if the Western Allies remained on the western bank of the Elbe. Hundreds of thousands—perhaps as many as a half-million—military and civilian casualties might not have occurred with a rapid U.S. capture of Berlin, though the specter of direct confrontation between the Western Allies and Soviet Union looms large in this option. If under these conditions Eisenhower stopped at the Havel River and left Berlin east of Spandau to fall as a *fait acompli* to the Soviets, then it stands to reason that a direct confrontation between the Western Allies and the Soviets Union might have been avoided, and the Soviet's post-war political clout might have been greatly diminished.

The captured German territory east of the Elbe held potential use in bargaining with Stalin before a withdrawal. This option only had potential, however, if this was part of a broader political agenda of Soviet containment by the Western Allies. There is precedence for this line of thought as the Soviet's acceptance of Western Allied occupation of the agreed upon zones in Berlin appears to have been predicated not on the wartime agreements, but on the U.S. withdrawal from Czechoslovakia and southern Germany after the war.[7] The United States, however, lacked the political will to pursue aggressive diplomacy against Stalin the remaining months of the war in Europe, or even immediately after. The Western Allies might have allowed the Soviets to occupy their zone in exchange for free elections in Poland or the return of the legitimate Polish Government in exile. Likewise, free elections might have been demanded in Czechoslovakia and other Eastern European states. Soviet post-war reconstruction relied heavily on German slave labor, and industry that was literally uprooted from Germany and brought back to Russia.[8] Soviet reconstruction efforts would have taken longer without the industrial base from the eastern half of Germany making this territory very valuable to Stalin.

Stalin's continued mistrust of the Western Allies coupled with his postwar agenda to allow Eastern Europe to turn Communist and bring it within the Soviet sphere of influence were among his chief reasons to capture Berlin before the U.S. or British. The prestige of Berlin's capture, Hitler's resulting death, and physical control of Germany east of the Elbe provided Stalin with considerable political leverage to ensure his postwar goals. There is no doubt that the course of European history in the latter half of the Twentieth-Century might have taken a myriad of unforeseen courses if Eisenhower crossed the Elbe River.

GERMAN STRATEGIC PLANNING

Hitler and the *German High Command* never developed a defensive strategy for Germany or Berlin. The failure of *Wacht am Rhein* January 1945 ended their ability to launch further strategic offensives that might split the Western Allies and grant Hitler breathing room to continue the fight against the Soviets. Only the capture of 'Eclipse' offered Hitler a road map to develop a defensive plan that might succeed in favorably changing the course of Germany's strategic position. The only course of action that remained was to deploy his forces on the Eastern Front to delay the Soviets and draw the Western Allies into the post-war Soviet Zone of Occupation in the hope that the two sides might clash, igniting open hostilities between the former Allies. Open hostilities between the Allies might allow a negotiated settlement with Hitler's Germany—preventing unconditional surrender. As unlikely as this may sound, this was the only strategic option open

Changing eras, changing icons. This rare photo shows the damaged Frederick II statue that sat just to the west of the Brandenburg Gate. On the pedestal reads "Frederick II, German Kaiser, King of Prussia." In the right background of the photo a crane can be seen placing the giant bronze Soviet soldier on the top of the Tiergarten War Memorial. Frederick II's statue was either buried or blown up by the victorious Soviets soon after this photo. Author's collection.

The Tiergarten Soviet War Memorials in Berlin, just west of the Reichstag, autumn 1945. The Soviets built this memorial very quickly using granite from Hitler's New Reich Chancellery and with an emphasis on completing the project by November 1945. This memorial was built in Berlin's Western Zone of Allied occupation and serves as an enduring reminder to the Western Allies who captured Berlin—the Soviets. Also note the Kroll Opera House and Ministry of Interior in the background. Both of those buildings were demolished by the Soviets after the war. Author's collection.

The Tiergarten Soviet War memorial as it looked in 2005. Nothing has changed, except that the Soviet Honor Guard is no longer present. There are two other grandiose Soviet War Memorials in Berlin that the Germans must maintain by treaty agreement signed during the unification of Berlin. These monuments are ever present reminders of who won WWII in Europe. Author's collection.

The conquerors of Germany—Zhukov and Eisenhower—pose for a postwar photograph in Berlin.
Photo courtesy of the Cornelius Ryan Collection, Mahn Center, Alden Library, Ohio University, Athens, OH.

Official Soviet victory parade held in August during the arrival of the Western Allies into Berlin.
Photo courtesy of the Cornelius Ryan Collection, Mahn Center, Alden Library, Ohio University, Athens, OH.

Zhukov and his staff in front of the Brandenburg Gate in May of 1945. Note that the barricade has been removed. Soviet Army
photo courtesy of the Cornelius Ryan Collection, Mahn Center, Alden Library, Ohio University, Athens, OH.

to Hitler. It was clearly a better option then to sit back and do nothing. Hitler, however, seemed destined to fall into strategic apathy. He left Germany's fate to providence until he found himself encircled in Berlin and at the center of a "decisive victory" planed by his senior commanders.

It was emphasized again and again [by Guderian] that above everything else this was the point of emphasis; the Oder line must be defended. Here the Russians must be brought to a final halt. No foot of German territory must be given up to them after what the eastern territories had experienced in the east [Russian atrocities]; then [the Western Allies] could move quite easily to the Oder and in this manner they would stand at the rear of the German troops who were posted on the Oder. Better that the Americans should come to Berlin but, in no circumstances, the Russians.[9]

The *German High Command's* planning and execution of the final "decisive" battle for Berlin demonstrates that the *OKW/OKH* staff had considerably more influence over Hitler than typically thought. They might have influenced the battle for Germany much earlier by developing a course of action that brought the remaining Wehrmacht divisions from the various fringes of occupied Europe to the main battle line of AGV with the mission to hold back the Soviets. The *German High Command* understood through the issues raised at Yalta that a political rift existed between the Western Allies and the Soviet Union. They also understood that this rift might be exploited along the Elbe River—the demarcation line outlined in 'Eclipse'—if they knew the demarcation line was real. Only when military events confirmed the correctness of the demarcation line did 'Eclipse' factor into the *German High Command's* strategic conduct.[10] They responded to the intelligence coup far too late to make a strategic difference. As *OKH* Chief of Operations, Guderian saw potential in 'Eclipse' and set into motion a plan not designed to split the Western Allies and Stalin, but in his mind, to save Germany and Berlin from Soviet vengeance he knew was at hand. Guderian

Soviet soldiers that participated in the assault on Berlin received a commemorative certificate like this one. Author's collection.

set the plan in motion but Heinrici bore the responsibility to carry it out. Heinrici continued to follow Guderian's guidance even after the latter's forced retirement by Hitler.

What is important to note is that Hitler had very little to do with the battle for Berlin, other than anchoring the defense to the city because he remained there while many of his inner circle fled to Bavaria. It was Keitel, Jodl, and Krebs that devised the final plan to defeat the Soviets outside the city in the hope of creating some form of victory that might be politically exploited by Germany. Likewise, Guderian, Heinrici, Manteuffel, Busse, and Wenck all exercised their own decisions when the time came, ignoring directives from both the *German High Command* and Hitler. What makes this so interesting is that most histories of this period tend to judge the Hitler-*German High Command* relationship as one where Hitler dominated, but in the last months of the war it is clear that many of his senior Generals drove the final strategic decisions.

ZHUKOV'S OPERATION 'SAVED' BY KONIEV

Berlin is often viewed as Zhukov's greatest military achievement. Even in Russia today, Berlin's capture is considered the crowning achievement of a military commander that never lost a battle. In his memoir Zhukov wrote the following about the Berlin Strategic Offensive Operation:

It had taken just sixteen days for the troops of three fronts—the First Byelorussian, the First Ukrainian and the Second Byelorussian—to crush enemy forces in the area of Berlin and to seize the German capital. The victory had been made possible by the fact that the Soviet Army neared the end of the war mightier than ever before, both materially and spiritually, surpassing the enemy substantially both in military mastery and in operational and strategic skill.[11]

His statement clearly lacks historical authenticity. It also undervalues his rival Koniev's impact on his operational plan.

Zhukov's operational plan to take Berlin was built on his belief that the Germans were already defeated. He based this assessment on his own faulty perception of reality influenced by the Vistula-Oder campaign of January. Zhukov did not expect the Germans to defend their own soil with the fanaticism he encountered. Even after the bitter fighting his forces encountered during their conquest of Prussia and Pomerania, Zhukov failed to appreciate what he was up against. On 8 March, a report to Hitler by *General* Eberhard Raus concluded that "as a peculiarity of the Pomeranian battle, I can report that of the 580 enemy tanks which have been knocked out up to this time, 380, or two-thirds, were destroyed by the *Panzerfaust*—that is, by the courage of the individual soldier. Never before has an army achieved so much success [than] with the *Panzerfaust*."[12] Yet the losses experienced by the Soviets never altered Zhukov's military view of what his forces might expect when they crossed into eastern Germany to assault Berlin.

Zhukov's primary concern was to take Berlin before the Western Allies while keeping to Stalin's schedule. All other considerations, including the lives of his men, were secondary. Once he realized that Koniev, his rival, entered the assault on Berlin, Zhukov ordered his forces to cross the established inter-front boundary within the city to prevent Koniev from reaching the Reichstag. He did not attempt to coordinate operations in Berlin with Koniev; he sought only to disrupt Koniev's advance, regardless of the Soviet fratricide that might be caused in the process.

Zhukov probably never understood or appreciated how Koniev's advance helped him in his goal to capture Berlin. Few historians have grasped the significance of Koniev's role in ensuring Zhukov's military victory of the operation. Popiel, the 1st Guards Tank Army's Operations Officer, wrote the following after the war:

> But, what really would have been the situation if the troops of the 1st Ukrainian Front had not helped us to cut off Berlin from the rest of Germany? The Hitlerites who were concentrating the *[12.] Armee* from the Western Front to [redeploy] against the Red Army would have been able to mount a formidable offensive against Berlin. And, the question was that they might have been able to surrender the city to the Americans. And in this case the commander of our Front Marshal Zhukov would not really have any opportunity to call himself the 'Victor of Berlin' and it wouldn't have been Koniev either, it would have been Eisenhower.[13]

Koniev's drive toward the southern suburbs of Berlin ensured that the *9.Armee* and *12.Armee* were prevented from direct involvement in Berlin's relief. Without Koniev's forces, Zhukov's 8th Guards Army might have been dispatched to tie down Busse's *9.Armee* leaving German forces in Berlin free to concentrate to the east and north. This would have left far fewer of Zhukov's forces to conduct urban operations in Berlin. In fact, Koniev's forces that entered Berlin effectively tied down at least one-third of Weidling's defenders in the city. This prevented key German units from maneuvering against Zhukov's forces. Zhukov's failure to quickly take Berlin might have forced Eisenhower over the Elbe River opposite Magdeburg to drive toward the Reich Capital or perhaps, as suggested by Popiel above, would have caused Weidling to offer Berlin's surrender to Eisenhower through Wenck—two dramatic political events with incalculable effects on post-war European history.

In a 1962 interview Koniev was directly questioned about his rival's publicized comments given in June of 1945 where Zhukov asserted that he alone was commander of all Soviet Fronts in the Berlin Strategic Offensive Operation. Koniev quickly replied that Zhukov was only speaking for his own two Soviet Fronts and immediately drew a distinction between Zhukov's and his own methods of combat in the operation. Koniev quickly ran down his method of breaching the Neisse River with two hours of artillery fire followed by a smoke screen, instead of using search lights in the opening phase of the offensive like Zhukov—alluding to the fact that even in the 1960s Soviet Union Zhukov's opening operational plan to take Berlin was considered a failure. Koniev, perhaps catching himself from stating anything too derogatory about Zhukov, simply ended the thought by stating "We give the opportunity to the historians to judge who's methods were more effective."[14]

GERMAN AND SOVIET OPERATIONS IN BERLIN

German operations in Berlin are characterized by asymmetric small unit actions. The defenders came together at a specific point, attacked, then dispersed back into the city's ruins. Operations of a division size were impossible inside the city. Weidling managed at least two regiment-sized counterattacks that were quickly stopped by massed Soviet firepower. The problem was that if the German defenders grouped into a large formation for any

Medal awarded to Soviet veterans of the assault on Berlin. Author's collection.

length of time they quickly became targets of dominant Soviet artillery and rockets. Another problem with the execution of large-scale counterattacks was the lack of command-and-control. Communication was accomplished almost exclusively by *Hitlerjugend* messengers. Messengers carried written orders through the ruins from Weidling's HQ to the tasked unit. This was an excruciatingly slow process that subjected the messenger to a variety of hazards from both the German and Russian sides. This method proved insufficient to coordinate operations effectively in an urban environment the size of Berlin. The other unique characteristic of Berlin's defense was the overlapping command structure. Everyone, it seemed, could issue orders to the troops and they did. Hitler, Goebbels, Mohnke, Sector Commanders, and others all issued their own orders contrary to the military needs of the appointed military commander of Berlin, Weidling.

Like the Soviet Army before the assault, German military training lacked any focus in urban combat operations. The Germans did have several distinct advantages; they were operating on interior lines that favored the defense, and many of the defenders knew the terrain and layout of the city. The placement of anti-tank guns was a key defensive asset. These weapons, especially the 8.8cm guns, were well concealed and often had a long field of view down broad avenues. Their fire was accurate and deadly. Likewise, the limited number of German Panzers performed the same function. The Panzers moved around as mobile firing platforms to engage Soviet tank breakthroughs. Arguably no other weapon system had a bigger impact on the battle then the *Panzerfaust*. A single soldier was now capable of destroying the largest Soviet tank at close range and be able to escape back into the ruins.

One Soviet veteran, Vladimir Pavlovich Rozanov, interviewed after the war provided insight into the tough opposition that the small scale German operations gave the assaulting Soviets. Rozanov was an infantryman who fought at Kursk and Warsaw prior to his participation in the assault on Berlin. As a member of a reconnaissance platoon for an artillery regiment, Rozanov engaged in much of the street fighting. He recalled how the "fighting was heavy and difficult. It was fighting for each street and each house. It meant getting into the cellars and it meant fighting for the floors and windows. Many of my friends were buried by ruins falling on them." He attributed much of his unit's difficulties to the German defenders' effective employment of *Panzerfausts*.[15]

Soviets tactics were inappropriate to conduct military operations in mainland Europe's largest urban complex. One German veteran provided his assessment of Soviet infantry tactics in Berlin after the war:

> Anyway, they didn't have to risk too much. Every time the Russians threw in men and they were seriously opposed, they always withdrew. [Author's note: after the withdrawal the Soviets often employed massive firepower on the suspected German positions]. Russians had a lot of *Panzerfausts*. The infantry would [fire] them into the ruins, explode them, and in the dust and wake of the explosion they would fan out into the wrecked buildings. It was sheer weight of men and a complete disregard for casualties. In the center of [Berlin] around the government areas they

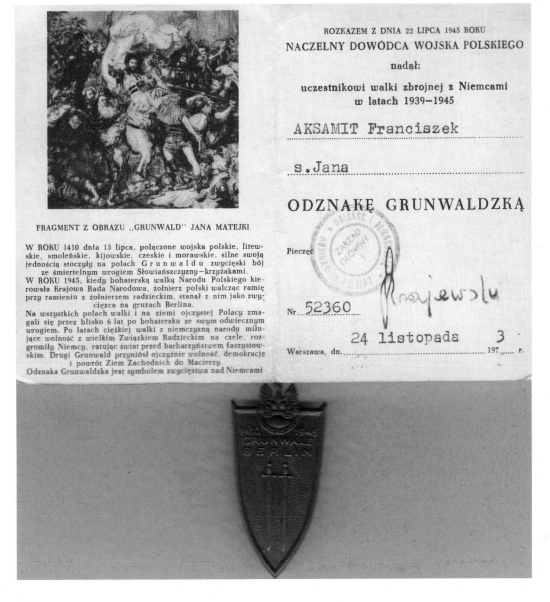

Medal awarded to Polish soldiers that fought in Berlin. This Polish medal traced its victory over Berlin back to the Battle of Grunwald (Tannenberg) 1410. During this battle a combined Polish, Lithuanian, and Mongol force under the command of King Wladislaw Jagiello narrowly defeated the smaller force of Teutonic Knights under the command of Grand Master Ulrich von Jungingen, killing the Grand Master in the process. The Polish victory was the precursor to the end of the Teutonic Knight's rule in Prussia and brought Poland national survival of their country. The postwar Polish government saw fit to link the military events of 1410 with those of 1945. Author's collection.

were very careful and not too eager to attack. In fact they moved slowly. They simply infiltrated during the evening and pummeled us all the time by mortar and shellfire.[16]

Soviet soldiers lacked street fighting skills, though it could be argued that there was no way to prepare them to fight inside a city the size of Berlin. Training before the battle didn't include essentials like infantry-armor coordination. The Russians tended to rely on massive firepower to blast out German defenders. This caused two secondary effects. First, it blocked roads from being used by Soviet tanks to advance, and second, it created fertile defensive terrain that was difficult for attacking forces to overcome. The Soviet rifleman had to quickly adapt to his combat environment.

The biggest problem for the Soviets was the poor use of tanks in urban terrain. The final assessment of the 11th Tank Corps offers an excellent view of the problems faced in the fighting for Berlin:

> The fire of the tanks was used generally for the destruction of barricades and for smashing passages through them, for destroying enemy manpower and his fire positions, for combat against his tanks and self-propelled guns, for destroying fire positions and for very many other tasks. The offensive was conducted along the line of the streets, in a majority of cases on the [sidewalks and pedestrian walkways]. During the course of the action in Berlin it was plain that in a single street it was impossible to employ more than a single company of tanks. In order to deploy the infantry they had to echelon. The infantry who were in action in co-operation with the tank corps had to be able to utilize the successes of the tanks and to guard the tanks against tank killers [*Panzerfausts*]. During the period of the fighting for Berlin, the tank brigades, which were specially employed [in order to guard them] against the tank killers, were attached to each of the Motor Rifle Battalions of the Motor Rifle Brigades of the Corps. This was called for since the infantry of the 5th Shock Army frequently did not protect the tanks. The infantry usually deployed itself into the cellars and into the parts of the houses. As a result of which the tanks were left on the streets without protection. As the tanks moved forward, the infantry hung back and the tanks, being forced to wait for them, suffered heavy losses.[17]

Two examples illustrate the losses faced by Soviet tank formations. By 2 May the 7th Guards Heavy Tank Brigade lost 391 personnel killed or wound, 28 JS–2s burnt out by German anti-tank guns, and 11 by *Panzerfaust*. Another 28 were damaged but returned to service. A heavy tank brigade averaged 65 tanks, meaning that this unit witnessed nearly 100% losses in tanks during the battle. The 67th Guards Heavy Tank Brigade did not fare better. This formation lost 343 personnel killed or wounded, 12 JS–2s burnt out by anti-tank guns and Panzer fire, while 18 were destroyed by *Panzerfaust*. An incredible 41 tanks were damaged but later repaired. This represented a 109% loss ratio, meaning that many tanks were repaired more than once.[18]

Only belatedly during the battle did independent thinking Soviet commanders employ small combined arms battle groups and design protective screens for their tanks to better enable urban combat operations and help reduce the effects of the *Panzerfaust* employed against their forces. Both of these innovations might have become critical tactical developments that the Soviet Army might have adapted to their advantage in later conflicts if not for the overall institutional inflexibility of Soviet Army's command structure and doctrine.

KONIEV'S CONCLUSION

Koniev's unpublished memoir provides a very frank assessment of Soviet operations. His account offers an interesting perspective from the Soviet side that is lacking in the accounts by his peers—most notably Zhukov, and Chuikov.

> The battles in Berlin itself lasted 'day and night' and here I want to dwell on the nature of the events of Berlin, with which we had to deal during these battles, without, so to speak, tying these observations down to a definite day.
>
> I have encountered opinions that the battles in Berlin could, they say, have been conducted with less fury, bitterness, and haste, and thus in the final analysis, with fewer losses. In these discussions an apparent logic is present, but they ignore the main thing—the real situation, the real tension of the battles and the real state of the spirit of the people. And our people had a fierce, violent, impatient desire to end the war as soon as possible. And those who want to judge the justification or lack of justification of some sacrifices or other, as to whether or not Berlin could have been taken a day or two later, they should remember this. Otherwise, in the situation of the Berlin battles it is impossible to understand literally anything ….
>
> Goebbels headed the organs of the civil authorities and was responsible for the training of the civil population of the city for defense. As for Weidling, when he was assigned the post of commander of the defenses of Berlin, he received from Hitler a quite categorical order: to defend the capital to the last man.
>
> The Germans had prepared Ber1in for a firm and fierce defense, calculated for lasting a long time and with a system of strong fire and strongpoints, as well as centers of resistance, all constructed. The closer we got toward the center, the denser the defense became. Massive stone structures, with a great thickness of their walls, were adapted to a prolonged defense. The windows and doors of many buildings were walled up – only loopholes for firing remained in them. [Author's note: Koniev overstates the German's preparedness.]
>
> Several buildings thus fortified formed a center of resistance. The flanks were covered by strong barricades, with a thickness of up to four meters. These barricades were simultaneously powerful anti-tank obstacles. Wood, earth, cement, and iron were all used in the barricades. Corner buildings were especially strengthened, making it possible to control flanking and indirect fire from them.
>
> All this, from the standpoint of the organization of the defense, was quite well thought out. All the centers of defense were saturated with a large quantity of *Panzerfausts* which, in a situation of street fighting, turned out to be dreadful anti-tank weapons.
>
> In the defense system, the Germans widely used underground structures, of which there were more than enough in the city. Bomb shelters, the tunnels of the subway, underground sewers, drainage ditches, and, in general, all types of underground passages were used both for maneuvering troops—making it possible to transfer troops under-

In the stark ruins of Berlin a broken bust of Hitler surveys all that remains of his 1,000 Year Reich. Author's collection.

ground from one place to another—and for bringing up ammunition to the front lines. By using the underground structures, the defenders of the city inflicted upon us an extraordinarily large number of unpleasantnesses. Our troops would take some center of resistance or other, it would appear, that at this point everything was finished, but the Germans, using underground passages, would throw into our rear their reconnaissance groups and individual saboteurs and snipers. Such groups of automatic riflemen, snipers, grenade throwers, and *Panzerfaust* operators, sent there through the underground communications, fired on motor vehicles, tanks, gun crews that were moving along streets already captured, interrupted lines of communications, and created a tense situation behind our front lines. [Author's note: This is modern asymmetrical urban warfare. Koniev's description is eerily reminiscent to the tactical hardships Soviet forces faced nearly 50 years later during the fighting in Grozny, the capital city of Chechnya.]

The battles in Berlin required a great amount of ability of our junior officers, who directly organized the battle in their sector, primarily from the commanders of regiments and battalions, because our assault groups most frequently were led by battalion commanders.

The movement of our troops in the street fighting was hampered also by a number of circumstances besides those that I have already mentioned. In Berlin, especially in its central part, there were many special reinforced-concrete shelters. The largest of them were reinforced-concrete bunkers on the surface, in which a large garrison of from 300 to a 1,000 soldiers could be stationed. Some of these bunkers had up to six stories each, and their height ran as high as up to thirty-six meters, while the thickness of their roofs varied from a meter and a half to three and a half meters, and the thickness of the walls, of one to two and a half meters, was practically invulnerable to modern field artillery. [Author's note: Koniev is referencing the three massive Flak Towers.]

On the grounds of these bunkers were usually several antiaircraft guns, operating simultaneously against aircraft, tanks, and infantry.

These bunkers were unique fortresses, included in the defense system within the city, and throughout all of Berlin there were about four hundred of them. In the city were also built many reinforced-concrete pillboxes of the field type, in which machine gunners could be stationed. Our soldiers, breaking through into an area on the territory of some plant or factory or other, frequently encountered fire in which the Germans were sending from these reinforced-concrete pillboxes.

Berlin also had much anti-aircraft artillery, and in the period of the street fighting it played an especially great part in anti-tank defense. If we do not consider *Panzerfausts*, the majority of our losses in tanks and self-propelled guns were suffered in Berlin precisely from German anti-aircraft guns.

During the Berlin operation, the Germans succeeded in destroying or knocking out a little more than 800 of our tanks and self-propelled guns. And the main parts of these losses were incurred in the battles in Berlin itself. [Author's note: Total losses in armor were significantly higher. See the Introduction.]

Striving to reduce losses due to *Panzerfausts*, during the battles we introduced a simple but very effective device – we created a so-called screen around the tanks: we hung sheets of steel or sheet iron over the armor. The projectiles of the *Panzerfausts*, hitting the tank, at first penetrated this first insignificant obstacle, and then beyond this obstacle there was an empty space, and finally, the projectile struck the armor of the tank, already having lost its reactive force, and most frequently ricochet, without inflicting any damage.

Why was this "screening" used so late? Apparently, because in practice we had not encountered such a wide-spread use of *Panzerfausts* in street battles, and in field conditions we did not especially consider them.

The battalions of the *Volkssturm*, in which elderly people and juveniles predominated, were especially widely armed with *Panzerfausts*. A *Panzerfaust* was precisely such a weapon which could create in people who where not physically prepared or trained for war a feeling of psychological confidence that, having become soldiers only yester-day, they today could really do something. And, I must say that these *Panzerfausts* operators, as a rule, fought to the end and at this last stage showed considerably greater firmness than German soldiers who had seen the sights, but were worn out by defeats and fatigue brought about by many years of service. [Author's note: Koniev is referring to the *Volkssturm* and Hitlerjugend recruits.]

The soldiers, as before, surrendered themselves as prisoners only when there was no other way out for them. The same thing should also be said of their officers. But already no fighting spirit remained in them. Only the gloomy, hopeless resolution to fight until an order for capitulation was received remained.

And in the ranks of the *Volkssturm*, in the days of the decisive battles for Berlin, a feeling dominated, as I have al-ready characterized, which could be called hysterical self-sacrifice. These last defenders of the Third Reich, including boys who were still very small, saw in themselves the personification of the last hope for a miracle, which, in spite of everything, at the very last moment must occur.[19]

Koniev's candid view of the Soviet assault written in the early 1960s is still very relevant today.

POSTWAR COMMUNIST DOMINATION OF EUROPE AND BERLIN

The human cost of WWII for Germany and Eastern Europeans did not end in 1945 with the fall of Berlin and the subsequent 8 May treaty ending hostilities in Europe.

Across Eastern Europe 16.5 million Germans were driven from their homes under the harshest of conditions. An estimated 2.2 million Germans lost their lives in a population shift that can only be termed as the largest ethnic cleansing operation in European history that resulted in the eradication of more than 700 years of German culture east of the Oder River. More German civilians died during the ethnic expulsions in the decade after the war, then during the war itself. Both at the Yalta Conference held on 1 February, and the Potsdam Conference held on 21 July, Stalin raised the issue of shifting Poland's borders west and in the process force out the Germans remaining there. When questioned at both conferences, by Churchill and Roosevelt in February and Churchill and Harry S. Truman (the new U.S. President) in July, about the fate of the Germans living in those territories, Stalin openly lied by stating that no Germans lived east of the Oder any longer as they were either killed during the war or fled west. Despite the protests of the Western Allies, Stalin was not only given a free hand to shift borders and whole populations, but in the case of Prussia, all three Allies agreed that this particular German State could no longer exist in Europe. By 1946 the elimination of Prussia had become policy, one that had already been pursued since the spring of 1945 when the Soviet captured K igsberg and began the cultural obliteration of the city. There was no accounting for political or social orientation during the expulsions, despite the fact that the various Eastern and Central European countries now under Moscow influence pursued the policy slightly differently. Germans, however, were not the only victims of Stalin post war agenda.

While Europeans west of the Elbe celebrated their new freedom, Stalin plunged Europe east of the Elbe into and era of Communist Dictatorship that brought suffering and death. Immediately the NKVD unleashed a bloody purge against civilians they believed were Nazi ollaborators, and ympathizers. The number of victims may have reached into the millions. Stalin needed men to rebuild his war torn country and there were simply not enough German POWs to do the work. An estimated 12,000,000 people transited to Soviet postwar labor camps, many of whom were citizens of the victorious Russia. More startling is the number of dead reportedly killed during Stalin reign over Eastern Europe from 1945-1953. In less than ten years it is estimated that the death toll may have reached 15,000,000, of which 3,000,000 were Eastern Europeans (it should be noted that these deaths are calculated separate from those caused during the German expulsions). The killing continued even after Stalin death in 1953 and would not end until 1987. These numbers are staggering, and rival those of the period of Soviet history known as the Great Terror. It should come as no surprise that under these circumstances armed insurgencies rose up in almost all Eastern European countries as the Soviet Army arrived on the heels of the retreating *Wehrmacht*. Men and women who survived the trials of Nazi occupation now sacrificed their lives to either shake off the yoke of a new conqueror and gain independence for their countries, or find a way to reach the West, and start a new life.

In the period from 1945-1961 2,500,000 people fled to the West through the borderless division between democracy and commu-nism that ran north-south through Berlin. Communist East Germany lost 15% of its population this way. There was no incentive to remain living in a tyranny when you could walk to freedom; that is until the Berlin Wall was constructed in 1961. The building of the Berlin Wall did not stop the desire of individuals to flee to the West, it only served to constrict the flow, forcing the desire for freedom to build like steam in a pressure cooker, waiting to burst the lid open.

During almost three decades after the construction of the Berlin Wall the pressure for freedom built behind the Iron Curtain until inside Berlin, where Stalin Soviet Union claimed their inheritance of conquest in May 1945 from the rubble of the destroyed capital of the Third Reich, came the sudden collapse of Europe second great tyranny; a collapse not heralded by the sounds of gun fire, clanking tank treads, or spent artillery shells striking the street pavement, but by the sounds of hammers and crowbars peeling back the enduring symbol of Communist oppression he Berlin Wall nd finally bringing unity to that divided city, freedom and self-determination to Europeans East of the Elbe River, and a final end to WWII.

Notes to Chapter 8

1 Army Battle Casualties and Non-Combat Deaths in World War II, Final Report, 7 December 1941-31December 1946, p. 5.
2 Tissier, Slaughter at Halbe, p. 212. The numbers of German casualties may actually be higher.
3 Tissier, Race for the Reichstag, p. 195.
4 Keegan, "Berlin," pp. 82-83.
5 Ambrose, p. 98.
6 Robert P. Grathwol, and Donita M. Moorhus, American Forces in Berlin: Cold War Outpost, p. 32.
7 Grathwol, and Moorhus, pp. 4, 6.
8 MacDonough, pp. 393-94.
9 Heinrici interview.
10 Schultz-Naumann, p. 192.
11 Zhukov, p. 288.
12 P. Tsouras, ed. Panzers on the Eastern Front, p. 220.
13 Popiel, p. 20.

14 Koniev interview.
15 Oder and Berlin Russian Participants interviews, (RC: 73/7).
16 Dr. Albrecht Lampe interview (RC: 67/10).
17 Platonov, pp. 29-30.
18 M. Baryatinskiy, The IS Tanks, p. 53.
19 Koniev memoir, pp. 162-165.
20 Macdonogh, p. 1. Total estimates of how many Germans died or were forced to move varies. One fact is clear, if you were German or of German descent, you were not wanted in Central or Eastern Europe.
21 Alfred-Maurice de Zayas, A Terrible Revenge, p84-85.
22 Christopher Clark, *Iron Kingdom*, p. 674-680.
23 Ronald Heidemann, *Verbotenes Ostpreu n*, pp. 15-33. Compare the before and after photos of the city and you can see how

thoroughly the Soviets attempted to destroy all aspects of German cultural in the city.
24 Rummel, p. 194.
25 Ibid, p. 198.
26 Ibid, p. 200. Rummel estimates are based on factual surveys of varying, available sources or what he terms *reasonable approximation*. As he states on p. 235 . . it must be clear at the outset that we cannot expect to determine the actual number of deaths. Even if all the Soviet archives opened and every record of those murdered by police, secret police, or the military available, we then might have a figure closer to the truth, although still probably off by millions.
27 Ibid, p. 220-221.
28 F. Taylor, *The Berlin Wall: A World Divided, 1961-1989*, p. XVIII.

APPENDIX A

U.S. ARMY INTELLIGENCE REPORT ON THE SOVIET ARMY IN BERLIN – 8 MAY 1945

What follows is an accurate assessment of the environment in Berlin immediately after the Soviet assault as reported by the first two U.S. Army servicemen to enter the defeated city. Their report written on 8 May, and supplemented by a follow-on interview in the 1960s, provides key impressions of what the city looked like, the violence of the street fighting, and the state of the Soviet Army.

On the 7 May General Oliver, commander of the U.S. 5th Armored Division asked Captain Charles Twohey and Lieutenant Peter Blake to cross the Elbe and invite the Russian Commanding General of the division on the opposite side of the river to join General Oliver for dinner. Captain Twohey had the direct responsibility for conveying the message and Lieutenant Blake was to act as translator as Lieutenant Blake was born in Berlin, spoke fluent German, and knew the area east of the Elbe River better than anyone in the division. They arrived in a jeep driven by a Chinese driver from San Francisco.

After crossing the Elbe and conveying the invitation to the Russians, Blake asked what would happen if they drove to Berlin. The Russian responded that they could do so but they would be "at their own risk." Twohey and Blake took off immediately and were the first U.S. Army soldiers in the city, arriving only 5 days after the fall of Berlin. Upon their return they compiled the below report. [*Author's note: all spelling mistakes are part of the original report and interview*].

REPORT
MII TEAM 440 – G
8 MAY 45

SUBJECT: VISIT TO BERLIN
TO: A C of S, G–2

We crossed the ELBE river at approximately 0700, 7 MAY 45 about two miles north of WITTENBERGE by ferry, having obtained permission to do so from the 84th U.S. Inf. Div. stationed in that sector. On arriving in WITTENBERGE we contacted the CP of the 32nd Russian Cossack Cavalry Division, and were given verbal permission to proceed toward and into Berlin along their MSR. We started out around 0800.

On leaving WITTENBERGE we discovered that the direct road to PERLESBERG was so badly pockmarked with shell-holes that we would have to take a detour by way of BAD WISMACK. This took us through some of the country south of WITTENBERGE, which showed evidence of fairly intense fighting, with several German RR guns and AA weapons abandoned in the woods. There were Russian cavalry units in practically all the villages, apparently divided up into groups of about company strength. Some Russian artillery in the woods, with medium caliber AA guns in evidence. Control of traffic — especially of civilian traffic — was well organized by the use of road barriers at the entrance to villages, but it was actually not very effective, since the guards at the barriers spoke no language other than Russian and could not effectively check travelers. Small bridges were blown and no effort had been made to replace them to date.

We reentered the MSR at KLETZKE and, from there on, followed this route # 5 all the way into Berlin. Along the road we found tremendous numbers of vehicles of all types, most of them horse-drawn, ramshackle carts and pre-Model T Russian Fords, with a sprinkling of modern Lend Lease trucks. There was apparently no organization to speak of, and we encountered several serious traffic jams, each over a mile in length, which were caused simply by lack of organization and common sense. Bridges were almost all blown, and replaced by the most primitive of dams. Vehicles regularly got stuck on these, and there was no control of traffic over these one-way bottlenecks. Large columns of German prisoners would be marched across these bridges in priority to supply trucks, and civilian refugees, going in all directions, were given preference over tanks. Frequently there would be three columns of traffic jammed against one of these bottlenecks, with two more columns stuck in the fields parallel to the road in an attempt to circumvent the jam. These conditions were aggravated by the fact that the MSR itself was cluttered up with broken down tanks, trucks, cars, carts and the carcasses of horses and cows, while many of the soldiers were herding along sheep and other cattle apparently requisitioned from German farms. Since the convoys, if they could be called that, often consisted of vehicles of very different speeds (tanks were mixed up with horse-drawn stuff and cavalry units), the average speed of these columns was very poor. They seemed highly vulnerable to air attack.

Among these convoys there was a great deal of artillery in evidence, and all the pieces, unlike their crews, looked extremely clean and well looked-after. None of the pieces we noticed were of greater caliber than 105 mm howitzers. Most of the tanks were T34s, but there were German, British and U.S. tanks in evidence also. The T34 chassis was used predominantly to carry SP artillery. It looks like a good tank, low silhouette and broad tracks, but the tracks are often much too loose. We believe we saw some of the Stalin tanks, and their guns make them look more impressive than the Panther and Tiger even. However, most Russian workmanship is not by far as highly polished as ours, though all the weapons, despite their rough workmanship, seem serviceable and good enough to do the job. The Russian soldier has a great many varieties of small arms, with Submachine guns very much predominant. The Submachine guns were similar to the British drum-type Tommy gun. The pistols were a little like our 45s, but of coarser workmanship. Rifles were long and of all types, very often. We saw hardly any Russians wearing helmets. Their uniforms are very colorful, often very dirty, and not very uniform. We saw a disproportionately large number of officers, and a great many woman-soldiers and some woman tank-drivers. There were also a great many woman "co-travelers." Discipline in the "garrison" sense of the word was absent. Truck drivers don't seem to have much mechanical know-how, since tires are often abandoned simply because they are punctured. Lend-Lease trucks look very well taken care of.

We met units of the two Polish armies fighting with the Red Army. The men are all well-dressed, well-disciplined and their convoys appear well-organized. They are a very good-looking outfit, with officers apparently capable and efficient. However, they do not have the Russian's reverence for the machine, and cavalry units were very large within Polish units that we saw.

In NAUEN, about half-way to Berlin, we found a group of American and British PWs, who are in none too good shape. Six of them, seriously injured fliers, had no medical attention worth speaking of, and we have dispatched an ambulance this morning to pick them up. The others were deliriously happy to see us. It seems that what Russian MG [Military Government] there is has not been able to help them at all, and it is most urgent to send out some trucks or make some arrangements with the Russians to pick up our men before they starve. Most of them are trying to make for the ELBE, but Russian guards along the roads are stopping them. It is only fair to mention that we are also trying to discourage such homeward traffic by Russians and Poles in our area. But food conditions among our men are bad. Many of them repeat rumors of Russian atrocities, but we were unable to verify any of them—we didn't try to, in any case. However, the German population seems desperately cowed and frightened. Most of them don't talk at all, but one or two said to us that "we came too late." In this context it might be worth mentioning that the Russians make them sweep the streets of all towns-a repetition in reverse of what the Germans did to thousands of Jews all over Europe. This mania for clean streets is rather amusing, since there is very little apparent attempt to clean up the serious obstacles—such as broken down vehicles and collapsed buildings and bridges. However, it is obvious that the Russians are making the master-race work and they have made their slaves work for all these years.

On approaching Berlin itself, we found more and more evidence of serious, close-hand combat, with many tanks knocked out and a great many 88s abandoned. Tanks had apparently been knocked out by *Panzerfausts* primarily, though there were some German 50mm AT guns and, of course, the 88s. STAAKEN airfield, just outside Berlin, is being

used by the Red Air Force, and we saw about a dozen biplanes (obviously artillery observation planes) and a great many blue-painted, modern-looking fighters—similar to the Hurricane but somewhat smaller. There were also some C–47s with Red Air Force markings. The Air Force organization, what we saw of it, seems good.

The suburbs of Berlin are about 50% livable, though practically every house has some machine-gun damage and blown-out windows. The racecourse at RUHLEBEN is pretty badly smashed, and the Olympic Games arena (we saw it from a distance) is damaged by shell fire at least. There is a great deal of evidence of serious bombing by the RAF and USAAF, with the former's bombing apparently more terrible from what civilians say. We first entered along the Hamburger Chausse, which showed the usual damage and wreckage, then found that we could not cross the bridge into Berlin (it was blocked by dozens of wrecked trolley cars), and we took the Charlottenburger and Spandauer Chaussee to enter the city. After passing the Luisen Schloss on our left, we turned off to the south along the Kaiser Friedrich Strasse. From the moment we crossed the bridge into Berlin we found ourselves in a tremendous pile of rubble. Every single house, without exaggeration, had been, first bombed, then shelled, and finally machine-gunned. The Luisen Schloss no longer exists. Neither does the Spandauer Chaussee. After we turned south, we hit what used to be the Bismarck Strasse. The Deutsche Opernhaus (German Opera) is wrecked. The Knie Square is unrecognizable. The Technische Hochschule (Polytechnic School) is non-existent. The Hardenberg Strasse, near which this writer was born, is beyond recognition. We continued toward the Grosse Stern Square, and into the Tiergarten. Mines and what sounded like small caliber artillery was still going off from inside this central Park of Berlin—but the detonations were infrequent. The Park is a battlefield, with heavy and medium artillery pieces strewn around grotesquely, and remnants of pillboxes smashed and adorned with twisted reinforcing rods. The Siegessäule (Column of victory), which we were now approaching, still stood, but its stern was cracked with artillery and its base chipped with bombs. The angel of victory on its top was waving a red flag. We were now directed by a woman police guard in Red Army uniform to take a right turn, and passed down toward the residential and embassy section of the Tiergarten. The Japanese Embassy still was there, though it had lost quite a lot of facade, but the staff was still operating it—more or less. The Italian Embassy next door was a shambles also. Farther on, some of the old government buildings were still recognizable by the general shape of their foundation walls.

On reaching the former Hermann Goering Strasse we again turned north and came to the Brandenburger Gate. The Nazis, in a rather idiotic gesture of defiance, had put an anti-tank barrier across it, which was now being hacked away by German civilians. The Gate itself is shell marked, but the Pariser Square beyond it is gone. The Adlon Hotel—the former Waldorf-Astoria of Berlin—is a burned out shell, half smashed, the rest blackened with smoke. We had now reached Unter-den-Linden, which had become a large parking area for Red Army vehicles. Civilians were sweeping the streets, and erecting Red Army propaganda posters in its center.

The entire complex of government buildings along Unter den Linden is no more. Neither are the Linden trees. Goebbels' Propaganda Ministry has gone the way of all propaganda. The Kaiser's elaborate Palace, the famous Zeughaus (a museum-like arsenal) are wrecked and their contents destroyed. The facades all along the street are smashed by high explosives. The broad square in front of the "Ehrenmal"— a kind of German Cenotaph, is destroyed, and the little Memorial building itself, where the Nazis had their elaborate parades and goose stepped to the sound of drums and guns and planes, is grotesquely shot to pieces, its little columns knocked out from under its roof. The Berlin Dome beyond it has had its cupola knocked off, and Red Army recruits are doing close order drill in front of the

Kaiser Wilhelm Palace—or what remains of it. Somewhere along the road lies a bronze statue of what seemed to be Frederick the Great, though since his nose was in the dust identification was difficult.

We turned back, and made for the Wilhelm Strasse. Hitler's old Chancellery, to which he added a new wing, is burned out and wrecked. The fantastic new Chancellery somewhere up along the road is relatively unharmed; it merely lost a couple of wings, and its interior seems burned out, but Russian soldiers were using parts of it as an aid station and for barracks. The golden eagles in front of the building have been partly shot off their pompous pedestals, and the balcony from which the Fuehrer used to survey his cohorts is hanging from the merest of supports, with its center, where Hitler stood once, knocked out by a shell. Two Germans were erecting a Red Army propaganda poster right in front of the building.

The Reichstag, whose cupola we saw on our return, has a red flag flying from its top. Down along the Charlottenburger Chaussee, some two hundred yards west of the Brandenburger Gate, Red Army soldiers were building a tremendous reviewing stand. They said that they expected a parade around May 27, and hoped Marshal Stalin would be present. German civilians were sweeping the streets in front of the new structure.

We turned back, taking the same route along which we had come originally. Outside Berlin, the traffic jams were still clogging up the MSR. We finally made our way back to the ELBE just before darkness came.

Among the observations we made during this trip we would like to stress the following particularly:

1. Our party was not readily recognized by the Russians. We were the first Americans they had seen, and though our jeep was familiar to them, our uniforms and helmets, generally speaking, were not. We had no American flag, so that we made ourselves known by signs and by answering "Amerikansk" whenever questioned. This usually released a stream of obviously benevolent greetings, endless handshakes and everything else including embraces. All without exceptions were very glad to see us, and two Russian officers insisted on taking pictures of us—the cameras were German, but we do not know for certain whether there was any film in them. In the middle of the Unter den Linden a Russian officer treated us to a large-sized glass of excellent rum. Whenever we were stopped for identification, the word "Amerikanski" would be a magic "Open Sesame." Everyone was very genuinely happy to see us, and we found no mistrust or unfriendliness. However, it is suggested for all future travelers' benefit that an American flag, as large as possible, be flown from their jeep. The Red Army soldiers like the sound of small arms fire.

2. Traffic control, while poor on the country roads, was excellent within Berlin, where Red Army Policewomen gesticulated wildly and smartly with a yellow and a red flag, and directed us firmly to wherever they wanted us to go. However, we were in no sense "made to see only certain things"—we could go anywhere we pleased, and did. The yellow and red signals, incidentally, are apparently of little consequence. We did not understand them when we entered Berlin, and we understand them less now.

3. Morale of the Red Army soldiers seems excellent. They sing, drink, make love and generally turn the war into a kind of carnival, in which traffic jams and road blocks are matters of very little importance.

4. Their artillery is often well dispersed, has rubber tires, and when self-propelled, looks very formidable and heavy. There is a great deal of it. Camouflage using natural concealment, is practiced very extensively. We saw several large Red Army units bivouac in the woods or make their way into a wooded area to escape possible aerial observation.

In conclusion, we would like to say that from all evidence, and from talking with many Red Army officers in Berlin, it appears that we were the first U. S. Army men to enter the German capital since its capitulation.

Charles K. Twohey
Capt.
Peter J. Blake
2nd Lt.   AUS

The above report is supplemented with the following interview conducted in the early 1960s. The first part is the interviewer's comments on Blake's recollections, followed by direct comments from Blake.

About half way to Berlin, at the town of Nauen, which had been the principal site for radio Berlin during the war, Blake ran across many American prisoners of war who had been in the area since they'd been captured in Africa. The PWs took Blake to a nearby hospital which held six very badly wounded U.S. fliers. (These are the fliers for whom Blake sent back an ambulance.) The GI/PWs had moved into various German houses throughout the town of Nauen. Blake asked if they wanted to go back with him across the Elbe and they thought that was a fine idea. But when Blake returned from Berlin the Americans all said they'd better stay. Blake asked why and the Americans said that they thought that their staying in the town would provide the German families who had sheltered them with some measure of protection from the Russians. The PWs had put lists of all the inhabitants of the people in each house on the doors and had hung makeshift American flags under the lists. The PWs were quite serious about staying and they said that when they had started to pack up the various German families had all tried to kill themselves and so the Americans decided to stay. (Later, these Americans all were reported to have made their way back to the Elbe and to the American side of the river.)

Another incident that Blake does not mention in his report was his impression of the general sense of demoralization of the Red Army. As Blake recalls it, there were sentries with sub-machine-guns at every roadblock. The only problem being that almost every sentry was blind drunk. They would point their guns at the stomach of anybody who approached them and Blake believes that they were totally incapable of making an intelligent decision. The traffic jams involving the Russian Army were fantastic. Bridge after bridge was blown and Blake would see Russian Generals arguing violently with ordinary GIs as to how the bridges could best be repaired.

Blake's comments follow:

"You simply cannot imagine what a mess it was," says Blake, "the chaos was fantastic. This was an army that could have been destroyed by 20 planes. Other things you were very conscious of were (1) the drunkenness, (2) the lack of discipline, (3) and the terribly brutality that the Russians showed towards their own people. We saw many wagons that were loaded with badly wounded- Russians. In some cases you could tell that the wounded had just been tossed on without any regard to their injuries. In other cases the wounded were strapped to the sides of tanks. If they died, they were simply rolled into a ditch. Most of the Red Army troops were from what I believe to be Asiatic areas and they were particularly curious about the Chinese soldier that was with me. There were still some bodies in the streets of Berlin when we got there. We were stopped by the Russians in the Tiergarten, and they offered us excellent brandy. We could still hear sporadic firing or it might have been land mines [see report above]. But I couldn't tell if there was any fighting still going on. As we drove off, one of the Russians stepped off the road onto the grass and there was an explosion. He fell over. We didn't stop to see if he had been wounded by the mine or whatever because we thought it would be best if we got out of there before we could be linked to an incident. The Chancellery and the Bunker areas were surrounded by Russian guards and it was impossible for us to go near them. The city of Berlin has always had an unusual odor. It's surrounded by pine forests and one could always notice the scent of the pine trees. Now it smelled like pine trees on fire and you could smell smoke drifting through the town. The most noticeable thing about the destruction of the city were the number of smashed self-propelled guns and tanks. Many were still on fire right in the middle of town. All through the city you could see completely wrecked tanks around which German women were sweeping and clearing the road. My evaluation of the fighting was that it was either very intense or the Russians simply went wild. Almost every wall had a spray of bullet holes on it.

From my judgment, the concentration of Russian troops was such that it appeared that they would attack to the west across the Elbe. Their dispersion, their camouflage, everything pointed to that. There was quite a bit of Russian artillery on railroad flat cars. And we were very conscious of the fact that we weren't supposed to be there so we made no effort to examine the Russian's emplacements. On the other hand of course it could have been simply the massing of troops in preparation for guerilla warfare. After all, that was what the Russians had done to the Germans and the Russians could expect the same in return. All of Berlin was full of big posters containing Stalin's quote: "Hitlers come, Hitlers go, but the German people will remain forever."

From the very beginning, I noticed that the Russians spread the story throughout Berlin that the major part of the damage had been done by the United States and British Air Forces. This was obviously an attempt to swing German public opinion towards the Russians.[1]

Blake's recollections in the 1960s provide more colour to his Berlin visit than officially contained by his joint report with Twohey in 1945. Blake's observations highlight significant issues of morale in the victorious Soviet Army at the time. In addition, he confirms—as an independent third party—the ferocity of fighting in Berlin, recounted in the previous pages by both German and Russian veterans.

Note to Appendix A

1   Ryan Collection, Box 46.

APPENDIX B

SOVIET ORDER OF BATTLE

The Soviet order of battle (OB) for the 'Berlin Strategic Offensive Operation' is immense. The listing below is not meant to be all inclusive of every formation that participated in the assault. Hundreds of rifle divisions, tank brigades, and artillery regiments took part in the assault. In order to keep the Soviet OB manageable, all Soviet Armies are detailed down to corps only, except for the 1st Byelorussian and 1st Ukrainian Fronts. I elected to detail the OB for these two Fronts down to division, tank and self-propelled (SP) artillery regiments for those armies that fought inside Berlin. I chose not to detail artillery units due to the large number of these units assigned to each Soviet Army. A few additional comments are in order. 'Self-propelled artillery' typically refers to the range of medium and heavy anti-tank armor like the SU–76 or ISU–152 models. They are referenced here because of their dual role as both anti-tank and indirect fire systems.

2ND BYELORUSSIAN FRONT – Marshal K. K. Rokossovskii

2nd Shock Army – Col Gen I.I. Fedyurinsky
    108th, 116th Rifle Corps
65th Army – Col Gen P.I. Batov
    18th, 46th, 105th Rifle Corps.
70th Army – Col Gen V.S Popov
    47th, 96th, 114th Rifle Corps
49th Army – Col Gen I.T. Grishin
    70th, 121st Rifle Corps
19th Army
    40th Guards, 132nd, 134th Rifle Corps
5th Guards Tank Army
    29th Tank Corps
4th Air Army – Col Gen K.A. Vershinin
    4th Air Assault, 5th Air Bomber, 8th Air Fighter Corps.

1ST BYELORUSSIAN FRONT – Marshal G. K. Zhukov

61st Army – Col Gen P.A. Belov
    9th Guards Rifle Corps – Lt. Gen. G.a. Halyuzin / Lt Gen A.D. Shtemenko
        12th, 75th Guards, 415th Rifle Divisions
    80th Rifle Corps – Maj Gen V.A. Vyerzhbitsky
        212th, 234th, 356th Rifle Divisions
    89th Rifle Corps – Maj Gen M.A. Siyzov
        23rd, 311th, 397th Rifle Divisions
1st Polish Army – Lt Gen S.G. Poplowski
    1st Polish Infantry Division 'Tadiuscz Kosciuszko'
    2nd, 3rd, 4th & 6th Polish Infantry Divisions
        4th Heavy Tank Regiment
        13th Self-propelled Artillery Regiment
        7th Independent Self-propelled Artillery Battalion
47th Army – Lt. Gen F.I Perkhorovitch
    77th Rifle Corps – Maj Gen / Lt Gen Y.S. Vorobyev
        185th, 260th, 328th Rifle Divisions
    125th Rifle Corps – Maj Gen / Lt Gen A.M. Andreyev
        60th, 76th, 175th Rifle Divisions
    129th Rifle Corps– Maj Gen / Lt Gen M.B Anashkin
        82nd, 132nd, 143rd Rifle Divisions
    70th Guards Heavy Tank Regiment
    334th Guards Heavy Self-propelled Artillery Regiment

    1204th, 1416th, 1825th, 1892nd Self-propelled Artillery Regiments
3rd Shock Army – Col Gen V.I. Kutznetsov
    7th Rifle Corps – Maj Gen V.A. Christov / Col Gen Y.T. Chyervichenko
        146th, 265th, 364th Rifle Divisions
    12th Guards Rifle Corps – Lt Gen A.F. Kazanin / Maj Gen A.A. Filatov
        23rd Guards, 52nd Guards, 33rd Rifle Divisions
    79th Rifle Corps – Maj Gen S.L. Perevertkin
        150th, 171st, 207th Rifle Divisions
    1203rd, 1728th, 1729th Self-propelled Artillery Regiments
5th Shock Army – Gen / Col Gen N.E. Berzarin
    9th Rifle Corps – Maj Gen / Lt Gen I.P. Rossly
        230th, 248th, 301st Rifle Divisions
    26th Guards Corps – Maj Gen P.A. Firsov
        89th Guards, 94th Guards, 266th Rifle Divisions
    32nd Rifle Corps – Lt Gen D.S. Zherebin
        60th Guards, 295th, 416th Rifle Divisions
    220th Tank Brigade
    89th Guards Heavy Tank Regiment
    92nd Engineer Tank Regiment
    396th Guards Heavy Self-propelled Artillery Regiment
    274th Independent Motorized Battalion
8th Guards Army – Col Gen V.I. Chuikov
    4th Guards Rifle Corps – Lt Gen V.A. Glazonov
        35th Guards, 47th Guards, 57th Guards Rifle Divisions
    28th Guards Rifle Corps – Lt Gen V.M. Shugeyev
        39th Guards, 79th Guards, 88th Guards Rifle Divisions
    29th Guards Rifle Corps – Maj Gen P.I. Zalizyuk
        27th Guards, 74th Guards, 82nd Guards Rifle Divisions
69th Army – Col Gen V.Y. Kolpakchi
    25th Rifle Corps
        77th Guards, 4th Rifle Divisions
    61st Rifle Corps
        134th, 246th, 247th Rifle Divisions
    91st Rifle Corps
        117th, 283rd Rifle Divisions
33rd Army – Col Gen V.D. Svotaev
    16th Rifle Corps
        323rd, 339th, 383rd Rifle Divisions
    38th Rifle Corps of
        64th, 89th, 169th Rifle Divisions

62nd Rifle Corps
    49th, 22nd, 362nd Rifle Divisions
2nd Guards Cavalry Corps
    3rd, 4th, 17th Guards Cavalry Divisions
16th Air Army – Col Gen S.I. Rudenko
    6th & 9th Air Assault Corps
    3rd & 6th Air Bomber Corps
    1st Guards, 3rd, 6th, 13th Air Fighter Corps
18th Air Army – AVM A.Y. Golovanov
    1st Guards, 2nd, 3rd, 4th Air Bomber Corps

Mobile Forces
1st Guards Tank Army – Col Gen M.Y. Katukov
    8th Guards Mechanized Corps – Maj Gen I.F. Drygemov
        19th, 20th, 21st Guards Mechanized Brigades
        1st Guards Tank Brigade
        48th Guards Heavy Tank Regiment
        353rd Guards Heavy Self-propelled Artillery Regiment
        400th Guards Self-propelled Artillery Regiment
    11th Guards Tank Corps – Col A. H. Babadshanian
        40th, 44th, 45th Guards Tank Brigades
        27th Guards Motorized Rifle Brigade
        350th Light Artillery Regiment
        362nd, 399th Guards Heavy Self-propelled Artillery Regiments
    11th Tank Corps – Maj Gen I.I. Jushuk
        20th, 36th, 65th Tank Brigades
        12th Motorized Rifle Brigade
        50th Guards Heavy Tank Regiment
        1071st Light Artillery Regiment
        1461st, 1493rd Self-propelled Artillery Regiments
2nd Guards Tank Army – Col Gen S.I. Bogdanov
    1st Mechanized Corps – Lt. Gen S. I. Krivosheina
        19th, 35th, 37th Mechanized Brigades
        219th Tank Brigade
        347th Guards Heavy Self-propelled Artillery Regiment
        75th, 1822nd Self-propelled Artillery Regiment
    9th Guards Tank Corps – Maj Gen A.F. Popov
        47th, 50th, 65th Guards Tank Brigades
        33rd Guards Motorized Rifle Brigade
        1643rd Light Artillery Regiment
        341st Guards Heavy Self-propelled Artillery Regiment
        369th & 386th Guards SP Artillery Regiment
    12th Guards Tank Corps – Maj Gen M.K. Teltakov/Col A. T. Shevchenko
        48th, 49th, & 66th Guards Tank Brigades
        34th Guards Motorized Rifle Brigade
        79th Guards Heavy Tank Regiment
        283rd Guards Light Artillery Regiment
        387th, 393rd Guards Self-propelled Artillery Regiments

FRONT RESERVES

3rd Army – Col Gen A.V. Gorbatov
    35th, 40th, 41st Rifle Corps
    2nd, 3rd, 7th Guards Cavalry, 3rd Guards, 8th Guards Tank Corps

1ST UKRAINIAN FRONT – Marshal I.S. Koniev

3rd Guards Army – Col Gen V.N. Gordov
    21st 76th, 120th Rifle Corps
    25th Tank Corps
13th Army – Col Gen N.P. Phukov
    24th, 27th, 102nd Rifle Corps
5th Guards Army – Col Gen A.S. Zhadov
    32nd, 33rd, 34th Guards Rifle Corps
    4th Guards Tank Corps
2nd Polish Army – Lt Gen K.K. Swierszczewski
    5th, 7th, 8th, 9th, 10th Polish Infantry Divisions
    1st Polish Tank Corps
52nd Army – Col Gen K.A. Koroteyev
    48th, 73rd, 78th Rifle Corps
    7th Guards Mechanized Corps
2nd Air Army – Col Gen S.A. Krasovsky
    1st Guards, 2nd Guards, 3rd Air Assault Corps
    4th, 6th Guards Air Bomber Corps
    2nd, 5th, 6th Air Fighter Corps

Mobile Forces
3rd Guards Tank Army – Col Gen P.S. Rybalko
    6th Guards Tank Corps – Maj Gen V.A. Mitrofanov
        51st, 52nd, 53rd, Guards Tank Brigades
        22nd Guards Motorized Rifle Brigade
        385th Guards, 1893rd, 1894th, Self-propelled Assault Artillery Regiments
    7th Guards Tank Corps – Maj Gen V.V. Novikov
        54th, 55th, 56th, Guards Tank Brigades
        23rd Guards Motorized Rifle Brigade
        384th Guards, 702nd, 1977th Self-propelled Assault Artillery Regiment
    9th Mechanized Corps – Lt Gen I.P. Suchov
        69th, 70th, 71st Mechanized Brigades
        91st Tank Brigade
        383rd Guards, 1507th, 1978th Self-propelled Assault Artillery Regiments
    16th Self-propelled Artillery Brigade
    57th Guards, 90th Independent Tank regiments
4th Guards Tank Army – Col Gen D.D. Lelyushenko
    5th, 6th Guards Mechanized Corps
    10th Guards Tank Corps

FRONT RESERVES

28th Army – Lt. Gen A.A. Luchinsky
    20th, 38th Guards, 128th Rifle Corps
31st Army – Lt Gen V.K. Baranov
1st Guards Cavalry Corps

APPENDIX C

GERMAN ORDER OF BATTLE

An accurate accounting of all formations that fought in and around Berlin is simply impossible due to the lack of primary documents. Many units were *ad-hoc* or *Kampfgruppe* formed from training units, or stragglers, and named after their senior commander then thrown into battle against the Soviets. Many of these units didn't survive the first attack, and those that did retreated until they were absorbed by a different unit, under a different commander's name. The German order of battle is detailed below down to division level for all major formations. Those units that fought inside Berlin are detailed down to regiment and battalion where appropriate.

HEERESGRUPPE VISTULA (Army Group Vistula)– Generaloberst Gotthard Heinrici

3.Panzer Armee – General Hasso von Manteuffel
    'Swinemunde' Korps – General Ansat
        402., 2.Naval Divisions
    XXXII Korps – General Schack
        'Voigt' Infanterie Division
        549.Volksgrenadier Division
        Stettin Garrison
        281.Infanterie Division
    'Oder' Korps – SS Obergruppenführer von dem Bach/Gen Hörnlein
        610., 'Klossek' Infanterie Divisions
    XXXXVI Panzer Korps – General Martin Gareis
        547.Volksgrenadier Division
        1.Naval Division
9.Armee – General Theodor Busse
    CI Korps – General Wilhelm Berlin/General Friedrich Sixt
        5.Jäger Infanterie Division
        606.Infanterie Division
        309.'Berlin' Infanterie Division
        25.Panzergrenadier Division
        '1001 Nights' Kampfgruppe
    LVI.Panzer Korps – General Helmuth Weidling
    9.Fallschirmjäger Division – General Bruno Braüer / Col Harry Hermann
        25, 26, 27.Fallschirmjäger Regiments
        9.Fallschirmjäger Artillerie Abteilung
        9.Panzerjäger Abteilung
    20.Panzergrenadier Division – Generalleutnant Georg Scholze
        76., 90.Panzergrenadier Regiments
        8.Panzer Abteilung
        20.Artilerie Regiment
    'Müncheberg' Panzer Division – Maj Gen Werner Mummert
        1., 2.'Müncheberg' Panzergrenadier Regiments
        I/29.Panzer Regiment
            1., 2.Panzer Abteilung
        920.Döberitz Panzerjäger Brigade
    XI SS Panzer Korps – SS Obergruppenführer Mathias Kleinheisterkamp
        303.'Döberitz' Infantry Division
        169.Infantry Division
        712.Infantry Division
        'Kurmark' Panzergrenadier Division

    V SS Mountain Korps – Oberstgruppenführer Friedrich Jackeln
        286.Infanterie Division
        32.SS '30. January' Volksgrenadier Division
        391.Sy Division

Frankfurt an der Oder Garrison – Generalleutnant Ernst Biehler

Army Reserve
    156.Infanterie Division
    541.Volksgrenadier Division
    404.Volks Artillery Korps
    406. Volks Artillery Korps
    408.Volks Artillery Korps

Army Group Reserve
III.SS-Germanic Panzer Korps – SS Obergruppenführer Felix Steiner (divisions later allocated to the 9.Armee)
    11.SS- Nordland Panzergrenadier Division – SS Gruppenführer Joachim
    Ziegler / Gruppenführer Dr Gustav Krukenberg
        23.Panzergrenadier Regiment Norge
        24.Panzergrenadier Regiment Danmark
        11.SS Hermann von Salza Panzer Abteilung
        s.SS.503.Panzer Abteilung
    23.SS-Nederland Panzergrenadier Division – SS-Gruppenführer Wagner
    (divisions later allocated to the 3.Panzer Armee)
        27.SS-Langemarck Grenadier Division
        28.SS-Wallonien Grenadier Division

OKW Reserve (later allocated to the LVI Panzer Corps, 9.Armee)
18.Panzergrenadier Division – Generalleutnant Josef Rauch
    30.Panzergrenadier Regiment
    51.Panzergrenadier Regiment
    118.Panzer Regiment
    18.Artilerie Regiment

12.Armee – General Walther Wenck
    XX Korps – General Carl-Erik Kohler
        'Theodor Körner' RAD Division
        'Ulrich von Hutten' Infanterie Division
        'Ferdinand von Schill' Infanterie Division
        'Schamhorst' Infanterie Division
    Sturmgeschütz Brigade 1170
    XXXIX Panzer Korps – General Karl Arndt
        'Clausewitz' Panzer Division
        'Schlageter' RAD Division
        84.Infanterie Division

XXXXI Panzer Korps – General Holste
  'von Hake' Infanterie Division
  199th Infanterie Division
  'V-Weapons' Infanterie Division
XXXXVIII Panzer Korps – General Maximillian Reichsherr von Edelscheim
  14.Flak Division
  'Leipzig' Kampfgruppe
  'Halle' Kampfgruppe

HEERESGRUPPE MITTE – Generalfeldmarschall Ferdinand Schörner

4.Panzer Armee – General Fritz-Herbert Gräser
  (later transferred to the 9.Armee)
  V.Korps – General Wagner
    35.SS-Police Grenadier Division
    36.SS-Grenadier Division
    275.Infanterie Division
    342.Infanterie Division
    21.Panzer Division

Ungrouped Formations

'Friedrich Ludwig Jahn' RAD Division – Oberst Gerhard Klein / Oberst Franz Weller (Remnants made their way to Armee Detachment Spree in Potsdam)
  'Potsdam' Infanterie Division – Oberst Erich Lorenz
  Kampfgruppe Möws
  Kampfgruppe Kaether
  II./ Panzer Regiment.36
  4./ Panzer-Regiment.11
  Panzergreandier-Kompanie Ülzen
  Panzer-Kompanie Kummendsdorf
  Panzerjäger-Kompanie Dresden
  schwere Panzerjäger-Kompanie.614

Kampfgruppe Ritter (Consolidated the remaining forces Kampfgruppe Möws and Kaether after their destruction on 22 April)

FORTRESS BERLIN

Volkssturm and Hitlerjugend Formations
  3., 16., 17., 39., 93., 103., 107., 109., 121., 205., 260., 721.,Volkssturm Bataillons
  57.Fortress Regiment
  3./115 Siemenstadt Volkssturm Abteilung
  2./Fortress Regiment 60
  Skorning Kampfgruppe
  Kampfgruppe Rossbach
  Hitlerjugend Gruppe 200
  Kampfgruppe Thiemer
SS Formations
  Leibstandarte SS Adolf Hitler (LSSAH) Wachregiment
  1./SS-Regiment 'Anhalt'
  2./SS-Regiment
  Leibstandarte SS Adolf Hitler (LSSAH) Ausbildungs-und Ersatz Bataillon
  Führer-Begleit-Kompanie
  Reichsführer SS-Begleit Bataillon
Other Combat Formations
  Wachregiment Grossdeutschland
Luftwaffe Formations
  1.Flak Division
  Kampfgruppe Müller (sent from Döberitz Training Area on 22 April into the northern suburbs of Spandau)
  Panzerjäger Brigade Krampnitz
  Pioneer Abteilung 968
  Machine-gun Abteilung116
  Regiment Solar (arrived on 22 April)
  Sturmbataillon Charlemagne (arrived on 24 April)
  Bataillon Fantasma (Spanish SS volunteers already in Berlin)
  SS-FusilierBattaillon15(Latvian volunteers)

APPENDIX D

MILITARY OFFICER RANKS

NATO	*Wehrmacht*	Waffen-SS
General of the Armies	*Reichsmarschall des Großdeutschen Reiches*	
General of the Army	*Generalfeldmarschall*	Reichsführer-SS
General	*Generaloberst*	Oberstgruppenführer
Lieutenant General	*General*	Obergruppenführer
Major General	*Generalleutnant*	Gruppenführer
Brigadier General	*Generalmajor*	Brigadeführer
Colonel	*Oberst*	Standartenführer
Lieutenant Colonel	*Oberstleutnant*	Obersturmbannführer
Major	*Major*	Sturmbannführer
Captain	*Hauptmann*	Hauptsturmführer
First Lieutenant	*Oberleutnant*	Obersturmführer
Second Lieutenant	*Leutnant*	Untersturmführer

BIBLIOGRAPHY

Primary Documents

US National Archives, College Park, Maryland

Record Group 226: Interagency Working Group (IWG), Boxes 440–442
Box 440
    NO 135 *"Possibility of Anglo-German Agreement March 1945"*
Box 441
    NO 841 *"German View of American Russian Relations Jan 1945"*
    NO 855 *"German view of Yalta Conference"*
    NO 880 *"German Evaluation of Allied Military Affairs Feb 1945"*
    NO 905 *"German account of Decisions Reached at Yalta Conference"*
Box 442
    NO 969 *"German Discussion of Yalta Conference Results"*
    NO 975 *"German Information on Yalta Decision"*
    NO 986 *"German Attitude Toward Alleged British Policy on Disagreement at Yalta."*

Record Group 242: National Archives Collection of Foreign Records Seized
T77 Records of Headquarters, German Armed Forces High Command (Oberkommando der Wehrmacht/OKW)
T78 Records of Headquarters, German Armed Forces High Command (Oberkommando der Heeres/OKH)
T311 Records of German Field Commands: Armies
T313 Records of German Field Commands: Panzer Armies
Record Group 331: Records of Allied Operational and Occupational Headquarters, World War II, 1907–1966, Supreme Headquarters Allied Expeditionary Force. G–2 Division.

Aerial Imagery
Flight Can #ON017070: Image Number 4013, 4305, 4309
Flight Can #ON017062: Image Number 3069, 3073, 3074, 3075, 3081
Flight Can #ON017056: Image Number 3202
Flight Can #ON017082: Image Number 3078
Flight Can #ON014065: 4176, 4175, 4177, 4172
Army Battle Casualties and Non-Combat Deaths in World War II, Final Report (Washington, D.C., Statistical and Accounting Branch of the office of the Adjutant General, Department of the U.S. Army: 1946)
MS # P–136 The German Defense of Berlin by Wilhelm Wilmer, Oberst a.d. (Historical Division, United States Army, Europe, 1953)
MS # D–189 The Pomeranian Battle and Command in the East (Historical Division, United States Army Europe, 1947)

Bundesarchiv-Militärarchiv, Freiburg, Germany
RH 10–173 *Panzerdivision Müncheberg*
RH 19 XV *Heeresgruppe Weichsel*
RH 20–9 *9. Armee*
RH 24–56 *LVI. Armeekorps*
RH 26–309 *309. Infanteriedivision bzw. Infanteriedivision Groâdeutschland*
RH 27–20 *20. Panzerdivision*
RH 27–18 *18. Panzerdivision*
RS 4 *Brigaden, Bataillons und Verbände der Waffen-SS*
RS 3–11 *11. SS-Freiwilligen Panzer-grenadier-Division (Nordland)*
RS 3–15 *15. Waffen-Grenadierdivision der SS (lett. Nr.1)*

Cornelius Ryan Collection, Mahn Center, Alden Library, Ohio University, Athens, OH

German Forces

Box 61
Folder 5
    Berlin districts by Army command
    Chronological listing of days and dates
    Organization of 3rd SS Panzer Corps, Apr 23, 1945

Folder 7
  Willemer, Wilhelm, "The German Defense of Berlin", OCMH, MS #P- 136

Box 62
Folder 2
  Bauer, Magna, "Ninth Army's Last Attack and Surrender Apr 21 – May 7, 1945", OCMH, MS #R–79, Apr, 1956
Folder 3
  Bauer, Magna, "The End of Army Group Weichsel and Twelfth Army, Apr 27 – May 7, 1945", OCNH, MS #R–69, June, 1956
Folder 5
  German messages, field commands and main events, Apr 20–29, 1945
Folder 6–7
  Army Group Weichsel war diary, Apr 20–29, 1945
Folder 8
  OKW messages and documents listing, Feb-Mar, 1945
Folder 9
  OKM messages, Apr 26 – May 15, 1945

Box 64
Folder 1
  OKW documents and messages, Feb – Apr, 1945
Folder 2–3
  Army Group Weichsel war diary, Apr 20–29, 1945
Box 65
  National (Alpine) Redoubt.
Folder 2
  Newspaper articles
Folder 3
  With 12th Army Group's Reorientation of Strategy, Mar 21, 1945
Folder 4
  Hq, 7th Army, G–2 Study on National Redoubt, Mar 25, 1945
Folder 5
  Hofer, Franz, "National Redoubt", OCMH, MS #B–458
Folder 6
  "The Alpine Defense-Line"/"The Alpine- Fortification", OCMH, MS #B-Folder 7
  Von Hengel, Georg R., "The Alpine Redoubt", OCMH, MS #B–461
Folder 8
  Von Hengel, Georg R., "Report on the Alpine Fortress", OCMH, MS #B–459
  Hitler's Bunker.
Folder 9
  Maps and floor plans of Fuhrerbunker
  Fuhrer messages and directives concerning defense of Berlin and transfer of command to Doenitz

Box 66
Folder 1
  Kratschmar, Heinz, Interview
Folder 2
  Lohmann, Hanns-Heinrich, Interview
Folder 3
  Voss, Lt Peter, Interview
  Hitler's Court.
Folder 15
  Erickson, "Conclusions re Hitler's death"
Folder 30
  Hitler files.
  Hitler: Forms for marriage
  Hitler: Political testament
  Hitler: Private will
  Hitler: Will

Box 67
OKW
Folder 1
  Schramm, Percy (ed), Excerpts from WAR DIARY OF THE ARMY HIGH COMMAND, v.4
Folder 5
  Schultz, Maj Joachim, "War Diary of Hq North (A)", Apr 20 – May 23
  Schultz, "The Battle for Berlin"
Berlin Command.

Folder 10
    Lampe, Lt Albrecht, Interview
Folder 11
    Refior, Col Hans, Interview
    Refior, "My Berlin Diary"
Folder 12
    Reymann, Gen Hellmuth, Interview
    Reymann, "I Had To Defend Berlin"
3.Panzer Armee.
Folder 14
    Muller-Hillebrand, Maj Gen Burkhart, Interview
Folder 15
    Steiner, Gen Felix M., Interview
Folder 16
    Von Manteuffel, Gen Hasso, Interview

Box 67
9.Armee
Folder 17
    Busse, Gen Theodor, Interview
    Busse, "The Last Battle of the 9th Army", MILITARY SCIENCE REVIEW, v.5, #4, Apr, 1955
    Bauer, Magna, "Ninth Army's Last Attack and Surrender", OCMH, MS #R–79
Folder 18
    Fritz, Lt Albert, Interview
    12.Armee.
Folder 23
    Reichhelm, Col Gunther, Interview
    Reichhelm, "The Last Rally: Battles Fought by the German 12th Army in the Heart of Germany, between East and West (13 April – 7 May 1945)", OCMH, MS #B–606, May 31, 1947
Folder 24
    Wenck, Gen Walter, Interview
    Ritter, H.W., "Factual Report of Interviews with General A.D. Walter Wenck"
    "Summary of Final Battles between the Order and Elbe in Apr/May 1945 (Especially the Battles of 12th Army)"
Army Group Weichsel (Vistula).

Box 68
Folder 2
    Eismann, Col Hans G., Interview
Folder 3
    Heinrici, Gen Gotthard, Interview
    Memoirs
    Army Group Weichsel command structure
    Map overlay
    Statement to Chief of Staff, Apr, 1945
    Weapon and equipment lists
Folder 4
    Heinrici diary
    History and account
    Jodl-Heinrici telephone conversation, Apr 26, 1945
    Army Group Weichsel war diary, Apr 20–29, 1945
LVI (56th) Panzer Corps.
Folder 8
    Bottcher, Lt Col Friedrich, Interview

Box 69
Folder 1
    Von Dufving, Col Theodor, Interview
    "Surrender of Berlin Garrison 1st and 2nd May, 1945"
Folder 2
    Weidling, Gen H., Russian interrogations
    Weidling, "The Final Battle in Berlin (April 23 to May 2, 1945", WEHRWISSENSCHAFTLICHE RUNDSCHAU, Jan-Mar, 1962
Folder 3
    Wohlermann, Hans-Oscar, Interview
    Wohlermann, "Commentary on General of the Artillery H. Weidling's: The Final Battle in Berlin", WEHRWISSENSCHAFTLICHE RUNDSCHAU, June, 1962
1st Flak Division.

Folder 8
　Von Zabeltitz, Capt Leonhardt, Interview
9th Paratroop (*Fallschirmjäger*) Division.
Folder 9
　Arnold, Lt Hans- Werner, Interview
Folder 10
　Hirsch, Lt Alfred, Interview
Folder 11
　Jansen, Lt Hans, Interview
Folder 12
　Rein, Lt Hans, Interview
　Nordland Division.
Folder 14
　Bensch, Sgt Willy, Interview
Folder 15
　Burghart, Cpl Roman, Inteview
Folder 18
　Haas, Cpl Fritz, Interview
Folder 19
　Hensler, Lt Hans, Interview
Folder 20
　Illum, Gunnar M., Interview
Folder 23
　Krukenberg, Maj Gen Gustav, Interview
Folder 24
　Scholles, Sgt Hans-Peter, Interview
Folder 25
　Timm, Lt Walter, Interview
Folder 26
　Winge, Pvt Hans-Joachim, Interview

Box 69
Volkssturm.
Folder 30
　Haaf, Oskar, Interview
Folder 33
　Hellriegel, Hermann, Interview
Folder 36
　Wrede, Fritz, Questionnaire Interview
Zoo Flak Tower.
Folder 7
　Ache, Capt Kurt, Interview
Hitler Youth.
Folder 11
　Bonath, PFC Herbert, Interview
Folder 12
　Feldheim, Willy, Interview
Folder 13
　Pienkny, Gunther, Interview
Folder 14
　Schulz, Aribert, Interview
Folder 16
　Wetzki, Hans J., Interview
Cab 81204

Maps.
Draw 8
　Supplement #1 to the report of Col Reichhelm on the battles of the 12th Army, Apr 13 to May 7, 1945: Starting position on Apr 12–13, 1945, scale 1:1,000,000.
　Supplement #2 to the report of Col Reichhelm on the battles of the 12th Army, Apr 13 to May 7, 1945: Starting positions on Apr 24, 1945, and development of enemy positions until Apr 29, 1945, scale 1:1,000,000.
　Supplement #3 to the report of Col Reichhelm on the battles of the 12th Army, Apr 13 to May 7, 1945: Position of the 20th A.K. on Apr 28–29 for regrouping and attack, scale 1:250,000 (2 copies).
　Supplement #4 to the report of Col Reichhelm on the battles of the 12th Army, Apr 13 to May 7, 1945: Position of the 12th Army from May 1 to May 7, 1945, scale 1:250,000.

Soviet Forces

Box 71
Folder 7
Chuikov, Marshal Vasili Ivanovich, Interview
Report from 150th Rifle Division concerning the seizure of the Reichstag
Chuikov, "The Assault on Berlin"
Duka, Maj Gen M., STORMING OF THE SPREE

Box 74
Folder 8
Ehrenburg, Ilya, WE COME AS JUDGES
Ehrenburg, PEOPLE, YEARS, LIFE v.3
Folder 9
Table of contents of SHTURM BERLINA
Red Army Order of Battle, Apr 15, 1945
Bocca, G., "Red Rape: The Final Agony of Berlin," TRUE (12p.),
Box 72
Folder 1
Golbov, Sergei Ivanovich, Interview
Folder 2
Ivanov, Maj Gen Georgy Vasilievich, Interview together with Lt Georgy Vladimirovitch Kilchevsky and Maj Aronvich Lazaris
Folder 3
Koniev, Marshall Ivan Stephanovich, Interview
Koniev, MEMIORS
Account of meeting with Stalin, Apr 1, 1945, from "Forty Five," NOVIY MIR, #5, 1965
Excerpts from THE GREAT FATHERLAND WAR OF THE SOVIET UNION 1941–1945
Folder 8
Neustroyev, Lt Col S.A., THE STORMING OF THE REICHSTAG
Neustroyev, SHTURM BERLINA
Box 74
Folder 10
Platonov, S.P. THE SECOND WORLD WAR 1935–1945
Yedenskii, THE BERLIN OPERATIONS OF THE THIRD SHOCK
Folder 12
Popiel, N. N. FORWARD TO BERLIN
Account of Stalin-Zhukov-Koniev meeting of Apr 1, 1945
Box 73
Folder 2
Notes of Seelow Heights Terrain
Russian book excerpts
Folder 3
Thirteen Leading Soviet War Correspondents, WHAT WE SAW IN BERLIN
Telpuchowski, Boris S., THE SOVIET HISTORY OF THE GERAT FATHERLAND WAR 1941–1945
Folder 4
Orders from the Supreme Soviet Command to Front Commanders, Apr 3–23, 1945
Notes on Russian army structure and officer personnel
SHTURM BERLINA table of contents and order of battle for April 15, 1945

Box 74
Folder 11
Zhukov, Marshal Georgi K., "TAKING BERLIN," MILITARY-HISTORCAL JOURNAL, #6, 1965

Allied Political and Military Leadership

Box 42
Folder 1–2
Allied War Diaries Sept 4, 1944 – June, 1945: messages, memos, reports, minutes between SHAEF and CCS
Folder 3–4
SHAEF files Nov 10, 1943 – Mar 31, 1945: letters, memos, messages, minutes, reports between SHAEF and CCS and SHAEF internal activities
Folder 5
"Report by the Supreme Commander to the Combined Chiefs of State on the Operations in Europe of the Allied Expeditionary Force", Feb 12, 1944

Box 43
Folder 3
> Background paper: "Political Decision-making Machinery for Germany/Berlin Question, with Special Reference to the British Position (1943–45)"
> "Instrument of Unconditional Surrender of Germany to the Supreme Commands of the United States of America, the United Kingdom, and the Union of Soviet Socialist Republics""
> G–3 SHAEF to Chief of Staff, GCT 384.1- 1/Plans, May, 1945, subject: Negotiations for the Surrender
> "Agreement between the Allied High Commands and Certain German Emissaries"
> "Act of Military Surrender"
> "Undertaking Given by Certain German Emissaries to the Allied High Commands"
> "Act of Surrender" (Rheims version)
> "Act of Military Surrender" (Berlin version)

Box B
Folder 7
> Eisenhower, Dwight D., Interview

Box 44
Folder 4
> Gillem, A.C. Interview
Folder 5
> Military orders concerning advance beyond the Elbe River.
> Hq, 9th Army to Corps commanders, Apr 15, 1945, subject: Future Operations
> Hq, 9th Army to Corps commanders, Apr 13, 1945, subject: Current Operations
> Hq, 12th Army, Letter of Instructions Number Twenty, Apr 4, 1945
> Hq, 9th Army, Letter of Instructions Number Nineteen, Apr 7, 1945 with Amendment Number One, Apr 11, 1945
> Hq, 9th Army, Letter of Instructions Number Eighteen, Mar 29, 1945
Operation ECLIPSE.
Folder 6
> SHAEF Appreciation and Outline Plan, Nov 10, 1944
> German translation of captured SHAEF Appreciation and Outline Plan, Nov 10, 1944
> English translation of German copy of captured SHAEF Appreciation and Outline Plan
Cab 81204
Draw 8
> Maps of Berlin, showing zones of occupation, scale 1:12,500, 1950.
> Germany, showing administrative zones of occupation, as of July 1, 1944, 1946.

Box 46
Folder 5
> Blake, Lt Peter J., Interview
> MII Team 440-G report, "Visit to Berlin", May 8, 1945

Published Works

Books

Abyzov, Vladimir, *The Final Assault, 1945* (Moscow: Novosti Press Agency Publishing House, 1985)

Altner, Helmut, *Berlin Dance of Death* (Hevertown, PA: Casemate, 2002)

Ambrose, Stephen E., *Eisenhower and Berlin, 1945: The Decision to Halt at the Elbe* (New York: W.W. Norton & Company, Inc., 1967)

Bahm, Karl, *Berlin 1945: The Final Reckoning* (St. Paul, MN: MBI Publishing, 2001)

Bartov, Omer, *Hitler's Army: Soldiers, Nazis, and War in the Third Reich* (New York: Oxford University Press, 1992)

Baryatinskiy, Mikhail, *The IS Tanks: IS–1, IS–2, IS–3* (Surrey, UK: Ian Allan Publishing Ltd, 2006)

Baumgart, Eberhard, *Jenseits von Halbe: Der Todesmarsch der 9. Armee in den "Morgenthau" Ende April/Anfang Mai 1945* (Germany: Druffel-Verlag, 2001)

Beevor, Antony, *The Fall of Berlin 1945* (New York: Viking, 2002)

Bessonov, Evgeni, *Tank Rider, Into the Reich with the Red Army* (London, UK: Greenhill Books, 2003)

Bracher, Karl Dietrich, *The German Dictatorship: The Origins, Structure, and Effects of National Socialism* (New York: Praeger, 1970)

Brownlow, Donald Grey, *Panzer Baron: The Military Exploits of General Hasso von Manteuffel* (North Quincy, Massachusetts: The Christopher Publishing House, 1975)

Chamberlain, Peter, Hillary Doyle, and Thomas Jentz, *Encyclopedia of German Tanks of WWII* (London, Weidenfeld Military; New Ed edition, 1999)

Chuikov, Marshal Vasili I., *The Fall of Berlin* (New York: Holt, Rinehart and Winston, 1967)

Clark, Christopher *Iron Kingdom: The Rise and Downfall of Prussia 1600–1947* (Cambridge, MA: Belknap Press of Harvard University Press, 2006)

Courtois, Stéhane, et al, Translated by Johnson Murphy and Mark Kramer, *The Black Book of Communism: Crimes, Terror, Repression* (Cambridge, MA: Harvard University Press, 1999)

Crofoot, Craig, *The Berlin Direction: April-May 1945: an Extraction of the Official Soviet Army Order of Battle of the Berlin Strategic Offensive Operation, April-May 1945* (West Chester, OH: The Nafziger Collection, 1999)

Davies, Norman, *Rising '44: The Battle for Warsaw* (New York: Viking Press, 2004)

de Zayas, Alfred-Maurice, *A Terrible Revenge: The Ethnic Cleansing of the East European Germans* (New York: Palgrave MacMillan, 2006)

Ditting, Dr. Wolfgang et al., *Sowjetische Gräberstätten und Ehrenmale in Ostdeutschland heute* (Berlin, Germany: Wostok, 2005)

Duffy, Christopher, *Red Storm on the Reich: The Soviet March on Germany, 1945* (New York: Da Capo Press, 1993)

Eberle, Henrik and Matthias Uhl, *The Hitler Book: The Secret Dossier Prepared for Stalin from the Interrogations of Hitler's Personal Aides* (New York: PublicAffairs, 2005)

Eilhardt, Hans Joachim, *Frühjahr 1945: Kampf um Berlin Flucht in den Westen* (Aachen, Germany: Helios Verlag, 2003)

Eisenhower, Dwight D., *Crusade in Europe: A Personal Account of World War II* (New York: Doubleday & Company, Inc., 1948)

Engelmann, Joachim, *Die 18. Infanterie und Panzergrenadier Division 1934–1945* (Eggolsheim, Germany: Dörfler im Nebel Verlag GmbH, 2004)

Erickson, John, *The Road to Berlin* (Boulder, CO: Westview Press, 1983)

Ethel, Jeffery and Dr. Alfred Price, *Target Berlin, Mission 250: 6 March 1944* (London, UK: Greenhill Books/Lionel Leventhal Ltd, 1981)

Fest, Joachim, *Inside Hitler's Bunker: The Last Days of the Third Reich* (New York: Farrar, Strauss and Giroux, 2004)

Fey, Will, *Armor Battles of the Waffen-SS 1943–45* (Winnipeg, Canada: J.J. Fedorowicz Publishing, 1990)

Fleischer, Wolfgang, *Panzerfaust and other German Infantry Anti-Tank Weapons* (Atglen, PA: Schiffer Military/Aviation History, 1994)

Foedrowitz, Michael, *The Flak Towers in Berlin, Hamburg and Vienna 1940–1950* (Atglen, PA: Schiffer Military/Aviation History, 1998)

Forbes, Robert, *Pour L'Europe: The French Volunteers of the Waffen-SS* (Robert Forbes, 2000)

Fritz, Stephen G., *Endkampf: Soldiers, Civilians, and the Death of the Third Reich* (Lexington, Kentucky: The University Press of Kentucky, 2004)

Gablentz, O.M. von der (ed.), *Documents on the Status of Berlin, 1944–1959* (München, Germany: R.Oldenbourg, 1959)

Gavin, James M., *On to Berlin: Battles of an Airborne Commander, 1943–1946* (New York: Viking Press, 1978)

Getman, A. L., *Tanks are Heading to Berlin*, (Moscow: Nayka Publishing House, 1973)

Glantz, David M., *Zhukov's Greatest Defeat: The Red Army's Epic Disaster in Operation Mars, 1942* (Kansas: University of Kansas Press, 1999)

_____, *Red Storm over the Balkans: The Failed Soviet Invasion of Romania, Spring 1944* (United States: University of Press Kansas, 2007)

Gorlitz, Walter, *The Memoirs of Field Marshall Wilhelm Keitel: Chief of the German High Command, 1938–1945* (New York: Cooper Square Press, 2000)

Gosztony, Peter, *Der Kampf um Berlin 1945* (Germany: DTV, 1975)

Gunter, Georg, *Last Laurels, The German Defence of Upper Silesia January-May 1945* (England: Helion & Company, 2002)

Hastings, Max, *Armageddon: The battle for Germany, 1944–1945* (New York: Alfred A. Knopf, 2004)

Heiber, Helmut and David M. Glantz eds, *Hitler and His Generals: Military Conferences 1942–1945: The First Complete Stenographic Record of the Military Situation Conferences from Stalingrad to Berlin* (New York: Enigma Books, 2003)

Heidemann, Ronald *Verbotenes Ostpreußen* (Düsseldorf, Germany: Droste Verlag GmbH, 1990)

Hillblad, Thorolf, ed., *Twilight of the Gods: A Swedish Waffen-SS Volunteer's Experiences with the 11th SS-Panzergrenadier Division "Nordland," Eastern Front 1944–45* (England: Helion & Company, 2004)

Holzträger, Hans, *In a Raging Inferno: Combat Units of the Hitler Youth, 1944–45* (England: Helion & Company, 2000)

Jentz, Thomas L., *Panzertruppen: The Complete Guide to the Creation & Combat Employment of Germany's Tank Force, 1943–1945* (Atglen, PA: Schiffer Military History, 1996)

_____, *Germany's Tiger Tanks: Tiger I & II: Combat Tactics* (Atglen, PA: Schiffer Military History, 1996)

_____, and Hilary L. Doyle, *Germany's Tiger Tanks: VK45.02 to Tiger II: Design, Production & Modifications* (Atglen, PA: Schiffer Military History, 1996)

Kampe, Hans Georg, *Zossen—Wünsdorf 1945: Die letzten Kriegswochen im Hauptquartier des OKH* (Berlin, Germany: Projekt + Verlag Dr. Erwin Meißler, 1997)

Kissel, Hans, *Hitler's Last Levy: The Volkssturm 1944–45* (England: Helion & Company, 2005)

Krivosheev, Colonel—General G. F. ed., *Soviet Casualties and Combat Losses in the Twentieth Century* (London, UK: Greenhill Books, 1997)

Kuby, Erich, *The Russians and Berlin 1945* (London, UK: William Heinemann Ltd., 1965)

Ladd, Brian, *The Ghosts of Berlin: Confronting German History in the Urban Landscape* (Chicago: University of Chicago Press, 1997)

Lakowski, Richard, and Klaus Dorst, *Berlin: Frühjahr, 1945* (East Berlin: Miltärverlag der Deutschen Demokratischen Republik, 1985)

_____, *Gedenkstätte/Museum Seelower Höhen* (Seelow, Germany: 1992)

_____, *Seelow 1945: Die Entscheidungsschlacht an der Oder* (Berlin, Germany: Brandenburgisches Verlagshaus, 1994)

_____, *Der Kessel von Halbe: Das letzte Drama* (Berlin, Germany: Brandenburg, 2001)

Landwehr, Richard, and Holger Thor Nielsen, *Nordic Warriors: SS-Panzergrenadier-Regiment 24 Danmark, Eastern Front, 1943–45* (Hailfax, UK: Shelf Books Ltd, 1999)

_____, *French Volunteers of the Waffen-SS* (Brookings, Oregon: Siegrunen, 2002)

Lehmann, Armin D., *Hitler's Last Courier: A Lift in Transition* (United States: Xlibris Corporation, 2000)

Luck, Hans von, *Panzer Commander: Memoirs of Colonel Hans von Luck* (New York: Dell Publishing, 1989)

Mabire, Jean, *Berlin im Todeskampf 1945: Französische Freiwillige der Waffen-SS als letzte Verteidiger der Reichskanzlei 1945* (Coburg, Germany: Nation Europa Verlag, 1995)

Macdonogh, Giles, *After the Reich: The Brutal History of the Allied Occupation* (New York: Basic Books, 2007)

Maier, Georg, *Drama Between Budapest and Vienna: The Final Battles of the 6. Panzer-Armee in the East – 1945* (Winnipeg, Canada: J.J. Fedorowicz Publishing, Inc., 2004)

Megargee, Geoffrey P. *War of Annihilation: Combat and Genocide on the Eastern Front, 1941* (Lanham, MD: Rowman & Littlefield Publishers, INC, 2006)

Michaelis, Rolf, *Die 11.SS-freiwilligen-Panzer-Grenadier-Division "Nordland"* (Berlin, Germany: Michaelis, 2001)

Michulec, Robert, Miroslaw Zientarzewski, *T–34: Mythical Weapon* (Gdynia, Poland: Armageddon & Airconnection, 2006)

Millet, Allan R. and Williamson Murray, ed., *Military Effectiveness: Volume III, The Second World War* (Boston: Unwin Hyman, 1990)

Müller, Rolf-Dieter, and Gerd Ueberschär, *Hitler's War in the East: A Critical Assessment* (New York: Berghahn Books, 2002)

Münch, Karlheinz, *The Combat History of German Heavy Anti-Tank Unit 653 in World War II* (Mechanicsburg, PA: Stackpole Books, 2005)

Naimark, Norman, *The Russians in Germany: A History of the Soviet Zone of Occupation, 1945–1949* (Cambridge, Massachusetts: The Belknap Press of Harvard University Press, 3rd Printing 1997)

_____. *Fires of Hatred: Ethnic Cleansing in Twentieth-Century Europe* (Cambridge, Massachusetts: Harvard University Press, 2001)

O'Donnell, James P. *The Bunker: The History of the Reich Chancellery Group* (Boston MA: Houghton Mifflin Company, 1978)

Pçtersons, Aivars, *Mums jâpârnâk: Latvieðu karavîripçdçjie Berlînes aizstâvji* (Riga, Latvia: Aplis, 2003)

Pierik, Perry, *From Leningrad to Berlin: Dutch Volunteers in the Service of the German Waffen-SS, 1941–1945* (Soesterberg, Netherlands: Aspekt, 2001)

Piotrowski, Tadeusz, *Poland's Holocaust* (New York: McFarland & Company, 1997)

Popiel, Nikolai, *Forward to Berlin,* (Moscow: ACT Publishing House, 2001)

Ramm, Gerald, *Gott Mit Uns: Kriegserlebnisse aus Brandenburg und Berlin* (Woltersdorf/Schleuse, Germany: Verlag Gerald Raum, 2001)

Rummel, R.J., *Lethal Politics: Soviet Genocide and Mass Murder since 1917* (New Brunswick, New Jersey: Transaction Publishers, 1996)

Ryan, Cornelius, *The Last Battle* (New York: Pocket Books, 1985)

Saft, Ulrich, *Krieg im Osten: Das bittere Ende jenseits der Weichsel bis Oder und Neiâe* (Walsrode, Germany: Militärbuchverlag Saft, 2002)

Schiefer, Joachim, *Historischer Atlas zum Kriegsende 1945: Zwischen Berlin und dem Erzgebirge* (Leipzig, Germany: Sax-Verlag Beucha, 1998)

Schneider, Russ, *Gotterdammerung 1945: Germany's Last Stand in the East* (Philomont, VA: Eastern Front/Warfield Books Inc., 1998)

Schneider, Wolfgang, *Tigers in Combat II* (Mechanicsburg, PA: Stackpole Books, 2005)

Schramm, Percy E. *Kriegstagbuch Des Oberkommandos Der Wehrmacht, 1940–1945 (Wehrmachtführungsstab): Band I-IV* (München, Germany: Bernard & Graefe Verlag, 1982)

Schultz-Naumann, Joachim, *The Last Thirty Days: The War Diary of the German High Command from April to May 1945* (New York: Madison Books, 1995)

Sharp, Charles C., *Soviet Order of Battle World War II: Volume II "School of Battle:" Soviet Tank Corps and Tank Brigades, January 1942–1945* (George F. Nafziger, 1995)

_____, *Soviet Order of Battle World War II: Volume III "Red Storm:" Soviet Mechanized Corps and Guards Armored Units 1942–1945* (George F. Nafziger, 1995)

_____, *Soviet Order of Battle World War II: Volume IV "Red Guards:" Soviet Guards Rifle and Airborne Units 1941–1945* (George F. Nafziger, 1995)

_____, *Soviet Order of Battle World War II: Volume VI "Red Thunder:" Soviet Artillery Corp, Divisions, and Brigades 1941–1945* (George F. Nafziger, 1995)

_____, *Soviet Order of Battle World War II: Volume X "Red Swarm:" Soviet Rifle Divisions Formed From 1942–1945* (George F. Nafziger, 1996)

_____, *Soviet Order of Battle World War II: Volume XII "Red Hammers:" Soviet Self-propelled Artillery and Lend Lease Armor 1941–1945* (George F. Nafziger, 1998)

_____, *Soviet Infantry Tactics in World War II: Red Army Infantry Tactics from Squad to Rifle Company from the Combat Regulations of November 1942* (George F. Nafziger, 1998)

_____, *Soviet Armor Tactics in World War II: Red Army Armor Tactics from Individual Vehicle to Company According to the Combat Regulations of February 1944* (George F. Nafziger, 1999)

Slowe, Peter and Richard Woods, *Battlefield Berlin: Siege, Surrender & Occupation, 1945* (London, UK: Robert Hale, 1988)

Spaeter, Helmuth, *The History of the Panzerkorps Großdeutschland vol. 1–3* (Winnipeg, Canada: J.J. Fedorowicz Publishing, 1995)

Stimpel, Hans-Martin, *Widersinn 1945: Aufstellung, Einsatz und Untergang einer Fallschirmjägerdivision* (Göttingen, Germany: Cuvillier, 2003)

Taylor, Frederick, *The Berlin Wall: A World Divided, 1961–1989* (New York: HarperCollins, 2006)

Tessin, Georg. *Verbände und Truppen der deutschen Wehrmacht und der Waffen-SS im Zweiten Weltkrieg 1939–1945. Bearbeitet auf Grund der Unterlagen des Bundesarchivs-Militärarchivs; herausgegeben mit Unterstützung des Bundesarchivs und des Arbeitskreises für Wehrforschung. 14 Bände + 3 Registerbände in mehreren Teilen* (Osnabrück, Germany: 1967–1998.)

Thorwald, Juergen, *Flight in the Winter: Russia Conquers—January to May 1945* (New York: Pantheon Books Inc, 1951)

Thrams, von Hermann, *Küstrin 1945: Tagebuch einer Festung* (Berlin, Germany: Landesverband Berlin, 1992)

Tieke, Wilhelm, *Das Ende Zwischen Oder und Elbe: Der Kampf um Berlin 1945* (Stuttgart, Germany: Motorbuch Verlag, 1995)

_____, *Tragedy of the Faithful: A History of the III. (germanisches) SS-Panzer Korps* (Winnipeg, Canada: J.J. Fedorowicz, 2001)

Le Tissier, Tony Le, *Zhukov at the Oder: The Decisive Battle for Berlin* (Westport, CT: Praeger, 1996)

_____, *Berlin: Then and Now* (London, UK: After The Battle Publications, 2000)

_____, *With Our Backs to Berlin: The German Army in Retreat 1945* (England: Sutton Publishing Ltd, 2001)

_____, *Slaughter at Halbe: The Destruction of Hitler's 9th Army, April 1945* (England: Sutton Publishing Ltd, 2005)

Tsouras, Peter G. ed, *Panzers on the Eastern Front: General Erhard Raus and his Panzer Divisions in Russia 1941–1945* (Greenhill Books/Lionel Leventhal Limited London, 2005)

Trevor-Roper, H.R.R, *The Last Days of Hitler* (New York: The MacMillan Company, 1947)

_____, H.R.R ed., *Blitzkrieg to Defeat: Hitler's War Directives 1939–1945* (New York: Holt, Rinehart and Winston, 1964)

Tully, Andrew, *Berlin: Story of a Battle: April—May 1945* (New York: Simon and Schuster, 1963)

Venghaus, Wolfgang, *Berlin 1945: Die Zeit vom 16. April bis 2. Mai: Eine Dokumentation in Berichten, Bildern und Bemerkungen* (Netphen: Venghaus, n.d.)

Voss, Klaus, and Paul Kehlenbeck, *Letzte Divisionen 1945: Die Panzerdivision Clausewitz und Die Infanteriedivision Schill* (Schleusingen, Germany: AMUN-Verlag, 2000)

Wallin, Erik, *Götterdämmerung: Schwedische und deutsche Freiwillige der SS-Division "Nordland" im Endkampf 1945 in Pommern und Berlin* (Pluwig, Germany: Munin Verlag GmbH, 2000)

Wegner, Bernd, *The Waffen-SS: Organization, Ideology and Function* (Cambridge, MA: Basil Blackwell Ltd., 1990)

Yelton, David K., *Hitler's Volkssturm: The Nazi Militia and the Fall of Germany, 1944–1945* (Kansas, University Press of Kansas, 2002)

Zhukov, Georgi K., *Marshal Zhukov's Greatest Battles* (New York: First Cooper Square Press Edition, 2002)

Ziemke, Earl F., *Stalingrad to Berlin: The German Defeat in the East* (New York: Barnes and Noble Books, 1996)

Articles

Bowen, Wayne H., "The Ghost Battalion: Spaniards in the Waffen-SS, 1944–1945," *The Historian*, 1/1/2001 from www.encyclopedia.com

Keegan, John., "Berlin," *MHQ: The Quarterly Journal of Military History*, NO. 11 (Winter 1990).

Novikov, A.A. "The Air Forces in the Berlin Operation," *Soviet Military History Journal*, May 1975

Rudenko, Air Marshal S.I. "On the Employment of Aviation in the Berlin Operation," *Soviet Military History Journal*, May 1985

Skorodumov, N. "Maneuvers of the 12th Guards Tank Corps in the Berlin Operation," *Soviet Military History Journal*, May 1978

Documentaries and Films

C. Barrand, K. Jan Hindiks, A. Uvarov, *Berlin: At All Cost!*, 1994

Mikhail Chiaureli, *The Fall of Berlin*, Mosfilm Cinema Concern: 1949

Websites

www.russianbattlefield.ru
"Development History of the JS–1/JS–2"